Thomas Henry Dyer

The History of the Kings of Rome

With a Prefatory Dissertation on its Sources and Evidence

Thomas Henry Dyer

The History of the Kings of Rome
With a Prefatory Dissertation on its Sources and Evidence

ISBN/EAN: 9783742801906

Manufactured in Europe, USA, Canada, Australia, Japa

Cover: Foto ©ninafisch / pixelio.de

Manufactured and distributed by brebook publishing software (www.brebook.com)

Thomas Henry Dyer

The History of the Kings of Rome

THE HISTORY

OF

THE KINGS OF ROME.

WITH

A PREFATORY DISSERTATION ON ITS SOURCES
AND EVIDENCE.

BY

THOMAS HENRY DYER, LL.D.
OF THE UNIVERSITY OF ST. ANDREWS.

LONDON:
BELL AND DALDY, YORK STREET
COVENT GARDEN.
1868.

PREFACE.

THE design of most of the recent historians of Rome appears to have been to obliterate as much as they could of its ancient history. "Negemus omnia; comburamus annales, ficta hæc esse dicamus"—such seems to have been the maxim of almost every critic and historian who has handled this subject since the days of Niebuhr. The Germans have of course taken the lead in this crusade, as in everything else connected with classical literature, and, in England at least, they have been almost implicitly followed; where the scholars who have ventured to assert any independence of thought are few indeed. Yet, after all, there is little originality in the German scepticism. All the chief objections to the early Roman history were urged by De Beaufort, a century before Niebuhr. The Germans following in his track have, with characteristic industry and perseverance, picked the bones of the quarry cleaner. And they have done worse than this. They have attempted to reconstruct, as well as to destroy, to dress out the skeleton with figments of their own, possessing generally not a tithe of the probability and consistency of the narrative which they are intended to supplant. We are thus threatened with a succession of Roman histories, each totally unlike its predecessor.

The work now offered to the public is written on a directly opposite plan. The object of it is to preserve, instead of to destroy, as much as it may be possible of the ancient history; and in this respect at least it may lay claim to comparative novelty. Neither labour nor expense is spared in endeavouring to rescue from oblivion the smallest material relic of antiquity; a statue, a picture, a gem, or even the meanest implement of household use; yet, in what regards the traditions of ancient times, we appear to pursue an entirely opposite course. Hence it appeared to the author that an attempt to rescue the early Roman annals from the oblivion with which they are menaced might at all events be a laudable one, and, if he should succeed only in some small part of his design, he will esteem himself abundantly recompensed for his labour. Such an undertaking necessarily involved a large amount of critical discussion. The narrative part of the book is, indeed, little more than a translation of Livy, intended only as a vehicle for the remarks appended to it. As a medium for these, Schwegler's "Römische Geschichte" has been selected, because it embraces in the completest detail all the objections which have been urged against the early history, and because it evidently suggested and partly supplied the materials for Sir G. C. Lewis's work on the "Credibility of the Early Roman History." The observations of the last-named writer, as well as those of other scholars, have been occasionally examined, where they appeared to supplement, or to offer any divergence from, Schwegler's arguments; and the author hopes it will be found that he has not evaded the discussion of any important objections. By way of introduction a dissertation on the sources of early Roman history, and on its internal evidence, has been prefixed to the book; since without an examination of these, any work on the subject must necessarily be incomplete.

LONDON, *October* 1887.

CONTENTS.

	PAGE
PREFATORY DISSERTATION ON THE SOURCES AND EVIDENCES OF EARLY ROMAN HISTORY	v—cxxxv

SECTION
I.—	THE EARLY POPULATION OF ITALY	1—23
II.—	FOUNDATION OF ROME	23—56
III.—	REIGN OF ROMULUS	57—135
IV.—	THE INTERREGNUM	135—147
V.—	REIGN OF NUMA POMPILIUS	147—160
VI.—	,, OF TULLUS HOSTILIUS	160—215
VII.—	,, OF ANCUS MARCIUS	215—230
VIII.—	,, OF TARQUINIUS PRISCUS	230—278
IX.—	,, OF SERVIUS TULLIUS AND INQUIRY INTO THE REGAL CONSTITUTION	278—364
X.—	,, OF TARQUINIUS SUPERBUS	364—440

A DISSERTATION

ON THE SOURCES OF EARLY ROMAN HISTORY, AND THE CREDIBILITY OF ITS INTERNAL EVIDENCE.

ANY inquiry into the authenticity and credibility of the History of the Roman Kings, as handed down to us by ancient authors, naturally divides itself into two parts,—namely, its external and its internal evidence. The first of these concerns the sources from which the history has been derived, such as annals, laws, treaties, and other written documents; to which may be added, as collaterally confirming them, public works and buildings, statues, and other monuments of the like kind. The second part of the inquiry concerns the probability of the narrative when tested by a critical examination of its consistency, as well with itself as with ordinary experience and the general tenor of political history. It is proposed to pursue, in this Dissertation, both these heads of inquiry in the order indicated. And first, of the

EXTERNAL EVIDENCE.

The gift of speech, without the art of writing, would be of comparatively little value in perpetuating the annals of mankind. Oral tradition, besides being short-lived and evanescent, is ever liable to change and falsification; against which the only safeguards are permanent records. Hence the first and most important questions which present themselves in the present inquiry are, Were letters known at Rome in the time of the kings? and, if they were, is there any reasonable ground for supposing that they were employed to record the political events of that period? For answers to these questions we naturally turn to ancient authority, and, unless this can be successfully impugned, we have no right to reject it.

In the opinion of some writers, the first Romans were little better than illiterate barbarians. This view, however, appears to be very unreasonable. The mere fact of building a city implies a very considerable degree of civilization. Not to mention architectural art, it implies agriculture and trade, laws, and the requisite intelligence for civil and political government. Rome, too, in comparison with many other cities in Italy, was founded at a late period, and, as we shall endeavour to show, by a Greek race. At that time, Greece had made great progress in literature and art; the influence of which, according to the opinion of Cicero, must have been felt in Italy. And, when we reflect that Cumæ had been founded on the Italian coast perhaps three centuries before the building of Rome, this opinion seems in the highest degree probable. "Atque hoc," says Cicero, "eo magis est in Romulo admirandum, quod ceteri, qui dii ex hominibus facti esse dicuntur, minus eruditis hominum sæculis fuerunt, ut fingendi proclivis esset ratio, quum imperiti facile ad credendum impellerentur. Romuli autem ætatem minus his sexcentis annis, *jam inveteratis litteris atque doctrinis*, omnique illo antiquo ex inculta hominum vita errore sublato, fuisse cernimus."[1] Whence Cicero evidently considered that the influence of Greek literature had been felt at Rome at that period; and we cannot consequently imagine him to have thought that the first Romans were ignorant of the art of writing.

But that letters were known at least in the time of Numa appears from more direct testimony. Not to mention Numa's reputation for learning, which was so great that he was thought, though wrongly, to have been a pupil of Pythagoras, we are expressly told that he committed his laws to writing.[2] Ancus Marcius subsequently caused these laws to be copied out from Numa's Commentaries into an album, and posted up

---

[1] De Rep. ii. 10, 18.
[2] "Eique (Marcio) sacra omnia exscripta exsignataque dedit."—Liv. i. 20.

in public;[1] a fact which not only shows the use of the art of writing, but also a reading public. In like manner the treaty made between Tullus Hostilius and the Albans is said to have been recited from writing.[2] If these accounts are true, no further proofs are wanting that letters were known at Rome in the time of the kings. We may, however, mention a few later instances, which rest not, like those just cited, merely on the testimony of historians, but consist of documents which survived till the imperial times, and were then seen by eye-witnesses. Such was the treaty of confederation made by Servius Tullius with the Latins, engraved in antique Greek characters on a brazen column, and preserved in the Temple of Diana on the Aventine, where it was inspected by Dionysius;[3] who draws from it an argument that the Romans could not have been barbarians. Also the treaty made by Tarquinius Superbus with the Gabines, written on an ox-hide stretched over a shield, and kept in the Temple of Sancus; which likewise appears to have been seen by Dionysius.[4] The same author mentions that the treaty made by Tarquinius Superbus with the Latins was engraved on brazen pillars, but says not that he had seen it.[5] Lastly, we may adduce the treaty between Rome and Carthage, executed in the first year of the republic, and preserved in the ærarium of the Capitoline Temple, where it was copied by Polybius; who remarks that the language of it was so ancient as to be difficult of interpretation even by the most learned in such matters.[6]

All the passages in ancient authors relating to the subject assume, either directly or by implication, the use of the art of writing in the kingly period; we are not aware of one in which it is denied or contested: the modern critic, therefore, who attempts to controvert it, is bound to establish his opinion

---

[1] "Omnia ea (sacra publica ut a Numa instituta erant) ex commentariis regis pontificem in album elata proponere in publico jubet."—Liv. i. 32.
[2] "Tabulis ceravc."—Ibid. 24.
[3] Lib. iv. 26. The use of the word *sevi*, for *sivi*, noted by Festus (p. 165, Ned) as appearing in some document in this temple, may, as Schwegler observes (R. L S. 16, Anm.), have been referable to this treaty.
[4] Lib. iv. 58. This treaty is also alluded to by Horace, Epp. ii. l. 25.
[5] Lib. iv. 45.   [6] Polyb. iii. 22, 26.

by the most irrefragable proofs. Schwegler has attempted to do so, but his arguments are based only on inference and probability. Thus he says:[1] "We are led to the same result—namely, that the history of the regal period had not been recorded by any contemporary annalist—in another manner, when we consider the age of Roman writing. It is not, indeed, precisely and credibly handed down at what time the Romans became acquainted with the use of letters: since Evander and Hercules, to whom the introduction of them is ascribed, cannot of course pass for historical personages. But since the Etruscans, who were earlier civilized than the Romans, according to tradition knew not the art of writing till about the 30th Olympiad, through the Bacchiad Demaratus, the father of Tarquinius Priscus; and as this tradition, so far at least as relates to the time, has every probability in its favour, we are warranted in assuming that the Romans also were unacquainted with letters before the epoch of the Tarquinian dynasty. We have the more ground for this assumption, since the Romans, as may now be regarded as proved, derived not their alphabet from the Etruscans, but apparently from the Greeks of Campania, and probably from Cumæ; and Rome's commerce with Campania did not begin before the Tarquinian dynasty. The oldest written monument at Rome mentioned by credible tradition is the document relating to the foundation of the Dianium on the Aventine in the time of Servius Tullius. But, if the Romans first became acquainted with writing only in the time of the elder Tarquin, it cannot of course be supposed that any extensive use of a new and difficult art could have been made during the whole regal period. It cannot indeed be doubted that, under the last kings, writing was used for monumental purposes,—such as the recording of public treaties and alliances, dedicatory inscriptions, &c.,—but not for literary purposes, or historical record. The want of writing materials forbids us to suppose that this could have existed. Besides brazen tablets or columns, the only materials employed for writing on in the very early times were wooden tablets, pieces of linen, the

[1] B. i. Sect. 13.

skins of animals, and tablets made of the bark of trees. It
is clear that such cumbersome and inconvenient materials
would place almost insuperable obstacles in the way of any
extensive use of writing; and, under such circumstances,
it is hardly possible to conceive any literature, properly so
called. If, therefore, what we cannot doubt, annalistic
records were made in the pre-Gallic times, they must have
been in the last degree jejune and meagre, and could have
contained only the very briefest abridgment of facts. A
real literature was impossible until the use of paper and
parchment became general; the former of which materials was first discovered, according to Varro, in the time of
Alexander the Great, the latter under his successors."

The first argument is, that the Etruscans had no alphabet
before the time of Demaratus; and, as the Etruscans were
earlier civilized than the Romans, the latter could not previously have known the art of writing. It is also insinuated
that the art must have been introduced at Rome by the
Tarquins.

The authority for Demaratus having introduced writing
among the Etruscans is contained in the following passage of
Tacitus:[1]—" At in Italia Etrusci ab Corinthio Demarato,
Aborigines Arcade ab Evandro didicerunt : et forma litteris
Latinis, quae veterrimis Graecorum."

Now we must take *the whole* of this passage as containing
the tradition; we cannot say, at our pleasure, that one-half
of it is tradition, and the other half not. The tradition, therefore, was, that the aborigines, under whom, in the view of
Tacitus, we must include the Romans, *did not* obtain their
alphabet from the Etruscans: consequently, it is quite beside
the purpose whether Demaratus introduced letters into Etruria
or not. According to tradition, Evander brought them into
Latium; and, whether Evander was a real personage or not,
still he was the hero, or symbol, of a very high antiquity.
Consequently the tradition amounts to this : that letters had
been known in Latium time out of mind, and long before the
arrival of Demaratus at Tarquinii. The assertion, therefore,

[1] Ann. iii. 11.

that the civilization of the Etruscans is of an earlier period than that of the Romans, is, so far as letters are concerned, entirely unfounded.

The anecdote about Demaratus is nothing but a sort of sidewind insinuation of Schwegler's; since he believes, as we shall see further on, that the Tarquins were a Latin family, and came not from Etruria. And he admits the futility of it when he observes that the Romans "derived not their alphabet from the Etruscans, but from the Greeks." This, indeed, cannot be denied; the passage in Dionysius already cited, where he speaks of the treaty in ancient Greek characters preserved in the Temple of Diana, is sufficient to prove it. And, as we hope to show in the course of this work that Romulus was the son, or at most the grandson, of a Greek, we need not go to Cumæ for the alphabet. It had, indeed, as we have already said, probably been naturalized in Latium long before the time of Romulus. That the Romans got their alphabet from Cumæ in the time of the Tarquins is a mere conjecture, at variance with tradition, utterly destitute of proof, and invented merely to prop a theory.

Dr. Mommsen, who has devoted great attention to ancient alphabets and writing, places at an immemorial period their introduction into Italy. Reasoning from the adoption of abbreviations, he observes:[1] "We must, both as regards Etruria and Latium, carry back the commencement of the art of writing to an epoch which more closely approximates to the first incidence of the Egyptian dog-star period within historical times, the year 1322 B.C. than to the year 776, with which the chronology of the Olympiads began in Greece. The high antiquity of the art of writing in Rome is evinced otherwise by numerous and plain indications." He then proceeds to instance the treaties, &c. of the regal period, to which we have already alluded, the primitive marking of cattle (*scriptura*), the mode of addressing the Senate (Patres conscripti), &c.

On the whole, the use of writing at Rome, from the very earliest period, is established on the best evidence that can

[1] History of Rome, B. i. ch. 14, vol. i. p. 221, Dickson's Trans.

reasonably be expected in a matter of such high antiquity. The argument drawn by Schwegler from the want of writing materials is absurd. Even allowing that the articles which he enumerates are all that could be employed for the purpose —and he omits the waxen tablets mentioned in a passage before cited from Livy[1]—still, if linen could be prepared for writing on, as the Libri Lintei show, then the early Romans had a very good substitute for paper; not to mention other substances, such as wooden tablets, the bark of trees, the skins of animals, &c. Nor can any argument be drawn, as is sometimes done,[2] against the use of letters, from the ancient law bidding the Prætor Maximus drive a nail into the right-hand wall of the Capitoline Temple on the Ides of every September. The annals of the Pontifex Maximus were not open to public inspection after the close of each year; and therefore the nail was a convenient mark to show the lapse of successive years. We may infer from Livy's account that the first nail was driven by the Consul M. Horatius, when he dedicated the temple in the year after the expulsion of the kings. But in fact it was a superstitious observance as much as anything else. And that it was not adopted as a substitute for writing is evident from the fact that it existed contemporaneously with the use of writing. For in the year B.C. 331, on the discovery of a system of poisoning among the Roman matrons, Cn. Quinctilius was created Dictator in order to drive a nail; and the precedent was taken *from the annals* in the time of the secessions of the *plebs*. (" Itaque memoria ex annalibus repetita, in secessionibus quondam plebis clavum ab dictatore fixum—dictatorem clavi figendi causa creari placuit."—Liv. viii. 18.) The driving of the nail was, therefore, *recorded in writing* in the annals of the time. And as it was necessary to refer to these annals, the precedent sought must have been beyond the memory of man, and would carry us up about a century. Now what is called the fourth secession—which, however, rests only on the authority of Ovid—occurred in B.C. 307, only thirty-six years before the period in question, and could not therefore have been the period alluded to by

[1] Above, p. xi.   [2] See Liddell's Rome, ch. xvi.; cf. Livy, viii. 3.

Livy; who, indeed, recognises no secession on this occasion, but says only that the matter came near to one.[1] The third secession happened in the year B.C. 449; and, even allowing that it is to this, and not an earlier one, that Livy is referring, then there must have been annals extant in B.C. 331 which reached back to B.C. 449, or more than half a century before the capture of the city by the Gauls.

We do not mean to impugn Livy's inference from this custom, that letters were rare at that period.[2] But to assert that they were rare implies that they existed, and shows that Livy did not consider their existence to be disproved by the driving of the nail. And we are ready to admit Schwegler's view, that letters were not used "for literary purposes," if by that expression is meant the works of professed authors, written and circulated for public use. But, in the absence of literary history, there might still be historical record for which those "rarae literae" would have sufficed. We wish it to be remembered that we are not attempting to prove that the ancient works on the subject are a full and complete history of Rome; on the contrary, we regard them as extremely deficient and fragmentary. All that we aim at establishing is, that the greater part of what we do possess is genuine, and that there are no good grounds for the sweeping charges brought against it by some modern critics and historians: as, for instance, when Niebuhr asserts that "the names of the kings are perfectly fictitious; no man can tell how long the Roman kings reigned, as we do not know how many there were;"[3] or when Dr. Arnold says, even of the latter part of the regal period, "the general picture before us is a mere fantasy."[4] We believe that, without the aid of oral tradition, there were records enough to certify the names and order of succession of the kings, and the general truth of the leading events of their reigns.

Before quitting this part of the subject, we may observe that Sir G. C. Lewis says little or nothing about the art of writing at

---

[1] "Prope secessionem plebis res venit."—Lib. vi. 42.
[2] "Quia rarae per ea tempora literae erant."—Ibid.
[3] Lectures, vol. i. p. 11.   [4] Hist. of Rome, vol. i. p. 49.

Rome, and expresses no opinion as to its antiquity; a clear proof that he thought the arguments in its favour incontrovertible, as he seizes every opportunity to damage the early history.

Assuming, therefore, that the art of writing was known at Rome from the earliest period, the next step in our inquiry is, For what kind of public records it was employed?

Of these the first in importance were the Annales Maximi. With regard to these Cicero observes: "Ab initio rerum Romanarum usque ad P. Mucium Pontificem Maximum, res omnes singulorum annorum mandabat literis Pontifex Maximus efferebatque in album et proponebat tabulam domi, potestas ut esset populo cognoscendi; iique etiam nunc Annales Maximi nominantur."[1] Hence we learn that from the very earliest times the Pontifex Maximus was accustomed to note down in a book all the public events, and thence to transfer, or, as we might say, post them into an album, or whitened tablet, which he set up before his house, so that everybody might read them. And these annals, as we perceive from the same passage, were still extant in the time of Cicero—"etiam nunc Annales Maximi nominantur." Their existence is further attested by other passages in the same author. Thus in the speech for Rabirius (c. 5): "Cum isto omnes et suppliciorum et verborum acerbitates non ex memoria vestra ac patrum vestrorum, sed ex annalium monumentis atque ex regum commentariis conquisierit." And in the De Legibus (i. 2, 6): "Nam post annales pontificum maximorum, quibus nihil potest esse jucundius" (or jejunius) "si aut ad Fabium . . . venias," &c., and in other places, one of which we shall have to cite further on. It must, however, be admitted, that when, in the passage first cited, Cicero says that these annals existed from the beginning of Rome—"ab initio rerum Romanarum"—he could not of course have meant any higher period than the reign of Numa; since the Pontifices, as he himself says in another place,[2] were first instituted by that king.

The existence of the Annales Maximi even down to the imperial times is attested by other authors. Thus Cato, as quoted by Aulus Gellius,[3] referred to them in his Origines.

[1] De Orat. ii. 12.   [2] De Rep. ii. 12.   [3] Noct. Att. ii. 28.

Dionysius of Halicarnassus cites them for the death of Aruns, son of Tarquinius Priscus, in the following passage: "ἐν γὰρ ταῖς ἐνιαυσίαις ἀναγραφαῖς κατὰ τὸν τεσσαρακοστὸν ἐνιαυτὸν τῆς Τυλλίου ἀρχῆς τετελευτηκότα παρειλήφαμεν,"[1] where by ἀναγραφαί Dionysius means public annals, or State registers: since he distinguishes them in the following passage from the χρονογραφιαί, or annals of such writers as Licinius Macer, Gellius, and others, and points to them as the source whence such writers drew: ἀλλ᾽ ἔοικεν ὁ πρῶτος ἐν ταῖς χρονογραφίαις τοῦτο καταχωρίσας, ᾧ πάντες ἠκολούθησαν οἱ λοιποί, τοσοῦτον μόνον ἐν ταῖς ἀρχαίαις εὑρὼν ἀναγραφαῖς, ὅτι πρέσβεις ἀπεστάλησαν ἐπὶ τούτων τῶν ὑπάτων εἰς Σικελίαν,"[2] κ.τ.λ. Pliny, in his Natural History,[3] quotes a passage from the Annales Maximi. Macrobius alludes to the privilege conceded to the Pontifices of keeping these annals, and says that they were called Maximi after the Pontifex Maximus.[4] But one of the most important passages as to their nature, and especially as to the form in which they were preserved and accessible to readers in later times, is the following from Servius:[5]— " Ita autem annales conficiebantur: tabulam dealbatam quotannis Pontifex Maximus habuit, in qua, præscriptis consulum nominibus et aliorum magistratuum, digna memoratu notare consueverat domi militiæque, terra marique gesta per singulos dies. Cujus diligentiæ annuos commentarios in lxxx libros veteres retulerunt, eosque a Pontificibus Maximis, a quibus fiebant, Annales Maximos appellarunt." From which we learn that the names of the consuls, or other annual magistrates, were prefixed to the events of each year; and consequently, in the regal period, the name of the reigning king would have been prefixed. Events were recorded under the days on which they happened; and it further appears, as we have before remarked, that the Pontifex Maximus kept books of the events ("annuos commentarios") besides inscribing them on the album for public perusal. And of these Annui Commentarii an edition was in later times published in eighty

[1] Lib. iv. 30.   [2] Lib. viii. 1.   [3] Lib. xxxiv. 11.
[4] Sat. lib. c. 2, sub fin.   [5] Æn. i. 373.

volumes; at what time we know not, but evidently before the time of Cicero. And in this edition the obsolete language and spelling were probably modernized.

Schwegler, however, contests [1] whether these annals were genuine, or, even if they were, whether they could have been of much service to an historian. He says: "These annals were at a later period copied, and thus multiplied, forming at last a collection of eighty books. Had these records been made with due completeness, and in the form of a connected historical narrative, they would have constituted an excellent source for later historians; but they were exceedingly meagre and concise; nothing, in short, but a dry record of external events and circumstances, and especially of prodigies and extraordinary natural appearances such as eclipses of the sun and moon, famines, pestilences, &c. Nay, it may be questioned whether political actions or resolutions of the popular assemblies and changes in the constitution were fully noted, and whether the prominent or even exclusive contents did not wholly consist of prodigies, or other like events, which appeared remarkable in a religious point of view; and whether it was not for this reason that the keeping of these annals was intrusted to the Pontifex Maximus. That a chronicle of such a kind could afford but few materials to later historians is evident at first sight; it could not have been possible to form from it a connected history; and we need not therefore be surprised that Livy and Dionysius made no use, or, at all events, no immediate use, of these annals; though mediately many accounts in Livy, and especially those regarding prodigies, may have been derived from the pontifical annals.

"Nevertheless, if these annals began from the foundation of Rome, they would have formed for later historians a desirable *point d'appui*, and would also have afforded a certain security that the general outlines at least of the primitive tradition are historical. But such an assumption is incorrect. Internal as well as external evidence makes it probable that the general pontifical annals do not reach

[1] Buch i. Sect. 1.

higher than the Gallic conflagration, still less to the regal period. Internal evidence; because it is precisely the chronology of the regal period which is so confused and so full of contradictions, and rests so evidently on a mere combination of numbers, and a subtle system of combination, that it is impossible to think it founded on a series of records annually made. External evidence; since it cannot be reasonably doubted that the wooden tablets on which the annals of the Pontifices were inscribed, perished in the Gallic conflagration. They were kept in the dwelling of the Pontifex Maximus, or the Regia, and in the hasty evacuation of the city were assuredly not saved, since even the sacred utensils of the Temple of Vesta could be preserved only by burying them. These assumptions from probability are raised to certainty by a passage in Cicero. That author says (De Rep. i. 16), that from the eclipse of the year 350, the first recorded in the Annales Maximi, the preceding eclipses were calculated backwards to that of the Ides of Quinctilis, when Romulus disappeared. But, if it was necessary to compute them, they could not have been recorded. It seems at all events as if, after the Gallic conflagration (365), an attempt was made to restore the annals so far backwards as the memory of the living generation served; but such restored annals could not of course have had the value of authentic documents. To what period they were carried back is uncertain. When Cicero affirms that the making of these annals began with the foundation of Rome, this means no more, though improbably enough, that the custom originated at that early period, and not that the annals with which he himself was acquainted reached so far back. On the other hand, a writer of the later imperial times assumes that they did; and it must at all events be accepted that the copies of the Annales Maximi then in circulation went back to that period. But a fragment of these restored annals, preserved by Gellius, and the only one which remains to us, betrays a tolerably recent origin.

"It is almost the antiquaries alone who have made use of the annals; we do not find in the historians any certain

traces of their direct use. This is particularly the case with
Livy and Dionysius, as we have before said. Even of the
antiquaries, Verrius Flaccus, so far as we know, was the last
who had them in his hands: for Gellius, who in all other
cases when he cites 'Annals' means the historical works
of the annalists, evidently took not his citation out of the
Annales Maximi, from these annals themselves, but from
Verrius Flaccus. Pliny also has no quotation from them, nor
does he mention them in the list of his sources. In general,
when merely 'Annales' are cited—citations which are frequently referred without ground to the Annales Maximi—
it is not these that are meant, but always the historical works
of the annalists."

To expect that the annals of the Pontifex Maximus should
have been made in the form of a "connected historical
narrative" is to expect that they should have been regular
history instead of the materials for it; nor can we conceive
a better source for later historians than these records in their
annalistic form. When Schwegler proceeds to say that they
contained almost, if not quite, exclusively only records of
natural appearances and prodigies, he asserts this only from
his own conjectures. For Servius, in a passage already
quoted,[1] says that they contained *everything worthy of note*
either in peace or war set down under the proper days.
This passage has been captiously interpreted as if Servius
asserted that there was an entry under every day; but he
only means those days on which something noteworthy—
dignum memoratu—was done. But, says Schwegler in a note,
it may be asked whether Servius saw them with his own
eyes. To which we answer, at all events in their public
form; while it is certain that Schwegler never saw them,
though he pretends to know so much about them. And if
Servius did not see them himself, he must have had better
information about them than we moderns possess. And the
fact that Dionysius cites them for the death of Aruns shows
that they recorded other events besides prodigies.

This passage, to which we have before referred, as well as

[1] See above, p. xviii.

one in Livy, which we proceed to quote, suffices to refute Schwegler's assertion that those historians made no immediate use of the annals. Livy says: "His consulibus cum Ardeatibus fœdus renovatum est: idque monumento est, consules eos illo anno fuisse, qui neque in annalibus priscis, neque in libris magistratuum inveniuntur."[1] Livy cannot be here referring to the annals of Fabius, Piso, and the other early historians: first, because by way of distinction he calls the annals which he cites *prisci*; secondly, because he is appealing to them as a work of high authority, coupling them with the Libri Magistratuum, another official record, and indeed naming them first, as the more important work. Livy proceeds to explain how the names of the consuls might have been omitted: military tribunes, he thinks, had been appointed at the beginning of the year; and the consuls, being *suffecti*, had not been mentioned. Why so? Because the magistrates appointed at the beginning of the year were, in fact, the date of it; and if two sets of magistrates had been named, the chronology would have been in confusion. But Livy's observations on this point further show that he is alluding to some *official* record; for, in a literary history, a motive like that alluded to for suppressing the names of the *consules suffecti* could not have existed.

We see by this example that, from the imperfect manner in which the early Roman records were kept, and especially from the want of a fixed chronological era, an historian who trusted to these official documents alone might easily be led into error. Thus, in the present instance, the consulate of L. Papirius Mugillanus and L. Sempronius Atratinus would have been unknown except for the renewal of the treaty with Ardea. In the time of the kings, matters must have been still worse, as there would have been no mark to distinguish one year of their reigns from another; their sum at the end of them is all that is given. In such a state of things, even with a knowledge of writing, the driving of a nail as a chronological mark was a contrivance not to be despised. We may well suppose that there were other points

[1] Lib. iv. 7.

in which those annals were imperfect; and we need not therefore wonder that, in spite of them, great variation and uncertainty prevailed in the early Roman history.

The few occasions on which the Annales Maximi are appealed to by ancient writers are no proof of their non-existence. It was not the custom of ancient historians to quote their sources; they refer to them only now and then in cases of doubt and difficulty. Schwegler's assertion, therefore, that Livy and Dionysius made no immediate use of them, is groundless, because it is impossible for anybody to say whether they did so or not.

Schwegler asserts in a note [1] that neither Livy nor Dionysius ever mentions the Annales Maximi; which may be true *literally*—that is, they are not found quoted under that precise name. But we have already produced passages from those authors which can have been derived from no other source. Schwegler then proceeds to adduce several passages from Livy (viz. ii. 54, iii. 23, iv. 20, iv. 23, iv. 34, vii. 21, viii. 18, xxxiii. 8), in which *annales* are mentioned, and denies that in any one of them the pontifical annals can be meant. That this is the case in the greater part of these passages we admit, but there are two of them in which we take it to be impossible that Livy can have been alluding to the *literary* annals of Fabius Pictor, Cincius Alimentus, and their successors. One of these is the following:—"Qui si in ea re sit error" (viz. that Cornelius Cossus was a Tribunus militum) "quod tam veteres annales quodque magistratuum libri, quos linteos in aede repositos Monetae Macer Licinius citat identidem auctores, nono post demum anno cum T. Quinctio Penno, A. Cornelium Cossum consulem habeant, existimatio communis omnibus est" (iv. 20). Now here, as in a case before adduced, the *annales* alluded to being again coupled with the Magistratuum Libri, being again placed before them in the order of precedence, and therefore, we may presume, of importance, and being further characterised by the very strong epithet "tam veteres," it is impossible to imagine that the annals of Fabius or Cincius can have been meant, and

[1] R. S. Anm. 4.

we are consequently driven to one of two conclusions: either that Livy must be here referring to the Annales Maximi, or at all events that there must have been other annals long antecedent to the time of Fabius, and the other reputed first literary annalists.

The following instance (from Lib. xxviii. 8) we take to be still more decisive. The story is this. C. Valerius Flaccus having obtained the office of Flamen Dialis, insisted on an ancient right attached to that priesthood of entering the Senate. But the Prætor, L. Licinius, ejected him, affirming that the law was not to be determined by examples that had become obsolete through the high antiquity of the annals which contained them—"non exoletis vetustate annalium exemplis stare jus voluit"—but by recent usage and custom; and that no Flamen Dialis had enjoyed the right in the memory of their fathers or grandfathers. Now this dispute occurred in the consulship of Q. Fulvius Flaccus in B.C. 209. Fabius and Cincius, the first literary Roman annalists, only flourished about this time. Licinius therefore could not possibly have been alluding to their annals, since those which he cites must have been at least a century older, going back beyond his grandfather. Besides, it would have been an absurdity to quote a literary history on a point of constitutional law, and not some authentic state-document. Licinius must therefore have been alluding either to the Annales Maximi, or at all events to the Commentarii Pontificum, which, as we shall show further on, were another documentary source of Roman history.

It is true that this example cannot be made, by strict demonstration, to carry us up beyond the Gallic conflagration; but it reaches demonstrably to within eighty years of it, and is therefore, at all events, a refutation of Sir G. C. Lewis's opinion that there was no *recorded*, and consequently no authentic, history before the time of Fabius.[1] But, by any

[1] On this subject we may quote the following from Niebuhr:—"We have no reason to deny that history was written at Rome previous to the banishment of the kings."—*Lect.* vol. i. p. 6. And: "The scepticism is contemptible which says that the Romans had no history before the time of Fabius."—Ibid. p. 21.

fair and candid interpretation, the words of Licinius carry us up a century or two higher; for it is not customary to speak of records only a hundred years old as quite obsolete and out of date on account of their antiquity.

But the previous passage respecting Cornelius Cossus carries us certainly higher than the Gallic conflagration. According to Livy, and the authorities which he followed, Cossus, being then a military tribune, but not *consulari potestate*, placed the second Opima Spolia in the Temple of Jupiter Feretrius in the year B.C. 437. But when Augustus Cæsar inspected that temple previously to rebuilding it, he found therein a linen doublet, having on it an inscription respecting the spoils, in which Cossus was styled "consul." In a later edition of his book, Livy deferred to the imperial critic, though not with a very good grace. Augustus had, indeed, a sort of personal interest in the question. In his fourth consulship, M. Crassus slew, with his own hand, Deldo, king of the Bastarnæ. But, though Crassus on this occasion commanded the Roman army, Augustus allowed him not the honour of the Opima Spolia, alleging that the victory belonged to himself as consul, having been achieved under his auspices;[1] against which decision the inscription on the doublet would have been a standing protest, if proof could have been drawn from it that Spolia Opima might be claimed by a subordinate officer.

But this by the way. For our purpose the material point is that an inscription placed in the Temple of Jupiter Feretrius forty-eight years before the Gallic conflagration had been preserved down to the imperial times. It appears further that there were Annals and Libri Magistratuum, quoted by Licinius Macer, from which it appeared, in contradiction of the assertion of Augustus, that Cossus did not become consul till nine years later, or in B.C. 428. These annals must undoubtedly have been contemporary, as may be inferred both from the way in which Livy characterises them—"tam veteres annales"—and from the consideration that he would not have been so silly as to appeal against the authority

[1] Dio Cass. li. 24.

of a contemporary document to annals which were compiled a couple of centuries later.

Among the instances which Schwegler adduces in the same note from Dionysius to show that he does not allude to the Annales Maximi, he omits that which we have already quoted from Lib. iv. 30, where it is hardly possible that anything else can be meant. In the following passage from Lib. i. 73: ἐκ παλαιῶν λόγων ἐν ἱεραῖς δέλτοις σωζομένων, Dionysius rather meant, as we shall see further on, the Commentarii Pontificum than the Annales Maximi. The passage in Lib. i. 74—ἐπὶ τοῦ παρὰ τοῖς Ἀγχισεῦσι κειμένου πίνακος—is corrupt; but whether, with Niebuhr, we should read ἀρχιερεῦσι we will not pretend to determine.

Schwegler proceeds: "Internal as well as external evidence makes it probable that the genuine annals of the pontiffs do not reach beyond the Gallic conflagration, and still less into the regal period." The internal evidence is derived from the alleged confusion and contradiction in the chronology of the regal period, and from its resting on mere combination of numbers, and a subtle system of computation. The chronology we shall have to examine further on, and need not therefore enter into the subject here. The combination of numbers and subtle system of computation arise, as we also hope to show, only from the fanciful views of German critics, and are not found in the ancient authors. But though Schwegler asserts that the genuine annals of the pontiffs do not reach beyond the Gallic conflagration, yet he soon afterwards quotes a passage from Cicero (De Rep. i. 16), in which that author says that an eclipse of the sun was noted down in the Annales Maximi in A.U.C. 350; that is, thirteen years before the capture of the city by the Gauls. And as Schwegler and other German critics use this passage as an argument against the existence of still earlier annals, they must of course consider it to be genuine; otherwise their reasoning is unfounded and absurd. But if this entry is genuine, there can be no reason why entries of much earlier date should not also be genuine: for, if this part of the annals had escaped the fire, the whole might have been saved. Moreover, we have already shown[1] that annals of some sort must have been extant in B.C. 449, or fifty-nine years before the Gallic conflagration; since they are quoted as furnishing a precedent for the driving of a nail by the dictator Quinctilius in B.C. 331.

Schwegler, however, ignores this evidence for the existence of annals before the conflagration, founding his argument, or rather we should say, his conjecture, on the other side on a mistranslation of Livy. "It cannot be reasonably doubted," he observes, "that the wooden tablets on which the Annals of the Pontifices were written perished in the Gallic conflagration. They were kept in the dwelling of the Pontifex Maximus,—that is, in the Regia, and in the hasty evacuation of the city were assuredly not saved; since even the sacred utensils of the Temple of Vesta could be preserved only by burying them."

This view, wrong and absurd as it is, has been adopted by all, or most, of the leading German critics; as Niebuhr, Becker, and others. Niebuhr remarks:[2]—

"Now I grant Antonius in Cicero says that this custom" (viz. of making annals) "had subsisted from the beginning of the Roman state: but it does not follow from this that Cicero meant to assert that the annals in possession of the Roman historians, who did not begin to write till so late, reached thus far back. Those of the earlier times may have perished; which Livy and other writers, without specific mention of the Annales Maximi, state as having happened at the destruction of the city by the Gauls: and certainly this fate may have befallen them at that time, as the tables perhaps were not yet transferred into books, and it is still less likely that any transcripts of such books should be in existence; besides they may not have been preserved in the Capitol, where the chief pontiff did not reside, and where he had no occasion to keep his archives like the duumvirs of the Sibylline books.

"I think we may now consider it as certain that those annals really met with such a fate, and that they were replaced by new ones."

[1] Above, p. xvi. [2] Hist. of Rome, vol. I. p. 212 (Eng. Trans.).

Let us advert for a moment to this curious specimen of argumentation, where a conclusion considered as "certain" is deduced from a series of the loosest conjectures. Thus it is said that the earlier annals *may* have perished; that Livy and other writers state this to have happened, but *without specific mention* of the Annales Maximi; that this fate *may* have befallen them, as the tables *perhaps* were not yet transferred into books, and it is *still less likely* that any transcripts of them were in existence; besides, they *may not* have been preserved in the Capitol. From which series of conjectures follow the very satisfactory conclusion that it may now be considered *as certain* " those annals really met with such a fate!"

But our main object in citing this passage is to show that Niebuhr was of opinion that the Pontifex Maximus noted down the events which formed his Annals at once, and in the first instance, on an album or whitened board; that these boards were kept year after year in the Regia, and consequently at the time of the Gallic fire, supposing that they began with the reign of Tullus Hostilius, would have amounted to nearly 300, or many cartloads; and, as they had never been copied into a book, and were too cumbersome to carry away, were then burnt.

To the same purpose Becker remarks:[1] "If the assumption of the existence of these annals in the earliest times, and especially in the regal period, is destitute of all probability, then Cicero's assertion, that they existed *ab initio rerum Romanarum*, becomes almost an impossibility by the fate which must and would have overtaken these tables. They were kept, according to the unanimous testimony of authors, in the dwelling of the Pontifex Maximus,—that is, in the Regia, hard by the Temple of Vesta on the Forum. We cannot suppose that there were any copies of them. The Regia was the only record-office at Rome; except, perhaps, that some religious corporations may have recorded a few things in separate commentaries. Now, even if we had no historical testimony to the fact, it would be very natural that

[1] Rom. Alterth. B. I. S. 7.

this ponderous history should have been destroyed in the Gallic fire. It is not to be conceived that in the hasty evacuation of the city any thought was taken for their preservation. In the midst of that panic the sacred utensils of Vesta's Temple were saved only by burying them; and it may even be doubted whether the Twelve Tables, that dearly purchased and most important monument, were not abandoned as a prey. Still less would those wooden tables have been thought of; and that they were not, that the chronicle of the city was then destroyed, is decisively recognised by some authors."

On this we may remark: first, that even had the Annales Maximi existed only on a quantity of boards, it by no means follows that they would have been destroyed by the Gauls; since, as a professed topographer like Becker should have known, the Regia was not burnt on that occasion, but existed till the fire in Nero's reign, when the destruction of that ancient monument is expressly recorded by Tacitus.[1]

But, secondly: although Niebuhr, Becker, Schwegler, and other German critics often accuse Cicero and Livy of not understanding their own language, yet their view of the history of the Annales Maximi—the egregious absurdity of which might, one would have supposed, have caused them to pause and inquire a little further—is founded on a gross mistranslation of a common Latin construction. Cicero, describing the manner of making the Annals, in the passage already quoted, uses the words, "Res omnes singulorum annorum mandabat literis (Pontifex) efferebatque in album:" that is, first of all he wrote the events down, and then transferred, or posted them, into an album. It is singular how such great critics should have missed the sense of so simple a passage. Two acts are plainly signified, as we see by the enclitic *que*: first the events were noted in a book kept by Pontifex, and were thence copied out into the album, for public inspection. The word *effero* admits no other mode of construing. To make this plain, we will cite from Livy[2] another passage, in

[1] Ann. xv. 41. [2] Lib. I. 32.

which it is similarly used: "Omnia en, *ex commentariis regis pontificem in Album data proponere in publico jubet*," where the matters in the album are posted (*data*) out of the commentaries of Numa.

Thus the conjectures and assumptions of these critics about the existence of cartloads of wooden tables, and about the non-existence of a copy of their contents, fall at once to the ground. The ponderous record is reduced to a portable volume or two, much more easily to be saved than the utensils of Vesta's Temple, and which, according to the best testimony of antiquity, *were saved*.

Becker, however, asserts that their destruction is "*decisively recognised*" by some writers. But those who have only glanced into Becker's books know that the worse case he has the more bold and confident—we had almost said arrogant— are his assertions. The chief writer whom he adduces in support of his view is Livy, in the well-known passage in Lib. vi. 1: "Et quod etiamsi quæ in Commentariis Pontificum aliisque publicis privatisque erant monumentis, incensa urbe pleraque interiere." In examining this passage we will quote Sir G. C. Lewis's remarks upon it. He is also of opinion that the Annales Maximi perished in the conflagration, though he does not appear to have thought that they were written only on wooden tablets.

"Livy tells us," says the author just mentioned,[1] "that most of the early records perished at this time; and if there was so important an exception as a complete series of contemporary national annals, he could scarcely fail to mention it. Hence Goettling, in his History of the Roman Constitution, expresses his opinion that the Annales Maximi were not preserved for the period antecedent to this event. It is even conjectured by Becker, in his work on Roman Antiquities, that the original brazen plates on which the laws of the Twelve Tables were engraved perished in this conflagration and ruin, and that the copy afterwards set up was a restoration. If a record of so enduring a nature as the Twelve

[1] Credibility of the Early Roman History, vol. 1. p. 158.

Tables did not survive this calamity, it is not likely the more perishable annals of the pontiffs should have weathered the storm."[1]

Sir G. C. Lewis is generally a closer reasoner than the German critics, in whose method it is truly wonderful how soon a mere conjecture, or series of conjectures, becomes a certainty, as in the specimen already given from Niebuhr. In a similar manner Sir G. C. Lewis here adopts Becker's *conjecture* that the brazen plates of the Twelve Tables were destroyed, and then proceeds to argue, that *if* a record of so enduring a nature *did not* survive, it is not likely that the more perishable annals survived. Where, letting alone the bad logic, we might ask why should not a portable book—and Sir G. C. Lewis seems to think that they were first entered in a book[2] —have as good, or better, chance of escape as a quantity of brazen tablets, fixed most probably on a wall, and difficult to be detached?

Sir G. C. Lewis thinks that, had the Annales Maximi been saved, Livy would not have failed to say so. We think the contrary view the more probable one,—that had they been lost he would assuredly have mentioned it. In the passage in question Livy is enumerating the *losses* by the fire; and, though he instances the Commentarii Pontificum, he says nothing about the Annales Maximi, a much more important document. The natural inference is, that they were saved. And it would have been supererogatory to mention a fact which must have been notorious to every Roman.

From what has been said, it appears that Becker's assertion that the destruction of the Annals is *decisively* recognised ("mit Entschiedenheit") by some authors, is at all events not applicable to Livy. And what else can be produced in support of his view? Only two passages from Plutarch, one of

[1] Yet in another place (vol. I. p. 112), Sir G. C. Lewis is of opinion that at least the authentic text was preserved.

[2] He does not expressly say so; but we infer from his description of the making of them that such was his conception: viz. that the Pontifex Maximus "used to commit all the events of each year *to writing*, to *inscribe them* on a whitened tablet, and to exhibit *this* record in his house" (p. 155), where the words *write* and *inscribe* seem to refer to two distinct acts.

which is an appeal to this very chapter of Livy, and therefore adds nothing to the evidence, for we can interpret Livy for ourselves. We shall only observe on it that Plutarch, by the use of the word ὑπομνηματισμούς, seems, like ourselves, to have construed Livy as referring only to the Commentarii and not the Annales. The other passage runs as follows:[1] Κλώδιός τις ἐν Ἐλέγχῳ χρόνων (οὕτω γάρ πως ἐπιγέγραπται τὸ βιβλίον) ἰσχυρίζεται τὰς μὲν ἀρχαίας ἐκείνας ἀναγραφὰς ἐν τοῖς Κελτικοῖς πάθεσι τῆς πόλεως ἠφανίσθαι· τὰς δὲ νῦν φαινομένας οὐκ ἀληθῶς συγκεῖσθαι, κ. τ. λ. But it is not certain that this Clodius, whom Plutarch mentions so disparagingly as some obscure writer (Κλώδιός τις), is speaking of the Annales Maximi; for these annals would hardly have entered into any question about the genealogy of Numa. Clodius was more probably speaking of the Commentarii Pontificum, which, as we shall show further on, contained a history of the city from the earliest times; and which, or the greater part of them, were no doubt burnt at the capture of the city, though they were afterwards probably restored so well as it could be done. But of this by and by.

The testimony of this obscure Clodius is eagerly grasped at by the critics, and especially by Sir G. C. Lewis. It is astounding what these sceptical critics will believe, provided only it can be turned against the received history. Sir G. C. Lewis, who refers the account of Clodius to the Annales Maximi, actually thinks it possible that so important a public document as these annals, extending over centuries, and always exhibited in public, might be forged with impunity and success. He observes:[2] "The account of the discovery of the books of Numa in a stone chest in the year 181 B.C. proves indubitably that documents on the most important subjects could be forged at that time with the hope of successful deceit, and be attributed to the ancient kings. The circumstances attending this supposed discovery, and its treatment by the Senate, are conclusive evidence that it was a deliberate imposture. Considering the reverence in which Numa and his ordinances respecting religion were held by the

[1] De Fortun. Rom. 13.   [2] Vol. i. p. 167.

Romans of this period, we may be certain the Senate would not have caused the books to be burnt, if their forgery had not been placed out of all doubt."[1]

Never was a bad argument supported by a more unfortunate example. No doubt the pretended books of Numa were "a deliberate imposture." No doubt, also, that the Senate was satisfied of the imposture when it caused them to be burnt. But what does all this prove? Why, that documents on the most important subjects, though they might be forged at that time, as they may at any time, with the *hope* of success, yet that the hope, as the event proved, was very ill founded. And if the forgery of some isolated books failed of success, how much more difficult would it have been to forge the whole annals of a nation! It was a plausible contrivance to dig up Numa's books on the spot where he was supposed to have been buried, nor would their contents have interfered with tradition, or with the pretensions of family pride. But how should those bulky annals, which ultimately, we are told, filled eighty volumes, have been suddenly brought before the public with any plausible account of their preservation and discovery? Or how should they have stood the test of other historical documents, such, for instance, as family memoirs, some of which reached to a very high antiquity? He who believes such a forgery could be successfully accomplished, believes a much more incredible thing than the preservation of the annals.

Schwegler, who is also of opinion that the Annales Maximi had been falsified, supports his view by observing that the fragment preserved by Gellius[2] betrays "a tolerably recent origin," and adds in a note: "As this fragment occurred in the eleventh book, it must have belonged to a rather early time, and therefore, as Becker justly remarks,[3] the smooth *senarius*, 'Malum consultum consultori pessimum est,' is all the more striking. In genuine annals of that time, a rude Saturnian verse could at most have existed." But it does not follow from the words of Gellius that the verse was in the

---

[1] See Livy, xl. 20; Plin. H. N. xiii. 27.   [2] S. 11, Ann. 10.
[3] Röm. Alterth. L 10, Anm. 4.

Annals. The passage runs as follows: "Tunc igitur quod in Etruscos haruspices male consultantes animadversum vindicatumque fuerat, versus hic scite factus cantatusque esse a pueris urbe tota fertur,

"'Malum consultum consultori pessimum est.'

Ea historia de haruspicibus, ac de versu isto senario, scripta est in Annalibus Maximis libro, undecimo, et in Verrii Flacci libro primo Rerum memoria dignarum." The story, then, had two sources, the annals and the work of Verrius Flaccus. The account of the haruspices, who, to the supposed detriment of the city, had directed the statue of Cocles to be placed in a lower position, was no doubt found in the annals; but that a public record of the driest kind should have contained verses is altogether incredible. This part of the story Verrius must have taken from another source, and probably modernised the verse in the transfer.

Another point to which the sceptical critics attach great importance, as showing the non-existence of the annals at a remote date, is the first registration of an eclipse of the sun. This point is urged, after Niebuhr, by Becker, Schwegler, and Sir G. C. Lewis. We subjoin what the last-named writer says:[1]

"There is likewise another argument against the existence of a complete series of the Annales Maximi from a remote date, upon which Niebuhr not undeservedly lays great stress. Ennius, as quoted by Cicero, spoke of an eclipse of the sun about the year 350 U.C. assigning its natural cause; namely, the interposition of the moon. 'Now,' says Cicero,[2] 'there is so much science and skill in this matter, that from this day, which we perceive to be recorded in Ennius, *and in the Annales Maximi*, all the preceding eclipses have been calculated backwards, up to that which occurred on the Nones of Quinctilis in the reign of Romulus, when Romulus was really slain in the darkness, though he was fabled to have been taken up to heaven.' Assuming the year 350 U.C. to correspond to the year 404 B.C.—fourteen years before the

[1] Vol. i. p. 159.   [2] De Rep. i. 16; cf. ii. 10.

capture of the city—it would follow that there was no contemporary registration of eclipses before that year; and we observe from this very passage of Cicero that in this year an eclipse of the sun was recorded in the Annales Maximi. Eclipses, moreover, are particularly specified in the fragment of Cato the Censor—an ancient and unimpeachable witness to such a fact—as among the prominent contents of the pontifical annals; and, indeed, without any specific testimony, we might safely assume that a prodigy so rare and so alarming as a visible eclipse, and one necessarily followed by national expiatory ceremonies, would be duly entered in this public record.

"Unluckily, however, in this, as in other instances, we feel sensibly the defective state of our information respecting a point of early history. We have not the entire passage of Ennius as cited by Cicero, and we cannot ascertain to what year he alludes. According to the Varronian era, the year 350 U.C. would correspond to the year 404 B.C.; but we do not know what era Ennius followed. In another part of his Annales, he spoke of the 700th year after the building of the city, though, according to the Varronian date, he wrote about the year 582."

"Niebuhr thinks that the allusion is to a solar eclipse, visible in the Mediterranean, which occurred on the 21st of June, in the astronomical year 399 B.C. This eclipse, however, was not visible at Rome, though at Cadiz the middle of the eclipse fell three minutes before sunset. Niebuhr believes that the Romans derived information from Gades of the day and hour when it occurred, and that this eclipse, visible at the extremity of Spain, but invisible in Italy, is the eclipse alluded to by Ennius."

"If this event had occurred during the Second Punic War, it would be conceivable that the Romans might have had precise information respecting the circumstances of an eclipse which was only just visible at Gades; but that in the year 399 B.C. during the siege of Veii, nine years before the Gallic invasion, they should have known and thought so much about an eclipse in that place as to afford the subject of an allusion to Ennius more than two centuries afterwards, is utterly incredible. The Romans did not obtain a footing in Spain, or acquire any accurate knowledge of it, until after the First Punic war. No allusion to an eclipse of the sun about the year 350 U.C. occurs in any of the historians, and therefore it seems impossible to fix the year of the eclipse to which Ennius alludes.

"Thus much, however, we may infer from the passage in Cicero,—namely, that the eclipses which had taken place at Rome in the first centuries of the city, had not been recorded in the pontifical annals, or in any other register, and that before the time of Cicero some attempts had been made, with such rude processes as the ancient astronomers were possessed of, to calculate these unregistered eclipses backwards. That the computation was not a scientific one may be inferred from the attempt to calculate the year in which the eclipse of Romulus occurred—an event wholly fabulous, and apparently not admitted into the most current version of the story of his death or apotheosis."

In this view of the matter Sir G. C. Lewis blindly follows his German guides, who have misled him partly by not giving a full and fair account of it, and partly, as in a former instance, by mistranslating a common Latin sentence. Had Sir G. C. Lewis turned to the chapter of Cicero which he quotes (De Rep. i. 16), he would have seen that the German critics have suppressed a very material part of it. Cicero there alludes to an eclipse which terrified the Athenians in the Peloponnesian war, in the lifetime of Pericles,[1] who is said to have dissipated their alarm by explaining to them the true nature of the phenomenon, which he had learnt from his teacher Anaxagoras. The eclipse at Athens appears to have taken place in the first year of the war, or B.C. 431.; that at Rome, as we have seen, in B.C. 404, according to the received chronology; or, if this chronology should have to be reduced according to a principle which will be explained in the sequel, some ten years later. Thus it appears that a phenomenon which first became commonly understood at Athens

[1] It seems to be the eclipse mentioned by Thucydides, ii. 28.

in B.C. 431, began to be known at Rome some twenty-eight or thirty-eight years later.

Now here we have a very natural explanation why this should have been the first eclipse recorded, in its true nature *as an eclipse*, in the Annales Maximi. Previous eclipses could not have been recorded, because they were not known to be such. But the matter being now reduced, as Cicero says, "to science and skill," previous eclipses could be reckoned backwards to that which happened at the death of Romulus. Before this time, eclipses could not have been *predicted* by the Romans, because the theory of them was not understood. Hence they would often have passed unobserved, especially when partial, and even total ones when the weather was cloudy; and, when observed, the phenomenon would not have been attributed to its right cause, nor called by its right name, but would have been ascribed to a cloud, or to some unknown cause. Thus, while Cicero attributes the darkness at the death of Romulus to an eclipse, Livy,[1] following no doubt the old annals, ascribes it to a storm.

This view is corroborated by the passage from Cato, which these critics mistranslate: "Non lubet scribere quod in tabula apud Pontificem Maximum est, quotiens annona cara, quotiens lunae, aut solis lumini caligo aut quid obstiterit."[2] These words do not mean, as Niebuhr and Sir G. C. Lewis represent, that the Pontifex Maximus recorded *eclipses* of the sun. Their literal meaning is: "I do not like to write such things as we see in the tablet of the Pontifex Maximus; as when corn was dear, *or when a darkness, or something or another*, intercepted the light of the moon or sun." The mistranslation is the more unpardonable, as Gellius proceeds to remark: "So little did Cato care to know or tell the true causes of the obscuration of the sun and moon" ("Usque adeo parvi fecit rationes veras solis et lunae deficientium vel scire vel dicere").

Now let us observe that this rude and unscientific mode of noting eclipses could hardly have been used after their true nature was understood at Rome,—that is, after the year

[1] Lib. i. 16.   [2] Orig. ap. Gell. II. 21.

B.C. 403; and Cato, therefore, must be referring to entries in the annals made previously to that date, which he selected apparently for their ignorance and uncouthness. The year mentioned by Cicero as that of the first scientific record of eclipses in the Annales Maximi ascends thirteen years above the Gallic capture; and, as Cicero says that he had seen this entry with his own eyes—" quem diem in Maximis Annalibus consignatum *vidimus*"—we have here another proof, in addition to those already cited from the same author, that the annals survived the conflagration. But the passage from Cato, for the reason assigned, carries us up to a much earlier period, and confirms the existence of very early Annales Maximi, by one of those traits of careless truth which it is impossible to invent; namely, that no eclipses were recorded in them before the year mentioned, for the simple reason that the theory of them was not understood; and therefore, when the darkness which they occasioned was observed, it was attributed to "something or another" unknown.

We need not discuss Niebuhr's notion that the eclipse alluded to by Cicero may have been one partially visible at Cadiz. No critic out of Germany would imagine that the Romans would have recorded an eclipse which they had not seen, even allowing it to be possible that they might have heard of it. But if, as we shall attempt to show further on, the Roman year consisted for a long period of only ten months, then the eclipse must be sought at a later time than that mentioned.

We have already remarked, with regard to Schwegler's assertion that we do not find in the historians any trace of the direct use of the annals, that it is impossible to say whether they used them *directly* or not. But we may affirm, without fear of contradiction, that there are numberless passages in the historians which must either have been taken directly from the annals, or at all events from earlier writers who had so taken them. The account of the treaty with the Albans in the reign of Tullus Hostilius,[1] which gives the

---

[1] Livy, i. 24.

names of the Fetialis and of the Pater Patratus, could hardly have been derived from any other source. In like manner, we find the names of the Albans who were made patricians.[1] Another proof is the prodigies recorded in the regal period and before the burning of the city.[2] Further, the accounts of pestilences, famines, droughts, dearness of provisions, and other matters which affect the domestic life of the city, which occur in the first five books down to the Gallic conflagration, and through the remainder of the decade, prove that the Annales Maximi, the proper register of such casualties, must have continued extant. There are more pestilences and famines recorded in Livy's first decade than in any of the rest, and nearly half of them occur in the first five books. Thus we read of pestilences in the reign of Tullus Hostilius, and in B.C. 463; in one accompanied with famine, which occurred in B.C. 453, the names of several distinguished persons who died of it are recorded; as Ser. Cornelius, the Flamen Quirinalis, Horatius Pulvillus, an augur, the Consul Quinctilius, and three tribunes of the people.[3] Such particulars could not have been preserved but by contemporary registration. It would be monstrous to suppose that Roman annalists made them out of their own heads two or three centuries afterwards. Such barefaced forgeries in an age that had little or no literature, and when consequently nothing was to be gained by them, cannot for a moment be supposed.

It is not very material whether Verrius Flaccus was or was not the last who had the Annales Maximi in his hands; for, as that writer lived in the age of Augustus, they would at all events have survived long enough for the purposes of authentic history. But we do not see how this opinion can be reconciled with the following passage from Pliny: " Invenitur statua decreta et Turaciæ Gaiæ, sive Suffetiæ, virgini vestali, ut poneretur ubi vellet; quod adjectum non minus

---

[1] Livy, l. 30.
[2] Ibid. i. 31, 55, 56; ii. 7, 42; iii. 5, 10, 29; iv. 21, &c. Others also in Dionysius. Yet Niebuhr asserts (Lectures, vol. i. p. 16) that "no prodigies are mentioned by Livy before the burning of the city by the Gauls!"
[3] Livy, iii. 32: cf. l. 31; ii. 9, 34; iii. 6; iv. 21, 25, 30; v. 13; vii. 1, 2, &c.

honoris habet, quod feminæ esse decretam. Meritum ejus in ipsis ponam Annalium verbis: Quod campum Tiberinum gratificata esset ea populo."[1] To quote the *ipsissima verba* of the decree would have been absurd had not Pliny taken them for some official source. Aulus Gellius also mentions that the name of Caia Tarratia appeared "in antiquis annalibus."[2] On the whole, the Annales Maximi having been edited and published, there seems to be no good reason why they may not have existed till a late period of the empire; and they were evidently seen by Servius.

The Annales Maximi would have established the leading historical facts of the regal period; the names of the kings and their order of succession, at all events from the time of Tullus Hostilius, and the principal events of their reigns. We will grant that they would not have sufficed to make any perfect history; nor have we any perfect history. The chronology would have been confused, because there would have been nothing to distinguish the different years of a reign, subsequently so well marked by the annual consulship. From this circumstance Schwegler has been led to conclude that registration did not begin till the time of the republic; but in fact this amended chronology is only the natural consequence of the altered form of government. The true inference lies the other way. The fact that we have the names of the consuls registered immediately on the establishment of the republic affords good ground for inferring that registration was still more ancient; that it was nothing but the continuation of a practice before observed under the kings, but rendered more conspicuous through its chronological definition by the annually elected consuls.

Besides the Annales Maximi, another source of history was the books kept by the subordinate pontiffs, called Commentarii Pontificum. Vopiscus alludes to the Pontifices being the regular historiographers of the city, as follows: "Quod post excessum Romuli, novello adhuc Romanæ urbis imperio, factum, pontifices, penes quos scribendæ historiæ potestas fuit, in literas retulerunt, ut interregnum, dum post bonum

[1] H. N. xxxiv. 11. [2] Lib. vi. 7, 1.

principem bonus alius quæritur, iniretur."[1] Vopiscus cannot here allude to the Annales Maximi, to which the name of history cannot be appropriately given; nor was the making of those annals intrusted to the Pontifices generally, but only to the Pontifex Maximus. Nor would the Annales Maximi have recorded the interregnum after the death of Romulus, because there was no pontificate, and consequently no contemporary record, till the time of Numa at least.

We will now endeavour to show that the Commentarii Pontificum were not only history, but also retrospective history.

Canuleius, in a speech to the plebs A.U.C. 310, says: "Obsecro vos, si non ad fastos, non ad Commentarios Pontificum admittimur; ne ea quidem scimus, quæ omnes peregrini etiam sciunt? consules in locum regum successisse? nec aut juris aut majestatis quicquam habere quod non in regibus ante fuerit."[2] He then proceeds to instance a great many facts of Roman history up to the time of Romulus. "Do we not know," he says, "that the kings were succeeded by consuls who inherited their prerogative; that Numa Pompilius was not only no patrician, but not even a Roman citizen; that L. Tarquinius was a Corinthian, Servius Tullius the son of a captive? &c. Do we not know all this, although we plebeians are not admitted to the Commentarii Pontificum?" which must therefore have been substantially a Roman history; and a retrospective one, as they entered into the genealogy of Numa. And though the plebeians were not allowed to see these commentaries, the facts no doubt transpired through the patricians: the principal ones, it appears, were known even to foreigners, and must therefore have been familiar to the great body of the Roman citizens.

Passages in Dionysius also show that these commentaries were both historical and retrospective. "The Romans," says that writer,[3] "have not a single ancient historian, or prose author; but, from ancient accounts preserved in their sacred books (ἐν ἱεραῖς δέλτοις), each of their writers formed his narrative." The "sacred books" here mentioned could have been no other than Commentarii Pontificum alluded to by

[1] Vit. Tac. 1.   [2] Liv. iv. 3.   [3] Lib. i. 73.

Canuleius. The account of Dionysius shows that they contained the Latin traditions concerning the descent of Romulus; a subject to which we shall have occasion to revert in the body of this work. Nor can it be doubted that Dionysius is referring to the same work, under the name of αἱ τῶν ἱεροφαντῶν γραφαί, as recording the apparition of the goddess Fortune;[1] and also under the name of βίβλοι ἱεραὶ καὶ ἀπόθετοι, when he quotes them on a question whether there were consuls or military tribunes.[2] In the last case Schwegler[3] takes him to mean the Libri Lintei; but these were neither sacred nor secret.

The German critics have not rightly apprehended the nature of these books: as, for instance, when Niebuhr says that they were an exposition of the early Roman constitution related in law cases;[4] or when Becker describes them as containing all that concerned, immediately or remotely, the Pontifices themselves and their office;[5] or when Schwegler characterises them as a collection of cases out of the old political and sacerdotal law, with the decisions of the Pontifices,—in short, a collection of precedents, which served as general rules of law for judges.[6] Sir G. C. Lewis also regards them in the same light. "The conjecture," he observes,[7] "which Niebuhr makes as to the contents of these books is probably not far from the truth: 'We can only conceive them,' he says, 'to have been collections of traditions, decisions, and decrees, laying down principles of law by reporting particular cases.'"

That civil and religious usages were noted in the Commentarii Pontificum we do not mean to deny. We see from Pliny that they contained a precept for taking the Augurium Canarium; "Ita enim est in Commentariis Pontificum: augurio canario agendo dies constituatur, priusquam

[1] Lib. viii. 56.   [2] Lib. xi. 62.   [3] R. I. S. 17, Anm. 1.
[4] Vorträge über Röm. Gesch. ap. Schwegler, R. I. S. 33, Anm. 8.
[5] "Die Pontifices noch besondere Bücher führten, in denen sie alles aufzeichneten, was in näherem oder entfernterem Bezuge auf sie und ihr Amt geschah."—Röm. Alterth. i. S. 12.
[6] Röm. Gesch. B. I S. 33.   [7] Credibility, &c. vol. i. p. 171.

frumenta vaginis exeant, et antequam in vaginas perveniant."[1] But, though such notices may occasionally occur, Becker seems right in remarking that the Commentarii are quoted *for facts*, while from the Libri Pontificii—a distinct work—only religious propositions are adduced.[2] Facts, for instance, like the following are not likely to have been found in a mere collection of legal rules and precedents: "(Possumus suspicari disertum) Tib. Coruncanium, quod ex Pontificum Commentariis longe plurimum ingenio valuisse videatur" (Cic. Brut. 14, 55): "Habetis in commentariis vestris C. Cassium Censorem de signo Concordiæ dedicando ad pontificum collegium retulisse, ei M. Æmilium Pontificem Maximum, pro collegio respondisse" (*Idem*, Pro Dom. 53, 136). In fact, the very name *commentarius* seems to indicate something more than a book of precedents, for, as Sir G. C. Lewis remarks:[3] "*Commentaries* means a memoir, memorial, note, or memorandum. Hence it may be applied to historical memoirs, such as those of Julius Cæsar, whose two works are entitled *Commentarii*. And in this sense it is equivalent to the Greek ὑπομνήματα."

But the strongest proof that the Commentarii Pontificum contained historical matter may be drawn from the fact that Livy names them first in enumerating the sources of history destroyed by the Gallic fire. He is explaining—we might almost say making a sort of apology—how he had included the history of the city down to its burning by the Gauls in only five books; which he ascribes to the obscurity naturally attaching to great antiquity, and to the rarity of literary documents in those early ages. "These," he observes, "whether contained in the Commentarii Pontificum, or in other public or private monuments, for the most part perished when the city was burnt." ("Et quod etiamsi quæ (literæ) in Commentariis Pontificum aliisque publicis privatisque erant monumentis, incensa urbe pleræque interiere," Lib. vi. 1.) These com-

---

[1] H. N. viii. 3, 3.
[2] "Wenigstens ist es auffallend dass aus den Libris Pontificiis nur religiöse Satzungen angeführt, die Commentarii nur in Bezug auf Thatsachen genannt werden."—S. 12, Anm. 18.   [3] Vol. i, p. 169, note 125.

mentaries are here specifically named and put prominently forward as one of the principal sources for the early history, thus confirming the testimony of Vopiscus, with which we headed this branch of the inquiry.

This account suggests one or two reflections, and the first and most important is, that the history of Rome down to its burning by the Gauls *did not rest on oral tradition*. The principal events had been recorded: first, on their occurrence, in the journal of the Pontifex Maximus, or the Annales Maximi; and secondly, they had been afterwards reduced to a more regular historical form by the other pontifices.

Before proceeding further, we will turn for a moment to what Sir G. C. Lewis says respecting the materials for early Roman history. "We have," he observes,[1] "in the three preceding chapters, attempted to ascertain what were the materials for the formation of a narrative of early Roman history at the command of Fabius Pictor, Cincius, and Cato when they began to write their accounts of that period in the Second Punic War. We have found that there was a continuous list of annual magistrates more or less complete and authentic, ascending to the commencement of the consular government; that from the burning of the city there was a series of meagre official annals kept by the chief pontiffs; that many ancient treaties and texts of law—including the laws of the Twelve Tables—were preserved; together with notes of ancient usages and rules of customary law—both civil and religious—recorded in the books of the pontiffs and some of the civil magistrates; and that these documentary sources of history, which furnished merely the dry skeleton of a narrative, were clothed with flesh and muscle by the addition of various stories handed down from preceding times by oral tradition. Some assistance may have been derived from popular songs, and still more from family memoirs; but there is nothing to show or make it probable that private families began to record the deeds of their distinguished

[1] Vol. I. ch. vii. p. 243.

members before any chronicler had arisen for the events which interested the commonwealth as a whole.

"The essential characteristic of the history of the first four and a half centuries of Rome—so far as it deserves the name of history, and is a veracious relation of real events—is, that it was not reduced into a narrative form by contemporary writers, but that the account of it was drawn up at a later period from such fragmentary materials as we have just described."

In examining this passage we will confine ourselves to what is said about the Annales Maximi and the Commentarii Pontificum. It is supposed that the first of these were not extant higher than the burning of the city; that the Commentaries of the priests were nothing but "notes of ancient usages and rules of customary law;" that the history had not been "reduced into a narrative form by contemporary writers," but that such a narrative was first framed at a later period—that is, in the time of Fabius Pictor, Cincius, and Cato—from the fragmentary materials described, and by adding to them various stories handed down by oral tradition.

Now, we submit that this account of the matter is totally at variance with all that can be gathered from ancient testimony. We have shown that evidence almost unanimously favours the preservation of the Annales Maximi; that only one insinuation from an obscure writer mentioned by Plutarch can be produced against it; and that even this insinuation more probably refers to the Commentarii than to the Annales. We have also shown from the testimony of Livy and Dionysius that the Commentaries were something more than notes of ancient usages, for in that case how could Canuleius have adverted to them as containing the facts of Roman history? Or how could Livy have set them down as the principal authority for it? Or Dionysius have quoted them for the history of the foundation of the city? There is no ground, therefore, for the assertion that the history had not been reduced into a narrative form by contemporary, or at all events very early writers, though not for the purpose of publication. Everything tends to show that the Pontifices had commenced a connected historical narrative soon after their institution, and at least in the time of Tullus Hostilius, so that the only reigns which rested upon oral tradition would have been those of Romulus, and partly perhaps of Numa. And this period of about half a century was so recent that the description of it by the Pontifices may almost be called contemporary, since it was not beyond the memory of man, but well within the period fixed by Sir G. C. Lewis and others as the limit of authentic oral tradition.

Well, then, if the principal affairs down to the burning of the city had been recorded in writing, the oral tradition of which Sir G. C. Lewis speaks as forming the chief foundation for the narratives of the first literary annalists would have taken its date from that catastrophe, and not from the time when the events occurred; so that oral tradition would have been responsible for less than two centuries, instead, for instance, of three centuries up to the expulsion of the kings, or four centuries and a half up to the reign of Tullus Hostilius. But can it be believed that a people which had a connected history of their affairs in writing down to the burning of their city, should have made no attempt to restore it while it was fresh in their minds? that a nation so proud of its former glories should have suffered them to sink into oblivion, or, what is about the same thing, should have intrusted them to oral tradition alone, although they still continued to record in writing the events which occurred after the fire? and that they should do this, although they were at the greatest pains to recover their domestic laws and their foreign treaties, and even published some of them for general use?[1] Or could these laws and these treaties have been fully understood unless illustrated by some narrative setting forth the occasions of them?

Fortunately, however, we are not reduced to an appeal to probability in support of the assumption that the Pontifices

[1] "Imprimis foederis ac leges (erant autem ex duodecim tabulis et quaedam regiae leges) conquiri, quae comparerent, jusserunt: alia ex iis edita etiam in vulgus."—Liv. vi. 1.

restored the history. The passage in Dionysius, to which we have already referred [1] as taken from "the sacred books," exhibits them as tracing the descent of Romulus and relating occurrences before the building of the city. Dionysius, it is true, does not quote them directly, or from personal inspection, but he says that the Roman historians of later times took their accounts from these books. They must, therefore, have named them as their sources, which is as satisfactory evidence of their existence, and of the nature of their contents, as if Dionysius himself had quoted them at first hand.

We are willing, however, to allow all due force to the objection that books thus restored from memory were not of equal value with the originals as historical memorials; and this circumstance may even have lent a colour to the charge of that "certain Clodius" that the books so restored were altogether false and forged. We will even concede that the Pontifices may have used the opportunity to introduce a few apocryphal stories to the advantage of Roman glory and of their own priestcraft, and especially that it may have been on this occasion that the story of the descent of Romulus from Æneas was introduced; though, at the same time, the true account was faithfully recorded of his having been the son, or grandson, of some Greek who had landed on the coast. But of this we shall have to speak in the sequel. In spite, however, of a few interpolations of this sort, it may be presumed that the main outlines of the history were faithfully recorded, so far as memory served. And memory would have been aided, as well as checked, by memorials which had not been destroyed, or which had been recovered; such as the Annales Maximi, laws, treaties, inscriptions, private memoirs, funeral orations, public buildings and monuments, &c. As we learn from a passage in Livy, before quoted, that even foreigners were acquainted with the history of Rome, we may conclude that a knowledge of it was too widely spread and too deeply rooted among the Romans themselves to have admitted any very important alterations. The share, moreover, which the great patrician houses had in the history of

[1] Lib. I. c. 73.

their country would have made them jealous and vigilant critics of the narrative, and thus have prevented the pontifical scribes from deviating very far from the truth.

After all, however, Livy's account of what was lost in the fire is very vague. The phrase "pleræque interiere" may allow of anything short of half, including half the Commentarii, being saved, and we all know with what licence such terms as *more* or *most* are used. Niebuhr observes that Livy's statement on this subject "is only half correct, or rather altogether false, and gives us an erroneous idea of the early history," adding, "When Livy, speaking of the times previous to the burning of the city, says, *per illa tempora litteræ raræ erant*, this is one of those notions in which he was misled by opinions prevalent in his own age, and which are only partially true."[1] When Niebuhr, however, makes Livy say that "*all* written documents were destroyed in the burning of the city," and that "history was handed down solely by tradition," this is founded only on his own misconstruction of Livy's words.

There are passages in Livy, relating to events previous to the Gallic conflagration, so dry and annalistic in their form that they seem to have been taken directly from those ancient books, or, at all events, through the earliest literary annalists. Take, for instance, the following passage: "Agitatum in urbe a tribunis plebis ut tribuni militum consulari potestate, crearentur; nec obtineri potuit. Consules fiunt L. Papirius Crassus, L. Julius. Æquorum legati fœdus ab senatu quum petiissent, et pro fœdere deditio ostentaretur, indutias annorum octo impetraverunt. Volscorum res, super acceptam in Algido cladem, pertinaci certamine inter pacis bellique auctores in jurgia et seditiones versa. Undique otium fuit Romanis. Legem de mulctarum æstimatione, pergratam populo, quum ab tribunis parari consules unius ex collegis proditione excepissent, ipsi præoccupaverunt ferre. Consules L. Sergius Fidenas iterum, Hostus Lucretius Tricipitinus. Nihil dignum dictu actum his consulibus. Secuti eos consules A. Cornelius Cossus, T. Quinctius Pennus iterum. Veientes in agrum

[1] Lectures, vol. i. p. v. seq.

Romanum excursiones fecerunt. Fama fuit, quosdam ex Fidenatium juventute participes ejus populationis fuisse: cognitique ejus rei L. Sergio, et Q. Servilio, et Mam. Æmilio permissa. Quidam Ostiam relegati, quod, cur per eos dies a Fidenis abfuissent, parum constabat. Colonorum additus numerus, agerque iis bello interemptorum assignatus. Siccitate eo anno plurimum laboratum est: nec cœlestes modo defuerunt aquæ, sed terra quoque ingenito humore egens, vix ad perennes suffecit amnes. Defectus alibi aquarum circa torridos fontes rivosque stragem siti pecorum morientium dedit; scabie alia absumpta: vulgatique contactu in homines morbi, et primo in agrestes in gruerunt, serviliaque: urbs deinde impletur."[1] And so through the whole chapter, which contains the events of four years. It is impossible that a passage like this, relating to events more than thirty years previous to the capture of Rome by the Gauls, could have been restored from memory; and it would be still more absurd to suppose it a deliberate forgery. Such is not the style in which literary forgeries are perpetrated, and especially in a comparatively illiterate age. If not taken from the Commentarii Pontificum its materials must at all events have been found in the Annales Maximi.

It has been a favourite method with the sceptical critics since the time of Beaufort[2] to compare the Roman history with the Greek. Although the Greeks, it is said, were a much more cultivated people than the Romans, and began to write history much earlier than they, yet they had no historian before Herodotus, who flourished in the fifth century before Christ. In like manner Sir G. C. Lewis observes:[3] "But even in Greece, the use of writing for the purposes of public historical registration was very limited at the time to which Livy refers. Thucydides describes the Athenians, in the year 415 B.C., as knowing their history during the Pisistratic period, which was about a century back, only by hearsay accounts, and not from written documents; and

---

[1] Liv. iv. 30.
[2] See his "Dissertation sur l'Incertitude des cinq premiers Siècles de l'Histoire romaine," p. 2, &c.   [3] Vol. i. p. 154.

the burning of Rome was in 390 B.C., only twenty-five years afterwards. Moreover, the Romans, though an enterprising and warlike people, were at this time far from equal to the Athenians in refinement and mental cultivation; and writing, which was still not in common use at Athens, was, we may be sure, still more rarely employed at Rome." Hence it seems necessarily to follow that it must have been long after this period that history began to be written at Rome.

This argument contains its own refutation; because if the Athenians in B.C. 415 knew their history for the preceding century only by hearsay, they could not have been more advanced than the Romans as regards, at least, historical knowledge; nay, if there be any truth in what we have said on this subject, they must have been a great deal behind them. In fact, the rise of literature at Athens was late and sudden. And though in polite literature they were immeasurably superior to the Romans, yet that circumstance by no means proves that they were more careful in recording political events. The practical turn of mind of the Romans seems here to have given them an advantage over the more refined and brilliant intellect of the Athenians. The Romans appear to have formed a different conception of history from the Greeks. They regarded it not as a matter of literary leisure and amusement, to be left to any casual writer who might be induced by a love of fame, or any other motive, to pursue it: they made it an affair of state, and charged the Pontifices not only with the care of noting down in the Annales Maximi the principal events as they happened, but also of drawing up in the Commentarii a connected history of the city. The result is what we see. For the early annals of Rome, however imperfect through the lapse of ages and the injuries occasioned by fire and other accidents, are still much more full and satisfactory than those of Athens or of any other Greek city. This respect for the past, this desire to be guided by example and precedent, is a striking characteristic of the early Romans, and appears to have been common to them with other Italian peoples. Thus we find Ovius Pactius, an aged Samnite priest, reading, in B.C. 293, *from an ancient linen book*, a formulary of sacrifice.¹ Aricia, Præneste, and Tusculum had their Fasti, which were cited by the antiquary Cincius,² and Dionysius mentions that the Sabines possessed annals from an early period.³

It seems probable that the Commentarii Pontificum were also known by the name of *Annales*, which was a common appellation for an historical work among the Romans; and the Commentarii were probably digested according to years, at all events after the establishment of the Republic. Hence when Quintilian says, "Quid erat futurum si nemo plus effecisset eo, quem sequebatur? Nihil in poetis supra Livium Andronicum, nihil in historiis supra Pontificum Annales,"⁴ he seems to mean the Commentarii; and the Annales *Maximi* were perhaps always cited under that precise title. So again, when Cicero, speaking of Pythagoras having been the teacher of Numa, says: "Sæpe enim hoc de majoribus natu audivimus et ita intelligimus vulgo existimari: neque vero satis id annalium publicorum auctoritate declaratum videmus,"⁵ he is probably referring to the Commentarii Pontificum, because the words *publicorum* and *auctoritate* seem to refer to a work of more weight than the early *literary* annals; and because he could hardly have meant the Annales Maximi, which, being merely a register of events as they occurred, would not have entered into the education of Numa. The following passage from Diomedes, the grammarian,⁶ also appears to show that the Commentarii Pontificum were sometimes called *Annales Publici*:—"Annales Publici, quos Pontifices scribæque conficiunt;" where, if he had been alluding to the Annales Maximi, he would have named only the Pontifex Maximus.

We will now discuss some objections which have been urged against the existence of any such historical sources

¹ Liv. x. 38.
² Macrob. Sat. i. 12. A portion of the Fasti Prænestini have been discovered, which mention the ancient Latin traditions respecting Mezentius and Acca Larentia. (Orelli, Inscr. Lat. iii. 368, 404.)
³ Lib. ii. 49.   ⁴ Inst. Orat. x. 2, 7.
⁵ De Rep. ii. 15.   ⁶ P. 180, ed. Putsch.

as those we have described. Schwegler remarks,[1] after Beaufort: "If we inquire for the sources of the older Roman history, we meet at the outset the surprising circumstance that no connected historical work was composed during the first five centuries of the city, which might have served as a foundation for later historians. The writing of history began at a very late period among the Romans. Livy complains more than once of the want of literature during the first five centuries; and, on the occasion of the controverted dictatorship of the year 432, he expresses his regret that the history of that period had not been handed down by any contemporary writer. Dionysius also, in enumerating his sources, remarks that Rome had not a single ancient historian. In fact, Fabius Pictor is the most ancient one we know of, and is expressly characterised by Livy as such."

We have explained, and need not here repeat, the difference between mere literary history and those annalistic records the keeping of which was among the Romans a function of state; and it follows from this explanation that it is false to imagine that the first literary historians had no foundation for their narrative. Nor is it true that Livy complains of an absolute want of literature (*Litteraturlosigkeit*), but only of its comparative rarity, as appears from the two passages adduced by Schwegler in proof of his assertion: "Quod parvæ et raræ per eadem tempora literæ fuere," vi. 1; and, "Quia raræ per ea tempora literæ erant," vii. 3. And if the literature was scanty, so the history is proportionably meagre and unsatisfactory: which is all that Livy means to say. The one bears a direct ratio to the other; for while Livy records the events of the first four centuries and more in ten books, the remaining period down to the death of Drusus, embracing less than three centuries, filled one hundred and thirty-two books.

With regard to the dictatorship of the year U.C. 432, we will give the whole passage from Livy, and not merely the concluding sentence, as quoted by Schwegler in a note:—

[1] Buch I. § 2. Compare Sir G. C. Lewis, vol. I. ch. iii. § 10, where much the same arguments are employed.

"Nec discrepat quin dictator eo anno A. Cornelius fuerit: id ambigitur, belline gerendi causa creatus sit; an ut esset qui ludis Romanis, quia L. Plautius prætor gravi morbo forte implicitus erat, signum mittendis quadrigis daret, functusque eo haud sane memorandi imperii ministerio, se dictatura abdicaret: nec facile est aut rem rei, aut auctorem auctori præferre. Vitiatam memoriam funebribus laudibus reor, falsisque imaginum titulis, dum familia ad se quæque famam rerum gestarum honorumque fallente mendacio trahunt. Inde certe et singulorum gesta et publica monumenta rerum confusa. Nec quisquam æqualis temporibus illis scriptor extat, quo satis certo auctore stetur." [1]

Let us observe, first of all, that writers were agreed that A. Cornelius was dictator in that year. The fact could not be denied, because no doubt his name appeared in the Annals, or in the Liber Magistratuum; which, however, did not assign the reason of his appointment. That his name so appeared is evident from Livy proceeding to say that, through family ambition, "et singulorum gesta et *publica monumenta* rerum *confusa*," for from these words it is evident that public records of the period existed. But though Cornelius was dictator, it was for so trifling a cause as rendered it an "imperium haud sane memorandum," and therefore the Annals, or Commentarii, said no more about him. But after his death, it seems to have been asserted by his family that he had been appointed dictator on account of the Samnite war; and this was proclaimed in his funeral oration, and inserted among the titles on his bust. Nor after all was the pretension so egregious, as Cornelius appears to have defeated the Samnites in his dictatorship a year or two before; though some writers claimed even this victory for the consuls.[2] Further, Schwegler's assertion of Livy's regret that the history of that period had not been handed down *by any contemporary writer*,[3] is totally unfounded, and springs from a misconstruction of Livy's words. For when that historian says, "Nec quisquam

---

[1] Lib. viii. 40. [2] Ibid. 38, 39.
[3] "Dass die Geschichte jenes Zeitraums von keinem gleichzeitigen Geschichtschreiber überliefert sey."—§ 2.

æqualis temporibus illis scriptor extat, *quo satis certo auctore nitatur*," his words necessarily imply that there were contemporary writers, but none whom he could sufficiently trust in this matter. Had he meant that there was absolutely no writer, to say that he could not sufficiently trust a writer who did not exist would have been utterly absurd.

Before proceeding any further, we will say a word or two about these funeral orations. The origin of them was at least almost coeval with the Republic, for in B.C. 480 the Consul Fabius Vibulanus made an oration over the bodies of his colleague Manlius and of his own brother Q. Fabius, who had fallen in the Etruscan war.[1] These orations, with the titles upon busts, sarcophagi, &c. must have constituted a sort of records dating from a very early period; but unfortunately, from the cause already adverted to, they could not be implicitly relied on. At the same time, let us recognise from their existence the desire which prevailed among the Romans of perpetuating the memory of the achievements of their ancestors, as a sure pledge that they would not have suffered the history of their country to fall into oblivion for want of a chronicler; for with it were intimately connected the history and the glory of the great patrician families. Nor after all, perhaps, was the vanity which prompted a little exaggeration in these funeral eulogiums and inscriptions a source of any very great depravation of the history; for the Roman historians were fully aware of it, and on their guard against it. This is shown by the passage just quoted from Livy, as well as by the following one from Cicero:—" Nec vero habeo antiquiorem (Catone) cujus quidem scripta proferenda putem, nisi quem Appi Cæci oratio de Pyrrho et nonnullæ mortuorum laudationes delectant. Et hercules hæ quidem extant: ipsæ enim familiæ sua quasi ornamenta ac monumenta servabant et ad usum, si quis ejusdem generis occidisset, et ad memoriam laudum domesticarum et ad illustrandam nobilitatem suam. Quamquam his laudationibus historia rerum nostrarum est facta mendosior: multa enim scripta sunt eis, quæ facta non sunt, falsi triumphi, plures consulatus, genera etiam falsa

[1] Livy, ii. 47; cf. ii. 61, &c.

et ad plebem transitiones."[1] But in most such cases the truth would have been elicited by comparing together the memorials of different families, and the whole with the public registers. Take, for instance, the account just given of the dictator A. Cornelius. Whether it was he or the consuls who defeated the Samnites might be matter of dispute between the gens Cornelia and the gentes Fabia and Fulvia; but the dispute itself is a proof that the Samnites were beaten, which after all is the main point; by whom was not of much importance, except to the families mentioned. And admitting that several minor errors of this description may have crept into the early Roman history, still this does not invalidate the great bulk of it, and reduce it to a mere fantasy.

The memoirs of some of the great houses must have been of much the same value as historical sources as these funeral orations, being liable to the same exaggerations. These memoirs occasionally claimed a very high antiquity. The gens Octavia, for example, must have possessed old family memoirs reaching up to the time of the kings, since we are told that it traced its origin to Velitrae, that it was elected into the Roman gentes by Tarquinius Priscus, into the Senate by Servius Tullius, and became ultimately plebeian.[2] But in general we may suppose that family memoirs hardly existed before the establishment of the Republic, and would not therefore have thrown much light upon the regal period. The Censorian families, in particular, appear to have kept such records, and Dionysius tells us[3] that they were carefully handed down from father to son. He even mentions having seen some which must have been previous to the Gallic conflagration, as they recorded the census taken in the consulship of L. Valerius Potitus and M. Manlius Capitolinus, which fell in the 118th year after the expulsion of Tarquin, and consequently two years before the burning of the city.

There is no force in Schwegler's concluding remark, that both Livy and Dionysius expressly call Fabius Pictor the

[1] Brut. 16. [2] Suet. Oct. c. 1, seq.
[3] Lib. I. 74.

oldest historian.[1] No doubt he was the first writer of literary history for the public; but we have already shown from both the writers named, that histories not intended for publication had been composed at Rome centuries before the time of Fabius.

Although Sir G. C. Lewis is of opinion that the early Roman history could have had little or no foundation but oral tradition, yet Schwegler is so convinced of the impossibility of its having been derived from such a source, that, as he rejects the preservation of any public annals, he is induced to assume the existence of certain private chroniclers. "Besides the annals of the priests," he observes,[2] "and unconnected with them, there must have been private chronicles. The Roman annalists from the time of Fabius Pictor evidently drew from older chronicles, which must have reached back beyond the Gallic catastrophe. For it cannot be supposed that the previous history, which has quite an annalistic form, the accounts of the Volscian, Æquian, and Veientine wars, with their frequently dry and wearisome details, or the history of the numerous prodigies, epidemics, and striking natural phenomena handed down from that epoch, were first recorded after the Gallic capture from memory and oral tradition. Most of these accounts must rest on contemporaneous and written record, or at all events nearly contemporaneous. Such annalistic records appear to have been begun not long after the overthrow of the monarchy, or at all events in the third century of the city, and appear to have been originally carried up to the foundation of the Republic. That they did not, at least originally, reach up to the regal period, is shown, as we have before remarked, by the unchronological character of the history of the kings, which excludes all possibility of annalistic record. Even the first score or two years of the Republic cannot have been recorded contemporaneously, but from memory, as may be perceived partly from the contradictions in the chronology—as, for instance, the battle of Lake Regillus is placed by some in the year 255, by others in 258—partly from the confusion of the Fasti during the first years

Livy, L. 44; ii. 10; Dionys. vii. 71.   [2] Buch i. § 5.

of the Republic, and partly from the legendary and unhistorical character of the traditions of that period. There must, moreover, have been several independent chronicles of this kind, as we sometimes find in the later historians one and the same fact related twice, or oftener, under different years, which can only have arisen from their having put together without any critical examination the varying accounts of different chronicles. Thus, for example, Livy relates four campaigns against the Volscians in the years 251—259, which doubtless are only variations of one and the same event. It was these chronicles which served as historical sources to Fabius Pictor, Cincius Alimentus, and the annalists of the sixth century, and give us a security that the traditional history, from about the time of the first secession, is in its general outline authentic. Even in the narrative of Livy we may, as Niebuhr justly remarks,[1] detect here and there the dry and halting style of the old chronicles, as, for instance, in the following passage:—" His consulibus Fidenæ obsessæ, Crustumeria capta, Præneste ab Latinis ad Romanos descivit;"[2] a brevity which strikingly differs from the long descriptions in other places of indecisive battles. Livy, however, had not seen these chronicles, as clearly appears from a passage in his work.[3] Nor had Dionysius; which, however, would not exclude the possibility that such chronicles were extant in the time of Varro and Verrius Flaccus, and were used by those learned antiquaries. Schwegler then proceeds to point out the similarity of such chronicles to those of the Carlovingian times: as, for instance, to a passage like the following:— " Carolus bellum habuit contra Saxones. Carolus mortuus est. Eclipsis solis. Fames valida."

The general view contained in this passage, namely, that there must have been records from which Fabius Pictor, Cincius, and the other early annalists drew their narratives, appears to us unanswerable. We have already endeavoured to show that such minute, and, we might say, commonplace details as sometimes appear in the early history could not possibly have been handed down by oral tradition, and are

[1] Rom. Gesch. II. 5.   [2] Lib. ii. 19.   [3] Lib. viii. 40.

still less likely to have been the produce of literary forgery. But with regard to Schwegler's opinion that these materials for history were not preserved in any official records, but in certain political chronicles kept by private individuals or families, we may observe: First, that this is mere conjecture, unsupported by a single scrap of authority; while, on the other hand, we have already shown, from the testimony of various authors, that the Annals and Commentaries of the priests contained the facts of the early history, and were, in all probability, in great measure preserved. Secondly, such an authentic source being in existence, it is difficult to see what motive could have induced a private individual to keep a similar chronicle, even if he had the requisite opportunity to do so; and at all events such a chronicle could have been little more than a transcript of the official one. Thirdly, if such private chronicles existed, how could Fabius and Cincius with propriety be called the first annalists? Fourthly, the chronicles, so frequently recording prodigies, epidemics, and striking natural phenomena, savour much more of records kept by priests than of the memoirs of a warrior or statesman. We are therefore of opinion that it is much more probable to assume the preservation of the Annales Maximi, partly also of the Commentarii Pontificum, than the existence of these private chronicles of the State.

At the same time it cannot be doubted that many of the great patrician houses kept family memoirs; and when we consider what a leading part some of these families—such, for instance, as the Fabii—played in the affairs of Rome, it is evident that a history, or chronicle, of the gens Fabia would, for a certain period, and to a considerable extent, be a history of Rome. It seems a probable conjecture of Bernhardy's[1] that the possession of such a chronicle and of numerous other historical documents by the Fabii may have been one of the motives which induced Fabius Pictor to write his work.

The answer to Schwegler's remarks about the unchronological character of the history of the kings, and the inference

[1] Grundriss der Röm. Lit. S. 175, Anm. 129; S. 205, Anm. 155.

thence drawn that contemporary record could not have reached up to the regal period, has been forestalled by showing that the better chronology of the republican period is merely a result of the annual consulship.

Sir G. C. Lewis remarks:[1] "If these writers (Fabius and Cincius) began to collect materials for their history of the First Punic War in the years 220—200 B.C., they might have obtained oral accounts of it from aged persons whose memory extended as far back as its commencement. . . . Fabius and Cincius might therefore have written as contemporaries themselves, or from information furnished directly by contemporaries, for the period including the first two Punic Wars, 264—201 B.C., and for any later time comprehended within their histories."

According to this an absolutely authentic history, or one founded on contemporary testimony, could not have reached beyond the First Punic War. And even at this late period, it is not supposed that any public records were made. The only materials used by Fabius and Cincius are conjectured to have been what they knew of their own knowledge, or had heard from old men; both which sources might not have been first-rate. But a page or two further on, this view is considerably modified, as follows:—

"When we consider the energy, intelligence, and systematic fixed principles of policy with which the Romans had not only conducted the two Punic Wars, but which they had exhibited in their resistance to Pyrrhus, we must feel satisfied that they could not have been indifferent about their own early history. A nation which held so strictly to legal and constitutional precedent in the administration of public affairs and to an established course of practice, must have possessed an accredited, if not an authentic and true tradition respecting its past transactions; respecting its former successes, dangers, and reverses; respecting its great men and their great deeds; respecting the origins of the political forms, the military regulations, and the religious institutes round which their patriotic feelings clustered, and which, in their belief, were

[1] Vol. i. p. 80.

the sources of their power and greatness. The leading families of the State, in whom the high and important offices, civil and religious, were almost hereditary, who furnished a succession of consuls, prætors, censors, quæstors, and pontiffs to the Roman people, and who successively contributed members to the dignified Roman Senate, were doubtless the depositaries of a traditionary belief respecting the past ages of the city.[1] How far this belief was authentic, and adequately supplied the place of a history written contemporaneously with the events, or taken down from the mouths of contemporaries, we shall inquire presently. But that such a fixed belief in the history of Rome, from its foundation up to the time of Pyrrhus, was then in existence among the more intelligent and instructed portion of the Roman people, and particularly among those who took a prominent part in the conduct of its public affairs, cannot be doubted by any one who considers the political and social state of Rome during the Punic Wars."[2]

We have here an admission very similar to that of Schwegler, to which we have just adverted. The Romans as early as the time of Pyrrhus, that is, nearly three centuries B.C., were not "indifferent about their own early history." Yet even then, and although it is not disputed by Sir G. C. Lewis that they possessed the art of writing, they are not supposed to have noted it down. Nay, though they were such lovers of constitutional precedent and an established course of practice, they are not supposed to have recorded even the events of their own times for the benefit of their posterity; for Sir G. C. Lewis, as we have seen, thinks that Fabius and Cincius, the first annalists whom he recognises, who flourished a century later, drew their narratives entirely from tradition and the memory of old men.

Sir G. C. Lewis's character of the Romans is in glaring

---

[1]. Here Sir G. C. Lewis adds in a note, "This system of practically confining the chief offices of the republic to a small number of Roman families must have tended, by preserving political traditions, and concentrating political interest, to perpetuate the history of the past."

[2] Vol. i. p. 83, seq.

contradiction with his estimate of their history. He admits
that they took the greatest interest in it, that they were
aware of its importance for the establishment of constitutional precedent, and yet they took not the slightest
care to preserve it from oblivion for the benefit of their
posterity!

But is it probable, after the many vicissitudes which
Rome had undergone, that this interest was first awakened
so late as the time of Pyrrhus? Or that in spite of "the
intelligence and systematic fixed principles of policy" of the
Romans of that time, these principles were founded on mere
romance? If it was from such materials that their constitutional precedents were drawn, they had better have been
without them; and the intelligence and energy attributed
to them seems to be nothing but a bitter irony.

Let us observe a few more contradictions. In vol. i. p. 119,
Sir G. C. Lewis affirms that the historical knowledge of the
best informed statesmen and pontiffs at the beginning of the
Second Punic War did not reach much beyond a century.
And in the next page he says: "Those who lived at the
beginning of the Second Punic War were doubtless better
acquainted with the constitution of that time and of the
century immediately preceding than the writers of the
Augustan age could be. Their knowledge of the earlier
times must, however, have been imperfect, faint, and confused, even where it was founded on authentic though meagre
traditions, and positively erroneous if an attempt was made
to fill up the outline. The Roman constitution had not,
indeed, undergone any fundamental change in the interval
of 230 years between the Decemvirate and the Second Punic
War (449—218 B.C.); but during this period the Canuleian
law of 445 B.C., the Licinian laws of 367 B.C., the laws of
the Dictator Publilius Philo, of 359 B.C., the Ogulnian law of
300 B.C., and the Hortensian law of 287 B.C., all formed important steps in the development of the Roman constitution."

That is, though the statesmen at the time of the Second
Punic War had only a confused knowledge of the history of
their country for the previous century, yet Sir G. C. Lewis,

even at this day, can go back and make a positive assertion respecting it for more than double that time, and can trace the successive measures by which the Roman constitution was developed during a period of 230 *years before* the Second Punic War!!

We agree with Sir G. C. Lewis's main position, that without record there can be no authentic history. But what were the laws here cited but records? And to suppose that these laws stood isolated and alone, and that all knowledge of the circumstances under which they were passed and of the objects which they were meant to attain was lost, is to suppose an absurdity.

Having attempted to show by arguments, some of which, we believe, have not been before employed, that direct and authentic sources for the early history of Rome existed in the Annales Maximi, the Commentarii Pontificum, and in family memoirs and records, we will now proceed to consider some other collateral sources, which might have served to check and confirm the history, and where needful, to suggest restorations. Among these we may first mention the Libri Pontificum, Pontificii, or Pontificales—which appear to have been distinct from the Commentarii—and the Libri Augurales. The contents of the latter may be inferred from their name. They were the registers of the college of augurs, and must have contained the laws and traditions of that priesthood. That they occasionally contained historical facts or constitutional precedents is shown by the following passage of Cicero: "Provocationem etiam a regibus fuisse declarant pontificii libri, significant etiam nostri augurales."[1] It is a fair inference from this passage that both the Libri Pontificii and Libri Augurales reached up to the time of the kings; at all events, they must have contained the traditions of the regal period. The antiquity of the Libri Augurales is supported by their obsolete language. Thus Varro remarks,[2] that they had *tera* for *terra*, and *tempestutem* for *tempestatem*. From another passage in the same books, we learn that a dictator was anciently called Magister Populi;[3] that is,

[1] De Rep. ii. 31. [2] Ling. Lat. v. 21; vii. 31. [3] Cic. De Rep. i. 40.

commander of the *whole army*, or people; while his subordinate officer was only Magister Equitum, commander of the knights, or cavalry. These books seem also to have been sometimes called Commentarii Augurum, as in the following passage: "Itaque in nostris Commentariis"—that is, of our college of augurs—"scriptum habemus: Jove tonante fulgurante, comitia populi habere nefas."[1]

We may suppose that the Libri Pontificales contained the pontifical laws and customs, just as the Augurales contained those of the augurs. Thus we find passages cited from them relating to observances at funerals,[2] at sacrifices,[3] on holidays,[4] &c. There were other sacerdotal books of this sort, as those of the Salii, called Agonenses,[5] and the Commentarii Quindecemvirorum.[6] The Commentaries of Numa probably formed the foundation of them. According to Servius, the Libri Pontificales were also called Indigitamenta: " Nomina hæc numinum in Indigitamentis inveniuntur, id est, in libris pontificalibus, qui et nomina deorum et rationes ipsorum nominum continent;"[7] though it may be suspected that the Indigitamenta were more particularly books containing the proper prayers to, and modes of addressing, the different deities, from *indigitare* == imprecari, incantare.[8] And so Macrobius: "Eadem opinio sospitalis et medici dei in nostrisque quoque sacris fovetur; namque Virgines Vestales ita indigitant: Apollo Medice, Apollo Pæan."[9] The language of the Salian books was so ancient that in the time of Quintilian it was no longer understood by the priests themselves.[10] Even in the time of Varro, Ælius, a distinguished student of Latin literature, passed over many obscure passages in interpreting them; and Varro considered them to be seven

---

[1] Cic. De Div. ii. 18.
[2] Varr. Ling. Lat. v. 23; Serv. Æn. xii. 603.
[3] Varr. Ib. 98. Festus, p. 189, *opima*.
[4] "Sane quæ feriæ a quo genere hominum, vel quibus diebus fieri permissum sint, si quis scire desiderat, libros pontificales legat."—Serv. Georg. i. 272; cf. Colum. R. R. ii. 21, 5.
[5] Varr. Ling. Lat. vi. 14.
[6] Censor. De Die Nat. c. 17.
[7] Ad. Georg. i. 21.
[8] Paul. Diac. p. 114.
[9] Sat. i. 17; cf. Schwegler, B. 52.
[10] Inst. Or. i. 6, 40.

centuries old.[1] Horace also notes their obsolete language in the following lines:—

> "Jam saltare Numæ carmen qui laudat, et illud
> Quod mecum ignorat solus vult scire videri."[2]

The Libri Lintei, or Libri Magistratuum, contained, as the second name shows, lists of the magistrates, while the first name indicates that they were made of linen. Becker, however, is of opinion, from a passage in Livy before quoted (Lib. iv. 7), that the Libri Lintei and Libri Magistratuum were distinct: because Livy there says that the consuls of that year were not mentioned in the Libri Magistratuum, though they were mentioned in the treaty with the Ardeates; and then adds that, according to Licinius Macer, their names appeared both in the Libri Lintei and in the treaty. But it by no means follows from this passage that the Libri Magistratuum were distinct from the Lintei. They are used here as convertible terms, and this is shown by other passages in which Livy so uses them. Thus in Lib. iv. 20, he says: "Quod tam veteres annales, quodque *magistratuum libri, quos linteos* in æde repositos Monetæ Macer Licinius citat identidem auctores." And another passage shows that the Libri Lintei really contained the names of the magistrates: "Nihil enim constat disi in libros linteos utroque anno relatum inter magistratus præfecti nomen" (Lib. iv. 13).

The first of the passages in which their authority is appealed to relates to A.U.C. 310, or B.C. 443, more than half a century before the burning of the city; and indeed it is not pretended that these books were destroyed on that occasion, since they were preserved in the Temple of Juno Moneta on the Capitol, which never fell into the possession of the Gauls. One would think from this circumstance that Livy might have satisfied himself on the point in question by consulting the books themselves; but from some cause or another—probably his idleness, of which we shall find more than this example—he does not appear to have done so.

[1] Ling. Lat. vii. 2, *sq.*   [2] Epp. ii. 1, 86.

We also hear of Commentarii Regum, as in a passage of Cicero's Oration for Rabirius already quoted.[1] Only those, however, of Numa and Servius Tullius are specifically mentioned.[2] But the substance of the Commentaries of Numa had doubtless been absorbed in the Libri Pontificales; for had they been extant in their original form, the forgery of them, to which we have already alluded, would not have been attempted. In like manner the Commentaries of Servius seem to have formed the groundwork of the subsequent Tabulæ Censoriæ. For, as Schwegler has pointed out,[3] Festus, in the following passage, refers the expression *procum* to Servius Tullius: "Procum patricium in descriptione classium, quam fecit Servius Tullius, significat procerum" (p. 49) while Cicero cites the Censoriæ Tabulæ for the same expression: "Jam ut Censoriæ Tabulæ loquuntur, fabrum et procum audeo dicere, non fabrorum et procorum."[4] The first Censoriæ Tabulæ, however, must have been those of Servius; and it is therefore, not altogether impossible that they may have been extant, and that both Cicero and Servius are alluding to them.

The Leges Regiæ were another collateral source of early history. They are frequently mentioned as extant by the best authorities. Livy expressly says[5] that some of the laws of the kings, besides the decemviral tables, were recovered after the fire; and they who make so much of his text as an authority for the loss of historical documents in that catastrophe, are surely bound to accept the exceptions which he specifies. L. Valerius, in his speech for the abrogation of the Lex Oppia, refers to the existence of such laws: "Hæc quum ita natura distincta sint, ex utro tandem genere ea lex esse videtur, quam abrogamus? An vetus regia lex, simul cum urbe nata,"[6] &c. And Cicero bears positive testimony to the

---

[1] Above, p. xvii.
[2] See Livy, L. 81, 32, 60. Cicero appears to quote some expressions from the Commentaries of Servius in the following passage: "In quo etiam verbis ac nominibus fuit diligens: qui quum locupletes assiduos appellasset ab ære dando, eos qui aut non plus mille quingentum æris aut omnino nihil in suum censum præter caput attulissent, proletarios nominavit."—De Rep. ii. 22.
[3] R. i. § 6.
[4] De Orat. 46, 155.
[5] Lib. vi. 1.
[6] Lib. xxxiv. 6.

existence of Numa's laws : " Et animos, propositis legibus his, *quas in monumentis habemus*, ardentes consuetudine et cupiditate bellandi religionum cærimoniis mitigavit :"[1] and again : " Illa autem diuturna pax Numæ mater huic urbi juris et religionis fuit : qui legum etiam scriptor fuisset, *quas scitis extare*."[2]

Schwegler, after Osann, thinks[3] that the word *fuisset* in the last passage shows that Numa's laws could not have been written ; that we must supply, Numa would have written them, if at that time writing had been in common use. The sentence is fragmentary, breaking off in the middle, so that we know not what Cicero was going to add. But we may be quite sure that it was not an objection to the possibility of Numa having written his laws, because in the passage first quoted Cicero speaks of their positive existence, and because, in a passage before cited, we see that Cicero believed *literæ* and *doctrinæ* to have been already *inveterata* in the time of Romulus.[4] And Livy, in a passage, also before quoted,[5] says that Numa delivered his laws written and signed to Marcius. Festus speaks of Numa's laws as written : " Itaque in Numæ Pompili regis legibus scriptum esse,"[6] &c. Tacitus alludes to a law of Tullus Hostilius, and speaks of Ancus Marcius and Servius Tullius as lawgivers.[7]

Schwegler infers that the laws of Numa had been absorbed in the Pontifical books, citing in support of this opinion Festus (p. 189, Opima) and Plutarch (Marc. 8). But the passage in Festus leads to a directly opposite conclusion. It runs as follows : " Testimonio esse libros Pontificum, in quibus sit : Pro primis spoliis bovem (bove) pro secundis solitaurilibus, pro tertiis agno publice fieri debere : esse etiam compelli reges (Pompilii regis ?) legem opimorum spoliorum talem: Cujus auspicio classe procincta opima spolia capiuntur, Jovi Feretrio darier oporteat," &c. Now, when a writer cites a passage from the Libri Pontificum, and then adds, there is also a law of King Pompilius (" esse etiam," &c.) on the same

---

[1] De Rep. ii. 14.
[2] Ibid. v. 2 ; cf. Dionys. ii. 24, 68, &c.
[3] R. i. 8. 25, Anm. 7.
[4] P. 178, Occinum.
[5] De Rep. ii. 10, 18.
[6] Lib. i. 20.
[7] Ann. iii. 26 ; xii. 8.

subject of Opima Spolia, the necessary inference is that these two documents were distinct.

Schwegler argues[1] that the decemviral legislation shows the want of previous written laws, and appeals to the testimony of Dionysius that, before the Twelve Tables, laws consisted only of the traditions of juristic practice, and that only a little having the force of law had been written down in certain sacred books, the knowledge of which was confined to the patricians. But the language of Dionysius is not half so strong as this. He only says that *all* law was not comprised in writing—οὐδ' ἐν γραφαῖς ἅπαντα τὰ δίκαια τεταγμένα (x. 1)—and this shows that some was. All that we are contending for is, that there were certain written laws of the kings, not that there was a complete body of them, which might have sufficed for all subsequent time. And to this point another passage of the same Dionysius may be cited, not mentioned by Schwegler, when that historian alludes to a law of the kingly period having been incorporated into the Twelve Tables, and quotes a passage from the *written* laws of Numa.[2]

On this subject Sir G. C. Lewis observes:[3] "It was easy for a pontifical scribe, who entered a rule of consuetudinary law in his register, to dignify it with the name of a *lex regia*, and attribute it to Numa, Servius, or one of the other kings." But it is still more easy to make a conjecture of this sort, though it is not only against all evidence, but against all probability. For to think that codes of law, the most sacred of all human institutions, could be trifled with—nay, could be forged—in this free and easy manner, and that too among a people who, as Sir G. C. Lewis tells us himself, "held so strictly to legal and constitutional precedent," is contrary to all experience, and in fact one of the most random and impossible suppositions that can be imagined.

It will, perhaps, at all events be allowed that what the Romans called their Leges Regiæ were older than the laws of the Twelve Tables; for it is not improbable that they had sense enough to discriminate whether they were prior or sub-

[1] R. L. B. 24.
[2] ἐν αἷς καὶ αὕτω γέγραπται—ὥσπερ καὶ ἐν ἐγραφεν. - ii. 27.   [3] Vol. i. p. 526.

sequent to that great epoch in their legislation. Nor would it have been easy after the promulgation of the Twelve Tables, by which their jurisprudence was reduced to a more exact science, to pretend that a law passed by the assemblies of the people was a regal law; neither is it very obvious what motive there could have been for making such an attempt. But the period which elapsed between the expulsion of the kings and the decemviral legislation is only about half a century, and therefore it requires no great stretch of faith to believe that the Leges Regiæ were really what they professed to be. It is not disputed that the laws of the Twelve Tables survived the Gallic conflagration. Sir G. C. Lewis observes: "That the decemviral legislation was preserved with perfect fidelity in the original authentic text cannot be doubted."[1] Where, then, is the improbability that laws only a century or two older may also have survived? On this subject Niebuhr observes: "It would be arbitrary scepticism to doubt that the early Roman laws were written long before the time of the Decemvirs,"[2] and, "The high antiquity of a collection of the laws of the kings compiled by one Papirius seems unquestionable."[3] Mere antiquity cannot be alleged as a reason why the laws of the Roman kings should have perished, for there are Anglo-Saxon laws extant that are ten centuries old, and the interval between Numa and the historical times is only about half that period.

Further collateral evidence in support of the history of the regal period is afforded by the treaties already mentioned, of Servius Tullius with the Latins, of Tarquinius Superbus with the Gabines, and the treaty between Rome and Carthage concluded in the first year of the republic. A treaty made with the Latins in the consulship of Cassius and Cominius in B.C. 493, only seventeen years after the expulsion of the kings, may almost be said to belong to this epoch. Cicero speaks of it[4] as extant in his time, engraved on a brazen column which stood behind the rostra. It is also alluded to by Livy[5] and Dionysius,[6] the latter of whom gives the sub-

[1] Vol. i. p. 112. [2] Lect. vol. i. p. 6. [3] Hist. vol. i. p. 211.
[4] Pro Balbo, 23. [5] Fab. i. 33.   [6] Lib. vi. 95.

stance of it. Schwegler's conclusion,[1] that it could not have been extant in the time of those historians because Cicero, in the passage cited, says that it had *lately* stood behind the rostra—" quod quidem nuper in columna ænea meminimus post rostra"—is not a very logical one, since its removal from that position does not imply its destruction.

These are all the literary monuments of the regal period which it may be necessary to mention. It appears to us that they might have sufficed to preserve the memory of the kings and the principal events of their reigns; at all events they might have prevented the history from being a mere blank, so that even the names of the kings should not be accurately known, and the whole narrative be nothing more than a fantasy. Schwegler, after reciting in the eighth section of his book, the treaties just mentioned, observes: " The importance of the documents just recited is not to be lightly prized from the point of view of historical criticism; they are boundary stones, which restrain an unbridled and measureless scepticism. The alliance of Servius Tullius with the Latins, the commercial treaty with Carthage, and the treaty of Sp. Cassius, will not be doubted by any discreet historical inquirer." But he has hardly uttered these words when he goes on to reverse his judgment by asserting that the traditional history gains nothing by these monuments, and concludes the paragraph by saying that, so far from supporting it, they rather serve to show how little authenticity it has? We shall inquire, in the course of the following work, how far this judgment may be well founded with regard to such of these documents as come within its scope.

Besides literary records, there were also other monuments, architectural and plastic, of the regal period. Such were the walls and gates of the Palatine and Servian cities, the Vetus Capitolium, the temples erected by Romulus, Tatius, and Numa, the Curia Hostilia, the Tullianum, the Cloaca Maxima, the Circus, the Capitoline Temple, &c. In the plastic way we may principally instance the statues of the kings which stood in the Capitol. These must have been erected before the

[1] S. 19, Anm. 5.

republican times, and most probably by Tarquinius Superbus when he finished the Capitol; they would have borne witness to the number and names of the kings, and would have formed a trustworthy record, dating only between two and three centuries from the foundation of the city. There were, besides, the statue of Junius Brutus, of Attus Navius, the carved wooden image of Servius Tullius in the Temple of Fortune, &c. All these monuments would have told their own tale, and have been indissolubly connected with the names of their founders and prototypes.

Such, then, were the principal materials with which we are acquainted, which might have been used by writers of a later period for the early history of Rome. In order to complete that portion of our dissertation which relates to the external evidence for that early period, it only remains to inquire how its history has been treated by the writers who made it their subject.

The first historians of Rome were Greeks. Hieronymus, of Cardia, in the Thracian Chersonese, who flourished in the fourth century B.C., appears to have been the first who gave a brief survey of Roman affairs,[1] in his history of the Epigoni, or Diadochi, as the successors of Alexander were called. His subject led him to treat of the invasion of Italy by Pyrrhus, and it was doubtless on this occasion that he adverted to the affairs of Rome. Timæus, of Tauromenium, in Sicily, was the next Greek writer who handled the same subject, in his history of Italian and Sicilian affairs, of which only a few fragments remain.[2] Timæus was probably born about the middle of the fourth century B.C., and consequently considerably less than half a century after the capture of Rome by the Gauls. His vicinity to Magna Græcia must have afforded him an excellent opportunity to become acquainted with Italian affairs in general, and his history probably contained some valuable information respecting the early times of Rome. He also wrote a history of the war of Pyrrhus with the Romans.

[1] Dionys. i. 6, sq.
[2] Suidas, Τίμαιος; cf. Gellius, N.A. xI. 1, "Timæus in historiis quas oratione Græca de rebus populi Romani composuit."

The great historians of Greece proper knew little or nothing about the Romans. Neither Herodotus nor Thucydides once mentions them, although the former historian spent the last years of his life at Thurii. The existence of Rome is, however, sometimes recognised by early Greek writers. Hellanicus, who flourished in the fifth century B.C., is said to have recorded in his chronicle of the priestesses of Juno at Argos, that Æneas was the founder of Rome.[1] Cephalon of Gergithes, Demagoras of Samos, and the Arcadian poet Agathyllus, seem also to have alluded to Rome; but though these were early writers, their exact date is uncertain.[2] Damastes of Sigeum, a contemporary of Hellanicus and Herodotus, also spoke of the foundation of Rome.[3] Antiochus of Syracuse,[4] and the geographer Scylax mentioned the name of that city.[5] Theopompus adverted to the capture of Rome by the Gauls.[6] Aristotle, who was a contemporary of Theopompus, mentioned the same event, and also adverted to the legend of the burning of the ships by the Trojan women on the coast of Italy.[7] Heraclides of Pontus also mentioned the Gallic catastrophe,[8] which would therefore appear to have created a great sensation in Greece. Theophrastus, the pupil of Aristotle, is said by Pliny[9] to have been the first Greek who treated Roman affairs at all diligently. Antigonus, Silenus, and Diocles of Peparethus, touched upon the same subject; but we have no accurate information of the nature of their works, or even of the period in which they lived.

Polybius, who flourished B.C. 204—122, is the first extant Greek historian from whom we derive any information at all valuable respecting the early history of Rome. Polybius was one of the Achæan hostages sent into Italy in B.C. 167, and he resided seventeen years in the house of Æmilius Paulus, at Rome. In his "Universal History" he treated of the Second Punic War, and prefaced it with a sketch of the early Roman history from the burning of the city; but the only part of

[1] Dionys. I. 72.   [3] Ibid.   [5] Ibid.
[2] Id. I. 12, 72.   [4] Peripl. 5.   [6] Plin. H.N. III. 9, 57.
[7] Dionys. I. 72; Plut. Cam. 22.   [8] Plut. ibid.
[9] H. N. III. 9, 57.

his work still extant that is of any use for the history of the kings, is the account of the Carthaginian treaty already alluded to, which, as we shall have occasion to show further on, confirms in general the accounts of the progress of Rome during the regal period.

We are now arrived at Dionysius of Halicarnassus, who, to judge from bulk alone, should be by far the most important of all the writers on early Roman history. Of the life of Dionysius little more is known than what he himself tells in the introduction to his work. The date of his birth is not exactly known, and has been placed in the rather wide interval between 78 and 54 B.C. He appears to have arrived in Italy soon after the battle of Actium (B.C. 31), and to have lived at Rome two and twenty years; during which period he made himself master of the Latin tongue, and employed himself in collecting the materials for his history, by studying the ancient annals, and conversing with the most learned of the Romans. He mentions in his preface[1] the second consulship of Claudius Nero, which fell in B.C. 7, and his book was therefore probably published about this time. He probably subsisted by teaching the art of rhetoric, which he professed; a calling which has not tended to enhance his merits as an historian.

It can scarcely be doubted that the work of Dionysius appeared after that of Livy; for Niebuhr's opinion that Livy did not commence his history till he was fifty years of age, is altogether untenable. The earlier portions of it must have been written before the conclusion of the civil wars. How else could he have said in his Præfatio: "Festinantibus *ad hæc nova*, quibus jam pridem prævalentis populi vires *se ipsæ conficiunt:* " or, " Ego contra hoc quoque laboris præmium petam, ut me *a conspectu malorum quæ nostra per tot annos vidit ætas, tantisper* certe, dum prisca illa tota mente repeto, *avertam!*" The forces of a people which are still employed in their own destruction, the desire to avert the eyes from misfortunes which had so long afflicted, and must have still continued to afflict, the state, can refer only to the civil wars. At the same time, the first book affords evidence that an edition of it must

[1] Lib. i. c. 3.

have been republished at a considerably later period. Thus on the question of the Spolia Opima achieved by Cornelius Cossus, Livy tells us that he had first related the story as he found it in previous writers, but afterwards he varied from it, when he heard that Augustus had inspected the linen breastplate of Cossus in the Temple of Jupiter Feretrius, and had in consequence introduced a new version.[1] The words in this chapter, from "Omnes ante me," evidently belong to a late edition. And because Livy in the nineteenth chapter of his first book adverts to the shutting of the Temple of Janus, after the battle of Actium in B.C. 29, saying that it was the second occasion of that ceremony since the reign of Numa, while he does not notice a subsequent closing of that temple by Augustus in B.C. 25, it has been concluded that this first book of the history was written between the dates mentioned. But another passage, towards the end of the same book, must have been added after the complete establishment of the empire. For Livy there suppresses some parts of Brutus's invective against Tarquinius Superbus, observing that the present posture of affairs rendered it difficult for writers to insert them.[2] But to return from this digression.

The main object of Dionysius in writing his book was, he tells us, to make the Greeks better acquainted with the Romans, to disabuse them of a prejudice that that people were no better than barbarians; nay, to show that they were not only Greeks, but even more Hellenic than the Greeks themselves.[3] His work embraced the history of Rome from the earliest times down to the First Punic War, and was intended as a supplement to that of Polybius, whose account of the events previous to that epoch was a mere sketch. Of the twenty books in which Dionysius comprised his history, only the first eleven are now extant, and the last two of these in a somewhat mutilated condition. Of the other nine books, only some fragments remain.

[1] Lib. iv. 20.
[2] "His, atrocioribusque, credo, aliis, quæ præsens rerum indignitas haud-quaquam relata scriptoribus facile subjicit, memorata."—Lib. i. 59.
[3] Thus Pyrrhus is made to speak of them as ἀσπόνδους ἐχθροὺς Ἑλλήνων καὶ βαρβάρους, Exc. ed. Dionys. lib. xix. 2; cf. l. 89, 90, &c.

f

With some of the German critics Dionysius is a great favourite, which may perhaps arise from a congenial turn of mind, for Dionysius possessed in an eminent degree the German talent for prolixity, and devotes four books to the history of the kings, which Livy had given in one. Schwegler cannot sufficiently praise this quality, though he admits in the same breath that it has been the source of some egregious faults and blunders. "The history of Dionysius," he remarks,[1] "is particularly distinguished by its great fulness. He has collected with the greatest care all that he found scattered in the annals of his predecessors. And if, in order to gather up all the crumbs, and let nothing be wasted, he sometimes gives two divergent narratives of the same occurrence, and relates them as two different events, this completeness affords, nevertheless, a real treasure of instructive and important accounts!"

Other items in the panegyric of the same critic are[2] that Dionysius is a very careful writer; that no important contradiction can be found in his work; that he detects the contradictions and absurdities of the Roman history; that he is very careful of chronology; that his study of sources was extensive, though he consulted documents only occasionally. Lastly, he was a highly conscientious writer, and we may be sure that there is in his work nothing of his own invention, except the speeches and the pragmatic reflections.

On this we may remark that our knowledge of early Roman history is not sufficiently complete to pronounce a confident opinion on the accuracy of Dionysius. But if the absence of contradictions, as asserted by Schwegler after Niebuhr, is to be the test of it, then the opinion breaks down. The work of Dionysius contains many contradictions, of which we will here instance a few by no means unimportant ones; others there will be occasion to notice in the sequel. In ii. 76 the institution of the *pagi* is ascribed to Numa, and in iv. 15 to Servius Tullius. In ii. 12 the Senate is represented as elected by the tribes and curiæ, yet in iii. 67 Tarquinius Priscus is described as choosing them, and in v. 13 the Consuls Brutus

---
[1] R. L. S. 100. [2] Buch ii. § 14.

and Valerius. In iv. 21 the constitution of Servius Tullius is said to have been a trick to deceive the people, while in other places he is represented as a most democratic king (iv. 34, 37, 40, &c.), and in v. 75 is called δημοτικώτατος βασιλεύς. In iv. 3 Tarquinius is made a patrician by the Roman people; while in iii. 41 we are told that he was elevated to that rank by King Ancus. In ii. 63 Julius is described as a descendant of Ascanius, and a Roman husbandman in the time of Romulus; while in iii. 29 the Julii are said to have first come to Rome after the capture of Alba Longa. In iv. 51 Fidenæ is Sabine, and in v. 40 revolts from Rome. In iv. 91 the last class is exempt from military service, and yet in the very same chapter it is said that each of the 193 centuries must furnish its quota of soldiers.

In fact, though Dionysius lived twenty-two years in Rome, he never obtained a critical knowledge of the Latin language; and to this defect many of his errors and contradictions must be attributed. Thus in describing the constitution of Servius,[1] he calls the last century of the people, or the *capite censi*, a *classis* (συμμορία) like the rest, although that term could be applied only to those who bore arms. In another place he says that Servius built a temple on the banks of the Tiber to Fortuna Virilis,[2] misapprehending the genitive of *fors* for that of *fortis*. Again, in ii. 12, he calls the Romulean senators Patres *Conscripti* (Πατέρες ἔγγραφοι), an appellation only given long afterwards to part of them.

These instances may serve to raise a doubt whether Dionysius deserves the character of a very accurate and careful writer. With regard to his chronology, though it has the appearance of great accuracy, from his comparison of dates with those of the Greeks, yet it is easy to see how it was manufactured. It was invented out of his own head. He took the Roman chronology as he found it, and comparing it with the Greek, put down the Olympiads, or the names of the Athenian archons, who by this method appeared to be contemporary with certain persons or events in the Roman

[1] Lib. iv. 18.
[2] Τύχῃ ἣν ἀνδρείαν προσηγόρευσεν, iv. 27; cf. Varr. L. L. vi. 17.

history. That this was his method may be shown as follows:—

During a scarcity which prevailed at Rome in the consulship of Geganius and Minucius, B.C. 492, envoys were despatched into Sicily to buy corn, with a supply of which they returned in the following year. Livy, in narrating this event,[1] mentions not the name of any Sicilian sovereign from whom the corn was procured, while Dionysius says[2] that Gelon was then tyrant of Syracuse. Now, on what authority did he name Gelon? Evidently on none at all. For he says that the Roman annalists who mentioned any Sicilian sovereign named Dionysius; and he conjectures that the first annalist, finding no name in the public records, but only the fact of the corn coming from Sicily, inserted the name of Dionysius at a guess, and without searching the Greek historians. But Dionysius flourished eighty-five years later, and therefore this account is impossible.

It appears from this passage that Dionysius did not find the name of Gelon in any Roman annalist, but that he "searched the Greek historians," and finding in them, as he supposed, from a comparison of the received chronology of Rome with that of Greece, that Gelon was contemporary with the event in question, he inserted his name: a synchronism, therefore, obtained like all his other ones, merely by construction and inference.

With regard to his extensive study of sources, we may remark that he himself records only the annalists who had preceded him, and conversations with learned Romans. Such conversations are not, perhaps, the best materials for history, while the annalists could have afforded nothing but the groundwork of a compilation. But perhaps Dionysius has here done himself an injustice, for it appears from some passages in his work that he referred sometimes to original documents, as, for instance, the Latin and Gabine treaties, and those references are perhaps the most valuable parts of his

---
[1] Lib. II. 34.
[2] Lib. vii. 1. According to Clinton, Gelon reigned B.C. 485 — 478; Dionysius places him a few years earlier.

work. For since, as Schwegler says, there is no reason to impugn his good faith, he has thus supplied us with valuable evidence on some important points of the early history.

His invented speeches and pragmatic reflections appear to arise from want of judgment, and, owing to his inaccurate knowledge, are most unfortunate specimens of his "invention." This is admitted by Schwegler, who, in spite of his previous panegyric, proceeds to make some remarks which entirely demolish the character of Dionysius as an historian. It is said that he exercised little critical judgment in selecting his materials; that his point of view was quite unhistorical, as shown by his *pragmatismus*,[1] of which Schwegler says in another place,[2] that by means of these arbitrary details and literary word-painting, he has placed all the early history in a false light. With regard to his speeches, some of them are quite impossible,—as, for instance, that which he puts into the mouth of Romulus, and most of them ridiculous and without any individuality of character. He had no historical view, and his idea of the Roman constitution especially is founded on erroneous assumptions. But of course his chief fault is that he believed the traditions of the regal period to be fundamentally historical. Where Livy doubts, Dionysius relates all with the confidence of an eye-witness.

There is much truth in this latter part of Schwegler's character of Dionysius. His speeches are below contempt; they are nothing but specimens of his art as a professor of rhetoric, and pay no regard either to time, or place, or character. His historical details are still worse, because they are often misleading. His want of sound historical judgment is manifest throughout his work, and throws a suspicion on his whole narrative. Hence when he differs from Livy or Cicero, we should in general reject his testimony; and when he supplies any facts not to be found in the Roman authors, we may in most cases abandon them without hesitation. Yet,

[1] This expression is untranslatable, but seems to mean the supplying of the details of a narrative not from authentic record, nor even from tradition, but from inference and construction,—that is, out of the writer's own head.

[2] H. ii. 3. 6.

such being the character of Dionysius, he has been a most serviceable instrument in the hands of the sceptical critics, who, by pointing out variations between his narrative and that of Livy or Cicero, have thus found a convenient method of attack, by attributing to the history itself faults which in fact belong only to the historian.

After what has been said, it will perhaps be only fair to insert Niebuhr's estimate of Dionysius. "I have been censured," says that writer,[1] "for wishing to find fault with Dionysius, but assuredly no one feels that respect, esteem, and gratitude towards him which I feel. The more I search the greater are the treasures I find in him. In former times, it was the general belief that whatever Dionysius had more than Livy were mere fancies of his own; but, with the exception of his speeches, there is absolutely nothing that can be called invented: he only worked up those materials which were transmitted to him by other authorities. It is true that he made more use of Cn. Gellius and similar writers than of Cato, and it is also true that he not unfrequently preferred those writers who furnished abundant materials to others who gave more solid and substantial information. All this is true, but he is nevertheless undervalued, and he has claims to an infinitely higher rank than that which is usually assigned to him. He worked with the greatest love of his subject, and he did not certainly intend to introduce any forgery."

This amounts only to saying that Dionysius was a compiler of the worst sort; that he preferred quantity to quality, and drew from Cn. Gellius, "a very prolix and credulous writer,"—"a second-rate historian, and no authority,"[2] rather than from briefer, but more judicious authors, like Cato.

Becker's character of Dionysius seems more justly drawn, and affords little room for objection. "A subtle grammarian and dialectician, and writing of the earliest times, about which numerous and important contradictions existed, he undertook the impossible task of reconciling, so far as it could be done, these conflicting accounts, and of extricating from the complication of legends what appeared true and credible. This

[1] Lectures, vol. i. p. 52.   [2] Niebuhr, ibid. p. 38.

pragmatismus, proceeding from a false view of legendary history, good-natured, but highly dangerous, and accompanied with a certain vanity and envy of others, had naturally an unfavourable influence as well on his historical narrative, as on his explanation of the oldest constitutional forms. Hence we must always use him with caution when he is not speaking of relations that continued to exist in his own time; and even these, perhaps, he has not always adequately comprehended. Although he lived twenty-two years in Rome, he never completely overcame the difficulties which a foreign language and foreign customs offer to a stranger. Hence we may point to some gross mistakes; as, for instance, when he translates *Templum Fortis Fortunæ* by ἀνδρείας Τύχης (iv. 27); or, speaking of the Colline Salii (ii. 70), ὧν τὸ ἱεροφυλάκιον ἐπὶ τοῦ Κολλίνου λόφου (if the reading be correct); or of Dius Fidius, ἐν ἱερῷ Διὸς Πιστίου, ὃν Ῥωμαῖοι Σάγκτον καλοῦσιν (iv. 58). The double narrative also concerning Cincinnatus (x. 17 and 24), is doubtless a misapprehension.[1] When such errors can be pointed to, we cannot avoid the suspicion that where his accounts are unsupported, or contradicted by those of other writers, a misapprehension may be possible. For the rest, his great industry, and his zealous desire to attain the greatest possible accuracy, deserve to be recognised. He seems, by his allusions to them, to have often consulted documents, when such existed; and this would appear still more plainly if that part of his work was extant which treated of the times when such public sources were more abundant. Nor did he neglect private documents, as he appeals expressly to the Commentarii Censorum."[2]

Sir G. C. Lewis also gives a depreciating character of Dionysius as an historian,[3] though he often avails himself of the authority of that writer to controvert a statement of Livy, or to found on the discrepancy of these two authors an imputation of discrepancy in the tradition. In fact, Dionysius has done more harm to the early Roman history by his inventions, mistakes, and *pragmatismus*, than he has done good by

[1] For other similar blunders see Wachsmuth, Aelt. Gesch. d. 2, St. S. 47.
[2] Röm. Alterth. B. i. S. 49, f.   [3] Credibility, &c. vol. i. p. 246.

the few additional sources that he has indicated, or by his testimony to the existence of ancient documents and historical memorials.

The remaining Greek writers of Roman history need not detain us. Diodorus, who was a somewhat older contemporary of Dionysius, probably gave an account of the Roman kings in the earlier books of his "Universal History;"[1] but of these a few excerpts are all that remain. Diodorus appears to have been as injudicious an historian as Dionysius, and we have not, perhaps, much reason to regret the loss of his account of the regal period.

Plutarch, several of whose biographies, as well as his "Roman Questions," and "Fortune of the Romans," relate to early Roman history and antiquities, was probably born about A.D. 46. Since by his own confession[2] he was only imperfectly acquainted with the Latin tongue, his writings cannot be regarded as an authentic source of Roman history. Owing to this defect, he had recourse chiefly to Greek writers for his materials; as Diocles of Peparethus, Zenodotus, Dionysius of Halicarnassus, and others; and especially to Juba II. king of Mauritania, who, among other things, wrote in Greek a history of Rome. Plutarch, however, sometimes cites Roman authorities; as Fabius Pictor, who also wrote in Greek, Calpurnius Piso, Valerius Antias, and Varro. His frequent use of the romancer Valerius Antias shows how little reliance can be placed on his judgment and knowledge. Niebuhr remarks of Plutarch: "He worked with great carelessness, and therefore requires to be read with much discretion."[3]

Appian, who lived a generation after Plutarch, gave in the first book of his Roman history an account of the regal period. It is lost, and, even if it had survived, it would hardly have been of much service, as it was probably a mere abridgment of Dionysius.

The only Greek work, besides that of Polybius, treating of the early period of Roman history, whose loss need occasion us

[1] Heyne, De font. Hist. Diod. in Diod. Opp. l. p. lxxvi. f. (ed. Bip.).
[2] Vit. Demosth. 2.   [3] Lectures, vol. l. p. 70.

much regret, is that of Dion Cassius. This author wrote in the early part of the third century. His history of Rome in eighty books began from the earliest period and was carried down to A.D. 229; but, unfortunately, of the first twenty-four books only fragments remain. Niebuhr says of him: "He did not acquiesce in the information he gathered from Livy: he went to the sources themselves; he wrote the early period of Roman history quite independent of his predecessors, and only took Fabius for his guide. The early constitution was clear to him, and when he speaks of it, he is very careful in his expressions. He has great talents as an historian."[1] But Niebuhr's assertion about his sources is evidently a random one; and other German writers are of opinion that he made, at all events, no critical use of the older writers.[2] Yet he appears not to have servilely followed either Livy or Dionysius.

Later Greek compilers, such as Zonaras and Lydus, it is not necessary to mention, and we will now advert to the Romans who have treated of their own history.

The first Latin literature, like that of most nations, was in verse, and its earliest productions were dramatic. Livius Andronicus first brought upon the stage a play in the Latin tongue about the year B.C. 240. He was soon followed by Nævius, and at a somewhat later period by Ennius, who is thought to have been born the year Livius began to exhibit. The last two poets are connected with our subject by their having written historical poems. Nævius composed a history of the First Punic War in Saturnian metre, and Ennius a history of Rome in eighteen books in hexameter verse, which he called Annales. The first Roman historians who wrote in prose, Q. Fabius Pictor and L. Cincius Alimentus, were about contemporary with Ennius;[3] but they adopted the

---

[1] Lectures, vol. I. p. 73.
[2] Becker, B. i. S. 53; Wilmans, De fontt. et auctorit. Dionis Cassil.
[3] We cannot here enter into the questions whether Q. Fabius Pictor wrote in Greek or Latin, or in both languages; or whether there was more than one annalist so named. Against the express testimony of Dionysius that he wrote in Greek (i. 6), we see but little force in the arguments from induction, most of which are very easily answered. On this subject see

Greek language; a fact which shows that no Latin prose literature yet existed.

It can hardly be doubted that the works of the first Roman historians contained the substance of the history of the regal period much as we find it in the narratives of later authors. The question therefore arises, From what sources did they derive their materials?

If there is any truth in the view which we have adopted, that there existed a collection of public annals, of which, at all events, a considerable part had escaped the Gallic conflagration, while that which was burnt had been restored so well as circumstances would permit, there will be no difficulty in answering this question. They must have drawn from the sources thus provided. Indeed, we have the express testimony of Dionysius that they did so.[1] Livy expressly testifies to the diligence of Cincius in consulting ancient monuments. From that annalist mentioning the driving of the *clavus* at Volsinii, it appears that his researches were not confined to Rome; and therefore, *à fortiori*, we may give him credit for an industrious use of Roman monuments. The assertion of Plutarch[2] that Fabius Pictor mostly followed Diocles of Peparethus—an author mentioned by nobody else, for the insertion of his name in Festus is the work of Scaliger or Ursinus—is too absurd to demand attention; though it is of course eagerly seized on by the sceptical critics.[3] If it be denied that any public or private monuments were in existence, or that they were used by the first literary annalists, then only two hypotheses remain by which we can account for the origin of the early Roman history: it must either have been founded upon popular tradition, or it must have been nothing but a fiction and a forgery. These two sources do not, of course, exclude each other, and it might be asserted

---

Vossius, De Hist. Lat. lib. i. c. 3; Closset, Historiogr. des Romains, Développement, No. ii.; Becker, Röm. Alterth. B. I. S. 39, Anm. 72, &c.

[1] As in a passage before quoted : τοσούτων μόνον ἐν ταῖς ἀρχαίαις εὑρὼν ἀναγραφαῖς. Cf. l. 73, ἐκ παλαιῶν μέντοι λόγων ἐν ἱεραῖς δέλτοις σωζομένων ἕκαστά τις παραλαβὼν ἀνέγραψε. [2] Rom. 3.

[3] See Becker, Röm. Alterth. I. 39. Becker's argument in support of it, from Fabius having written in Greek, is in the highest degree absurd.

that the history is partly traditional, partly feigned or forged. The examination of these two hypotheses belongs properly to the internal evidence, and we therefore postpone it to the second part of this dissertation.

The next two Roman historians in the order of time were C. Acilius and A. Postumius Albinus. They were contemporary with Cato, and flourished in the earlier part of the second century B.C. These annalists also wrote in Greek. M. Porcius Cato was the first author who attempted a Roman history in Latin prose. Yet what a predilection for Greek literature still lingered among the Romans may be inferred from the well-known fact that Cato, with all his national prejudices, applied himself at an advanced age to the study of it. It was also at this period of his life that he wrote his Origines, so called, according to Cornelius Nepos,[1] because in the second and third books was contained an account of the origin of the Italian cities. The first book comprised the history of the kings of Rome, the fourth book contained the First Punic War, and the remaining books contained the history down to Cato's own time. The industry and diligence of Cato are commended by ancient writers;[2] his strong practical sense, and blunt and honest character, forbid us to think that he introduced any inventions into his writings, or adopted accounts which he did not sincerely believe to be genuine: though his historical judgment is, of course, open to criticism, and he seems to have adopted too readily the legends respecting the foundation of the Italian cities. The elevated rank of the first Roman annalists is, in some degree, a guarantee of their good faith. They were not authors by profession, writing for profit, or even mere literary fame; their motive rather was to give their countrymen an account of those events in which their ancestors and connexions had played an honourable part. It was not till the declining days of the republic that historical writing fell into meaner hands. L. Otacilius Pilitus, who had been tutor to Pompey, was the first libertinus who composed a history.[3]

[1] Vit. Cat. 3.   [2] Nepos, loc. cit.; Vell. Pat. i. 7, 4.
[3] Suet. De Clar. Rhet. c. 3.

Cato was soon followed by other Latin annalists, of whom we shall mention only the principal. One of the first of these was Lucius Cassius Hemina, who wrote a history of Rome from the earliest times, in four books. He was followed by L. Calpurnius Piso Frugi, who flourished in the time of the Gracchi, whom he appears to have opposed. He was consul in B.C. 133, and censor in B.C. 120. Contemporary with him was C. Sempronius Tuditanus, consul in B.C. 129, whose work also commenced from the earliest times.

All the works hitherto mentioned appear to have been written in the shortest and driest manner, and in a certain rude and ancient simplicity of style. Cn. Gellius, who was contemporary with Piso and Hemina, was the first who wrote a voluminous Roman history, which must have treated copiously of the regal times, as the treaty of Romulus with Tatius was not related till the third book. This prolixity savours more of the author by profession; nor does it appear that Gellius held any high post in the state. We may conclude that his work somewhat resembled in style that of Dionysius; and—what does not give us any high idea of the value of his work—he seems to have rationalized and modernized the early history. Valerius Antias, who flourished a little later, was a writer of the same, or perhaps rather a worse, stamp. Livy gives him a very bad character, and accuses him of falsehood, invention, and exaggeration.[1] At the same time lived Q. Claudius Quadrigarius, whose narrative, however, does not seem to have embraced the period before the capture of Rome by the Gauls. Also C. Licinius Macer, who was impeached by Cicero for extortion in his prætorship in B.C. 66, and escaped by suicide a sentence of condemnation. Macer would appear from notices in Livy to have diligently consulted ancient records and monuments, though he appears not to have been altogether free from the prevailing inclination to modernize the ancient history.

Cicero also claims a place among the Roman annalists, on account of the short sketch which he gives of the early history in the second book of his Republic. It is valuable

[1] See Livy, lii. 5, 8, 31; xxvi. 40; xxxiii. 10, &c.

in spite of its briefness, as being the only extant account of that period, though in a mutilated condition, from the hand of a Latin writer before the time of Livy. From a passage in it some writers have concluded[1] that the substance of it was taken from Polybius; but all the inference the passage justifies is, that Cicero followed the chronology of the Greek historian. Niebuhr, on the other hand, is of opinion[2] that Cicero derived the greater part of his information from Atticus, who had likewise investigated Roman history. We may at all events conclude that Cicero did not make any original researches for so slight a sketch. Its chief value therefore is, that it shows Cicero's notions of the early history to have agreed in most of the essential points with the narrative of Livy: though there are a few marked discrepancies, and probably mistakes, which perhaps arose from carelessness. Occasional references to Roman history are also found in Cicero's other works; but he does not seem to have made a thorough study of it, or even of the Roman constitution.

About this time a vast number of historians ("scriptorum turba," Liv. Praef.) appears to have arisen, each endeavouring to throw some new light on Roman history; but for the most part their works have perished, and the names only of a few, with some fragments of their writings, have come down to us. M. Terentius Varro, a contemporary of Cicero, styled from his great learning "doctissimus Romanorum," wrote many books on Roman antiquities. The only works of his which could really be called historical were his Annales, which must have been tolerably copious for the early history, as it appears from Charisius[3] that the reign of Servius Tullius occurred in the third book; and a history of the Second Punic War. His other works cannot properly be called historical, though they contained valuable materials for history. Such were his De Vitâ Populi Romani, De Initiis

---

[1] See Schwegler, R. L. S. 94. The passage, which refers to the years of Numa, runs as follows: "Sequamur enim potissimum Polybium nostrum, quo nemo fuit in exquirendis temporibus diligentior," Rep. ii. 14; cf. Becker, I. 68.
[2] Lectures, i. 45.
[3] Lib. I.

Urbis Romæ, De Rebus Urbanis, De Republicâ, De Rebus Trojanis, &c.; some of which, however, were probably only portions of his Antiquitates. His book De Linguâ Latinâ, of which a considerable part is extant, contains many notices of Roman antiquities.

Titus Pomponius Atticus, the friend of Cicero, appears to have drawn up a scheme of Roman history apparently in a tabular form, which he called Annalis. It recorded in chronological order every law, every treaty, and every war, while the histories of distinguished families were interwoven in it.[1] He seems also to have written the history of several Roman families separately, as that of the Gens Junia, at the request of Brutus; of the Marcelli, Fabii, Æmilii, &c. Materials for such biographies must therefore have been extant. It may be said that such sources were polluted by partiality and family pride; but one biography of a leading family would be corrective of another, and there would always be critics enough to denounce and expose pretensions that were too egregious. Indeed Pliny tells us that Messalla Corvinus, who flourished in the reign of Augustus, wrote his book De Romanis Familiis for that very purpose.[2]

About the same time, Q. Ælius Tubero wrote a history of Rome from its origin, which is sometimes quoted by Livy and Dionysius. The work of Sallust did not touch upon the early period of Rome. Cornelius Nepos, the friend of Cicero, Atticus, and Catullus, wrote an epitome of universal history, in which the facts of the early Roman history must have been inserted.

We are now arrived at the greatest of the Roman historians, whose authority and reputation have been so much attacked in recent times. As Livy is the chief and best source for the history of Rome, his work has, of course, been subjected to the most minute and searching examination by the sceptical critics. That from such an ordeal it should have come out totally unscathed was hardly to be expected. Livy's materials, in the earlier part of his subject, were too scanty and unsatisfactory not to leave here and there a loop-

[1] Corn. Nep. Att. 18. [2] H. N. xxxv. 2, § 8; cf. xxxiv. 38.

hole for attack; and yet we will venture to say, that the success of his assailants has not been very great or astonishing. A considerable part of their charges is founded on their own misconceptions of the Roman history and constitution. Thus we find Schwegler enumerating[1] among Livy's "blunders" that he holds the Patres who assumed the government when the throne was vacated to have been the Senate (Lib. i. 17, 32); that the Patres Auctores who confirmed the resolutions of the people were also senators (Lib. i. 17); that he misunderstands in like manner the term *patres*, when he considers Patres Minorum Gentium to be the hundred new senators created by Tarquinius Priscus. Both these acts, it is said, cannot have been identical, because Tarquin, according to consentient tradition, doubled the patrician races (the Patres), but augmented the Senate only by a third.

We have examined these points in their proper places in the sequel of this work, and need not therefore enter here into a discussion of them. We have endeavoured to show that the Patres who became Interreges were really the Senate; that the Patres who gave their *auctoritas* were also the senators, as well as the Patres Minorum Gentium created by Tarquin; that it is not true, nor handed down by "consentient tradition," that Tarquin doubled the patrician races, or stem tribes, and augmented the Senate only by a third.[2] It may be true, as Schwegler goes on to complain, that Livy, when speaking of ancient matters, sometimes uses phrases pertaining to them in the more modern sense which they had in his own time; but the question is, whether such a use of them would for a moment have puzzled a Roman, though such may be its effect upon us, who know the language only through dictionaries. We cannot believe that Livy should not have known the true meaning of such words as *concilium*, *populus*, *contio*, &c., and the imputation on his knowledge is probably only the result of our own ignorance. It would be impossible within our limits to examine every charge of this

---
[1] R. i. S. 108, f.
[2] See below, p. 139, *sq.*; 254, *sqq.*; 287, *sq.*; 347, *sq.*

sort; such an undertaking would rather belong to a regular edition of Livy; and even if it should be proved that he may now and then have inadvertently used a word improperly, still, in any candid view of the matter, this forms no serious drawback to the general value of his testimony.

Nor will we enter into the question whether Livy's conception of Roman history was that of a philosopher or a statesman. For the purpose of the present volume it suffices to inquire whether he related the facts of the early history with good faith and also with discrimination. His work is universally allowed to be characterized by simplicity, candour, and a love of truth; and those qualities are better guarantees for the fidelity of his narrative than all the philosophy in the world. His pre-eminent merit, so far as our object is concerned, is, that he faithfully followed the ancient sources. This is admitted by Schwegler, who says: "Er gibt die alte Sage verhältnismässig treu und unverfälscht wieder."[1] To the same effect Lachmann observes, in his elaborate treatise on Livy and his sources: "Summa in eo erat rerum et auctorum antiquorum reverentia, et fides ac religio, qua eos sequutus est, nec nova mirabilisque narrandi, nec causas rationesque rerum ex suo ingenio addendi cupiditate, neo præjudicatis opinionibus partiumque studio corrupta" . . . "Cum fide antiquos sequitur, et veritatem sub mythorum involucris latentem non eruit sed illæsam servavit, ubi Dionysius recentiorum exornationes aut ingenium suum sequutus omnia auxit et ipsis verbis recentiora tempora produxit."[2] Wachsmuth admits that Livy's annalistic method, though not philosophical, is a proof that he followed his sources, and hence accords to him an authority equal to that of the old annalists.[3] And Sir G. C. Lewis is also of opinion[4] that Livy framed his narrative after Fabius Pictor, Cincius, and Cato, quoting in corroboration of it the following sentence from Niebuhr: "One may assume that Livy took every circumstance in his narrative from some of his predecessors,

[1] B. I. S. 105.
[2] De Fontibus Hist. T. Livii, Pars Prior, p. 63.
[3] Aeltere Gesch. S. 37, 42.   [4] Credibility, &c. vol. I. p. 248.

and never added anything of his own except the colouring of his style."

We may consider, then, that we possess in Livy's narrative of the regal period the substance of the history as given by the earliest annalists; and its general resemblance to what we find in other authors—as, for example, Cicero and Dionysius—confirms this assumption. In this view of the matter, the credibility of the early Roman history rests almost entirely on the good faith of the annalists in question, a subject to which we have already alluded, and to which we shall again have occasion to advert in the second part of this dissertation. But in Livy's work we also possess the advantage of having these early traditions winnowed from the heap after a searching critical examination. This is evident from a comparison of his narrative with that of Dionysius. Livy was a highly judicious, not to say sceptical, writer. His incredulity has, in fact, been of no slight service to the assailants of the history, who have eagerly caught at all his doubts and admissions in support of their arguments. But this scepticism renders what remains all the more valuable. And though we find in Livy's work some of those fables which his countrymen believed to be inseparably connected with their glory, yet the attentive reader will easily discriminate what traditions the historian himself accepted, and what he rejected.

Of the remaining Latin historians of Rome it is not necessary to speak. Those of any note that are still extant contain only passing allusions to the earlier history; while such compilers as Florus, Eutropius, Orosius, and others of the like stamp, merit not the attention of the critical inquirer. We will therefore pass on to the second part of the subject of this dissertation, and proceed to examine the internal evidence connected with the early Roman history.

INTERNAL EVIDENCE.

The critics who deny that the early Roman history was derived from the sources before enumerated are necessarily bound to show in what manner it originated. For this purpose several hypotheses have been formed. They rest, of course, on an examination of the history such as it has come down to us in the works of the extant historians, and are therefore for the most part founded on inference and conjecture; supported, so far as it may be possible, by any passages in ancient authors that may seem to favour these conjectures. The objections to the extant history, which are supposed to be fatal to the assumption that it can have been founded on any authentic records, are drawn from its alleged general improbability, and sometimes even impossibility, which are said to be displayed in the supernatural events which it records, in the contradictions which it contains, and in the confusion which marks its chronology. The extant history being deemed, from these considerations, to be in great part, if not wholly, fictitious, though some small part of it may possibly rest on oral tradition, some critics are of opinion that the great bulk of it must have been derived from ancient poems, others that it is a downright forgery, and others again—which seems to be now the favourite hypothesis—that it is founded on ætiology and symbolization; that is, either on fables intended to explain the origin and causes of the different names that are found in the early history, or of stories invented to symbolize some abstract ideas which the early Romans are supposed to have been incapable of expressing in words. We will examine each of these hypotheses in their order, and we will then proceed to investigate the charge of improbability or impossibility.

The theory that the early Roman history is founded on ancient poems was brought forward by Niebuhr,[1] and enjoyed awhile immense favour. We may be indebted to it in this country for Dr. Arnold's "History," and for Lord Macaulay's "Lays of Ancient Rome." But it is now going out of fashion,

[1] It did not altogether originate with Niebuhr; Perizonius had alluded to such a source in his Animadvv. Hist. c. 6. See Niebuhr's Röm. Gesch. B. L S. 255, ff. (4te Aufl.) and his Lectures (Eng. transl. edited by Dr. Schmitz), vol. L pp. 12, 17, &c.

and indeed, as we shall endeavour to show, it is altogether untenable.¹

One sort of historical songs, according to Niebuhr, were those sung at banquets in praise of distinguished men, as we learn on the authority of Cato, quoted in the following passage from Cicero:—" Gravissimus auctor in Originibus dixit Cato, morem apud majores hunc epularum fuisse, ut deinceps, qui accubarent, canerent ad tibiam clarorum virorum laudes atque virtutes."² The custom is also alluded to by Varro:³ " (Aderant) in conviviis pueri modesti ut cantarent carmina antiqua, in quibus laudes erant majorum, assa voce, et cum tibicine." The proper office of the Camenæ was supposed to be to sing the praises of the ancients.⁴

But, among his quotations on this subject, Niebuhr has omitted one which shows that this kind of songs, and the singers of them, were held in no great esteem. Cicero, in another passage of his Tusculan Questions, says:—" Quamquam est in Originibus, solitos esse in epulis canere convivas ad tibicinem de clarorum hominum virtutibus: honorem tamen huic generi non fuisse declarat oratio Catonis, in qua objecit, ut probrum, Marco Nobiliori, quod is in provinciam poetas duxisset."⁵ But if in these songs the Roman history was embodied, Cato could hardly have objected to them, who was fond of that subject, and wrote a book upon it. Nor does his account of them convey the remotest hint that they were in any way connected with history. That they were lyrical songs, and not epic rhapsodies, appears from the fact of their being sung to the flute; and no connected history could have been conveyed in snatches of songs after dinner.

¹ For a more elaborate refutation the reader may consult Sir G. C. Lewis, Credibility, &c. vol. i. ch. 6, n. 5; and Schwegler, Röm. Gesch. Band. i. Buch i. § 23.
² Brutus, 19; Tusc. Q. iv. 2. ³ Ap. Non. H. 70, assa voce.
⁴ "Camenæ, musæ, quod canunt antiquorum laudes."—Paul. Diac. p. 43, "Camenæ." When Niebuhr adds: "and among these also of kings," he does not state on what authority he makes that addition. It is not in Paulina. That Ennius sang the kings, and that Lucretius mentions them with honour, are no proofs that they were celebrated in these banqueting songs.
⁵ Tusc. Q. i. 2.

Besides, the narrative of the regal period is for the most part exceedingly prosaic. The chief exceptions are some parts of the reign of Tarquinius Superbus, which contain materials that might be adapted to a poetical subject, just like the reign of Mary Queen of Scots, and several other modern sovereigns. What, for instance, could prove a more striking or better defined rhapsody in a national epopee than the Hundred Days, Bonaparte's escape from Elba, his landing in France, his march to Paris, his final struggle and overthrow, and his banishment to St. Helena? Yet these are facts which have occurred in the memory of the present generation, or, at least, of the more elderly among them. But to sing the reign of Tarquin would not agree with Cato's description, which was to sing the *virtues* of famous men, a description which unfortunately at once banishes from these songs a great part of history, the actors in which are frequently more remarkable for their vices than for their virtues. And though it may be allowed that the Romans had a few songs concerning historical personages, as those in honour of Romulus, mentioned by Fabius Pictor as still sung in his time,[1] yet these would be very far from making a history.

Niebuhr discovers another sort of historical songs in the *nœniæ*, or dirges, sung at funerals. But the Romans could not have been always singing funereal dirges. They would not have formed very lively entertainments at a dinner-party, nor can we imagine any other occasion, except the actual funeral, on which people would have assembled for the pleasure of hearing them. The *præficæ* and their pipers would have to be hired, and the whole affair would have been a sort of profanation of a sacred rite. These nœniæ, therefore, however great the individual in whose honour they were sung, could not have been very extensively known among the people at large, and consequently could not have formed the basis of any popular history. Niebuhr thinks he discovers such nœniæ, or remnants of them, in the inscriptions found in the tombs of the Scipios. But, even allowing this to be so, when they began to be engraved they ceased to be only songs,

[1] Dionys. l. 79.

and might take their place, for so much as they were worth, among written funeral orations, busts with titles, and other family records, as materials for history. All that we contend for is that, in the shape of songs, they could have afforded no such materials.

Besides these festive and these funereal songs, Niebuhr thinks that the whole history of the kings was conveyed in a series of rhapsodies.[1] The reign of Romulus formed of itself an epopee. Numa was celebrated only in short songs. Tullus, the story of the Horatii, and the destruction of Alba, formed an epic whole, like the poem of Romulus; nay, we have even a fragment of it preserved in Livy,[2] in the "lex horrendi carminis." After this, however, there is unfortunately a gap. The reign of Ancus has not the slightest poetical colouring, and the question how it came down to us must therefore remain, according to this hypothesis, a mystery. But the poetry begins again with L. Tarquinius Priscus, forming a magnificent epopee which terminates with the battle of Regillus. Its parts are, the arrival of Tarquin at Rome, his deeds and victories, his death, the supernatural history of Servius, the criminal marriage of Tullia, the murder of the righteous king, the whole history of the last Tarquin, the tokens of his fall, Lucretia, the disguise of Brutus, his death, the war of Porsena, and lastly, the quite Homeric battle of Regillus. These formed a poem which in depth and brilliancy of fancy far surpassed anything that Rome afterwards produced. Deficient in the unity of the most perfect Grecian poem, it is divided into sections, which correspond with the adventures of the Niebelungenlied; and should any one, says Niebuhr, have the boldness to restore this poem, he would commit a great error if he chose any other plan than this noble form.

On this we may remark, that for the existence of the banqueting songs and the nœniæ before spoken of there is at least some evidence; but where shall we find any for the existence of these supposed epopees? To use a slang quasi-philosophical phrase of the day, Niebuhr seems to have

[1] B. i. S. 272, f.   [2] Lib. i. 26.

developed them out of his "inner consciousness." The only passage which he adduces in support of his view is the following one from Ennius:—

> "Scripsere alii rem
> Versibu', quos olim Fauni Vatesque canebant
> Quom neque Musarum scopulos quisquam superarat
> Nec dicti studiosus erat."

But the *rem*, or subject, here alluded to cannot be any of these ancient epopees, because the word *scripsere* can refer only to some written poem, and indeed a passage in Cicero's Brutus[1] shows that Ennius was referring to the poem of Nævius on the First Punic War. The whole value of the passage, therefore, in relation to Niebuhr's view, is that there existed long before the time of Ennius verses sung by Fauni and Vates— Fauns and poets, or prophets. Now these surely were not epopees. For the verses of the Fauns, as we learn from Varro, were those in which they delivered their oracles in woods and solitary places; and they were in the rugged Saturnian metre, in which Nævius had composed the poem alluded to.[2] The "annosa volumina vatum" mentioned by Horace,[3] are also cited by Niebuhr in support of his view,[4] though with the admission that these were probably prophetical books, like those of the Marcii—an admission which is doubtless correct. For such is the view taken by Cicero of what Ennius meant by the word *vates*, as appears from the following passage:—"Eodem enim modo multa a vaticinantibus sæpe prædicta sunt neque solum verbis, sed etiam

> 'Versibu', quos olim Fauni vatesque canebant.'

Similiter Marcius et Publicius vates cecinisse dicuntur."[5] Ennius therefore was alluding to the metrical predictions of Marcius and Publicius, of the former of which we have a specimen in Livy,[6] and not to any historical epopees.

Moreover, had these epic poems ever existed, it is most

---

[1] Cap. 19, 75, *sq*.
[2] "Fauni dei Latinorum, ita ut Faunus et Fauna sit; hos versibus, quos vocant Saturnios, in silvestribus locis traditum est solitos fari futura a quo fando Faunos dictos."—L. L. vii. 36.
[3] Epp. ii. 1, 26.   [4] R. i. S. 274, Anm. 688.
[5] De Div. i. 50, 114, *sq*.   [6] Lib. xxv. 12.

extraordinary that they should not only have entirely disappeared, but that not even a hint of their former existence should be found in any ancient author. Niebuhr would fain point to some traces of them in the "lex horrendi carminis," quoted by Livy in his narrative of the trial of Horatius; and he has taken the liberty of altering it a little, *sub silentio*, in order to make it square with his theory. But *carmen* is a common expression for any legal, constitutional, or religious formula;[1] nor can the substance of the law, even with Niebuhr's *ad libitum* emendation, be tortured into metre. Its form, though perhaps rather more antique, very much resembles that of the specimens of Roman laws given by Cicero in the third book of his De Legibus. We might as well contend that Livy's history was originally written in hexameters, because his preface opens with an imperfect one,[2] as infer a metrical history from a law like this. The assumption of such a history is quite at variance with the unpoetical nature of the Roman mind, and especially in the earlier days of Rome. But we need not any longer detain the reader with an examination of this theory. It was partially abandoned, or at all events very extensively modified, by Niebuhr himself, at the beginning of his second volume, and we believe that it is now pretty universally rejected by scholars.

Some authors are of opinion that the early Roman history, or at all events the best materials for it, is a direct and barefaced forgery. Thus Sir G. C. Lewis remarks:[3] "It has been already mentioned that Clodius, the author of a work on Roman chronology, described the early records as having perished in the Gallic conflagration, and as having been afterwards replaced by registers fabricated with the view of doing honour to particular persons. We have likewise cited Cicero's account of the early eclipses having been calculated back from a certain solar eclipse recorded in the Annales Maximi. These testimonies lead to the inference that, after the early annals had been destroyed, or when a demand arose for annals

---

[1] See the authorities collected by Sir G. C. Lewis, vol. i. p. 224, note 126.
[2] "Facturusne operæ pretium sim," &c.
[3] Credibility, &c. vol. i. p. 165, seq.

which never had existed, forgeries were executed, by which a record of this kind for the early period of Rome was supplied."

"Ecce iterum Crispinus!" This Clodius is too valuable a witness to let drop, though nobody knows who he is, and though the only voucher, even for his existence, is such a writer as Plutarch. But it is evident, even from the testimony of Clodius himself, that there had once been annals, or how could they be said to have been destroyed? Sir G. C. Lewis has two strings to his bow, for fear that one should break; but it only makes his weapon the weaker. For if there were no annals, as Sir G. C. Lewis in another place has attempted to show, from the passage in Cicero about eclipses, which we have already examined,[1] then the inference from Clodius that they were *replaced* by fabricated ones is absurd; and if there were annals, then the inference from Cicero that they did not exist is good for nothing. It is evident that either the one or the other of these witnesses must be discarded; either Clodius, who says that annals once existed, were destroyed, and replaced by forged ones, or Cicero, who, by inference and construction, is supposed to say that they never existed at all. But we have shown before that the passage in Cicero will admit of no such interpretation.

We will assume, however, for a moment, even for the sake of Sir G. C. Lewis's hypothesis, that early annals had existed and been destroyed; at what period could it have been that a demand arose for them, which was supplied by means of forgery? and who could have been the forgers?

It is plain that a demand for annals must have existed from the very first day that a line of them was written, or why should they have been kept at all? Sir G. C. Lewis, however, appears to think that nobody cared anything about them, till certain persons took it into their heads to write a Roman history for the public; and as they wanted materials for the earlier part, they must have applied to the Pontifex Maximus, and that personage, not having any Annales earlier than the Gallic conflagration, very obligingly supplied them

[1] Above, p. xxxvii. *seq.*

with a forged set! For it is evident that no private individual could have forged them, since, first, there would have been no demand for such things—that is, in the sense meant by Sir G. C. Lewis—before the commencement of historical writing for the public; and, secondly, Fabius Pictor, Cencius Alimentus, Cato, and others, must have been very foolish persons, to say no worse, if, knowing that the Pontifex Maximus was the only person privileged to keep such annals, they had accepted any from a private individual.

It might be said that the early history, as recorded by the first writers, was a forgery of a different kind; that it was not founded on any documents or records at all, but was, for the most part at least, a pure literary invention. But such a supposition is at once overthrown by considering the essential agreement in the narratives of the earliest writers. It is impossible that several authors, writing independently, should have adopted almost exactly the same tale, even if we could imagine that a grave author like Cato, for instance, should have lent himself to such a thing. Nor does the character of the history bear the appearance of invention. Much of it is dry detail, which even the most impudent forger of a highly literary age would not have had the hardihood to invent. Any motive for such a forgery could only have been the gain expected from it. But it is impossible to attribute such a motive to the first Roman annalists, who were men of distinction, and not needy and venal *littérateurs*, seeking a living by their pen.

Another hypothesis is, that the early Roman history was entirely derived from Greek writers. This view has been adopted by A. W. Schlegel,[1] and other German critics; but, with all our respect for Schlegel's critical talents, we must avow our entire disbelief in his theory. According to him, the early Roman history is nothing but a "Greek romance," derived by the barbarous Romans from Greek writers, when, after the war with Pyrrhus, they came to be better acquainted with that nation. But the early Roman history, even that of

[1] Werke, B. xii. S. 447, sqq., 486, sqq.; cf. Dahlmann, Forschungen auf dem Gebiete der Gesch. ii. 1, S. 129, f.

the kings, contains many details concerning constitutional, legal, consuetudinary, and topographical points, which could not possibly have proceeded from any but a native pen. We mean not, however, to deny that some particulars may have been supplied by Greek writers, and especially, as we have already observed, by Timæus. But whatever in Timæus, or in any other Greek writer, would have approved itself to a Roman understanding, must have been derived, immediately or remotely, from a Roman source. Schlegel's idea that the Romans could have been indebted for any part of their history to the needy Greeks who flocked to Rome about the age of Augustus, is altogether preposterous.

We will now proceed to examine Schwegler's view of the origin of the early history. It is constructed with much plausibility, and as it has to a considerable extent been adopted by Sir G. C. Lewis, we will give it at length in a translation:[1]—

"The true and genuine tradition of the foundation of Rome, and of its earliest fortunes,—if indeed such a tradition ever existed,—appears to have been soon lost. And this could scarcely be otherwise. Being neither secured against destruction or falsification by being committed to writing, nor having become the subject of popular poetry, and thus obtained a firm traditional form at least in song, it must, from the nature of the case, have become mute and been extinguished in the course of generations. It is very possible, nay probable, that in the time of the Decemvirs the Romans no longer knew anything certain respecting the origin of their city. But in this ignorance they did not acquiesce. It was felt necessary to say something more definite respecting a period and events of which no historical knowledge existed; and therefore, on a foundation of obscure remembrances and unconnected legends which had been preserved, a history was subtly constructed from proper names, monuments, institutions, and usages, wherewith to fill up the gap of tradition. In this process, conscious deceit and designed falsification are not for an instant to be imputed; on the contrary, a full persuasion was

[1] See Röm. Gesch. Buch i. § 20.

entertained that in these narratives the real course of events had been felicitously divined, and the original history reconstructed. It is of course to be understood that a history devised in such a manner was not at first a connected whole, such as is presented to us in the works on Roman history. This whole,—in which the legend of Æneas' settlement is brought into pragmatical connexion with the foundation and history of Alba Longa, and the line of the Alban kings with the foundation of Rome, so that the story, from the landing of Ancus to the overthrow of the younger Tarquin, is strung together by the thread of a continuous, unbroken historical narrative,—this systematic whole was of course first developed by a knitting of it together, and a common working at it, and partly also, no doubt, by literary industry and reflection.

"If we resolve this history into its component parts, and examine each separate part by itself, with regard to its origin and genetic motives, it appears that the Roman legends and traditions are of very different growth, and require very different explanations.

"And first of all it must be recognised that certain fundamental things in the traditional history of the kings are historical, and derived from historical memory. Some remembrance, though a very confused one, of the principal points in the development of the Roman constitution was preserved till the literary times. Hence we cannot withhold from the constitutional traditions a certain degree of credibility. The united kingdom of the Romans and Sabines ; the three stem-tribes, and their successive origin ; the three centuries of knights ; the successive augmentation of the Senate till it reached the number of three hundred ; the addition of a plebs ; the creation of the gentes minores ; the introduction of the census ; the overthrow of the monarchy and the foundation of a republic—these fundamental points of the oldest constitutional history are in all probability essentially historical ; although the details, and especially the numerical ones, with which they are related, as well as the causal connexion in which they are placed by the historians, may nevertheless be invented or formed by construction. But over this foundation of facts a rank and luxuriant growth of invention has entwined itself; a growth of legends which we must now more closely examine, and lay them bare in their germs.

"A distinction has in general been rightly drawn between myth and legend. Legend is the memory of remarkable occurrences propagated from generation to generation in the mouth of the people, particularly in national songs, and decked out by the imagination, more or less arbitrarily, but without any conscious design, so as to become wonderful. A myth is exactly the opposite of a legend. If the kernel of a legend is some historical fact, only adorned by the inventions added to it, and thus quantitatively exaggerated, so on the contrary some definite idea is the kernel and genetic motive of the myth, and the actual occurrence only the stuff, or means, which the poet uses in order to bring the idea into view and contemplation.

"If we apply this view to early Roman history, it cannot be denied that it contains both legends and myths, in the strict sense of them just laid down. To give some examples: the heroic deeds of an Horatius Cocles, a Mucius Scævola, a Clœlia, may pass for legends; Brutus is a legendary figure; the battle of Lake Regillus is depicted in a legendary manner; and in like manner the victorious career of Coriolanus; the destruction of the three hundred Fabii; the expedition of Cincinnatus to the Algidus. On the other hand the procreation of Servius Tullius by the Lar of the palace is a specimen of a myth; in which is expressed the idea that the innermost spirit of the Roman monarchy became incarnate in this king. Further, the contest of Hercules (that is, of the heavenly god Sancus) with Cacus, breathing smoke and fire, is a pure myth, proceeding from an ancient symbolism of nature. Again, the reference of the disparate elements of the Roman national mind in which political and warlike capacity were so remarkably blended with religious veneration, to the disparate personifications of two original founders, of whom one, a warlike prince, regulates the civil and military affairs of the State, the other, a prince of peace, those of religion and divine worship, is an historical myth.

"The greater part of the Roman traditions, however, fall neither under the definition of legend nor under that of pure ideal myth: they are rather, to use such an expression, ætiological myths: that is, they relate events and occurrences which have been imagined or subtly invented in order to explain genetically some given fact, or the name of a custom, usage, worship, institution, place, monument, sanctuary, &c. The ætiological myth is a peculiar subordinate sort of myth. It is a myth in so far as the actual event in the narrative of which it consists is a freely imagined one; but it differs from the true myth insomuch as its motive, and the point whence it proceeds, is not an idea, or an ideal contemplation, but one empirically given, which through this narration is explained and referred to fundamental causes. The ætiological myths are the oldest and indeed for the most part childish attempts at historical hypotheses. The early Roman history is rich in such ætiological myths. The settlement of Evander, the presence of Hercules in Rome, the story of the Potitii and Pinarii, the taking possession and saving of the Palladium by the Nantii, the sow with the thirty pigs, the rape of the Sabines, the beautiful bride of Talassius, the fable of Tarpeia, the founding of the Temple of Jupiter Stator, the traditions respecting the origin of the name of the Lacus Curtius, the miraculous deed of Attus Navius, and other traditions of this sort, may serve as examples of them, and will be explained from this point of view in the course of the following disquisition. Plutarch's 'Roman Questions' contain a rich and instructive collection of such ætiological myths.

"The etymological myth is a subordinate kind of the ætiological, which takes as its point of departure some given proper name, and seeks to explain its origin by suggesting for it some actual event. The early Roman history is also very rich in myths of this sort; a heap of the fables which it contains has been spun out of proper names. Such is the fable of Argos, the guest of Evander (whence the name of

Argiletum, Serv. Æn. viii. 345), and the Argive colony at Rome; the birth of Silvius Posthumus in the wood; the relation of Evander, the good man, to Cacus, the bad man; the suckling of Romulus; the relation of the sucklings to the ruminal fig-tree; the reputed origin of the Fossa Cluilia; the extraction of the Tarquins from Tarquinii; the discovery of the head of Olus; the birth of Servius Tullius from a slave; the building of the Tullianum by the like-named king; the idiocy of Brutus; Scævola's burnt right hand; the conquest of Corioli by Coriolanus, &c.

"There is still another sort of Roman tradition, to be distinguished from the ætiological and etymological myths; such traditions as may be described as mythical clothings of actual relations and events, which thus occupy a middle place between myth and legend. To this head belongs, for example, the legend of the Sibyl who comes to Rome in the reign of the younger Tarquin, offers this king nine books of divine prophecies at a high price, being ridiculed by him burns three of them, and then another three, before his eyes, and lastly sells to the king the three still left at the price originally demanded for the nine. An actual occurrence lies doubtless at the bottom of this legend; the fact that the Sibylline prophecies were probably brought to Rome from Cumæ in the reign of the second Tarquin; but the clothing of this fact is invention, a mean between legend and myth. Perhaps it is the same with the making of the Roman kings seven in number; these seven kings represent the seven fundamental facts of the older (pre-republican) history of Rome which remained in historical remembrance.

"In general the Roman myths have the peculiar and characteristic property, that as a rule they are not unlicensed invention, nor creations of the fancy; and particularly, not like the greater part of the narratives of the Greek mythology, myth from natural philosophy, or resting on a symbolism of nature, but that they are historical myths, that a certain aspect of actual relationships and real events lies at the bottom of them. The figures of Romulus and Tatius, for example, are indeed mythical: they never really existed;

but their reputed double rule contains nevertheless historical truth: it is the mythical expression of a real historical relationship, of the united Latino-Sabine twofold state. The contest of Tarquinius Priscus with the augur Attus Navius is to be similarly judged: it is scarcely historical in the manner in which it is related; at all events, the story of the whetstone is an evident fable: nevertheless a real event is mirrored in it; the historical conflict of the pre-Tarquinian sacerdotal state with the political ideas of the Tarquinian dynasty. In most of the legends and myths of the ancient Roman history, historical remembrances and appearances constitute in like manner the foundation; they may be detached from it if one refers each myth to the general fundamental representation which forms its genetic motive.

" It can scarcely be necessary to justify this conception of the early Roman history, and especially the idea of the myth, against such objections as have been recently brought against it, in which the 'levity' and the 'vain and idle play of thoughts,' of such mythic creations have been found irreconcilable with the moral earnestness and the practical turn of mind of the ancient Romans. This objection would then only hit the mark if the myths were arbitrary and conscious inventions,—if, in short, they were wilful lies. They are, however, so little such, that they are rather the only language in which a people in a certain grade of civilization can express its thoughts and ideas. Thus, for example, the Latin language, at that point of civilization which the Romans had attained at the time when such myths were invented, was unable to express exhaustively the historical conflict between the pre-Tarquinian and Tarquinian idea of a state; wherefore the conception was aided by symbolizing and bringing into view in a single significant scene this contest and the general events connected with it: a scene which, empirically taken, is at all events unhistorical, but in its foundation is historically true. Let us figure to ourselves a people, which, having reached a certain stage of culture, feels the want of bringing under its contemplation its primitive existence, of sketching for itself a picture of its original condition, of which it has no longer any historical knowledge, of tracing the causes of its present institutions and circumstances, of its political and sacerdotal traditions: how will it be able to satisfy this want in any other way than by the invention of myths? What out of its present consciousness it expresses about its origin it will be obliged—so long as it is not yet intellectually ripe enough to give these expressions in the form of historical hypotheses—to express in the form of images, that is, in mythic language.

"In what precedes we have laid down the various motives and modes of origin of the Roman legends and traditions. The legends which arose in this manner were then further spun out by intelligent reflection, and connected with one another; and thus by degrees arose that complete whole of Roman tradition which the Roman historians found and noted down. The legend of Silvius Posthumus, the ancestor of the Alban Silvii, may serve as an example of such myth-spinning. Silvius, it is said, obtained that name because he was born in a wood—evidently an etymological myth. Thus —it was further inferred—his mother Lavinia must have sojourned in the wood at the time of his birth: she had therefore doubtless fled thither; hence probably after the death of her husband Æneas; thus probably for fear of her step-son Ascanius. That all these accounts rest not on real tradition, but on pure invention, is manifest. In like manner the reputed origin of the Roman population from a runaway rabble, and the account that it was on this ground that the envoys of Romulus, who proposed *connubium* to the neighbouring peoples, were repulsed with contemptuous words, were certainly only inferred from the purely mythical narrative of the rape of the Sabines. The reputed despotism exercised by Romulus in the later years of his reign, and the body-guard with which he surrounded himself, are nothing but inferences drawn from the legend of his dismemberment (which was also mythical in its origin) in order to explain by them that enigmatical act.

"It is of course understood that every single trait of the traditionary history cannot any longer be elucidated; but the whole manner of its coming into existence will have become by these preliminary remarks sufficiently clear."

This hypothesis is, at all events, more plausible than the preceding ones; yet we do not think that it is a whit more true.

We may observe at the outset that it is a mere guess or conjecture, unsupported by a single scrap of authority. We may further remark that it is needlessly invented; for, as we have already shown, there were other methods, the existence of which rests on the best ancient testimony, by which the Roman history may have come down to us,—namely, through the Annales Maximi, the Commentaries of the Pontifices, &c. The hypothesis of Schwegler, therefore, is not only a guess, but a superfluous one.

Schwegler's motive for choosing the decemviral period as that in which he thought the history first began to be constructed is plain enough. The use of writing could no longer be denied, because the laws of the Twelve Tables were incontestably written laws. But, as we have seen, letters were known long previously; and if they had been first introduced at this late period, some record of their introduction could hardly have been wanting. It does not, however, appear very clearly whether Schwegler supposes that the history thus invented was now first written down, or that it was merely constructed orally, and transmitted in the same manner. But to both these assumptions there are insuperable objections. For if history now began to be written, then—excluding always the Commentarii Pontificum, which Schwegler does not appear to contemplate—Fabius Pictor and Cincius Alimentus were not, as they are universally allowed to have been, the first annalists; and if it was not written, then it is quite impossible that such a body of history, containing many minute details, could have been handed down orally.

We may next remark that, if the theory were tenable, it would still provide us with a good deal of credible history of the regal period. For the decemvirs were appointed only about half a century after the expulsion of the kings; and

h

oral tradition, it is commonly allowed, may be relied on for a century, and even a good deal more, when connected with and supported by usages, laws, monuments, &c. Especially a full and authentic account might be supposed to have come down of the last Tarquin, whose history must have been in the memory of many men still living. Yet of all the kings, at all events after Numa, the reign of the last Tarquin is precisely the one which is said to bear the most traces of falsehood and poetical invention.

Schwegler indeed acknowledges that certain fundamental points of the regal period may be considered as historical; and especially a certain degree of credibility is not to be refused to constitutional traditions. Among such historical things he classes the united state of the Romans and Sabines, the three original tribes, the three centuries of knights, the introduction of the census, the fall of the kings, &c. In short, he allows the main facts of the history, but not the manner in which they are related to have come to pass; though the facts and the method of their accomplishment rest on precisely the same testimony. But round these facts, it is asserted, had entwined itself a rank growth of inventions and falsehoods, the origin of which he proceeds to discuss; and he divides them into legends and myths.

Now we do not mean to assert that the Roman history is altogether free from fiction. If the exaggeration of some actual occurrence constitutes a legend, then no doubt legends are to be found in it, as they are in the early history of most nations. The progress of a story in passing from mouth to mouth is proverbial; nor do we contend that the Romans were free from a natural, we might almost say an inevitable, failing. All we contend for is that these exaggerations do not invalidate the main outlines, the grand features, of the history. On the other hand, we altogether doubt whether it contains myths that come under Schwegler's definition; namely, narratives of occurrences invented merely to typify some abstract idea. We agree with the objectors alluded to by Schwegler, that such inventions are entirely foreign to the Roman turn of mind. The example proposed in the story of Attus Navius is in the highest degree improbable. The invention of a symbolical story of that nature would imply a far higher degree of intellectual refinement and subtlety than the capacity to understand, and, consequently, to express—for if it could not be expressed it could not be understood—the difference between two forms of government. Indeed, a political myth appears to us altogether an absurdity. Schwegler is obliged to confess that it can be found only among the Romans, and that even with them there is some true historical fact at the bottom of it. If it be accompanied with preternatural incidents—as, for instance, the cutting of the whetstone by Attus Navius—which give it a mythic colouring; this circumstance admits of an easy explanation. We shall discuss this point presently, when we come to consider the objections which have been brought against the history on the ground of the supernatural events which it contains. Every supernatural appearance, or supposed appearance, is not necessarily connected with a myth. Thus, for instance, the story of the phallus seen in the fire, to which was attributed the generation of Servius Tullius, may have been the result of fancy, or superstition, or many other causes. It is an extremely far-fetched and improbable supposition, that it was invented in order to express the idea that the spirit of the Roman monarchy became incarnate in Servius; perhaps, of all the Roman kings, the one least fitted to be a type of the monarchy.

Schwegler admits that the greater part of the traditional history of Rome cannot be brought under the definition either of pure myth or even of legend; and he has therefore discovered for them an origin in what he calls the ætiological myth. The ætiological myth is a story subtly invented in order to account for the existence of certain usages, worships, institutions, monuments, &c. Now we will not deny that some inventions of this kind are to be found in the early Roman history, and especially in that portion of it which is prior to the foundation of the city; and it is to this period that the instances cited by Schwegler chiefly belong. It was a common practice among the ancients to magnify their origin and their primæval history. "Datur hæc venia antiquitati, ut, miscendo humana divinis, primordia urbium augustiora faciat," says Livy in his Preface. But we do not believe that any ætiological myths of this description are to be found after the foundation of the city, or at all events after the reign of Numa. We may further remark that the ætiological myth cannot have been altogether baseless. For if usages, worships, &c. had come down to be explained, they must have formerly existed. It is true, however, that in the narrative they may have been altered and exaggerated; and thus a settlement of Arcadians may have been attributed to Evander, of Argives to Hercules, and so forth.

Perhaps the most plausible part of Schwegler's theory is that of the etymological myth, a subordinate kind of ætiological myth, invented to explain the origin of proper names. This part of the theory has been very extensively adopted by Sir G. C. Lewis. But it is a purely arbitrary conjecture. If the principle is good for anything, it may be carried a great deal further than the author has carried it, and quite into the historical times. If it be asserted that the conquest of Corioli was invented to explain the name of Coriolanus, the story of Mucius burning his left hand to explain the name of Scævola, the account of Junius's idiocy to explain the name of Brutus, &c., then on the same grounds we may affirm that the conquest of Africa was imagined to explain Scipio's name of Africanus, the wisdom of M. Porcius to explain the name of Cato, &c. In fact the theory amounts to this, that no person can ever be named after a place, nor after some peculiarity; whereas nothing can be more natural and common than the imposition of such names. The greater part of our English surnames have no other origin; as John Carpenter, James Butcher, William Colchester, William Rufus, John Lackland, &c. So also it might be said that the story of a Danish settlement was invented to account for the names of St. Olave's, St. Clement Danes, &c.

Further, Schwegler neglects to observe that tradition has handed down many things that are not necessarily connected with any proper name, usage, institution, &c., and the origin of which cannot be explained by any ætiological myth. Thus the religious system of the Romans, the Cloaca Maxima, the circus, the census, the Capitoline temple, &c. are not necessarily connected with the names of Numa, of Servius Tullius, of the Tarquins, nor can they be referred to those sovereigns by the invention of an ætiological myth. There must, therefore, have been a substantive tradition, unconnected with, and independent of, mere names. Occasions will present themselves in the sequel of this work for further examining this ætiological theory—as, for example, in its application to the story of the Horatii and Curiatii[1]—and we need not, therefore, pursue the subject here.

Having thus considered the causes which have been assigned for the existence of the Roman history, we will next proceed to examine the arguments which have been brought forward against its authenticity from its alleged general improbability.

One of these arguments is based on the supernatural occurrences which it relates. Schwegler, after examining the sources of Roman history, observes:[2] "By the preceding exposition we think it has been sufficiently shown what the case is with regard to the testimony of the earliest Roman history; and that if this history has been recently claimed as 'attested,'[3] a very confused idea of historical 'attestation' lies at the bottom of such a notion. What does it signify to assert over and over again that it was once historically handed down, and that the Romans themselves believed it? By the same maxim, anybody might claim the whole Grecian mythology as history, since that was also handed down, and also at one time believed. By this maxim Romulus was actually the son of Mars, and Picus, Faunus, and Latinus were once really kings of Laurentum. Even Dionysius says:[4] 'At that time Faunus reigned over the aborigines, a man of action as well as great wisdom;' and later authors even give the years of the three Laurentine kings.[5] If we are to admit at once as

---

[1] Below, p. 190, sqq. [2] Buch i. § 19.
[3] The author seems to be alluding to the History of Gerlach and Bachofen.
[4] Lib. i. 31. [5] Eusebius, Hieronymus, Syncellus.

historical all that the Roman historians relate in good faith; if we are to suffer ourselves to be led in the representation of the deeds of the Romans by the Roman standard of knowledge and belief; it is much more consistent to accept, with Theod. Ryck, even Janus and Hercules as historical persons, than to draw the boundary line between the mythical and the historical so arbitrarily as it is drawn in the most recent defences of the history. This boundary line must be drawn somewhere else; it must be drawn where the supernatural events cease: for the miraculous, the 'dearest child' of popular belief, is the surest criterion of invention. Where miracles cease, there history begins."

On this it may be remarked that if the line is to be drawn where the supernatural ceases, then it must be placed a great deal lower than where Schwegler draws it. It is commonly allowed that the narrative of the Second Punic War is historical. Yet it was a general belief among the Romans that Hannibal was conducted over the Alps by some divine being.[1] Livy records many prodigies that occurred in the year B.C. 169—as a torch in the heavens, a speaking cow, a weeping statue of Apollo, showers of stones and blood, &c.[2] Such prodigies continued to be publicly recorded and expiated down to the imperial times. It is related that, a few months before the murder of Julius Cæsar, there was discovered at Capua, in the reputed tomb of Capys, its founder, a brazen tablet with a Greek inscription, purporting that when the bones of Capys should be disinterred it would happen that a descendant of Julius would be killed by the hands of his relatives, and would be presently avenged amidst great calamities of Italy. This was no mere vulgar report. It rested on the testimony of Cornelius Balbus, the friend and biographer of Cæsar.[3] The horses which Cæsar had consecrated on passing the Rubicon, and released from further service, were seen before his death to abstain from food and to weep abundantly. The arms of Mars, which were in his house as Pontifex Maximus, were heard to clatter in the night, and the folding doors of the chamber in which he slept

[1] Polyb. iii. 48. [2] Lib. xliii. 13. [3] Suet. Cæs. 81.

opened of themselves. A wren with a laurel branch seeking refuge in Pompey's curia was torn to pieces by other birds. There were also the omens of his wife's dream, of the soothsayer's warning, of his own abortive sacrifices, &c.[1] We might even go down to the reign of Constantine, and instance the labarum and the hosts of celestial warriors seen in the sky. Now these portents are quite as wonderful as those recorded in the regal period,—such as the eagle which lifted the cap of Tarquin the Elder, the story of Attus Navius and the whetstone, the miraculous generation of Servius Tullius, the apparition of Castor and Pollux at Lake Regillus, &c.; yet nobody thinks on that account of rejecting the fact of Hannibal's passage of the Alps, or of Cæsar's assassination, or of Constantine's conversion to Christianity.

The boundary line between history and myth cannot, therefore, be drawn where miraculous events cease to be related; for it is plain from these instances that they may be mixed up with the most genuine and incontestable history. It may be allowed, indeed, that as a people becomes more intellectual and rational, such events become fewer and fewer, and at last, perhaps, almost vanish altogether. But this fact militates, not for Schwegler's view, but against it. History is written from the point of view of the historian, which varies in different ages. When a German rationalist now sits down to recompose a history of early Rome, he of course omits all miraculous tales; but the history, for all that, is not half so credible as the old one that it is trying to supplant. In like manner, if the early history had been invented, according to the notion of Sir G. C. Lewis and other critics, in the latter centuries of the republic, we may be sure that we should not have found half so many miracles in it. The occurrence of them is a proof of its genuineness: they show that it was written when such things were currently believed; that it was noted down contemporaneously, or nearly so, by the pontiffs. Such miraculous events, therefore, instead of being "the surest criterion of invention," are a sure criterion of the absence of invention; that is, in the

[1] Suet. Cæs. 81, and Dion Cass. xliv. 18.

writers of the history. But we are not bound to believe these stories, like Theod. Ryck, because the Romans believed them; nor to reject the history because they believed them. In fact, the educated Romans of the later ages, like Livy, did not believe them; but they did not on that account reject the remainder of the history. Schwegler's argument on this subject is altogether beside the purpose. The Grecian mythology never pretended to be composed, like the Roman history, from records. It is not necessary for us to believe that Romulus was the son of Mars, but only that the Romans, or a great part of them, believed him to be so. If later authors have accepted some of these fables, that is an argument against their judgment, and not against the early history. Dionysius, who was an injudicious historian, believed a great many things that Livy rejected. We need not, therefore, suffer ourselves to be led "by the Roman standard of knowledge and belief," and follow Theodore Ryck; but neither, at the same time, need we be led by the standard set up by the modern rationalistic critics, and reject everything indiscriminately on account of a few wonderful tales.

After enumerating several of these supernatural events in the early history, Schwegler proceeds to remark:[1] "Nobody at present any longer believes these traditions to be historical facts; yet many still entertain the childish notion that we have only to reject these too manifest fables, and to strip off from the mythic narrative what is evidently exaggerated and impossible, and so find in the remainder genuine and actual history. They reflect not that the wonderful and supernatural is the very life, soul, and genetic motive of the myth —not the husk, but the kernel; and that when this is stripped away the remainder is merely the *caput mortuum* of the old poetic legend, and the farthest possible from an historical fact. And, in general, what right have we to regard a narrative which is everywhere interwoven with manifest inventions, as perfectly historical in all those points where the invention is not palpable, which contain nothing absolutely impossible? Such a narrative must rather, on account of its

[1] R. i. Buch i, § 21, S. 51.

connexion with what is indubitably unhistorical, pass at least for problematical, even where it contains nothing impossible in itself."

The force of this reasoning depends on the following assumptions: that the early Roman history is mythical; and that the wonderful and supernatural stories which we find in it prove it to be so. This involves the assertion that all events connected with any supernatural story must necessarily be fabulous; but we have already seen in the case of Cæsar, &c. that this assertion is not true.

The resolution of the question here involved depends on that of another—what was the true origin of the early Roman history? If it was nothing but a myth, then we may admit that, when it is divested of the wonderful and supernatural, the residue will be nothing but a *caput mortuum*. But even Schwegler himself has not ventured to assign to it a purely mythical origin. Thus in a passage in his twenty-sixth section, which we have already translated,[1] he says: "It must be recognised that certain fundamental things in the traditional history of the kings are historical, and derived from historical memory.... But over this foundation of facts a rank and luxuriant growth of invention has entwined itself; a growth of legends which we must now more closely examine," &c.

It follows, then, from Schwegler's own words, that if we strip off the rank and luxuriant inventions, the residuum will be something more than a *caput mortuum*: it will be, on his own showing, genuine history.

In fact, there is no ground at all for assuming the early Roman history, after the foundation of the city, to be mythical. The supernatural occurrences bear, after all, a very small proportion to the mass of prosaic details which it contains; details as far removed as possible from poetical invention. The miracles are only such as might very readily spring up among an illiterate and superstitious people, especially when the belief in them was encouraged and propagated by priestcraft. The exploits of the Maid of Orleans are historical; yet few, perhaps, will believe the supernatural details with

[1] Above, p. xcix.

which they are connected: her commission from heaven to achieve Charles VII.'s coronation at Rheims, her revelation to that monarch of a secret which he believed to be confined to his own breast. The story of Jeanne d'Arc is as romantic and incredible as anything in the early Roman history; and in like manner its supernatural details are doubtless the product either of enthusiasm or craft.

Another argument against the authenticity of the history is derived from the contradictions which it is alleged to contain. On this head Schwegler remarks:[1] "A further proof of the little authenticity of the earliest history of Rome is the striking contradiction of the accounts: a contradiction which displays itself in numberless points; and not only in minor details, but also often in important facts; and thus places the whole history of that period in a doubtful light. A period whose history is so anomalous and contradictory cannot possibly pass for historical. Take, for instance, the astounding jumble in the traditions concerning Romulus's descent! How can these traditions, which make the founder of Rome sometimes the son, sometimes the grandson, of Æneas, and sometimes represent him as born five hundred years later, claim the slightest pretension to historical credibility? Concerning the birth of Servius Tullius, and mediately concerning his attaining of the throne, four different traditions are preserved, of which precisely the two that are relatively the best attested, the national Roman tradition and that of the Tuscan Annals, are separated from each other by an immeasurable chasm, that cannot be filled up. We cannot here instance all these contradictions of tradition; they will be spoken of in their proper places: we may only remark here that the fragment of Dionysius recently found has afforded a new proof how low the variation and uncertainty of tradition reaches; since that the second dictatorship of Cincinnatus and all connected with it is a fable, can no longer be the subject of any well-founded doubt. What in this point chiefly excites suspicion against the common tradition is, that it is found to be in contradiction with the documents,

[1] B. i. Buch i. § 16.

where any of these have chanced to be preserved. Neither the alliance of the younger Tarquin with the Gabines, nor the first commercial treaty with Carthage, nor the treaty of confederacy of Sp. Cassius, can be brought into accordance with the traditional history; and we may suspect that this tradition might be shown to be falsified in other points in case more documents had come down to us."

Let us here again remind the reader that it is far from our purpose to maintain that every incident of the early Roman history is strictly historical. It would be absurd to claim for a narrative coming down from comparatively rude and illiterate times, and in so fragmentary a form, the same historical authority which may be accorded, for instance, to the history of England during the last two or three centuries. All that we contend for is that there is evidence enough to establish the main outlines of the narrative after the foundation of the city; to prove the names of the seven kings, their order of succession, and the principal events of their reigns; and thus to vindicate the history from being, as some modern writers have called it, a mere fantasy, or to justify its being treated as Dr. Mommsen has done in his recent work, where the individuality of the kings is completely ignored; and though many of the events of the history are accepted, yet they are interpreted and reconstructed in a manner often entirely new, and quite unjustified by any sound critical principles.

But, after all, these alleged contradictions have been very much exaggerated, as we shall endeavour to show in the proper places, with regard to those instances which fall within the compass of the present work. Many of them arise from the absurdity and ignorance of Dionysius and Plutarch; but if those writers, from their inadequate acquaintance with the Roman history and constitution, as well as their imperfect knowledge of the Latin tongue, made statements which are at variance with those of Latin authors, this forms no just ground of charge against the history. We will not deny that the carelessness of Livy may now and then lend a colour to the same charge; but such instances are rare and of minor importance.

With regard to the instances of contradiction alleged in the paragraph just translated, we may remark that we abandon at once the whole history before the foundation of the city. It was invented, though perhaps from some obscure vestiges of tradition, in order to carry up the Roman lineage to Æneas. Hence the difference of some five centuries in the birth of Romulus; who, as we shall endeavour to show in the proper place,[1] was probably the son, or grandson, of a Greek who had landed on the Italian coast not a great many years before the foundation of Rome. Of the birth of Servius Tullius, and the mode in which he obtained the throne, we shall also speak in the proper place. The next instance of contradiction, regarding the second dictatorship of Cinciunatus, falls beyond the limits of the present work. But that the fragment of Dionysius lately discovered can be said, on any sound critical principles, to prove the account a fable, we altogether deny. All it proves is that one or two annalists related the matter differently, and so improbably that even Dionysius himself rejected their version of it.

The other instances adduced by Schwegler will be examined in their proper places; where in particular we shall endeavour to show that the commercial treaty with Carthage, so far from being inconsistent with the traditional history, confirms its main features in a most remarkable manner. But it will be evident that to enter further here into this subject would be to anticipate the scope of the following book.

One of the chief arguments brought against the early Roman history is founded on its chronology. On this subject Schwegler remarks:[2] "The seven kings are related to have reigned altogether 240 or 244 years. It has been frequently remarked that this number contradicts all experience and probability. It gives on an average thirty-four years for the reign of each king; whilst in Venice, from the year 805 to the year 1311, that is in five centuries, forty doges reigned;[3] each therefore having a reign of 12½ years, or about a third part of the average of the reigns of the Roman kings. The examples which have been

---

[1] See below, sec. II. p. 23, sq.; 28, sq.
[2] Buch xviii. § 20, S. 806. [3] Niebuhr, Rom. Gesch. i. 301, Anm. 912.

adduced to justify the traditional chronology are not to the purpose, inasmuch as the Roman kings did not succeed to the throne by birth, but obtained it by election; and consequently not as boys or youths, but in the age of manhood. Besides, it must be remarked that, of the whole seven kings, only two died a natural death, and that the last survived his overthrow about fifteen years. The traditional chronology also stands in irreconcilable contradiction with the remaining tradition; and if Tarquinius Priscus actually reigned thirty-eight years, Servius Tullius forty-four, and the younger Tarquin twenty-five, there arises, as we have already shown,[1] a chain of absurdities and impossibilities. Lastly, the number of 240 years, which the older tradition gives for the regal period, stands in such a mathematical relation to the number 120, the period which elapses between the expulsion of the kings and the Gallic catastrophe, as justly to excite suspicion; especially if one views in connexion with both numbers the twelve Romulean birds of fate.

"Under these circumstances the age of Rome cannot at all be determined. But that the origin of the city is to be dated higher than it is placed by tradition, has been rightly inferred from the Tarquinian buildings, and especially from the Cloaca Maxima.[2]

"The traditional years of each king's reign are of course

[1] In Buch i. § 20.
[2] See Scipio Maffei, Diplomatica che serve d' Introduzzione all' Arte Critica, 1727, p. 60; Levesque, Hist. crit. de la Rép. Rom. 1807, i. p. 52; Niebuhr, Vortr. über Röm. Gesch. i. 128. When Schwegler cites the authority of Maffei, he could not have referred to his work, for at p. 60 of the edition of 1727, which reference is copied from Levesque, there is nothing at all relating to the subject. After long hunting for it we found the following passage, which we suppose is the one meant, at p. 253: "Le Cloache di Roma fatte in tempo di Tarquinio Prisco, opera descritta da Plinio (xxxvi. 15) per massima di tutte l' altre, e di cui recano ancora maraviglia i pochi avanzi, non mostrano per certo una Città cominciata cencinquant' anni avanti, ma più tosto resa già grande in longo corso d'età, per numeroso popolo e per richezza." We have nothing here but an ipse dixit of Maffei, copied by Levesque, founded on the false view that the builders of Rome could have been nothing but barbarians. The assumption rests altogether on a wrong idea of the constructive art among the ancient peoples. And let it be remembered that, though the Cloaca is certainly a noble sewer, it was originally of no great length, extending only to the Forum, which it was intended to drain.

invented. On what principle the Pontifices proceeded in the fixing of them cannot now be entirely discovered. We can only see thus far, that they placed Numa's death at the end of the first physical sæculum, and that of Tullus Hostilius at the end of the first civil sæculum."[1]

On this we may remark, that it is of no use to give us the average reigns of forty Venetian doges, unless their age at the time of their accession is also given. We know that most of the Roman kings were young men when they began to reign. Romulus was only eighteen. Numa is said to have been born on the day that Rome was founded; and therefore, as Romulus reigned thirty-eight years, and as there was an interregnum of a year, he would, by the common computation, have been thirty-nine when he was elected. But in the time of Romulus, at all events, the year consisted of only ten months—an allowance, by the way, which is never made by the critics, though it suffices of itself to throw out all the fine calculations about the sæculum. Deducting, therefore, one sixth from his reputed age, Numa would have been thirty-two at his accession, and there is nothing improbable in his long reign. Tullus Hostilius was a young man—"tum ætas viresque, tum avita quoque gloria, animum stimulabat"[2]—the grandson of a contemporary of Romulus. There is nothing by which we can determine the age of Ancus at the time of his election; but as he was the the grandson of Numa, and as, from the active duties required of him, the Romans appear to have preferred a young man for their king, we may conclude that he was not very far advanced in life; but even if he was, he may very well have reigned the twenty-four years assigned to him. Tarquinius may probably have reached middle age when he ascended the throne; but there is still room for a reign of thirty-seven years. The birth of Servius Tullius is narrated when the reign of Tarquin was well advanced, and therefore he must have been a young man when he seized the throne.

---

[1] See more in Niebuhr, Röm. Gesch. I. 253, Vortr. über Röm. Gesch. I. 84; and Schwegler, p. 557. The sæculum civile consisted of 110 years, and Tullus Hostilius died in the year of Rome 110 (=38 + 1 + 39 + 32).

[2] Liv. I. 22.

Tarquin the Proud reigned only twenty-five years, and consequently there is no occasion to compute his age at his accession.

The principle of election, therefore, if youth and strength were among the elements which determined it, was, contrary to the assertion of Schwegler, more favourable to length of reign than hereditary succession. A father, son, and grandson, even under favourable circumstances, can hardly expect to reign more than a century, which, at an equal average, would fix the age of accession at thirty-three. But the greater part of the Roman kings acceded considerably below that age; and if most of them met a violent death, it must be also remembered that it was at an advanced period of life, and when they had long filled the throne.

The objections to the chronology of the Tarquins will be examined under the reigns of those sovereigns. The objection about the mathematical proportion between the period of the kings' reigns and that between their expulsion and the destruction of the city is nothing but what a popular writer would call a German "cobweb." For, first of all, the duration commonly assigned to the regal period is not 240 years, but 244; and the former number is obtained by striking off, after Polybius, four years from the reign of Numa. Again, when this is done, we must strike off at all events six or seven years from the reign of Romulus, which would reduce the kingly period either to 238 or 234 years, and again destroy the supposed mathematical proportion. The connecting of these years with the twelve vultures is another "cobweb,"[1] as well as Niebuhr's hypothesis about the chronology having been invented according to the reckoning of the Quindecemvirs of the physical and civil sæculum. On this subject

[1] There was an old Roman prophecy, derived from the Romulean augury, about the duration of the Roman State for twelve centuries. See Censorinus, De Die Nat. c. 17 (who took it from Varro); Claudian, De Bell. Get. v. 265, &c. But it is difficult to see what connexion there is between the expulsion of the kings and the capture of the city by the Gauls, or what ratio the 360 years from the foundation of Rome to its capture—even if we admit that calculation—bears to the twelve vultures. For though 360 may be divided by twelve, leaving a quotient of thirty without remainder, the meaning of such a quotient is not at all obvious to untranscendental minds.

Schwegler remarks:[1] "That the reigns of the first two kings form a peculiar order of things, separated from the later history, is in a certain manner shown by tradition, which makes the first sæculum of the city expire with the death of Numa. For the first secular festival after the expulsion of the kings was celebrated, according to the Commentaries of the Quindecemvirs, in A.U.C. 298; and if from this point we calculate the sæculum of 110 years backwards, the beginning of the second sæculum falls in A.U.C. 78, and this very year was according to Polybius, who is followed by Cicero, the first year after Numa's death. Consequently the year of Numa's death was the last year of the first sæculum. The old tradition that Numa was born on the day of Rome's foundation has the same meaning.[2] For, according to the doctrine of the Etruscan rituals, the first sæculum of a city ended with him who, of all those born on the day of its foundation, attained the greatest age. Hence Numa's death, as this tradition appears to intimate, forms the line of demarcation between two epochs. And, indeed, with his death the purely mythical epoch of Rome expires, and the half-historical time, the dawn of history, begins: while, on the other hand, the first two kings—the one the son of a god, the other the husband of a goddess—evidently belong to a different period of the world than the ordinary one."

The last sentence of this paragraph would lead us to suppose that the Quindecemviri looked upon the early Roman history with as sceptical an eye as a modern German critic; that they set down the first two kings as mythical, and on that account fixed on the close of the second king's reign as a chronological epoch. That, however, was not the only reason for choosing that epoch; for the German critics are always abundantly supplied with reasons for their theories: there was another, which, by a very singular coincidence, also pointed to the same period, namely—that Numa, who, by Plutarch at least, is said to have been born on the day when Rome was founded, then closed his life. We will not stop to

---

[1] D. L. S. 557. [2] Plut. Num. 3; Dion Cass. Fr. 6, 5.

remark that, however mythical the foundation of Rome and the reigns of the first two kings may be said to be, they are nevertheless here made the data for a very precise chronological computation, but will pass on to the general drift of the paragraph.

And first we will ask whether we are to suppose that the early Roman history was written in accordance with these data of the Quindecemviri? The seventeenth chapter of Censorinus, "De Die Natali," from which all this ingenious web is spun, shows clearly that it was not. The Quindecemviri stood quite alone in their opinion about the secular games having been celebrated, or at all events about their celebration being due, at the expiration of every 110 years. Their calculation is evidently an arbitrary one, made at the time when the secular games were celebrated by the order of Augustus, and confirmed by a decree of that emperor. The Quindecemviri had superseded the Decemviri only about sixty or seventy years previously—in the time of Sulla; so that if it had been an old opinion among the interpreters of the Sibylline books, the authority of the Decemvirs, and not of the Quindecemvirs, would have been cited for it. But the old annalists —the supposed inventors of the early Roman history and chronology—from whom Livy and the other historians drew, flourished long before this time, and formed quite a different opinion of the chronology of these games; so that the early chronology could not have been invented according to the Quindecemviral sæculum of 110 years. We subjoin the two statements. According to the Quindecemvirs, the games were celebrated as follows: A.U.C. 298, 408, 518, 628, 737.[1] But according to Valerius Antias, Varro, Livy, and the historians generally, the period for the recurrence of the games should have been a century, though they were actually celebrated as follows: A.U.C. 245, 305, 504, 605,[2] 737. After

[1] This seems to be a year short of the usual period. But perhaps Julius Cæsar's year of confusion, consisting of fifteen months, must be taken into the account. The period is confirmed by Horace's Carmen Seculare: "Undenos decies per annos orbis."

[2] There was a slight difference with regard to this celebration; some annalists, as Piso, Cn. Gellius, and Cassius Hemina, placing it three years later, or in

the reign of Augustus the celebration took place at much shorter intervals.

We may remark on the above that Valerius Antias and the other historians placed the first celebration in the year after the expulsion of the kings, which agrees with the account in Valerius Maximus,[1] that they were first publicly instituted by Valerius Publicola in his first consulship. The games, with sacrifices at the altar of Dis and Proserpine, at a place in the Campus Martius called Tarentum, or Terentum, had indeed been previously celebrated by an individual named Valerius, out of gratitude to, and by direction of, the gods, for the recovery of his children from a pestilential disease by drinking of some warm springs at that spot; but this was a private matter, totally unconnected with the state; and the celebration of the games by the Consul Valerius was, as we have said, the first public one. The Quindecemvirs placed their origin still lower, or in A.U.C. 298. Yet Niebuhr dreams about carrying them up to the origin of the city, and thus making them a festival commemorative of the age of Rome. With this view, Niebuhr,[2] who is followed by Schwegler in the passage already cited, mistranslates the following sentence of Censorinus: "Primos enim ludos sæculares exactis regibus, post Romam conditam annis ccxlv. a Valerio Publicola institutos esse, Valerius Antias ait; ut xv-virorum Commentarii annis cclxxxxviii. M. Valerio, Sp. Verginio Coss. :" by rendering "the *first* secular festival *after the expulsion of the kings* was *celebrated,*" &c. instead of, "the first secular festival was *instituted* after the expulsion of the kings;" the first method of translation assuming that there had been celebrations during the regal period; the second, which is the only correct one, excluding any such assumption. And this mistranslation is made in contradiction of a direct statement of Censorinus only a page further on, viz.: "Cum

---

603; and as Hemina lived at this time, he ought to have known. But the discrepancy probably arose from some difference in fixing the foundation era.

[1] Lib. II. c. iv. s. 6.

[2] B. i. S. 353: "Das erste Säcularfest nach Verbannung der Könige sey im Jahr 298 gefeyert worden," u.s.w.

ab urbis primordio ad reges exactos, annos ccxliv., (ludos), factos esse, *nemo sit auctor.*" So that this attack on the Roman chronology is founded on the mistranslation of a common Latin book like Censorinus!

In fact the festival had, properly speaking, no immediate connexion with the age of Rome. And this was most distinctly the opinion of Censorinus himself, who says, after recording the different æras of celebration before given: "Hinc animadvertere licet, neque post centum annos, ut hi referrentur ludi, statum esse, neque post centum decem. Quorum etiamsi alterutrum retro fuisset observatum, *non* tamen *id satis argumenti* esset, quo quis his ludis *sæcula discerni* constanter affirmet, præsertim cum *ab urbis primordio, ad reges exactos*, annos ccxliv. *factos esse, nemo sit auctor.* Quod tempus proculdubio naturali majus est sæculo. Quod si quis credit, *ludis sæcularibus sæcula discerni*, sola nominis origine inductus; sciat, sæculares dici potuisse, *quod plerumque semel fiant hominis ætate.*" Yet it is in the face of this opinion, and from the very same chapter which contains it, that Niebuhr, and after him Schwegler, have derived their fanciful theory! in aid of which it was necessary to cut off four years from the received chronology of the kings, and to assume that the Tuscan notion of the physical sæculum was adopted by the Romans, of which there is not the slightest evidence.

It is plain, therefore, that the early Roman chronology was not manufactured in any such capricious manner as that hero assumed. That it contains serious errors and defects,—that it is, in short, the weakest point in the history,—must be acknowledged; and it were only to be wished that a portion of the superfluous ingenuity which has been expended in not very happy attempts to explain the supposed method of its invention, had been employed rather in investigating whether there might not be some way of reconciling it with the probability of the history. This is the very difficult task which we here propose to ourselves; and we must therefore claim for the attempt the candid consideration of the reader.[1]

[1] The writer has before slightly touched upon the subject in the Introduction to his "History of the City of Rome."

The idea of a complete astronomical year, at the end of which the sun is found in the same position in the heavens as he occupied at the beginning, is so familiar to us that it is difficult to conceive a period at which any other notion prevailed. But when we reflect on the vast amount of science and observation required to determine this year with any approach to accuracy, we shall not be surprised to find that among rude and imperfectly civilised nations the grossest deviations from this standard prevailed. The period of the natural day is a measure of time that is forced upon us involuntarily. Next to this, the revolutions of the moon afford the most striking indication of the lapse of time; and hence days and months become necessary units in all calculations where time is concerned. But the duration of the astronomical year is not so easily ascertained, and especially in southern latitudes, where the difference between the seasons is not so strongly marked as in more northern ones. Ten months may perhaps have been first assigned for the sun's annual course by a rude guess; or because the scanty decimal arithmetic of a half-civilised people—counting on the ten fingers—rendered them unequal to, or indisposed for, a longer calculation; or they may have been satisfied with such a measure, and utterly regardless of a scientific accuracy—which, indeed, they had no means of attaining—although in a few revolutions of the sun the same month which had been midsummer would have become midwinter. And we know the force of habit. When such an imperfect year had become habitual among a people; when contracts and all the usages both of civil and religious life had come to be regulated by it; it would have been difficult to change it for a more accurate and scientific year, even if the means for calculating such a one had been at hand.

Hence we are not surprised to learn that among the nations of antiquity years of various duration had been in use, and even among the Italian people. Thus the Ferentines, the Lavinians, and the Albans are said to have had different years;[1] and Laurentum, which, as we shall show, was probably the

[1] Censorin. De Die Nat. c. 20.

mother city of the Romans, had a year of ten months, extending from March to December, since we learn from Macrobius that the Laurentines sacrificed to Juno, who was with them equivalent to Luna, on all the kalends of those months.[1] It was almost generally agreed among the authors of antiquity that the Roman year also, as well as the Laurentine, at first consisted of only ten months. The only authors who dissented from this view appear to have been Licinius Macer and Fenestella,[2] whose opinion was followed by Scaliger, in his "Emendatio Temporum." But it is far outweighed by more numerous and better authorities; as Junius Gracchanus, Fulvius, Varro, Suetonius, Livy (who says that the year of twelve months was introduced by Numa), Ovid, Aulus Gellius, Macrobius, and others, with whom Censorinus agreed. On the subject of the year Ovid says:—

> "Nec totidem veteres, quot nunc, habuere kalendas,
> Ille minor geminis mensibus annus erat.
> Nondum tradiderat victas victoribus artes
> Græcia, facundum, sed male forte genus.
>   .   .   .   .   .   .
> Ergo animi indociles et adhuc ratione carentes,
> Mensibus egerunt lustra minora decem.
> Annus erat decimum quum Luna repleverat orbem,
> Hic numerus magno tunc in honore fuit
> Seu quia tot digiti per quos numerare solemus," &c.

The question is, How long this year of ten months lasted? The lines of Ovid would seem to imply that the astronomical year was not introduced till Greece had been conquered by the Roman arms; but that appears to be too late a period. The time of the Decemvirs might be a probable epoch, and they are said to have made some regulation respecting intercalation; but there are indications that the year of ten months must have lasted beyond their time. The same indications seem to show that two sorts of years were in use at the same time at Rome; one a moon-year, consisting of 355 days—the introduction of which is attributed by some writers to Numa, by others

---

[1] "Sed et omnibus kalendis, a mense Martio ad Decembrem, huic Deæ kalendarum die supplicant."—Sat. l. 15.
[2] Censorin. De Die Nat. c. 20.

to Tarquinius Priscus or Servius Tullius—and the Romulean year of 304 days. The knowledge of the former year, and, indeed, the regulation of the calendar altogether, seems to have been confined to the priests. How ignorant the laity were of the lapse of time and revolutions of the year appears from the circumstance that, far into the republican times, the consuls, or a dictator created expressly for the purpose, were accustomed to drive a nail into the wall of Minerva's cell in the Capitoline temple, on the Ides of every September, in order to mark the lapse of time, and perhaps to serve as a sort of check upon the priests. The monopoly of knowledge on the part of the priests is also shown by the circumstance that it was they who proclaimed the new moon and fixed the Ides, and who retained to themselves the knowledge of the Dies Fasti and Nefasti. After the time of Servius Tullius the celebration of the lustrum every fifth year, or every sixth Romulean year, brought the two years into some kind of harmony; but, as is well known, the calendar was a heap of confusion down to the time of Julius Cæsar.

It cannot be imagined that the Romulean year ceased to be observed, for civil purposes, after the time of Romulus, or indeed for a long while afterwards. There were certain inveterate customs connected with it relating to some of the most habitual and important acts of life, which must have required a long period to take so firm a root. As Niebuhr has pointed out, a year of ten months was the period during which widows mourned their husbands:[1] it was also the term for the payment of portions bequeathed by will, for credit on the sale of yearly profits, for loans, and for calculating the rate of interest. Some of these things would hardly have been known in the reign of Romulus. A passage in Macrobius illustrates still more strikingly the year of ten months. That author relates[2] that in March the matrons waited on their slaves at supper, as their masters did in the Saturnalia of December, in order that the honour thus accorded to them at the beginning of the year might incline them to be obedient; for which, at the end of it, they were rewarded by the

---

[1] Hist. of Rome, vol. i. p. 342.   [2] Sat. i. 12.

Saturnalia. But there could have been few, if any, slaves at Rome in the time of Romulus. The fact of the asylum is totally at variance with the existence of any considerable slave-population.

That the year originally began with March is shown by the names of several of the months; as Quintilis, Sextilis, September, &c.: for Quintilis, afterwards Julius, was the fifth month from March; Sextilis, afterwards Augustus, the sixth, &c.: January and February were *added to the end* of the year. Thus Varro:[1] "Ad hos qui additi, prior a principe Deo Januarius appellatus; posterior ab diis inferis Februarius." Cicero[2] also calls February the last month of the year: and the same fact is apparent from its being made the intercalary month; for it was natural to add the extra days at the end of the year.

There are several passages in Livy which show that, down to a very advanced period of the republic, the lustrum recurred not every fifth but every sixth year, or consulship; and that, consequently, the two years, the priestly year of twelve months and the civil one of ten months, must during that time have co-existed. There are distinct traces of the Romulean civil year having existed down to B.C. 293. That year was the consulship of L. Papirius Cursor and S. Carvilius Maximus, and in it the lustrum was performed by the censors, P. Cornelius Arvina and C. Marcius Rutilus.[3] But the preceding lustrum had been celebrated in the *sixth* previous consulship, that of M. Fulvius Pætinus and T. Manlius Torquatus,[4] by the censors, P. Sempronius Sophus and P. Sulpicius Saverrio, in B.C. 299, according to the ordinary chronology. Therefore the lustrum, which was a period of five astronomical years, contained six consulships, or, what is the same thing, six civil years of ten months. The consulships are as follows: —B.C. 299 (lustrum), M. Fulvius Pætinus, T. Manlius Torquatus; B.C. 298, L. Cornelius Scipio, Cn. Fulvius; B.C. 297, Q. Fabius, P. Decius; B.C. 296, L. Volumnius, Ap. Claudius; B.C. 295, Fabius and Decius again; B.C. 294, L. Postumius Megellus, M. Atilius Regulus; B.C. 293 (lustrum), L. Papirius

[1] L. L. vi. 34. [2] De Leg. II. 54. [3] Liv. x. 47. [4] Ibid. c. 9.

Cursor, S. Carvilius Maximus. The Fasti place this last lustrum in the preceding consulship, but our statement is taken from Livy.

So also, according to Livy, six consulships before that of Fulvius Pætinus and Manlius Torquatus, or in the consulship of Arvina and Tremulus, in the reputed year B.C. 305, M. Valerius Maximus and C. Junius Bubulcus were censors;[1] but it is not said that the lustrum was celebrated. The lustrum, however, is no sure test. Its celebration, for some reason or other, was frequently omitted. Thus, for instance, in the year of Rome 294, though the census was taken, the lustrum was not celebrated, from religious scruples, because the Capitol had been taken and one of the consuls killed.[2] This census, which was not completed till the following year by the celebration of the lustrum, is said by Livy to have been only the tenth;[3] though in due order more than twenty should have been celebrated. And from the first lustrum, celebrated by Servius Tullius, and the last, celebrated by Vespasian in A.U.C. 827, a period of about six centuries and a half, there had been only seventy-five lustra,[4] giving an average interval of between eight and nine years between them. But it may be assumed that censors were appointed every five years—or, in the early times of the republic, in every sixth consulate—as the duties of their office, such as fixing the taxes, &c., could not well be postponed.

In the period between B.C. 305 and 299, we find, indeed, another pair of censors recorded by Livy; viz. Q. Fabius and P. Decius, in the consulship of Sulpicius Saverrio and Sempronius Sophus, in B.C. 303;[5] but these were created not for taking the census, but for an extraordinary occasion,—the creation, namely, of some new tribes, in order to put an end to forensic tumults. At this period, by the Lex Æmilia, the duration of the censorship was limited to eighteen months. The censorship of Valerius Maximus and Junius Bubulcus would therefore have expired; and unless these extra censors

---

[1] Liv. ix. 43.   [2] Id. iii. 22.   [3] Ibid. 24.
[4] Censorin. De Die Natal. c. 18: cf. Ideler, Handb. der Chronologie, ii. 79, f.
[5] Liv. ix. 46.

had been appointed, the forensic disturbances must have continued three or four years longer, till in the regular course the censors of B.C. 299 were appointed.

It is not easy to trace the censorship backwards in Livy beyond the year B.C. 305. He mentions the celebrated censorship of Appius Claudius Crecus, but with an interval of only five consulships, instead of six, reaching backwards from B.C. 305. The Fasti, however, give a year in this period—B.C. 309—in which there were no consuls, but only a dictator; and thus we are again brought to a term of six (civil) years. But the strongest proof that Livy considered the censorship as recurring in early times every sixth consulate, is the following passage in the last chapter of his tenth book:—"Lustrum conditum eo anno est (B.C. 293) a P. Cornelio Arvina, C. Marcio Rutilo censoribus: censa capitum millia ducenta sexaginta duo trecenta viginti duo. Censores vicesimi sexti a primis censoribus; lustrum undevicesimum fuit." We here have another example that the lustrum did not keep pace with the censorship. But if these were the twenty-sixth censors—that is, *bona fide* censors for taking the census, without reckoning those appointed for extraordinary occasions—then, as the first censors were created in B.C. 443, there were twenty-five censors—for we must strike off either the first or last—in the period between 443 and 293, which amounts to 150 years. And 150 divided by 25 gives a quotient of six years for the regular recurrence of the censorship.

We may conclude then that, in Livy's view, down to the year of Rome 459, B.C. 293, six consulships only equalled five years. In the remaining portion of his work the censorships follow at an interval of five years; but as the second decade is lost, we cannot precisely tell when this change was effected, and the duration of the consulship extended to twelve months. It seems probable, however, that it was made at, or soon after, the close of the first decade, in the before-mentioned year B.C. 293. Our reasons for this opinion, or rather we should say for this conjecture, are, that Livy's recapitulation of the years of the preceding censorships at this juncture seems to denote that it was the beginning of another system. And it is remarkable that L. Papirius Cursor, who was one of the consuls in B.C. 293, set up the first sundial that had been seen at Rome.[1] As it had not been constructed for the latitude of Rome, and therefore did not show the time correctly, it can only be regarded as a sort of monument, which might appropriately commemorate the change from the civil to the solar year. The place in which it was erected, before the Temple of Quirinus, or Romulus, the introducer of the civil year, seems to be not without significance. It may also be remembered that, only a few years before, the scribe C. Flavius, by publishing the calendar which he had surreptitiously obtained, had robbed the priests of their secret of the Fasti, and had thus deprived them of any interest which they might have had in opposing a change of style.

That Livy did not adopt the ordinary Roman chronology, founded on a comparison with that of Greece, may, we think, also be shown by other circumstances. First of all we may remark that he takes no notice of the Olympiads, like Polybius and Dionysius, and even Cicero, as a means for fixing the early Roman chronology. Again, in the few synchronisms which occur at an early period between Greek and Roman history, his statements appear to show that he adopted a much lower era than the common one, which can be explained only on the supposition that he deducted one-sixth part from the years before A.U.C. 459 or B.C. 293. To illustrate this we subjoin a comparative table of the received chronology and one reduced in this proportion. The first column contains the usual chronology, the second the reduced:—

Rome founded	B.C. 753	678
Accession of Numa	716	646
,, Tullus Hostilius	673	610
,, Ancus Marcius	640	582
,, Tarquinius Priscus . . .	616	562
,, Servius Tullius	578	531
,, Tarquinius Superbus . . .	534	494
Expulsion of the kings	510	474
Rome captured by the Gauls	390	374
End of Livy's first decade	293	293

[1] Pliny, H. N. vii. 60.

We will compare with this table a few reputed synchronisms.

Cicero says that Pythagoras came into Italy in the fourth year of Tarquin the Proud, and that he was there in the time of Junius Brutus.[1] His arrival in Italy, and the commencement of the reign of Tarquinius, occurred, he says, in the same Olympiad, the 62d; according to which computation Tarquin began to reign in B.C. 532, which agrees with Cato's era, and Pythagoras came into Italy in B.C. 529. Now this accords with all the accounts of his life. Thus, according to Aristoxenus,[2] Pythagoras quitted Samos in the reign of Polycrates, at the age of forty; which, as he is supposed to have been born in B.C. 570, would have been in the year B.C. 530; and he might therefore have very well arrived in Italy in the following year. This account also tallies with the chronology of Polycrates, who reigned in Samos from B.C. 532 to B.C. 522; and consequently Pythagoras must have quitted that island in the second year of his reign. The variations respecting the date of Pythagoras' birth do not affect the question. According to some authorities he was born in B.C. 608 or 605; which dates are adopted by Bentley and Larcher, while Dodwell prefers that of B.C. 570. But all testimonies make him contemporary with Polycrates. Of the dates of his birth the latter seems the more probable one, as according to the other he would have been ninety-six years old at the expulsion of Tarquin, and ninety-eight when he is said to have urged the Crotoniates to a war with Sybaris, in B.C. 510!

These variations, however, are of no consequence, as there is no difference of opinion about the date of his arrival in Italy. But while Cicero places it in the fourth year of Tarquinius Superbus, Livy[4] assigns it to the reign of Servius Tullius. Now, according to the ordinary chronology, Servius died in B.C. 534, or five years before Pythagoras' arrival. Livy must therefore have adopted a different mode of computation; and it will be seen that by the reduced table

[1] De Rep. ii. 15; Tusc. L 16, iv. 1: cf. A. Gell. N. A. xvii. 41.
[2] Porphyr. Vit. Pyth. c. 9.
[3] See Clinton, Fasti Hellen. [4] Lib. I. 18.

the year B.C. 529 would have been the second year of the reign of Servius. Livy adds that Pythagoras arrived more than a hundred years after Numa—"centum amplius post annos;" that is, of course, after the time when Numa could have been his pupil, before he became king of Rome. But, according to the ordinary chronology, it would have been 167 years, for which term such an expression would be absurd. And even from the death of Numa it would have been 144 years, too long a period to be so described. By the reduced computation it would have been 117 years from Numa's accession to B.C. 529, which agrees with Livy's mode of speaking.

Take another instance. Livy[1] places the first invasion of Italy by the Gauls in the reign of Tarquinius Priscus, at the time when the Phocæans were founding Massalia. Now, as we have shown in the body of the work,[2] Massalia was founded a few years after B.C. 546. But, according to the common chronology, Tarquin the Elder died in B.C. 578. We must, therefore, resort to the reduced chronology, which shows his reign to have lasted from B.C. 562 to 531; and the foundation of Massalia would then have occurred about the middle of it.

Could any undoubted synchronisms be shown between the early Roman history and the Greek, in which the received Roman chronology tallied with the Olympiads assumed to correspond with it, there would of course be an end to the question; but, so far as we are aware, none such are to be found. The marking of the Olympiads in Polybius and Dionysius is obtained empirically, by assuming that the Roman year, or consulate, always consisted of twelve months, and then placing the two chronologies in co-ordination: thus Dionysius, in a passage to which we have before adverted,[3] endeavours to make out a synchronism between the consulship of Geganius and Minucius in B.C. 492, when envoys were despatched into Sicily to buy corn, and the reign of Gelon at Syracuse. But we have shown that this pretended synchronism is a mere invention of that author. The year B.C. 492 would, in the

[1] Lib. v. 34.   [2] See p. 83, sqq.   [3] See above, p. lxxvi.

reduced chronology, be B.C. 459, and thus fall in the period when the chief man in Sicily was Ducetius, whose reign was in B.C. 466–440; and it is not improbable that some of the Roman annalists may have confounded his name with that of Dionysius of Syracuse. But at all events the error was not adopted by Livy, nor can Dionysius' amendment of it be accepted.

But if the early Roman year was one of ten months, then the duration of the regal period would have to be reduced by one sixth, thus making it only 203 years, a period often equalled in the reigns of seven consecutive sovereigns. And thus one of the tritest objections to the early history would be removed.

To recapitulate.—As the art of writing appears to have been practised at Rome in the very earliest times, there is no reason to doubt the testimony of the best ancient writers that public records had been kept almost from the foundation of the city; especially as such a practice accords with that love of precedent, as well as of national glory, which is admitted to be a characteristic of the Romans. And although a considerable part of these records may have perished in the Gallic conflagration, yet the fact of their existence down to the middle of the fourth century of Rome shows that its history during that period did not rest on oral tradition: it might, therefore, have been easily reconstructed after that catastrophe—or at all events its leading facts—from memory, aided by such documents as had escaped the fire. To suppose that it was not so reconstructed and preserved is not only at variance with the character of the Romans, as shown by the preceding records, and as painted by the sceptical critics themselves, but also with the fact that enough must have remained to substantiate the leading events, and with the evidence we possess of the pains taken to recover what laws and treaties had been destroyed.

Further: if we deny the preservation of any public or private records, then there remains no probable method by which we can account for the existence of the early history. The first *literary* annals of Fabius, Cato, and the rest, could

not have been founded on oral tradition, which would have
been totally incompetent to hand down such a mass of details,
often of the most prosaic nature. That they were the product of forgery or invention is still more improbable. The
high character of these early writers, who were not needy
littérateurs, but men of distinction; the minor differences
sometimes found in their narratives, yet the general resemblance of them on the whole, showing that they drew independently from sources of recognised authority; and the
check that must always have been upon them from the
jealousy of the great patrician houses, could not but have
insured their accounts from any flagrant perversions of historical truth. The methods which have been *invented* in
order to account for the existence of the history are not only
destitute of all evidence, but also inadequate and improbable.
Niebuhr's theory of a poetical origin is unauthenticated, improbable, and in great part abandoned by the author himself.
The ætiological hypothesis is also a mere invention, and
altogether inadequate to account for the far greater portion
of the history, which no ingenuity can torture into an
ætiological origin.

To conclude: the objections which have been urged against
the history on the ground of its internal improbability are
altogether insufficient to invalidate its origin from contemporary record. The argument drawn from the supernatural
accounts which it contains is futile, since similar accounts are
found in much later, and unquestionably authentic, history.
Their greater frequency in the early period confirms, instead
of invalidating, its authenticity, as showing it to have been
written in the superstitious and comparatively illiterate times
which it records. Its alleged contradictions are chiefly the
result of the paucity of materials, of their partial destruction,
of our own ignorance, as well as the ignorance and want of
judgment of Dionysius and Plutarch; but, after all, these
contradictions have been much exaggerated, and are not of
a nature to obliterate the general historical picture. Lastly:
the arguments adduced against the history from chronology
are also often the result only of our own ignorance, or are

founded on the mistranslations, misapprehensions, and whimsical fancies of the sceptical critics themselves. But though this part of the history is undoubtedly the weakest, yet it is not of a nature to invalidate the whole narrative, nor to leave us without hopes that by careful investigation we may ultimately succeed in clearing it up.

THE HISTORY OF THE KINGS OF ROME.

SECTION I.

THE EARLY POPULATION OF ITALY.

To determine how Italy was first peopled seems a hopeless task. Of the first immigration into that peninsula there is not, as Dr. Mommsen has observed, even a legend. All that can be said upon the subject must consequently rest upon inference and conjecture, and we shall therefore content ourselves with a brief outline of some of the theories respecting it.

That Italy was peopled at a comparatively late period seems highly probable. No vestiges, it is said, are found there, as in Germany, France, England, and Scandinavia, of a savage race that subsisted by hunting and fishing, that knew not the art of working metals, and used implements of flint and bone. The geographical features of the Italian peninsula might lead us to the same conclusion. Surrounded on three sides by the sea, on the fourth by almost impassable mountains, Italy must in a barbarous age have been excluded from all commerce with the rest of the world. The wandering tribes that first overspread and peopled Europe, knowing not what they might find on the southern side of the Alps, would hardly have been tempted to encounter the difficulties and dangers of surmounting that stupendous barrier rather than direct their onward course over the plains of Germany and France.

One thing seems tolerably certain—that the great bulk of the early Italian population belonged to a race allied to the Greek. Niebuhr held this race to have been Pelasgians, who once, he thought, occupied the peninsulas both of Greece and Italy, till they were overwhelmed by the incursions of other tribes, and left behind them only partial traces of their existence; just as the physical features of a country are overwhelmed by a deluge, except a few hill-tops, which here and there lift themselves above it. But this theory is now exploded. Schwegler has refuted it with regard to Italy,[1] and Dr. Mommsen, one of the latest historians of Rome, does not once mention the name of the Pelasgians.

The last-named writer, to whom we thus advert *par excellence*—for Niebuhr's star is setting, and that of Mommsen is in the ascendant, with the last new version of Teutonic-Roman history—is nevertheless of opinion that Italy was first peopled by a Greek race, and that they entered the peninsula by crossing the Alps. At the period of their immigration they had, he thinks, arrived at that stage of civilization which is implied in the practice of agriculture; an opinion formed on certain analogies in the Greek and Latin languages. But, generally speaking, an agricultural people ceases to wander. Its next stage is to found large and opulent cities, and if these are near the sea, to enter upon a commercial life. As the Greeks were pre-eminently a maritime people, it seems much more likely that whatever Hellenic elements may be discovered in Italy were introduced by sea, and that the population which entered by the Alps were of the Celtic stock; of whose language traces have been pointed out in the Italian dialects by modern inquirers.

The balance of probability whether Italy was peopled entirely by immigrants who crossed the Alps, or partly also by sea, must in a great measure depend on the antiquity of navigation. That the Greeks were capable of making long voyages at least as early as the time of the siege of Troy, is attested by the account of Ulysses having sailed to that city from Ithaca, and of his long wanderings over the sea after its

[1] Römische Geschichte, Buch iii. § 4.

fall. It is nothing to the purpose to object that these are mere poetical legends. We do not here cite them as historical facts, though we believe them to be founded on real occurrences. We allude to them here merely to show that a poet who lived a great many centuries before the Christian era, believed such voyages to be possible twelve centuries before that era. On the other hand, Dr. Mommsen argues[1] that Italy must have been totally unknown to the Hellenes in Homer's time, because he does not once mention its name. But to prove this point, a negative suffices not. An expedition of the Greeks towards the east called not for any mention of Italy; while, if we allow Homer to have been the author of the Odyssey, he appears to have been acquainted with the still more distant Sicily, which he speaks of under the name of Thrinakia.[2] The Siculi are several times mentioned in the same poem;[3] and Strabo is of opinion[4] that, under this name, he may allude to the people who inhabited the extremities of Italy. Such a people were at all events entirely unknown in Greece. The name of Epirus, which signifies the "mainland," in contradistinction to the islands which lie off it, appears in the Iliad.[5] But to suppose that a seafaring people, acquainted with Epirus, should not have also known the coast of Italy, which is only about forty miles distant, is utterly incredible.

Dr. Mommsen's opinion on this subject is altogether incomprehensible and self-contradictory. In fact, he confutes himself out of his own mouth. At the beginning of his tenth chapter he tells us that, at the time when the Homeric songs were composed, the Greeks had no certain knowledge of Italy and Sicily, though they might have heard of their existence from some storm-tossed mariner. But at the time when Hesiod's Theogony was composed, they knew, he says, the whole Italian coast, and not long afterwards they may have begun to make settlements upon it.

The different theories respecting the period when Homer flourished embrace a period of no fewer than five centuries, and Dr. Mommsen tells us not what date he selects. We

[1] Röm. Gesch. B. I. Kap. 2.   [2] Odyss. xii. 127.
[3] Odyss. xx. 383; xxiv. 211, &c.   [4] Lib. i. c. 1, § 10.   [5] Il. 635.

will, however, assume that he takes the earliest, according to which Homer flourished within a century after the Trojan war, or towards the end of the eleventh century before the Christian era. There is also a difference of more than a century in the computations of Hesiod's date; but here also we will take the highest calculation, which places him in the middle of the ninth century B.C. Now, on Dr. Mommsen's own showing, the Italian coast must not only have been known to, but even colonized by the Greeks long before this period. For Sybaris was, as he rightly tells us, founded in Olympiad xiv. 2, or B.C. 723; and in the same paragraph he further tells us, also in all probability correctly, that Cumæ was founded three centuries before Sybaris;[1] which would be B.C. 1023, or nearly two hundred years before the time of Hesiod, at the very least, and within about half a century of the very highest date assigned to Homer, who is said to have been ignorant of the existence of Italy! It matters not whether the Cumæan Greeks were, as Dr. Mommsen says, merchants, and the Sybarite Greeks agriculturists; though it is probable that the Greeks had sailed to, and traded with, Italy, long before they began to settle there.

When it is considered that the Phœnicians were a great maritime and commercial nation many centuries before the reputed era of the Trojan war, it is difficult to believe that a clever and enterprising people like the Greeks should not have acquired from them the art of navigation long before that famous siege. Herodotus, who lived in the fifth century B.C., and who may therefore be supposed to have been a better judge of the capabilities of ancient navigation than we can possibly pretend to be at this day, tells us[2] that a crew of Cretans—in whose island there are traces of Phœnician settlements—were, on their return from Sicily, driven by stress of weather on the coast of Iapygia, the Roman Calabria, and

---

[1] "Kyme dreihundert Jahr alter ist als Sybaris"... "Die Gründung von Sybaris fällt Ol. 14, 2, oder 23 der Stadt," s. 89. We perceive that, in the English translation, the text is much altered here; and, instead of the first sentence, we find only, "There is a further credible tradition that a considerable interval elapsed between the settlement at Cumæ and the main Hellenic emigration."—Vol. i. p. 140.   [2] Lib. vii. c. 170.

there established themselves. This happened in the reign of Minos, king of Crete; that is, in the mythical period before the Trojan war. Having no means of returning to their own country, they built, where fortune had cast them, the town of Hyria; thus becoming, says Herodotus, Iapygian Messapians instead of Cretans. Whether this story be an historical fact or not, it at least exhibits the opinion of a very ancient and very inquisitive historian as to the antiquity of Greek navigation, and of Greek settlements on the Italian coast.

The Iapygians, or Messapians, settled in this south-easternmost peninsula, or "heel," of Italy, Dr. Mommsen considers to have been the primitive inhabitants, or reputed autochthons, of the country; the main reason for that opinion appearing to be that though they had come in over the Alps, they had, as usually happened, been thrust down to this extremity of the land by constantly succeeding swarms of new immigrants. The only remains by which their ethnology can be traced are a few inscriptions in a Greek character, and bearing apparently some analogy to the Greek language; but they have never been deciphered and, according to the opinion of Dr. Mommsen, never will be. The names of certain Greek divinities, αρτεμες, δαματρια, αφροδιτα—that is, Artemis, Demeter, Aphrodite[1]— show, we think indubitably, that the authors of the inscriptions must have been of an Hellenic race; but who shall tell us whether they were the original, or autochthonic inhabitants, or immigrant Greeks, such as the Cretans mentioned by Herodotus, speaking a very primitive Hellenic dialect, corrupted perhaps by intercourse with barbarians? so that the Messapians were universally regarded by the later Greeks as a barbarous people.

Besides the accidental visits and settlements of the more southern and maritime Greeks, such as that just alluded to, we think it highly probable that southern Italy may also have been partly colonized at a very early period by immigrants from Epirus and the western coasts of Greece. It is true that we have no historical record, or even tradition, of any early contact between Greeks and Italiots at this point; and,

[1] Mommsen, Die Unteritalische Dialekte, p. 64.

considering the state of our knowledge respecting the early history of Italy, it would be surprising if we had. But when the same names of places and tribes are found in two countries, there is room, at all events, for a very strong presumption that one of them was peopled from the other. It can hardly be accidental that we should find in both countries a race called Chaones, or Chones, a town called Pandosia, and a river called Acheron. And if these names afford evidence of a connexion between the two lands, it is difficult to believe that it could have been established in any other way than by the sea.

At the same time we are willing to allow that in ancient times there was not probably much intercourse between Greece and Italy across the Adriatic. The Epirots were a pastoral race, not much addicted to the sea; though, with the length of coast which they possessed, it would be strange if they did not sometimes venture upon it, and even a fishing-boat might come within sight of Italy. The seafaring Greeks, however, capable of making what in those days were considered long voyages, dwelt in the Peloponnesus, in the islands of the Archipelago, on the eastern coasts of Greece, and on the shores of Asia Minor. Hence it is easy to see that no Greek navigators, with the exception, perhaps, of those dwelling on the western coast of Peloponnesus, and especially the Corinthians, would, in steering westward for Italy, have anything to do with the Adriatic. On such a course, a vessel from any part of Greece eastward of Cape Tænarum (now Cape Matapan), would have to double that promontory, and would thus find itself considerably to the south of Cape Pachynus (Cape Passaro), the southernmost point of Sicily. Under these circumstances, her course would be across the Ionian Sea for Sicily; whence she would reach the western coasts of Italy either by circumnavigating that island, or what is more probable, by passing through the Straits of Messina. That this was the usual course of Greek navigation, is evident from the situation of their Italian colonies. Leaving Iapygia, or Messapia, and Venice out of the question, there is not a single Greek colony on the eastern coast of Italy, except Ancona;

and this we know was settled by refugees from Sicily as late as the fourth century before the Christian era. In Sicily, and on the southern and western coasts of Italy, the Greek colonies were numerous, while the Adriatic was but little known to and less explored by the greater part of that nation. The Corinthians alone, from their geographical position, their gulf opening out not far from the entrance of that sea, seem to have visited it, and to have planted a few colonies on its eastern shores; but even they appear to have abstained, from what cause we cannot explain, from colonizing the Italian coast of the Adriatic. Now, if such was the usual course of Greek navigation during the historical times, or, in other words, when the colonies of Magna Græcia were founded, there seems to be no reason why it should not also have been pursued at an earlier period, provided always that the Greeks had become sufficiently skilful sailors to make so long a voyage; and that they had attained this skill in very remote antiquity we have already endeavoured to show. Here, then, might have been another source of Italian population, and the many legends which we have of Greek settlements in the neighbourhood of Rome before that of the people which actually built that city, seem to point to such a source. We are also of opinion that several of the races which we hear of in southern Italy, and Sicily, as the Ænotrii, Siculi, Itali, &c., probably Pelasgic tribes, might have been introduced by sea.

We shall content ourselves, however, with indicating the possibility that some portion of the early Italian population might have been so introduced without discussing at any length how Italy was peopled. As the main object of the present work is to endeavour at ascertaining what truth there may be in the early history of Rome, it will hardly be expected that we should enter into the still more obscure question of Italian ethnography, a subject upon which, the more we investigate it, the more incompetent we feel to pronounce any decided opinion. If, as is supposed, there is not evidence enough to establish the history of the first few centuries of Rome, of which at all events there profess to be some records, how should it be possible to give a satisfactory account of a long antecedent period, of which there are only a few traditions, and those of the most divergent and contradictory nature? This circumstance, however, has not deterred writers of Teutonic-Roman history of the Niebuhr school, who profess to reconstruct it by a process of "divination,"[1] from proposing the most confident theories, built, of course, on the vaguest inductions. "When we come to examine the evidence," observes Sir George Cornewall Lewis, "on which the ethnological theories of the majority of antiquarian treatises are founded, our wonder at their wide, and indeed almost unlimited divergences, is at an end. No probability is too faint, no conjecture is too bold, no ethnology is too uncertain to resist the credulity of an antiquarian in search of evidence to support an ethnological hypothesis. Gods become men, kings become nations, one nation becomes another nation, opposites are interchanged at a stroke of the wand of the historical magician. Centuries are to him as minutes; nor, indeed, is space itself of much account when national affinities are in question."[2]

In the absence of all records or traditions, the great modern method of comparative philology may undoubtedly teach us something respecting ancient ethnography. It has been used with some success in discriminating the different races which, during the historical period, inhabited the Italian peninsula, but it has not as yet made much progress in demonstrating their immediate origin. For this purpose the method is so comprehensive that it teaches little or nothing specific. It is now, we believe, decided that all the peoples of ancient Italy, including the Etruscans, were of what is called the Indo-European family: that is, they spoke languages the roots of which may be traced up to the Sanscrit. This description contains within its comprehensive boundaries tongues now so widely different as the Greek, the Latin, the Teutonic, the Erse, the Gaelic, and several more. As these nations, however diverse their dialects, had all some words, fewer or greater in number, which belonged to them in common, it is easy to see how this fact complicates, instead of removing, the difficulty

[1] Hist. of Rome, vol. i. p. 152.
[2] Credibility of Early Roman History, vol. i. p. 270.

of settling, from philological induction, the ethnology of the early Italian races. There is, for instance, a considerable similarity between the Latin and Greek languages; yet this would not justify us in concluding, as was formerly done, that Latin and Greek stood in the relation of mother and daughter, and that one of the races speaking those languages must have been immediately descended from the other. For if both sprung in a very remote age from a common stock, what words they had in common might be derived from that stock, though the Italians had never been in Greece, nor the Greeks in Italy. Both peoples might have passed independently into Italy and Greece at different and very remote periods, as we believe is now the favourite theory, carrying with them their common language, more or less altered and modified, yet still retaining considerable resemblance, although no intercourse might have taken place between them for a score of ages. Reasoning in the same manner, there would be no conclusive grounds for assuming that a German or a Celtic race had settled in Italy at a very early period because the Latin happens to have some Celtic and Teutonic words.[1] Such words, it may be said, were their joint property, because in a very remote age they all sprung from the same stock; and if they had not some such common words, they could not be ranged under the general category of Indo-European. Thus, as soon as we have so ranged them, we have gone a great way towards rendering it impossible to trace the immediate origin of specific races by means of language.

The best way of meeting this difficulty, and endeavouring to make philology yield some historical results, seems to be that of classing rather than counting the words, which certain nations may possess in common; that is, to judge by their quality rather than their number. Dr. Mommsen has adopted this principle in his second chapter, where by a comparison

[1] Professor Newman contends (Regal Rome, ch. 2), that Latin is nearer to the Gaelic and Celtic than either to the Greek or German. Mommsen, on the other hand, says (Rom. Gesch. B. I. Kap. 2, § 14), that Greek and Latin are nearer to each other than either tongue is to German or Celtic, but that German is next to them.

of certain classes of Greek and Latin words with one another, and with their parent Sanscrit, he has attempted to trace the progress of those peoples. This method may, indeed, be liable to some objections, and lead to not a few fallacies. From their long intercourse with the Greeks, and because their literature was almost entirely modelled on the Grecian, the Romans no doubt adopted, at a late period, many Greek words into their language, which could not be originally found there. There is a great probability, too, as we shall endeavour to show further on, that Rome itself was a Greek settlement, which would account for a great many of the Greek words found in the Latin language. Hence in any comparison of the Italian dialects with those of Greece for ethnological purposes, Latin, it seems to us, should be omitted, and the comparison made between Greek and the Umbro-Sabellian dialects. Waiving, however, for the moment these objections, the results of the process alluded to appear to be that when the Græco-Italians separated from the parent stock they had arrived at nothing more than pastoral life, since the words which they possess in common with the Sanscrit do not go further than this stage in the progress towards civilization. Mommsen next supposes that after this separation, and while the Græco-Italians still continued to dwell together, they arrived at the stage of agriculture, as he infers from the agricultural words which they had in common. They have also common words for things relating to domestic life, and to some elementary principles of religion, but here also religion of the more domestic kind; as for instance the worship of Vesta, the goddess of the hearth, was known both to Greeks and Italians. Here Dr. Mommsen stops short, for further than this a comparison of the Greek and Latin will not carry him.

It is obvious, however, that though the preceding investigation may tend to show an original community of race between the Greeks and Italians, it affords no insight whatever into what, in an historical point of view, is much more important—their political life. The Greek and Latin terms for civil and military affairs are for the most part quite different; and what is singular, the Latin bear a very striking resemblance to the Gaelic and Welsh. Professor Newman has collected some of these words in the work before referred to,[1] from which we extract a few that have the most striking resemblance. In military terms we find—Latin, arma, G. *arm*;[2] gladius, G. *claidheamh*, W. *cleddyr*; telum, G. *tailm*; gules, E. *galia*; caterva, W. *catorva*; sagitta, G. *saighead*; lorica, G. *luireach*; balteus, G. *balt*; murus, W. *mur*; vallum, W. *gwal*, G. *fal* and *balle*; præda, W. *praidh*, spolia, G. *spuill*; corona, G. W. *coron*; gloria, G. *gloir*; &c. In civil affairs we have—Latin, rex, G. *righ*; populus, W. *pobl*, G. *pobull*; senatus, G. *scanadh*; carcer, W. *carchar*; ordo, W. *urdh*; and several more. Now as it is natural that victors should impose upon the conquered their names for military affairs and for civil government, we might hence infer that the original Italian tribes had been subdued by Celtic invaders. Dr. Prichard, in his "Physical History of Mankind," and other modern writers, have maintained that the Umbrians were a Celtic race, and this opinion is in some degree supported by an obscure tradition to the same effect mentioned by some of the later Roman writers;[3] an opinion, however, which philological researches into the Umbrian dialect have not tended to confirm. On the other hand, it might be said that the Celtic nations derived these words from the Romans during their long struggle with and partial subjugation by that people. This, however, does not account for the manner in which the Romans came by them; and, besides the terms of war and politics before alluded to, there are many others relating to mere natural objects which are common to the Latin and Celtic, and not to the Greek, such as the names for *earth, sea, mountain, wind, storm, &c.*[4]

But we abstain from pursuing any further these general observations, and will content ourselves with recording the most generally received results of modern inquiry with regard to the ancient populations of Italy.

[1] Regal Rome, ch. 4. [2] The letters G. W. E. stand for Gaelic, Welsh, Erse.
[3] Solinus, II. § 11; Serv. ad Æn. xii. 753; Isidore, Orig. ix. 2.
[4] See the list in Newman's Regal Rome, p. 20, seqq.

There can be no doubt that, leaving aside the Ligurians, of whom little or nothing is known, the Italian peninsula was for the most part occupied, at the time when Rome was founded, by three races, distinguished from one another by their language; namely, the Iapygians, or Messapians, the Etruscans, and a collection of tribes called Umbro-Sabellian, speaking a cognate dialect.

Of the Iapygians we have already spoken. Respecting the origin and ethnological affinities of the Etruscans, little or nothing can be established. The remains of their language cannot be interpreted; but enough is known of it to decide that it was entirely different from any other Italian dialect, yet that the Etruscans nevertheless probably belonged to the Indo-European family.[1] As no clue to the origin of the Etruscans can be derived from their language, so also tradition is so various that it leaves us in an equal state of uncertainty. One of the most commonly received accounts is, or rather was, that of Herodotus,[2] who represents them to have emigrated, under the pressure of famine, from Lydia, then called Mæonia, into Italy. Tursenus, one of the sons of Atys, king of Mæonia, was the leader of this expedition; he conducted half the nation to Smyrna, where they embarked, and landed at last in the country of the Ombrici, or Umbrians.

This account seems to have been almost universally received among the Romans. Dionysius of Halicarnassus appears to be the only ancient author who disputed it; but his argument that the Etruscans could not have been Lydians, because in his time they entirely differed from that people in language, customs, and religion, is eminently absurd.[3] It assumes that two nations which must have been separated from each other twelve or fifteen centuries,[4] and had both undergone during that long period extreme vicissitudes, should have retained unaltered their customs and their language. In fact, the

---

[1] Mommsen, Röm. Gesch. B. i. § 81.   [2] Lib. I. c. 94.
[3] Ant. Rom. l. 30.
[4] The emigration mentioned by Herodotus must have taken place more than twelve centuries before the Christian era, as the dynasty of Atys was previous to that of the Heraclidæ.

ORIGIN OF THE ETRUSCANS.   13

original emigrants were not, properly speaking, Lydians, but Mæonians; and although Herodotus considers these two peoples to have been identical, there is good reason to believe, as Niebuhr has shown from other ancient authors, as well as from the fact of their change of name, that they were distinct races, and that the Mæonians were conquered by the Lydians.[1] Subsequently, Lydia endured many revolutions, among which was subjugation by the Persians, and by the Greeks; so that, as Strabo tells us,[2] the Lydian language had in his time entirely disappeared. Yet Dionysius, who lived at the same time as Strabo, is still seeking it![3] The Lydians in Italy must in their turn have endured equal vicissitudes. Nevertheless, the argument on which Dionysius seems to lay even more stress than on the dissimilarity of their language to that of the Lydians, namely, their dissimilar customs, appears to be contradicted by the researches of modern inquirers.[4]

A custom common to the Etruscans with the Lydians is so singular, as well as abominable, that the coincidence could not well have been the work of chance; the custom, namely, alluded to by Plautus,[5] of prostituting their daughters for the sake of procuring them a dowry.

Several modern writers, and among them Dr. Mommsen, have also disputed the probability of the account given by Herodotus, on the ground that it would have been impossible to convey so numerous a people so far across the sea. This difficulty, however, occurred neither to Herodotus himself, nor to his critic Dionysius, who, though he disputes the story, does not employ this argument against it. These ancient writers were better acquainted with early navigation than their modern critics are. In fact, if the Greeks could people

---

[1] Hist. of Rome, vol. I. p. 32 : Lect. on Anc. Hist. vol. I. p. 87.
[2] Lib. xiii. ch. iv. 17, p. 631.
[3] He uses the present tense : ἀλλὰ γὰρ ἐκείνους ἀμφηλεγοῦσί εἰσιν, loc. cit.
[4] See especially Mr. Dennis's Etruria, vol. I. ; who points out many similarities in the customs of the Etruscans with those of their reputed forefathers in Asia Minor.
[5]   "Non enim hic est nisi ex Tusco modo
    Tute tibi indigna dotem quæras corpore."—Cistell. II. 3, 20. '
Cf. Herod. L. 93.

the coasts of Magna Græcia and Sicily, why might not this have been performed in Etruria some centuries before, provided navigation had made adequate progress? And that this was the case at a very early period we have already endeavoured to show.

But the Lydian immigrants need not have been so very numerous. Herodotus, indeed, speaks of half the people; but in ancient times a people was often composed of a city or a tribe. Nor is it necessary to suppose that they all came in one fleet. A few thousand immigrants may under favourable circumstances soon grow up into a great nation; and though the Lydians may not at first have formed any great portion of the people afterwards called Etruscans, yet, from their superior civilisation they may have succeeded in imparting many of their customs and much of their language to the more barbarous people among whom they landed, and perhaps even their name.

It is evident that other settlements had also been made on the coast of Etruria by an Hellenic race. Such were Pisæ, Telamon, Agylla or Cære, with Pyrgi, its port, and others. The name of Pyrgi (Πύργοι, the towers) of itself denotes its Greek origin; which is further shown by its containing a temple to Eileithyia, a purely Greek goddess, who presided over child-birth. The circumstance that Cære had a treasury at Delphi, affords also a strong presumption in favour of its Grecian origin. Telamon and Pisæ are Grecian names: the Greek origin of the latter was almost universally recognized in antiquity; Cato, the only author who ascribes to it an Etruscan foundation, admits at the same time that its site had been previously occupied by a people speaking a Greek dialect.[1] These Greek settlers appear to have spread themselves a considerable distance into the interior. Dionysius of Halicarnassus relates[2] that even in his time vestiges of an Hellenic race might still be traced in the Etruscan towns of Falerii and Fescennium. Such were their Argolic shields and lances and other weapons, their religious rites, the method in which their temples were constructed, &c. But the

[1] Apud Serv. ad Æn. x. 179. [2] Lib. I. ch. 21.

strongest evidence was a temple at Falerii exactly like that of Here, or Juno, at Argos, in which similar sacred rites were performed; among which may be more particularly distinguished the basket-bearing virgin (κανηφόρος) who inaugurated the sacrifices, and the chorus of girls who sung their traditionary hymns to the goddess. Livy, in relating the treachery of the Faliscan schoolmaster, who offered to give his pupils into the hands of the Romans, remarks that it was a Greek custom to commit several boys to the care of one master.[1] Moreover, some Etruscan words connected with religion, as *haruspex* and *hariolus*, are, as Mr. Newman observes,[2] manifest corruptions of the Greek ἱεροσκόπος and ἱερεύς. There were also traces of the Argives at Rome, as we shall see further on.

It seems highly probable that the aid which the early Romans occasionally received from Etruria, and the Etruscan settlements made in that city, were derived from the Grecian population of Etruria, and were prompted by a community of race. It was probably also the Pelasgic, or Hellenic, portion of the Etruscan population that became by their piracies the terror of the seas. Piracy, as we know from Thucydides, was a favourite pursuit of the more ancient Greeks, and regarded by them as an honourable one. The great bulk of the Etruscans do not seem to have been a maritime people. At all events, the leading cities of the Etruscan confederacy were inland: not one of the twelve was seated on the sea.

But of what was the great bulk of the Etruscan population composed? Of the Umbrians, whom the Lydians are said to have found there on their arrival?[3] Or of a distinct race, that called by Dionysius *Rhasennæ*?[4] It is evident that no

---

[1] "Mos erat Faliscis, eodem magistro liberorum et comite uti: simulque plures pueri, quod hodie quoque in Græcia manet, unius curæ demandabantur."—Liv. v. 27.

[2] Regal Rome, p. 109. Whatever Tarquin may have done at Rome, it is evident that he could not have introduced the religious usages above adverted to at Falerii.

[3] This is the opinion of Lepsius in his "Tyrrhenische Pelasger in Etrurien" (8vo. Leipsic, 1842, 2 Bände).

[4] Lib. i. c. 30.

mixture of Hellenes and Umbrians could have produced a language totally unintelligible to the Romans, which has defeated all the efforts of modern philologists to interpret it. There must, therefore, have been a third element, and the question is whether this was Lydian or Rhasennic? The latter race, however—if indeed it be a distinct race at all, instead of only another name for the Etruscans—is known only from Dionysius, and is mentioned by no other ancient author. How they came into Italy, if their existence as a separate race is to be allowed, it is impossible to ascertain. The Etruscans appear at one time to have occupied the plains of Lombardy, where they must have subdued the Umbrians, till they were themselves driven out in turn by the Celts or Gauls, about the time of Tarquinius Priscus; when part of them appear to have taken refuge in the mountains of Rhætia, and the remainder, we may presume, proceeded towards the south.[1] Hence some modern writers, from the resemblance of the names *Rhætia* and *Rhasenna*, have been led to conclude that the Etruscans entered Italy from the Alps, which had been their primitive abode. But this is quite at variance with the account of Livy. That historian tells us that, before the above-mentioned invasion of the Gauls, the Etruscans occupied both sides of the Apennines, that towards the Adriatic, and that towards the Tyrrhenian Sea, having in each district twelve cities. The twelve *original* cities were those on the Roman side of the Apennines, and the twelve on the further, or northern side, were colonies from these. The latter occupied all the territory beyond the Po as far as the Alps, except the district belonging to the Veneti. Hence, also, the origin of the Alpine races, especially the Rhætians; who became barbarized in these countries, retaining nothing of their ancient cultivation except their language, and even that corrupted.[2]

[1] Plin. H. N. lii. 20, § 21; Justin, xx. 5.
[2] Liv. v. 33. Livy does not explain whether the Etruscans were driven into the Alps, or went there voluntarily in the progress of colonization. But the latter supposition is quite improbable, while the former agrees with the accounts of Pliny and Justin. It may be observed that Livy's account is at

ORIGINAL SEAT OF THE ETRUSCANS.

From this account we see that the universal opinion among the Romans respecting the Lydian origin of the Etruscans did not rest only on the authority of Herodotus, but was also supported by historical tradition, which represented the original Etruscan settlements to have been on the southern, or Roman side of the Apennines; that is, in Etruria proper. Hence they pushed forward their colonies northwards to the Alps; facts which show that they did not enter Italy by those mountains, but by the sea. And it must be remembered that this tradition belongs to the historical times, the Gallic invasion which drove the Etruscans from North Italy having occurred so late as the reign of Tarquinius Priscus.

On the whole, therefore, it seems to us most probable that the greater part of the population of Etruria was composed of Umbrians, whom the Lydians had reduced to a state of subjection; since we find that when the Gauls invaded Northern Italy, about the time of Tarquinius Priscus, they not only drove out the Etruscans, the dominant race, but also the Umbrians, who were their subjects; a fact which Livy seems to mention with some surprise,[1] and in a way which would lead us to suppose that the first Celtic tribes which passed the Alps had suffered the Umbrians to remain in the districts between those mountains and the Po, but that subsequent invaders had expelled even them as well as the Etruscans. In fact, a semi-barbarous race, as the Gauls then were, would not have had much occasion for the services of a people that must have resembled them, while the more civilized Lydians knew how to convert them into useful dependants and servants.

Besides the Lydians and the Umbrians, another element of the Etruscan population was the Greeks settled on the sea-coast and in the southern parts of Etruria. In the course of

---

direct variance with Mommsen's assertion (Röm. Gesch. B. I. Kap. 9, S. 82), that in historical times the Etruscans moved from north to south. That the Etruscans were first driven into Rhætia by the Gauls is also the opinion of Schwegler (Röm. Gesch. I. 269).

[1] "Penino deinde Boii Lingonesque transgressi, quum jam inter Padum atque Alpes omnia tenerentur, Pado ratibus trajecto, non Etruscos modo, sed etiam Umbros agro pellunt: intra Apenninum tamen sese tenuere."—Lib. v. c. 35.

time, when the Etruscan dominion had been limited to Etruria proper, or the country between the Magra on the north, the Tiber on the south, the Apennines on the east, and the Tyrrhenian Sea on the west, all these elements, being confined to narrower limits, became gradually more and more fused together, and the language and customs of the Lydians, the governing race, obtained the predominance. How the nation thus formed obtained the name of Etruscans it is difficult to say, but it is hard to believe that it should not have been imposed by the dominant race. The Umbrians, to judge from the Eugubine Tables, appear to have called them *Turaci*, which, by an easy transposition of the *u* and *r*, became *Trusci*, and by the addition of *e*, probably an article, *Etrusci*. *Tusci* and *Etruria* are perhaps Roman corruptions. The name of *Rhasenae*, mentioned only by Dionysius, may rest on some mistake of that author. The root of *Turaci* is perhaps to be sought in *Tyrrhenus*, the name of the leader of the Lydian emigration.[1] The appellation can hardly have been derived from the Tyrrhenian Pelasgians as founders of the Hellenic portion of the Etruscans; and the name of Mare Tyrrhenum, for the Lower Sea, seems to have been chiefly confined to Greek writers. The Etruscans, however, when in possession of Northern Italy, appear to have given name to the Adriatic through their colony of Adria, near the mouths of the Po.

Besides the Iapygians and Etruscans, Ancient Italy was inhabited by various other nations, which, as they spoke cognate dialects, are supposed to have been originally descended from one common stock. Their remote stock is universally agreed to have been Indo-European; whether their more immediate stock was Greek, Teutonic, or Celtic, has been differently determined, according to the judgment or

[1] May not the name Τυρσηνός be composed of Τυρσ, whence the Tursci of the Umbrians, and ηνός, a significant particle, meaning in Lydian son, or something analogous? Hence we might explain such Etruscan names as Pors-ēna (or Porsenna), Vib-ena, &c. The making of the *e* short seems to be a licence taken by some, not all, of the Latin poets. Greek authors write Πορσηνός or Πορσηνας. Virgil, the most learned of the Latin poets, has Porsēna (Æn. viii. 646).

the prejudice of inquirers. These various races are commonly ranked under the three grand divisions of Umbrians, Sabellians, and Latins; though some writers, as Dr. Mommsen, recognise only two, including under the Umbrians those races which others call Sabellian. The Sabellian races included the Sabines and the Samnites, with the tribes which sprung from them, as the Marsi, Marrucini, Peligni, Picentes, Hirpini, and others. The near connexion between the Sabines and the Samnites is shown by the fact that the latter called themselves *Safini*,[1] with a change of *b* into *f*. And that the term *Sabellus* was applied both to Samnites and Sabines appears from several passages in ancient authors. Horace uses it of both races.[2] Pliny says that the Samnites were called Sabelli,[3] and Livy identifies the Sabellian territory with that of Samnium.[4]

The Sabines, the Samnites, and their cognate races occupied the greater part of Central Italy, from the Nar and the Æsis on the north to Lucania and Apulia on the south, and from the Adriatic on the east to Latium and Campania on the west. North of these lay the Umbrians, who, in very early times, probably occupied the whole of Northern Italy, from sea to sea, and as far as the Alps, with the exception of Liguria on the west, and the territory of the Veneti on the east. At the time when Rome was founded they still continued to occupy these regions; for they had not yet been driven from the north by the invasion of the Gauls and the establishment of Gallia Cisalpina. But, for the most part at all events, they were no longer independent. They had been subdued by the Etruscans, who appear to have held as conquerors, as we have already observed, the greater part of the Umbrian territory as above defined, as far south at least, as Felsina, or Bononia, which they appear to have

---

[1] Mommsen, Unterit. Dial. S. 101.
[2] Of the Samnites, Sat. II. 1, 36 : of the Sabines, Od. iii. 6, 38 ; Sat. 1. 9, 29, &c.
[3] H. N. III. 12, 17. ; cf. Strab. v. 12, p. 250.
[4] " Alteri Consuli Æmilio, ingresso Sabellum agrum, non castra Samnitium, non legiones usquam oppositæ."—Lib. viii. c. 1.

founded. In the south-east the Umbrians seem to have maintained their independence; but after the Gallic invasion they were reduced to a small strip of land between Etruria on the west, and the central chain of the Apennines on the east, and from the sources of the Tiber on the north, to the Sabine territory on the south.

If the Umbrians are to be regarded as the most ancient of the Italian races, as they are universally represented to be by ancient authors—though this hardly agrees with the theory that Italy was peopled exclusively by land, since in that case we might expect them to have been thrust towards the south—then they must be regarded as the progenitors of those Umbro-Sabellian tribes before alluded to, who spoke cognate dialects. And this seems to be confirmed by philological researches, facilitated by the celebrated Tables found at Gubbio, the ancient Iguvium, containing tolerably long specimens of what, from the place of their discovery, is considered to have been the ancient Umbrian dialect.

The southern extremities of Italy, besides the Iapygians, seem, in very ancient times, and before the foundation of Rome, to have been inhabited by various Grecian or Pelasgic tribes,[1] such as the Œnotrians, or Itali, the Daunians, Siculi, &c., whose history and ethnological affinities are so obscure and perplexed, that it would altogether exceed the scope of the present work to attempt to unravel them. Only as the name of the Itali, who are supposed to have been identical with the Œnotrii, has become famous by being extended to the whole Italian peninsula, we may mention that originally they seem to have occupied only the extremity of the toe of Italy, or Bruttium, southwards from the Tarinæan and Scyllætian Gulfs. Hence the race and the name spread northwards over the territory subsequently occupied by the Lucanians, a Samnite race, who with the Bruttii seem to have subdued the Itali. How, after this catastrophe, the

---

[1] Among other evidences of Greek colonization at a very remote period, may be mentioned the Scyllæan promontory in Argolis, and the promontory of the same name on the coast of Bruttium, or Italia, alluded to by Homer (Odys. xii. 73, 235, &c.).

name came to be preserved, and ultimately to have been adopted for the whole peninsula, from the Alps to the southernmost extremity, is a problem which we are unable to solve. It appears to have been applied in that extended signification at least as early as the time of Polybius,[1] or more than a century and a half before the Christian era; though its meaning does not seem to have been quite settled even in the time of Augustus, as Dionysius thinks it necessary to define what he comprehends under the name.[2]

All this southern part of Italy came afterwards to be called Magna Græcia, from the numerous Greek colonies founded along its coasts. North of the Itali, or the more modern Lucania, extending from the river Silarus on the south to the Liris on the north, and bounded on the west by the sea, on the east by the country of the Sabines, lay the district known in later times as Campania, but inhabited at an early period by the Ausonians, Opicans, or Oscans, who, if not identical, were probably only different tribes of the same people.

It remains to give some account of Latium, the most important of all the Italian districts, as the country of the Latin race, and the seat of Rome. The boundaries of Latium were at first uncertain, except where they are marked by the Anio, the Tiber, and the sea. On the east and south the Latins were surrounded by hostile nations, the Sabines, the Hernici, Æqui, and Volsci, and their limits seem to have varied with their success in war.

The early history of Latium is as obscure as that of the other Italian nations, and even more so, from the figments respecting it handed down by ancient authors. It appears to have been inhabited at an early period by the Siculi, who, perhaps, also had possession of Campania, and were probably a Pelasgic or Greek race nearly allied to the Œnotrians or Itali. These tribes would then have held possession of the southern and western coasts of Italy, as far north as the Tiber, till they were, for the most part, driven out or subdued by the advancing Sabellian nations, when they retired into Sicily, and gave name to that island. Their presence in

[1] Hist. II. 14.   [2] Ant. Rom. I. 10.

Latium seems to be attested by some words common to the Latin with Sicilian Greek.[1] Pliny enumerates the inhabitants of Latium in the following order: Aborigines, Pelasgians, Arcadians, Siculians, Aurunci, Rutulians.[2] The Aurunci seem to have been identical with the Ausones. The Pelasgians and Arcadians must have been colonists from Greece, who settled in Latium at a very remote period. The Latin traditions conveyed an indistinct memory of them in the stories of Hercules and the Pelasgian Argives founding a Saturnian city on the Capitoline Hill, of the Arcadian Evander building another on the Palatine, and of a third called Antipolis on Mons Janiculus. These settlements, however, were abandoned, from what cause cannot be said, and the inhabitants probably proceeded further inland, or joined their Hellenic brethren in the south of Etruria. It is possible that the inconvenience of the situation may have led to their abandonment; for Rome was the last city built in this district, by a necessity apparently which left no choice, all the surrounding parts being then thickly studded with towns. Dr. Mommsen, indeed, in his history, rejects all these accounts of Grecian colonists, and considers the Latins to have been a pure and unmixed Italian race. Yet his opinions as a philologist differ from those which he holds as an historian. For in his work on the dialects of Lower Italy, he maintains that the Arcadian refugee Evander brought the Greek alphabet to the inhabitants of Latium, and that his mother Carmenta formed out of it the oldest Latin one, in order to commit to writing the holy formulæ, or Sacra Carmina, over which she presided. Dr. Mommsen does not, indeed, say that Evander founded a colony; but, on his own showing, Evander and his mother must have exercised a very considerable influence; and that they could have come into Italy at all is a very

[1] Mommsen, Röm. Gesch. B. I. Kap. 3, quotes a few of them, and thinks they may have resulted from the commerce between Rome and Sicily. But there are more than he cites, and some of these latter could have had no reference to commerce; as *gela, campus, nepotes*, &c. See Newman, Regal Rome, p. 11, and Müller, Etrusker, p. 12.
[2] H. N. iii. 9.

important admission from one who elsewhere so stoutly denies the possibility of such a visit in the state in which navigation was in that very remote period.[1]

SECTION II.

FOUNDATION OF ROME.

THE constancy with which tradition asserts the foreign origin of Rome forbids us to think that it could have been founded by native Latins; while the name itself ('Ρώμα = Valentia, strength) points directly, like *Pyrgi*, or *Neapolis*, to Greek founders. The traditions respecting its origin are, however, so numerous and so divergent as to deprive them, for the most part, of any historical value; and the fact that they are almost wholly found in Greek authors tends the same way. Any Latin traditions would naturally be more trustworthy; and such fortunately have been preserved by Dionysius. They were taken, it appears, from the sacred, or sacerdotal, books; and as such books could not, of course, have been in existence before the time of Numa, we may infer, from their mentioning antecedent events, that the Pontifices were not, like the Pontifex Maximus, mere registrars of contemporary occurrences, but composed a sort of chronicle, resembling those of the monks in the Middle Ages, and that in fact, in the absence of a cultivated and reading public, pro-

---

[1] "Insofern hat also die Sage durchaus Recht, wenn sie die Einführung der litteratura in Rom dem Evander oder dem Herkules zuschreibt. Von den Pelasgern in Arcadien sei die Schrift nach Latium gekommen, nicht lange nach dem dieselbe den Arkadern selber bekannt geworden; der Arcadische Flüchtling Evander habe von dort das griechische Alphabet den Aboriginern mitgebracht und dessen Mutter Carmenta daraus das älteste Lateinische gebildet (graecas literas in latinas commutavit, Hygin.) ohne Zweifel zunächst zur Aufzeichnung der heiligen Formeln, der Sacra Carmina, denen Carmenta vorstand."—Die unteritalischen Dialekte, S. 28.

Indeed Dr. Mommsen is as great a stickler for the antiquity of Italian literature as he is a determined opponent of early Greek navigation. Thus, in the work just cited (p. 3), he holds that the Samnites brought their alphabet with them when they immigrated at some remote and unknown period over the Alps into Italy. It is difficult to conceive how a writer who holds such opinions should consider the early Roman history to be entirely fabulous.

fessional authors, and an established book-selling trade, they were the recognised historiographers of the Roman city.[1]

After giving the Greek traditions respecting the foundation of Rome, Dionysius proceeds as follows:[2]—

"I could adduce many other Greek writers who record various founders of the city; but, not to be tedious, I will come to the Roman authorities. The Romans have not, indeed, a single ancient historian, or prose writer: but they are accustomed to draw from the ancient sources preserved in their sacerdotal books (ἐν ἱεραῖς δέλτοις). Now some of the writers who drew from these books say that Romulus and Romus, the founders of Rome, were the sons of Æneas; while others say that they were the children of his daughter, without specifying their father; and that Æneas gave them as hostages to Latinus, king of the Aborigines, when the treaty was made between them. Latinus not only treated the youths kindly, but, dying without male issue, made them heirs of part of his dominions. Others say that on the death of Æneas, Ascanius, who had succeeded to all his dominions, divided all the Latin territory into three parts, sharing them with his brothers Romulus and Romus; that Ascanius himself built Alba and some other cities, while Romus founded Capua, which he named after his great-grandfather Capys; Anchise, so called after his grandfather Anchises; Ænea, afterwards Janiculum, after his father; and Rome, which bore his own name. This last remained some time deserted, till the Albans sent another colony thither, led by Romulus and Romus, when its ancient form was revived. Thus it appears that Rome was founded twice; first a little after the Trojan war, and again fifteen generations later."

We have here a strange jumble of traditions, from which, however, it may not be impossible to extract a kernel of truth.

First of all it must be laid down that the traditions about the appearance of Æneas in Italy are nothing but pure fable. Homer, who is the best authority concerning him, knows nothing of his wanderings, but appears to have conceived that he reigned over the Trojans after the death of Priam,

[1] See the Preliminary Dissertation. [2] Lib. I. ch. 73.

This conclusion, indeed, is drawn from a sort of prophecy uttered by Poseidon in the council of the gods, which does not state *where* Æneas was so to reign: but any fair and natural interpretation of the passage will, we think, show that Homer meant at Troy,[1] and Strabo appears to have accepted the words in that sense.[2] As Schwegler observes,[3] Homer cannot mean, by any common exegetical method, that Æneas was to reign, after many years of wandering, over a small remainder of the Trojans in a distant and barbarous land. Further, that as all poetical prophecies of this kind are *vaticinia ex eventu*, there can be little doubt that this particular one had fulfilled itself when the Iliad was written, and that its fulfilment was known to Homer's audience. That the Æneadæ reigned in the Troad after the death of Æneas is also shown from several prose writers.[4] It would be superfluous, however, to refute at any length a fable which is, we believe, now almost universally exploded.[5] The origin of it among the Romans has been ingeniously referred by O. Müller[6] to the bringing of the Sibylline Books to Rome. There can be little doubt that these books alluded to Æneas. Dionysius appeals to them in corroboration of the story of Æneas's arrival in Italy, and relates that the portent about the Trojans eating their tables was foretold to them by the Sibyl at Mount

---

[1] Νῦν δὲ δὴ Αἰνείας βίῃ Τρώεσσιν ἀνάξει
Καὶ παίδων παῖδες, τοί κεν μετόπισθε γένωνται.—Il. xx. 307.

[2] Lib. i. xiii. § 53.   [3] Röm. Gesch. B. L. 8. 293.

[4] As Strabo, xiii. § 52, *sq.*; Conon, Narr. 41; Acusilaus, Fr. 26, ap. Müller, Fr. Hist. Gr. t. L p.103; and anonymous writers alluded to by Dionysius, Ant. Rom. I. 53. It also appears from this same passage of Dionysius that many ancient authors either denied that Æneas had come into Italy, or asserted that it was another Æneas, and not the son of Venus and Anchises.

[5] One of the most important works on the subject is Klausen's Æneas und die Penaten, Hamb. 1839, 2 Bde. 4to. which unites the merits and defects so often found in German works of great learning, and considerable but often overstrained acuteness, with obscurity, fancifulness, and tedious prolixity. The reader will find a short but satisfactory refutation of the legend of Æneas in Schwegler's Römische Geschichte, Buch v.; or in Sir G. C. Lewis's Credibility of the Early Roman History, vol. i. ch. 9.

[6] In a paper in the Classical Journal, 1822, vol. xxvi. No. 52: Explicantur causæ Fabulæ de Æneæ in Italiam adventu, pp. 308—318.

Ida.[1] All the Greek Sibylline oracles originated with the Teucrian Sibyl, who delivered her prophecies in the ravines of Ida. According to the legend she was born at Marpessus, a place not far from Gergis, in the Troad, where her tomb was shown in the Temple of Apollo. The principal subject of her prophecies was the race of the Æneads, which ruled in Mount Ida over the remnant of the Teucrians. The Sibyl and her prophecies was afterwards transferred to Erythræ, where, as the Erythræan Sibyl, she attained her greatest renown. It was this collection of prophecies that was offered to Tarquinius Superbus, having come no doubt by way of Cumæ, which had indeed a celebrated Sibyl, but no oracles, of its own;[2] and appears therefore to have used the Gergithean collection. That this had been brought to Cumæ is inferred from the circumstance that the Campanian Cumæ was partly founded by the Æolian Cymæans, among whom some Teucrians of Gergis dwelt.[3]

We have inserted this account partly for its ingenuity, and partly because, as the Sibylline books offered to Tarquin will occur again further on, it may not be amiss to know something of their contents and their reputed origin. That they were originally of Trojan growth is shown by the circle of gods to which they appear to relate, as Apollo, Lato or Latona, Artemis or Diana, Aphrodite or Venus, and Pallas or Minerva, all which deities belong to the native worship of Mount Ida; but more particularly is it shown by their inculcating the worship of the Idæan mother, as appears from the fact that it was at their bidding the Idæan mother was brought to Rome from Pessinus, A.U.C. 549.[4] Nevertheless we are of opinion that the legend of Æneas, and, in connexion with it, the history of the Alban kings, by which the Romans traced their origin to him, obtained a footing in Rome in a less recondite manner. It was a common practice of antiquity to refer the foundation of cities to some hero or demigod. Hercules, Diomede, and Æneas were favourite personages for

---

[1] Lib. i. c. 49, 55.
[2] Pausan. x. 12, 8.   [3] Athenæus, vi. 68; xii. 26.
[4] Liv. xxix. 10; cf. Schwegler, B. i. S. 315.

this purpose; and the ambiguity of Homer's language left at least a peg on which to hang the fiction of the wanderings of Æneas, who is reputed to have founded several cities, besides being the remote founder of Rome. Nay, it is even possible that the Sibyl—who was evidently a mercenary impostor—may have been induced to bring her wares to Rome, from a knowledge that the Romans claimed descent from Æneas, which would render the books more saleable.

It is evident that the legend of Æneas was not credited by educated Romans of the later times. Cicero, in the short sketch which he gives of early Roman history in the second book of his Republic, says not a word about it, but passes on at once to the foundation of Rome. Livy, as we have before taken occasion to remark in the Introduction, considered, as appears from his Preface, the whole history before the time of Romulus, as it was commonly received, to have been fabulous. But the story of Æneas had then taken such hold of the public mind, and was so intimately connected with the glory of the Julian race, that he consulted perhaps both his literary popularity and his favour with the imperial family, by abstaining from refuting it.[1] He accepted the story as it stood, without inquiring into it critically, resigning on this occasion his functions of historian. Hence Sir G. Cornewall Lewis is rather hard upon him when he observes that "at the outset of his history he speaks of the exception made in favour of Æneas and Antenor, after the capture of Troy, by the victorious Greeks, as a certain fact;"[2] thus charging him with inconsistency in varying from what he had said in his Preface. But we think that the very words which Sir Cornewall Lewis adduces in support of this assertion prove the contrary. Livy does not say, "jam primum omnium constat," as he would

---

[1] "Ea nec affirmare, nec refellere in animo est."—Praef. How grateful the story was to the Imperial mind is shown by the splendid fiction of Virgil, the flatterer of Augustus, who also gratified the popular taste by pressing into it, against all the laws of chronology, the tale of Dido, and by many passages calculated to flatter the national self-love. But the Æneid could hardly have been published when Livy wrote his Preface and earlier books, at least.

[2] Credibility, &c. vol. i. p. 311, note 199.

have done in announcing a *certain* fact; but he qualifies the word "constat" with "satis"—"jam primum omnium *satis* constat"—"it is tolerably certain." Sir Cornewall Lewis proceeds to charge him with saying of Ascanius that he was *certainly* the son of Æneas—"certe natum Æneâ constat," though he had not ventured to decide whether by Creusa or Lavinia. Livy, however, is here also quite consistent. He knew very well that the true Ascanius could not have been the son of Lavinia; but he was quite justified in calling him the son of Æneas, for which he had the authority of all antiquity. It was delicate ground. The whole passage was cautiously framed, so as not to question too rudely the imperial pedigree; or may even have been a delicate and latent satire upon it. "I will not pronounce for certain," says Livy, "whether it was Ascanius, or an elder than he, born of Creusa before Ilium fell, and afterwards the companion of his father's flight, whom, as Iulus, the Julian family claims as the author of its name."[1] In fact, Livy knew that Ascanius and Iulus were two distinct personages, born many centuries apart; as we shall proceed to show.

The true tradition, that Rome had been founded only a generation or two after the settlement of some Greek colonists on the coast of Latium, had been preserved in the pontifical books; but these unfortunately had been burnt when Rome was taken by the Gauls. It can hardly be doubted, however, when we see what pains the Romans took to recover their old laws after that catastrophe,[2] that the priests re-wrote their *Commentarii* at that epoch; for, if they had not done so, how should subsequent authors have been able to find in their books, as Dionysius assures us they did, accounts relating to a period antecedent to the foundation of Rome? In thus re-writing their books, they must, no doubt, have trusted to their memory, unless where documents were still extant that might have guided them; such as the *Annales Maximi*, laws, treaties, inscriptions, domestic histories, &c. The *Commentarii*, however, down to the burning of the city, were not probably very voluminous; and when we consider that there were five

[1] Liv. i. 3.   [2] Ibid. vi. 1.

pontiffs, including the Pontifex Maximus, we are perhaps justified in thinking that, with one another's assistance, they may have restored pretty accurately a work which must have been one of their chief employments, and also in those days, when there was no public literature, one of their chief amusements, and must consequently have remained pretty deeply impressed upon their memory. It must be allowed also, that the original work, down perhaps to the time of Tullus Hostilius, must have rested on tradition. But for a century or two even tradition may be trusted, with regard at least to leading political events; and if the immigrants who founded Rome landed only a generation or two before its foundation, not more than a century and a half, at most, might have intervened between that event and the reign of Tullus.[1]

Meanwhile, however, between the first edition of these books and their restoration after the Gallic conflagration, the story of Æneas's arrival in Latium and its consequences, together with the miraculous birth of Romulus, had taken firm hold of the public mind. To trace the line of their kings to some god was as favourite a practice among the ancients as to refer the foundation of their city to some demigod or hero. Thus the founder of the Sabine town of Cures is related to have been, like Romulus, the offspring of Mars and of a noble virgin, who in a moment of divine enthusiasm, it is said, had incautiously entered his penetralia.[2] To run counter to stories like these would have been an unpopular act on the part of the pontiffs; nor were the stories themselves ill calculated to promote superstition and priestcraft. They were therefore

---

[1] Both Nævius and Ennius adopted the tradition that Romulus was the grandson of Æneas by his daughter Ilia. See Serv. Æn. l. 273. Yet Ennius had also adopted the story of Mars being the father of Romulus and Remus, the exposure of the twins, the suckling of them by the wolf, &c. Ennius (ap. Varro, R. R. lil. 1, 2) also held that Rome was only about 700 years old in his time, which would be very far from reaching up to the Trojan times; while at the same time, as he died before the end of the sixth century of Rome, that computation would exceed by more than a century the received date for the foundation of the city. These contradictions it is impossible to reconcile.

[2] Dionys. ii. 48, after Varro.

accepted in the new edition of the *Commentarii*. At the same time, however, the pontiffs were honest enough to insert the original story containing the authentic version of the very speedy foundation of Rome after the arrival of the Greek colony; and hence the inconsistent stories of two Æneases, two Romuluses, the confusion between Ascanius and Iulus, and a double foundation of Rome.

The story, however, derived some support from the Pelasgian or Grecian settlements which had been made, some centuries before the foundation of Rome, on the Capitoline and Palatine Hills and on Mons Janiculus. There is no good reason to doubt that such settlements may have been made, when we find that Cumæ was, in all probability, founded three centuries before the era commonly received for the foundation of Rome, and that the Greek colonies in Etruria must also have been planted long before that event. That at least a strong tradition of such settlements prevailed is evident from the circumstance of Romulus retaining certain memorials of them, and even consecrating them by religious observances: that of an Argive settlement, under the reputed leadership of Hercules, whose worship Romulus established by consecrating to him the Ara Maxima, and appointing an hereditary priesthood for his worship; and that of an Arcadian settlement under Evander, who was also honoured, and more especially in the person of his mother Carmenta. Why these settlements should have been abandoned it is impossible to say, but much perhaps may be attributed to the nature of the site. To fresh comers, who had no experience of it, this site may have appeared attractive enough. Isolated, craggy hills, which a broad and rapid river further helped to defend, offered at least a secure stronghold, a point of no small importance to settlers in a strange country. But these advantages were soon discovered to be counterbalanced by equal defects; among which the unhealthiness of the air, and particularly the overflowings of the Tiber, which must have often rendered the surrounding neighbourhood a complete swamp, are sufficiently obvious. It seems not improbable that these early colonists, when they abandoned the site

which they had first chosen, may have betaken themselves to
the Alban Mount, and there have founded Alba Longa. It
lies within about twelve miles of Rome; its elevated situation
also offered a strong position, while its distance from the
Tiber and its floods rendered the site both more healthy and
more convenient. Hence from the mixture of this Greek
race with the original inhabitants of Latium, whom they had
subdued, arose the first Latin race, distinguished from the
later one by the name of Prisci Latini.

It was soon discovered by the Romans that the man whom
they called Æneas could not possibly have been that hero;
he had landed on their coast only a generation or two before
the foundation of their city; and, as they got wiser and more
learned from a further acquaintance with Greek traditions,
they began to perceive that their tale contained an anachronism of many centuries. But they were naturally unwilling to abandon it, and, in order to retain it, they adopted
the expedient of connecting the genealogy of their founder
with that of the Alban kings. There were many difficulties
in the way, which, however, they heeded not. Alba had
become thoroughly Latinized long before the foundation of
Rome, as is seen by its very name, as well as by the names
of its kings, which, besides having a Latin signification, are
also double; that is, they had a gentile name besides their
individual one, as Æneas Silvius, Latinus Silvius, &c.; whilst
the name of Rome, as we have seen, is Greek, and the name
of its founder, after the Greek fashion, single, without the
gentile addition of Silvius, which might have shown him
connected with the royal family of Alba. This is a botch
which betrays the rent between the two stories.

That Rome was a colony of Alba is also destitute of all
historical probability. The reasons against it may be summed
up as follows:[1] first, immediately Rome is founded, Alba
for a long time altogether vanishes—there are no traces
of any connexion as between a colony and its mother city;
secondly, had there been such a connexion, Rome would have
had the *jus connubii*, not only with Alba, but also with all the

[1] See Schwegler, Röm. Gesch. B. i. Buch viii. S. 24.

Latin towns, and had not needed to resort to the stealing of women. It is no valid objection to this view to say that Rome must have had the *jus connubii* with Alba before the reign of Tullus Hostilius, since the Horatii and Curiatii who fight on either side are cousins; because this *jus* might have been acquired by treaty, although there is no special record of such a treaty in the early history. Moreover, no invitations to the Consualia are despatched to Alba Longa; and again, in the war with the Sabines, when the Romans are on the brink of destruction, no aid is asked from, or offered by, Alba, the pretended mother city. Dionysius, indeed, has a story to the contrary,[1] which is also to be found in Paterculus;[2] but the way in which this author speaks of it, viewed in connexion with all the circumstances which render any connexion between Rome and Alba so utterly improbable, shows that it was invented for the purpose of propping up what was considered to be a weak point. Another objection, first started, apparently, by Beaufort,[3] is, that Romulus never appears to have made any claim to the kingdom of Alba after Numitor's death, which so warlike a prince would hardly have failed to do had he really been Numitor's grandson.[4] Again, Rome at first is entirely estranged from Latium, which would not have been the case had she been an Alban colony; in which case she would have been a member of the Latin league. The badness of the site on which Rome is built is also sometimes adduced as an argument against its having been colonized from Alba; but we are unwilling to lay any great stress upon it: Rome was founded at a very late period, probably the very latest of any city in Latium; all the territory around

---

[1] Lib. II. c. 37.

[2] "Id gessit Romulus, adjutus legionibus Latinis avi sui. Libenter enim his, qui ita proliferant, accesserim; cum aliter firmare urbem novam, tam vicinis Veientibus aliisque Etruscis ac Sabinis, cum imbelli et pastorali manu vix potuerit."—Paterc. lib. I. c. 8, § 5. Paterculus, therefore, believed it, not because he considered it an authentic tradition, but because he considered it necessary to probability.

[3] Dissert. sur l'Incertitude, &c. p. 183.

[4] Plutarch, Rom. 27, mentions an improbable and unsupported story that Romulus, after Numitor's death, voluntarily renounced the succession.

was thickly studded with towns, and the adoption of such a site seems to have been not a matter of choice, but of necessity.

The notion that Rome was a colony regularly planted by Alba seems, for these reasons, to be now pretty generally abandoned. Some scholars, however, have imagined a compromise, which indeed has more probability, and have considered that, instead of being planted in the regular manner, it was founded in consequence of civil dissensions at Alba, and by a secession of part of its inhabitants, under the conduct of Romulus.[1] There are not wanting passages which might lend a colour to these reputed dissensions at Alba; but, on the other hand, it may be remarked that such an origin of Rome is entirely at variance with, or at all events wholly unsupported by, the ancient tradition. But what we take to be the strongest argument against an Alban origin in any way is, that Rome, as we shall endeavour to show, bears indubitable marks in its institutions of having been founded by Greeks who had not very long before landed in Italy, and had not yet forgotten their language and their customs.

The foundation of Rome is probably placed the better part of a century too high, and should fall, perhaps, as we have already observed in the Introduction, in the first half of the seventh century before Christ, instead of the middle of the eighth. Greek colonization on the Italian coast was remarkably active in the latter half of the eighth century, when Rhegium, Sybaris, and Tarentum were founded. This colonization went on two or three centuries longer. Thus we find Hyele, or Velia, founded in B.C. 544, and Buxentum even so late as B.C. 470. Hyele was founded by Phocaeans, who also founded Massalia, probably about the same time. When Phocaea was besieged, in B.C. 546, by Harpagus, the general of Cyrus, the inhabitants embarked on board their fleet, and endeavoured to form a settlement in the islands of Œnussae, belonging to Chios; but being repulsed by the Chians, they proceeded to Alalia, in Corsica, a colony which they had

---

[1] This view has been adopted by Rubino, Röm. Staatsverf, § 112, Anm. 2; Göttling, Gesch. der Röm. Staatsverf, § 44, and others.

founded about twenty years before. After staying there five years, they went to Rhegium, and soon after founded Hyele, or Velia.¹ Herodotus, who relates these events, mentions nothing about their founding Massalia; but Pausanias represents these same fugitives from the Medes as settling there after defeating the Carthaginians in a naval battle.² It can hardly be doubted that this is the same battle alluded to by Herodotus and by Thucydides.³ There is, however, other evidence to fix the foundation of Massalia, which is incidentally of some importance to the early chronology of Rome. Justin, the epitomizer of Trogus Pompeius, tells us that the Phocæans, on their way, entered the mouth of the Tiber, in the reign of King Tarquinius, and contracted an alliance with the Romans; and thence, sailing into the furthest gulfs of Gaul, founded Massilia among the Ligurians and the savage Gallic races.⁴ Justin, of course, means Tarquinius Priscus. His testimony is confirmed by Livy, who relates that when the Gauls were passing into Italy, in the reign of Tarquinius Priscus, they heard on their way that the Massilienses from Phocæa were attacked by the Ligurian tribe of the Salyes.⁵

But how shall we reconcile this account with the ordinary chronology of Tarquinius Priscus, which fixes his reign from B.C. 616 to 578? If the Phocæans only took to their ships in B.C. 546, and founded Massalia some years afterwards, it is evident that they could never have arrived in Italy in the lifetime of the elder Tarquin. There is, indeed, an account in Scymnus Chius, which professes to be taken from Timæus, of a previous foundation of Massalia one hundred and twenty years before the battle of Salamis, or B.C. 600.⁶ But that work

¹ Herod. i. 163—167.   ² x. 8, § 6.   ³ Lib. l. c. 13.
⁴ "Temporibus Tarquinii regis ex Asia Phocæensium juventus ostio Tiberis invecta amicitiam cum Romanis junxit: inde in ultimos Gallis sinus navibus profecta Massiliam inter Ligures et feras gentes Gallorum condidit."—Lib. xliii. c. 3.   ⁵ Liv. v. 34.
⁶
Μασσαλία δ' ἐστ' ἐχομένη
Πόλις μεγίστη Φωκαίων ἀποικία.
Ἐν τῇ Λιγυστικῇ δὲ ταύτην ἱστέον
Πρὸ τῆς μάχης τῆς ἐν Σαλαμῖνι γενομένης
Ἔτεσιν πρότερον, ὥς φασιν, ἑκατὸν εἴκοσι·
Τιμαῖος οὕτως ἱστορεῖ δὲ τὴν κτίσιν.—Vers. 208, seqq.

has been shown to be spurious;[1] besides, the Phocæans who visited Tarquin are expressly said to have been those flying from the Medes. Herodotus, who mentions Alalia, knows nothing of a previous Phocæan colony. Nor does Justin—or, rather, Trogus Pompeius, whom he abridged,—who, being of Gallic descent, was likely to have taken a strong interest in such a subject, and gives the longest account of it which we possess, recognise more than one foundation of Massalia. And if, as we have shown on other grounds, the date of the foundation of Rome is to be placed seventy or eighty years lower than the era commonly received, then the account of this visit tallies very well with the chronology of Tarquin, and, in fact, may be regarded as forming a corroboration of it.

Our main object in adverting to this account of the foundation of Massalia, and to the Greek colonies planted on the coast of Italy at that time, and a couple of centuries earlier, is to show that the establishment of one in the neighbourhood of Rome during this period is by no means improbable. Collaterally, it has also served to show that there really was such a king as Tarquinius Priscus, whom it is now the fashion to regard as a mythical personage; for it is impossible to believe that two independent notices of him by two different authors, both on the occasion of the same event, but of different phases of that event, were the result either of accident on the one hand, or of a fictitious combination on the other.

Where the colony which ultimately founded Rome first established itself, we will not pretend to say. We will only observe that there seems to be the same ambiguity between Lavinium and Laurentum as between the two Æneases, the two Romuluses, and the two foundations of the city. Thus the retainers of King Tatius are represented to have struck the ambassadors of the *Laurentines;* yet the insult is avenged by the murder of Tatius at *Lavinium*.[2] May not this ill-feeling between the *Sabine* Tatius and the Laurentines have

---

[1] By Meineke, in his edition of Scymnus (Berlin, 1846).
[2] Liv. i. 14.

arisen from the latter having been the progenitors of the Græco-Roman portion of his subjects?[1] On this occasion Romulus forbears to punish, and renews—for what reason does not appear—a former treaty between Rome and Lavinium. It is possible that a body of Laurentines may have gone to Lavinium to murder Tatius. The more ancient Greek colony, which subsequently migrated to Alba Longa, was first, perhaps, established at Lavinium; for it is incredible, if they originally settled at Laurentum, that they should have removed to another place, of much the same kind, only four or five miles distant. Lavinium was probably the cradle of the *Prisci Latini*, the founders of Alba, and Laurentum that of the more modern Latins represented by the Romans. In process of time, as the Romans confounded their early history with that of Alba, so also they would naturally confound the two cradles of the races; and Lavinium came, at length, to be looked up to as the original settlement of Æneas, the abode of the Penates, and, as it were, the birthplace of the whole Latin race.

The above remarks are merely offered as conjectures. They do not pretend to any historical authority; for it would be idle in a modern writer to seek any in a subject abandoned by Livy as mythical. There were, however, certainly such towns as Lavinium and Laurentum, and there were also certain traditions connected with them; and, in so famous a subject, the imagination may please itself awhile in endeavouring to select and arrange the vestiges of probability. After the foundation of the city, tradition becomes more firm and consistent; for it is still to tradition that we must look for, perhaps, three-fourths of the first century of its existence. But it is now confined to a definite place, and is aided by walls and temples, and other monuments; in short, it has emancipated itself from that period which the Roman historian considered as fabulous.

It seems probable that Romulus, before he built his city, had contracted an alliance with some of the Grecian cities of

[1] The name Laurentum is perhaps derived from the Greek λαύρα, a street or village, a small place, such as would be founded by new colonists.

THE ORIGIN OF ROME. 37

Etruria, which, though belonging to the Etruscan confederacy, continued to retain their Hellenic customs. These Etruscan cities, when the general interests of the league were not in question, seem to have acted pretty independently. To some such alliance we must refer the circumstance of his building Rome with Etruscan rites, and his adopting the Etruscan ensigns of regal power; as well as the aid which he appears to have received from Etruria in his struggle with the Sabines, to which we shall have occasion to advert further on. He must also have conciliated the shepherds who fed their flocks on the future site of Rome, and who probably belonged to the Latin race. Whether they had been previously connected with Alba, it were useless to inquire.

But before proceeding any further, let us relate the story which obtained almost universal acceptance, if not belief, among the Romans themselves. It plays so great a part in their traditions, it has been the subject of so much of their poetry, and is in itself so pleasing and poetical, that it is absolutely necessary for the student of Roman history and literature to be acquainted with it.

After the fall of Troy, Æneas is supposed to have embarked upon his fleet, and to have visited successively Pallene and the shores of Northern Greece, the islands of Delos, Crete, and Zacynthus. Hence, after touching at Leucas, Buthrotum, and other places, he makes the Italian shore at the Iapygian promontory, and, coasting along its southern extremity, arrives off Sicily, and proceeds to Drepanum at its western end. The storm which overtook the Trojans on sailing from this port forms the opening of the Æneid. They are described as driven by it to the coast of Africa, for the purpose of introducing into the Latin version of the story the famous anachronism of Æneas's visit to Dido; an episode, however, which does not appear to have been invented by Virgil, but to have been introduced by Nævius, in his poem on the "First Punic War,"[1] some two centuries before Virgil's time. Varro seems also to have recognised the story of Æneas's visit to Carthage,

[1] See Nævii Fragmenta, ed. Klussmann, p. 38, seqq.; Lewis, Credibility, &c. vol. l. p. 316, note 76.

though he makes Anna, Dido's sister, and not the Carthaginian queen herself, enamoured of the Trojan hero;[1] but the account of Æneas being driven to the African coast is ignored both by Livy and Dionysius.

After leaving Carthage, Æneas again visits the western point of Sicily, and founds the town of Segesta, and a temple of Venus at Eryx. Then, having left a portion of his followers in Sicily, he sails for the Italian coast. Points on this coast which have become famous through Virgil's poem are Cape Palinurus, between the gulfs of Laus and Pæstum, so named from Æneas's pilot, who there fell overboard and was drowned; the islands and promontory of the Sirenusæ, the abode of the Sirens; Cape Misenum, at the northern extremity of the Gulf of Naples, the burial-place of the trumpeter Misenus; Cumæ, where Æneas's visit to the Sibyl gives occasion to one of the finest episodes in the poem; and lastly, Cajeta, the southernmost promontory of Latium, so named after the nurse of Æneas.

The Trojans are supposed to have finally landed at Laurentum, some ten miles southwards of the mouth of the Tiber. Here the prediction was fulfilled, according to which the place where they consumed their tables—which they did here either by eating the parsley on which they were reposing, or the slices of bread on which they had laid their meat—was to be the term of their wanderings. To the spot where they landed they are said to have given the name of Troy; but any village of that name, which may have existed there in later times, was probably the result of the legend. So also Antenor, who, like Æneas, is said after the capture of Troy to have sailed with the Ileneti to the top of the Adriatic, and to have established there the Venetian people, is related to have founded a town named Troja.

When Æneas landed in Italy, the aborigines or native inhabitants of Latium, near the spot, at all events, where he disembarked, were ruled by King Latinus, the fourth of a dynasty whose founder was Saturn. The reign of Saturnus was the golden age of Italy. It was fabled to enjoy all the

[1] Apud Serv. ad Æn. iv. 682; v. 4.

blessings of civilization, without the evils which it brings in its train. There was wealth and abundance, but it was all enjoyed in common; the public felicity was consequently undisturbed by theft or violence, and the precautions taken to prevent or repress them were utterly unknown. Saturnus had his dwelling on the Capitoline Hill, which hence obtained the name of Mons Saturnius. Over against him, on a hill on the other side of the river, dwelt Janus, a still more ancient king than he, and apparently belonging to the aborigines, whereas Saturnus was an immigrant, to whom Janus extended his hospitality. Saturnus was succeeded by Picus, and Picus by Faunus. It was during the reign of Faunus that the Arcadian Evander came to Latium, and formed a settlement on the hill next Mons Saturnius; which by some is thought to have derived its subsequent name of Mons Palatinus either from Pallantia, a daughter of Evander, or from the Arcadian town of Pallantium.[1] Evander, like most of these ancient founders, was descended from the gods, being the son of Mercury by Carmenta, an Arcadian nymph and prophetess, who was afterwards regarded with great veneration by the Romans, till she was superseded by the Sibyl.

It was also in the reign of Faunus, and only a few years after the Arcadian settlement, that Hercules arrived in Italy, bringing with him from Hesperia the oxen of Geryon, which he was conveying to Argos. Here he was robbed of some of them by Cacus, a ferocious robber of the Aventine, a legend so prettily told in the verse of Ovid. Dionysius of Halicarnassus[2] represents Hercules as taking possession of Mons Saturnius; but this version seems at variance with the more

[1] There are various other etymologies; as from Pallas, son of Hercules, by Lanna, a daughter of Evander; from Palanto, either mother or wife of King Latinus; or from Palatium, an aboriginal colony near Reate. Others seek the origin of the name etymologically; as from *balare*, or *palare*, the bleating or the wandering of sheep; or from *palus*, a stake, supposing the hill to have been originally fortified with palisades. But perhaps the most probable derivation is from Pales, the god, or goddess, of shepherds and flocks. The foundation of Rome is said to have taken place on the festival of that deity, the Palilia, celebrated on the 21st of April.

[2] Lib. i. c. 34, sqq.

commonly received account. The legend of the arrival of
Hercules in these parts made, however, a deep impression on
the public mind, and was perpetuated by Roman institutions
and temples in his honour.

All the settlements and events which we have just recorded
occurred before the time of the Trojan war. It was in the
reign of Latinus, the successor of Faunus, that the siege of
Troy took place; and when Æneas arrived in Latium, Latinus
was already an old man. On the landing of the Trojans, he
turned his arms against them. Both the Trojans and the
Latin king are, however, warned in a dream to forbear from
hostilities; and Latinus, after a colloquy with Æneas, agrees
to assign to him forty stadia of ground around the hill which
he had occupied, on condition that he should lend his aid
against the Rutuli. A radius of forty stadia, or five miles all
round, seems to be about the usual average of territory possessed by these primitive cities.

In pursuance of this treaty, the Trojan leader completes
the foundation of Lavinium, at a spot to which he had been
directed by the flight of a white pregnant sow, which, while
he was offering his first sacrifice, had escaped from the hands
of the priests, and rested not until she had reached this place.
The new town was called Lavinium, after Lavinia, the daughter
of Latinus, whom Æneas had received in marriage. Hence,
as the first stable resting-place of the Trojan Penates after
their long wanderings, Lavinium was in after ages a place of
peculiar veneration for the Romans; and it became customary
for the consuls, prætors, and dictators of the republic to offer
sacrifice there when they entered on their magistracies to the
Penates and to Vesta.[1] These deities show that it was the
first *home* of the Trojans on Italian soil; and they could
not therefore have founded Laurentum, which was a later
settlement.[2]

But Lavinia had been promised to Turnus, king of the
Rutuli, a neighbouring people, who, enraged at being thus

[1] Macrob. Sat. lib. iii. c. 4.
[2] So Varro: "Oppidum, quod primum conditum in Latio stirpis Romanæ Lavinium; nam ibi dii penates nostri."—Ling. Lat. v. § 144.

supplanted by a stranger, made war upon Æneas and Latinus. In a battle which ensued the Rutuli were defeated, but the Trojans and aborigines purchased their victory with the loss of Latinus. Turnus and the Rutuli now had recourse to Mezentius, king of the Etruscan city, Cære, who, jealous of the intrusion of the Trojans into Italy, readily joined his arms with those of Turnus. Such is the account of Livy.[1] But as Cære was a Greek colony, and could hardly have been founded long at the time of the supposed arrival of Æneas, the story of Virgil seems to be constructed with more probability, who represents Mezentius as having been driven from his dominions by his subjects on account of his cruelty and tyranny, and as having taken refuge with Turnus.[2] In the face of this danger, Æneas, in order the better to unite his subjects, gives them not only laws in common, but also a common name, calling them, after his father-in-law, Latins. Æneas defeats Turnus and Mezentius, but is himself killed, or disappears in some mysterious manner. According to some accounts, he was drowned in the river Numicius, and at all events he is said to have been buried on its banks. After his death he was ranked among the gods, and received the name of "Jupiter Indiges," or the native Jupiter.

Ascanius, the son of Æneas and Lavinia, was not of an age to assume the reins of government at the time of his father's death, and his mother therefore took the direction of affairs during his minority. There is a doubt, however, as we have already intimated, whether the name of this young prince was Ascanius or Iulus, and whether he was the son of Creusa or Lavinia. Ascanius, when he came of age, finding that Lavinium had a superabundant population, abandoned it to his mother, or stepmother, and migrating with a part of the people to Mons Albanus, which is distant only a few miles from Lavinium, founded there, according to a usual custom in those early times, a new city, which, from its being seated on a long ridge, was called Alba Longa. This event

[1] Lib. i. c. 2.
[2] Æn. viii. 470, sqq. Virgil, too, with more consistency, gives the town its ancient name of Agylla.

took place thirty years after the foundation of Lavinium, which are supposed to represent the thirty pigs littered by the sow. We shall not inquire into the natural history of this miraculous parturition. Alba Longa is thought to have occupied the ridge which overhangs the eastern side of the lake of Albano, where massive fragments of what are supposed to have been its walls still remain. Its name is by some derived from the white sow; but it is difficult to see the animal's connexion with Alba, which more probably took its name from the nature of the place. Varro combines both these etymologies.[1] The new city seems to have been founded without molestation, for the power of the Latins, particularly after the defeat of the Etruscans, had so much increased, that none of the surrounding peoples ventured to attack them. Agreeably to the treaty of peace with the Etruscans, the river Tiber, then called the Albula, was to form the boundary between the two nations.

Ascanius was succeeded on the throne by his son Silvius Postumus; a name which is accounted for by his having by some chance been born in the woods. It remained the family name of the Alban kings. The next two in hereditary succession—for, unlike Rome, Alba was an hereditary monarchy —were Æneas Silvius and Latinus Silvius. The latter planted some colonies, whose inhabitants, according to Livy,[2] were called *Prisci Latini;* but it seems a more probable account that the Prisci Latini were the more ancient Latins, before the foundation of Rome.[3] The successors of Latinus Silvius were Alba, Atys or Epytus, Capys, Capetus or Calpetus, Tiberinus—who gave name to the Tiber from being drowned in it—Agrippa, Romulus or Aremulus Silvius, Aventinus—who was buried on the Aventine, and bequeathed his name to it—Procas, Numitor, and Amulius.

The reigns of these sixteen Alban and Trojan kings, from Æneas to Numitor, both inclusive, occupy a period of 432

---

[1] "Propter colorum suis et loci naturam Alba Longa dicta."—Ling. Lat. v. § 144.
[2] Lib. i. c. 3; cf. Dionys. i. 45.
[3] Paul. Diac. p. 226; cf. Serv. ad Æn. v. 598.

years,[1] giving an average of twenty-seven years to each hereditary reign. If we add this term to 753, the Varronian era (B.C.) for the foundation of Rome, we have 1185 years, which exceeds by one year the era of Eratosthenes for the capture of Troy (B.C. 1184), and makes besides no allowance for the time of Æneas's wanderings.

Amulius was a usurper who dethroned his elder brother, Numitor, put Numitor's sons to death, and compelled his daughter, Rhea Silvia, to become a vestal, in order that she might have no offspring. But Silvia was deflowered by Mars and brought forth male twins: whereupon Amulius cast her into prison, and directed that her babes should be drowned in the river. It chanced that the Tiber had overflowed its banks, and the slaves to whom had been committed the execution of this cruel order, exposed the boys in their cradle at a spot on the Palatine Hill, subsequently marked by the Ficus Ruminalis. The neighbourhood was at that time a vast solitude. Presently the flooding waters began to recede into their channel, leaving the cradle high and dry, when a she-wolf, that had come thither to slake her thirst, was attracted by the cries of the children, and gave them suck. At this juncture, Faustulus, a herdsman of the king's, arrived at the spot, and found the wolf licking the babes with her tongue. So he took them from her, and carried them to the cattle-sheds, where he gave them to his wife Larentia to nurse. Some have explained the miraculous story by saying that Larentia was called *lupa*, or wolf, from her prostitute life.

As the boys grew up they took to hunting, instead of slothfully tending the cattle; and having thus acquired strength both of body and mind, instead of pursuing wild beasts they began to attack robbers laden with booty; for Italy seems to have been almost as much infested with brigands in those remote ages as it is at present. What spoil they took they divided with the other shepherds; and with the band of youths who grew up with them, and increased in number daily, they celebrated various sports and festivals. Among

[1] The years are given by Dionysius and Diodorus; Livy says nothing about them.

these was the Lupercal, which was celebrated on the Palatine Hill. It is said to have been an Arcadian solemnity, instituted by Evander when he had possession of this district. Naked youths ran about in it sportively and wantonly in honour of the Lycean Pan, afterwards called Inuus by the Romans. These sports recurred at certain fixed periods; and the brigands, who were enraged at the loss of their prey, availed themselves of the opportunity to make an attack on Romulus and Remus; for such were the names of the two youths. Romulus managed to defend himself; but Remus they took, and brought him before Amulius—for they sometimes showed themselves in the towns just as they do now—and they accused him, as well as Romulus, of carrying off booty from Numitor's fields. They appear even then to have stood pretty well with the authorities, for their story was believed, and Remus was handed over to Numitor for punishment.

Faustulus had all along suspected that the youths whom he was educating were of the royal race; but he determined not to reveal his thoughts till a proper occasion should present itself: and thinking that this had now arrived, he opened the matter to Romulus. Numitor also, on hearing the story of the youths, had begun to suspect the same thing; and so far from punishing Remus, was on the point of acknowledging him as his grandson. Under these circumstances, Romulus having collected together a band of shepherds, and being aided by Remus with another band, they made themselves masters of Alba,[1] and put to death Amulius.

Numitor, at the beginning of the tumult, exclaiming that enemies had entered the city, had drawn away the Alban youth under pretence of defending the citadel; but when he beheld Romulus and Remus, after they had killed Amulius, approaching him with congratulations, he at once called a council, to whom he explained the whole story of his brother's wickedness, the origin, education, and discovery of his grandsons, and the death of the tyrant, of which he declared him-

---

[1] Cic. De Rep. lib. II. c. 2.

self the author. Then Romulus and Remus saluted Numitor
as king, and the whole council did the like.

Numitor being thus reinstated in his kingdom, Romulus
and Remus were seized with a desire to build a city at the
spot where they had been exposed and educated. The project
was favoured by the superabundant multitude of Albans and
Latins; the shepherds also were numerous, so that it seemed
probable that Lavinium and Alba would be but small cities
in comparison with that which they should build. But these
plans were disturbed by ambition, the hereditary curse of
their family. Being twins, their pretensions as to which of
them should give name to and reign over the new city could
not be decided by priority of birth; so they resolved to consult by means of augury the will of the gods; to which end
Romulus chose the Palatine Hill as a temple, and Remus
the Aventine.

As they thus stood surveying the heavens, six vultures
appeared to Remus; but presently after a dozen showed
themselves to Romulus. Hereupon the followers of each
saluted him king: Remus, because the vultures had appeared
first to him; Romulus, because he had seen the greater
number. Hence a quarrel and a fight; blood was shed, and
amidst the tumult Remus was killed. A commoner version
of the story, however, is that Romulus slew his brother for
having contemptuously leapt over the rising walls of his city.
Romulus, thus become sole master, built a city on the
Palatine, and named it after himself.

Such was the most commonly received legend of Rome's
foundation; into the different versions of it we shall not
enter. The list of the Alban kings has all the appearance of
having been invented in order to carry up to the Trojan times
the lineage of Romulus; though it is not improbable that a
dynasty of the name of Silvius may have reigned at Alba.
The story, however, acquired a firm hold on the popular
belief, and, being received into the sacred books, to doubt it
became a sort of heresy. So also *Valentia*, the equivalent
Latin name of *Roma*, was forbidden to be whispered; for it
might have betrayed to the ignorant the recent Greek origin

of the city, and have upset the story of its Trojan foundation through the Alban dynasty.

How and when Rome's foundation legend was invented, what grains of truth there may be at the bottom of it, it is impossible to say. We have already surmised that it may have found its way into the Pontifical Commentaries at a very early date; but all that is certainly known is, that it must have been rooted in the popular mind as an article of historical belief at least as early as the year of Rome 458 (B.C. 295), since in that year the Ædiles Cn. and Q. Ogulnius caused to be erected at the Ficus Ruminalis images of Romulus and Remus sucking the wolf.[1] This fact at once upsets Plutarch's account[2] that the story was first introduced to the Romans by Fabius Pictor, who took it from one Diocles of Peparethos, since Fabius Pictor flourished at least half a century later than B.C. 295. Indeed, as Schwegler remarks,[3] it has all the characteristics of home growth, and could not possibly have been of Greek invention. Into the allegorical meanings which have been attributed to the legend we shall not enter;[4] though it is probable enough that it symbolizes in general the warlike character of Romulus and the early Romans.

The testimony of all antiquity that the original Roman city stood upon the Palatine has been confirmed by modern excavations; and, to whomsoever we may attribute its foundation, there can be no reasonable doubt that on this hill stood a town, or citadel, which formed the proper nucleus of Rome, and was in process of time developed into the magnificent city which became the mistress of the world.

We will here pause a moment to survey the general condition of Italy at this period; for unless we obtain a correct notion of the state of civilization and society when Rome was founded, we shall be apt to form very incorrect ideas of early Roman history.

The essential step towards civilization—which in its proper and primary signification means the dwelling together in

[1] Liv. x. 23. [2] In Romul. c. 3, 8. [3] R. L. S. 412.
[4] The German writers are, of course, great on this head

cities and communities—is agriculture; for, without the supplies derived from this source, it is impossible for men to live together in any great numbers. But, having these supplies, they begin to build cities for their mutual protection; the division of labour is established, the useful arts of life are invented, and by degrees, as wealth begins to accumulate in a few hands, and thus to afford the means of leisure, literature and the finer arts are cultivated, the manners of society become more refined and polite, and violence and crime are repressed by laws and civil institutions. But it is soon discovered that the accumulation of wealth gives birth not only to domestic fraud and violence, but also to foreign aggression. Hence a wider horizon opens on the view of rulers and legislators; they become politicians as well as lawgivers—that is, they begin to consider the relations of cities and communities to one another, and to establish alliances, leagues, unions, and confederacies, and thus arise the first beginnings of a State. The third and last step in what may be called the political progress of civilization is the formation of large kingdoms and empires. At the time when Rome was founded, neither Greece nor Italy had reached this stage. It was only in the East, which had been much earlier civilized, that great monarchies had arisen, as the kingdom of Egypt and the Assyrian and Median empires.

At the period alluded to, Italy was far behind Greece in political development. This is shown, among other things, by the superabundant population of the Greek cities, which long before and long after the foundation of Rome led them to plant colonies in Italy, then comparatively uncivilized and but scantily peopled. And though Greece had not yet arrived at that stage when single cities are swallowed up by, and amalgamated with, a great empire; yet this perhaps partly arose from Greek habits of mind, as well as from the nature of their country, whose mountainous character and numerous bays helped cities to maintain their independence. Yet they had recognised the unity of the Hellenic race by a community of religious festivals, and by their Amphictyonies.

In Italy the second stage of political existence had hardly

been reached at the time when Rome was founded, except in Etruria. Even in that country, however, though there can be little doubt that the Etruscan confederacy had been formed before the foundation of Rome, the different cities which belonged, or were nominally subject to it, appear to have acted a very independent part, and were probably not called upon to perform any federal duties, except when some extreme and common danger threatened the well-being of the whole confederacy. This may be seen in the wars waged between Rome and Veii, in which the latter city does not appear to have been supported by the Etruscan confederacy, even when the Romans deprived it of great part of its territory. We hear also of a Latin League, but this appears to have been of the same, or even, perhaps, a still looser description. Of the political constitution of the other nations which bordered upon Latium, such as the Sabines, the Hernici, the Volsci, and others, we know little or nothing; but it seems probable that their chief, if not sole, bond of union lay in community of race.

We have, therefore, to figure to ourselves Rome in its early days as closely surrounded by a vast number of small yet virtually independent cities, whose political views were almost entirely confined to their own preservation or advancement. These cities had all been established before Rome, which, as we have before intimated, was probably almost the last founded in Latium. They appear to have been, like the original Rome itself, small places,—in fact, little more than modern villages of a few thousand inhabitants; though we are apt to form a higher idea of their importance because they were walled and fortified, and were in general ruled by a magistrate who had the title of "king." Thus, besides the Alban and Roman kings, we hear of kings of such places as Cœnina, Cures, Ardea, &c. Even Alba, the ancient metropolis of Latium, was so small a city that all its population, when transferred to Rome, could be accommodated on the Cælian Hill. These cities, as we have before observed, possessed a territory of some ten miles in diameter; a fact which we not only know from tradition, but of which we may immediately convince ourselves by inspecting a map of ancient Latium, when we shall see that, if they had had a larger territory, there would not have been room for them.

Thus Strabo points out that what were originally called the towns of Collatia, Antemnæ, Fidehæ, Lavicum, &c. were only thirty or forty stadia (four or five miles) distant from Rome, and had in his time become mere villages owned by private individuals.[1]

It is important to bear these circumstances in mind, because some authors would assign for the growth of a town like these as long a period as would be necessary for the development of a large kingdom, and hence have been led to regard as improbable the comparatively rapid progress of Rome.

It seems probable that the band of Romulus, including the shepherds whom he had enlisted in it, did not exceed about 1,000 men, at which number they were stated by Plutarch.[2] When Dionysius[3] calls them 3,000 foot and 300 horse, he evidently takes that number, by a *prolepsis*, from the 30 curiæ of 100 men each, subsequently established by Romulus; for such, as we learn from Varro, was the total of the primitive Roman army after the Sabine union, consisting only of one legion, to which each of the three tribes contributed 1,000 foot soldiers, and 100 horse.[4] The recent excavations on the Palatine, conducted by Signor Rosa for Napoleon III., have shown that the Romulean city was confined to the western portion of the hill, or that occupied by the Farnese Gardens; and the same fact, as the author has endeavoured to prove in another work,[5] is further shown by the circumstance that all the memorials of Romulus are confined to this district. So

---

[1] τὰς δὲ κώμας, κτήσεις ἰδιωτῶν.—Lib. v. c. 3, s. 2.
[2] In Rom. 9.
[3] Lib. ii. c. 2. Dionysius (ii. 6) makes Romulus establish these curiæ before the amalgamation of the Romans with the Sabines; but Livy and Cicero agree that it was done afterwards.
[4] "Milites, quod trium millium primo legio fiebat, ac singulæ tribus Titiensium, Ramnium, Lucerum millia singula militum mittebant."—Ling. Lat. v. 89. "Turma, quod ter deni equites ex tribus tribubus Titiensium, Ramnium, Lucerum fiebant."—Ibid. 91.
[5] Hist. of the City of Rome, p. 18, seq.

small an area would hardly have sufficed to accommodate 3,000 persons, but it was amply large enough to serve as a fortress or citadel for some thousand men. We must remember that the followers of Romulus were probably all young men. When the population of a colony such as that of Laurentum, or at whatever place on the coast the original Greek settlement may have been made, began to overflow its narrow boundaries—and in the course of even less than half a century this might easily happen—it was the youth that went forth to seek for themselves new homes. The Romulean emigration was forced to content itself with the site of Rome for their settlement, for it was in fact the only choice they had, the surrounding country being now fully occupied with cities. But from the nature of the place, and with the help of a wall, 1,000 soldiers, without apparently women or other incumbrances, might easily defend themselves against any force which a neighbouring town might have thought it worth while to direct against them.

Such, then, was the original Rome; the western half of the Palatine Hill with a wall erected round its base in a quadrangular, or rather lozenge-like, form; whence the name of *Roma Quadrata*. The wall, according to the well-known description of Tacitus,[1] was built with Etruscan rites; the *pomœrium*, or sacred space around it, being marked out by a furrow made with a plough drawn by a cow and a bull; the clods being carefully thrown inwards, and the plough being lifted over the profane spaces necessary for the gates; whence, according to Cato, the name of *porta, a portando*, because the plough was carried.[2] We are thus to consider a city founded with these religious rites as a sacred enclosure, in fact a *templum*, whose limits, the *pomœrium*, marked the extent of the city's auspices.[3] This enclosure was under the protection

---

[1] Ann. xii. 24.   [2] Ap. Isidor. xv. 2, 3.

[3] A *templum terrestre* was always of a square form—Aurelius, Plut. Rom. 22; Cam. 32; Nägele, Studien, S. 127; ap. Schwegler, B. L S. 448; Anm. 12. But there was also within the Palatine city, in the Area Apollinis, a *mundus*, or small square walled place, in which were deposited things considered to be of good omen in founding a city; which place was also called Roma Quadrata. (Fest. p. 258.)

of a presiding deity, or deities, as Rome was—or at all events the Tarquinian Rome—under that of Jupiter, Juno, and Minerva. So also Veii was under the safeguard of Juno, and could not be taken, it was thought, till the deity had given her consent.

Such was the original Rome; a little fortress on a hill. That it could ever have entered the head of any writer that such a city founded in such a place could have been intended for a great commercial emporium, as is maintained in a work that has attained great popularity both in this country and in Germany,[1] surpasses all belief, and seems to betray total want of historical judgment. A mixed race of shepherds, we are told, partly Latin, partly Sabine, and partly of another nation represented under the name of Luceres, but also supposed to be Latin, had long dwelt together in concord and amity on these hills, till at length this pastoral people resolve to turn merchants. They choose for their place of commerce a hill-top, which, though it is, indeed, near the Tiber, yet on that side, and indeed on three sides, was a mere swamp, subject to continual inundations, which could never have presented any convenient landing-place, or wharf, at all events till it was drained by the Cloaca Maxima. That this sewer, which still remains one of the *material* evidences of early Rome, should have been coeval with the foundation of the city will, we presume, be hardly maintained even by those who reject all historical tradition. Indeed, Dr. Mommsen is inclined to assign it, at least in its finished state, to the republican times,[2] and consider the Palatine in the regal period to have been almost entirely surrounded with marsh. A fine situation for a great commercial city!

Dr. Mommsen's account of the origin of the founder and inhabitants of the city is just as incredible as that of the city itself. He accepts the tradition of early Roman history that there must have been a union between a Roman and a Sabine

[1] Dr. Mommsen's Hist. of Rome, B. I. ch. 4.
[2] B. I. ch. 5, p. 47. Dr. M., who does not even know the number or names of the kings, yet is certain that *peperino* was not employed in building in their period!

race. The evidence is here too strong for him; but he rejects the method in which tradition tells us it was accomplished, and invents one of his own, which is not a hundredth part so probable, or rather which is utterly incredible.

"That the Ramnians," says Dr. Mommsen,[1] "were a Latin stock, cannot be doubted, for they gave their name to the new Roman commonwealth, and therefore must have substantially determined the nationality of the united community."

That in a certain sense the Ramnians were a Latin stock we will allow. That is, they were a *new* Latin stock, arising from the fusion of a tolerably recent Greek colony with the people of that part of Latium where they settled. That the Ramnians gave name to Rome we will also allow, but not in the sense that the author means. We do not believe that the words *Ramnes* and *Romani* are identical because both have an *r* and an *m*. *Ramnis* or *Ramnes* is evidently a Greek name, 'Ραμνούς, the last syllable having become Latinized, just as πούς becomes *pes*. We shall not claim for these Ramnes an origin from the Attic *demus* Rhamnus; although there is a tradition which might render such an origin not altogether improbable. Emigrants from Athens, it is said, went first to Sicyon and Thespia, whence a large portion of them afterwards proceeded to Italy, and founded on the Palatine Hill a city named *Valentia*; which name, when Evander and Æneas with many Greeks arrived at the same place, was changed into *Roma*. However absurd this story may be thought, which, by putting the Latin name first, places the cart before the horse, it nevertheless shows that, in the opinion of antiquity, its etymon was the Greek word ρώμη, and not the gentile appellative Ramnia. This account is given by Festus[2] from an author of Cumæan history; who, after the Latins, may be thought to have had the best information about Rome. Without, however, claiming an Attic origin for the Romans, it is enough that their name, before the founding of the city, was evidently Greek, derived at all events, probably like that of the Attic borough, from ῥάμνος, *brier*; a characteristic of a country which may have given

[1] Vol. I. p. 45, Engl. transl.   [2] Voc. Romam, p. 266.

name to more than one town in Greece. We agree therefore with Dr. Mommsen, that the Romans, before the foundation of their city, were called Ramnians; probably also after, by those who wished to distinguish the Romans according to their original tribes; but we cannot admit that *Romani* comes from *Ramnes*, when it is evidently the ethnic name of those who dwell in *Roma*.

We also agree that the Ramnians "substantially determined the nationality of the united community;" though, according to Dr. Mommsen's hypothesis, it is strange how he could have come to that conclusion. For he tells us in the next page—"It would appear, therefore, that at a period very remote, when the Latin and Sabellian stocks were, beyond question, far less sharply contrasted in language, manners, and customs than were the Romans and the Samnites of a later age, a Sabellian community entered into a Latin canton union; and as in the older and more credible traditions, without exception, the Tities take precedence of the Ramnians, it is probable that the intruding Tities compelled the older Ramnians to accept their *synoikismos*."

According to this account, the Tities, or Sabines, are the conquering race; for it is only those who are superior who can compel others to a *synoikismos*; as Athens did in Attica. Yet we have just been told that it was the Ramnians who determined the nationality; and the author goes on to compare this Sabine invasion with the voluntary settlement of Attus Clauzus, or Appius Claudius, with his few thousand followers, in the Roman territory many centuries afterwards, when they were received by the Romans and formed into a rural tribe; that is, he compares a people who came in sufficient numbers to be victorious, and who must have had all the power and pride of conquerors, with a small tribe forming not a twentieth part of the Roman people, who came into their territory as refugees, and were glad to be received there!

How far the Latin and Sabellian stocks differed in language and customs, "at a very remote period," we do not pretend to tell; nor do we believe that Dr. Mommsen can tell. We only see that his views are not always consistent, but vary according to the point that he wishes to prove. For, in his second chapter, in which he treats of the most ancient immigrations into Italy, and therefore, we presume, of a very remote period, he separates the Latins from all the other Italian races, which he classes under the term Umbro-Samnite, and tells us that the Latin dialect formed "a marked contrast" to the dialects of these races.[1]

It is hardly worth while to pursue in detail a theory which rests on nothing but the wildest conjectures. We shall only briefly observe that if, as Dr. Mommsen supposes, the Sabines had been the superior race in pre-Roman times—though, indeed, it is difficult to determine whether he considers them superior or inferior—no town taking its name from the Romans would have been built. Further, it is impossible to suppose that such a city should have been founded by the Latin confederacy for trading purposes; because, as we have said, the Latin League was but very loosely bound together, and would not have united for such a purpose; and because during the early days of the city we can trace no connexion between it and the Latins. Had there been this connexion, would the Latin Confederacy have suffered the Sabines to oppress the Ramnians, and, as we are told they did, force upon them their *synoikismos*? But the strongest reason against this commercial hypothesis is perhaps the fact of the total repugnance of early Roman manners and institutions to a commercial life; though in process of time, and when she had extended her empire to the mouth of the Tiber, Rome to some extent engaged in foreign commerce.

Dr. Mommsen, indeed, is of opinion that the Romans possessed from the earliest times the country on both sides of the Tiber down to the sea, as well as the port of Ostia; though we do not see what strength this adds to his commercial theory. According to him, one of the reasons for choosing

---

[1] "Innerhalb des Italischen Sprachstammes aber tritt das Lateinische wieder in einen bestimmten Gegensatz zu den umbrisch-samnitischen Dialekten."—R. I. S. 11; cf. Transl. I. p. 53. We have already seen that both Samnites and Sabines were Sabellian, and in fact almost identical.

Rome as an *entrepôt* was, that being so high up the river it was out of the way of pirates. But if Ostia was to be a landing-place—and if the assumption does not mean that, it means nothing—this advantage vanishes at once.

As a matter of fact, however, and on Dr. Mommsen's own showing, the Romans could not have originally possessed the territory down to the sea. "We have evidence," he says, "more trustworthy than that of legend, that the possessions on the right bank of the Tiber must have belonged to the original territory of Rome; for in this very quarter, at the fourth milestone on the later road to the port, lay the grove of the creative goddess (Dea Dia), the primitive chief seat of the Arval Festival, and Arval Brotherhood of Rome."[1]

Now the Ambarvalia were a festival of boundaries, and even in the time of the Empire, when Rome was mistress of the greater part of the world, they were celebrated at the *original boundaries* of the Roman State. Thus we learn from Strabo[2] that, in the time of the Emperor Tiberius, the Ambarvalia continued to be celebrated at various places on the borders of the primitive Ager Romanus, and among them at Festi, which lay on the road to Alba, about five or six miles from Rome. The grove on the right bank of the Tiber, at the fourth milestone, shows, therefore, that the primitive Roman territory did not reach a quarter of the way to the sea. And this agrees with the account of Livy,[3] who tells us that the Veientines ceded to Romulus a tract on the right bank of the Tiber; and that the whole territory down to the sea was not acquired till the time of Ancus. According to tradition, it was Romulus who founded the Arval Brotherhood, of which, indeed, he is himself said to have been a member.

On modes of thus reconstructing ancient history like that adopted by Dr. Mommsen, Sir G. Cornewall Lewis has passed a very sensible judgment, which we shall here extract. In such attempts, he observes, "We are called upon to believe that a modern historian is able to recast the traditions which were thus preserved through the dark ages of Rome, and to

[1] Engl. Trans. vol. I. p. 49. [2] Lib. v. c. 3, s. 2.
[3] Lib. I. 15, 83.

extract the truth which is imbedded in them, although in their existing form they are false. We are first to believe that a tradition was, in substance, faithfully conveyed from the eighth century before Christ to the Second Punic War, and then to believe that, although it is not literally true, it is typical of some truth which can be discerned under its covering for the first time by a writer of our own age. This doctrine of historical types is more difficult to reconcile with reason and experience than even the supposition that some authentic facts may have been preserved through a long series of years, in an unaltered state, by oral tradition. It is in fact nothing more than an ingenious and refined application of the rationalist method of interpreting the marvellous legends of mythology, so much employed by the ancient historians. It is only another form of the system of reduction, by which the god Mars in the sacred grove was converted into an armed man in disguise, who overpowered Ilia, and the wolf of Romulus was transmuted into a courtesan. One imitation may be executed by a coarse and clumsy hand; the other may be performed with all the resources and skill of modern learning; but still they are both no better than historical forgeries."[1]

Nothing can be truer than these remarks, in their general scope. We must either take the early Roman history as it stands—or nearly as it stands, rejecting only those figments which are evidently the natural product of an illiterate and superstitious age—or we must abandon it altogether, as no better than a romance from first to last. Our only hope of escape from this last alternative, lies in the circumstance that it may not rest so entirely on *oral tradition* as Sir G. C. Lewis supposes.

[1] Credibility, &c. vol. i. p. 110, sq.

SECTION III.

THE REIGN OF ROMULUS.

THE PERSONALITY OF ROMULUS.

ROMULUS, it is said, is no real person, but a fictitious eponymous hero, and this is shown by the etymology of his name. The name of Roma could not have been derived from the name of Romulus, as we are told by ancient authors, but, *vice versa*, the name of Romulus must have come from Roma. The former derivation is a grammatical impossibility; for the name of a city taken from that of Romulus would have been Romules, or Romulia, not Roma. Had tradition called Rome's founder Romanus, instead of Romulus, nobody would have doubted for an instant that it was a name derived from the city. But Romulus is just as much a derivative from it as Romanus, and has in fact the same meaning. Thus we find in the poets such expressions as "Romula tellus," "Romula hasta," "Romula gens," "Romula virtus," &c. with the same meaning as Romana. The city Roma, therefore, must have existed before the man, or reputed man, Romulus, and consequently he could not have been its founder.[1]

REMARKS.—To this we answer, that the real name of Rome's founder was not Romulus, but Romus ('Ρῶμος). He was a Greek, or at most the second in descent from a Greek, and is called Romus in most of the Greek traditions. We will here venture a suggestion, that the story of the city having been founded by twins may perhaps have had its origin in this double name of Romulus. Romus, indeed, seems to have been identical not only with Romulus, but also with Remus, which are only different forms of the same name. Thus the latter is called Romus, as we have seen above,[2] in the Latin tradition given by Dionysius of the foundation of Roma. In Greek writers the form Remus hardly ever appears; the deeds attributed

---

[1] Schwegler, 1 Abth. B. viii s. 9.   [2] Page 24.

to him are done by Romus. Cicero, in his account of the foundation of Rome,[1] makes no mention of Remus, though he is aware that Romulus had a brother of that name; and the Roman poets frequently consider Remus as identical with Romulus; as "Remi nepotes," "domus Remi," "turba Remi," "plebs Remi," &c.[2] Romulus is only a Latinized form of Romus. It was natural for the Latins to give it this form; not so much, perhaps, as Servius says, as a diminutive and by way of endearment,[3] but because such a termination was agreeable to the genius of their language, as is shown by the many words they have with such an ending. Like their descendants, the modern Italians, they loved *parole sdrucciole*—long, slippery, well vocalized words that tripped nimbly and smoothly off the tongue. Thus they changed the Greek word *circus* into *circulus*, just as they had the name of Romus. The name of Porta Romanula, instead of Romana, for the ancient gate on the Palatine, affords another striking instance. So also Tusculum, Janiculum, several rivers Albula, &c., all names belonging to early Latin times. Romulus, however, as the Latins called him, kept closer to his own Greek name of Romus when he gave it to his newly-founded city; for 'Ρῶμος, if not itself actually derived from ῥώμη, was at all events near enough to suggest it. Had his name been derived from the city by Latin inventors of a later age, he would doubtless have been called Romanus, to make him the eponymous father of the Romans, just as King Latinus was of the Latins.

We do not, therefore, see any valid etymological grounds for rejecting the almost universal testimony of antiquity, that Rome was named after its founder. We might further urge how incredible it is that the Romans, who possessed from the earliest times the art of writing, should have forgotten in the course of a century or so the name of their founder, and been obliged to invent a new one for him. Why, any of the neighbouring cities, which were in existence long before Rome, could in all probability have refreshed their memories, had it been necessary.

As Romulus is a fictitious person, so all the deeds attributed to him are mere abstractions. That the founder of Rome institutes its fundamental military and political regulations, wages the first wars

[1] De Rep. II c. 2, seq.
[2] See Catull. lvi. 5; Prop. iv. 1, 5; Juv. x. 73; Mart. x. 76, 4.
[3] "Ut pro Romo Romulus diceretur, blandimenti genere factum est, quod gaudet diminutione."—Ad Æn. L 273.

with the neighbouring cities, celebrates the first triumph, wins the first *spolia opima*,—all these, it is said, are abstractions arising from the idea of a founder of warlike Rome.[1]

From this idea, then, we learn, at all events, that the old Romans did not consider their early city to have been a commercial one.

But on what grounds are we to assume the events alluded to to have been mere abstractions? The founder of every city must, we presume, lay down some rules of civil and military conduct; it is not unlikely that he may have to contend with offended, jealous, and suspicious neighbours; it is far from improbable that Romulus may have been in general victorious, otherwise we do not see how his infant state could have maintained itself; and if he was victorious, it is not altogether incredible that he may have instituted the triumph. To assert that these acts were not real, but invented, is to beg the whole question. It is a good specimen of that magisterial *ex cathedrâ* dictation which too often characterises German critics—as if they had just come down from the skies. The only colour for it must be derived from the assumption that Romulus was a fictitious personage, whan his deeds must also be fictitious. But we have already seen that the arguments to prove him so are altogether inconclusive.

Nor do the miraculous circumstances which are said to have attended his birth and death prove him to have been an unhistorical person.

Besides abstraction, it is said, the other element that goes to make up the history of Romulus is myth—the wolf that gives suck, the Lupercal, the Ruminal fig-tree, the stepfather Faustulus, the stepmother Acca Larentia, the laceration of Romulus at the Goat-lake on the day of the Caprotine Nones. These mythological ideas are evidently taken from the worship of Faunus Luperous, who, *as we must assume*, had the cognomen of Rumus, or Ruminus. This fecundating goat-god, Ruminus-Faunus, appears in the traditional legend to have been fused into one person with Romulus, the eponymous founder of Rome.

Here it occurs to ask, if the Romans considered Romulus to be identical with Faunus, how came it that they also made him a mere name, derived from the name of the city, as we have just been told they did? The two views are utterly incompatible.

The whole induction, it will be seen, rests on two conjectures:

[1] Schwegler, B. I. S. 425.   [2] Ibid. *sq.*

first, that Faunus had the name of Rumus; second, that Rumus is, or was supposed to be, identical with Romus, or Romulus.

If we ask for the evidence for Faunus having borne the name of Rumus, or Ruminus, we are told[1] that two other German authors, Schwenck and Zinzow, had "conjectured" the same thing; and that Schwegler himself had "conjectured," a few pages before, that Rumia, or Rumina, was perhaps identical with Fauna Luperca. With such evidence are these critics contented who reject, on most occasions, the much more sensible evidence of the Roman historians!

If we inquire how Romulus is connected with *rumus*, we find, indeed, traces in the ancient authors of some such connexion, or rather confusion. Thus Festus[2] says that some derived his name from the Ficus Ruminalis; others—which is nearly the same thing—from the teat (*ruma*, or *rumis*) of the wolf by which he had been nourished. Plutarch has a notice to the same effect. Other authors reverse the derivation, as Servius,[3] who says that the Ficus Ruminalis was named after Romulus; and Livy gives a notice to the effect that the Ficus Ruminalis is a corruption of Romularia.[4] So that the theory gains nothing here; or rather, the balance of evidence is against it.

It would be mere learned trifling and battling with the wind to proceed with such an inquiry. It is, of course, necessary to Schwegler's theory to connect *ruma* with Roma. Roma, he says, has a name of the same meaning with Palatium; it is *ruma*, the "nourisher," just as the name of the Palatine is derived remotely from the shepherd-goddess Pales, whose root is *pal*, from the Sanscrit *pâ* (to nourish, feed).[5] But, viewed with regard to its meaning, Ruma, the "nourisher," is by no means so appropriate a name for a citadel as Roma (strength, a stronghold); and, viewed etymologically, it requires the *u* to be changed into *o*, while Roma requires no change at all, ῥῶμα being the old Greek form for ῥώμη. The same remark applies to Dr. Mommsen's odd derivation from *Rama*,[6] and this apparently from *ramus*; since he considers it to mean the wood, or bush-town. Surely, the Greek name, ῥώμη, adopted by Niebuhr, is a hundredfold more appropriate than these.

[1] Schwegler, B. i. S. 426; Anm. 26. [2] P. 266.
[3] Ad Æn. viii. 90; cf. Plut. Rom. 4, 6.
[4] "Ubi nunc ficus ruminalis est (Romularem vocatam ferunt)."—L 4.
[5] Schwegler, B. I. S. 420, 444; Anm. 10.
[6] R. l. c. 4.

ETYMOLOGIES OF ROMULUS AND ROMA.

Of course all or most of the circumstances connected with the birth of Romulus are fabulous; we have already admitted it. Livy had said so before us; but he does not conclude, on that account, that all the circumstances of his reign are fabulous. It is impossible to say how the legends of Romulus's birth and education may have arisen; but it is not improbable that they may have sprung from old traditions connected with the Palatine Hill. It would be just as irrational, however, to reject the historical existence of Romulus, because these traditions have been tacked to his name, as it would be to doubt the existence of Edwy and Elgiva, because the monkish legends attribute some supernatural acts to St. Dunstan. Every age treats history according to its own views and convictions. A superstitious age, or an illiterate but poetical age, will invent and believe many things which would be at once exploded in more cultivated times; but it does not follow thence that the ordinary transactions of life in those periods are also to be regarded as fabulous. Nay, we will go further, and say that these miraculous additions are a proof of good faith, and show that the tradition first arose in the times to which it relates, because it is framed in the spirit of the age. If of these early times a purely rationalistic account had been transmitted to us, such as a German professor or historian might have written in his study at Berlin or Leipsic, we should at once pronounce it to be the forgery of a later age.

ROMULEAN CONSTITUTION.

Romulus, having thus built a city on the Palatine, and named it after himself, proceeded to endow it with laws and religious ceremonies. The latter were to be performed with Alban, that is, Latin rites,—a concession, no doubt, to the usages of his Latin subjects. The only Greek rites which he retained were those in honour of Hercules; and it is difficult to perceive why he should have preserved even these, except that he was himself of Grecian descent. The worship of Hercules was kept up in after times, and especially in the neighbourhood of the Palatine; under which, in the subsequent Forum Boarium, was the Ara Maxima, besides one or two temples dedicated to that demi-god. Romulus then called his subjects together, and dictated to them certain laws.

According to this account the Roman sovereign was an absolute king, the head both of Church and State. He ruled by divine right, for the gods had given him the kingdom by augury. Livy has represented these matters correctly, but Dionysius of Halicarnassus quite erroneously,[1] when he describes Romulus as calling the people together and leaving to them the choice of a constitution. The Roman king, like those of ancient Greece, was irresponsible; his power was an ἀρχὴ ἀνυπεύθυνος,[2] which it would hardly have been had it been delegated to him by the people. And though after Romulus the kings were elected by the people and senate, yet the same, or very nearly the same, absolute power which he had enjoyed appears to have passed on to them; as may be seen, for instance, in the example of Servius Tullius, who bestows a new constitution of his own free will and absolute power.[3] In order to render his person more venerable, Romulus assumed certain badges of authority and command; as a more august dress, and especially the attendance of twelve lictors. Some have supposed that the number of these was taken from the vultures seen by Romulus; but Livy thinks it more probable that it was derived from the Etruscan practice; in which nation each of the twelve cities of the confederacy supplied a lictor. This agrees, too, with the circumstance that the *sella curulis* and *toga prætexta* were borrowed from the Etruscans.

The Romulean kingdom was theocratic; almost as much so as that of the Jews, if the comparison of the latter with a Pagan government may be admitted. Not only is the king appointed by the will of the gods, as manifested by augury, but all the institutions of the state, the senate, the centuries

---

[1] Ant. Rom. lib. ii. c. 3. See Rubino, Röm. Staatsverfassung.
[2] See Wachsmuth, Hellenische Alterthumskunde, Th. L Abth. I. S.
[3] "Nobis Romulus, ut libitum, imperitaverat; dein Numa religionibus et divino jure populum devinxit: repertaque quædam a Tullo et Anco; sed præcipuus Servius Tullius auctor legum fuit, quîs etiam reges obtemperarent."—Tac. Ann. iii. 26.

of knights, and the whole constitution, are founded on the same divine sanction.[1] Hence its conservative nature even under the popular forms of a republic. For the grand plea of the patricians against the plebeians was always their sacred character, the possession of the auspices. This conservative character is manifested by the tendency to retain, in name at least, institutions which had been virtually abolished. Thus, after the expulsion of the kings a Rex Sacrificulus was appointed for certain functions, which none, it was thought, but a royal priest could properly discharge; and long after the real power of the Comitia Curiata had vanished, they still nominally retained their original power of sanctioning and confirming.

But the chief characteristic of the early monarchy is, that the king is the general of his people, their leader in war; and that the people are but an army, whose principal duty it is to be prepared to obey the first summons to take the field. Thus, during the first interregnum, the chief fear of the senate is, "Ne civitatem sine imperio, *exercitum sine duce*, multarum circa civitatum irritatis animis, vis aliqua externa adoriretur."[2]

THE ASYLUM.

After awhile other spots beyond the city walls began to be occupied and fortified, but rather to provide for the expected increase of the citizens, than because the present limits were too small. Among the places thus occupied was the Capitoline Hill; since it was on this hill, at the spot called *Inter duos lucos*, in the depression between the two summits, that Romulus opened his Asylum. This was a place of refuge for fugitives from other communities; a contrivance not unfrequently adopted in ancient times by the founders of cities, in

---

[1] "Hunc (senatum) auspicato a parente et conditore urbis nostrae institutum ... accepimus."—Tac. Hist. L. 84. "Id (centurias equitum) quia inaugurato Romulus fecerat."—Liv. i. 36. "Omnino apud veteres, qui rerum potiebantur, iidem auguria tenebant. Ut enim sapere, sic divinare regale ducebant. Testis res nostra civitas, in qua et reges augures, et postea privati eodem sacerdotio praediti rempublicam religionum auctoritate rexerunt."—Cic. Div. i. 40.   [2] Liv. L 17.

order to augment the population. Such refugees were of course commonly of the lowest class; and hence, Livy suggests, may have arisen the fable of populations that sprung from the earth.

REMARKS.—The asylum is of course regarded by the sceptical critics as a pure invention. First, it is said, such an institution is entirely at variance with all that we know of the manners of the times. "All the peoples of antiquity lived under strong and stable regimen (in *festen Formen*); the civic communities were always organized down to the lowest classes; and the more remote the times, the more binding were these regimens, the more compact all the relations of civil life. Under these circumstances it is difficult to see how these bands of adventurers, vagabonds, and dissolute fellows could have come together, which, according to the common tradition, flocked to Rome from the neighbouring towns and tribes."[1]

This, we must confess, appears to us a new idea of these ancient times, and hardly to be realized in any, except, perhaps, the Golden Age, those Saturnia Regna which had long passed by in Italy. It assumes that there were no such persons as insolvent debtors, brigands, pirates, criminals of all sorts, runaway slaves, persons dissatisfied with the government or with their own lot, or desirous of a change merely for the sake of novelty. We certainly hear of such classes in the ancient authors, and think it not improbable that they might have been found at the time of Rome's foundation, just as they may now and probably ever will be.

That the Roman nation should have sprung, it is further said, from a band of robbers, is contradicted by the entire character of the old Roman state.[2] The original state was a family state. Such a one can be made neither by legislation nor by military

[1] Schwegler, B. I. S. 465.
[2] We do not see how this view agrees with the passage quoted from Hegel (Philosophie d. Gesch. S. 345 f.) in support of it. Hegel appears to us to accept the robber-state, and, by means of it, to account for the severity of Roman discipline. This is precisely contrary to Schwegler's view. His words are: "Dass Rom ursprünglich eine Räuberverbindung war, und sich als Räuberstaat constituirt hat, muss als wesentliche Grundlage seiner Eigenthümlichkeit angesehen werden. Dieser Ursprung des Staats führt die härteste Disciplin mit sich. Ein Staat, der auf Gewalt beruht, muss mit Gewalt zusammengehalten werden. Es ist da nicht ein sittlicher Zusammenhang, sondern ein gezwungener Zustand der Subordination."

force, still less could it be constituted out of a rabble of refugees. If it be true that the character of every state is determined by its origin, then it is certain that a community so strongly organized as the old Roman, so closed against what was external to it—as seen by the word *hostis*, which signifies both stranger and enemy—could not possibly have arisen from a mass of refugees.

On this we may remark that nobody, we suppose, would maintain that Rome *sprang* from a band of robbers. The refugees would have formed only a small portion of its citizens, especially after the Sabine union; and even of this small portion, only a few, it is to be hoped, were robbers. And if it was a family state— that is, we presume, somewhat aristocratic as times then went—so much the more need would there have been of persons to do the hard and dirty work. But the assertion that Rome was shut against strangers is founded on a total misconception of early Roman history. This question is not to be settled by the etymology of a word, but by the tale told by her annals, from which we learn that her gates were always open to strangers. Witness the Tuscan and Latin colonies which she received within her walls, the Tuscan king which she placed upon her throne. This policy was, in fact, the secret of her rapid advance.

That, in so old a matter, the name of the divinity who presided over the Asylum should be unknown, or forgotten, will hardly be regarded as a serious argument against its existence.

The last objection which Schwegler brings against the asylum is, that it is not a Roman or Italian institution, but entirely a Greek one.[1] No other example of it can be pointed to in the whole course of Roman history till we come to the Temple of Divus Julius; and Dion Cassius tells us that this was unexampled since the time of Romulus. For though the asylum of that king continued to exist after his death, yet it had been enclosed in such a manner that nobody could enter it.[2]

Dr. Ihne has adopted the same line of argument in a paper in the "Classical Museum"[3] on the Asylum of Romulus. He observes that not only are there no traces of the institution of sacred places of refuge in any Italian state, or in Rome itself, except this asylum of Romulus, but also that there is not even a word in the Latin language to designate the Greek ἄσυλον.

[1] Schwegler, R. I. S. 466. [2] Dio. Cass. xlvii. 19; cf. Tac. Ann. III. 36.
[3] Vol. III. p. 190.

On this we will observe: first, that the Romulean Asylum could not then have possibly been a fiction and invention of the Romans, for no people invent an institution as established among themselves which is entirely foreign to their habits, and for which their language has not even a name.

Secondly, it could not have been invention, because the place where it stood continued to retain its name even down to the imperial times. The long survival of such names is by no means uncommon or unparalleled. We have still in London, in the Church of St. Clement's Danes, a memorial of the Danes settled in that neighbourhood more than eight centuries ago,[1] as well as several others in London and other parts of England. This is a longer period than that between Romulus and the imperial times. And being called the "Asylum of Romulus," it was indissolubly connected with his name, and helped to hand it down to posterity, as that of the first Roman king; being in this way as good a voucher of that fact, or even a better, than any written document.

Thirdly, it is not likely to have been an invention, as it reflects no great credit upon the Roman people. A nation is not apt to invent stories that in some degree dishonour it, however prone it may be to the opposite course, and to imagine for instance, as the Romans did, a descent from Æneas.

But if an asylum existed at Rome, it could have been no other than that of Romulus, for, as Schwegler says, the whole course of Roman history knows of none other. And here we have a natural explanation of it; for Romulus, as we have seen, was to all intents and purposes a Greek; and in instituting the asylum he was only following a custom of his own country. And he gave it a name from his own language, since he could find no Latin name, just as he called his city by a Greek name.

Dr. Ihne, who of course supposes that the founder of Rome was a Latin, calls it a "preposterous supposition" to believe that Romulus had sufficient connexion with and knowledge of Greece, to adopt this foreign institution. We have endeavoured, and shall further endeavour, to show that he had such connexion. How much force there may be in Dr. Ihne's remark that " even this would prove useless, for Romulus would surely never have been able to attract many suppliants from the neighbouring states, if the asylum had been something new, which nobody knew of, and to

[1] See Worsaae's Danes and Norwegians in England, &c. p. 16, sqq.

which nobody could trust," we must leave the reader to determine. How "many" he attracted it is impossible to say, but, though the institution was a novelty, we think it would have been readily discovered, easily understood, and eagerly embraced by the class of persons for whom it was intended.

THE ROMAN SENATE.—THE CONSUALIA.

The city having been thus founded, its boundaries enlarged, and its population augmented, Romulus created a council, or senate, to guide him with their advice in the ruling of it. It consisted of a hundred members, a number probably deemed sufficient, or it may be that there were not more whose age and rank entitled them to enter it. These senators were called *Patres*, or fathers, by way of honour or affection; their families were to bear the title of *patricii*, or patricians, to distinguish them from the *plebs*, or general mass of the people. The functions of this new senate were merely to advise; they shared no portion of the royal power; their influence arose from the respect due to their judgment, which was called *auctoritas*, or authority.[1]

A city formed in the manner which we have described was necessarily ill provided with women; and, as it did not enjoy the privilege of intermarriage with the surrounding cities, although in warlike power it was quite equal to any of them, it was evident that it could last but a single generation. In order to remedy this defect, Romulus, by the advice of his senate, sent ambassadors to the surrounding peoples, to request their alliance and *connubium*, or the right of intermarriage; a process which seems somewhat to have resembled the recognition of a new state in modern times. But the application was everywhere scornfully rejected. The new city was not only despised, it was also feared, and its increasing strength

---

[1] Cicero, De Rep. ii. 8, represents Romulus as instituting the senate after the Sabine War, in conjunction with Tatius, and at the same time when he divided the people into tribes and curiæ; while Dionysius relates that both the senate and the curiæ were established before the Sabine War. The account in the text is taken from Livy; but it seems probable that the full complement of the senate was at least not completed till after the Sabine union.

was looked upon as dangerous. The refusal was frequently accompanied with insult, and the ambassadors were asked, "Why they did not open an asylum for women? In that manner they would find suitable wives."

The Roman youth could not brook this insult; it was evident that the matter must end in war and violence. Romulus was willing to encourage this temper, but at the same time determined to provide a fitting place and opportunity for its manifestation. He therefore dissembled his anger; and in the meantime busied himself in preparing some solemn games in honour of the Equestrian Neptune, which he called *Consualia*. He then directed the spectacle to be announced among the neighbouring people; and the games were prepared with all the magnificence then known, or that lay in his power, in order to give them renown, and cause them to be looked forward to with interest and curiosity.

REMARKS.—Whether the exact nature of these games has been correctly handed down to us does not seem to be a point of very vital importance as to the general credibility of the early Roman history. On such a subject tradition may naturally have varied a little; and we do not pretend that before the time of Tullus Hostilius the history rested on anything but tradition. Nevertheless, we do not think that the story is amenable to all the charges that modern critics have brought against it. First, it is objected[1] that the games of the Circus were not introduced till the time of Tarquin the Elder, and indeed could not have taken place in the reign of Romulus, when the site of the Circus was nothing but a marsh. But the two professed historians of Rome, Livy and Dionysius of Halicarnassus, say not a word about the Circus. They merely state that Romulus gave some games at Rome in honour of Neptune.[2] It is probable enough that posterity may have regarded these games as the origin of those of the Circus; and it is at all events quite certain that there could have been none earlier at Rome. It is only Cicero, amongst the classical Roman authors, who, in the slight sketch which he gives of Roman history in his *De Republica*,[3] and perhaps by a slip of the pen, says that they actually took place in

[1] Schwegler, B. I. S. 471. [2] Liv. I. 9; Dionys. II. 30.
[3] Lib. II. c. 7.

the Circus. For though they are also alluded to by Valerius
Maximus,[1] and Virgil,[2] under the name of *circenses*, those authors
say nothing about the Circus. Now Romulus must of course have
prepared some space where the chariots were *driven round*, the only
method in which they could have been conveniently viewed by the
spectators; and this place he called in his mother tongue κίρκος,
a circus, or ring. In the Latin tongue he would have said *orbis*.
Hence these were really the first Circensian games, though not
performed in the place afterwards expressly provided for them,
but, it may be, in the Campus Martius, or some other suitable spot.
It is further objected: How should the pastoral folk of the Palatine city, an inland town without navigation or commerce, have
come to celebrate a festival to Neptune, of all the gods? Where
has ever a shepherds' festival—and such originally were the Consualia—concerned Neptune? Further; an Equestrian Neptune is
found only in the Greek mythology; the Italian Neptune has no
relation at all to the taming of horses. And so in the Circus
Maximus, it was not Neptune, but Consus, that was honoured.
The interpretation of Consus as Poseidon Hippios is therefore
altogether unauthorized; a mere subtlety of later archæologists,
who knew perhaps that in Greece, and especially in Thessaly and
Bœotia, it was customary to give horse-races in honour of Neptune
as the breeder and tamer of horses; and accordingly they transferred the games and races on horseback and in chariots, exhibited by Romulus on the festival of the Consualia, to Poseidon
Hippios. But this interpretation is only a new proof how completely incapable the later Romans were of understanding their
antiquities.[3]

Now of course nobody would presume to say that an old Roman
knew so much about his language and antiquities as a modern
German, although he might have had many sources for studying them
which are now lost, and might, therefore, possibly have had some
way of connecting Consus and the Equestrian Neptune with
which we are unacquainted. We see, at all events, as much difficulty as Schwegler does in connecting horse and chariot races
with a shepherds' festival, as in connecting them with anything
in the world, and therefore with Consus, whoever he may have
been.

We might leave Dr. Mommsen and his followers in the mar-

---

[1] Lib. ii c. iv. s. 4.   [2] Æn. viii. 636.   [3] Schwegler, B. I. S. 472.

cantile theory to settle the objection about the pastoral inhabitants of the Palatine city celebrating a fête to Neptune, except for that second objection, that it was the Greek Equestrian Neptune; for the Mommsenites are all pure Latins, and know nothing about a Greek mixture in Latium. But according to our theory that Romulus was a Greek by descent, we find no difficulty whatever in this Equestrian Neptune; nay, it only adds to the probability of our view.

It is said that the *Consualia* were originally nothing but a shepherds' festival, in which they rolled or jumped upon hides. The authority for this is Varro, *De Vit. Pop. Rom.*, quoted by Nonius, voc. *Cernuus*, p. 21:—" Etiam pelles bubulas oleo perfusas percurrebant, ibique cernuabant. A quo ille versus vetus est in carminibus: Sibi pastores ludos faciunt coriis consualia." But against Varro in Nonius we may set the same Varro in his book *De Lingua Latina*, where he says:—" Consualia dicta a Conso, quod tum feriæ publicæ ei deo, et in circo ad aram ejus ab sacerdotibus ludi illi quibus virgines Sabinæ raptæ."[1] Here Varro, like all the other best Roman authorities, connects Consus with the Circus, and with the rape of the Sabines. And we will here venture a conjecture, which may reconcile Varro with himself, and which is at all events as well founded as Schwegler's, that the *Consualia* were *originally* (ursprünglich) a pastoral fête—for Varro does not bear him out in saying that such was *their origin* —namely, that the shepherds, after seeing Romulus' chariot races, made for themselves a sort of Consualia—" *sibi* ludos faciunt Consualia "—in which they ran about on oiled hides and skins, in racing fashion, as they had seen the chariots run. Such a piece of mimicry would be quite in the Italian character.

There can be no doubt that there was an Ara Consi in the Circus, for it existed there, at all events, down to the time of Tertullian. It appears to have been underground, and was kept covered and concealed, except at the festival of the Consualia, when, as we understand the words of Varro, the priests gave some games there in imitation of those which accompanied the Sabine rape.[2] From

---
[1] Lib. vi. s. 20 (ed. Müll.).
[2] So also Dionysius: τὴν δὲ τότε τῷ Ῥωμύλῳ καθιδρυθεῖσαν ἑορτὴν ἔτι καὶ εἰς ἐμὲ ἄγουσι Ῥωμαῖοι διετέλουν, Κωνσουάλια καλοῦντες, ἐν ᾗ βωμός τε ὑπόγειος ἱδρυμένος παρὰ τῷ μεγίστῳ τῶν ἱπποδρόμων, περισκαφείσης τῆς γῆς, θυσίαις τε καὶ ἀπαρχαῖς γεραίρεται, καὶ δρόμος ἵππων ζευκτῶν τε καὶ ἀζεύκτων ἐπιτελεῖται.—Lib. ii. c. 31. Dionysius, therefore, had seen them.

this underground site of the altar, Hartung,[1] and other German critics, who are followed by Schwegler, infer that it was consecrated to Consus as an infernal deity. This view is supported by adducing the circumstances that the offering at his altar was made by the Flamen Quirinalis and the Vestal Virgins; and that on the festival of the Consualia, horses and mules were released from work and decked with garlands, while mules were used in celebrating the games in the Circus Maximus. For the horse stood in near relation to the infernal world, and mules especially were acceptable to the infernal deities, on account of their unfruitfulness; for which reason it was a custom and a sacred precept not to harness mules on the occasion of the *feriæ denicales*, or solemnity for the purification of the family of a deceased person, —a parallel, it is said, which exactly suits the Consualia.[2]

How an occasion on which mules were not harnessed can be a suitable parallel to another on which they were harnessed, as they must have been to perform the games in the Circus, it is rather difficult to perceive. These were the games alluded to by Varro, in the passage before quoted, as performed by the priests in commemoration of the rape of the Sabines. Why they used mules instead of horses it is impossible to say, but the former have always been a sacerdotal kind of animal. Schwegler has expended a great deal of misplaced ingenuity in trying to prove Consus an infernal deity, when all the circumstances which he adduces may be satisfactorily explained, in conformity with the account of the Roman historians.

For, in the first place, it is the most natural thing in the world that the Romans should have placed there an altar to the god whom their traditions connected with the origin of their horse-races. It was also natural that the horses and mules should enjoy a holiday on this occasion, much as they do at the present day at Rome on the feast of St. Antony, when they are also decked with garlands and ribbons; a practice, however, which seems to us of rather too cheerful a nature for an infernal ceremony. The altar was underground and concealed, not because Consus was an infernal deity, but because it was thus typical of the secret design of Romulus in instituting the games. It was revealed only at the time when they were performed, just as the counsel of Romulus had been. This agrees with the explanation of Servius in a

[1] Religion d. Römer. B. II. S. 87.   [2] Schwegler, ib. S. 474.

passage which we look for in vain among those cited by Schwegler: "Consus autem est deus consiliorum, qui ideo templum sub tecto in Circo habet, ut ostendatur tectum debere esse consilium."[1] Nay, we learn from a passage in Tertullian, that the following inscription to the same effect, which he probably saw with his own eyes, actually stood upon the altar:—" Et nunc ara Conso illi in Circo defossa est ad primas metas sub terra cum inscriptione hujusmodi: Consus consilio, Mars duello, Lares comitio (or coillo) potentes:"[2] where we have a history in brief of the whole transaction; the design of Romulus, the war which ensued, and the subsequent reconciliation with the Sabines, and union with them in domestic life. And now we see the reason why the Flamen Quirinalis, or of Romulus deified as Mars, and the Vestal Virgins, should have offered the sacrifice; the former in reference to the war, the Vestals with reference to the union of the Sabines and Romans under the Lares of a common city.

The inscription shows what sort of idea at least the Romans themselves entertained of the god. How or at what time Consus became the eponymous deity of this festival, instead of Poseidon Hippios, it is impossible to say; but it is natural that a Grecian deity should have ultimately given place to a Latin one. When the Latin writers use the term *Consualia* in speaking of the games given by Romulus, this is a *prolepsis;* they employed the name that was most familiar to them. Whether the Romans derived the name of Consus from *consilium*, we shall not stop to inquire. If they did, perhaps the similarity of sound sufficed them; for we are constantly told that they were very bad etymologists. But though the ancient authors use the name of Consus in conjunction with *consilium*, they do not say that it was derived from it.

Schwegler having satisfied himself for such reasons as we have seen, and against the concurrent testimony of antiquity, that Consus was an infernal god, proceeds to argue that such gods were closely related to fruitfulness, though he has just before told us that mules were used in these games because their unfruitfulness was acceptable to the infernal deities! For this reason Consus was to be conciliated with games, races, and the like festivities, and for this reason also he was connected with the first Roman marriages and the rape of the Sabines! We shall not abuse our readers'

[1] Ad Æn. viii. 636.   [2] De Spect. 5.

patience by going through his arguments on this subject, which occupy two pages,[1] but will proceed with the history of Romulus.

THE RAPE OF THE SABINES, AND SABINE WAR.

The proclamation of the games naturally excited great curiosity among the surrounding peoples, who flocked to Rome with their wives and children in great multitudes, not only from the desire of beholding so novel a spectacle, but also of viewing the new city itself. The greatest number came, of course, from closely adjoining places, as the Latin cities Cænina, Crustumerium, and Antemnæ, which lay within a few miles of Rome; but there was also a vast quantity of Sabines. They were hospitably received and lodged, and were conducted round the city, when they could not help admiring its rapid increase in so short a period. When the time for the spectacle had arrived, and when the eyes and minds of the guests were completely absorbed by it, the stratagem was carried into execution. At a given signal the Roman youths rush upon them and seize the unmarried women. The greater part were carried off indiscriminately; but some of the more beautiful, who had been allotted to the principal patricians, were conveyed to their houses by plebeians, to whom that business had been intrusted. It is related that one of them, conspicuous above the rest for her form and beauty, was carried off by a band of a certain Talassius; and these men, to many inquiries for whom she was destined, in order to prevent her from being snatched from them, called out "Talassio;" whence the use of that word in nuptial ceremonies. The consternation produced by this act interrupted the games. The parents of the ravished virgins fled, filled with grief and indignation, and calling upon the god to whose solemnity they had been invited to avenge upon their perfidious hosts the violated laws of hospitality. The ravished virgins were equally desponding and indignant. But Romulus went round among them, explaining that they must attribute what had happened to the pride of their fathers in refusing their neighbours the right of intermarriage. Let them consider that by becoming

[1] S. 175 f.

the wives of Romans, they would share in all the fortunes of the city, and consequently of their children, the dearest of all ties to the human heart. He persuaded them to lay aside their anger, and to give their affections to those to whom fortune had given their persons. He represented to them that a wrong by no means barred love from following it; and that they would find their husbands all the more kind and affectionate, because every one of them would endeavour by attentions to make them forget their parents and their country. These arguments were seconded by the caresses and flatteries of the husbands, who excused their act by alleging irresistible love; an apology which to a female mind is ever the most efficacious.

By these means the women were gradually pacified; but not so their parents; who, going about in mourning attire, endeavoured by their tears and complaints to excite their respective cities to avenge their cause. And not their own cities alone. They gathered about Tatius, King of the Sabines, to whom also embassies were despatched on the subject; for Tatius was the most renowned sovereign in those parts. But he and his Sabines appearing too slow in the matter, the Cæninenses, Crustuminians, and Antemnates, who, as we have said, had also shared in the injury, made a league among themselves and prepared to go to war. But the Cæninenses found even their allies too slow; they therefore took the field on their own account, and invaded the Roman territory. But they began to devastate and pillage without order and discipline, and so became an easy prey to Romulus, who fell upon and routed them at the first onset. He then pursued their flying host, killed their king in combat, and possessed himself of his spoils; and the enemy having thus lost their leader, he took their city at the first rush. Then he marched home with his victorious army; and as he was as ostentatious of his deeds as he was great and admirable in their accomplishment, he ascended the Capitoline Hill, bearing the spoils of the slain king on a frame adapted to the purpose. Here he deposited them by an oak, regarded as sacred by the shepherds; and at the same time he marked out in his mind the limits for a temple to Jupiter, adding an appropriate name for the god.

"Jupiter Feretrius," he exclaimed, "I, the victorious King Romulus, here bear to thee these royal arms, and dedicate to thee at this spot a temple which I have determined in my mind, to be for posterity, after the example I now set, a receptacle for *spolia opima*, or those spoils which are taken from a slain king or leader of the enemy." Such is the origin of the first temple dedicated at Rome. The gods have willed that the words of its founder should not be altogether vain, when he mentioned the future dedication of such spoils, nor at the same time that the reputation of such an offering should be made too common by the number of the dedicators. Although since that time down to the establishment of the empire so many years have elapsed, so many wars have been waged, only twice have such spoils been subsequently dedicated. So rare has been the fortune of so great an honour!

Whilst the Romans were thus employed in celebrating their victory, the Antemnates seized the occasion of their borders being left defenceless to make a foray over them. But they committed the same mistake as the Cæninenses: while they were spread in disorder through the fields, Romulus suddenly attacked them with his legion, routed them on the first onset, and captured their city. Hersilia, the wife of Romulus, at the intercession of the ravished brides, besought him to pardon their fathers, and to receive them into his city; and thus, by means of coalition and concord, to strengthen and augment the state; and Romulus, though flushed with his double victory, readily acceded to the request. A most important tradition, and the secret of Rome's future greatness; for it cannot be doubted that the Romans acquired their empire as much by their policy of conciliating and amalgamating the vanquished, as by their valour in subduing them. The policy is expressed in Virgil's line—

"Parcere subjectis et debellare superbos."[1]

---

[1] Compare the speech of the Emperor Claudius to the Senate: "Quid aliud exitio Lacedæmoniis et Atheniensibus fuit, quamquam armis pollerent, nisi quod victos pro alienigenis arcebant? At conditor noster Romulus tantum sapientia valuit, ut plerosque populos eodem die hostes, dein cives habuerit."
—Tac. Ann. xi. 24.

Romulus now marched against the Crustuminians, who were preparing to attack him. His victory in this quarter was still more easy than the preceding ones, for the Crustuminians had become completely demoralized by the defeat of their allies. Romulus having thus vanquished his more immediate enemies, planted colonies at Crustumerium and Antemnæ. We may suppose that these were only a few hundred soldiers, who served to keep the conquered cities in check; whilst a considerable migration to Rome, especially of the parents and relations of the ravished brides, tended to fuse together Rome and her conquests.

The last war against the Sabines was the most formidable of all. For that people did not follow the mere blind impulse of anger and cupidity; they carefully matured their warlike preparations, and concealed their design to enter upon hostilities till they were thoroughly prepared to carry it out. Stratagem was added to counsel. Tatius bribed the daughter of Sp. Tarpeius, the commander of the Roman citadel on the Capitoline, who had proceeded beyond the fortifications to fetch water for some sacred solemnities, to admit the soldiers into the fortress. The Sabines, on being admitted, overwhelmed and killed her with their arms; either to make it appear that the citadel had been taken by force, or for the sake of example, and to show that treason can never rely upon impunity. The story is embellished by relating that Tarpeia had stipulated for the heavy golden bracelets which the Sabines commonly carried on the left arm, and their rings beautifully set with gems; when, instead of these, the Sabines heaped upon her their shields. Some say that in the agreement for what they had in their left hands, her object was to get possession of their arms; and that her fraudulent intention being perceived, she was made the martyr of it.

The Sabines, however, in whatever manner, had got possession of the citadel; nor on the following day did they come down into the level ground between the Capitoline and Palatine hills, till the Romans, incited by rage and the desire of recovering their citadel, were preparing to mount to the assault of it. The principal leaders were, on the side of the Sabines Metius Curtius, on that of the Romans Hostius Hostilius. Hostius, planting himself in the van, sustained awhile by his courage and audacity the fortunes of the Roman host, which was arrayed on very unfavourable ground; but no sooner did he fall than the Roman line was immediately broken and driven back to the ancient gate of the Palatine. Romulus himself was carried away in the crowd of fugitives; when, lifting up his hands towards heaven, he exclaimed, "O Jupiter, it was by the command of thy auguries that I laid here on the Palatine the first foundations of the city. Already, through fraud and corruption, the Sabines are in possession of the citadel; and now they have crossed the valley, and are hastening to attack the Palatine. Drive them at least hence, O father of gods and men; arrest this panic of the Romans and stop their foul flight. I here vow to thee, as Jupiter Stator, a temple, which shall be a monument to posterity that the city was preserved by thy present aid." So saying, as if perceiving that his prayer had been heard, he exclaimed, "From this spot, Romans, Jupiter Optimus Maximus commands you to stand and renew the fight!" By these words was the flight of the Romans arrested, as if they had heard a voice from heaven; and Romulus flies to their head. Metius Curtius was leading the Sabines. Charging down from the citadel, he had driven the Romans from him the whole length of the Forum; and he was now not far from the Palatine gate, exclaiming: "We have conquered our perfidious hosts and cowardly enemies! They have learnt that it is one thing to ravish virgins, another to fight with men." While he was thus boasting, Romulus set upon him with a band of his boldest youth; and as Metius happened to be on horseback he was the more easily driven back. The Romans pursued him as he fled; whilst another Roman band, inflamed by the king's courage, breaks the Sabines. Metius, whose horse was frightened by the cries of the pursuers, threw himself into the marsh; but animated by the shouts and gestures of the Sabines, he managed to get through. The Romans and Sabines renew the fight in the valley between the hills; but the Romans were now evidently superior.

At this juncture the Sabine women, by the injury inflicted upon whom the war had arisen, throwing aside womanly fear at this terrible sight, ventured, through the thick of the flying missiles, to throw themselves between the combatants and to pacify their rage, appealing on one side to their fathers, on the other to their husbands, imploring them, as the case might be, not to stain themselves with the blood of a father or a son-in-law and contract the stain of parricide. "If you regret this relationship, this marriage, turn your anger against us; for we are the cause of this war, and of the mutual wounds and slaughter of husbands and parents. It will be better for us to perish than, either as orphans or as widows, to live deprived of you."

The sight of the women, their pathetic entreaties, touched both the common soldiers and their leaders. The fray ceased all at once, and the tumult of strife was succeeded by a profound silence; amidst which the leaders on both sides stepped forth for the purpose of making a treaty. In this was included not only a peace, but the converting of the two cities into a common one. The two kings agreed to share the royal power; but the entire government was assigned to Rome. The city being thus doubled, in order that the Sabines might not seem to be neglected, they were called Quirites, from the town of Cures. A monument of that battle is the lake called Curtian, so named from the spot where the horse of Curtius, having at length emerged from the deep bog, bore him safely to the margin.

REMARKS.—The rape of the Sabines, and the war which ensued, terminated by a peace which fused the two peoples together, form one of the most important traditions of early Roman history. It involves the questions whether the Romans were a pure or a mixed race; and if the latter, whether the mixture was effected by treaty and agreement, or, as some have supposed, by the actual subjugation of the Romans. That the tradition is accompanied with some fabulous circumstances must be at once admitted; but it would be unreasonable to reject it on this account, if the principal fact rests on evidence that must be considered as almost irrefragable. It would be preposterous to expect that early history should be handed down in all that connexion of events, and with all that array of evidence, which characterise modern historical compositions. The work of Herodotus, for instance, contains no doubt a vast substratum of truth, though mixed up occasionally with what appear to us to be the most ridiculous and childish fables. This characteristic arises not unfrequently from the simplicity of ancient manners. The ancients were the children of the world; they often regarded things in a simple and credulous manner; and they are not, therefore, to be regarded as wilfully palming untruths upon us, but rather as transmitting to us truths accompanied with extraordinary and fabulous circumstances, such as they themselves, or the great majority of them, believed. That such fables should particularly attach themselves to the more striking and important events of early history is natural enough. It was these that made the deepest impression upon the popular mind; that were the constant topics of conversation; that were the subjects of such songs and poetry as might then have existed; and were hence accompanied with exaggerated details, and embellished with pleasing fictions, which have not only depreciated, but actually destroyed, their historical value in the eyes of modern critics. The Sabine War was pre-eminently an event of the kind just alluded to, and a natural subject for embellishment and fiction. We will endeavour to eliminate what traits of this sort, or what other incongruities, may have attached themselves to it, and will then proceed to examine the main subject of the tradition.

Among the objections to the story of the rape of the Sabines are the dates at which the event is placed, and the varying numbers of the ravished virgins.[1] According to Fabius Pictor,[2] the rape took place in the fourth month after the building of the city. Nothing, it is said, can be more simple than the way in which this calculation was made. The *Consualia* fall on the 18th of August, and consequently in the fourth month after the *Palilia*, or festival of the foundation of the city. Other writers, to whom this period seemed too short, as Cn. Gellius, quoted by Dionysius,[3] arbitrarily converted it into four years. These variations compel us to conclude that the date of the event was unknown; but it does not necessarily follow that it did not take place.

The original tradition gave the number of the ravished Sabines

[1] Schwegler, Buch ix. S. 7.   [2] Ap. Plut. Rom. 14.
[3] Lib. II. c. 31.

at thirty; which number was evidently taken from the thirty curiæ, to which the names of Sabine women are said to have been given. But as this seemed too small, another tradition assigned it only to the women who had sued for the peace;[1] which is evidently only a rationalistic version of the original account. When other traditions make the number of the women 527, or 683, or 800,[2] these are the purest and most arbitrary inventions, and only serve to show with what levity the most positive data were invented by the later annalists.

It may be that the number thirty was taken from the number of the curiæ; but it is quite evident that this could not have been the whole number of the ravished women. For those who gave names to the curiæ were all Sabines, besides whom, women from the three Latin towns also fell into the hands of the Romans: though from the intimate connexion which subsequently ensued between the Romans and Sabines, it was natural that the Sabine women should have almost engrossed the tradition. The whole thirty curiæ, however, were not named after the Sabine women. Ten of them must have existed before the Sabine union; and that this was so, appears from the circumstance that, among the few names of these curiæ that have been preserved, two or three are evidently Romulean. These names are Forienais, Rapta, Veliensis, Velitia, in Festus;[3] Titia, in Paulus Diaconus, as among the new curiæ;[4] Faucia in Livy;[5] and Acculeia in Varro.[6] Of these the Curia Veliensis is evidently named from the Velian Hill, and was therefore Romulean; while the Titia is as evidently Sabine. The Acculeia was also probably Romulean; as a sacrifice was offered in it to Angerona, the Goddess of Silence, particularly as regarded the forbidden utterance of the secret name of Rome. Macrobius[7] indeed makes the sacrifice performed in the chapel of Volupia, which stood near the Porta Romanula; but the curia and sacellum very probably adjoined each other. The Roman and Sabine names lend some confirmation to the old tradition.

It seems probable that even the Sabine women must have been

[1] Cic. De Rep. II. 8; Dionys. II. 47.
[2] Dionys. ii. 30, 47; Plut. Rom. 14; comp. Thes. et Rom. 6. But the number, "nearly 800," appears to be a slip of memory on the part of Plutarch for "nearly 700;" alluding to the number 683.—See Lewis, vol. II. p. 421, note 61.
[3] Page 174. [4] Page 366. [5] Lib. ix. c. 88.
[6] Ling. Lat. vi. 23 (ed. Müll.). [7] Sat. I. 10.

considerably more than thirty in number; and it is not unlikely that, with those of the Latin cities, the whole number may have reached 500 or 600. There is nothing in which oral tradition is more subject to err than numbers; but this affords no valid ground for disputing the fundamental truth of the tradition. Nay, on such grounds we might dispute the truth of many well-known facts which have occurred in the memory of some of the present generation; and from the mendacious bulletins of the first Buonaparte—which are *written*, not *oral*, testimony—we might conclude that some of his most famous battles had never been fought.

The whole story of the rape of the Sabines is, it is said, an ætiological myth,[1] invented to explain certain Roman marriage customs. With most of the peoples of antiquity, marriage was originally a robbery, or rape, and many reminiscences of this custom survived after the custom itself had become obsolete. Thus, in Roman nuptials, the bride was torn from the arms of her mother; she was lifted over the threshold by those who came to take her; the spear, also, with which the bride's hair was parted, indicated that marriage was a work of arms and force; while the custom of not celebrating marriages on a festival, or holiday (*die feriato*), points the same way, since to commit violence on such days was an act requiring expiation.[2] All these traits were referred by the Romans themselves to the rape of the Sabines, and especially the cry of "Talassio," uttered by the party who escorted the bride from the house of her parents to that of her husband. But concerning this Talassius there was a great difference of opinion. Some thought that he was a distinguished youth, whose people carried off for him the most beautiful of the maidens; others that he was a man who had been so peculiarly fortunate in his marriage that his name was called out by way of good omen; whilst some, again, were of opinion that it was the word agreed upon by Romulus as the signal for the attack. It is clear, therefore, that there was no real tradition about it, and that those fables have only been invented in order to explain the customary but enigmatical cry of "Talassio." Like the other wedding customs, it was not derived from the pretended fact of the rape of the Sabines, but, *vice versâ*, the fact was deduced from the customs. While among the Romans marriage passed for a robbery, so it was concluded that the first marriages at Rome were effected in that manner.

[1] Schwegler, Buch ix. 8. 6.   [2] See Macrob. Sat. L 15.

Before we address ourselves to these objections, let us remark that the name Talassius is evidently a Greek one,—θαλάσσιος, "pertaining to the sea." How the Latins should have adopted a Greek word in their marriage customs it is not very easy to say, unless it came down to them from the time of Romulus, who, as we have seen, was a Greek; a word, moreover, appropriate to a festival of the Equestrian Neptune. The Ramnes had evidently not yet forgotten their long wanderings over the sea.

That there was a difference of opinion about the origin of the cry Talassius is nothing to the point. There is a difference of opinion about the manner in which the Order of the Garter was instituted, and whether the story about the Countess of Salisbury be true; but nobody doubts on that account that the Order was instituted by Edward III.

It is allowed that the Roman wedding customs were not mere arbitrary inventions, but were really derived from some ancient practice; and, indeed, it is contrary to all experience of human nature to suppose that such observances as these, which have penetrated deeply into the habits of a people, could have originated from a mere idle story. But if this be so, we think it speaks very much in favour of the old tradition, and the unanimous opinion of the Romans themselves concerning it. If it be admitted that the Romans at one time stole their wives, we see no more convenient epoch to which to refer the practice than where tradition places it, at the commencement of their history. That the practice obtained among "most of the people of antiquity," is an exceedingly round assertion. The Spartans only seem to have retained in their marriage ceremonies some traces of such a practice;[1] and, as Dionysius makes Romulus excuse his act by alleging that it was an ancient Greek custom,[2] we may conclude that he considered it as unknown in Italy. The same passage tends to confirm our theory of the Greek origin of Romulus.

But we have shown that the festival of the Consualia was also connected with the tradition of the rape of the Sabines. Thus we have two very prominent usages, one in the public life, the other in the domestic and daily customs of the Romans, both referring to a tradition which, according to the "ætiological" school of critics, was nothing but pure invention. That there should have been two customs of so different a nature, yet at the

[1] Plut. Lyc. 15; cf. Herod. vi. 65.   [2] ii. 13.

same time capable of being joined together as cause and effect, is most extraordinary, and we should say unexampled. And further, that they could have both been connected with the rape of the Sabines, unless there had previously existed a deeply-rooted tradition of that event among the Roman people, we confess ourselves unable to understand. To suppose that a story invented from these two customs at a comparatively late period should have met with the universal acceptance which that of the rape of the Sabines appears to have done, seems to us utterly incredible.

If the rape of the Sabines is mythical, continues Schwegler,[1] it could not have been the occasion of the wars which Romulus is said to have waged with some neighbouring cities, and afterwards with the Sabines. There is no historical ground for the wars with Cænina, Crustumerium, and Antemnæ; they are invented for the purpose of displaying Romulus as a victorious warrior, as celebrating the first triumph, and winning the first *spolia opima*; attributes which, on account of their ominous character, it was necessary to assign to a founder of Rome. But the Sabine war has a sure historical ground.

We have assigned some reasons for thinking that the Sabine rape may not be altogether mythical. The details of the wars which ensued may perhaps be exaggerated or misrepresented; but to say that they are altogether invented is a mere conjecture and gratuitous assertion, made for the purpose of supporting a preconceived theory. The Sabine war and its issue, as described by Livy, are probably made much too favourable to the Romans. In order to extenuate their defeat, the most is made of the careful and secret preparations of the Sabines. The pretty story of Tarpeia, which Livy himself calls a fable, and of which there were several different versions, is an evident invention to salve the wounds of national self-love. That the Sabines should have marched without let or hindrance to the foot of the Capitoline and have taken it on the first assault betrays their superiority, and suggests the idea that the Romans had previously met with some defeats which their vanity has concealed. The war, however, was much longer than it appears to have been in the narrative of Livy, where we have only the decisive results; a circumstance characteristic of tradition, and especially of a tradition derogatory to the national reputation. But it seems probable, from the consequences, either that the last battle

[1] Buch ix. S. 8.

was a drawn one, or that peace and union were effected between the two nations, by the intervention of the women, or in some other manner.

Before examining these consequences, we will advert for a moment to the wars, and one or two of their incidents. That Rome, soon after its foundation, should have had to contend with some of the surrounding cities, seems sufficiently natural, and that in these struggles it should in general have proved victorious is shown by the fact of its existence. We think that the Temple of Jupiter Feretrius, which continued to exist to a late period, undoubtedly belonged to the very early times of Rome. This is shown by its small and insignificant dimensions, as well as by its Greek name, derived from φέρετρον, which carries it up to Romulus. There is no Latin word from which Feretrius can be derived, the term for φέρετρον in that tongue being *ferculum*. The Temple of Jupiter Stator may be a more doubtful matter. The Consul Atilius in the Samnite war, A.U.C. 458, is also said to have vowed a temple to that deity.[1]

Almost every writer on Roman history admits a Sabine war and union. Even Mommsen allows such a union, though before the foundation of Rome; and, as he describes it as a *forced* union, we may suppose that it was preceded by a war. But his account of the matter, besides being unsupported by a single scrap of evidence or tradition, is in the highest degree improbable. Sir G. Cornewall Lewis is, so far as we know, the only writer who, consistently with his principle of regarding the entire early history of Rome to be without foundation, withholds his assent to the Sabine war, and consequent union.[2]

The amalgamation of two races into one nation is an historical event so striking and important, that, among a people who were not absolutely barbarians, the memory of it, even if they possessed not, as the Romans did, the art of writing, may be supposed capable of surviving several centuries, merely by oral tradition. And the value of the tradition is greatly enhanced when we find it preserved, if not exactly by the conquered nation, at all events by that on which the union had been forced. The national vanity of the Romans would doubtless have willingly ignored the event, had not the memorials of it been too numerous and too strong to be set aside.

[1] Liv. x. 36, 37.   [2] See Credibility, &c. vol. I. p. 438.

We will here enumerate some of the *material* evidences of the union, without going into those which must have manifested themselves to every Roman in their language, customs, laws, religious observances, in the name Quirites coupled with and equivalent to that of Romani, &c. On the Quirinal Hill, which had changed its ancient name of Mons Agonus to the Sabine one of Collis Quirinalis,[1] were—besides the Capitolium Vetus and its temple to Jupiter, Juno, and Minerva, showing the city on the Quirinal to be a substantive city, distinct from Rome—the following temples or fanes, sacred to Sabine deities: that of Quirinus, or the Sabine Mars, from which the hill derived its name; that of Semo Sancus, the Latin Dius Fidius, and those of Flora, Salus, and Sol.

This Sabine city on the Quirinal could not have existed, as Niebuhr supposes, before the foundation of Rome. It is the height of improbability, that Romulus on the one hand should have attempted to found a city in such near proximity to a foreign one, or, on the other, that Tatius and the Sabines should have permitted him to do so. There is no probable way of accounting for two distinct cities being found so close together but that handed down by tradition; namely, that the Sabine city arose after the two peoples had been united by agreement and compact.

The Sabines continued to retain possession of the Capitoline, which they had conquered, and, indeed, it was then united to the Quirinal by a tongue of land, subsequently removed in order to make way for Trajan's Forum. Hence the Janus Geminus at the north-eastern foot of the Capitol, afterwards converted by Numa into a temple, the famous index of peace and war, must, from its situation, have originally formed an entrance to the Sabine city, and this is certified by the additional name of Janus Quirinus, which we frequently find attached to it.[2] For Quirinus was the peculiar deity of the Quirinal Hill; and therefore his name would hardly have been given to the gate had it been a gate of Rome, as Schwegler supposes.[3]

The same author admits the storming and taking of the Capitoline by the Sabines.[4] But if the Sabines were settled on the

---

[1] Festus, p. 254.
[2] Suet. Oct. 22; Hor. Car. iv. 15, 9; Macrob. Sat. i. 19. The view in the text does not run counter to Macrobius's explanation that Janus was called Quirinus, "quasi bellorum potens, ab hasta quam Sabini *curim* vocant."
[3] Buch. L. 8. 481. [4] Ibid. S. 484.

Quirinal previously to that event, as he and Niebuhr assume, it is still more improbable that they should have allowed the Romans to settle on the Capitoline than on the Palatine. For, as we have seen, the Capitoline and the Quirinal were then virtually one hill. The old tradition that the settlement on the Quirinal was made *after* the war is the only probable one.

We will now continue the history after the amalgamation of the two peoples, down to the death of Tatius.

THE SABINE UNION AND CONSTITUTION.

The joyful peace so suddenly effected by the Sabine women after so terrible a war rendered them still dearer to their husbands and parents, and above all to Romulus himself, on which account he affixed their names to the thirty curiæ into which he divided the people. The number of the women was undoubtedly larger than this; but it has not been handed down to us how the thirty were selected, whether according to age, or the position and dignity of their husbands, or simply by lot. At the same time were enrolled three centuries of knights, called Ramnenses, Titienses, and Luceres. The Ramnenses were named after Romulus; the Titienses after Titus Tatius, the Sabine king. The cause and origin of the name Luceres is doubtful.

So far Livy. Cicero further says that Romulus also divided the people into three tribes, named after himself, Tatius, and Lucumo, who was an ally of Romulus, and fell in the Sabine war.[1] And as Livy himself afterwards mentions the existence of these three tribes,[2] we may suppose that he knew that they were instituted at this time; and, indeed, there is no other period to which we can conveniently assign their institution. The names of them appear to have been rather loosely used. The members of that named after Romulus were sometimes called Ramnes, sometimes Ramnenses. The former name appears in the passage just quoted from Livy, and both in the

[1] De Rep. ii. 8.
[2] "Ut tres antiquae tribus, Ramnes, Titienses, Luceres, suum quaeque augurem habrent."—Lib. x. c. 6.

subjoined passage of Varro.[1] Those named after Titus Tatius we find called Tatienses, Titienses, and Tities. The first two of these names occur in the passages already quoted. The name of Tities is found in Varro, in the passage cited below.[1] Of the Luceres we will speak in the Remarks.

After the amalgamation of the two peoples, the reign of the two kings was not only common but concordant. After a few years had elapsed, some relations of King Tatius struck the ambassadors of the Laurentines; and when these demanded the redress due to them by the law of nations, Tatius was deterred from affording it by the entreaties of his relatives and the love which he bore towards them. But by this conduct he only brought down upon his own head the punishment due to them: for, having gone to a solemn sacrifice at Lavinium, he was set upon and killed. Romulus is said to have borne this matter with more equanimity than became him; either because he thought that Tatius had been not unjustly killed, or because a partition of the supreme power can never be trusted.

REMARKS.—Schwegler observes,[2] that the tradition makes the union very speedily completed, and that, according to all inner probability, it must have taken a much longer time to effect it. He does not, however, bring forward this as an objection to the fundamental truth of the story, which, on the contrary, he accepts. We are of opinion that objections like this sometimes arise from want of considering the simplicity of early ancient life as compared with our own, and the small numbers which are dealt with. It is possible, however, that the time may have been longer, and that tradition has given us only the results.

The same author thinks that the relation of the two united

---

[1] "Ager Romanus primum divisus in parteis tris, a quo TRIBUS appellata Tatiensium, Ramnium, Lucerum, nominatæ, ut ait Ennius, Tatienses a Tatio, Ramnenses a Romulo, Luceres, ut Junius, a Lucumone."—Ling. Lat. v. § 55 (ed. Mull).

[2] "Tribuni militum, quod terni tribus tribubus Ramnium, Lucerum, Titium olim ad exercitum mittebantur."—ibid. § 81; cf. § 91. Though some MSS. have an a here—taclum, taeclum, tatium. From this passage we may infer that the institution of the tribes was for military purposes.

[3] Buch ix. S. 11.

peoples was at first only federative and isopolitical; they did not form a single state in common, but a confederacy. This is apparent from the fact that each state retains its own king. Moreover, a credible, or at all events a sensibly devised, tradition tells us that the two kings did not immediately consult together about their common affairs, but that each of them had his own senate of one hundred men, with whom he first took counsel apart; and it was after this that they met together for the purpose of coming to resolutions in common. If this is well founded—and internal probability speaks in its favour—then the later constitution, which recognises only one king, one senate, and one assembly of the people, was a work of gradual assimilation, and must have been produced by a series of mediations. It must have taken much longer time to accomplish the religious union of the two peoples. It may have been centuries before all differences on this subject were reconciled, and the Roman sacra completely fused with the Sabine.

On this we may remark that there are no traces of a double kingdom, except for the short period of the life of Tatius. It can hardly be imagined that if the double kingdom had lasted a considerable time, tradition should have preserved no memory of it. After the death of Tatius we hear only of single kings, alternately Sabine and Roman; but this alternation of the two races shows that there could have been no motive for concealing a joint reign, had there really been one. It is impossible to draw any conclusion from the symbolical empty throne, with sceptre and crown, which, according to a tradition preserved by Servius,[1] Romulus placed next his own. Servius himself assigns the empty throne to Remus; Schwegler,[2] after Niebuhr, considers that it represented the dormant right of one of the two peoples. But even if this view be the true one, it admits that there was actually only one king of both Romans and Sabines. The "sensibly devised" tradition—it is astonishing how readily the sceptical critics adopt such traditions when favourable to their own views—of each king having held his own separate senate, rests only on the authority of Plutarch, and his follower Zonaras,[3] and is totally incompatible with the other accounts of this period, such as the institution of the curiæ, &c. How long it may have taken to effect the complete religious union of the two peoples it is impossible to say; but, with the easy-going

[1] Ad .En. i. 2 ; vi. 780. [2] S. 488; Anm. 3.
[3] Plut. Rom. 20; Zonar. vii. 4.

faith of paganism, the participation of such sacra as were necessary to equal political rights, was probably immediate. Cicero, at least, who must have been a better judge of such a subject than a modern writer, finds no difficulty in this way.[1]

In their relation also as towns, Schwegler proceeds to observe, the original separation only gradually ceased: Rome and the Quiritian settlement may have existed for a long while side by side as separate towns. Niebuhr has given several examples of towns so separated by walls: as the Phœnician Tripolis of the Sidonians, Tyrians, and Aradians; in the Middle Ages the old and new towns of Dantzic; and the three independent towns of Königsberg, &c.[2] Dionysius tells us,[3] that after the union the swampy valley between the Capitoline and Palatine was filled up with earth and converted into a market-place; which may be true, but we must not think of a Forum in the proper sense of the term. We must also suppose that, after the complete union of the two towns, a new Pomœrium was drawn, and a new mundus laid; but it may be questioned whether the Temple of Vesta was first placed outside of Roma Quadrata after this enlargement. Tradition also refers the Sacra Via to the union of the two races; but it does not appear that this explanation is well founded.

We may ask whether the relations of the two peoples were, from the commencement of their union, on a footing of political equality?[4] Tradition assumes that they were; and it is, at all events, an incontestable fact that the Ramnes and Tities were subsequently on such a footing. This appears from the double kingdom, from the alternation of Roman and Sabine kings which followed it, and from the equal representation of both races in the Senate, the equestrian order, and the priesthood. The Luceres, on the other hand, appear to have been an inferior race.

It is another question whether this equality was not the fruit of a long struggle. And it cannot be denied that there are many traces of the Romans having been originally subordinate to the Sabines. In favour of this view there is, first, the general proba-

[1] "Quo fœdere et Sabinos in civitatem ascivit, sacris communicatis."—De Rep. ii. 7.
[2] Niebuhr, Röm. Gesch. B. i. S. 305 f.
[3] Lib. ii. c. 50.
[4] The assertion of Servius (ad Æn. viii. 709) that the Sabines had all the rights of Roman citizenship, except the suffragium for the creation of magistrates, seems undeserving of attention.

bility that the little town upon the Palatine would, in the long run, have been as little able to resist the victorious advance of the Sabines as the other towns of the valley of the Tiber and the Anio. This idea seems even to have occurred to some of the ancient writers; and thus, for instance, Velleius Paterculus[1] thinks, that to have averted such a catastrophe, Romulus must have been aided by the legions of his grandfather, Numitor. Niebuhr is of opinion that Rome must have been subject to the Sabines.[2] The same state of things is apparent through the veil which the common tradition endeavours to throw over these events: the Sabines have seized the citadel, and Rome stands on the brink of destruction. It is probably from the memory of this subjection that Tatius appears to have been hateful to the Romans; Ennius[3] calls him "tyrant;" and, from his refusal to punish a breach of international law, he is slain at Lavinium, the city of the Lares and Penates of Latium. It has also been observed by Huschke, and others, that when all the three tribes are mentioned together, the most knowing archaeologists, as a rule, place the Tities first: an order of precedence which does not seem to be altogether accidental, as the Luceres, for instance, are as regularly put last.[4] A still more decisive proof of the subjection of the Romans at first would be the collective name of Quirites, if it could be shown that this name originally belonged only to the Sabines of the Quirinal; for otherwise the conqueror always imposes his name on the conquered. Lastly, the name of Quirinus, given to the deified Romulus, is a significant indication of the original precedence of the Sabine race.

Schwegler is also of opinion, with Niebuhr, that the tradition of the rape of the Sabines shows a time when the city on the Palatine did not enjoy the right of *connubium* with the city on the Quirinal, and therefore must have been inferior to it; till at length subjected Rome extorted the right,—that is, political equality,—by arms.

But, however this may be, it is significant, and doubtless not without a deep historical ground, that the Roman tradition always takes its stand on the Palatine city, and not on that of the Sabine conquerors. We must conclude from this that the Palatine Rome was at least the stem and stock on which the rest was grafted.

[1] Lib. I. 8, 5.
[2] Röm. Gesch. I. 305; cf. Ihne, Forschungen, S. 33.   [3] Ann. l. 151.
[4] The remark, however, does not hold good universally, as Schwegler himself mentions in his note, and as we have already seen from the quotation from Varro, L. L. § 81, where the Tities are put last. Above, p. 87, note 2.

With a good deal of these remarks of Schwegler's we entirely concur. We think that Livy's assertion, that the whole government was assigned to Rome, is the reverse of the truth; and that the Romans, though not actually conquered, were placed, during the reign of Tatius at least, and perhaps for a considerable period afterwards, in a subordinate position.[1] To the reasons adduced by Schwegler for this view, the following may, we think, be added.

The tradition that makes the Sabine women rush in between the combatants was probably adopted by Livy for two reasons: first, it is picturesque, and secondly, it obviates the embarrassing question, Why, if the Romans were thus driving the Sabines before them, did they stop short in their victorious career, and not complete their success by regaining possession of the Capitoline? There is another tradition adopted by Cicero, that after a battle of varying success and undecided result, thirty of the Sabine women were despatched, with the consent of the Roman Senate, to beg a peace from their countrymen.[2] This seems more accordant with the state of things which we find afterwards. Thus, when the people are distributed into Curiæ, these are designated not by Roman but by Sabine names, showing the predominance of the latter race. In like manner Tatius dedicates in *all* the curiæ a table, or altar, to Juno Quiritia, or Curis, which tables, Dionysius tells us, were extant in his time.[3] Again, all the transactions during the joint reign of Romulus and Tatius are conducted by the latter monarch, and Romulus retreats quite into the background. Thus it is Tatius who receives the Laurentine ambassadors; it is to Tatius, and not Romulus, to whom the Laurentines apply to redress the insult which their ambassadors had received; and it is Tatius also who proceeds to the solemn sacrifice at Lavinium, though that was a town peculiarly Latin, if not Roman. Dionysius, indeed, tells of a joint expedition by Romulus and Tatius against the Alban town of Cameria,[4] which they subdued and converted into a Roman

---

[1] How much more the later Romans prided themselves on their Ramnensian origin, than on their other progenitors, appears from the speech of Canuleius: "Hoc si polluit nobilitatem istam vestram, quam plerique oriundi *ex Albanis et Sabinis*, non *genere nec sanguine*, sed per co-optationem in Patres habetis," &c.—Liv. iv. 4.

[2] "Matronis ipsis, quæ raptæ erant, orantibus," De Rep. ii. 7; and, "ex Sabinis virgines raptæ—oratrices pacis et fœderis," ib. c. 8; cf. Dionys. ii. 45.

[3] Lib. ii. c. 50. [4] Loc. cit.

colony, transferring 4,000 of the inhabitants to Rome. But we read of this event in no other author, and Dionysius is little to be trusted except when he speaks of things that came under his own knowledge and observation. His evidence on this occasion is particularly suspicious, as we find him afterwards mentioning Cameria as reduced by Tarquin, and again by the Consul Verginius.[1] Besides, a joint military expedition of this kind proves nothing as to the relative superiority or inferiority of the two kings in the internal government of Rome.

For these reasons, as well as for some of those stated by Schwegler, we are inclined to think that Romulus was quite subordinate during the lifetime of Tatius. But we cannot go so far as Ihne, Ampère,[2] and other writers, who are of opinion that Rome was absolutely conquered. Had that been the case its name would have ceased to exist, and instead of a history from the Roman point of view, we should have had one from the Sabine point of view. The resumption of the sole power by Romulus, after the death of Tatius, and the recurrence after Numa of a Roman king, show that the Roman power and influence, though for a time inferior, had not been annihilated.

We may here remark, that originally the curiæ were evidently a Romulean institution; however, after the Sabine union, they may have been altered and adapted to the new circumstances, and their number increased. The early Roman constitution was little more than a division of the people for military purposes. In fact, the Romulean population were to all intents and purposes an army, of which Romulus was the supreme and irresponsible commander. The term *populus* itself seems to have originally signified the army. It was the fighting men alone who at first enjoyed any civil rights at Rome, in the same manner as the ancient Germans; among whom it was only the warriors who administrated the affairs of State.[3] In process of time, these rights were gradually extended to citizens who did not belong to the army, and hence the original military signification of *populus* became ultimately quite obsolete, and denoted the Roman people instead of the Roman army. Its ancient signification, however, was still retained in some cognate words, as *populare*, to lay waste; *populatio*, a laying waste or plundering, &c.

---

[1] Lib. iii. 51, v. 40, 49. [2] L'Hist. Rom. à Rome, t. I. p. 112, sq.
[3] "Nihil enim neque publicæ neque privatæ rei nisi armati agunt."—Tac. Germ. 13.

Before the Sabine union, the army of Romulus consisted probably of only about 1,000 men, distributed into ten curiæ, each containing 100 men under a *curio*, or captain; and this company again divided into tens under a *decurio*. Hence the name of *miles* for a soldier— one of the thousand. When we consider that this was not a standing army, but composed of men engaged in agricultural and pastoral pursuits, such an arrangement appears an excellent one both for summoning an army quickly to the field, and for keeping it well in hand when on service: but for civil purposes it would have been totally useless and inexplicable.

The word *curio* evidently comes from the Greek κύριος, a lord or master, thus showing the institution to be Romulean. Each curia formed a sort of clan, under the *curio* as its head. It had common *sacra*, and hence the *curio* was also its priest. The head-quarters or places of assembly for these clans were also called curiæ. Thus we find on the Palatine hill the Curiæ Veteres; the position of which shows that they were Romulean, while the epithet *veteres* proves that they were antecedent to the curiæ erected after the Sabine union. The men who formed the ranks were called *clientes*, from the Greek κλύω, to *hear*, which is synonymous with *obey*. Another proof of the Greek origin of the institution.

We must not, however, confound the *populus*, or primitive Roman army, with the *exercitus* of later times. It rather resembled a feudal militia. All were bound to do military service, when required, under their lord; but in peaceable times they cultivated their fields. Hence they also became involved in civil affairs, by the expenses and risks of agriculture, losses, disputes, lawsuits, &c. To help them in these conjunctures with advice and money, they had recourse to the head of their *gens*, or clan, whom they regarded as a sort of father, and called *patronus*. These last relations between patron and client continued to subsist to a late period, long after the primitive relation of captain and common soldier had become obsolete and forgotten.

There can be no doubt, as we shall show further on, that the clients gave their votes in the Comitia Curiata, or assemblies of the curiæ. But the clients were certainly not patricians, and consequently, in opposition to the dictum of Niebuhr, the term *populus* must always have included some plebeians. That the clients, although they voted in the curiæ, were plebeian, appears from a passage in Cicero, where he tells us that Romulus distributed the *plebs* into *clientelæ* of the leading men, or patricians.[1] The clients, however, could not have constituted the whole of the *plebs*. There must have been other plebeians of a lower grade, who did not belong to the army, or *populus*, and who had not the franchise.

The division of the people into curiæ was an arbitrary political regulation; the division of them into three tribes was dictated by the nature of the population. This may be the reason why Livy did not think it necessary to mention the formation of these tribes.[2] There is no difficulty about the Ramnes and Tities; the former being the original Greek stock of Romulus, the latter the Sabines of Titus Tatius. But of what the Luceres were composed, and what was the origin of their name, have been matters of dispute. Livy confesses his ignorance on the subject.[3] Many writers derive the name from "Lucumo," an Etruscan, and ally of Romulus, who fell in the Sabine war;[4] some from the Lucus Asyli, the origin of the refugee part of the population;[5] and one[6] from Lucerus, a king of Ardea, who aided Romulus in his war against Tatius. It is evident that these are mere guesses founded on a similarity of name; and Livy, therefore, very sensibly left the point undecided. The second of the proposed derivations might seem the most probable; since besides the Ramnes, or immediate followers of Romulus, and the Sabines of Tatius, the early Roman population must have also had an element composed of the shepherds who joined Romulus, and the refugees who flocked to his asylum. This part of the population would naturally have been considered inferior to the rest; and such was the estimation in which the Luceres stood. It is, however, not improbable that among these refugees was an Etruscan Lucumo named Cæles Vibenna, or Cælius Vibennus, with some followers—(*cum sua manu*)—to whom the Mons Querquetulanus was assigned as a place of residence, and derived from him the name of the Cælian Hill.[7] We can hardly imagine that Romulus had formed any regular Etruscan alliance at this early

---

[1] "Et habuit plebem in clientelas principum descriptam."—De Rep. ii. 9, 16.

[2] It is extraordinary how Schwegler (S. 498, Anm. 2) can charge him with being ignorant of the existence of these tribes, when in the same note he quotes the passage in which Livy speaks of them as such. (Lib. x. c. 6.)

[3] Lib. i. c. 13.

[4] Cic. De Rep. ii. 8; Varr. L. L. v. 55; Prop. iv. 1, 29, &c.

[5] Plut. Rom. 20; Schol. Pers. i. 20.   [6] Paul. Diac. p. 119.

[7] Varr. L. L. v. s. 46.

period; while at the same time the Mons Cælius appears to have obtained its name before the time of Numa, as we find it mentioned in the sacred books relating to the Argive chapels.¹ The assertion of a certain tragic poet named Volnius, recorded by Varro,² that all the three names of the tribes were Tuscan, is altogether absurd and inadmissible.

The arguments brought by Schwegler against the Luceres having been thus composed, do not appear to us to be of much weight. He is of opinion that the formation of a tribe out of such fugitives, with land assigned to it, and furnishing members to the Equites, is not to be thought of.³ But among these fugitives may have been political refugees of condition, like Cæles Vibenna. It is, at all events, as likely that one of the Roman tribes should have been formed out of these persons, whom Romulus had invited to his hospitality, as subsequently out of the conquered Albans, which is Schwegler's improbable supposition. In order to support that position, Schwegler can point out what a subordinate place the Luceres held; and shows, that though they were admitted among the knights, yet a king was never taken from them, as from the other two tribes, and that they were not represented in the senate or the priesthood.⁴ But these arguments are equally good for the Luceres having been refugees.

Schwegler's arguments, derived from there being no traces of early Etruscan influence in the Latin language or religion,⁵ do not affect our view; because we do not assume that a large Etruscan colony settled at Rome on this occasion, but only, among other refugees, though perhaps the most distinguished of them, an Etruscan Lucumo with a few followers. The circumstance of there having been a second and more regular Etruscan settlement at Rome would be no good argument against a former one; and in such remote traditions that the name of Cæles Vibenna may have been connected with both is not very extraordinary.

The division of a people into three tribes merely for political and administrative purposes, and not from any difference of race, appears to have been a frequent Grecian practice, and especially among the Dorians.⁶ We might avail ourselves of this circumstance in support of our theory of the Grecian origin of Rome. We are

¹ Varr. L. L. v. 47. ² Ibid. s. 55. ³ B. I. S. 500.
⁴ Buch. I. S. 514. ⁵ Ibid. 509, seq.
⁶ See the examples collected by Schwegler, D. ix. §. 14.

of opinion, however, as we have said before, that this threefold division arose at Rome from an actual diversity of race. That the Romans had been divided into three tribes before their union with the Sabines, though asserted by Dionysius in his imaginary sketch of the Roman constitution, is, as Schwegler has shown, entirely contrary to the remainder of the tradition. The thirty curiæ cannot be brought into accordance with the hundred patres of the Romulean senate, or the thousand original settlers on the Palatine. The notion is also confuted by the undoubted identity of the Tities with the Sabines; whilst Dionysius nowhere ventures to give the names of the three Romulean tribes.[1]

A better argument for Grecian origin may be derived from other parts of the Romulean constitution; and the Romans are particularly said to have imitated the Lacedemonians.[2] It was not, however, imitation, but hereditary custom. Dionysius has pointed out several particulars in which the Romulean constitution resembled the Spartan: as the division of the people into curiæ, with common sacra for each, a curia, or curial house, in which they feasted together on festivals, and a hall, like the Greek *Prytaneu*, common to all the curiæ. The body-guard of Romulus had also a Spartan prototype. Dionysius likewise found a resemblance between the relations of Romulus and the Spartan kings to their senates; but on this point we shall not insist, as he totally misunderstood this part of the Roman Constitution.[3] The number three, combined with ten, 3, 30, 300, also plays a great part in the institutions of both peoples.

We will here add a few words respecting the agrarian constitution of Romulus.

Dionysius tells us[4] that Romulus, after setting apart a portion of the Roman territory for the support of the crown and of the service of the temples, and another portion as common land, divided the rest into thirty equal parts, and assigned one of them to each of the thirty curiæ. We are disposed to believe this account because it tallies with scattered notices which we find in Latin authors. Thus Cicero says, that large tracts of arable land, pasturage, and wood, were set apart as royal, and were cultivated for the use of the

[1] Schwegler, Band I. S. 504; cf. Dionys. II. 7.
[2] μιμησάμενοι κατὰ πάντα τὴν Λακεδαιμονίων πολιτείαν οἱ Ῥωμαῖοι.—Athen. vi. 106.
[3] See Dionys. lib. ii. c. 13, 14, 23.   [4] ii. 7; iii. 1.

kings, in order that they might not be distracted, by the necessity of providing for their own support, from devoting their whole attention to the affairs of the people, and more particularly to the administration of justice, of which they were the fountain.[1] The division of the land among the people is confirmed by Varro and others.[2] To each member of a curia were allotted two *jugera*, which, because on the death of the holder they fell to his heir, were called *heredium*.[3]

Schwegler objects to this account[4] that it is merely adopted by the Roman writers from the ancient practice in founding colonies, when to each man was assigned a couple of acres; and that this practice has been retrospectively attributed to Romulus. But it seems much more probable that the practice may have descended from antiquity than that a variety of writers should have conspired to attribute to more ancient times a comparatively modern custom. Objections like this arise only from a settled determination to represent every circumstance of the ancient history as forged or invented. In fact, we know that the Roman colonies were imitations in miniature of Rome itself, and that all their institutions were modelled after those of the metropolis.[5]

Before we quit this part of the subject, we must say a few words about the name of *Quirites*.

Livy tells us,[6] that by way of concession to the Sabines they were called *Quirites*, from the town of Cures. This is of a piece with the rest of his history of the Sabine war and union, in which he endeavours to extenuate—though perhaps in this following his ancient authorities—all that might tend to the humiliation of the Romans. Cures is the name of a place, and, according to all accounts of the place, whence the victorious Sabines came; and accordingly such a concession would amount only to this, that the Sabines, who evidently had the upper hand, were allowed to retain

---

[1] "Jus privati petere solebant a regibus: ob easque causas agri arvi et arbusti et pascui lati atque uberes definiebantur, qui essent regii, qui colerenturque sine regum opera et labore, ut eos nulla privati negotii cura a populorum rebus abduceret."—De Rep. v. 2.

[2] "Bina jugera a Romulo primum divisa viritim," &c.—R. R. L. 10, 2. "Bina tunc jugera populo Romano satis erant, nullique majorem modum attribuit (Romulus)."—Plin. N. H. xviii. 2; cf. Paul. Diac. p. 53.

[3] Varr. loc. cit.   [4] R. L. S. 450.
[5] See Gellius xvi. 13, 8.   [6] Lib. l. c. 13.

their own name, instead of being compelled to assume that of the Romans, who were evidently inferior.

Another difficulty is, why, if Tatius was king of Cures, should he have abandoned his sole and ancient monarchy, only to share the regal power with Romulus at Rome?

But the ancients had another derivation of *Quirites* from *quiris*, a spear;[1] whence the name would signify "spearmen," or "warriors." Such a derivation is much more befitting the warlike Sabines; and after all it would only put them on a level with the Romans, seeing that the term "Populus Romanus" meant the Roman army. Professor Newman, who maintains a Gaelic, or Celtic mixture in the ancient Italian populations, observes on this subject "We happen here to have a clue which the Romans had not. The Gaelic language has numerous words in common with the Latin; and gives us Coir (sounded Quir), *a spear;* Curaidh, *a warrior;* the similarity of which to Quir and Quirite sets at rest the question what Quirite meant."[2] The analogy is certainly striking; but as the author had just before observed, "that until it is shown that Cures cannot also have come from the same root, there is no proved disagreement in the two explanations," it is, perhaps, going too far to say that the question is entirely set at rest.

On the whole, however, we accept as much the more probable one the derivation from *curis*, or *quiris*, a spear. The Sabines were enrolled, together with the Romans and Luceres, in the thirty curiæ, which now formed the military force of the entire city of some 3,000 men, with 300 horse. But as this force no longer consisted only of the Populus Romanus, that name was not, indeed, abolished, but was accompanied with one of equal extent and honour taken from the Sabine tongue, and the whole army was called "Populus Romanus Quirites."

It is a nice point whether this may have meant "the Roman people *and* the Quirites." The omission of the copula is not at all unusual in Latin, and is constantly seen in the familiar address "Patres Conscripti," standing for "Patres et Conscripti." But we think that in the present case there is a mere apposition, and not an

---

[1] Ovid. Fast. ii. 475; Paul. Diac. p. 49, *curis;* Plut. Rom. 29; Macrob. Sat. i. 9, &c. We learn from Dionysius (L. 48 *fin.*) that Varro also knew this derivation (χύρεις γάρ οἱ Σαβίνοι τὰς αἰχμὰς καλοῦσιν), but it does not appear in his extant works, except mediately through Quirinus; which he derives from Quiritibus.—Lib. v. 8, 73.

[2] Regal Rome, p. 65, *seqq.*

addition. This is shown by the formula which frequently occurs of "Populus Romanus Quiritium,"[1] where the Romani and Quirites are identified. Nor can this latter form be a corruption, as some critics have thought, since in the following passage of Livy we also find the two words identified, though in a different manner. It relates to the Patres devoted to death at the time of the Gallic invasion: "Sunt, qui M. Fabio Pontifice Maximo præfante carmen, devovisse eos se pro patria Quiritibusque Romanis, tradant,"[2] where *Romanis* is evidently an adjective—the Roman Quirites. We might here also add the many occasions on which Quirites stands for the whole of the Romans.

In fact, after the amicable union of the Romans and Sabines, it would have been keeping up a memory of their ancient feud to call one part of the people Romans and another Quirites. As individual citizens the name Romanus was naturally applied to all, both Romans and Sabines, because the name of the city continued to be Roma, and an inhabitant of it must therefore have been a Romanus. But this common name for Romans and Sabines individually is another presumption that they had not separate names collectively.

In process of time, however, and when the constitution of the army had been altered, the name *Quirites*, like *Populus*, entirely lost its military signification, and retained only its civil meaning, to denote those who enjoyed civil rights, as the *suffragium*, &c.; which were originally vested only in the men who bore arms. Thus it became at last the usual appellation of the Romans, when addressed collectively in their civil capacity; probably because it was shorter than "Populus Romanus Quirites," and because *Quirites* was more direct and personal than *Populus*. Nay, the word not only lost its original meaning of "warrior," or "soldier," but became at length entirely opposed to it; as we learn from the anecdote of Cæsar quelling a mutiny and insubordination of the Decumani, merely by calling them *Quirites* instead of *milites*; which so hurt their military pride that they became as docile and obedient as lambs.[3]

On the whole, the names *Romani* and *Quirites*, which remained in the language many centuries, and were pretty nearly equivalent, must be regarded as the strongest possible proof of the truth of the accounts of the Sabine union given by the historians. There is no probable way of accounting for this double name,

---

[1] For instances see Becker, Handb. der Röm. Alt. B. ii. L 21, ff.
[2] Lib. v. c. 41. [3] Suet. in Jul. c. 70.

except by the union of two peoples; and that a union effected by treaty and agreement, and not by force; for in the latter case, which would have been one of conquest and subjugation, the name of the conquered nation would have vanished, and that of the victors would alone have been preserved.

We will now return to the course of the history after the death of Tatius.

REMAINDER OF THE REIGN OF ROMULUS.

Romulus abstained from avenging the death of Tatius by a war; though to expiate the wrong suffered by the ambassadors, and the murder of the king, he renewed the alliance which existed between Rome and Lavinium. On this side, therefore, there was an unexpected peace; but another and much nearer war broke out almost at the gates of Rome. It was, indeed, this close vicinity that occasioned the hostilities.[1] For the Fidenates, thinking that the neighbouring city was growing too strong, seized the occasion to make war before Rome should have arrived at that pitch of strength which it promised to attain. Wherefore they made a sudden incursion into the Roman territory, and on the side of the Tiber laid waste all that lies between the two cities; then, turning to the left, they continued their ravages, to the great alarm of the rural population. The tumult and trepidation of the husbandmen, as they rushed into the city, brought the first news of the matter. Romulus at once led forth his army, and indeed so close a war admitted of no delay. Having pitched his camp about a mile from Fidenæ, and left a moderate garrison to guard it, he took the field with all his remaining soldiers. Placing a part of them in ambush at a spot concealed by thick brushwood, with the greater part of his troops and all his horse, he approached Fidenæ; and by sending his cavalry up to the very gates, and threatening a tumultuous and disorderly attack, he obtained his object of drawing out the enemy. This display of a cavalry engagement made the flight which it was his design to feign less

[1] Fidenæ was only five miles from Rome, on the same bank of the Tiber, but higher up, at the present Castel Giubileo.

-urprising. Whilst his horse seemed hesitating between attack and retreat, the foot also began to give way; when the enemy rushing suddenly forth from the crowded gates, and driving before them the Roman line, are drawn by the ardour of pursuit to the place of ambush. The Romans concealed there suddenly rise, and charge the pursuing enemy in flank; whose panic is increased by seeing the garrison that had been left in the camp advancing to the attack. The Fidenates, terrified by the danger which threatened them on all sides, took to flight almost before Romulus and his cavalry could wheel round their horses; and they endeavoured to regain their city in a much more disorderly rout than the feigned one of the Romans; for theirs was real. But they could not escape their pursuers. Romulus was close at their heels, and, before they could close the gates, broke in with them in one troop. Thus was Fidenæ taken, and made a Roman colony.[1]

The Veientines were contagiously irritated by this war, as well as from their consanguinity to the Fidenates; for according to Livy the Fidenates were Etruscans, though most other writers make them Latins. The proximity of the war also served still further to irritate them, as the Roman arms seemed to threaten hostility to all who were nearest them. Resolving, therefore, to bring matters to a settlement, they invaded the Roman territory more in the manner of a depredatory incursion than of regular warfare. They neither pitched any camp nor awaited the Romans, but returned to Veii, carrying off with them the booty which they had seized in the fields. The Romans hereupon, finding no enemy in their territory, pass the Tiber, resolved and intent upon war to the last extremity. But when the Veientines heard that they were pitching a camp, and intended to attack their city, they went forth to meet them, preferring to try the fortune of the open field, to contending within their walls for their homes and hearths. In the battle which ensued, Romulus was victorious, without having recourse to any

---

[1] Livy does not state so here (lib. i. c. 14); but it is mentioned by Dionysius (lib. II. c. 53); and we find Fidenæ alluded to by Livy as a Roman colony a little further on (c. 27).

stratagem, and merely through the superior qualities of his veteran troops. He pursued the routed enemy to their gates, but abstained from attacking so well fortified a town, and one, too, that was defended by its very site. So he contented himself with laying waste the Veientine territory, as he returned, from a motive of revenge rather than the desire of booty. The Veientines, tamed no less by their losses than by their defeat, sent ambassadors to Rome to beg a peace. A truce of a hundred years was granted them, but they were mulcted in part of their territory. Dionysius says[1] that the district ceded was the Septem Pagi, and that the treaty was engraved on columns.

Such were the domestic and military transactions of the reign of Romulus; in which, whether we consider his courage in recovering his grandfather's kingdom—as the ordinary tradition relates—or his wisdom in building his city, and in strengthening it by his wars and treaties, there was nothing at variance with the belief of his divine origin or of his own apotheosis after death. From such beginnings Rome grew so strong, that during the forty ensuing years she enjoyed uninterrupted peace. Romulus was more beloved, however, by the populace than by the patricians, but most of all was he endeared to the soldiers. It was perhaps on this account that, in peace as well as war, he had always a body-guard of 300 armed men, whom he called Celeres.

Romulus, after performing these immortal works, had assembled a *concio* at the lake, or marsh, of Capre, in the Campus Martius, for the purpose of reviewing his army. While he was thus employed, a terrible tempest of thunder and lightning suddenly arose, and covered the king with so thick a darkness that the assembly could no longer discern him. Nor was he again seen upon earth. The Roman youth having recovered from their alarm, when the storm had passed over and was succeeded by a calm and brilliant sunshine, beheld the royal throne vacant. The Fathers, who had stood near the king, told them that he had been carried up to heaven in the tempest; but, though they doubted not this affirmation,

---

[1] Lib. II. c. 55. The same author makes the war last two campaigns.

they remained for some time dejected and sorrowful, as if they had suddenly become orphans. At length the whole of them, following the impulse of a few, hail Romulus as a god, the son of a god, the king and parent of Rome; they implore his favour, and pray that he will ever be propitious towards them, his offspring. I believe, however, that there were already some who suspected that he had been torn to pieces by the hands of the Fathers; for an obscure report of this kind has been handed down. But admiration of the man, as well as the fear and awe with which they were overcome, caused the other account to prevail. The belief of it, moreover, was strengthened by the contrivance of one Proculus Julius; who, perceiving the sorrow of the citizens for the loss of their king, and their anger against the Fathers, stepped forward in an assembly of the people, and trusting that his authority would add weight to his words, even in so extraordinary a matter, said: "O Quirites, Romulus, the parent of this our city, having suddenly descended from heaven, appeared to me this morning at the break of day. Struck with awe and veneration, I stood still, and humbly implored that I might lift up my eyes towards him. Then Romulus said: 'Go tell the Romans it is the will of the gods that Rome, which I have founded, should be the head of all the earth. Let them therefore cultivate the art of war; let them know, and transmit to their posterity, that no human power can resist the Roman arms.' Having thus spoken, he again ascended into heaven." It is wonderful what belief this story acquired; and how much the regret of the army and the *plebs* for Romulus was mitigated by the certainty of his immortality.

The reign of Romulus lasted thirty-seven years.

As a ruler, the two great works of Romulus were the foundation of the Auspices and of the Senate. He is represented as always listening to the counsels of the latter.[1] He kept the people in order by mulcting them in cattle rather than by severe corporal punishments.[2] He was the

[1] "Patrum auctoritate consilioque regnavit."—Cic. De Rep. ii. 8.
[2] Ibid. 9.

founder of the Roman military system, and has the reputation of having been a very warlike prince; which must be attributed to his military success, and his personal prowess; for, according to the accounts transmitted to us, he did not enter upon a single aggressive war. All his wars were in self-defence; though he may be said to have brought upon himself the earlier ones by the rape of the Sabines.

REMARKS.—On the end of Romulus Schwegler remarks:[1] "One who had been born in so wonderful a manner could only leave the earth by miracle. In order to enhance the miraculous nature of these occurrences, the moment both of his conception and of his death is marked by an eclipse; a coincidence which has been already observed by Dionysius[2] and Plutarch.[3] The Greek mythology affords a parallel in the story of Hercules; for Hercules also is borne to heaven by a thunder-cloud; where he is reconciled to his enemy, Hera, and marries her daughter Hebe. This, or a similar, story of the Greek mythology was certainly present to the minds of the Roman poets; since the idea of an apotheosis in this form is originally as foreign to the Italian religion as the idea of sexual intercourse between gods and men, and a begetting of men by gods. Both ideas are derived from the Greek mythology; and it was doubtless Ennius, who had received a Greek education, who first invented the apotheosis of Romulus in such a form, and domesticated the idea among the Romans."

To the same effect Mommsen:[4] "The Greek hero-worship is entirely foreign to the Romans; and how recently and clumsily the Romulus legend was invented, is shown by his quite un-Roman metamorphosis into Quirinus. Numa, the oldest and most honoured name in Roman tradition, was never worshipped as a god at Rome, like Theseus at Athens."

Nobody, of course, believes in the actual apotheosis of Romulus; the only question is, whether such a belief was congenial to, and might have prevailed in, the times in which Romulus lived?

The very argument which Dr. Mommsen uses against the story proves that it could not have been a late invention, as a very little reflection might have shown him. No inventor of a story invents

[1] Buch x. § 10.
[2] De fort. Rom. 4.
[3] Lib. ii. c. 56.
[4] Kap. 12, p. 113.

one that runs counter to the manners of the people among whom he lives. For, first of all, such an invention would not occur to him; there would be nothing to suggest it. Again, an inventor naturally wishes his story to be believed; but how should it gain credit if it was totally foreign to the customs of the people whom he wishes to believe it? These reflections show that the story must have been the product of the age of Romulus, who with many of his followers was of Greek descent.

In the very same page in which Dr. Mommsen makes this objection to the legend, he mentions, without a word of comment, the worship of Hercules by the Romans, as a well-attested part of the Roman religion. But who was Hercules but a deified man? And what was his worship but hero-worship? This worship, as we have seen, had been instituted by Romulus, and is another proof of his Greek extraction.

The argument that Numa was never worshipped by the Romans is a strange one in the mouth of Dr. Mommsen, who does not believe in his existence. But the difference is easily accounted for. Romulus was a semi-Greek, Numa a pure Sabine. The followers of Romulus, especially the Ramnes, for whom probably his deification was principally intended, might readily believe it. Not so the Sabines of their king. And during the reign of Numa, Rome became thoroughly *Sabinized*.

The tradition, therefore, instead of being a late and clumsy invention, bears on its face the evidence that it was not invented at all; though of course the apotheosis itself was invented by those who had a purpose to serve. The tradition was handed down from that early period when alone hero-worship was practised, and could not have been invented at a long subsequent period, when it was not practised.

The same answer which we have given to the objections of Dr. Mommsen applies to those of Schwegler. The latter writer, though he adduces the story of Hercules from the Greek mythology, as suggesting to Roman inventors the apotheosis of Romulus, forgets that Hercules had been early naturalized at Rome. The Ara Maxima dedicated to him was undoubtedly one of the oldest fanes in the city. It required, therefore, no Ennius to introduce among the Romans the idea of apotheosis. And it is incredible that any poet should have been able to establish such an article of popular belief among them, especially if it was quite contrary to their way of thinking. But, in fact, that the deification of Romulus was known among the Romans long before the time of Ennius appears from the circumstance that the temple dedicated to him is mentioned in the sacred Argive books: "dictos enim collis plureis apparet ex Argeorum sacrificiis, in quibus scriptum sic est:

"'Collis Quirinalis, terticeps cis aedem Quirini.'"[1]

Schwegler himself recognises the high antiquity of the division of the city, according to these books;[2] divisions which must of course have preceded those of Servius.

We are of opinion, however, that though the belief in the apotheosis of Romulus originated at the time of his death, yet that the story of Julius Proculus, or at least his prediction, is a more modern addition. The prophecy that nothing could resist the Roman arms, and that Rome was to be the leading city of the world, is evidently a *vaticinium ex eventu*, which must have been invented, at all events, after Rome had made considerable progress in the conquest of Italy, and was perhaps inserted by Livy himself, as a rhetorical flourish and *ad captandum vulgus*. During the reign of Romulus there was nothing to suggest or to justify such a prediction. There is nothing of the sort in the tradition as given by Cicero; according to whom, Romulus appeared to Proculus Julius, on the Quirinal Hill, and merely requested that a temple might there be built to him; for that he was now a god and called Quirinus.[3]

That a simple and primitive people like the early Romans should have believed in the deification of Romulus is nothing surprising. Many centuries afterwards, amidst all the enlightenment of the imperial times, Julius Caesar was, like his successors, translated among the gods, not only, says Suetonius, by the mouths of those who decreed him that honour, but also in the belief of the vulgar.[4]

The descent of Romulus from a god, his own apotheosis, the colloquies of Numa with Egeria, and other supernatural events of this description, are eagerly seized upon by the sceptical critics as

---

[1] Varr. L. L. v. 52. The same books also mention an Ædes Romuli on the Germalus (ib. § 54); but it is possible this may have been the same as the Casa Romuli.

[2] R. I. S. 330, Anm. 11.

[3] De Rep. ii. 10, 20. So also Dionysius, lib. ii. c. 63.

[4] "In deorum numerum relatus est, non ore modo decernentium sed et persuasione vulgi."—Jul. Cæs. c. 88.

proofs of the falsehood of early Roman history. But in fact such objections only prove the thorough misconception of these critics of ancient character and manners, and especially of the ancient notion of deity. On this point we will transcribe the words of an eminent German scholar: "Notwithstanding that the use and meaning of the word *deus* is sufficiently known, yet we do not think it superfluous to remind our readers that when they are thinking of the Latin *deus*, they must quite throw aside the notion of the German word *Gott* (or the English word *God*). For it would lead us to very false ideas of the religious views of the ancients, if, for instance, we should regard the deification of Roman emperors according to our notions of a divine being. A *deus* is far from being so much as a *saint*; since every person's soul, after quitting the body, and after the performance of ceremonies like those employed in the apotheosis of an emperor, became a *deus*. The invisible guide assigned to every man by heaven, was called *deus*; a word which denoted not only a good, but also a wicked being. According to this view, the word *deus* denoted in general only an invisible, or spiritual, personality. These spiritual beings were as numerous as the corporeal appearances which presented themselves to the senses; since not only every man, but also every plant, every place, nay, every property of these creatures and objects, had, in the belief of antiquity, their spiritual counterparts."[1]

According to this view, it would be as rational to doubt the existence of St. Augustine, St. Jerome, or any other saint in the Roman calendar, because they have been placed among the heavenly choir, as to doubt the existence of Romulus because he had been deified. And if that king is to be regarded as a mythical personage on account of his apotheosis, so also must Julius Cæsar and the succeeding emperors, though their reality is amongst the best attested facts of history. It is true that we find no deifications during the republic; but this happened partly because, after the Sabine mixture, superstition ran less that way, and partly because it was difficult to find anybody to deify in that period of equality. But no sooner had the empire, or the rule of a single person, been re-established, than the practice was immediately revived. For the Cæsars, like Romulus, claimed a divine origin, through Venus and Æneas. There were, perhaps, fewer persons in that period who believed in the deification. The higher classes, at all events, had

[1] Hartung, Religion der Römer, B. i. S. 31.

grown more sceptical and rationalistic; but the mass of the people were still not much advanced above the superstition which prevailed under the kings.

We will now proceed to examine the remaining occurrences of the reign of Romulus.

Although Tatius, it is said,[1] can as little pass for an historical personage as Romulus—for he is the hero eponymous of the Tities, as Romulus is of the Romans—yet there seems to be some historical ground for the double kingdom which the legend offers as the oldest constitution of the federated state. It is quite possible that a contemporary reign of a king from both races may have preceded the alternate rule of Roman and Sabine kings. The tradition preserved by Servius of the double Romulean throne, with a sceptre and crown, which were always placed near Romulus when he was giving his sanction to anything, seem to point this way, though others refer them, not to Romulus and Tatius, but to Romulus and Remus.[2]

Can anything be more perverse than reasoning like this? It is quite possible that there may have been *a* reign of which tradition says nothing, like that of Romulus and Tatius, only it could not be *the* reign of those monarchs, of which tradition tells something! Surely such arguments are begot in the very spirit of contradiction.

The facts are admitted, but the persons to whom they refer are rejected as unhistorical. Why? We have already examined this question in the case of Romulus. The reason for rejecting Tatius is, that he is the eponymous hero of the Tities. Now, if there was otherwise any weight in such an argument, let us observe that the parallel does not hold. The Romans were a nation, the Tities only a city tribe, and wanted no eponymous hero; though it was natural enough that its name should have been taken from Tatius. But if that king had been an eponymous hero at all, it would surely have been of the Sabines, or Quirites, as a nation.

Let us observe that the body of Tatius was brought to Rome and buried in a magnificent tomb on the Aventine,[3] where public

---

[1] Schwegler, B. x. § 5.

[2] "Ob quam rem sella curulis cum sceptro et corona et ceteris regni insignibus semper juxta sancientem aliquid Romulum ponebatur, ut pariter imperare viderentur."—Serv. Æn. I. 276; conf. *id.* vi. 780. But Servius also in these places refers the double insignia to Romulus and Remus.

[3] "In eo (Aventino) Lauretum, ab eo quod ibi sepultus est Tatius rex, qui ab Laurentibus interfectus est, vel ab silva laurea."—Varr. L. L. v. § 152. *Adversus*

libations still continued to be made to his manes, at least down to the time of the empire; since Dionysius of Halicarnassus tells us that the practice existed in his time.

Here, then, we have evidence, not only of the existence of Tatius, but also collaterally of his having perished in the way tradition tells us. For it can hardly be believed that the Romans were so besotted as to make these libations for centuries to an imaginary king, or to have made them at all, except to expiate his untimely death, which Romulus had left unavenged. For this neglect having been punished by a devastating pestilence, Romulus took this method of appeasing the anger of the gods.[1]

The performance of these annual rites must have been handed down from the regal period; for it is impossible to imagine that they should have been established during the republic in favour of a king, and by no means a popular one.

Be it remarked that the testimony of Dionysius on this subject is only incidental. He had no point to prove, no theory to make out, for in his time nobody doubted the existence of Tatius. His merely accidental notice of the matter is, on that account, all the more valuable.

Schwegler rightly observes that when Plutarch, in the passage just quoted, connects these rites to Tatius with those performed at the grove of Ferentina, on the occasion of the meeting of the Diet, or Confederate Council of Latium, this explanation is no doubt quite groundless. There appears not to have been the slightest connexion between Rome and Latium, as a confederate state, during the reigns of the first two kings of Rome. The text of Plutarch is doubtless corrupt. It runs thus in the vulgate: καὶ καθαρμοῖς ὁ Ῥωμύλος ἥγνισε τὰς πόλεις, οὓς ἔτι νῦν ἱστοροῦσιν ἐπὶ τῆς Φερεντίνης πύλης συντελεῖσθαι. There was no Porta Ferentina at Rome; wherefore Becker[2] would adopt either the emendation of Doujatius, ὕλης for πύλης, or that of Cluver, πηγῆς; so that the expiatory rites were performed either at the grove or the fountain of Ferentina, which are both frequently mentioned. But this removes the scene of them entirely from Rome and the Aventine; where we know, from the passages of Varro and Dionysius just quoted, that Tatius was buried, and that such rites were performed. The

---

[1] εἰς Ῥώμην κομισθεὶς ἐντίμῳ ταφῇ, καὶ χοὰς αὐτῷ καθ᾽ ἕκαστον ἐνιαυτὸν ἡ πόλις ἐπιτελεῖ δημοσίας.—Dionys. lib. ii. c. 52.

[1] Plut. Rom. 24.   [2] Röm. Alterth. B. I. S. 177.

cities alluded to by Plutarch are only Rome and Laurentum, which, as we have said, had then nothing to do with the grove of Ferentina. It is evident, therefore, that Plutarch requires still further emendation. Nor need we scruple to apply it. Either through his own ignorance, or the blunders of his transcribers, he makes sad havoc with Roman topography; witness his discovering a spot on the Palatine called καλὴ ἀκτή, or Pulcrum Littus, which nobody ever heard of elsewhere, and which is evidently a mistake for Scalæ Caci. We should read, ἐπὶ τῆς Λαυρεντίνης ὕλης, at the Lauretum, or the Laurentine grove on the Aventine. It is possible that the grove may have derived its name from Tatius, and his connexion with Laurentum, rather than from its consisting of laurel-trees.

It will not be necessary to examine Schwegler's conjectures respecting a symbolical meaning in the whole history of this affair; that Tatius's violation of the law of nations towards Laurentum and Lavinium, towns which contained the Latian Lares, and the vengeance which the Laurentines took upon him, typify bloody conflicts which had taken place between the Sabine and Latin races. It is wonderful what hidden meanings these æsthetical critics discover in the commonest occurrences, and how they overlook the most obvious things that stare them in the face. Nor need we go into the fanciful resemblance between Tatius and Remus. All these things have no connexion with the credibility of the early Roman history.

In a similarly ingenious manner Schwegler goes on to suppose,[1] after Buttmann, that in the first two kings of Rome the myth has personified the two fundamental, though at first sight disparate, elements of Roman existence—the warlike spirit of the nation, and its *deisidæmonia*—or, if we may be allowed to borrow a word from the Latin, its *religiosity*. "Hence the first king, who founded the Roman state by force of arms, must have inspired it with the lust of conquest, the ambition of military superiority; whilst the second regenerated it, and founded it anew by religion and morals. Thus warlike activity is the central point of the acts of Romulus, and an exhortation to a zealous exercise of the military art is the last word which he addresses to the Romans, as if it were his political testament."[2]

We have already intimated our opinion that the warlike character

---

[1] Buch x. § 6; cf. Buttmann, Mythol. ii. 85.
[2] Schwegler, B. I. S. 521.

of Romulus has been much exaggerated. All his wars are defensive, and necessary to the maintenance of the new state; he undertakes none from the lust of conquest, and therefore could not have inspired his subjects with it; and this is shown by the extraordinarily long peace which followed his reign. His military character arises from the bravery and skill which he displays in the wars that are forced upon him, and more particularly, perhaps, from his being reputed the son of Mars. His last years are spent in almost ignoble peace; and this very circumstance is seized by the æsthetical critics as an objection against the length of his reign. His "political testament," as Schwegler calls it, is evidently the figment of a later age, found only in Livy, as we have already intimated. According to Cicero, in a passage to which we have before alluded, the two grand characteristics of Romulus's reign were religious and civil— the Auspices and the Senate—and it is to these, and not to his wars, that Cicero ascribes his apotheosis.[1] In fact, Romulus, as the first king, was necessarily the founder of *all* the institutions of the state, political, civil,[2] religious, and military, and, therefore, it is preposterous to contrast him with Numa, and to maintain that both had a peculiar and separate mission. Such a contrast is drawn merely with the view of colouring the assertion that both kings are the creatures of invention.

Besides the political institutions of the senate, the patricians, and the curiæ, Romulus also founded the Equites, or knights, at first 300 in number; that is, 100 from each tribe, or ten from each curia. Besides these, Livy mentions,[3] as a distinct body, 300 Celeres, which formed the king's body-guard. But the Celeres appear, in fact, to have been the same as the Equites. They are only two different names for the same class, *Celeres* being the Greek, or Romulean, name, afterwards superseded by *Equites*. And perhaps it was this double name which led some authors to think that they were different bodies; but Pliny acquaints us with their identity.[4] The name *Celer* seems to be derived from κέλλω, to run,

---

[1] "Ac Romulus, quum septem et triginta regnavisset annos, et hæc egregia duo firmamenta rei publicæ peperisset, auspicia et senatum, tantum est consecutus, ut, quum subito sole obscurato non comparuisset, deorum in numero collocatus putaretur."—De Rep. II. 10.

[2] So Livy: "jura dedit," lib. I. c. 8.

[3] Lib. i. c. 15.

[4] "Celeres sub Romulo regibusque appellati sunt (equites)."— N. H. lib. xxxiii. 2, § 9.

τάλης, a runner, or race-horse, in the Æolic dialect κέλης. *Celsus* is the same as *Celer*, and, therefore, also identical with *Eques*.[1] This may serve to explain the line in Horace:

"Celsi praetereunt austera poemata Ramnes."[2]

Here the word *Celsi* is commonly taken for an adjective, and commentators have racked their brains to explain it by supposed equivalent epithets, such as *elati, fastidiosi, sublimes*, &c. But *Celsi Ramnes* means the Roman, or rather the Ramnian, knights, the true old Romulean stock; for *Ramnes* by itself could not mean *knights*. Ramnes, or Ramnenses,—for both forms, in the same way as Tities and Titienses, are used indifferently,[3]—is, like other ethnic nouns, an adjective, and here stands for *Romani*, but with the stronger meaning of original or genuine Romans. It should be observed that the Tribunus Celerum was the next person in power and dignity to the king, and in his absence had the privilege of assembling the Comitia.

The wars of Romulus, it is said,[4] are a poor invention, and, like many other pretended events of the regal period, are borrowed from occurrences of the historical times. In support of this assertion, it is affirmed that Romulus's campaign against Fidenæ is a manifest copy of that of the year 328.

It is not our intention to affirm that the wars of Romulus are literally true, and that all the events of them occurred exactly as they are described. Allowance must be made for so high an antiquity, and for the circumstance that for the greater part, perhaps, of the first century of Rome, its history rested on oral tradition. But we do not think that they are inventions. They are rather meagre and fragmentary accounts of wars that really occurred; which, through the original want, or subsequent loss, of details, have an unconnected, desultory, and unhistorical appearance. The affirmation that the campaign against Fidenæ is a copy of that of 328, is quite unfounded, as anybody may see who will take the trouble to compare them.[5] The only resemblance is that in both the Romans rush into the town with the flying enemy; an event

---

[1] Paul. Diac. p. 55. "Celsus a Græco ἄλλως dictus." "Celsi in genere dicuntur omnes equitantes. ... Sed propria ratione sic dicuntur equites Romani" .. "*Celerres* und *celri*, die Ritter, ἄλκτεϛ."—Doed. Etym. p. 32; Koen. ad Greg. Dial. p. 140, sqq.; Serv. Æn. xi. 603.
[2] Ars. Poet. 342.
[3] See Varr. L. L. v. 55.
[4] Schwegler, Buch i. § 9.
[5] Liv. L 14; iv. 31, sqq.

which in the mode of ancient warfare may very easily have occurred, not only twice, but many times. All the other events of the campaign, including the ambush, are quite different. Had the incident of the torches been repeated, there might have been good grounds for assuming imitation. That there should have been many wars with Fidenæ, and that Veii, its neighbour, should have often combined with it against Rome, is nothing extraordinary; but it would have been truly wonderful if Rome had quelled two cities as strong, or stronger, than herself at one stroke. The hundred years' truce with Veii is, it is said, a random invention; but as the termination of it falls in the times of record, this is some guarantee for its truth; not to mention the account of Dionysius, that it was engraved upon a column. That author may be trusted as a witness to anything that fell under his own knowledge and eyesight; but he does not affirm that he saw this column. In other respects, he has incalculably damaged Roman history by his absurd accounts. And if he contradicts himself by asserting in one place that the Veientines ceded the salt-works to Romulus, while in another he represents the whole right bank of the Tiber as in the possession of the Etruscans long after,[1] that is no objection against Roman history, but only against the historian, Dionysius. Livy, as we shall see, represents the salt-works as first acquired by Ancus Marcius.

Schwegler then proceeds to object the improbability that only these two short campaigns against Fidenæ and Veii should have filled up the reign of so warlike a prince as Romulus, after the death of Tatius. But as we have already touched upon this point, we shall not again enter into it, and shall content ourselves with observing: first, that we do not know the date of the Sabine union, nor of the death of Tatius, nor consequently the length of Romulus's reign afterwards; and secondly, that all Romulus's campaigns are probably curtailed of their just proportions; for tradition fixes only on the more striking incidents and the results, and easily suffers the more ordinary details, as well as dates, to sink into oblivion.

It is impossible to say how Romulus came to be identified with Quirinus. According to a passage in Varro,[2] the Sabine god, Quirinus, was worshipped before the death of Romulus, since Tatius erected an altar to him. It is probable that he was not so identified before the time of Numa, whose care it was, as we shall have to show, to

[1] See lib. II. c. 55; lib. III. c. 45.   [2] Ling. Lat. v. § 74.

amalgamate as much as possible the Sabines and the Romans, and to remove all differences of creed and manners. But it is no objection to the general truth of early Roman history that we are unable to explain the origin of every early religious observance among that primitive and superstitious people. The same remark applies to the festival of the Populifugia, the Caprotine Nones, &c. There is nothing singular, however, in the circumstance that the two festivals just named should have fallen on the same day, since Romulus may have purposely chosen a holiday to review his army at the Palus Caprea. Nor shall we inquire into the nature of the Caprotine festival, or whether it resembled the Lupercalia. No conclusion can be drawn from the discussion of such points, though they admit of many fanciful interpretations, with which the German critics abound. But when Schwegler says,[1] that it would have appeared much more natural if the disappearance of Romulus had been assigned to the Quirinalia, on the 17th of February, instead of the Nones of Quinctilis, or July, we see at once that the old tradition is much more consistent than the modern critic, since in the time of Romulus there was no month of February. Had the story been *a modern invention*, the occurrence in question would probably have been placed on the Quirinalia, which, as Schwegler observes, would have looked "more natural;" but the way in which it stands is more consistent with the genuine antiquity of the tradition.

Schwegler proceeds to argue that the connexion of Rumus, or Romulus, with the festivals of the Lupercalia and Caprotine Nones, shows that he was an ancient and obsolete being of the Roman religion, that can only be dimly recognised from certain ancient sacred ceremonies. But we must leave him and his followers to reconcile this with his other theory, that Romulus is the eponymous hero of Rome, from which his name is derived. One or the other of these theories proves too much.

Schwegler is further "convinced" that the story of Romulus having been torn to pieces by the senators, also arises from some obsolete or misunderstood religious worship. But as his only ground of "conviction" is that Orpheus and Pentheus were also torn to pieces, we shall perhaps be excused from laying much weight on it.

We ourselves think that the tearing to pieces is very problema-

[1] R. L. S. 534, Anm. 21.

tical; though it is likely enough that Romulus may have met with a violent death, and that the lacerating part of the story is one of those popular exaggerations which so readily attach themselves to any remarkable occurrence. On this point Schwegler is more historically critical.[1] "Of course it was necessary," he observes, "to assign a motive for so horrible an outbreak of the deepest and bitterest hatred, as that murderous attack in the bosom of the Senate. Hence, it was invented (*gedichtet*), that the rule of Romulus became at last despotic and oppressive, that by insufferable pride and hateful ostentation he alienated all hearts from him; indecently slighted the Senate, consulting it only for the sake of appearance, and often not at all; as, for instance, when he divided the conquered lands among his troops, by his own supreme will, and restored the Veientine hostages against the opinion of the Senate; that he treated the new citizens in a contemptuous and overbearing manner; administered justice arbitrarily, and punished offences cruelly; and having made himself hateful by this despotic and violent conduct, out of a well-grounded suspicion surrounded himself with a guard of 300 men. All this, about which the old tradition knows nothing, may serve as a proof how little the Roman historians were at a loss for causes, when they were in want of them for their *pragmatismus*."

Exactly so. But who are "the Roman historians" who *pragmatize* in this manner? They are exclusively Greek—Dionysius, Plutarch, and their followers.[2] And so Roman history is to suffer because these rhetoricians wanted to make a pretty book for their countrymen!

It is a pity that Schwegler's critical acumen did not lead him to reject these accounts as worthless. But they told against early Roman history, and that was enough. He inserts them in a manner to make the reader believe that the faults of those historians are the faults of the history.

Yet he proceeds to give the Latin view as follows: "According to the old tradition, which is represented by Ennius, the rule of

[1] S. 535 f.
[2] The authorities quoted by Schwegler for the above "Inventions," are Plutarch, Rom. 26, 27, Num. 2; Dionysius, II. 56; Zonaras, vii. 4; Joann. Antioch, Fr. 32; App. B. C. II. 114; Dio. Cass. Fr. 5, 11. The only Roman authority that can be adduced for any one of the assertions is Livy for the body-guard. But it has been before shown that Livy wrongly distinguishes the Celeres from the Knights. This is also the view of Schwegler.

Romulus was just and mild; after his death his people lamented him as a father.¹ Even Cicero says, in complete contradiction to the above views—that is, the views of the Greek historians—that Romulus continued throughout on a good understanding with the Senate, and punished the offences of his subjects, not cruelly, but with a wise moderation."²

The drift of this passage is of course to show that Romulus, having behaved well towards the Senate, they had no reason to kill him, and that consequently the story, or rather the suspicion, of his having been put to death by them must be totally unfounded. But it is quite possible that Romulus may have behaved very handsomely to the Senate, and yet that from the desire of a revolution they may have put him to death. Louis XVI. behaved most kindly towards his subjects; yet he ended his days on the scaffold; while Louis XV., who really deserved that fate, died in his bed. And when we quote an author to support a view, we should quote him fairly, and not pick out passages that make for it, and leave out others that make against it. Cicero says, a little further on, that Proculus Julius told his vision of Romulus at the instigation of the Fathers, in order that they might deliver themselves from the hatred of having killed him—" impulsu patrum, quo illi a se invidiam interitus Romuli pellerent."³ And the proof that the Senate desired a revolution is the attempt to keep the supreme power in their own hands after the death of Romulus; to which Cicero alludes as if it were a base and ungrateful return for his kindness.⁴ In fact, the popularity of Romulus, as Livy says, lay with the mass of the people, and not with the Senate, as we also see by the conclusion of the passage just quoted.

The connexion of Julius Proculus with this story is not of much historical importance, except so far as relates to the family of the Cæsars. Schwegler observes;⁵ " The tradition represents the elevation of Romulus to be the god Quirinus as first revealed to Proculus Julius, and communicated by him to the rest of the people. This

¹ Enn. Ann. L 177 ff.
² De Rep. IL p. 8, seq.   ³ Ibid. 10, 20.
⁴ "Ergo quum illo Romuli Senatus, qui constabat ex optimatibus, quibus ipse rex tantum tribuisset, ut eos patres vellet nominari patriciosque eorum liberos, tentaret post Romuli excessum, ut ipse gereret sine rege rempublicam, populus id non tulit desiderioque Romuli postea regem flagitare non destitit."—Ibid. c. 12.
⁵ B. l. S. 536, sqq.

trait is not without significance. In it is reflected that familiarity of the Julian race with the gods, which marks its prominent and hereditary character. It is striking, on the other hand, that this Julius Proculus appears as a Roman citizen, while, according to the ruling tradition, the Julii did not come to Rome till later, in the reign of Tullus Hostilius. Can the former version of the story have proceeded from the Julii themselves, who may have set some value on having belonged to the original stock of the Roman people, and having been settled at Rome from the very beginning? And may it consequently have happened that Livy, out of respect for Augustus, mentions the Tullii, instead of the Julii, among the Alban families transplanted to Rome by Tullus Hostilius?"

What Schwegler here calls "the ruling tradition" is only the unsupported assertion of Dionysius,[1] that the Julii were transplanted to Rome after the reduction of Alba; an assertion which is not only contradicted by Livy, who names the Tullii on that occasion instead of the Julii;[2] but also, what is not unusual, by Dionysius himself, who, in the passage where he relates the apparition of Romulus, mentions that the person to whom he appeared was named Julius, and, in order that there may be no mistake about the identity, adds that he was a descendant of Ascanius![3] Such is the worth of this Greek authority. Nor can any inference on the subject be drawn from Tacitus,[4] who, though he mentions the Julii as coming from Alba, does not say at what time. But Schwegler's question, whether the former version may not have been invented by the Julii themselves, is answered by Cicero,[5] who, like Livy and Dionysius, mentions Julius Proculus as the person to whom Romulus appeared. Now Cicero assuredly did not invent the story to flatter Julius Cæsar; but must have taken it from some old annalist, as innocent of that intention as himself. And the same fact will exculpate Livy from an insinuated forgery.

We will now proceed to examine some objections brought by the late Sir G. Cornewall Lewis against the history of Romulus.[6] They are urged with more force than by the German writers, and are not disfigured and weakened by attempts to explain away facts by

---

[1] Lib. III. 29. [2] Lib. I. 30.
[3] Παρελθὼν τις εἰς τὴν ἀγορὰν Ἰούλιος ὄνομα, τῶν ἀπ' Ἀσκανίου.—Lib. ii. c. 63.
[4] Ann. xi. 24. [5] Rep. ii. 10, 21.
[6] See Credibility, &c., vol. I. chap. xi. § 9.

finding for them supposed resemblances in the Greek mythology. Nevertheless we think they are equally inconclusive.

The narrative, observes Sir G. C. Lewis, "does not profess to be derived from historians who were either contemporary, or who lived near the time; nor are any of its main facts supported by contemporary documents or inscriptions. It is totally devoid of all credible external attestation. On examining the texture of the history, we find that it is, with few exceptions, a mosaic, or patchwork, of explanatory legends, pieced together, and thrown into a narrative form. These legends are partly political and institutional; partly monumental and local; partly religious and ritual."

The question of contemporary historians we have discussed in the Introduction, where we have endeavoured to show that, though there were no *literary* historians at Rome, in the modern sense of the term, till about two centuries B.C., yet that the Annales Maximi and the Commentarii Pontificum supplied their place; that the books of the latter began at least as early as the reign of Tullus Hostilius; that they were *retrospective*, and contained an account of the city from its foundation. Thus the reign of Romulus may possibly have rested on tradition for not more than about half a century.

It does not follow that the history was not, *at one time*, supported by contemporary documents or inscriptions, because we cannot point to them *now*. This arises from the ancient method of writing history. The ancients did not, like most modern historians, cite their authorities at the bottom of the page, as vouchers of the truth of their information, or at all events of the source whence they derived it; though they now and then allude to them in the body of the work. On the same grounds we might question, for instance, the authenticity of the histories of Thucydides or Tacitus. We see from the correspondence of Tacitus with the younger Pliny respecting the eruption of Vesuvius, what pains he took to collect authentic information; yet, if we possessed that part of his history which contained an account of the eruption, we should not probably find in it the name of the younger Pliny.

It is affirmed, or assumed, universally by the ancients, that the art of writing was known at Rome from its very foundation; and the same fact is allowed by the best modern authorities. We have examined this question in the Introduction. But to suppose that the Romans never used an art which they knew is absurd; and to suppose that they never used it for public purposes is incredible. It cannot be doubted that there were public documents and inscriptions in the time of Romulus, or that they survived till the times of record. Dionysius, in a passage to which we have already referred, speaks of the treaty with Veii being engraved on a column. Other material and tangible evidences of the history would be the walls and buildings on the Palatine and the Quirinal, the Vetus Capitolium, the Sabine Temples on the Quirinal, the Temple of Jupiter Feretrius, &c.; not to speak of religious and domestic customs, as the festival to Consus, the marriage rites, the funeral libations to Tatius, and other matters of the like nature. It cannot be said, therefore, that the history was "devoid of all credible external attestation."

The assertion that the history is "a patchwork of explanatory legends" is quite gratuitous, and a begging of the whole question. But before entering upon this subject, we will advert for a moment to the objection drawn from Romulus's youth.

"In spite of his youth (for he was only eighteen years old when he founds Rome), and his early life passed among herdsmen and in rustic pursuits, Romulus appears from the very commencement of his reign as a wise legislator, versed in all the arcana of political science. Dionysius, indeed, intimates more than once that he acts upon the advice of his grandfather, Numitor; this expedient, however, does not substantially diminish the improbability and inconsistency of the received account. The history is evidently constructed upon the principle of collecting all that is characteristic and excellent in the primitive institutions and condition of Rome, and attributing it to the invention of the founder Romulus. The narrative is formed in the same manner as the Cyropædia of Xenophon and Plutarch's Life of Lycurgus, as in those works the institutions are real, but the account of their original establishment is fictitious, and the motives and reasons attributed to the founder are conjectural. Thus Cicero considers the formation of the Roman state as due to the wisdom of Romulus alone. Consistently with this view, he enumerates all the natural and political advantages of the site of Rome, which he attributes to the foresight of Romulus, in selecting so highly favoured a position, and one so well fitted to become the capital city of a great empire. The story of the birth of the twins, indeed, implies a different cause for the site of Rome, for, according to this fable, it is founded on the spot where they were exposed, suckled by the wolf, and discovered by Faustulus."

It is rather damaging to this argument from the youth of Romulus that the author should, in a note in the same page, have adverted to the parallel of Augustus. That emperor, at the time of his uncle's death, was precisely of the age of Romulus when he founded Rome; yet, in spite of the opposition which he experienced, he succeeded in seizing the sceptre of the world. This surely is a much more extraordinary feat than the founding of what was at first only a small city.

We have seen that the story of Romulus's life among the herdsmen is part of the invention necessary for tracing his descent from Æneas; and for the same reason we may dispense with Dionysius's *pragmatical* account of his acting on the advice of his grandfather, Numitor. We are not concerned about Cicero's praises, which are no doubt rhetorically exaggerated, and, under the name of Romulus, are only a panegyric upon Rome itself. There can be little doubt that Romulus was compelled to found his city where he did by necessity; for it was about the only vacant space left in the neighbourhood.

But the comparison of the early history of Rome to Xenophon's Cyropædia, or Plutarch's Life of Lycurgus, is certainly a most unfortunate one. Both these works are the productions of a highly literary age; while all that is told of the age of Romulus is rude and fragmentary. Neither the Asylum, nor the rape of the Sabines, could have been invented by way of models worthy of imitation; and, in fact, Cicero feels himself obliged to offer a sort of apology for the latter.[1] We need not here advert to the silly speeches which Dionysius puts into the mouth of Romulus, such as his discourse upon government, founded upon a complete mistake of the Romulean constitution; though we suppose it is the flourishes of this rhetorician that have partly suggested the comparison with the Cyropædia.

The assertion that the history is written on the principle of collecting all that is characteristic and excellent in the primitive institutions and condition of Rome, and attributing them to Romulus, is not only unfounded, and in the highest degree improbable; it is also contrary to what the author has just before

[1] "Novum quoddam et subagreste consilium."—De Rep. ii. 7.

laid down, that the history is a patchwork of explanatory legends, "partly political and institutional, partly monumental and local, partly religious and ritual." Which of these two contradictory hypotheses are we to accept as the author's *real* view? The institutions are admitted to have existed; the legends respecting them either existed, or they did not. If they existed, then the story of Romulus was not imagined in an after age like the Cyropædia; if they did not exist, then the history could not have been formed out of an explanation of them. One of these two hypotheses must necessarily be false; but we believe them to be both false.

"In pursuance of the same general view," continues Sir Cornewall Lewis, "Romulus is represented as dividing the people into tribes and curiæ, as creating the Senate, as organizing the military force, as originating the institutions of the Triumph, the Spolia Opima, and the colonial law, as laying the foundations of all the religious system, and as establishing the law of marriage and of filial relations. In all these matters his wisdom is highly commended, and he is shown in the character of the ideal king, equally prudent in council, and brave in war. At the same time, as scarcely any laws bore his name, it was necessary to say that his ordinances were for the most part unwritten: if any laws attributed to Romulus appeared in the digests of *Leges Regiæ* which existed in the Augustan age, they were only ancient legal rules, registered by the official scribes, and arbitrarily attributed by them to the founder of the state."

The institutions here ascribed to Romulus, as if they were the inventions of some ideal king, are for the most part absolutely necessary to all states; neither Rome nor any other city could have continued to exist without them. As Romulus was so young, he certainly wanted a Senate to guide him with their advice; a militia, or military force, must be organized for defence, and for that purpose it was necessary to institute certain divisions of the people, so that they might be assembled, at a short notice, from their daily occupations. All the other things enumerated were also absolutely necessary, except, perhaps, the Triumph and the Spolia Opima; and yet it is not improbable that the first king may have laid the foundation even of these. Neither are the institutions of Romulus pretended to have been absolutely perfect. His constitution was only adapted to the present state of the city; so that in the time of Servius Tullius it was necessary to construct a completely new one. Nor is it pretended that he founded *all* the religious system, as Sir G. C. Lewis says; on the contrary, his share in this appears to have been extremely small. In this way, Tatius did almost as much as he, and Numa a great deal more. Into the question about his laws we shall not enter, as we do not perceive how it affects the credibility of early Roman history, whether they were written, or unwritten.

"Another class of legends," continues Sir G. C. Lewis, "woven into the story of the reign of Romulus, are those which explain the origin of public buildings and monuments, and other local denominations, such as the Asylum, the Temples of Jupiter Stator and Jupiter Feretrius, the Tarpeian Rock, the Cœlian Hill, the Porta Pandana, the Lacus Curtius, the Comitium, the Forum, the names of the Curiæ. A third class are the legends of a religious or sacred character, such as those explaining the origin of the Consualia, the Matronalia, and the Populifugia."

Before we call the accounts handed down of the origin of these things legends invented to explain them, we are bound to show that they could not possibly have originated or existed in the way in which tradition tells us they did. If we deny, for instance, that Romulus opened an asylum at Rome, we are bound to prove that he could not possibly have done so; or, at all events, that his doing so is improbable to such a degree as to be wholly incredible. But this, we submit, has not been done. Therefore, to say that the tradition respecting the asylum is an ætiological legend is nothing but a conjecture, or guess; and, indeed, as we have before shown, not a very plausible one.

At the same time we will admit that, in some of the instances mentioned, as the Tarpeian Rock, the Porta Pandana, and the Lacus Curtius, the ancient explanations are probably mere guesses to account for a name the real origin of which had fallen into oblivion. These, however, are not connected with any very material point of Roman history; while the various explanations of them show that they rested not on any constant tradition. But the case is very different with the Asylum. Here tradition is constant; there are not two explanations of it. And, as it concerned a very important point of Roman history, it is all the more likely to have been correctly handed down. The Temple of Jupiter Feretrius was certainly, that of Jupiter Stator probably, Romulean; also the name of the Cœlian Hill, as we have shown, and the names of the Curiæ. The

Comitium, as the place where Romulus and Tatius met, appears, we believe, only in Greek writers, certainly not in Livy. The Forum is more doubtful; for when Livy speaks of the Forum in the battle between the Romans and Sabines, it is only by a *prolepsis*, and to make the account more intelligible to his readers.[1] It is possible, however, that there may have been the rudiments of a forum, as a mere market, in the time of Romulus, and even of the Comitium, as a place of general assembly for the Comitia Curiata.[2] The Consualia, as we have shown,[3] are certainly Romulean, and relate to a very important historical event, about the substance of which tradition is unvaried. The Matronalia and Populifugia are more uncertain. The latter, in fact, is decidedly not Romulean; it is only, we believe, Dionysius[4] who attributes it to the flight of the people on the death of Romulus; on which occasion, however, there was no flight.

"The ancient institutions of Rome," continues Sir G. C. Lewis, "both civil and religious, as well as the names of many remarkable buildings and public monuments, were anterior to a regular contemporary registration; or, if any authentic records of them had ever been made, they had for the most part perished in the Gallic conflagration, and through other casualties, before the Second Punic War."

Contemporary registration, as we have shown in the Introduction, began at all events in the reign of Tullus Hostilius, perhaps in that of Numa; therefore, not long after the origin of the earliest Roman institutions and buildings. And, though "the names" of some remarkable public monuments may have been anterior to contemporary registration, yet surely these must have formed of themselves a very valuable kind of registration. We have also shown that the Annales Maximi did not perish in the conflagration, and that what records did perish were restored from memory, and in other ways. But to continue our extract.

"Even before Rome had become a great imperial power, the curiosity of her citizens would naturally be excited about the origins of her institutions, usages, and buildings; and after she had extended her dominion, and acquired a vast renown, the desire to learn the history of a system which was seen to exercise so great an influence, would naturally increase. We may therefore assume

---

[1] "Et effusus egerat Romanos, toto quantum Foro spatium est."—Lib. i. 12.
[2] Varro, L. L. v. 155.   [3] Above, p. 63, s. 77.   [4] Lib. ii. c. 56.

it as certain, that such explanatory legends began to arise at a comparatively early period, and that the supply was multiplied as the demand increased."

These remarks are illustrated and enforced by a quotation, in a note, from Huc's *Travels in Tartary*. M. Huc, it appears, came in his travels upon a ruined and abandoned city, where he found a Mongol shepherd, who knew only that the place was called "The Old Town." Sir G. C. Lewis concludes the note by observing: "In a country inhabited by wandering pastoral tribes, such a state of incurious and satisfied ignorance respecting ancient monuments may exist; but where there are persons having a fixed habitation in the vicinity of a striking relic of antiquity, and living as its neighbours, their curiosity respecting it is excited; and if the true history of it has perished, a fabulous legend soon springs up to satisfy the cravings of the appetite for information."

To make the parallel complete, it was incumbent on Sir G. C. Lewis to show that Rome had been reduced to a state of solitude. As it is, he makes people constantly living in the vicinity of "some striking relic of antiquity"—say, Tarquin's Temple of Jupiter, or even Numa's Temple of Vesta—forget altogether who founded them, or for what purpose, although the proper service for which they were destined had never ceased to be performed in them; till at last, after a lapse we will say of two or three centuries—we cannot go beyond three, for there is less than that space between the foundation of the Capitoline Temple and the rise of literary historical writing at Rome—curiosity begins to revive, and some stories are invented to explain the origin of these monuments! Now would it not be just as reasonable to suppose that the people living in London should have forgotten for some centuries the foundation, say, of Westminster Abbey, and that it was designed for a place of worship, though service was continually performed in it, till, curiosity at last reviving, stories were invented to gratify it, that it was originally a church dedicated in the sixth century by King Sebert to St. Peter, on the site of which the abbey was subsequently erected by Edward the Confessor!

The same illustration will apply to institutions and usages, as well as buildings; for these, like them, must have been in daily use, and familiar knowledge.

In fact, we are too apt to suppose that the antiquities of Rome were as antique to the Romans as they are to ourselves, after the lapse of a further twenty centuries, and when most of the things have perished which served to identify them.

As we have said, there are less than three centuries between the building of the Capitoline Temple and the time of Fabius Pictor, the first *literary* Roman annalist. And as it is certainly assumed that "explanatory legends began to arise at a comparatively early period," we can hardly place this period at less than a century and a half before the time of Pictor. The origin and founder of this famous temple would therefore have been forgotten in less than a century and a half! Whereas it is allowed by the author that the mere oral tradition of events that are unsupported by the evidence of monuments may be accurately preserved for a period exceeding a century.[1]

The same reason will apply, with a little allowance for higher antiquity, to all the other monuments and institutions of the kingly period; as the Cloaca Maxima, the Forum, the Circus, &c. According to modern views, all these were the works of imaginary kings, even the very names of whom are not certainly known. But to proceed with our quotations.

"As the remote past was unrecorded and unremembered, the invention of the ætiologist was fettered by no restrictions; he had the whole area of fiction open to him, and he was not even bound by the laws of nature. His story was only subject to the condition that it must afford an apparent explanation of the custom, object, or proper name in question; and that the thoughts, manners, and circumstances introduced must agree with the peculiarities of the Roman people. We find accordingly that the utmost licence prevailed in the fabrication of these antiquarian legends; and that the merest resemblance of sound, or usage, were sufficient to suggest the idea of a real connexion. Thus, because the manners of the ancient Sabines were severe and simple, and their habits warlike, they were said to be colonists of the Lacedæmonians, who were distinguished by similar characteristics; although there was no historical proof of any such connexion, and it was quite unknown to the early Greek writers."

Thus we have the Romans painted as the greatest simpletons that ever existed on the face of the earth, ready to believe any idle story that might be palmed upon them, and accept it for their genuine history, which was entirely composed of these tales; for there is not a single old Roman monument or institution the origin

[1] Credibility, &c. vol. i. p. 101.

of which, according to modern critics, is not an ætiological myth. We know not of any other nation so civilized as the Romans were from their very origin that possessed, like them, an entirely imaginative history. And yet the Romans were not particularly distinguished for imagination.

That they were superstitious, however, and ready to believe many wonderful things in connexion with the supernatural world, must be allowed. But such a temper is not incompatible with the shrewdest practical sense. Louis XI. of France was one of the most sagacious monarchs that ever sat upon the throne. The Duke of Burgundy, indeed, once overreached him; but on the whole we hardly have a more striking instance of worldly wisdom. Yet Louis was the prey of the most abject superstition. So the Romans might have believed many miraculous and incredible things on points connected with religion, and yet have not been so easily imposed upon in matters which concerned their every-day life.

Sir G. C. Lewis, however, needed not to have reserved the proviso that the explanations of the ætiologist "must agree as to thoughts, manners, and circumstances with the peculiarities of the Roman people." The Asylum, the rape of the Sabines, the deification of Romulus were certainly not in accordance with the thoughts and manners of that later generation for whose edification they are said to have been invented. And this circumstance, as we have already endeavoured to show, is a proof that they were not invented at all.

An ethnographical hypothesis is not a legend; and if some of the Romans, misled by "the merest resemblances of sound or usage," thought that the Sabines were descended from the Lacedæmonians, we are afraid that the same reproach will touch now and then even some eminent modern ethnographers and philologists, who, in investigating modern subjects, would not readily admit an interpolation into the history of England or Germany.

"On similar grounds of apparent affinity, Dionysius affirms that Romulus copied the relation of the Roman king to the Roman Senate, and the institution of the Celeres, and of the common table of the Curiæ, from Lacedæmon."

Romulus, as we have endeavoured to show, being of Greek descent, had no need to borrow these institutions from the Spartans.

"We must suppose that the legends which were worked up into

the history of Romulus were originally independent and unconnected, and referred only to the peculiar subject which they served to illustrate. At what time they were moulded into a continuous narrative, such as is now presented to us, we have not the means of discovering; but we cannot doubt that the account of Romulus from his birth to his death—from his Alban origin and his foundation of the city to his political measures, his wars, and lastly his apotheosis—was substantially related by Fabius, and the earliest historians, in the form in which it has descended to us. This narrative was not, like the early British history of Geoffrey of Monmouth, for the most part a purely original fiction; the materials of it were, to a great extent, derived from oral legends, which were incorporated into the history. At the same time the connexion and the details must have been supplied by the first compilers; thus the story of the Asylum was some local legend; that of the rape of the Sabines illustrated the origin of the festival; that of the intervention of the Sabine women was probably a separate story; but in the narrative, as we read it, the Asylum is the cause of the rape of the Sabine women, and the rape of the Sabine women is the cause of their interposition between the hostile armies. The three events, once independent of each other, have become continuous links in the same historical chain."

Although in this paragraph Sir G. C. Lewis appears to be uncertain at what time "the legends" were formed into a continuous narrative, yet the whole context shows him plainly enough to have been of opinion that it was done by Fabius and the earliest historians. For he says that "the connexion and the details must have been supplied by the first compilers;" and these could have been no other than Fabius and the earliest historians. If this be not so, then there must have been historians, or compilers, before the period of literary history, or of history written and published for the public; which is quite at variance with the views of Sir G. C. Lewis, though, for our part, we think it probable enough.

The theory, then, stands thus: about two centuries before the Christian era there was no account whatever of the origin and progress of Rome; only some scattered oral legends without any connexion whatever between them; the first compilers adopted these, and worked them into "continuous links in the same historical chain."

It is truly surprising that a people which appears to have endeavoured at least to preserve some memory of their affairs—since there must at all events have been a list of consuls from the expulsion of the kings down to the time of Fabius, a period of more than three centuries—should have been in such utter ignorance of their history.

But, passing this over, let us observe that the theory involves two most extraordinary facts: first, that these scattered legends, which were wholly unconnected, were still capable of being placed together in an intelligible relation of cause and effect; and second, what is still, perhaps, more astonishing, that the first compilers should have agreed in weaving them together in the same connexion. The two earliest known writers of Roman history, Fabius and Cincius Alimentus, were contemporaries, and were speedily followed by other writers, in whose time the oral legends, if such they were, must have still survived; yet all these writers agreed in representing Roman history substantially in the same manner, and with only those slight divergences which show that they drew from independent sources! Surely this is much more incredible than to suppose that some sort of history, or at all events the materials for it, had been handed down.

But as we have touched upon this subject in the Introduction, we need not here dwell upon it.

"But although there is a continuity of narrative," proceeds Sir G. C. Lewis, "running through the story of Romulus; though the successive events stand to one another in an intelligible relation of cause and effect; yet we can trace throughout the deliberate invention of the ætiologist; we can perceive that each subject is treated after the manner of Ovid's Fasti. The story is formed by an aggregation of parts: there is no uninterrupted poetical flow or epic unity. Instead of resembling a statue cast, in one piece, in a foundry, it is like a tesselated pavement, formed into a pattern by stones of different colours. Even Niebuhr, who conceives the story of Romulus to be founded on a heroic lay, is forced to acknowledge that parts of it 'are without the spirit or features of poetry.'"

It is difficult to perceive how a narrative which is admitted to have "continuity," and "the successive events of which stand to one another in an intelligible relation of cause and effect," should resemble a tesselated pavement. If it does so—for we must confess that we do not exactly see the resemblance—it may be ascribed to want of art in the early historians; for, by the critic's own admission, they had all the materials with which to construct a narrative of uninterrupted flow. And this want of art is the best proof of their good faith. If we had had of these early times an elaborate, easy-flowing narrative, we might with good reason have suspected it to be a literary invention. The early writers, who are reflected in Livy, took the narrative as they found it. Tradition, adding perhaps a little embellishment, had seized upon only the more striking events, which accordingly may stand out rather too prominently, and obscure the connecting causes. These, however, did not the less exist; and we would therefore rather compare the history to a pearl or diamond necklace, in which the thread is hidden by the jewels which it connects.

Into the next paragraph of Sir G. C. Lewis's remarks, beginning at p. 437 with the words, "The great majority of the modern critical writers," and ending at p. 441 with the words, "no better than historical forgeries," we need not enter, because with the substance of it we cordially agree; and have indeed already quoted the concluding portion of it to support our reprobation of the practice of *reconstructing* history. The tenor of the paragraph in question is a brief but sensible condemnation of this practice in writers like Niebuhr, Mommsen, and Schwegler, who, though they condemn *in toto* the accounts of the reign of Romulus, and indeed of the kings in general, as false and fictitious, nevertheless select from it materials with which they build up a version of their own. There can be no third method. We must either show, as we have attempted to do, that early Roman history may really rest on authentic record, or tradition converted into record before it had grown obsolete, and therefore, making due allowance for such early times, that it may in the main be true; or, with Sir G. Cornewall Lewis, we must entirely reject it.

That writer proceeds to say: "Nothing consistent or intelligible can be extracted from the representation of the political history of Romulus as it is given in the received narrative. He is described as an elective king, and yet his chief title to the throne seems to be that he is of the royal family of Alba. His powers are, under the constitution formed by himself, extremely limited. There is a popular assembly, with extensive privileges; a Senate, of whose decrees he is merely the executor. Yet all the organization of the state is derived from him alone; he is the author of all the civil

K

and religious institutions; no person is named as taking any independent part either in the Senate or in the popular assembly. He is represented as governing mildly and in the spirit of a constitutional king in the early part of his reign; but as afterwards becoming despotic, although he meets with nothing but obedience at home and successes in war, and there is nothing to arouse his fears or awaken his jealousy. The joint government with Tatius, which is described to have lasted in the utmost harmony for five years, is only conceivable on the supposition that the offices of the two kings were honorary, and unaccompanied with real power—a supposition altogether inconsistent with the spirit of the old narrative. Even the Spartan kings, small as were their powers, lived in perpetual discord; and it may be safely affirmed that such a relation as is described in the received account to have existed between Romulus and Tatius, is unexampled in authentic history."

These objections are a good example of that mode of criticism which saddles on the history the faults of an historian, and charges it with inconsistencies which do not belong to itself, but to one or two of the writers who have undertaken to give an account of it. What Sir G. C. Lewis here calls "the *received* narrative" of the political history of Romulus, is the account of Dionysius of Halicarnassus, a Greek imperfectly acquainted with the Latin tongue, a rhetorician who frequently invented out of his own head speeches that could never have been delivered and events that could never have happened, and who was in particular notoriously ignorant of the Roman constitution. When Sir G. Cornewall Lewis accepts the description of Romulus having been an elective king, of his powers having been extremely limited, of his having been merely the executor of the decrees of the Senate, one would have thought that his suspicions might have been awakened by what he himself adds afterwards, that all the organization of the state is derived from him alone, that "no person is named as taking any independent part either in the Senate or in the popular assembly." But no; he accepts these flat contradictions in the lump, without stopping to inquire how they arose; he considers this *imbroglio* an actual part of the history, and then proceeds to make it an argument against its credibility. Now suppose a foreigner settled in London, imperfectly acquainted with our language, and still more imperfectly with our institutions, should have written for his countrymen a history of England full of the most glaring blunders; would posterity, from observing the contradictions between his work and those of better informed historians, be justified in pronouncing the whole history itself fictitious? Yet this is precisely what Sir G. Cornewall Lewis does in the present case.

The account which that writer accepts of the early Roman constitution is that of Dionysius,[1] the errors of which have been pointed out by Rubino[2] and other writers. Dionysius, who seems to have formed his idea of the reign of Romulus from those of the subsequent kings, who were certainly elective, or at least were so constitutionally, there makes Romulus summon the people together and address them in a long speech, which he says was suggested by his grandfather Numitor, but which could have existed nowhere but in the head of the writer. In this speech Romulus leaves to the people the choice of a monarchy or a republic; to which the people reply in another speech by electing him king. This is Sir G. C. Lewis's authority for Romulus being described as an "elective" king; but when he adds that "his chief title to the throne seems to be that he is of the royal family of Alba," this is a complete misconception of the Romulean constitution. Romulus rules by divine right. He is king by the will of the gods, manifested by augury, agreeably to the representation of Livy.[3] So also Ennius[4] represents the people passively awaiting which king the issue of the quarrel between Romulus and Remus may give them:

"Sic expectabat populus, atque ora tenebat
Rebus, utri magni victoria sit data regni."

Parker, indeed, affirms,[5] that the portent of the twelve vultures concerned only *the building* of the city. But this is a direct contradiction of Livy, who says: "Intervenit avitum malum, *regni cupido;*" and further on: "ut dii, quorum tutelae ea loca essent, auguriis legerent, qui nomen novae urbi daret, *qui conditam imperio regeret,* ... ad inaugurandum templa capiunt."[6]

The matter is further illustrated by another passage in Livy: "Vocata ad concilium multitudine .... jura *dedit;* quae ita sancta

[1] Lib. II. c. 3, seqq.
[2] Röm. Staatsv. B. I. S. 7, Anm. 1; and the Second Section, "Von dem Königthume."
[3] Lib. i. c. 6; cf. c. 18, "sicut Romulus *augurato* urbe condenda regnum adeptus est."
[4] Ap. Cic. De Div. I. 48.
[5] Röm. Alterth. II. L R. 291; Anm. 602.
[6] Lib. I. 6.

generi hominum agresti ratus fore, si se ipse venerabilem insignibus imperii fecisset, quum cetero habitu se augustiorem, tum maxime lictoribus duodecim sumptis, fecit." Whence, as Rubino observes it appears clearly enough that he did not mean to establish his ordinances by the consent of the people, but by the awe inspired by his dignity. Such is the view of all the best ancient writers. Romulus is an absolute monarch, ruling by divine right, the fountain of all law and justice, the supreme commander, the chief priest of his people, amenable to no tribunal but that of public opinion.[1] The Senate are only his advisers; it is he who has *created* them for that purpose, and to suppose that he was merely the executor of their decrees is one of the greatest possible mistakes. Cicero clearly discriminates their functions as those only of a council, and *head of Senate*.[2] Dio Cassius, who was much better informed than Dionysius respecting the early Roman constitution, in a passage which Sir G. C. Lewis himself has already quoted, makes Romulus tell the Senate that it was his office to command them, and not theirs to control him.[3] Even Dionysius himself, as usual, is not consistent; for in another place he tells us that in the regal times there was neither equality of right nor freedom of speech, that the kings out of their own will decided all suits, and that whatever they determined was law.[4] A passage upon which Rubino remarks that it is so unlike Dionysius's usual manner that he must have copied it from some *Roman* source; which is only saying that he did not, on this occasion, make it out of his own head. Nay, even Sir G. C. Lewis himself brings forward a sample of these contradictions, and remarks: " Dionysius seems to forget his account of the limited powers of the Roman king; for he describes the Interrexes as possessing an absolute authority: ἔπειτα διακληρωσάμενοι τοῖς λαχοῦσι δέκα πρώτοις ἀνέδωκαν ἄρχειν τῆς πόλεως τὴν αὐτ-

---

[1] "Nobis Romulus, ut libitum, imperitaverat."—Tac. Ann. iii. 26. "It privati petere solebant a regibus."—Cic. De Rep. v. 2.

[2] "Itaque hoc consilio, et quasi senatu fultus et munitus," &c.—De Rep. ii. 9, s. 15.

[3] καὶ τέλος εἶπεν ὅτι ἐγὼ ὑμᾶς, ὦ πατέρες, ἐξελεξάμην οὐχ ἵνα ὑμεῖς ἐμοῦ ἄρχητε, ἀλλ' ἵνα ἐγὼ ὑμῖν ἐπιτάττοιμι.—Fr. t. i. p. 7 (ed. Bekker).

[4] οὔτω γὰρ τότ' ἦν οὔτ' ἰσονομία παρὰ Ῥωμαίοις, οὔτ' ἰσηγορία, οὐδ' ἐν γράμμασιν ἅπαντα τὰ δίκαια τεταγμένα· ἀλλὰ τὸ μὲν ἀρχαῖον οἱ βασιλεῖς ἐφ' αὑτῶν ἵστων τοῖς δεομένοις τὰς δίκας, καὶ τὸ δικασθὲν ὑπ' ἐκείνων, τοῦτο νόμος ἦν.—Lib. x. c. 1.

[5] Röm. Staatsv. B. i. S. 125; Anm.

ἀμέτροπα ἀρχήν."[1] Yet such is the author from whom he takes the "received history!"

The account of Romulus having been despotic in his later days rests only, as we have already shown,[2] on the authority of Dionysius, Plutarch, and other Greek authors. The absurdities of these writers are intolerable. Thus, Plutarch represents that in the battle with the Veientines, fourteen thousand of them fell, and more than one-half of them by the hand of Romulus himself![3] In all probability, the whole population of Veii—men, women, and children—did not amount to more than fourteen thousand. Dionysius[4] has a still more absurd exaggeration when he states, that at the death of Romulus the Romans had an army of 46,000 foot and 1,000 horse! Such are the authors on whom Sir G. C. Lewis founds the *received* history of Rome.

The same writer objects to the joint government of Romulus and Tatius, because there is no example in authentic history of any joint reign lasting in harmony for five years. Such is the hard lot of early Roman history! if it relates anything that has a parallel, it is immediately said to be copied; if it relates something that has no parallel, it is said to be unexampled, and therefore incredible. Nay, although it may have a parallel from which it could not possibly be copied—as, for instance, the achievements of so youthful a king as Romulus, the history of which was in existence long before the time of Augustus—that will not save it from being rejected. Thus, relate whatever it may, it cannot escape censure. But we do not think that the present instance "is only conceivable on the supposition that the offices of the two kings were honorary, and unaccompanied with real power." We are of opinion, as we have endeavoured to show, that Romulus, during the reign of Tatius, was in reality quite subordinate; that he was a king only by sufferance, and, if not actually conquered, yet reduced to a condition that was not very different. It was the harmony, therefore, of the superior and the inferior; of the man who could command, and the man who knew only to obey.

We have now gone through, we believe, all the objections that have ever been brought against the history of Romulus, certainly all that have been urged by Schwegler and Sir G. C. Lewis.

[1] Credibility, &c. vol. L p. 432, note 109; Dionys. ii. 57.
[2] Above, p. 115.   [3] Rom. 25.   [4] Lib. ii. c. 16.

It has been subjected to the most searching ordeal by men of great learning and acuteness; it has been examined and cross-examined like a witness in a court of justice; all its weak points have been probed to the very bottom, and yet we are of opinion that nothing has been established to shake its general probability and truth.

With regard to the results of the inquiry, we think it may be affirmed that such a king as Romulus actually existed, and that he was the founder of Rome. If he was invented as its founder, the invention was a very clumsy one; for, unless facts had not been too strong for them, the Romans, with their desire to trace back their origin to the heroical ages, would have done better to go at once to Æneas or Ulysses, just as the Tusculans claimed Telegonus, or the Venetians Antenor. But Rome was a late-founded city, the very latest indeed in those parts; Alba Longa, and probably several other cities in the neighbourhood, had been in existence several centuries before it. In the face of these facts, it was impossible to place its foundation in the Trojan times. The memorials of Romulus as its founder were too recent to be obliterated or forgotten. There were considerably less than two centuries of astronomical years between the death of Romulus and the completion of the Capitoline Temple by Tarquinius Superbus; perhaps not more than a century and a half, if, as is very probable, the length of the reigns of the first two kings has been exaggerated. For though it is possible that the death of Numa may have been recorded in the Annales Maximi, which were preserved, yet the death of Romulus and the accession of Numa could not have been so recorded; and hence there was an opportunity to exaggerate the length of the reign of these two kings; which could not be done with those of their successors. And in the Capitol Tarquinius placed the statues of all the kings that had reigned before him. Livy, a judicious and sensible, not to say somewhat sceptical writer, intimates no doubt that Rome was founded by Romulus, though he rejects all that precedes its foundation as a tissue of fables; and indeed well might he reject so clumsy a contrivance as the connecting of Rome's history with that of Alba; a city with which the Romans appear to have had no connexion till the time of their third king, and then a hostile one. But it was their only chance of tracing their descent from the heroical ages.

If they had an inducement to invent this part of their story, they could have had none to invent the facts of the reign of

Romulus, several of which redound very little to their glory. The opening of an asylum for fugitives and vagabonds, the rape of the Sabines, the partial subjugation of their city by Tatius, are events which are very likely to have taken place in those days in a newly-founded state; but they are not such as a man, forming a history of his countrymen from imagination, would have been likely to invent. The reign of Tatius especially, whose name appears to have been very unpopular among the Romans, must have been highly unpalatable; and nobody who wished his story to be accepted would have ventured on imagining it.

The events just enumerated we believe to be true in the main; also the institutions of Romulus, and his wars, in their general outline, but not perhaps in detail. In many of the circumstances of his reign there may, perhaps, be some exaggeration; and the supernatural parts of it are of course false in themselves, but not false as viewed in relation to the ideas and manners of the age, and what the Romans were then capable of believing. On the whole, we think that the history has suffered more from oblivion and obliteration of parts, which render it sometimes obscure, than from invention and interpolation.

We will now proceed with the course of the history.

SECTION IV.

THE INTERREGNUM.

No sooner was Romulus dead than disputes about the supreme power, and a desire to seize it, arose among the Fathers. These factions were not excited by individuals, for, as among a new people, there was nobody who was particularly eminent; they arose rather among the different orders of the state. The Sabine part of the population, which since the death of Tatius had not been represented by a king, desired one to be chosen from among them, lest they should be deprived of their just share of power; while the old Romans, on the other hand, disdained a foreign sovereign. Yet, though views were divided on this point, the kingly form of government was universally desired, since there was no experience of the liberty enjoyed under a commonwealth. In this state of things the Fathers became alarmed lest, as the disposition of many of the surrounding cities was hostile towards Rome, some attack from without should be made upon it, while it was thus without a government, and the army without a general. All thought that some head should be appointed, yet none could prevail upon himself to concede that post to another. As a method of compromise, therefore, the hundred Fathers agreed to take the government upon themselves; dividing themselves into ten decuriæ, in each of which certain individuals should be appointed in whom the supreme power was to be vested. Ten ruled by turns, but only one among them had the lictors and the ensigns of royalty. His reign lasted five days, and was enjoyed by all in turn. This mode of government lasted a year, and, from its occurring between the reign of two kings, was called the *Interregnum*, a name which it still retains. But now the plebeians began to show symptoms of discontent, and loudly complained that their servitude was multiplied, that they had a hundred masters instead of one. When the Fathers became aware of this feeling, they resolved to gain the favour of the people by offering spontaneously what they would otherwise be forced to concede; and while they gave the supreme power into the hands of the people, they at the same time retained as much privilege as they bestowed. For they decreed that whomsoever the people[1] chose for a king should be confirmed in that dignity, if they ratified the choice by their authority. The same rule is observed now[2] in proposing laws and magistrates, though the force of it is destroyed. For the Fathers give their authority before the people give their votes.

Then the Interrex, having called an assembly, addressed it as follows:—"Choose a king, Quirites; such is the decision

[1] These passages show that the *populus* might include some *plebeians*. It is the plebeians who begin to murmur, "fremere deinde *plebs*," and they are pacified by the election of a king being referred to the *populus*, "adeo ki gratum plebi fuit," &c.—Liv. l. 17. The *populus* was the army—those who had a right to vote—and among these the clients were plebeians. Though there were also, perhaps, other plebeians who formed no part of the *populus*. The sequel of the passage shows that the Senate reserved a *veto* on the choice of the people.   [2] That is, in Livy's time.

of the Fathers; and may your choice be auspicious. The Fathers will give it their authority, provided you shall elect a king who may be worthy of succeeding Romulus." The people were so gratified by this proceeding that, not to appear behindhand in liberality, they merely passed a resolution that the Senate should name the person who was to rule over them.

It happened that there was then living at Cures, in the Sabine territory, a man named Numa Pompilius, famed for his justice and piety. He was also as perfectly skilled as it was possible to be in that age, in all law, both divine and human. His teacher, because no other can be pointed to, is falsely said to have been the Samian Pythagoras; but it was certainly more than a hundred years later, in the reign of Servius Tullius, that Pythagoras gathered round him a crowd of studious youths in the furthest part of Italy, about Metapontum, Heraclea, and Crotona. From which distant places, even if he had been contemporary with Numa, how could his fame have reached the Sabines? or how, as he taught in a language they were ignorant of, could any among them have desired to become his pupil? or with what guard could a single man have arrived there, who would have had to traverse the territories of so many races, differing in language and manners? I am of opinion, therefore, that Numa derived his virtues from his own mind and temperament, and that his knowledge and wisdom were not so much the fruits of foreign learning, as of that severe and rugged discipline which distinguished the ancient Sabines, formerly the least corrupted of all peoples.

The Roman Fathers, on hearing the name of Numa, did not venture to prefer any one of their own faction, nor any one of the other Fathers or citizens, to him; and although they were aware that, by choosing a Sabine king, they should add great weight to that party, yet they unanimously decreed that the crown should be offered to Numa.

Dionysius says [1] that the Romans and Sabines had agreed that the one race should choose a king among the other, and

[1] Lib. II. c. 58.

it is possible he may here be right, as Livy says that the choice was made by the Roman Fathers only. This would account for the alternation of Roman and Sabine kings—Romulus, Numa Pompilius, Tullus Hostilius, Ancus Marcius.

REMARKS.—Schwegler postpones his remarks about the interregnum till he comes to review it as part of the Roman constitution.[1] With respect to its historical worth, he observes that those who see in Romulus and Numa only imaginary personages cannot doubt that the interval between them is also devoid of authenticity, and that all that the historians say about it are mere abstractions from the later constitution. This is the more certain, as the elaborate (*durchdachte*) system of politico-religious ideas out of which the peculiarly Roman institution of the Interregna proceeded, could not possibly have existed in the first beginnings of the city, but could only have been gradually developed. Lastly, it appears from the contradictions of the historians, that their accounts of the details were not taken from authentic tradition, but were constructed by them. And he illustrates this by remarking, in a note, that Livy does not agree with Dionysius, nor these two with Plutarch; and that Zonaras, who copies Plutarch, must have found a different account in Dio Cassius, since he says that he knows of other things having been said respecting the interregnum.

Schwegler's position, that those who do not believe in Romulus and Numa will not believe in the interregnum, will not be disputed, but is not conclusive for those who do believe, nor convinces them that it is a mere abstraction. Nor will they be convinced by considering the elaborateness of the system; for the rule of ten senators in turn seems a simple contrivance enough, and the most natural one to have been adopted in the abeyance of a king. That Dionysius should disagree with Livy may not seem extraordinary after what we have already seen of the former historian, nor does it afford any conclusive argument against the truth of the history. But the fact is, that in this case they substantially agree, as Sir George Cornewall Lewis acknowledges,[2] and Cicero[3] also agrees, though in general terms. They differ only in the number of the senators, which Livy makes 100, and Dionysius

[1] Buch xlv. § 15.   [2] Credibility, &c. vol. I. p. 442, note 109.
[3] De Rep. II. 12.

200. The subject of the number of the Senate we shall examine in another place. We need hardly trouble ourselves about Plutarch, or Zonaras, who copies him; and if the latter found in Dio Cassius something that differed from Plutarch, it was probably the more correct accounts of the Latin historians, for Dio Cassius is a much better source than Plutarch.[1]

Schwegler goes on to suppose that the annalists—meaning, we suppose, Fabius Pictor, Cincius Alimentus, and the earliest writers of Roman history for the public—had related the first interregnum only briefly and obscurely, just as Livy relates the two following interregna. "They related summarily," he says,[2] "how after the death of Romulus the power of the state returned to the Patres, and how the Patres conducted the interregnum, until an agreement was come to about the election of the new king. The later historians, each interpreting the brief account of the annalists in his own fashion, have by the term *patres* understood the Senate. But as in the time of the republic it was not the Senate, or the patrician part of the senators, but the whole body of patricians to whom during an interregnum the ruling power devolved, and who chose the Interrex, so we may suspect that these writers, misled by the later method of speaking, misunderstood the term *patres*, which they found in their sources, and erroneously referred it to the Senate, instead of the whole body of patrician citizens. This assumption has the less difficulty, since Livy has made the same mistake with regard to the *patrum auctoritas*, and Cicero with regard to the *patres minorum gentium*."

In this very modest paragraph, *all* the ancient writers who have described the first interregnum are set down for ignoramuses, while a few German critics, like Becker and Schwegler himself, are alone in the right. Among these blundering writers, Schwegler enumerates in a note Livy, Dionysius, Plutarch, Appian, Vopiscus, Eutropius, Sextus Rufus, Servius, and Suidas. The reputation of some of those writers we will not undertake to defend; but we will add another to the list, whom Schwegler has not thought fit to mention. Cicero also is of opinion that the first interregnum was conducted by the Senate. For he tells us:[3] "Ergo quum ille Romuli *senatus* ... tentaret post Romuli excessum ut ipso gereret sine rege rempublicam," &c. And a few lines further: "Quum prudenter

[1] Plutarch absurdly states that each interrex ruled only for six hours of the day, and six hours of the night. [2] R. L. S. 657. [3] De Rep. ii. 13.

illi principes novam et inauditam ceteris gentibus *interregni incundi* rationem excogitaverunt, ut, quoad certus rex declaratus esset, nec sine rege civitas, nec diuturno rege esset uno," &c.

From this consentient view of the best authorities, an unprejudiced person might be inclined to suspect that it is not they, but the German critics, who are in error. And there are a few considerations which suggest that this may really be the case.

First, if these authorities were misled by the following later usage in their interpretation of the term *patres*, and referred it to the Senate instead of the whole patrician body, it is only natural to suppose that they would also have been misled by later usage *in the thing itself*, as well as the term; and that, in accordance with the more modern custom, they would have referred the interreges created after the death of Romulus to the whole patrician body, and not exclusively to the Senate. But here their account is at variance with the custom of their own times. They do not, *by construction*, refer a usage that prevailed under the republic to the times of Romulus. It is the German critics themselves who are guilty of this very unhistorical and uncritical method, which they are so ready to charge against the ancient writers; and who infer, *by construction*, that a practice which existed under the republic also existed at the very beginning of the monarchy.

But, secondly, there must have been a vast difference between the patrician body in the time of Romulus, and in the time of the republic, or even of the subsequent kings. It had in the time of Romulus only just been created. Besides the senators themselves, the remaining patricians were their own children, young men who, according to the severe Roman laws of paternity, were entirely in their power; whilst in a few generations not only would this near relationship have in a great measure ceased, but also the patrician body not included in the Senate would have become much more numerous and powerful. And here we have a reason why the Romulean Senate may have asserted an authority which they could not maintain in later days.

It will be seen that we here adopt the view of the ancient writers, that the patrician body sprung from the senators created by Romulus. Our reasons for thinking that this was their real origin, and that they did not consist of the whole body of citizens, will be given further on, when we come to treat of the early Roman constitution; where also we hope to show that it is not Livy and

Cicero, but the German critics, who have "made mistakes" about the *patrum auctoritas* and the *patres minorum gentium*.

Lastly, the Interreges who succeeded Romulus were entirely different in character from those of later times, when the office had become a merely formal one (though containing, perhaps, at the same time, a sort of protest, or latent claim, in favour of patrician privilege), for the purpose of naming a king, or other supreme magistrate. It was the design of the Senate, after the death of Romulus, to rule without any king at all; to be themselves kings by turns. Properly speaking, therefore, they were not Interreges; and that term can have been applied to them only *retrospectively*, after the people had compelled them to abandon that attempt, and to permit another king to be chosen. Hence it appears how erroneous it would be to argue backwards, as the German critics do, from the subsequent practice to the primitive fact.

From these considerations, and without insisting on the weight of ancient testimony, which, we are aware, is now considered mere dust in the scales, we are, nevertheless, of opinion that even the balance of mere probability is in its favour, when it tells us that the first Interreges were in the Senate, and created by the Senate.

"The method of proceeding in the election of a king," continues Schwegler, "was, according to the description of Livy[1] and Dionysius,[2] as follows: The Interrex summons an assembly of the people, to which, after previous consultation and agreement with the Senate, he proposes somebody for election: the people decide, and the Patres then confirm the person elected. Cicero apparently relates the proceeding differently:[3] the Interrex proposes (*rogat*), the Populus, assembled in Curiate Comitia, elects; and the elected person then obtains from the Curiæ the *imperium*, by means of a *lex curiata*. But though the account of Cicero differs in expression from that of Livy and Dionysius, it agrees entirely in substance. What the latter call *auctoritas patrum*, Cicero calls the *lex curiata de imperio*: both expressions signify the same thing, in so far as the confirmation of the Patres consisted in the conferring of the *imperium*. Though Cicero's account is more correctly conceived, because it clearly shows that the same curiæ which had elected the king, also conferred upon him the *imperium*; while the other account (even when we correctly take the expression *patres* of the

---

[1] Lib. i. 17, 22, 32, 47; iv. 3. [2] Lib. ii. 60; iii. 1, 36, &c.
[3] De Rep. ii. 13, 17, 18.

whole patrician body) presents a false appearance, as if the elective
assembly (the *populus*), and the confirming assembly (the *patres
auctores*), were different assemblies; although at that time there
was still only one kind of popular assembly—the Comitia Curiata.

The "false appearance" here imputed to the accounts of Livy
and Dionysius, exists only in the brain of the critic. For those
authors really meant that the electing assembly and the confirming
assembly were *different* bodies; that the first was the Comitia
Curiata, and the second the Senate. According to Schwegler's view,
the Comitia Curiata both elected and confirmed. A more absurd
blunder it is impossible to commit; a more preposterous assertion
cannot be made than that the *auctoritas patrum* and the *lex curiata*
were identical. It is on this ground that Schwegler reconciles the
accounts of Livy and Dionysius with that of Cicero. But the
accounts of these authors may be reconciled in a very different way;
namely, by a passage in Cicero which the German critics take care
to keep in the background, or at all events never quote at full
length. It is the following:—"Quibus quum esse præstantem
Numam Pompilium fama ferret, prætermissis suis civibus regem
alienigenam *patribus auctoribus* sibi ipse *populus ascivit;* eumque
ad regnandum Sabinum hominem Romam Curibus accivit. Qui ut
huc venit, quamquam populus curiatis cum comitiis regem esse
jusserat, tamen ipse de suo imperio *curiatam legem tulit*."[1]

Here we have the *patrum auctoritas* and *lex curiata* mentioned
as separate and distinct things. And while Cicero thinks it necessary to explain why Numa should have resorted *twice* to the same
body, the Comitia Curiata, first for his election, then for the *imperium*, he would certainly have explained further why he should
have gone to them *thrice*, if the *patres auctores* whom he mentions
were nothing else but these same Comitia. But we will not enter
further into these questions at present, as we shall have to consider
them again in the sequel.

Sir G. Cornewall Lewis observes[2] on the interregnum : "The form
of government which is recorded to have succeeded the death of
Romulus, and to have lasted for a year, is equally inconsistent with
experience, and its duration for so long a period is quite inconceivable. The senators, whether 100, 150, or 200 in number, are
related to have divided themselves into Decuriæ or companies of
ten; the order of precedence of each decuria was then determined

[1] De Rep. II. 13.   [2] Credibility, &c. ch. xl. § 10.

by lot; and each of the ten senators successively exercised the entire powers of king for five days, with the title of Interrex. According to this arrangement, seventy-three senators would have filled in turn the regal office during a year of 365 days. That so many transfers of the supreme power should, at a time when all constitutional and legal checks were in a very rude and inofficient state, have been quietly made, is wholly incredible. Even a community much more civilized than Rome could have been in the eighth century before Christ, above a hundred years before the legislation of Solon, could hardly pass with success through such an ordeal. A similar interregnum is related to have occurred between the reigns of Numa and Tullus Hostilius, and between those of Tullus Hostilius and Ancus Marcius; but in each case to have been of short duration. Dionysius says that the form of government was found to fail, on account of the difference of character and policy, in the successive Interreges; that in consequence the Senate consulted the people, whether the power should be placed in the hands of a king, or of annual magistrates; and that the people referred the matter back to the Senate, who decided in favour of a king. He does not, however, state (what would inevitably have happened) that this form of government led to civil discord, and to a successful attempt of some powerful and ambitious senator to retain his office for more than five days. This would be the certain result if such a polity were attempted as a permanent mode of government. Livy finds another cause for the discontinuance of the inter-regal form of government: he describes the people as complaining that they had a hundred masters instead of one, and as declaring that they would not endure any king in whose election they had no voice."

Let us observe, first of all, that the Romulean year is said to be of 365 days, though it is notorious that the astronomical year of twelve months was not introduced at Rome till the reign of Numa, and did not even then, probably, supersede the year of ten months in civil affairs, as we have endeavoured to show in the Introduction. But, though there can be no doubt about the Romulean year, at least, having had only ten months, yet that allowance is never made by modern critics.

Sir G. C. Lewis proceeds to observe that, under such a form of government as the interregnum, "some powerful and ambitious senator" would inevitably have succeeded in retaining his office for more than five days. Upon which we will observe that here also the ancient tradition is much more consistent and probable than the modern criticism. Among so recent a people there was not, as Livy expressly says, and could not possibly have been, any one senator much more powerful than the rest; and this was the reason, as Livy also tells us in the same passage, why none of the senators had aspired to be king.[1] In fact, if we consider that Rome had existed only thirty-one years—for we must deduct a sixth from the thirty-seven years ascribed to Romulus—and if we further reflect that the whole polity had, as it were, to begin anew after the Sabine invasion, we shall see that there had not been time for any one man or family to acquire vast possessions and a preponderating influence.

"A community much more civilized than Rome" would have had a much worse chance than she of passing through such an ordeal. It is by fortunate generals aided by mercenary armies, or by men whose families have accumulated great wealth and influence through a long series of years, that the supreme power in a state is commonly seized. The "constitutional check" at Rome was the best that could possibly be devised. *The people were the army.* Sir G. C. Lewis himself has shown, after Livy, that they were not disposed to endure any but a king of their own creating, though they did not actually *declare* so, as he makes them.[2] If, under such circumstances, an ambitious senator could have seized the throne, that, indeed, would have been a wonder.

And when we reflect how many consuls and dictators held the supreme power, not for five days, but for months and years together —for several of the consuls were elected three or four times over— and yet that, with two or three exceptions,[3] no attempt was made during centuries by any one of them to become absolute master or king, is not that, though not only true but indisputable, much more surprising than that not one of these five-day Interreges should have attempted it ! . Truly there is something in the old Roman character which we moderns do not quite understand.

[1] "Necdum a *singulis*, quia nemo magnopere eminebat in *novo populo*, provenerant factiones;" although, "certamen regni ac cupido patrum animos versabat."—Liv. l. 17.
[2] "Nec ultra nisi regem, et ab ipsis creatum, *videbantur passuri.*"—Lib. l. 17.
[3] Sp. Cassius, Maelius, and Manlius are said to have aimed at the regal power. But with respect to Maelius the charge seems to have been unfounded, and is not entirely certain with regard to the other two.

"The existence of the name and institution of the interregnum in the historical age of Rome," continues Sir G. C. Lewis, "may be considered, however, as a proof of its derivation from the regal period. We can only account for it on the supposition that it was an old constitutional form, which survived as a relic of a former state of things. It implies an elective royalty; for hereditary succession such an institution is not needed. The period of five days really existed in the historical time; and it was probably the term actually prescribed and observed under the kings, its shortness being dictated by motives of jealousy, and being intended to prevent any Interrex from acquiring a dangerous power. 'If it was known that the election of a king was impending, the security would in general be adequate; the parties contending for the throne would take care to prevent usurpation; but a permanent government of successive five-day kings would be an impossibility, if the king was really at the head of the state, and was not a mere honorary officer."

We have no remarks to make on this paragraph, in which Sir G. C. Lewis goes a great way to refute all that he has said before.

"It may be observed, likewise," proceeds that author, "that the name of *interrex* and *interregnum* is an absurdity as applied to the original institution, after the death of Romulus, in the form described by Cicero, Dionysius, Livy, and Plutarch. The reign of one of these five-day kings was only an interregnum in the sense that it came between the reign of a king and of another Interrex, or between the reigns of two Interregns. It was not conceived as intervening between the reigns of two kings."

Surely the whole space between the reigns of Romulus and Numa was an interregnum, whatever was the number of Interreges that filled it. And each of these individuals was therefore an *interrex*, and not a *rex*—for we must call him either one or the other. For as *rex* answers to *regnum*, so *interrex* answers to *interregnum*; and it would indeed have been an absurdity to call an *interrex* a *rex*.

"Dionysius, as we have seen, attributes the dislike of the people for the interregal system to the changeable character of the government. Cicero refers it to their love of royalty (*De Rep.* ii. 12), while Livy describes it as arising from a jealousy of the power of the Senate. Livy proceeds to say that the Senate conceded the election to the people, but retained a veto upon their choice. He believes that the formal confirmation of the Senate, given in later

L

times to the decision of the popular assembly even before it was made, had its origin on this occasion."

The object of this paragraph seems to be to throw discredit on the history by showing that the historians differed in opinion about the interregal system. Here, however, there is no question of *facts*, but only of *motives*; the fact is plain, that the people from whatever motive disliked the government. Livy, however, agrees with Cicero in representing the people as lovers of royalty.[1] Nor does he ascribe the resistance of the people to *jealousy* of the Senate. This is an interpolation of the critic's. What they complained of was the tyrannical nature of the government—they had a hundred masters instead of one;[2] which agrees very much with Dionysius's complaint of the changeable character of the government. Cicero also says that the people could not bear the interregal government.[3] And so, after all, the three authors do not vary widely differ.

In a note Sir G. Cornewall Lewis says :—"A fabulous account of the government of Œnarea, in Etruria, in Aristotle (*Mirab. Aus.* 94), may be compared with the description of this interregal government. The city in question is reported, from fear of falling under a single despot, to have placed the government in the hands of emancipated slaves, and to have changed them every year."

Contrasted would surely have been a better word than *compared*. The Romans wanted "a single despot;" and so far from placing their government in the hands of emancipated slaves for a year, would not trust it in the hands of their senators for five days.

"The election of the new king," continues Sir G. C. Lewis,[4] "is described as made by the Senate. Dionysius and Plutarch say that it was the result of a compromise between the old Roman and new Sabine senators : the former were to make the choice, but the person chosen was to be a Sabine. The regal office was accordingly offered to Numa Pompilius, a native of the Sabine town of Cures, the son of Pompilius Pompo. He was born on the natal day of Rome, and was therefore thirty-eight years old : his manners were simple and austere ; and he was renowned for his wisdom, and for his piety to the gods. At first with philosophic indifference to

[1] "Regnari tamen omnes volebant."—Lib. i. 17.
[2] "Fremere deinde plebs, multiplicatam servitutem, centum pro uno dominos factos."—Ibid.
[3] "Quum ille Romuli Senatus . . . tentaret post Romuli excessum ut ipse gereret sine rege rempublicam, populus id non tulit."—De Rep. ii. 12.
[4] Chap. xi. s. 11.

greatness he declined the proffered honour; but at last he yielded to entreaties, and was unanimously elected king by the Senate and the people. The ceremony by which the auspices in confirmation of this election were taken is minutely described by Livy."

If Numa was born in the same year that Rome was built, he was not thirty-eight years old when he was elected, but only thirty-two. For the Romulean year was incontestably one of ten months, and Romulus died after having reigned thirty-seven of such years, and the interregnum lasted one year. The paragraph offers no other subject of remark.

We will now return to the history, commencing with the ceremony just mentioned of Numa's installation.[1]

SECTION V.

REIGN OF NUMA POMPILIUS.

WHEN Numa arrived at Rome, he directed that the gods should be consulted by augury concerning his reign, just as Romulus in building the city acquired the kingdom by taking the auspices. He was therefore conducted to the citadel by an augur—who thereafter, by way of honour, obtained the augurship as a public and perpetual priesthood[2]—where he sat on a stone seat with his face turned towards the south. The augur, with his head veiled, took his seat on Numa's left hand, holding in his right hand a curved rod or sceptre, without any knot in it, which is called a *lituus*. Then, after a prayer to

---

[1] Sir G. C. Lewis's note at vol. i. p. 446 (No. 118), treats of a constitutional point which does not affect the credibility of the history, and to which we shall have an opportunity of returning.

[2] There must of course have been augurs at Rome before the arrival of Numa, or he could not have been consecrated by one; besides, Romulus himself was an augur. We make this remark because another passage in Livy (iv. 4) has sometimes been quoted as contradictory of the present one: "Pontifices augures, Romulo regnante, nulli erant: ab Numa Pompilio creati sunt." But of course Livy only means here that there was no public priesthood, or college, of augurs, in the time of Romulus; which is consistent with the present passage, in which he tells us that such a priesthood was established. According to Cicero (Rep. ii. 14), Numa also added two augurs to the former number, making five.

the gods, taking a view over the city and surrounding territory, he marked out and determined the regions from east to west; and he called the parts to the south, right, and the parts to the north left. He also determined in his mind, as a sign, some object opposite to him as far off as the eye could reach. Then, transferring the *lituus* to his left hand, and placing his right on Numa's head, he uttered the following prayer:—" O Father Jupiter, if it be lawful that this Numa Pompilius, whose head I hold, should be king of Rome, declare it unto us by sure and certain signs within those boundaries which I have marked out." Then he recited the auspices which he desired to be sent; on the appearance of which Numa was declared king, and descended from the temple.

Having thus obtained the throne, Numa prepared, through laws and customs, to found, as it were, anew the city which had been only so recently established by force of arms. He considered that it would be one of the best means to this end to mitigate the fierce disposition of the people by accustoming them to peace, for nothing tends more than war to render the mind ferocious. With this view, he established the Janus at the lowest part of the Argiletum, as an index of peace and war; so that when it was opened it signified that the city was at war, and when shut, that there was peace with all the surrounding nations. After the reign of Numa, it has only been twice shut: once in the consulship of T. Manlius, after the end of the first Punic war; and again, by a grace which the gods have reserved for our age, by the Emperor Cæsar Augustus, peace having been established both on sea and land after the battle of Actium. The Janus, therefore, being shut, and all the surrounding peoples being conciliated by alliances and treaties, Numa had to provide lest, in this absence of all external danger, the minds of the citizens, which had been hitherto restrained by fear of the enemy and military discipline, should luxuriate in idleness. Therefore he thought that the first thing to be done was to inspire them with fear of the gods—the most efficacious of all methods with a rude and uneducated multitude, as in that age they were. But as this could not be impressed upon them without

the contrivance of some miracle, he pretended that he had
nocturnal interviews with the goddess Egeria; that it was at
her bidding he instituted the sacred rites most acceptable to
the gods, and appointed for each divinity the proper priests.
And the first thing he did was to divide the year into twelve
lunar months. But as the moon does not complete thirty
days in a month, and as there are some days wanting to fill
up the whole year according to the course of the sun, he so
contrived, by interspersing intercalary months, that in every
twentieth year the days should come back to and agree with
the same place of the sun from which they had started, the
true period of all the years being thus completed. At the
same time he appointed the days called *fasti* and *nefasti*,
because it would be sometimes convenient that nothing should
be transacted with the people.[1]

Then he applied his mind to the creating of priests, although
he himself performed many sacred rites, and especially those
which belonged to the *flamen* of Jupiter. But as he thought
that in a warlike city there would be more kings like Romulus
than like himself, and that they would take the field themselves,—lest on such occasions the sacred rites discharged by
the king should be left unperformed, he created a regular *flamen*
of Jupiter, and appointed that he should wear a splendid vest-
ment, and should have the privilege of the royal curule chair.
He also appointed two other *flamines*, one to Mars, the other
to Quirinus. He also chose Vestal virgins, a priesthood that
had originated at Alba, and one not alien to the founder of
the state. To these he gave a stipend from the public money,
so that they might assiduously conduct the worship of the
temple; and he rendered them holy and venerable by the
vow of chastity, and by other ceremonies. Numa also built
himself a dwelling, or small palace, close to the Temple of
Vesta, which lay under the northern side of the Palatine
Hill, about midway between the Porta Mugionis and Porta

[1] That this new calendar was kept secret is evident because the people did
not know the *dies fasti* and *nefasti*. Hence we may infer that in popular use
the old calendar, and consequently the old civil year of ten months, went on.
We have adverted to this subject in the Introduction.

Romanula. This appears to have been his official abode as chief priest, as well as king; for he had also another residence on the Quirinal.[1] He also chose twelve priests of Mars Gradivus, called Salii, giving them the distinction of an embroidered tunic, and over that a brazen breastplate; and he appointed that they should carry those celestial shields called *ancilia*, and should make procession through the city, singing certain verses, accompanied with *tripudia* and a solemn dance. He then appointed as Pontifex Numa Marcius, the son of Marcus, one of the Fathers, and delivered to him all the sacred rites, written out and sealed. These directed with what victims, on what days, and in which temples, the sacrifices should be performed, and whence the money should be taken to defray the expense of them. And he subjected all other sacred rites, both public and private, to the decrees of the Pontiff; so that the people might have somebody to consult, and the confusion of the sacred law be prevented, either through neglecting the hereditary rites or adopting foreign ones. Nor was the jurisdiction of the Pontiff to be confined to celestial ceremonies, but was to extend to the due performance of funerals, and the rites for appeasing the Manes: also as to what prodigies, manifested either by lightning or in any other manner, were to be attended to and expiated. And in order to elicit them from the divine will, he dedicated on the Aventine an altar to Jupiter Elicius, and consulted that deity, by auguries, which prodigies were to be attended to.

The minds of the people being thus turned from arms and war to give their attention to these things, had something wherewith to occupy them: while the constant care of the gods, who seemed to be always present in human affairs, imbued the breasts of all with such a piety, that faith and the sanctity of oaths seemed to govern them, backed by fear of the laws and retributive justice. And as the manners of the citizens seemed to form themselves after the unique example of their king, so the neighbouring nations, who had before thought that a camp, rather than a city, had been placed in the midst of them, to disturb the peace of all, now

[1] Solinus, i. 21.

began to respect it, and to think it a wickedness to use violence towards a people that was totally occupied in the worship of the gods.

There was a grove near Rome through which ran a stream proceeding from a perennial fountain which burst forth in a dark cave. Here Numa frequently repaired alone, as if to meet the goddess, and dedicated it to the Camenæ, because their councils with his wife Egeria were held there. And he instituted a solemn worship to Faith alone; and bade the *flamines* repair to her temple in a carved chariot, and perform the service with the hand covered as far as the fingers, to show that faith was to be observed, and that it had a consecrated seat in the right hand. He also appointed and dedicated many other sacrifices, and places for performing them, which the pontiffs call Argei. But the greatest of all his works was the preservation of peace throughout his reign. Thus two kings in succession contributed, in different ways, to the augmentation of the city: one by war, the other by peace. Numa reigned forty-three years, according to Livy and Dionysius of Halicarnassus, and thirty-nine according to Cicero and Polybius.[1]

Cicero adds[2] to the above account, that Numa divided among the people the lands which Romulus had conquered; that he made the sacred rites which he instituted difficult to be learnt, from the number of observances, but easy to be performed on account of their cheapness: both which things would tend to enhance the character and influence of the priesthood, by the mystery in which it involved them, and by the inducement which it offered to the people to perform the rites. The same authority says that he also instituted markets, games, and other opportunities for the bringing of men together.

REMARKS.—The pacific, inert, and somewhat shadowy character of Numa, the attention which he directs almost exclusively to religious matters, and his reputed commerce with Egeria, have afforded the best handle to the sceptical critics for attacking the

[1] Cic. De Rep. II. 14. [2] Ibid.

early Roman history, and for attributing to it, as well as to Numa himself, a mythical character. We are nevertheless of opinion that there really was a king of that name, and that his reign occupied the space between that of Romulus and Tullus Hostilius. Our chief reason for this opinion—besides the constancy of tradition, which in the reign of Numa, or directly after, began to be fortified by record—is the improbability that the Romans in the age of Tarquinius Superbus, who erected in the Capitol statues of all his predecessors, should have forgotten the kings who reigned during the two preceding centuries, including Romulus as their founder. Further, if the history were fictitious, it is not to be believed that the Romans would have invented Numa, a Sabine king, and therefore a strong proof of enduring Sabine influence, if not domination, as the founder of their religious institutions. If they had had the liberty of choice, they would doubtless—as the history is confessedly written from the Roman point of view—have selected for this purpose a Roman; and, according to the hypothesis that the whole is a myth, it would have been just as easy for them to do this as to invent Numa.

Schwegler indeed remarks:[1] "If Numa appears as a Sabine, this has its motive not so much in the character of the worship which he established, since this—as, for example, the worship of Vesta, the Salii, &c.—is by no means peculiar to the Sabines. It was rather done because the Sabine race was renowned for its piety, and therefore a Sabine seemed best suited for the part of a Numa."

But, if the worship which he established was as much Roman as Sabine, that was a further reason for the myth to have preferred a Roman for its founder. And if a Sabine was selected because that race was conspicuously pious, then the Romans had already had a Sabine ruler in King Tatius; and the myth might have fathered the institutions upon him, without perpetuating a Sabine dynasty. But, in truth, Numa was the second King of Rome, because it was the turn of the Sabine part of the population to be represented on the throne. His piety is only a secondary and accidental consideration; though no doubt it might have been a motive with the Romans to elect him. Nor do we think that the objections brought against the history conclusively prove Numa to have been a mythical person, or even all the institutions established by him to have been false. These objections we shall now proceed to examine.

[1] S. 522, Anm. 1.

"We have already intimated," says Schwegler,[1] "how Numa is to be estimated. He is the counterpart, or, if you will, the complement, of Romulus. As the myth after which the early Roman history was constructed set out from the assumption that Rome began entirely afresh, brought with it absolutely no politico-religious dowry, but produced out of its own bosom its jurisprudence, its constitution, its religion, its worship, it became necessary to refer the introduction of its religious forms, as well as the establishment of the state, of the military system, and of the constitution, to some known individual. But the dissimilar qualities of a warlike hero and a religious founder could not be attributed to the same person, the first king, without the greatest improbability. In order to escape this, the myth attributed the foundation of Rome to two individuals, one of whom, a warlike prince and conqueror, founds the state; while the other, a peaceful prince and model of piety, a favourite and confidant of the gods, founds its religion and morals."

We have here an admission that it is more probable and conformable to truth that the political and military institutions of a state and its religious institutions should be introduced by two different persons than by the same person; and, therefore, the history as it stands is more probable and conformable to truth than if it had ascribed them all to Romulus. And we shall show further on that this was not necessarily an invention.

It is self-evident, and needs no argument to prove, that every city composed, as Rome is said to have been, of a mixture of different peoples,—Ramnes, shepherds, fugitives, Sabines, and others,—must begin with new institutions, and we have already pointed out that those introduced by Romulus were absolutely indispensable. If all these dissimilar elements had been described as united under a ready-made constitution, that assuredly would have been a myth. But the assertion that Romulus brought no politico-religious principles with him is quite unwarranted. We have already endeavoured to show that he had such principles by his Greek descent and education, and that he applied them both to his civil and religious institutions.

"That the state of the case with Numa," continues Schwegler, "was such as we have described, that he was no more an historical person than Romulus, is manifest from the abstract nature of his personality. He is nothing but the founder of the Roman religion

[1] Buch xi. § 6.

and ceremonial law. In this are included all his acts, his whole personal existence. For the rest he is quite a shadowy being, void of all individuality. The myth indicates this by saying that Numa was grey from his childhood. This trait is the more remarkable and instructive as the same thing is said of the dæmon Tages; who, as founder of the Etruscan discipline, is quite an analogous figure to Numa."

We may well doubt the critical judgment of an author who can assert that Tages is quite an analogous figure to Numa. Tages is a boy ploughed up in the fields, who, after delivering his precepts, vanishes as suddenly as he had appeared; Numa, when elected King of Rome, is a mature man, who has gone through a long course of education and discipline, and reigns many years over the Romans. Tages founds the new discipline of the Aruspices; Numa founds nothing new at all, but only establishes ceremonies and priesthoods in honour of gods already existing. The story of Numa's early greyness is found only in Servius;[1] it is not mentioned by the Roman historians, and is probably an absurd exaggeration.

Why nothing is attributed to Numa but his religious acts, we shall consider further on.

"The idea of a religious founder," continues Schwegler, "such as forms the groundwork of Numa's character, is, especially in its application to the age with which we are concerned, an utterly unhistorical and almost childish representation. Religious rites and usages are the oldest hereditaments of nations, and are found in the first dawn of history: no single individual has founded the religion of the Umbrians, the Sabines, or Latins. Still less can it be believed that, as is related of Numa, a single lawgiver should, in an already existing state, have introduced and founded the whole form of religious worship."

And yet there are instances of this having been done even in modern times. Luther introduced and established the whole form of the Lutheran worship; Calvin, that of the Presbyterian Church; and the founders of the Church of England, that of the Anglican Church. Mahomet founded the substance as well as the forms of the Mahometan religion; not to speak of Moses and the Jewish religion.

All forms of religious worship, even the oldest, must have had an origin, and have been founded by some person or persons.

[1] Ad Æn. vi. 809.

NUMA AS A RELIGIOUS FOUNDER. 155

Rome was a new nation, and, from the mixed character of its population, must have required some lawgiver of this kind. Romulus, as Schwegler shows, was not a particularly religious person; nor would his frequent wars and the pressing necessity of regulating the civil and military constitution of the state have allowed him much time for the affairs of religion. Nor is it true that Numa is supposed to have founded the *whole* form of religious worship. There must have been forms for those Greek and other deities already established by Romulus; and for those Sabine ones established by Tatius on the Quirinal. Nor were the forms introduced by Numa altogether new, as Schwegler himself will tell us immediately.

"The legend of Numa," proceeds that author, "is further refuted by the following consideration. Had Numa really established the observances and institutions which tradition ascribes to him, these must have been peculiar to the Romans; or where they are found among other nations, these nations must have borrowed them from the Romans. Now they are all found among one or the other of the two races composing the Roman nationality, although it is incapable of proof, and indeed is not even probable, that either of the races derived them from the Romans. Thus Numa is said to have established the worship of Vesta, and appointed the first Vestal virgins. But the worship of the goddess of the hearth was common to the Latins and Sabines from the very beginning; it belongs to the earliest and most widely disseminated worship of the whole Italo-Hellenic race; and the priesthood of Vesta was one of the oldest priesthoods of the Latins. It is, therefore, incredible, whether Rome was a colony of the Alba Longa or not, that the service of Vesta should have been introduced at Rome by the second king, a Sabine; on the contrary, the original settlement on the Palatine must have had this worship, and have possessed a common hearth of the city. In like manner the institution of the Salii, and the establishment of the Pontifices and Flamines, are ascribed to Numa; but all these priesthoods can be shown to have been old Latin institutions; and Salii especially are found at Alba Longa, at Tibur, and Tusculum. It is further said, that Numa established the worship of Quirinus in honour of the deified Romulus. But Quirinus appears before this among the gods to whom King Tatius erects altars; he was an ancient national deity of the Sabines, and his worship was certainly older than the foundation of Rome. The same may be said of the worship of Terminus, which Numa is related to have introduced; while, according to another tradition, Tatius had already built an altar and founded a chapel to that god. Lastly, the institution of the Fetiales is attributed to Numa, though it was from ancient times common to all the Italian peoples of the Latin-Sabine stock. The opinion, therefore, must be abandoned that all these institutions proceeded from the second King of Rome. Rather, according to all probability, the original settlers on the Palatine, and the first immigrants on the Quirinal, must have brought the one or the other of these worships with them, and the amalgamation of them into the Roman religion must have been a work of gradual mediation and reconciliation."

This agrees with what we have already said, that Numa was not so entirely the founder of the Roman religion as is asserted by those whose object it is to make him appear, on that account, a mythical person. We are of opinion, however, that it did not take a very long while to reconcile all these different worships, and that Numa may have done a great deal in this way. Paganism, having no dogmas, was not shocked by a variety of rites, but easily admitted them all.

The first part of the paragraph just quoted contains a palpable fallacy. It does not follow that the institutions which Numa established must have been peculiar to the Romans, and whom they are found among other nations must have been borrowed from them. This might be true if Numa had *invented* these institutions; but nobody says that he did. The worships which he established were not new. His great work was the establishment of a hierarchy to superintend the religious services in general, and the appointment of regular priests for the service of those deities whom he found already established, or whom he introduced, at Rome.

Among these, it is not incredible that Numa may have introduced the worship of Vesta. If that worship was a Latin as well as a Sabine institution, and even more Latin than Sabine, yet, as we have endeavoured to show that Romulus was of Greek descent, this may not affect the question. Besides, in the early part of his reign at least, when there was such a dearth of women, he would not have been much inclined to devote any of them to a life of chastity. Nor, if there was any truth in the scandal about his mother, might he have felt much reverence or liking for the institution. Moreover, Schwegler himself shows in a note[1] that the near connexion of the Flamen Quirinalis—whose institution is universally attributed to Numa—with the Vestals, strengthens the probability that the latter also may have been instituted by him. Thus, as Schwegler points out, it is the Flamen Quirinalis who accompanies the Vestals to Cære, and it is in his house that the sacred utensils of Vesta's temple are buried.[2] To which may be added that it was the Flamen Quirinalis and the Vestals who offered the sacrifice at the Consualia.[3] The connexion of the Flamen Quirinalis with the Vestals may have arisen either from the reputed origin of Romulus, or because Romulus, as the founder of the city, was necessarily connected with the public hearth of the city.

It is nothing to the purpose to show that the worship of Quirinus and Terminus, and the institutions of the Salii, Pontifices, and Flamines, may have existed elsewhere than at Rome, and before the time of Numa; since he is not said to have invented them, but only to have established them. And, indeed, the circumstance that these institutions were not original, but copied, tells very much against the argument for making Numa a mythical personage, and shows him only a careful, plodding, commonplace sort of king.

"The Roman tradition," continues Schwegler, "shows by its inconsistencies that the attributing of these institutions to Numa rests not on any certain historical grounds, but is a mere inference from probability. The introduction of the Fetial ceremonies, for instance, is not universally attributed to Numa, but by some writers to Tullus Hostilius, by others to Ancus Marcius. The motive for these different accounts is clear. The introduction of the institution was ascribed to Numa as the founder of the Roman sacred law, of which the Fetial law formed part. Others, on the contrary, considered that so peaceable a prince as Numa, who never went to war, would not have introduced the institution of the Fetials, and regulated the forms for declaring war, but rather his warlike successor, Tullus Hostilius. From both these considerations together proceeded the account which attributed them to Ancus Marcius, who, according to Livy,[4] had a temper between that of Numa and Tullus, and was therefore a likely person to institute

[1] S. 554, Anm. 2.   [3] Liv. v. 40; Val. Max. L. 1, 10.
[2] Above, p. 71, sqq.   [4] Lib. i. 32.

warlike ceremonies. There is the same variance about the worship
of Vesta, which is sometimes attributed to Numa and sometimes to
Romulus, and about the institution of the augurs, which is also
ascribed to both those kings; whilst sometimes Numa and sometimes Tatius is represented as introducing the worship of Quirinus.
The same also holds good with respect to Terminus. The introduction of the year of twelve months is ascribed by others to
Tarquinius Priscus; the division of the Roman territory into districts or *pagi* with their proper magistrates, to Servius Tullius, as
well as the founding of the trade guilds. Tradition, in referring
these institutions to Numa, did not do so on precise and certain
historical evidence, but only because the character of these institutions seemed to suit the general idea formed of Numa."

It may be asked why, if the author really thought that there was
any weight in these objections, he should have before represented
Numa as so entirely the founder of the Roman religion, and even
on that account have compared him with the supernatural Tages?

If some of the institutions mentioned were referred to Numa on
account of his general character, that is enough to show what his
general character was; and in a matter of such high antiquity this
may suffice. It is no fatal objection that the origin of some of his
institutions was disputed by Roman antiquaries. In what country
that has an ancient history have not such matters been disputed?
On the other hand, we do not find it doubted that he was the chief
founder of the Roman priesthood, and of the sacerdotal system, and
the only founder of the Roman sacred law. These are his chief and
most important characteristics, and in comparison of them it is of
little moment whether he may or may not have introduced a few
ceremonies and worships. That he was the founder of the religious
law there was indeed documentary evidence, which must have been
in existence at least down to the Gallic conflagration; for he had
written it out and attested it, and delivered it into the custody of
the chief pontiff. Yet, though this document must have lasted
centuries, it is denied that the early Roman history was at all
supported by documentary evidence, that there was anything to
show that Numa was not a mythical personage, and even his name
an invention!

But, even about the institutions in question, more contradiction
has been imputed than really exists. Although there appears to be
a discrepancy between Cicero and Livy, respecting the origin of the

declaration of war by Fetiales, the former referring it to Tullus Hostilius, the latter to Ancus Marcius;[1] yet Livy does not contradict himself, as Schwegler intimates.[2] The Fetiales which that historian introduces in the reign of Tullus Hostilius[3] are not employed in declaring war, but in making a treaty. Livy, in the preceding chapter, represents the Romans and Albans as going to war without any previous declaration: and the Fetiales are only employed to draw up the treaty containing the conditions to be imposed by the result of the combat between the Horatii and the Curatii. It is very likely, therefore, that Numa, as Dionysius and Plutarch state,[4] may have introduced Fetial laws, though they did not extend to the particular case of declaring war; a circumstance which agrees with his peaceable reign, for he made many treaties, though he made no wars.[5] Livy, in describing the Fetial ceremonies introduced by Ancus Marcius, expressly limits them to the declaration of war.[6] But it is inconceivable, if the institution had been altogether new, that Livy should not have also mentioned its other and more peaceable functions. The declaration of war was only something superadded to the already existing functions of the Fetiales. That Livy knew of their previous existence is evident from his mentioning them under the reign of Tullus; and there is, therefore, no ground for charging him with contradicting himself in the course of a few pages. This gradual development of the Fetial law, moreover, may have contributed to throw some obscurity over its origin; and Cicero finding the Fetials employed for the first time—for Numa made no wars—under Tullus, in the war between Rome and Alba, may have inadvertently concluded that they had their origin then. If there is any truth in these remarks, then Schwegler's ingenious invention of a motive for these different accounts falls to the ground.

The controversy about the foundation of the Temple of Vesta was an idle one. Cicero and Livy, the two best authorities for the early

[1] Cic. De Rep. ii. 17; Liv. i. 32.
[2] S. 555, Aum. 2.
[3] Ibid. c. 24.
[4] Dionys. ii. 72; Plut. Num. 12.
[5] "Quum omnium circa finitimorum societate ac foederibus junxisset animos."—Liv. i. 19.
[6] "Ut tamen, quoniam Numa in pace religiones instituisset, a se bellicae cerimoniae proderentur; nec gererentur solum, sed etiam indicerentur bella aliquo ritu; jus ab antiqua gente Æquicolis, quod nunc fetiales habent, descripsit, quo res repetuntur."—Lib. i. 32.

history of Rome, both affirm that it was founded by Numa.[1] Some nameless writers, indeed, without consulting any evidence, inferred merely from the presumption that, as Romulus was reputed to have sprung from Alba, and as the worship of Vesta was established there, he must have introduced it at Rome; but Dionysius, who appears to have examined this question with more than usual diligence, calls their writings empty and foolish.[2] And he adduces as a conclusive argument against them the situation of the Temple of Vesta; which stood not within the walls of Roma Quadrata, or the original Romulean city, and could not, therefore, have been founded by Romulus. No argument, then, can be adduced against the credit of the history from such a variation as this, which is no real one; any more than it would be an argument against the truth of English history, if some silly writer should deny the Norman Conquest.

The difference about the augurs being instituted by Romulus or Numa arose, as we have already shown, merely from a misapprehension of terms. There were no doubt augurs in the time of Romulus; but it was Numa who first formed them into a college, or priesthood. The same answer may be made to the objection about Quirinus. Tatius may have consecrated an *altar* to him as an old Sabine deity;[3] yet it was Numa who first made his worship a more regular service, dedicated a *temple* to him (*ædes Quirini*), and appointed a Flamen Quirinalis. How Romulus came to be identified with Quirinus is quite another question, and involves a mystery to which we have no clue. But there is no difference of opinion on this point; all the authorities are unanimous. And perhaps it may have arisen from Romulus being reputed the son of Mars. Terminus also may be placed in the same category as Quirinus. It was only an altar, as Varro tells us (*loc. cit.*), that Tatius dedicated to this deity; and, with several more vowed by that monarch, it was on the Capitoline Hill. But when it was to have been exaugurated, in order to make room for the Capitoline Temple, we find that it was something more than an altar; it was then a *fanum*.[4] Now *fanes*, Varro tells us,[5] must be consecrated by the Pontifices, and in the reign of Tatius there were no Pontifices.

[1] Cic. De Rep. li. 14; Liv. l. 20.
[2] τοὺς δὲ οἱ τὰς αἰτίας οὐκ ἐξετάσαντες καλῶς, ἐλεωτέρας ἐξεηγήσαντο τὰς γραφάς.—Lib. ii. 64.
[3] Varro, Ling. Lat. v. 74.
[4] "Aves in Termini fano non addixere."—Liv. l. 55. [5] Ling. Lat. vi. 54.

Therefore Numa must have made some addition to the worship of Terminus, and, indeed, Plutarch[1] says that he erected *a temple* to that deity.

So, after all, we find that the charge against the history, on account of variation in the traditions respecting the religious institutions of Numa, amounts to little or nothing. With regard to his civil institutions, we find only one author, Junius Gracchanus,[2] who attributes the introduction of the year of twelve months to Tarquinius Priscus instead of Numa. If Dionysius has contradicted himself in attributing the division of the Roman territory and the institution of *pagi* both to Numa and Servius Tullius, this is no more than what that author frequently does; and there is no such contradiction in the Latin sources, although Plutarch also attributes the *pagi* to Numa.[2] Dionysius has here confounded the Terminalia with the Paganalia. He says that Numa caused the boundaries of private fields to be marked out by *termini*, sacred to Jupiter Terminalis; that he also marked out the public territory in the same manner, and instituted the festival of the Terminalia. And of Servius Tullius he says, that he caused the Roman territory to be divided into tribes, and instituted *pagi*, or places of refuge for the rustic population in case of hostile invasion, with proper magistrates, and instituted the festival of the Paganalia.[4] So far there is no contradiction; but two chapters further on (ii. 76), Dionysius also attributes the institution of the *pagi* to Numa. Neither Livy nor Cicero says that Numa instituted the trade unions or guilds, unless we are to include them under Cicero's general expressions, that he instituted markets, games, and all kinds of occasions for the people to meet together.[5] Guilds, however, are mentioned as the institution of Numa by Pliny and Plutarch.[6] Schwegler, by way of making a contradiction, asserts that one author—Florus—ascribes them to Servius Tullius. But, in reality, Florus does no such thing, as will be seen from the passage on which this assertion is founded, which we subjoin in a note.[7]

---

[1] Num. c. 16.   [3] Ap. Censorinum, De Die Nat. c. 20.
[2] Num. c. 16.   [4] Dionys. II. 74; iv. 15.
[5] "Idemque mercatus, ludos omnesque conveniendi causas et celebritates invenit."—De Rep. ii. 14.
[6] Plin. N. H. xxxiv. 1, § 1; xxxv. 46, § 159; Plut. Num. 17.
[7] "Ab hoc (Servio Tullio) populus Romanus relatus in censum, digestus in classes, decuriis atque collegiis distributus: summaque regis sollertia ita est

Florus is describing the centuries instituted by Servius; and by *collegiis* he only means—as indeed Schwegler himself seems to suspect in a note—the centuries of carpenters and smiths attached to the army, and not such trades as potters, or dyers, or goldsmiths, who would have been of no use in war.

And thus the accounts of Numa's civil institutions are not more contradictory than those of his religious institutions.

"If we subtract," continues Schwegler, "from the traditional history of Numa, which almost wholly consists of an enumeration of his religious and civil regulations, all those worships and institutions which he cannot have founded, since they existed before his time, as well as those regulations which tradition has ascribed to him merely from combination and inference, there remains nothing but the abstract idea of a religious founder; and even this idea of the second king is undoubtedly of mythical origin."

The main gist of this paragraph has been already answered, by showing that there are not many institutions that can be fairly abjudicated from him. But we do not see, even if we should deprive him of the greater part of them, how it follows that nothing would remain but "an abstract idea." And to ascribe this abstract idea to a myth seems to be to assign two origins for it that are wholly incompatible.

"In its other traits also," Schwegler proceeds to say, "the tradition of King Numa proves itself a fiction. An unbroken peace of forty-three years, which no neighbouring people ventures to break, out of reverence for the godly reign of so pious and just a king—such a period of peace and undisturbed equity is a beautiful dream, but no history. It is the more incredible in that age of violence, if Numa was really the successor of the warlike and conquest-loving Romulus. Numa's marriage with Egeria justifies the same conclusion; a trait which alone sufficiently proves that this portion of Roman history is still half mythology, and not real history. The person of Numa is no more historical than that of his consort Egeria."

There is a difference about the length of Numa's reign. Some authors place it at forty-three years, some at thirty-nine; and if

ordinata respublica, ut omnia patrimonii, dignitatis, ætatis, artium, officiorumque discrimina in tabulas referrentur, ac sic maxima civitas minimæ domus diligentia contineretur."—Lib. i. c. 6, s. 3.

these sums be reduced by one-sixth, they will be respectively thirty-six and thirty-three. And we are of opinion that even then the length of it may have been exaggerated.

That a peaceable sovereign may have remained at peace for some thirty years does not seem impossible, nor even highly improbable. The Romans, mindful of the reign of Tatius, had been careful to choose for his Sabine successor an unwarlike monarch, a sort of King Log, who they knew would employ himself in pottering about his priests and altars. James II. reigned twenty-two years without going to war, though he had much to provoke him to it. The situation of Rome at Numa's accession was, as Livy tells us, favourable to peace. The warlike prowess of the Romans had made a strong impression on their neighbours. Veii had been reduced to beg a peace, which was to last one hundred years, or eighty-three astronomical years. The Sabines, the most dangerous neighbours of the Romans, seeing a portion of their own race established at Rome, under a Sabine king, would not have been inclined to initiate a war against her. This motive continued to operate with them even as late as the reign of Tullus Hostilius, with whom they chose not to go to war till they had secured foreign aid, as Tatius had planted part of their own force at Rome.[1] The Latins might even have regarded the rising city with satisfaction, as a bulwark interposed between them and the Etruscans. The fear which the Latins entertained of the Etruscans is shown by the speech of the Alban Dictator, Fuffetius, to the Roman king, Tullus Hostilius, previously to the treaty respecting the issue of the combat between the Horatii and Curiatii; and the proposal that the two cities should be amalgamated rather than exposed to an attack from that quarter.[2] And Numa strengthened all these favourable conditions at his accession by concluding treaties with the surrounding cities.[3]

The fable of Egeria does not invalidate the personality of Numa. Such supernatural beings were in accordance with the belief of the age; the notion of his commerce with the gods would lend authority to his holy institutions; and it was with this view, we are

[1] "Sabini, haud parum memores et suarum virium partem Romæ ab Tatio locatam, et Romanam rem nuper etiam adjectione populi Albani auctam, circumspicere et ipsi externa auxilia."—Liv. i. 30.
[2] Liv. i. 23.
[3] "Quum omnium circa finitimorum societate ac fœderibus junxisset animos."—Liv. i. 19.

told, that the fable was invented. So, as Schwegler himself tells us further on, Minos received his laws from Zeus in a cave, Lycurgus his from the Delphic god, and Pythagoras his precepts from the Delphic priestess Themistocleia. If we reject the history on this account, we might on the same grounds reject the greater part of all ancient history, and especially of all Roman history. Down to a late period the affairs of the Romans were directed, or supposed to be directed, by the visible interposition of the gods, as manifested by augury and other means.

It must be acknowledged, however, that the reign of Numa is more shadowy and unsubstantial than those of the other Roman sovereigns. It seems probable that this characteristic may be due to the fact that the priests were the historiographers of Rome. They have no doubt exaggerated the virtues and concealed the defects of their founder, and have endeavoured to represent him rather as a lawgiver sent by heaven, than as an ordinary prince ruling by the dictates of worldly policy. But, though a halo may be thus flung around him, we do not think that it conceals his real personality, or invalidates the fact that the greater part of the institutions ascribed to him were really his.

"That the reigns of the first two kings," continues Schwegler, "form a peculiar order of things quite distinct from the later history, is shown in a certain manner by tradition, which makes the first sæculum of the city end with the death of Numa. The first secular festival after the expulsion of the kings was celebrated, according to the minutes of the Quindecemviri, in A.U.C. 298. If from this point we reckon back the sæcula at 110 years[1] each, then the beginning of the second sæculum is A.U.C. 78; and this year was, according to Polybius and Cicero, the first year after Numa's death; viz. Romulus 37 years, Interregnum 1 year, Numa 39 years = 77 years. Consequently, the year of Numa's death was the last year of the first sæculum. The old tradition, that Numa was born on the day of Rome's foundation, has the same meaning. For, according to the doctrine of the Etruscan Rituals, the first sæculum of a city ended with the death of him who, of all that were born on the day of its foundation, had attained the greatest age. Thus Numa's death forms, as this tradition seems to point out, the boundary between two epochs. And, in truth, with his

[1] As they are given by Censorinus, De Die Nat. c. 17; and also by Horace, Carm. Sec.

death the purely mythical period of Rome expired, and the half-historical period, the dawn of history, begins; while on the other hand the first two kings—the one the son of a god, the other the husband of a goddess—evidently belong to a different order of the world than the common one."

We have already had occasion to examine this paragraph in the Introductory Dissertation, and need not therefore dwell upon it here. The calculation is Niebuhr's,[1] and is founded, as we have shown, on a misinterpretation, as well as a very palpable mistranslation, of Censorinus. The story of Numa's having been born on the day Rome was founded, as asserted by Plutarch and accepted by Niebuhr and Schwegler, is doubtless a fable;[2] and all this ingenious calculation falls to the ground when it is considered that the Romulean year consisted of ten months, that Numa therefore, if born as stated, was thirty-two years old when he began to reign, and consequently, even if we take the years of his reign as astronomical years, was only seventy-one at the time of his death. And if it should be said that the year of ten months is to be carried on beyond the reign of Romulus, and beyond the celebration of the games in A.U.C. 298, which we willingly accept, then we further remark that no calculation at all can be founded on the Ludi Sæculares, which, in spite of their name, were celebrated at very irregular intervals.

And thus, too, the ingenious surmise that tradition pointed to Numa's death as forming the boundary between two epochs, also falls to the ground. Though so far we agree with Schwegler, that after this period tradition became more steady, as being supported by *contemporary* record.

We need not enter into Schwegler's seventh section, which concerns Numa's intercourse with Egeria; a subject on which we have already said enough, and on which no new light is here thrown, so far as the credibility or incredibility of the history is concerned.

In the following section Schwegler says: "The old tradition made Numa the disciple of Pythagoras. That, for chronological reasons,

[1] Röm. Gesch. i. 254, ff.
[2] Dionysius (ii. 58) says that he was not far from forty when elected, which would throw his birth a year or two before the foundation of Rome, even on the received calculation. The same author says (ii. 76) that he lived eighty years and reigned forty-three, which would make him thirty-seven at his accession, a year short of the age of Rome. Livy (i. 21) also gives his reign at forty-three years; and he would, therefore, have died in the year of Rome 81.

this could not have been so, was no secret to the later Romans; we can therefore only ask, how the existence of this tradition is to be explained?"

Schwegler then devotes four or five pages to this explanation; into which, however, we shall not follow him, as it seems to be a mere waste of time to seek conjectural reasons for the possible origin of what is universally admitted, by ancients as well as moderns, to have been a mistake.

The only point worth noticing in this paragraph is that Schwegler, with the view of course of damaging the early history, attributes the mistake to the "old tradition" ("die alte Sage"). In support of this assertion, he even misconstrues Plutarch. That author says: Ὥστε συγγνώμην ἔχειν πολλὴν τοῖς εἰς τὸ αὐτὸ Πυθαγόρᾳ Νομᾶν φιλοτιμουμένοις συνάγειν ἐπὶ τοσαύταις ὁμοιότησιν.[1] Which Schwegler renders: "One should pardon *tradition* if it has brought Numa into personal relation with Pythagoras" ("man müsse es der Sage zu gut halten, wenn sie den Numa in persönliche Verbindung mit Pythagoras gebracht habe"); when Plutarch only says, those *persons* or *writers*; and he concludes the section by saying that we may assume the tradition of Numa's Pythagorismus to have arisen in Rome about the time of the Samnite War, or at all events before the pretended discovery of Numa's writings in A.U.C. 573 (B.C. 181).

Before examining this subject, we will insert what Sir G. C. Lewis says upon it, as follows:[2]—"Owing to the popular conception of him (Numa) as a philosopher and wise man, he was represented as the scholar of Pythagoras, whose fame was doubtless more widely spread in Italy than that of Thales and other ancient philosophers of Greece and Asia Minor. This belief seems to have been prevalent at Rome from an early time, and was doubtless recognised by Fabius and other ancient historians. It was embodied in the forged books of Numa's religious laws, which were brought forward as having been found in his tomb on the Janiculum in 181 B.C. about twenty years after the end of the Second Punic War. When, however, Polybius and other careful historians came to compare the time assigned to Numa with the date of Pythagoras, they perceived that the disciple must have lived above a century and a half before the master, and therefore that the story was false. The anachronism is as if it were said that James I.

---

[1] Plut. Num. 22.   [2] Credibility, &c. vol. i. p. 449, *seqq*.

derived his maxims of government from Adam Smith, or Henry IV. from Montesquieu. As this legend could not have arisen till the age of Pythagoras, and the fact of his being contemporary with the last king, or with the first years of the Republic, had been forgotten, we can hardly suppose it to have been much earlier than the capture of Rome by the Gauls."

Now let us remark the inconsistencies of this statement. It assumes, first, that the *true* tradition, that Pythagoras was contemporary with the last King of Rome, who was expelled in B.C. 510, must have been forgotten before the capture of Rome by the Gauls, which happened in B.C. 390; or, in other words, that it must have been forgotten in less than 120 years. It assumes, secondly, that the *false* tradition, which arose before B.C. 390, must have survived till B.C. 181, when the pretended books of Numa were found,—that is, for a period of more than two centuries! The tradition was, of course, according to Sir G. C. Lewis's view, *oral;* and the first assumption is not inconsistent with his theory, that oral tradition cannot last much more than a century. But how shall we reconcile the second assumption with that theory which makes a false tradition, therefore an invention, and one after all of no great importance to the facts of Roman history, last more than two centuries?

That the story of Numa's Pythagorismus is an invention is admitted on all hands; that it was invented from some real or fancied similarity between Numa and Pythagoras we agree with Schwegler and Sir G. C. Lewis in thinking;[1] but we do not agree with the first of these writers, in placing its origin in the Samnite War, and still less with the second, in placing it before the capture of Rome. We think it was of a much more recent date, when the Romans had acquired a taste for literary discussion, and that it was probably invented, as it was almost certainly adopted, by the first Roman historical writers, Fabius, Cincius, and the rest. It is no objection to this view that Cicero makes Manilius exclaim, "Dii immortales, quantus iste est hominum *et quam inveteratus error!*" For these feigned interlocutors are mere puppets; Cicero is really speaking in his own person, and as the scene of the *De Republicâ* is laid in the Consulship of Sempronius Tuditanus and M. Aquillius, in the year B.C. 129, it might still even then be called an "inveteratus error," if it had originated at the beginning of that century. That it was at least adopted by the first Roman

[1] Schwegler, D. i. S. 561; Credibility, &c. vol. I. p. 452, note 137.

historians is, as we have seen, recognised by Sir G. C. Lewis as a matter beyond doubt. The true date of the origin of the story is not of much importance, but it could hardly have found that universal acceptance among the Romans which Cicero tells us it did,[1] unless it had appeared in their written and published historics. It is, however, objected to the story, in the same passage, that it was not confirmed by the authority of the STATE ANNALS,[2] by which must be meant the Annales Maximi and the Commentarii Pontificum. For, had Cicero been speaking of the works of Fabius and his contemporaries, he would have called them simply *Annales*. The words *publici* and *auctoritate* show that he meant something of more weight than these literary historics.

And even if it should be contended that *publicus* is not here to be taken in its usual sense of *public* or *state*, but merely means *published*, and that Cicero, in the person of Manilius, is only referring to the annals of Fabius and his contemporaries; still even that method shows that the mistake concerning Numa's Pythagorismus is not to be fathered, with Schwegler, on the "old tradition." For those writers, according to this mode of construing Cicero, would have mentioned no such story. Wherefore, in this view of the matter, it must have been a very recent invention; and the attacks of Schwegler and Sir G. C. Lewis on the early history on account of it fall therefore utterly harmless.

Schwegler's ninth and concluding section of this book is occupied with relating and discussing the discovery of the reputed books of Numa in the grounds of the scribe Petillius on the Janiculum. As these books were undoubted forgeries, and as they were publicly burnt by order of the Senate, it is impossible that they should throw any light on the history of Numa; and therefore we may be excused from following Schwegler into this subject. We shall only observe that his assertion that none of the Roman historians expresses any doubt of the authenticity of the books, is hardly true; since Livy, in a passage which Schwegler himself quotes, by mentioning that the books had the appearance of being quite new,[3] virtually implies, if he does not actually state, that they were

---

[1] "Et ita intelligimus vulgo existimari."—De Rep. ii. 18.
[2] "Neque vero satis id annalium publicorum auctoritate declaratum videmus."—Ibid. We have examined the chronological question in the Introduction.
[3] "Non integros modo sed recentissima specie."—Lib. xl. 29.

forgeries. And though Petersen, in his *Dissertatio de origine Historiæ Romanæ*, may claim them as genuine, yet we abandon them altogether, notwithstanding that their genuineness would have established at once the personality of Numa, as well as that he was the founder of the Pontifical law. At the same time we cannot admit the validity of one of Schwegler's reasons for rejecting them; namely, that writing was not practised at Rome in the time of Numa. We have endeavoured to show in the Introduction that such an assumption is contrary to all evidence. But we will allow that the writing would have been of a character so antique as not to have been so easily read as these pretended books are said to have been; but rather it must have resembled that of the treaty between Rome and Carthage in the first year of the Republic, which the most learned of the Romans in the time of Polybius could hardly make out.

We will now resume the history.

SECTION VI.

TULLUS HOSTILIUS.—THE ALBAN WAR.

ON the death of Numa, there was another interregnum till the people elected Tullus Hostilius king; a choice that was ratified by the Senate. Tullus was the grandson of that Hostilius who had fought so bravely against the Sabines at the foot of the citadel. He was not only unlike his predecessor in temper, he was even more ferocious than Romulus. His youthful age, his strength of body, the warlike fame of his ancestor, all stimulated him to deeds of glory. The peaceful state of the city seemed to him to resemble the decay of old age, and he therefore looked about on all sides for some occasion of war. Now, it happened that the Roman peasants were at that time accustomed to make depredations on the Alban territory, and those of Alba, in their turn, on the Roman. C. Cluilius then reigned at Alba; and in this state of things, it occurred that ambassadors were despatched on both sides, at about the same time, to demand restoration of the booty made. Tullus had instructed those whom he sent to lose no time in making their demands, judging that the Alban sovereign would surely refuse them, and that he might thus declare war without offending against the divine laws. The Albans managed the affair more leisurely. Tullus succeeded in entertaining and amusing them; and it was not till he had ascertained that his own ambassadors had declared war against Alba, to commence in thirty days, that he granted the Alban envoys an audience for business. No sooner had they explained their mission, than Tullus (in the manner of the first Bonaparte) upbraided them with the dismissal of the Roman ambassadors from Alba, and called the gods to witness that on the heads of those who had first taken this step would be all the slaughter and calamities of the war.

Such was the origin of what may almost be called a civil war, waged between parents and children, since both peoples traced their origin to Lavinium. Each side entered on it with the greatest ardour and most elaborate preparations. It turned out, however, less deplorable than might have been anticipated, since it was concluded without any pitched battle; and though one of the cities was ultimately razed, yet this calamity was compensated by the amalgamation of the two peoples. The Albans first took the field. They invaded the Roman territory with a large army, pitched their camp only five miles from Rome, and surrounded it with a fosse, or ditch, which, during many centuries, was called *Fossa Cluilia*, after the Alban leader; but, in time, both ditch and name have disappeared, and are forgotten. Whilst the Alban army was encamped here, Cluilius suddenly died; upon which the Albans created Mettius Fuffetius their dictator. This event augmented the courage and ferocity of Tullus. He gave out that the gods, having begun with the leader of the Albans, would take vengeance on the whole race for this iniquitous war; and, marching out in the night, and passing by the enemy's camp, he proceeded into the Alban territory, laying it waste as he advanced. This proceeding induced Mettius to leave his camp. He led his army as near to the enemy as he could, and then

sent an envoy to Tullus to demand a conference, in which, he
said, he was certain that he could communicate matters of no
less importance to Rome than to Alba. He appears to have
learnt that the Veientines and Fidenates had combined to
attack both Romans and Albans whilst they were destroying
one another; and some authors say[1] that the same piece of
intelligence had also reached Tullus. However this may be,
the proposal was not rejected by the Roman king. The two
armies were drawn up in line confronting each other, and
both leaders, accompanied by a few of their principal officers,
proceeded into the space between. Here the Alban leader
candidly confessed that though the refusal to restore plundered goods, as they ought to have been restored, according
to a treaty made between the two cities in the reign of
Romulus, served as a pretext for this war between two cognate
and neighbouring peoples, yet there could be no doubt that
the lust of empire was the real cause of it on both sides. He
then pointed out—what indeed was well known to the Romans
—the great power of the Etruscans, both on land and still more
at sea; and affirmed that they were only awaiting the result
of this battle to attack both the conquerors and the conquered
—an assertion which he seems to have proved by producing
letters. He then proceeded to advise the adoption of some
method by which the dispute whether Alba or Rome should
enjoy the supremacy might be settled without much loss or
bloodshed. To this proposal Tullus assented, though apparently with some reluctance, as the ferocity of his temper had
been still further inflamed with the hope of victory.

After several proposals regarding the manner in which the
question should be decided had been discussed and rejected,
it was at length resolved to stake the issue on the result of a
combat between three champions selected from each side.
It happened that in both armies were three brothers, fairly
matched in ages and strength, each triplet the offspring of a
single birth. Their names were the Horatii and the Curiatii;
but which were the Roman, which the Alban champions, has

---

[1] Diony., iii. 7.

been a subject of some doubt, arising probably from the clashing pretensions of those who bore the same family names at a long subsequent period. Livy, however, is the only author who mentions this doubt, and he admits that the greater number of authorities state that the Roman champions were called Horatii. The young men were easily persuaded by the leaders on each side to enter the lists, in order to decide by their skill and valour whether Rome or Alba should be mistress. But, before the signal was given for the combat, a treaty was entered into between the Romans and the Albans, to the effect that, whichever city's champions gained the victory, that city should peaceably assume the supreme government of both. However the conditions of treaties may vary, yet they are all concluded in the same manner; and as this is the earliest treaty which remains on record, we shall take the opportunity to describe the method of it. The Fetialis who acted on this occasion was M. Valerius, who had constituted Sp. Fusius Pater Patratus, by touching his head and hair with verbena. The Fetialis first put the following question to King Tullus: "Dost thou command me, O King, to make a treaty with the Pater Patratus of the Albans?" And Tullus having given orders to that effect, the Fetialis continued: "Then I demand of you, O King, sacred herbs." To which the king replied: "Take them fresh (*puram*)." Then the Fetialis, having brought some fresh grass from the Capitol, proceeded to interrogate the king: "Dost thou constitute me thy ambassador, as well as of the Roman people and Quirites, sanctioning also my utensils and my companions?" To which the king replied: "I do, so far as it may be done without detriment to myself and to the Roman people and Quirites." Then the Pater Patratus, who is constituted for the purpose of sanctioning the treaty by an oath, did so by a long formula in verse, which we need not here repeat; after which, having recited the conditions of the treaty, he exclaimed: "Hear, O Jupiter! hear thou, also, Pater Patratus of the Albans! and ye, O Alban people! the words and conditions, first and last, which have been recited from those tablets, or wax, with perfect good faith, and as they are this day most clearly understood, shall never be first violated by the Roman people. And if it shall first violate them by solemn and public counsel, and with fraudulent intent, then, O Jupiter, strike the Roman people as I shall strike this swine; and strike it so much the more, by as much as thou art greater and more powerful than I." Whereupon he struck the swine with a huge flint stone. In like manner the Albans performed their formularies and oaths, through their dictator and priests.

When the treaty had been concluded, the combatants on each side armed themselves, and proceeded into the middle space between the two armies; who, filled with anxiety, though exempt from personal fear, had sat down before their respective camps to view a struggle in which the prize of empire depended on the valour or the fortune of so small a number of champions. These, whose native courage and ferocity had been still further excited by the exhortations of their countrymen, reminding them that their country and its gods, their fellow-citizens as well as their fellow-soldiers, were all looking anxiously for the result of the combat, joined battle at a given signal; forgetful of their own danger while engrossed by the thought that public empire or public servitude depended on their efforts, and that they were now to decide the future fortunes of their country. As their swords flashed in the sun, and resounded on the armour of their adversaries, a shudder ran through and seemed to paralyse the spectators, so that they uttered not a word, and could hardly draw their breath. The agitation increased as the motions of the combatants, the movements of their swords or their shields, and then the sight of blood and wounds, cast a doubt upon the issue. At length two of the Romans are seen to fall amidst the exulting shouts of the Alban army; but all the three Albans are wounded, and breathless anxiety pervades the Roman host for the fate of their only remaining champion, now menaced by the three Curiatii. He chanced to be unhurt, and thus, though no match for the three Albans together, a formidable adversary for any one of them alone. In this state of things the Roman flies, thinking that each opponent would follow as his wounds permitted; and so it happened. For when he turned after running a while, he found that one of the Albans was close upon him, while the other two were following at considerable intervals. The first pursuer is soon despatched, and Horatius proceeds to meet the second, encouraged now by the shouts of his fellow-soldiers, which were all the louder and more animating as hope had succeeded to despair. The second Curiatius is also despatched before the third could come to his aid, though he was not far off. The combatants, therefore, are once more equal in point of number, but quite unmatched in strength and confidence: the Roman unharmed, exulting in a double victory; the Alban badly wounded, exhausted by the pursuit, and dejected by the slaughter of his brothers. Then Horatius, exultingly exclaiming, "Two have I despatched to satisfy my brothers' manes: the third I sacrifice to the cause of this war, that the Roman may rule the Alban!" thrust his sword downwards into his opponent's throat, who had no longer strength to lift his arms in self-defence. Having achieved this victory, Horatius, after despoiling his adversary, hastens to join his fellow-soldiers, by whom he is received with extravagant joy; and both sides, agitated by the most opposite feelings, proceed to bury their dead at the spots where the combatants fell. The tombs of the two Romans are close together, in the direction of Alba, while those of the Albans are in the direction of Rome, with intervals between them.

Before the armies and their two leaders separated, Mettius asked King Tullus whether, according to the tenor of the treaty, he had any commands to give; when Tullus instructed him to keep the Alban youth under arms, as he should want their assistance in case of a war with the Veientines. Then both armies marched homewards, Horatius in front of the Romans, bearing before him the threefold spoils which he had won. As they drew near the city, his sister, who had been betrothed to one of the Curiatii, came forth to meet him; and when she beheld on her brother's shoulders the military robe of her affianced husband, which she had worked with her own hands, she tore her hair, and with sobs and lamentations invoked the name of her slain lover. This distress, so inopportune in a great public rejoicing and his own glorious victory, enraged the youth to such a degree that, drawing his sword, he stabbed his sister to the heart, at the same time exclaiming, "Begone with thy preposterous love, forgetful alike of thy country, of thy dead brothers and thy living one. Such be the fate of her who shall lament an enemy of Rome!"

The deed appeared horrible both to patricians and plebeians; and though it was in a manner sheltered by the recent deserts of Horatius, yet he was brought before the king to be tried. Tullus, in order to avoid giving so melancholy a judgment, which would necessarily be unpalatable to the populace, and pronouncing the punishment which must follow it, called a council of the people, and addressing them said that he had appointed duumvirs according to law, to try Horatius as a criminal against the state. The law was of dreadful tenor: "Let duumvirs judge the crime of high treason. If the accused should appeal from the duumvirs, let the appeal be heard; if the verdict of the duumvirs is confirmed, let him be hanged with a rope from a gibbet, with his head veiled, and let him be scourged either within or without the pomœrium." The duumvirs created under this law, thinking that according to its tenor they could not acquit even an innocent person, condemned him; and one of them said: "Publius Horatius, I find you guilty of high treason. Lictor, handcuff him." The lictor was about to perform this office, when Horatius, at the suggestion of Tullus, who interpreted the law mercifully, exclaimed: "I appeal." And so the appeal was referred to the people.

In that solemn judgment the minds of men were chiefly swayed by the father of Horatius proclaiming that he thought his daughter had been lawfully killed; that if such had not been his opinion, he would have punished his son by his own paternal authority. And then he implored the people not to render completely childless one whom they had seen only a little before at the head of so fine a family. And while he uttered these words he embraced his son; and pointing to the spoils of the Curiatii displayed at the place now called Pila Horatia, he proceeded to exclaim: "Will you bear to see, Quirites, this man scourged and tormented under the gallows, whom only just now you beheld adorned with triumphal spoils, and rejoicing in his victory? The eyes of the Albans themselves could hardly endure so sad a spectacle. Go, lictor, bind the hands which but just now achieved empire for the Roman people. Go, veil the head of the deliverer of this city; suspend him on the gallows-tree; go scourge him within the pomœrium, only let it be among the spoils and arms of the enemies whom he has slain; or without the pomœrium, among the sepulchres of the Curiatii. For whither can you lead this youth where his glorious deeds will not vindicate him from the foul disgrace of such a punishment?"

The people could not resist either the tears of the father or the courage of the youth, whose bearing remained unchanged in that extremity of danger; and they acquitted him more from admiration of his valour than from the justice of his cause. Yet, in order that a manifest murder should have some atonement, the father was directed to expiate his son at the public expense. Horatius, therefore, after making some piacular sacrifices, which became hereditary in that family, erected a beam across the street, and made his son pass under it, with his head veiled. This beam, called the Sororium Tigillum, exists to the present day, being constantly repaired at the public expense. The tomb of Horatia, constructed of solid masonry, may also be seen, at the spot where she was killed.

REMARKS.—On this epoch, Schwegler remarks:[1] "The day of Roman history begins to dawn with Tullus Hostilius. The two kings before him are purely fictitious; Romulus is a god and a son of a god; Numa, a mortal, indeed, but married to a goddess. There is nothing of this mythical character in the person of Tullus Hostilius, and there is no reason that compels us to deny that a king of this name may at some time or other have reigned at Rome.

[1] Buch. xii. § 9.

"Still we are far short of the assumption that with the third king we have reached the ground of authentic and credible tradition, and have from this date a genuine history, unmixed with falsehood. General probability would be against such an assumption, since a completely historical age does not immediately follow a mythical age. It is also opposed by the following consideration: the oldest historical records made in Rome were annalistic; and Roman history bears this annalistic and chronicle-like character from the time when it becomes purely historical, or from about the period of the first secession. The traditional history of the regal times, on the contrary, is not found in the form of annals; while, as we have before shown, it is filled with so many contradictions of fact and chronology as to exclude all possibility of contemporary annalistic record. Consequently, it must proceed not from written, but only from oral, tradition. But, a history whose source is oral tradition alone, or popular legend, cannot pass for genuine and testified history; and the less so in proportion as the interval is greater between the event related and the written record of it. Even the history of the last two kings is shown by a near examination to be altogether legendary. How great, for instance, is the contradiction in the accounts of the origin of Servius Tullius? How full of fiction the history of the last Tarquin? We must conclude, hence, that what is still earlier must be much less trustworthy.

"The history of the last five kings thus stands in the period of transition from the mythical to the historical time; and this epoch of Roman history may be called the mytho-historical. A kind of history now begins; the events henceforth related are for the most part not invention, nor miracles; their foundation is mostly historical; but we have not sufficient certainty respecting any one of these events, whether it is placed in the right light, or in the right sequel of causes; whether it is not arbitrarily altered by popular tradition, and inserted in the wrong place. The destruction of Alba Longa, for example, and the settlement of the homeless Albans at Rome, are without doubt historical events; but the manner in which they are connected with the third Roman king is probably fictitious. So also the wars waged by Ancus Marcius with the surrounding Latin cities are in their general traits certainly historical; they have evidently quite a different character from the campaigns of Romulus against Cænina, Crustumerium, and Fidenæ: but there is good ground for doubting whether they are to be ascribed entirely to the fourth Roman king; and how much of the details with which they are related may be historical must at least be left undetermined. The separation of the historical and unhistorical in this epoch is very difficult, often impossible, and, for the most part, a matter for individual subjective determination; but that this is so, that conjectures and hypotheses widely differ, is, of course, no ground for assuming the historical nature and complete credibility of the common tradition."

On this we shall observe, that we are also, like Schwegler, inclined to draw a line between the reigns of Numa and Tullus Hostilius; not, however, so strong a one as he draws, and upon quite different grounds. We do not think that the two kings before Tullus are purely fictitious, nor that the supernatural events connected with their reigns at all prove them to be so. If such events are not found, or at least not so often found, in the later history, it is simply because the age had grown less superstitious. They recur, however, again, as in the reign of Servius Tullius, and, after the expulsion of the kings, in the apparition of the Dioscuri at the battle of Lake Regillus; and therefore their disappearance cannot be said to form any very marked division of the history here. But we have already touched upon this subject more than once, and need not enter upon it again.

The true reason why the history after Numa comes out more clearly and distinctly is, that contemporary record had begun. Numa had instituted the Pontifices, who became the historians of the city. The annals of the Pontifex Maximus, though only a brief and dry record of facts, were necessarily an authentic record, and an invaluable guide for the succession of events. The Commentarii of the Pontifices were evidently more discursive, and made some approach to regular history. We have already shown this from the fact of their tracing the history beyond the foundation of Rome. And though the Commentarii, or the greater part of them—but not the Annales Maximi—probably perished in the conflagration of Rome, yet it is impossible to suppose that the Pontifices should have forgotten their contents, and highly improbable that they should not have attempted to restore them. And, indeed, we have already shown, from the fact of Dionysius citing them for præ-Roman history, that the Pontifices must have done so.

The treaty with the Albans before the combat of the Horatii

and Curiatii is evidently from record. Livy[1] says that it is the oldest treaty remembered, which must mean whose forms were recorded; for he has himself alluded to many treaties made before this time. The addition of the names of M. Valerius as the Fetialis, and Sp. Fusius as the Pater Patratus, are strong additional proofs of record. It is not thus that the poet or the literary forger invents; the former disregards such details, the latter avoids them, as they might prove an easy means of detection. The forms of trial of Horatius are also evidently from record.

When Schwegler observes that the oldest records made in Rome were annalistic, we perfectly agree with him; but when he says that the history does not assume this form till the period of the first secession, we cannot perceive any grounds for that assertion, nor does he state any. The history has the form of annals from the first establishment of the consulship, simply because the consuls were annual magistrates, and their election marks the beginning of a new year. But the office of king being for life, there was no event to mark the termination of each year. The early writers, who set not that value on chronology which it was found to have when history became more of a science, neglected to discriminate the separate years of the kings, and contented themselves with stating the whole sum of each reign at the end of it. That the Annales Maximi were digested according to years is shown by their very name; and if they had not been so during the regal period, Cicero would have been unable to demonstrate the mistake respecting the chronology of Pythagoras by referring to them.[2]

The alleged contradictions in fact and chronology we have examined in the Introduction; and if our view be admitted, then the history does not rest on oral tradition. And that it does not so rest is shown by Schwegler's own estimate of oral tradition. For he says that the older oral tradition is, the less authentic it is, which is very true; and then he proceeds to say that the history of the sixth and seventh kings is altogether legendary, while he admits that the reigns of Tullus Hostilius and Ancus Marcius, the third and fourth kings, who reigned half a century earlier, are at least semi-historical! But we shall show that the reigns of the last two kings are not legendary.

That all the details of early Roman history are literally authentic

---

[1] Lib. i. 24, "Nec ullius vetustior foederis memoria est."
[2] See above, p. 158.

we have never undertaken to establish. Schwegler admits that its events have henceforth an historical foundation, that they are not mere inventions; though we hardly see how this agrees with his character of the last two reigns. But his fears about their proper sequence are groundless, as that would have been secured by the fact that "the oldest historical records made in Rome were annalistic."

Schwegler then proceeds to remark in his tenth section: "If we examine the figure and position of Tullus Hostilius more closely, we cannot but perceive that he answers to Romulus, just as his successor, Ancus Marcius, answers to Numa. The contrast of the first two kings is repeated in the relation of the third king to the fourth. Even the old tradition adverts to this parallel by characterising Tullus as the very image (*Ebenbild*) of Romulus, and Ancus Marcius as the imitator of Numa, and following in his track. Tullus, like Romulus, is the warlike prince, wholly and exclusively intent upon enlarging his dominions and promoting the glory of his reign: his god is also Mars, the god of war; he also forms a contrast, like Romulus, to the pontifical Numa, nay, a still sharper one, as he ridicules the pious institutions of his predecessor, and finds his death through the same invocation of Jupiter Elicius which Numa had made with impunity."

"But it is not only in character that the second pair of kings resemble the first: Ancus Marcius is the grandson of Numa, while Tullus Hostilius is not, indeed, the grandson of the deified Romulus, who left no heirs of his body, but of that Hostius Hostilius who appears in the van in the great battle against the Sabines, and also grandson of Hersilia, who also appears as the wife of Romulus. It is clear that this genealogy rests not on any actual historical tradition, that it is not an actual fact, but merely expresses an ideal relation: and in this view it is very remarkable that Ancus Marcius is constantly called "grandson of Numa;" nay, that it is expressly handed down that only his grandfather is known, and not his father. But since the contrast of the first two kings, of the warlike Romulus and priestly Numa, is decidedly mythical, a well-grounded suspicion arises that the analogous parts in which the two following kings appear, in like manner rests not on historical tradition, but on construction.

"The history of the third king, moreover, shows itself in another point to be constructive. The first four kings, for instance, as we

have already remarked, represent the four component parts of the
Roman nation, the three original tribes and the *plebs*; and this in
such a manner that the creation of the third tribe and the addition
of a *plebs* are placed in causal connexion with the rule of the third
and fourth kings. Tullus Hostilius is the founder of the Luceres,
Ancus Marcius of the *plebs*. By virtue of this construction, the
rasing of Alba Longa and the settlements of the Albans (the subsequent Luceres) at Rome are ascribed to the third king: this fact
is the central point and tenor of his reign. But if it bears the
assigned relationship to this connexion, it follows of itself, without
regard to the objections which will be developed further on, that
the manner in which Tullus Hostilius is connected with the destruction of Alba Longa cannot pass for completely historical."

To this we reply, that if there is any general resemblance in the
Roman kings among themselves, and in the Sabine kings among
themselves, this arises from national character. It was natural
that the Romans, who had to fight their way in the world, and to
establish a new state, should have made military affairs their para-
mount consideration. The Sabines, on the contrary, who had been
long established in Italy, had not this pressing necessity to devote
their attention almost exclusively to war. They appear, besides,
to have been naturally of a religious temper; and thus we find that
even Tatius, during his short reign, founded as many, or more,
worships than Romulus; the mind of Numa was wholly devoted
to religious affairs, and Ancus paid more attention to them than
Tullus. This general resemblance, therefore, instead of being an
argument against the truth of the history, is an argument in its
favour, because it is true to nature. And if these resembling
kings come in alternate pairs, that arises from the agreement by
which the sovereign was to represent the Romans and Sabines in
turn.

But though there is a general national resemblance in the characters of the Roman kings and Sabine kings, it is by no means so
close as Schwegler pretends it to have been. How can Tullus be
called the "very image" of Romulus, when the tradition tells us
that he was still more ferocious?[1] Romulus had paid a great deal of
attention to civil affairs, and some to religion, which we do not find
in Tullus Hostilius. And how can Ancus Marcius be said to have
been the mere imitator of Numa, when, according to tradition,

[1] "Ferocior etiam quam Romulus fuit."—Liv. L. 22.

confirmed by the annals of his reign, his character was a mixed one, partaking of that of Romulus and that of Numa." [1]

It is hardly worth while to answer the objection that Ancus is the grandson of Numa. Where is the improbability that a grandson of Numa should have been elected king? But the critic must have been pushed to great extremities for an argument, when he tries to connect Tullus Hostilius with Romulus, because he was the grandson of Hostius Hostilius, who distinguished himself in the Sabine War? By the same method we might connect William Pitt with King George the Second, because his father, Lord Chatham, distinguished himself in that reign. Tradition varies as to whether Hersilia were the spouse of Romulus or of Hostilius;[2] but we cannot confound both these traditions, as Schwegler here does for the sake of bolstering up his theory, and make Hersilia at once the wife of Romulus and the grandmother of Tullus Hostilius. If she had been the wife of Hostius Hostilius, she might have been the grandmother of Tullus; but if she had been the wife of Romulus, she would have been the grandmother of nobody at all, for Romulus had no children. And it does not follow, because tradition varies on this point, that it therefore expresses a merely ideal relation. On the contrary, the doubts about the genealogy rather show the good faith of the tradition: the father of Tullus, not having been eminently distinguished, had slipped out of memory; but, if the story had been a myth, it would have been easy to invent a father for him. The same answer applies to the objection about the father of Ancus being unknown. A similar objection had been raised as early as the time of Cicero, who in his *Republic* introduces Lælius as making it; to whom Scipio replies: "Exactly so; but in those times the names of the kings were almost the only ones that became known and famous."[3]

And thus the whole argument falls to the ground. For it is not proved that the first two kings are mythical, or that the second

[1] "Medium erat in Anco ingenium, et Numæ et Romuli memor."—Liv. i. 32.

[2] She is represented as the wife of Romulus by Livy, i. 11; Ovid, Met. xiv. 830; Sil. Ital. Pun. xiv. 812, and others; as the wife of Hostilius by Dionys. iii. 1; Macrob. Sat. i. 6, &c.

[3] "Læl.: Sed obscura est historia Romana; siquidem istius regis matrem habemus, ignoramus patrem. Sc.: Ita est, inquit; sed temporum illorum tantum fere regum illustrata sunt nomina."—De Rep. ii. 18.

two are counterparts of them, and present the same contrast to each other as the first two.

The next argument drawn from the first four kings representing the constituent parts of the nation, is founded on one of those far-fetched and mysterious constructions which seem peculiar to the Teutonic mind. In answer, it suffices to say that it does not rest on facts. Tullus Hostilius is not the founder of the Luceres, nor Ancus Marcius of the *plebs*. It was Niebuhr[1] who first invented this theory, which is, we believe, now almost universally abandoned. The attempt to prove from Livy that the Luceres were the Albans[2] planted on the Cælian Hill,[3] is quite abortive. Livy had before described the Luceres as forming the third stem-tribe of the Roman nation in the time of Romulus.[4] Therefore, when he says, respecting the location of the Latins by Ancus: "Et quum circa Palatium sedem veteres Romanorum, Sabini Capitolium atque arcem, Cælium montem Albani implessent: Aventinum novæ multitudini datum" (i. 33), he cannot possibly mean, as Schwegler would make him,[5] that the Romans, Sabines, and Albans were the three *oldest* component parts of the Roman people; and that hence it is no far-fetched conjecture ("es ist hiedurch die Vermuthung nahe gelegt") to conclude that they were the three stem-tribes. A conclusion which he has rightly characterised; for it rests only on the *conjecture* of a few German scholars; while that the three tribes existed in the time of Romulus is confirmed by the best Roman authors; not only by Livy, but also by Cicero,[6] and by implication by Varro. For when that author mentions the Ager Romanus as *at first* divided among the three tribes of the Tatienses, Ramnes, and Luceres,[7] he evidently means that they arose *at the same time;* since if the Albans were the Luceres, they would have obtained their share by *addition* and not by *division*.

As Tullus Hostilius was not the founder of the Luceres, so

---

[1] Röm. Gesch. I. 312.   [2] Schwegler, R. L. S. 512, ff.
[3] Lib. I. 30, 33.
[4] Lib. I. 13. Livy, indeed, there mentions only the three centuries of knights; but as these centuries were taken from the tribes, and bore the same name, it is impossible that Livy should have been ignorant of the existence of the tribes at that time. We have already adverted to this.
[5] Ibid. S. 514.
[6] "Romulus populum in tribus tres descripserat."—De Rep. ii, 8.
[7] "Ager Romanus primum divisus in parteis tres, a quo tribus appellata Tatiensium, Ramnium, Lucerum."—Ling. Lat. v. 55.

neither was Ancus Marcius the founder of the *plebs*. On this subject Sir G. C. Lewis very justly remarks:[1] "Livy likewise represents Ancus as granting the right of citizenship to a large body of Latins, and settling them in the city on and near the Aventine. This statement is considered historical by Niebuhr, who supposes that the Latin settlers in question were the origin of the Roman *plebs*, and that Ancus was the founder of the plebeian order. For such an hypothesis there does not appear to be any foundation; no peculiar importance is attached to these Latin settlements by Livy: they are not mentioned by Dionysius, who describes the Latin War at some length; and the ancients know nothing of Ancus in the character which is attributed to him by Niebuhr. The plebeian order is treated by them as coeval with the very existence of the Roman state: thus Dionysius describes Romulus as dividing the people into patricians and plebeians, while Cicero speaks of his distributing the plebeians as clients among the several nobles."[2]

Sir G. C. Lewis, in a note, confirms these authorities by two citations from Livy. "Livy," he says, "speaks of Romulus being 'multitudini gratior quam patribus' (i. 15); and in c. 18, of Numa. 'neque se quisquam, nec factionis suæ alium, nec denique *patrum aut civium quemquam* præferre illi viro ausi.' To these two quotations we will add two more from the same author, both under the reign of Romulus, in which the existence of the *plebs* is not merely implied, but actually expressed: 'Quasdam (Sabinas) forma excellentes, primoribus patrum destinatas, *ex plebe homines*, quibus datum negotium erat, domos deferebant' (i. 9): 'Mirum, quantum illi viro (Proculo Julio), nuntianti hæc, fidei fuerit; quamque desiderium Romuli *apud plebem* exercitumque, facta fide immortalitatis, lenitum sit' (i. 16)."[3] This will suffice at present, as the whole question of the early Roman population, whether wholly patrician, or patrician and plebeian mixed, will be discussed more at length further on.

As, therefore, the assertion that the first four kings represent the four component parts of the Roman people is unproved and groundless, no argument can be derived from it to show that the

[1] Credibility, &c. vol. I. p. 468.
[2] Cic. De Rep. ii. 9; Dionys. ii. 8.
[3] On the same subject, the reader may consult in the Classical Museum (vol. vi. p. 15 *sqq.*) a review by Professor Newman of Dr. Ihne's Treatise on the Roman Constitution.

history of the third king is not genuine, but only constructive, that is, invented.

Schwegler, after these general objections, then proceeds, in the eleventh section of his twelfth book, to examine the details of the history of the third king: "If," he observes, "we examine more closely the traditionary history of Tullus Hostilius, his war with Alba Longa demands our particular attention. In this war, Alba Longa emerges for the first time out of the darkness and oblivion into which it had sunk, after its momentary appearance at the time of Rome's foundation. Its internal and external relations, it is true, still remain quite obscure. Livy calls Cluilius a king, Cato, a Prætor; and his successor in office, Fuffetius, who is chosen in the camp by the army, is called Dictator. It is clear that these contradictory accounts are not grounded on authentic tradition. When Licinius Macer says that after the death of Numitor annual dictators were elected at Alba, because the royal line had become extinct with this prince, this account is doubtless only an inference drawn from the circumstance that no kings of Alba appear after Numitor, and Mettius Fuffetius is commonly called a dictator, after the analogy of the later Latin dictators. But in this the fact is overlooked, that after the death of Numitor a scion of the Silvian house was still in existence, namely, Romulus. Plutarch, or his authority, has considered this circumstance; and he relates that, after Numitor's death, Romulus did not indeed succeed to the Alban throne, but that from this time he appointed every year a chief magistrate of the Albans. But if this was the case, and if, after Numitor's death, Alba became politically dependent upon Rome, how is it that it suddenly appears again independent and self-governed, without any event having been mentioned which could have produced this alteration? How comes it that Tullus Hostilius did not enforce his ancient pretensions and rights? These questions cannot be answered, because the account of Plutarch, which has occasioned them, is as arbitrary an invention as all the rest that is handed down concerning the relations of Alba Longa at that period. The account of Plutarch is contradicted by that of another antiquary (Cincius), that Alba Longa enjoyed the supremacy over the Latin states till the time of Tullus Hostilius."

We agree with Schwegler in thinking that the account in Plutarch, like many other things in that author, is an arbitrary and foolish invention, and we prefer, like him, the statement of Cincius,[1] as more conformable to the real state of things. We do not do so, however, because we think, with Schwegler, that his own questions are unanswerable: on the contrary, we think that they might be very easily answered. For it might be replied that, after the death of Numitor, the appointment of magistrates at Alba fell to Romulus by right of his royal blood; that his death was the event which made Alba independent; and that Tullus Hostilius, not being of the Silvian race, could not claim any rights over that city.

But, as we have said, we not only abandon Plutarch's story, which is unsupported by any good authority, but also, as we have already done, the whole account of Rome's early connexion with Alba,[2] and of its having been a colony of that city. And this absence of all connexion is confirmed by the " darkness and oblivion" which we find respecting Alba in the early Roman history; a state of things which could not have supervened if Rome and Alba were really so closely connected as they are related to have been. And under these circumstances it is not surprising that the Romans should not have been very well informed respecting the government of a foreign city. We think, however, that Licinius Macer was probably right, or at all events that Alba was governed, at the time of the war with Tullus, by a chief magistrate somewhat analogous to the Roman dictator or prætor; for in early times *prætor* was the name of the chief magistrate. Our reasons for this opinion are, that if Alba had been under royal government, the Alban army would not have proceeded to elect a dictator on the death of Cluilius; that at all events he would have been nominated from Alba, which was only six or seven miles off; that the preponderance of evidence tends to show that Cluilius was only a dictator; and that Livy himself varies somewhat in speaking of the office. Thus he uses *imperitabat*, not *regnabat*, to denote the rule of Cluilius at Alba; in the next chapter he calls him *dux*; though he also styles him *rex*.[3] We may add that neither Livy nor Dionysius, in their accounts of the transplantation of the Alban families to Rome, drop a word about there having been any royal family there; while it is hardly possible to suppose that, if there had been an Alban royal family, those writers would not have

---

[1] Apud Fest. p. 241, Prætor.　　[2] See above, p. 31.
[3] Lib. vi. c. 22, 23.

distinguished them from the rest.¹ On the whole, we may conclude that the exact nature of the chief magistrate's office at Alba was not very clear to the Romans; but this is a point of minor importance, and does not affect the credibility of their early history.²

"After the breaking out of the war," proceeds Schwegler, "the Albans pitch their camp at the place called Fossa Cluilia. This is the same trench at which Coriolanus also halts after taking from the Romans all their conquests. Hence we may presume that this trench once formed the boundary of the primitive Roman territory. It was five miles from Rome, and Strabo gives the same distance for the original Roman border.³ If this conjecture is right it explains at once why the old tradition placed the camp of Coriolanus, the camp of the Albans, and the combat of the Horatii and Curiatii at this spot. But when tradition ascribes the origin of the Fossa Cluilia to the Alban prince Cluilius, this is undoubtedly an etymological myth. Fossa Cluilia simply means a drain, or sewer; it is therefore quite superfluous to have invented an Alban prince to explain the name. That Cluilius appears only for the sake of the trench is evident from his sudden death: he dies in the camp over night to make room for Mettius Fuffetius, who doubtless was alone mentioned in the old tradition as the opponent of Tullus Hostilius."

The real etymology of the name of Fossa Cluilia is a piece of antiquarianism not very important to the history. As to its uses, Schwegler assigns two, that of a boundary and that of a drain, which he unites. But neither of them, we think, is very probable. We do not read anywhere that the Roman boundary was marked out by a fosse; and that there should have been a sewer in that rural district, midway between Rome and Alba, and that before the Cloaca Maxima had been constructed even at Rome, as Schwegler, after Hartung,⁴ supposes, is a highly singular and Teutonic supposition. We think that the fosse was most likely the remains of a camp; but whether Cluilius was invented to explain the name we

---

[1] Liv. i. 30; Dionys. iii. 29.

[2] It seems probable that the Romans may have derived their name of *rex* from the Sabines, and these from the Celtic.—See Newman's Regal Rome, p. 60, seqq.

[3] Liv. i. 23, ii. 59; Dionys. iii. 4; Strabo, v. 3, 2.

[4] Religion der Römer, ii. 250. Hartung derives the name *cluilia* from *cluere*, which anciently meant *purgare*. But it means other things besides.

will not attempt to fathom, but will content ourselves with observing that it seems hardly worth while.

"The decision of the war," continues Schwegler, "is left by agreement on both sides to a duel. Duels of this kind, which are in some degree to be ranked with judgments of God, are not infrequent in antiquity; and in this point of view the combat of the Horatii and Curiatii may not be unhistorical. But that there should have been triplets, or three children born at one birth, in both camps at the same time, and that their mothers should also have been twins, seems very improbable. And the story appears more certainly an invention, the more the mythical character of the accounts is laid bare. For in the twin sisters is certainly symbolized the relationship of the two sister nations, and in the triplet brothers the circumstance of their being composed of three stem-tribes.[1] The names also of the two pairs of brothers seem to have a symbolical meaning; and the Horatii especially call to mind Horatius Cocles, who likewise appears as the champion of the Roman boundaries. Under these circumstances it is a question whether this combat is an historical fact, or whether it is not rather a mythical representation of the decisive struggle between Rome and Alba Longa."

The main point to be considered here is whether the strife between the two cities was decided by some such combat as that of the Horatii and Curiatii; the details are of minor importance. Schwegler allows that, according to ancient manners, such a combat may be historical; but he adopts in preference the fanciful explanation of Niebuhr, that the whole story is merely symbolical. This explanation, however, which assumes a relationship between the Horatii and Curiatii, rests only on the suspicious testimony of Dionysius; for Livy knows nothing of the mothers of the combatants having been twins; and thus also a great part of Schwegler's objection, from the miraculous nature of the tale, vanishes. Even that the brothers were triplets is probably an exaggeration; they were more likely only brothers of about the same age, or even may only have belonged to the same *gens*. That there were more Curiatii at Alba appears from the fact of their having been transplanted to Rome at the destruction of Alba.[2] It is more consistent with experience that narratives of this kind are exaggerated and embellished than that they are entirely invented. Nay, we have a

---

[1] See Niebuhr, Röm. Gesch. I. 365; Anm. 871.   [2] Liv. I. 30.

very probable clue to the origin of the exaggeration: Trigeminus appears to have been a cognomen of the Curiatii. Thus we find a consul named P. Curiatius Fistus Trigeminus, in a.c. 453.[1] It may be objected indeed that the Curiatii may have affected the name of Trigeminus, in memory of the combat of their ancestors. But if they were the conquered party, this seems hardly credible. And, granting that the Curiatii affected the name, then we have collateral testimony to the tradition about two centuries after the combat, and sixty-three years before the Gallic conflagration; and indeed in all probability a great deal earlier. For it is not likely that the consul in a.c. 453 was the first Curiatius who bore the name of Trigeminus; though from his magistracy he is the first who is known to have done so. It is more probable that it had been handed down hereditarily from the period of the combat, even if the three champions themselves did not bear it. And thus their family name of Trigeminus may have caused them to be taken for *trigemini fratres*, or triplets.

The battles of the ancients, from the absence of firearms, were less noisy than modern ones; for the same reason the hostile forces approached each other more nearly; and thus there was more opportunity for parley, and for arranging the decision in the manner described. The same cause rendered personal prowess, and the heroism of the leaders of more importance; hence a greater disposition to refer the result to single combat.

It may seem strange that Livy should intimate a doubt whether the Horatii or the Curiatii were the Roman champions; a point not adverted to either by Schwegler or Sir G. C. Lewis. But this may be only an instance of that confusion which Livy himself complains of, as introduced into Roman history by family memoirs and funeral orations; the great houses sometimes seeking to appropriate honours which did not properly belong to them.

Schwegler in his critique of the reign of Tullus does not advert to the tombs of the five slain combatants, to that of Horatia, the Pila Horatia, and the Sororium Tigillum; all of which, Livy tells us, were extant in his time, and formed so many records of the history to which they related. As Schwegler had adopted Niebuhr's hypothesis that the whole history is symbolical, he could not resort, without damaging that hypothesis, to his favourite

---

[1] See the Fasti, a.u.c. 300; and Rubino, Röm. Staatsv. S. 492, Anm.

explanation, that it is ætiological. But the existence of the monuments is thus left unexplained.

Sir G. C. Lewis, however, adopts the ætiological theory. "A large part of this narrative," he observes,[1] "comes before us in the suspicious form of explanations of certain names of places and buildings; of topographical and monumental legends. The Fossa Cluilia, the tombs of the Horatii and Curiatii, and also the tomb of Horatia, the Pila Horatia, the Sororium Tigillum, the altars of Juno Sororia, and Janus Curiatius, and the piacular rites of the Horatian family, are the several pegs to which a large portion of the story is attached. The trial of Horatius likewise serves as an occasion for introducing the primitive right of appeal to the people in capital trials for homicide. Again, the story of the demolition of Alba explains the existence of temples on the ancient site of the town, and enables certain Roman families to trace their origin to families of Alba. Some of these memorials have been regarded as conclusive of the realities of the events which they are supposed to record; but the existence of the tombs of the Horatii and Curiatii, and of the Sororium Tigillum, for example, is not a better proof of the celebrated combat to which they referred, than the tools of Epeus at Metapontum are of the Trojan Horse, or of the pickled sow at Lavinium of the prodigy seen by Æneas. Some trustworthy contemporary testimony is necessary in order to prove the occurrence of an event before the connexion of the monument with that event can be established. Where the contemporary testimony implies the continued existence of a monument, its existence in later times is a powerful confirmation of the truth of that testimony. Thus the clear extant remains of a canal across the promontory of Athos serve to corroborate the account in Herodotus of its excavation by Xerxes. In like manner the ancient accounts of the construction of the Flavian amphitheatre at Rome are supported by the vast ruins of the Coliseum. On the other hand, the statements of several ancient writers respecting the gigantic size of the walls of Babylon, are rendered improbable by the entire absence of all traceable remains of those supposed bulwarks; if their extent, height, and thickness were what they are reported to have been, it seems incredible that every vestige of them should have disappeared. But where the event which serves to explain the monument is unrecorded by independent credible evidence, the mere existence of

[1] Credibility, &c. vol. I. p. 462.

the monument is not a proof of the event. The true origin of the monument may have been forgotten, and its unexplained existence may have served as an inducement to invent a legend in order to account for it. Such ætiological legends may, as is proved by many examples in the Greek mythology, and in Ovid's Fasti, be imaginative and poetical; they are, however, necessarily insulated and unconnected, until, by the skill of the subsequent compiler, they are woven into the texture of a consecutive historical narrative."

The conditions here laid down for the credibility of the history attached to any monument are, first, that it should have been contemporaneously recorded; second, the existence of the monument in later times. We can hardly suppose that by "later times" Sir G. C. Lewis meant our own times, so that we might see it with our own eyes; though the only two examples which he gives of a perfectly credible monument, those of Xerxes' canal and the Coliseum at Rome, would almost lead us to think so. But this would reduce the ancient monuments to a very small number indeed; and those connected with the story of the Horatii and Curiatii were not of a kind likely to survive to our own times, like those gigantic ones just mentioned. Such a method would even play great havoc with some modern ones. Thus, for instance, there are many even of the present generation who have never seen old London Bridge, and would be justified on this principle in disbelieving its existence. It was on the same principle that Juvenal, as Sir G. C. Lewis shows in a note, ridiculed the existence of Xerxes' canal as a figment of Greek mendacity; though, in this case, he might have convinced himself of its reality, had he taken the trouble to go to Athos and make the necessary researches.[1] By "later days," therefore, we presume that Sir G. C. Lewis only meant—as any fair critic would mean—the historical times; and then the condition would be, that the monument and its history should have been contemporaneously recorded; that the record should have survived a certain number of centuries, as well as the monument, and that the latter should have been seen and attested by some credible witness, whose testimony has come down to us. Now the monuments in question may be said to fulfil both these conditions. For the balance of probability and evidence is in favour

[1] "Creditur olim
Velificatus Athos, et quicquid Græcia mendax
Audet in historia."—Sat. x. 173, sqq.

of record having begun in the reign of Tullus Hostilius; while the existence of the monuments in the reign of Augustus Cæsar is attested both by Livy and Dionysius.[1]

Sir G. C. Lewis in the above paragraph places all ancient monuments on the same level, whether they relate to the wholly supernatural and incredible, as the sow of Æneas, or to the highly improbable, as the tools of Epeus, or are quite ordinary and natural ones, as tombs, and altars, and a beam of wood. But surely this does not show much discrimination; nor is it very good logic to argue that, because some miraculous relics have been invented, we are therefore to reject even those monuments against which no improbability can be urged, but rather have all the appearance of truth in their favour. This is to reverse the celebrated maxim, "Credo quia impossibile est," into its opposite, "Non credo quia possibile est."

But what shall we say of Sir G. C. Lewis's ætiological explanation of the monuments? Is it more natural and credible than the account handed down to us? We are of opinion that it is a great deal more difficult to believe. The monuments and usages relating to the story of the Horatii and Curiatii are exceedingly numerous. We have the sepulchres of the five combatants, the tomb of Horatia, the Sororium Tigillum, the Pila Horatia, the altars to Janus Curiatius, the piacular sacrifices of the *gens* Horatia, &c. To suppose that all these could have been woven into one story, so as to stand to one another in the connexion of cause and effect, as we are told was also done with the certainly fewer incidents of the Asylum, the rape of the Sabines, &c., surpasses all belief. The Romans, according to these ætiological theories, appear to have had one of the most singular histories in the world. They possessed a great many usages and monuments which nobody is believed to

---

[1] "Sepulcra *extant*, quo quisque loco cecidit: duo Romana uno loco propius Albam, tria Albana Romam versus; sed distantia locis, ut pugnatum est."—Liv. l. 25. "Spolia Curiatiorum fixa eo loco, qui nunc Pila Horatia appellatur."—Ib. 26. "Id (tigillum) *hodie* quoque publice semper refectum manet."—Ib. ἔστι δ' ἐν τῷ στενωπῷ τῷ φέροντι ἀπὸ Καρίνης αὐτὰ τοῖς ἐπὶ τὸν Κύπριον ἐρχομένοις στενωπὸν, ἕνθα οἵ τε βωμοὶ μένουσιν οἱ τότε ἱδρυθέντες, καὶ ξύλον ὑπὲρ αὐτῶν τέταται δυοῖ τοῖς ἀντικρὺ ἀλλήλων τοίχοις ἐνηρμοσμένον, ὃ γίνεται τοῖς ἐξιοῦσιν ὑπὲρ ἀσφαλῆς, καλούμενον τῇ Ῥωμαίων διαλέκτῳ ξύλον ἀδελφῆς. τοῦτο μὲν δὴ τὸ χωρίον τῆς συμφορᾶς τοῦ ἀνδρὸς μνημεῖον ἐν τῇ πόλει ἔτι φυλάττει, θυσίαις γεραιρόμενον καθ' ἕκαστον ἐνιαυτόν. ἕτερον δὲ τῆς ἀρετῆς μαρτύριον ἡ γωνιαία στυλίς (Pila Horatia), κ. τ. λ.—Dionys. lib. 22.

have known the origin of; and at the same time they had several ingenious writers—for a history so composed can hardly be attributed to one person—who were capable not only of arbitrarily uniting these together in different plausible stories, but of obtaining for these stories the implicit belief of their countrymen!

A favourite mode of objection to the accounts of the early history is, "Show us anything parallel in the history of other nations." We may retort this objection on the ætiological critics, and request them to point out any nation, of equal standing with the Romans, that has a history entirely composed of ætiological myths. Many nations have an early mythological history—in even the wildest fables of which are perhaps some grains of truth; but that a nation should have many tolerably old customs—for, after, all the antiquity of Rome, from its foundation to the historical times, is as nothing compared with that of many other peoples—and many tolerably old monuments, and yet that the traditions respecting these customs and monuments should be only a series of tales invented to explain them, we take to be without a parallel. We might also ask the same critics for an example of any sane nation—and the Romans were a sane nation—which perpetuated the memory of some political event—observe, we say *political* event, not any religious creed or worship—by keeping up for centuries, at the public care and expense, the monument which attested it. Yet this the Romans did with the Sororium Tigillum. As we are writing these lines, the fireworks are celebrating the two hundred and sixty-first anniversary of the Gunpowder Plot; and there seems to be no reason for doubting that the same custom may be observed two or three centuries longer, should the Pope last as long, and England remain Protestant. Now it would be about as reasonable to say that the story of Guy Fawkes was invented to explain this custom, as to affirm that the tale of Horatius is nothing but an ætiological myth attached to the Sororium Tigillum.

While we are upon the subject of the monuments of this reign, we will say a word or two, by anticipation, about the Curia Hostilia, or senate-house built by Tullus Hostilius after he had elected the chief persons among the Albans into the Patres. This building lasted till the year B.C. 53, when it was burnt during the funeral of Clodius. We must infer, therefore, that it was large and handsome; such a senate-house, in short, as did not disgrace the majesty of the Roman Republic in the greatness and splendour which it had attained at the period of its accidental destruction, since no project had hitherto been entertained of erecting a new one. There could be no doubt about its origin; no ancient writer has ever uttered one. Had it been erected and dedicated by any eminent magistrate during the Republic, we should certainly have heard of it; for that was an honour greedily sought after, and the memory of which no family would have willingly let die. Nothing is better attested than the origin of the public buildings at Rome. We know the names of nearly all their founders or dedicators, even of those buildings that had perished before the imperial times, as it is natural we should, since these names must have been recorded, not only on the structures themselves, but also in the Annales Maximi, and this of itself is a strong proof of contemporary registration. The antiquity of the Curia Hostilia must have been attested by its architecture, as well, no doubt, as by the inscription which it bore. Sir G. C. Lewis and Schwegler are silent about this building. It would, no doubt, have been difficult to torture it into the ætiological theory; it might have been too bold an affirmation that King Tullus Hostilius was invented to explain its existence. Yet we are to believe that an age capable of erecting such a structure could hardly read and write; that it neglected all memory of the past, all record of its own actions, for the benefit of posterity!

On the whole, therefore, we are inclined to regard, with M. Duruy,[1] the structures and observances transmitted from the reign of Tullus Hostilius, as "irrécusables monuments de la vieille histoire Romaine."

In the fourteenth section of his twelfth book, Schwegler proceeds to examine the trial of Horatius. "We shall say only a few words," he proceeds, "about the trial of Horatius, a closer examination of which belongs to the history of the Roman criminal law. The most accurate, and to all appearance the most authentic, representation of the trial is given by Livy. He, doubtless, took it, like other accounts in his first book concerning Roman legal and sacred antiquities, which are peculiar to his work, from the Commentaries of the Priests; a legal collection, in which we may conjecture that the principles and the traditions of the law were exhibited, in the shape of examples from legal cases that were related, and in which may have been thus exhibited, for example, the

[1] Hist. des Romains, t. I. p. 99.

oldest process of trial and appeal in the case of Horatius. In this respect, Livy's account has an incontestable value; but we must not think that we possess in it a true and documentary narrative, trustworthy in all its details. The trial of Horatius lies far beyond the historical times of Rome; it belongs to an epoch when the art of writing was far from being yet known or used, and concerning which, therefore, there is no genuine historical tradition. It is impossible to assume that a single legal trial of this period has been truly and credibly handed down; and therefore the narrative of the trial of Horatius can only be received as the immemorially oldest example of trial and appeal. It must, therefore, in the present case, be left undetermined how high this memory reaches, what is the age of the forms handed down, and whether the case is not anachronistically dated back in the regal period. On the whole, the trial is too isolated, too little authenticated in its details, and is also too variously related to afford a sure and convincing answer to the numerous questions respecting the history of Roman law which it calls forth."

The author then proceeds to give several examples of such questions; but, as these relate only to points of Roman law, and have nothing to do with the credibility of the story itself, we need not here enter into them.

It is highly probable, as Schwegler supposes, that Livy took his account from the Commentarii Pontificum; and if these were, as he further supposes, a collection illustrating by examples the principles and traditions of the Roman law, he comes to a right conclusion in saying that it has an incontestable value. But we do not see how this agrees with what he goes on to say, that, though taken from what must have been the highest legal source, it has no true and documentary character; nor how, if Livy had so taken it, but, what seems to be Schwegler's meaning, had altered and mutilated it, and transferred it anachronistically to the regal times,—a proceeding which would show Livy a common forger, and quite unworthy to be called an historian,—it could have any value whatever.

We do not think, however, that the Commentarii Pontificum were a mere legal collection. We believe that they contained the history of Rome. How else should Livy mention their destruction in the Gallic conflagration—or rather, the destruction of the *greater part* of them—as a loss of one of the sources of Roman history, of the "*memoria rerum gestarum?*"[1] But we have already treated on this subject in the Introduction and elsewhere, and need not enter upon it here; nor upon the antiquity of the art of writing, upon which Schwegler holds opinions that are contrary, as we have shown, to all evidence and probability.

The Libri Pontificii, which were different from the Commentarii and the Annales, appear to have contained law-cases, as we see from the passage in Cicero, quoted by Schwegler in a note: "Provocationem etiam a regibus fuisse declarant Pontificii Libri;"[2] which shows that law-cases must have been recorded in the time of the kings. But it is quite impossible, as Schwegler there supposes, that Cicero can have been alluding to this trial of Horatius. The appeal in that case is not from the king, but from the duumvirs. The narrative of Livy would rather tend to show that there was no appeal from the king. Tullus Hostilius appoints these duumvirs because he does not wish to be the author of an unpopular judgment, and of the punishment which would follow it; whence we may presume that no appeal would have been allowed from his sentence: he could not constitutionally refer the matter to the people. But he had a means of escape from this disagreeable position by appointing, as the constitution allowed him, duumvirs from whom there was an appeal. We may infer, then, that Tullus Hostilius inherited all the absolute power of Romulus, and that Cicero may have been alluding to a case under one of the later kings, when this power may have been somewhat modified.

In saying that the case is "variously related," Schwegler must be alluding to the account of Dionysius,[3] which agrees in its general tenor with that of Livy, but differs in the details. According to Dionysius it is also the people that acquit Horatius; though not through an appeal from the duumvirs, but from the king referring the matter to them. This variation, however, on the part of such a writer as Dionysius affords no ground for doubting the narrative of Livy; the accuracy and credibility of which are moreover strengthened by his citing the actual words of the law. The making of the crime of Horatius high treason (*perduellio*) instead of murder or manslaughter seems also to bear out this view. The institution of the duumvirs was, in the case of high treason, a method of preventing the king being judge in his own cause. The case of Horatius was probably made high treason by

[1] Liv. vi. 1. [2] De Rep. II. 31. [3] Lib. iii. c. 22.

a somewhat arbitrary construction: that in killing his sister he had taken the law into his own hands, and thus usurped the royal prerogative.

Sir G. C. Lewis observes:[1] "The entire story of the Horatii and Curiatii, including the murder of the sister, has the air of romance;" and adds in a note: "It does not appear that there is any instance of the murder of a sister by a brother in authentic history. It is possible that some cases may have occurred in oriental palaces; but the sanguinary ostracism of Asiatic despotisms has usually been limited to brothers. Olympias, the mother of Alexander the Great, murdered the daughter of Cleopatra, Alexander's step-sister, in her mother's arms; this was an act of feminine vengeance: Alexander had contented himself with the murder of his step-brother Caranus, her other child. See Justin ix. 7; xi. 2. The murder of a sister by a brother seems to be extremely rare, if not unknown, in the records of criminal courts."

If such crimes are fortunately rare, they are the less likely to be invented; and this rarity does not make them impossible. Nor, we will add, in this case highly improbable. For we must picture to ourselves a ferocious youth, whose nerves had been wound up to the highest pitch by the excitement of the combat; who had just escaped an imminent death by the achievement of a glorious victory; who in this state of excitement and exultation suddenly encounters the tears of a sister, instead of joy and congratulation. Upon some tempers, under such circumstances, the effect described, however dreadful and abominable, may not improbably have been produced.

We will now proceed with the history.

THE WARS OF TULLUS HOSTILIUS—DESTRUCTION OF ALBA LONGA.

The Alban peace was not of long duration. The dictator had incurred the hatred of the commonalty because he had committed the public fortunes into the hands of three soldiers. This circumstance quite addled the little understanding that he had; and as he had lost his popularity because good counsels had been unsuccessful, he determined on regaining it by adopting bad. Wherefore, as he had before sought peace in

[1] Credibility, &c. vol. l. p. 464.

war, so he now sought war in peace. But, as he saw that his own city had more courage than strength, he incited other nations to open and proclaimed war; reserving for his own, under the form of alliance, the opportunity for treachery. The Fidenates, who were a Roman colony, taking the Veientines into their counsels and alliance, are incited to war by an agreement that the Albans should desert to them. No sooner was the revolt of Fidenæ ascertained than Tullus, having summoned Mettius with his army from Alba, marched against the enemy, crossed the Anio, and pitched his camp at the point where it falls into the Tiber. The army of the Veientines had passed the Tiber between this spot and Fidenæ; hence in the line of battle they formed the right wing, near the river, while the Fidenates occupied the left towards the mountains. Tullus opposed the Roman troops to the Veientines, and the Albans against the legion of the Fidenates. The Alban leader was as cowardly as he was faithless, and, neither venturing to hold his ground, nor openly to go over to the enemy, he drew away gradually towards the mountains; and, not being able to make up his mind, he kept manœuvring his troops, by way of wasting the time, intending to join with his forces the side which should prove superior. The Romans who were posted in that quarter were at first surprised on perceiving their flank left exposed by the departure of their allies; till, at length, a knight galloped off to the king, and told him that the Albans were marching away. In this sudden danger, Tullus made a vow of twelve Salii, and of fanes to Pallor and Pavor. Then, upbraiding the knight with a loud voice, so that the enemy might hear, he bade him return to his post: "There was no cause for alarm; it was by his command that the Alban army was being led round to attack the Fidenates in rear." At the same time he told him to order the cavalry to raise their spears. By this method a great part of the Roman foot were prevented from seeing the departure of the Alban army; while those who were nearer, and had beheld it, having heard the king's words, fought all the more vigorously. The terror was now on the side of the enemy; for they had heard what the king had said, and a great part of the Fidenates, being Roman colonists, understood Latin. Wherefore, fearing lest they should be cut off from their town by a sudden descent of the Albans from the hills, they began to retreat. Tullus pursued, and completely dispersed them, and then returned to charge the Veientines, already shaken by the panic of their allies. They also could not resist the attack, but the river behind them prevented a disorderly flight. Thither, however, lay the only chance of escape. When they arrived at the river, some threw away their arms, and rushed blindly into the water; others were killed on the bank while they stood deliberating whether they should fight or fly. Never before had the Romans fought so terrible a battle.

After it was ended, the Alban army, which had been merely spectators of it, were led down into the plain; when Mettius congratulated Tullus on his victory, while Tullus, on his side, conversed with him in a friendly manner. Then he ordered the Albans to encamp by the side of the Romans, and prepared a lustral sacrifice for the following day. When morning dawned, and all had been prepared, he commanded both armies to be summoned to a *concio*, in the customary manner. The heralds, beginning from the extremities, first summoned the Albans, who, excited by the novelty of hearing the Roman king speak, gathered close round him. Then, as had been arranged, the Roman legion, all armed, surrounds them; the centurions having first received instructions to execute the king's orders without delay. Tullus then spoke as follows: "Romans! if there was ever an occasion, in any war that we have waged, to return thanks, first to the immortal gods for their goodness, and then to your own valour, it was the battle fought yesterday. For you had to contend not only with your enemies, but—what is much more terrible and dangerous —with the perfidy of your allies. For, to undeceive you of a false opinion, it was not by my command that the Albans retreated to the mountains. The orders which I gave concerning it were nothing but a pretence, in order that, being ignorant that you were deserted, you might not lose courage for the fight, and that the enemy might be struck with terror, and incited to fly, by the opinion that they were taken in the rear. Nor is the crime which I am denouncing that of all the Albans. They did but follow their general, as you yourselves would have done, had I wished to lead you away. It was Mettius who led them off—Mettius, the contriver of this war—Mettius, the violator of the treaty between Rome and Alba. I must make a signal example of him to all the world, or somebody else may again venture to do the like."

At these words the armed centurions surrounded Mettius, and the king proceeded to conclude his speech as follows: " I have in my mind a design which I pray may be a happy one, and of good omen, both to the Roman people and to myself, and to you, O Albans! It is to convey the whole Alban people to Rome; to give the franchise to the plebeians, to elect the leading Alban classes into the Roman patricians, and thus to make one city and one state, reuniting the peoples which, being formerly one, were divided into two." At these words the Alban youth were agitated with a variety of conflicting emotions; but, as they were unarmed, and surrounded by armed men, their common danger compelled them to be silent. Tullus then proceeded as follows: " Mettius Fuffetius, if it were possible for you to learn to be faithful, and to observe treaties, I would have suffered you to live, and been your instructor in that way. But, since your disposition is incorrigible, I will teach men, by making an example of you, to hold sacred those engagements which you have violated. Wherefore, just as your mind was lately wavering between the Fidenates and the Romans, so shall your body be now torn asunder." In pursuance of this sentence, two *quadrigæ* were brought, Mettius was bound upon the chariots, and then the horses were urged in different directions, carrying off in both chariots parts of the lacerated body and the limbs which had been retained in the chains, while all averted their eyes from so dreadful a spectacle. This was the first and last example among the Romans of a species of execution which regarded not the laws of humanity. In other respects, we may boast that no nation has contented itself with milder punishments.

While these things were still going on, the cavalry had been despatched to Alba to conduct the population to Rome; after which the legions were marched thither to destroy the town. Very different when they entered it was the spectacle from that usually presented by captured cities. There was none of that tumult and consternation which are seen when the gates have been broken in, or the walls levelled with the ram, or the citadel taken by assault, with hostile shouts and charges of armed men through the streets, and everything mingled in one common ruin, either by fire or sword. Instead of these reigned a mournful silence; a sorrow that found no vent in words seemed to paralyse the minds of all; in the forgetfulness of an absorbing fear, they hesitated as to what they should leave, what they should carry off; some were inquiring of others, or lingering on their thresholds, or wandering over their houses, which they were to see for the last time. It was not till the shouts of the horsemen were heard, commanding them to depart, and the noise of the falling houses which were being pulled down in the further parts of the city, and the dust which, though rising in distant places, had covered everything with a sort of cloud, that they tore themselves from their hearths, and their household gods, and the houses in which they had been born and brought up, hastily seizing and carrying off what articles they could. And now the roads were filled with an unbroken line of emigrants, shedding fresh tears at the sight of their common misery; while lamentations arose, and especially from the women, in passing the august temples now occupied by armed men, and leaving, as it were, their captured gods behind. After the Albans had quitted the city, the Romans levelled all the buildings, both public and private, with the ground; and thus in a brief space was destroyed the work of four centuries, for so long had Alba stood. The temples of the gods were alone preserved, agreeably to the king's orders.

REMARKS.—On this narrative Schwegler observes:[1] "According to tradition, the conflict of the two states ends with the destruction

[1] Buch xii. s. 11, S. 587.

of Alba Longa. That this destruction, like Alba's former existence as the capital of Latium, is an historical fact, cannot be reasonably doubted. It is irrefutably testified by the continued existence of the temples and worships of the destroyed city; and especially the continuance of the Alban priesthood of Vesta, which existed in the last days of heathenism." Schwegler then cites in a note the following authors for the fact that the temples were spared: Livy, i. 29; Dionysius, iii. 27 and 29; Strabo, v. 3, 4; p. 231. And for their continued existence, and the worships attached to them, the following passages, which we give at length:—Cicero (*pro Mil.* 31, 85), "Vos Albani tumuli atque luci, vos, inquam, imploro atque testor, vosque Albanorum obrutæ aræ, sacrorum populi Romani sociæ et æquales, quas ille (Clodius), cæsis prostratisque sanctissimis lucis, substructionum insanis molibus oppresserat;" Livy (v. 32), "Majores nobis sacra quædam in monte Albano Laviniioque facienda tradiderunt;" Lucan (*Phars.* ix. 990), where Julius Cæsar says—

"Di cinerum, Phrygias colitis quicumque ruinas,
Æneæque mei, quos nunc Lavinia sedes
Servat et Alba Lares, et quorum lucet in aris
Ignis adhuc Phrygius;"

Statius (*Silv.* v. 2) "Qua prisca Teucros Alba colit Lares;" Mommsen (*Inscriptiones Regni Neapolitani*, No. 1435), "pontifex Albanus minor;" Juvenal, (*Sat.* iv. 60)—

"Utque lacus suberant, ubi, quamquam diruta, servat
Ignem Trojanum et Vestam colit Alba minorem."

A Vesta Albana is also mentioned in an inscription in Orelli, (*Corpus Inscr.*, No. 1393); "Virgo Vestalis maxima Albana," (*ibid.* No. 2240); and in the inscription in Marini, (*Atti*, &c. p. 654); and Virgines Albanæ by Asconius (Ad Cic. *Mil.* p. 41). That the Alban priesthood of Vesta continued to exist in the time of Symmachus we see from the following passages: (*Ep.* ix. 128), "Primigenia, dudum apud Albam Vestalis antistes," and (*ib.* 129), "Primigenia virgo, quæ sacra Albana curabat."

Schwegler then proceeds to observe: "It is another question whether the destruction of Alba took place as tradition records, and especially whether it was accomplished by Rome. We have the weightiest grounds for answering this question in the negative. If we take our stand on the common tradition, Rome, in the first years of its third king, not yet three generations old, and remaining without external increase during the long reign of Numa, must have been a state of very moderate extent, and very humble military power. It was only through the conquest of the surrounding Latin territory, which, however, falls in the reigns of the fourth and fifth kings, that it attained a more respectable position. Before the Tarquinian foundations, it was quite an insignificant place, of which we can only form the most paltry idea. It is not to be thought that this Rome, which even in the time of the Æquian and Volscian wars was often compelled to exert itself many years to conquer and hold a hostile city, which centuries later contends for years with Veii, Antium, Præneste, Velitræ, should have been strong enough under its third king, that is, in the time of its infancy, without any external aid to level to the ground the ancient metropolis of Latium. And at what a small price, how easily, and as it were in sport, does it obtain this immense success! M. Horatius, with a chosen body of cavalry, is sent before, presses through the open gates into the unguarded and undefended town,[1] and announces the king's command. Nobody thinks of resistance. The procession of emigrants takes its departure, and the town vanishes in dust and ashes. It is a further improbability that the rest of Latium is so completely unconcerned in this conflict. The contest does not go beyond Rome and Alba; the rest of Latium vanishes out of sight. But, if Alba Longa was really the capital of the Latin League, its destruction affected the whole constitution of the League, and it is not credible that the rest of the confederate towns would have looked upon this event without taking any part in it. In short, whoever regards the traditional narrative of Alba Longa's fall, not in a sort of half dream, or state of somnambulism, but with a sober and practical estimate of the circumstances, their connexion, their possibility and probability, cannot for a moment doubt that he has no history before him, but only tradition mixed with invention.

"No human acuteness can of course now discover from what causes and under what circumstances the downfall of Alba occurred. We can only conjecture that the destruction of the former capital of Latium was the result of a conflict which must have struck deep into the relations of the Latin League. By whom Alba was destroyed also remains uncertain. Niebuhr assumes by Rome, in common with the surrounding Latins; yet holds it to be possible

[1] Dionys. iii. 31.

that Rome had no part at all in it; that the Latins alone destroyed Alba, and that the Albans sought refuge at Rome, and were there received as fugitives.[1] The latter assumption appears to us by far the more probable; seeing that the Albans settled at Rome were incorporated as one of the tribes of the Roman people, and that, at least according to tradition, they appear to have been represented from the beginning in the order of knights. According to the law of conquest of those times, a conquered people would not have been so treated.

"Moreover, if Rome was really a colony of Alba Longa, as tradition says, the razing of it was, according to the mode of thinking of the whole ancient world, a sort of parricide which we cannot suspect so pious a people as the ancient Romans to have been capable of committing; and the more revolting, as, allowing that Mettius Fuffetius was a traitor, Alba itself was not implicated in his crime."

We do not attach so much weight as Schwegler does himself to the reasons which he brings forward for disputing the tradition respecting the fall of Alba Longa. The question as to whether Rome would have been able to reduce Alba depends on their relative strength, which we have no means of ascertaining, except so far as tradition may throw some lights upon it. But as the whole Alban population could be settled on the Cælian Hill, Alba could not have been a very large and important place. The same fact is another proof of the very small number of inhabitants contained in these primitive towns. We may admit that Rome under Tullus Hostilius was probably not remarkable for architectural beauty, to which Schwegler seems to allude in talking of the Tarquinian foundations, though the Curia Hostilia shows that it was beginning to make some progress even in this direction; but military strength does not depend on this circumstance. The Sabine union would have been a source of great power; that it was so, we have already seen, from the respect in which Rome was held by her neighbours, so that during the reign of Numa none cared to attack her. And though that long peace, as Schwegler observes, must have prevented her from making any addition to her strength from without,

---

[1] Niebuhr draws this conclusion from the circumstance that, after the destruction of Alba, it is not the Romans but the Prisci Latini who are in possession of the Alban territory; and it was here, at the fountain of Ferentina, that they thenceforth held their assemblies.

it must have wonderfully developed her resources within. The increase of population, and also of wealth, must have been large and rapid. If, as Schwegler admits, Ancus Marcius, the successor of Tullus, could reduce the greater part of Latium only thirty or forty years afterwards, there seems to be no good reason for doubting that Tullus might have been able to conquer a single Latin city. This conquest, and the transplantation of the Albans to Rome, would have facilitated the success of Ancus, not merely by removing one obstacle out of the way, but also by actually increasing the Roman strength in the same proportion. It was so much taken from the Latins, and so much added to Rome. It is, therefore, a highly natural incident in the history, and renders the subsequent conquests of Ancus all the more probable.

Schwegler endeavours to throw a doubt upon the fall of Alba, by placing it in a different light from that in which tradition presents it to us. He ignores altogether, in his critical remarks just quoted, the fact that Alba, before its destruction, had become subject to Rome, through the event of the combat between the Horatii and Curiatii. He views, indeed, the tradition of that combat as merely symbolical, for which, as we have shown, he has no sufficient grounds. For while he admits that there is no *à priori* improbability in it, he at the same time ignores the monuments which attested it; and he grounds his symbolical interpretation on a circumstance which has no true historical foundation. To view the relations between Rome and Latium fairly, we must view them in the connexion in which they are presented to us by tradition; first, the subjugation of Alba by Rome; then its destruction by Tullus, caused by the treachery of Mettius, and the transference of its inhabitants to Rome; finally, in the next reign, the wars of the Romans with the Latins.

In pursuance of this misrepresentation, Schwegler makes Horatius merely ride into Alba with his cavalry and communicate the king's orders; adding, "nobody thinks of resistance." But it would have been a great deal more extraordinary if the Albans *had* thought of resistance; for Schwegler suppresses two somewhat important facts—that Tullus had surrounded and disarmed their army, and put their dictator and general, Mettius Fuffetius, to death.

The story of the first encounter between the Romans and Albans also throws some light upon the relations of Alba to the what is called the Latin League, and therefore we cannot suffer its consideration to be omitted here in its connexion with the whole story. Mettius Fuffetius, in his interview with Tullus before the combat, evidently does not reckon on the least support from the Latins in case of Alba being attacked by the Etruscans. He does not once mention them, but considers that the whole brunt of such an attack would have to be borne by Rome and Alba. This would lead us to suppose that the Latin League, like the Greek Amphictyonies, was rather merely a recognition that the cities composing it were of the same race and religion, than a confederation for political purposes. This recognition consisted in the performance of certain established religious rites in the temples of Alba Longa; which was thus, as well as from the circumstance that many of the Latin cities were her colonies, regarded as the metropolis of Latium.

This view derives some confirmation from the fact that Tullus, who was not a very religious prince, but rather decidedly the reverse, should have spared the Alban temples. This was a stroke of policy. He avoided provoking the anger of the other Latin cities by their destruction. Nor did he attempt to occupy the town as a Roman colony. Instead of this he conveys the inhabitants to Rome, leaving the temples and free access to them, so that the Prisci Latini are subsequently found there, holding their assemblies as usual.

Nor, even allowing that the Latin League was decidedly political, does it follow that one of its cities may not have been engaged in a private war without involving the rest. Rome was engaged many years in wars with Veii without the other Etruscan cities interfering; nay, not even to avenge her fall. There is something in the nature of these ancient leagues that we do not sufficiently understand to be able to draw an argument from them against the truth of the history.

Moreover, by the treaty between Alba and Rome after the combat of the Horatii and Curiatii, Alba had placed herself at the disposal of Rome, had alienated herself from the Latin League, and had deprived the Latins of all pretence for interfering, even had they been so inclined.

It may be added that one of the reasons why the Latins did not come to the rescue of the Albans may have been that Tullus had made a treaty with them, as appears from a passage in Livy's account of the reign of Ancus Marcius.[1] This treaty was most probably the sequel and result of the submission of Alba.

There is no ground whatever but conjecture for Niebuhr's assumption that Alba was destroyed by the Latins. The old tradition, supported by the testimony of historians, is infinitely more probable. Yet Schwegler, though he adopts this hypothesis, that the Latins destroyed their own metropolis, makes it an argument against the history that they are not represented as having defended it! Truly, if some of these critics had written the history of Rome it would not have been so consistent as it is.

Nor can we reconcile his surprise that the Albans were so leniently treated, and even admitted to the honours of Rome, with his following observation that Alba was not implicated in the treason of its dictator, and that therefore the proceeding of Tullus was a revolting act of parricide. Tullus was clearly aware of the distinction between the leader and his people. He had stated it in his speech on the morning following the battle. His whole conduct was political. He did not choose to leave a town so close on his flank whose conduct might be dubious: but he had no cause for anger against the inhabitants; he therefore transferred them to Rome, and, following the precepts and example of Romulus, by which Rome ultimately became so great, he gave them the privileges of Roman citizens. The history is highly consistent. Tullus acquires the right of sovereignty over Alba by the result of the combat between the Horatii and Curiatii, and the treaty between Rome and Alba, which depended on it. But finding that he could not rely upon this sovereignty, that it lay at the mercy and caprice of any treacherous commander, he did what, under the circumstances, he was perfectly justified in doing; he insured his sovereignty by transferring the Albans to Rome.

The story of Rome having been a colony of Alba we have already disposed of, and therefore of the argument about the impiety of the Roman people in destroying it. Instead of any argument being drawn from that story against the truth of these transactions of Tullus, those transactions, on the contrary, are only another proof of the falsehood of the story. In the time of Tullus it was not, perhaps, even invented. No inference on this head can be drawn from the speeches in Livy; since it was customary with the best ancient historians, even Thucydides for example, to insert speeches

---

[1] "Latini, cum quibus, regnante Tullo, ictum fœdus erat."—Lib. L 32.

which were assuredly never delivered, or at all events not in the form in which we read them.

While Schwegler believes in the existence and destruction of Alba, but not in the way recorded by history, Sir G. C. Lewis, perhaps more consistently, but we think not more reasonably, doubts its existence altogether.

"Niebuhr considers," writes that author,[1] "the fact of the destruction of Alba, in the reign of Tullus Hostilius, to be historical. He nevertheless rejects the circumstances of the received account; for he conjectures either that Rome, in conjunction with the Latin towns, took Alba, and divided the conquered territory and people; or that Alba was destroyed by the Latins, not by Rome. (*Hist.* vol. i. p. 350 *seq.*) That the Romans, from the dawn of their historiography, believed in the former existence of a city of Alba, on a site marked by an extant temple of Vesta, and that they regarded it as the metropolis of Rome, may be considered as certain. It is possible that the connexion may have been real, and that its memory may have been preserved by annual rites performed under the direction of the Roman state. At the same time it is difficult to affirm that the historical existence of a city near the Alban lake, said to have been demolished in the year 665 B.C. rests on a sure basis of evidence. We must, in order to be satisfied on this point, suppose that the memory survived its downfall about four centuries and a half, before it passed from oral tradition into written history. With respect to the internal evidence, the wars of Tullus Hostilius present nothing which offends the laws of probability; but the entire story of the Horatii and Curiatii, including the murder of the sister, has the air of romance; and the account of the death of Tullus by lightning is avowedly related as an example of the direct interposition of Jupiter."

On this we will observe that it may at least be regarded as certain that where the temples stood there must once have been a city: first, because temples dedicated to Vesta were not erected in solitary isolated places but in towns; secondly, because the remains of the walls of an ancient city may still be seen at the spot where Alba Longa is reputed to have stood.[2] That this does not absolutely prove it to have been Alba Longa we will admit; but it must have

---

[1] Credibility, &c. vol. i. p. 162.
[2] See Mr. Bunbury's article, "Alba Longa," in Smith's Dict. of Anc. Geogr. vol. i. p. 88.

been a Latin city, and if it was not Alba Longa, we cannot even conjecture what else it could have been. That Roman history consisted of nothing but oral tradition till the first literary historians put it into writing about two centuries B.C. is a point of course on which we are completely at issue with Sir G. C. Lewis, and which we need not here touch upon again. But, even had there been no written history, a temple with a regular service attached to it would, we think, have been its own record among any people that had continued to inhabit the same city, and had not degenerated into perfect barbarism. Sir G. C. Lewis himself seems to allow this when he observes that the memory of the connexion between Rome and Alba "may have been preserved by annual rites performed under the direction of the Roman state."

Whether the story of the Horatii and Curiatii be a romance we have already considered; the account of the death of Tullus we will examine presently.

The twelfth and thirteenth sections of Schwegler's twelfth book we need not examine. They consist of an attempt to prove that the third stem-tribe of the Roman people, that of the Luceres, with the knights selected from it, consisted of the Albans transplanted to Rome, and did not therefore exist before the time of Tullus Hostilius. Consequently these sections affect not the fundamental credibility of the early Roman history; rather in fact they assume it; for they suppose the existence of three tribes and the transplantation of the Albans to Rome: only they would assign a different origin to the third tribe from that handed down by tradition. It is an attempt not to confute, but to alter, Roman history in a way inconsistent with the testimony of all the ancient writers. We shall therefore content ourselves with saying, especially as we have before touched upon this subject, that Schwegler advances nothing in these sections that might not be very easily answered.

We now return to the course of the history.

LAST WARS AND DEATH OF TULLUS.

Meanwhile, Rome grew apace through the ruin of Alba. The number of the inhabitants was doubled, and for their accommodation the Cœlian Hill was included in the city. In order to render this new quarter more popular, Tullus chose it as a site for a palace, and fixed his residence there. He appears to have previously lived upon the Velia;[1] and this circumstance is sometimes absurdly brought forward as a contradiction to the account of Livy and Dionysius, that he built a palace on the Cælian: as if he must not have had some dwelling before the destruction of Alba.[2] And in order that the patrician class should be increased proportionally with the increase of the people, Tullus elected into it the chief Alban families: the Tullii, Servilii, Quinctii, Geganii, Curiatii, and Cloelii.[3]

The Senate being thus increased, Tullus built a temple for their accommodation, which continued to bear the name of Curia Hostilia down to the time of our fathers.[4] And in order that all ranks in the state might receive some addition from the new population, he chose ten troops of knights from among the Albans. He filled up the old legions in the same manner, and enrolled new ones.

Relying on this augmentation of force, Tullus declared war against the Sabines, a nation, in those times, second only to the Etruscans in military power. Injuries had been inflicted on both sides, and reparation demanded in vain. Tullus complained that certain Roman merchants had been arrested in open market at the fane of Feronia, a sanctuary in the territory of Capena, not far from Soracte, where a kind of fair of the neighbouring peoples appears to have been held. The Sabines, on their side, asserted that some of their people, who

---

[1] Varro ap. Non. p. 531; Cic. Rep. II. 31; Solin. i. 22.
[2] Liv. L. 30; Dionys. iii. 1; cf. Schwegler, R. I. S. 574, Anm. 3.
[3] There is some little difference here between the accounts of Livy (I. 30) and Dionysius (iii. 29). Dionysius substitutes the Julii for the Tullii; calls the Quinctii, Quintilii, and adds another family, the Metilii, who are unknown to the Roman Fasti. Of the Julii we have already spoken (above, p. 117, where they appear among the original followers of Romulus. It seems probable, however, that they were originally from Alba Longa, but through its colony, Bovillæ; where was discovered an ancient altar, with the following inscription:—" Vediovei patrei genteiles Juliei, leege Albana dicata." (Orelli, Corp. Insc. No. 1287). See on this somewhat curious subject, Tac. Ann. ii. 41, xi. 24, xv. 23; Suet. Oct. 100; Klausen, Æneas, ii. 1086; Gell, Topog. of Rome, p. 124; Ritschl, Monum. Epigr. Tria, 1852, p. 29; Nibby, Dintorni di Roma, t. I. p. 302, seq.; Orelli, Corp. Insc. Nos. 119 and 2252; Schwegler, B. I. S. 575, Anm. 2.
[4] Livy is speaking of his own time.

had previously taken refuge in the Asylum at Rome, had been detained there. Such were the causes given out for the war. The Sabines, who too well remembered that part of their force had been established at Rome by Tatius, and that the Roman state had likewise been lately increased by the addition of the Alban population, began to look around for external assistance. Etruria was nearest to them, and the Veientines were the nearest of the Etruscans. Hence they drew some volunteers; for many of the Veientines had a grudge against Rome from the recollection of the former wars; and some vagabonds of the destitute class were even enlisted for pay. But they were not publicly aided by the state; and Veii preserved inviolate the truce she had entered into with Rome.

Active preparation for war was now made on both sides, and, as the issue seemed to depend on which should first appear in the field, Tullus took the initiative by invading the Sabine territory. There was a hard-fought battle at the place called Silva Malitiosa, where the Romans were superior, not only by their infantry, but also more particularly through the late increase in their cavalry. The Sabine ranks were broken by an unexpected charge of horse, so that they could neither maintain the battle nor effect a retreat without exposing themselves to terrible slaughter.

According to the narrative of Livy, which seems rather abrupt, the Sabines were subdued by this engagement. That historian seems to have given only the last decisive battle; for, according to Dionysius,[1] the war had lasted two or three years, with varying success. The victory over the Sabines not only threw a great lustre on the reign of Tullus, and on the whole Roman state, but also increased their power. Soon afterwards we find mentioned, for the first time, one of those portents which so often appear in Roman history, the notice of which could hardly have been preserved except through record. The king and Senate were informed that a shower of stones had fallen on Mons Albanus. The matter appeared incredible, and some persons were therefore despatched thither

[1] Lib. III. 32, seq.

to ascertain the truth, who brought back word that they had seen the stones fall, just like a hailstorm. They seemed also to hear a loud voice from the grove on the summit of the mountain, commanding that the Albans should perform their sacred rites after the manner of their forefathers. This they had neglected to do, and seemed indeed to have quite forgotten them; for as if they had left their gods at the same time as their country, they had either adopted Roman rites, or, out of spite as it were against fortune, had wholly abandoned divine worship. The Romans also made a public religious festival for nine days, on account of the same prodigy; either having been admonished to do so by the same celestial voice from the Alban mount, or at the suggestion of the Haruspices. It is certain, at least, that whenever a prodigy of the same kind was announced, a festival of nine days was observed.

Shortly after, Rome was attacked with a pestilence. Hence an indisposition for military service. But a warlike king like Tullus would permit no respite, especially as he believed that the youth was more healthy in the field than at home: till at length the king himself was seized with a lingering distemper. Together with his body, his ferocious mind grew so debilitated, that he who had previously held nothing to be less worthy of a king than to attend to sacred matters, became all at once so altered, as to become the very slave of all kinds of superstition, and to occupy the people also with religious observances. It now became the general opinion that the only method of escape from the sickness was by obtaining peace and pardon from the gods, thus seeking to restore the same state of things which had existed under Numa. It is related that the king, on turning over the Commentaries of Numa, discovered an account of certain secret and solemn sacrifices, that were to be made to Jupiter Elicius, and withdrew into privacy in order to perform them. But these rites were either not properly adopted, or not accurately performed. Not only was he unfavoured with any celestial appearances, but through the anger of Jupiter, who had been supplicated with a false worship, he was struck with lightning, and consumed along with his house. Tullus had reigned two-and-thirty years, with a great warlike reputation.

REMARKS.—Neither Sir G. C. Lewis, nor Schwegler, makes any observations on the wars of Tullus Hostilius after the fall of Alba Longa, and we may therefore conclude that nothing can be said against their internal probability; indeed this is acknowledged by Sir G. C. Lewis, in a passage already quoted.[1] But though the account of these wars, as given by Livy, seems, as far as it goes, to be genuine, it is evidently very fragmentary. It appears as if the history of them had come down in a very mutilated and questionable shape, and that Livy had selected only those occurrences which he considered to be certain, though it is evident from his own testimony that Tullus must have had more wars, or, at all events, that they must have been of longer duration, than those which he records. Thus, for instance, he remarks that Tullus during the pestilence would give the Roman youth no respite from war,[2] though he mentions none in which they might have been engaged after the overthrow of the Sabines, which preceded the pestilence. But Dionysius, besides describing the Sabine War as lasting through several campaigns, as we have already said, makes the conclusion of it followed by a war with the Latins.[3] Fifteen years, it is said, after the overthrow of Alba, Tullus demanded of the Latins that in right of that conquest they should acknowledge Rome as their head, in place of Alba. But in a council of the League held at the Lacus Ferentinæ,[4] the Latin cities resolved not to subject themselves to Rome. Upon this a desultory war ensues, which lasts five years; but it is a merely predatory sort of warfare, without any pitched battle or siege, except that of Medullia, which place, according to Dionysius, had been made a Roman colony by Romulus, but had revolted back to the Latins. This is the only event of the war at all memorable, and, as Livy places it under Ancus instead of Tullus, it may be that from the paucity of events of the rest of the war, he did not think it worth recording, in the slight sketch which he gives of the early history,[5] though, as we have said, he seems to hint at such a war.

[1] Above, p. 208.
[2] "Nulla tamen ab armis quies dabatur a bellicoso rege."—Lib. I. 31.
[3] Lib. III. 24.   [4] Dionysius places it at Ferentinum, ib.
[5] "Legationem plerisque festinantibus ad hæc nova."—Præf.

Varro, Pliny, and Festus also mention a war of Tullus Hostilius with the Etruscans; but we have no other notice of it, and as these writers were not historians, the account probably originated in some mistake.[1]

The reign of Tullus, besides the acknowledgment of the critics that his wars have the internal stamp of probability, is important with regard to the credibility of the early history, as being the first which bears evident marks of contemporary record. This is consistent with the account that the Pontifices were the annalists and historiographers of Rome, and that they were instituted by Numa, the preceding king. We have already pointed out, as instances of record, the treaty between the Romans and Albans, with the names appended of the Fetialis, M. Valerius, and of the Pater Patratus, Sp. Fusius: to which may be added the law of *perduellio*, the list of Alban families transferred to Rome, the prodigy of the shower of stones, the *novendiale sacrum* instituted on account of it, and the subsequent pestilence. The three last are precisely the kind of events which would have been recorded in the Annales Maximi, from which they were evidently taken: the preceding ones were probably recorded either in the Commentarii Pontificum or Libri Pontificii.

The only other event, besides the combat of the Horatii and Curiatii, which Sir G. C. Lewis finds at all doubtful in the history of Tullus Hostilius, is his death. That the manner of it is somewhat mysterious must be allowed; but there may have been reasons of state for keeping it so, and this was easily effected when there was no public literature. The precise manner of the death of Richard II. is unknown; but the accounts of his reign are not, therefore, to be regarded as unhistorical. One account represents Tullus as having been murdered, and his house burnt down, by his successor, Ancus Marcius;[2] but the objection of Sir G. C. Lewis is grounded on the circumstance that his death by lightning is "related as an example of the direct interposition of Jupiter." There is nothing, however, in the manners of those times which renders the belief, and consequently the assertion, of such an interposition incredible; on the contrary, such a belief is quite consistent with them. Nor is it altogether improbable that Tullus may have

[1] Var. in Fert. p. 348, Septimontio; Plin. H. N. ix. 63, s. 136; Macrob. Sat. i. 6; cf. Schwegler, B. i. S. 577, Anm. 2.
[2] Dionys. iii. 35.

perished as related in some attempt to draw down lightning from heaven. The thunderstorms at Rome are frequent and heavy, and very different from those which we experience in this climate; and it is not impossible that Numa, with his science and his devotion to religion, may have contrived some conducting rod by which to elicit the will of Jove, as manifested by his bolts. The epithet of "Elicius," applied to Jupiter in this connexion, seems to point that way.

But to proceed with the history.

SECTION VII.

ACCESSION AND WARS OF ANCUS MARCIUS.

On the death of Tullus, the government again devolved to the Patres, according to the original institution; who thereupon appointed an Interrex. In the Comitia held by this magistrate the people appointed Ancus Marcius king, and the Patres ratified their choice. Ancus Marcius was the grandson of Numa Pompilius by his daughter. It was natural, therefore, that he should bear in mind what had formed the peculiar glory of his grandfather's reign; and as he observed that the preceding reign, though glorious in other respects, had been unprosperous in a religious point of view, either through the neglect of sacred rites or the improper performance of them, he determined at the very commencement of his reign that he could do nothing better than restore the public sacrifices just as they had been instituted by Numa. With this view he directed the Pontifex to extract from the Commentaries of that king the method of performing them, and to write it down on an album, which was to be fixed in some public place, so that everybody might read its contents.

These proceedings inspired not only the Romans, who were desirous of peace, but also the surrounding cities, with the hope that Ancus would follow in the footsteps of his grandfather. The Latins, therefore, began to take courage, and made a foray into the Roman territories; and when a demand was made for the restitution of the booty, they returned a haughty answer, thinking that the Roman king would pass his reign among his chapels and altars. But the temper of Ancus was a mixture of that of Numa and Romulus. And, though he thought that peace had been a necessity for his grandfather's reign over a new and ferocious people, yet he was of opinion that he should not be easily able to maintain the peace which Numa had enjoyed with impunity; that his patience would be worked upon, and then despised; and that the present time required a king like Tullus rather than Numa.

But, as his grandfather had instituted religious ceremonies that were to be observed in peace, he determined to establish certain warlike ones. With this view, in order that war should be declared with fixed rites, he copied from the ancient nation of the Æquicoli the law still observed by the Fetiales in demanding restitution. According to this, the ambassador on arriving at the frontier of the people from whom reparation is demanded, having first veiled his head with a woollen fillet, speaks as follows:—"Hear me, O Jupiter! Hear me, boundaries"—naming the nation whose limits they form—"Hear me, Equity! I am the public messenger of the Roman people; my mission is a just and pious one, therefore let my words be trusted." Then he recites his demands, and calling Jupiter to witness, says: "If it is impiously and unjustly that I demand these men and these things to be given up to the Roman people and to myself, then suffer me not to return to my country." Such is the demand, which he makes on crossing the boundaries to the first man he meets, repeating it when he passes the gate of the city, and when he enters the Forum; only altering, according to circumstances, a few words of its tenor and of the form of the oath. If those whose restoration he demands are not given up within three and thirty days—for such is the usual term—he declares war as follows: "Hear! O Jupiter, and thou, Juno, and Quirinus, and all the celestial, all the terrestrial, and all the infernal gods, hear me! I call you to witness that this people" (which he then names) "is unjust, performing not what right requires. But concerning these matters we will consult at home our elders, by what means we may obtain our rights."

Then the envoy returns to Rome for instructions; whereupon the king immediately takes the opinion of the Senate, in the following form of words:—"Respecting the things, the disputes, and the causes thereof, the Pater Patratus of the Roman people of the Quirites hath spoken with the Pater Patratus of the ancient Latins, and with the ancient Latins themselves—which things should have been given up, done, and paid for, but which they have neither given up, done, nor paid for,—say, what is your opinion?" Then the first person whose opinion is thus asked, replies: "I consider that they should be recovered in pure and holy warfare, to which I consent and agree." Then the rest are asked in turn; and if the greater part of those present are of the same opinion, war is resolved on. Then it is customary that a Fetialis should carry to the boundaries either an iron-headed lance, or one burnt at the top and bloody, and in the presence of not less than three adult persons, should say: "Whereas the peoples of the ancient Latins, and the ancient Latins as individuals, have done certain things, and committed certain offences against the Roman people of Quirites, and whereas the Roman people of Quirites hath decreed a war against the ancient Latins, and the Senate of the Roman people of Quirites hath determined on, consented, and agreed to a war with the ancient Latins; now, therefore, I and the Roman people do declare and make war upon the peoples of the ancient Latins, and the ancient Latin men:" and having thus spoken, he hurls the lance over their boundaries. Such was the mode in which reparation was demanded from the Latins and war declared against them; and the custom has descended to posterity.

Then Ancus, having relinquished the care of religion to the Flamens and other priests, and having enrolled a new army, marched forth, and took by assault Politorium, a Latin city; and following the example of his predecessors, who had increased the Roman state by receiving into its bosom its conquered enemies, he transferred the whole of its inhabitants to Rome. And as the ancient Romans occupied the Palatine, the Sabines the Capitol and citadel, and the Albans the Cælian Hill, the

Aventine was assigned to the new comers. More new citizens were not long afterwards located at the same spot through the capture of Tellenæ and Ficana. But Politorium had to be twice reduced, as the ancient Latins had again occupied it after its desertion; and for this reason it was now razed, lest it should be a continual receptacle for enemies. The whole brunt of the Latin War centred at last about Medullia, and was waged there with doubtful and varying success. For the town was well fortified, and defended by a strong garrison; insomuch that, pitching their camp in the open field, the Latin army sometimes contended with the Romans in a regular battle. At length, making an effort with his whole forces, Ancus defeated them in the field, and, having captured a vast booty, returned to Rome. On this occasion also many thousand Latins were received into the city, to whom habitations were assigned in the valley of Murcia, so as to connect the Aventine with the Palatine. The Janiculum was also added to the city, not for want of space, but for fear it should be seized by enemies as a citadel. It was then connected with the city, not only by a wall, but also, for the convenience of passing thither, with a wooden bridge, the first thrown over the Tiber. The Fossa Quiritium is also the work of King Ancus, no trifling defence for those parts of the city which, from the level nature of the ground, are easy of access. The city was thus immensely increased, and as in such a multitude of men, clandestine crimes, from the difficulty of detection, were constantly perpetrated, in order to repress by terror this increasing audacity, a prison was built in the middle of the city overhanging the forum. Nor was it the city alone which increased under this king, but also its territory and boundaries. For the Silva Mæsia having been wrested from the Veientines, the Roman dominion was extended to the sea: Ostia was built at the mouth of the Tiber, and salt-works established round about it. The Temple of Jupiter Feretrius was also enlarged, on account of the splendid successes which had been obtained in war.

Besides the wars just related, which are taken from the narrative of Livy, Ancus Marcius is also said to have fought against Fidenæ, which had revolted, and against the Sabines, who had twice broken the treaty made with King Tullus. These wars are related by Dionysius;[1] but they contain nothing at all remarkable except the reported capture of Fidenæ by means of a mine; while the wars with the Sabines consist only of incursions, without a single pitched battle of which the place is named; though they suffered so much at the hands of the Romans that they were obliged to sue for peace. It was probably this dearth of incidents that induced Livy to omit all notice of them, as they would have made no figure among the warlike annals of the Romans, with which his subsequent pages were to be filled. As we have seen, however, he just drops a hint of a war with the Veientines, by mentioning that the Mœsian Forest was wrested from them, and the Roman Empire extended on this side to the mouth of the Tiber and the sea. The account of this Veientine War by Dionysius[2] must therefore be regarded as a supplement to Livy. According to this, the Veientines had begun the war by an incursion into the Roman territories. Marcius attacks them near Fidenæ, overthrows them, and takes their camp; for which victory he celebrates a triumph. Two years afterwards the Veientines again break the treaty, and Ancus once more defeats them in a still more decisive action at a place which Dionysius calls Allæ, but which is not mentioned by any other writer. In this campaign Tarquinius, who afterwards became King of Rome, achieved great distinction as commander of the cavalry. He had also served in some of the previous wars. Dionysius also mentions a war with the Volsci, and the capture of Velitræ, their capital, which we do not hear of anywhere else, and which seems hardly probable.

Tarquinius, whom we have just mentioned, was an active ambitious man, and powerful from his wealth, who settled himself at Rome, in the hope and desire of obtaining honour, which there was no means of acquiring in his native town, Tarquinii; for there was he born, though of a foreign family. He was the son of the Corinthian Demaratus; who, being driven from home by political faction, had chanced to

---
[1] Lib. iii. cc. 39—42.   [2] Ibid. c. 41.

fix his abode at Tarquinii. Here he took a wife, who bore him two sons, Lucumo and Aruns. Aruns died before his father, leaving his wife pregnant; but Lucumo survived, and became the heir of all his property. Demaratus had died very soon after his son Aruns, and, being ignorant that his daughter-in-law was in the family-way, he left nothing to his posthumous grandson; to whom was given, on account of his poverty, the name of Egerius. Lucumo was elated by the enormous wealth of which he had thus become possessed, and his pride was further stimulated by his wife Tanaquil, who belonged to the first family in the state, and was not disposed to suffer that her position by marriage should be inferior to that which she claimed by birth. But there was no prospect of rising at Tarquinii, as the Etruscans despised Lucnmo as the son of a foreign exile. Tanaquil could not brook this indignity, and, forgetting all love for her country provided she could see her husband honoured, she formed the resolution of migrating from Tarquinii. Rome seemed to be the place best suited to such designs. Among a new people, where all nobility must be recently acquired, and the fruit of valour, some place would be found for a brave and active man. She considered that the Sabine Tatius had reigned there; that Numa had been called to the Roman throne from Cures; that Ancus himself sprang from a Sabine mother, and could trace his pedigree no further back than Numa. It was not difficult to persuade her husband to fall into these views, both because he was desirous of distinction, and because Tarquinii was his country only on his mother's side. He therefore repaired to Rome with all his property. He was travelling with his wife in an open carriage, and had arrived at the Janiculum, when an eagle, swooping gently down, carried off his cap. The bird then, with much clamour, accompanying the course of the carriage, as if it had been dispatched from heaven on this mission, at length replaced the cap on Lucumo's head, and took its flight into the air. Tanaquil, who, like most of the Etruscans, was skilled in the interpretation of celestial prodigies, was overjoyed at this augury. Embracing her husband, she bade him raise his hopes high, seeing from

TARQUINIUS MIGRATES TO ROME.

what region of the heavens, and from what god, the bird was a messenger; that the omen was manifested on the highest part of him, his head; that the bird had removed a mere human ornament, in order to restore it by divine interposition. It was with such thoughts and hopes that they entered the city; and having procured a house there, Lucumo assumed the name of L. Tarquinius Priscus. Here he attracted the notice of the Romans, as well from his wealth as from the circumstance of his being a stranger. Nor was he backward in pushing his fortunes by conciliating all the friends he could, by his affable address, by the banquets which he gave, and by the benefits which he conferred. At length his fame reached the palace; and, having obtained the notice of the king, by a skilful use of this opportunity, and by discharging dexterously and liberally the offices with which he was entrusted, he soon obained so large a share of the royal confidence and friendship, that he was consulted on all business, both public and private, both foreign and domestic; and at last, having thus been proved in all sorts of ways, the king appointed him by will the guardian of his children.

Ancus reigned four and twenty years with as much conduct and glory, both in peace and war, as any of the former kings.

REMARKS.—"We have already observed," says Schwegler,[1] "that Ancus is the reverse of Tullus and the very image of Numa. In this peculiar character he cultivates religion, restores the neglected worship of the gods, brings the precepts of Numa again into force and to public knowledge, and is by temper peaceable and averse to war. On the other hand, as the fourth king, he is the founder (*Stifter*) of the *plebs*. Hence he makes war upon the surrounding Latin territory, conquers their towns, transplants the inhabitants to Rome, and thus lays the foundation of the Roman *plebs*. As creator of the *plebs*, Ancus appears also as their patron, just as, later on, conquered towns and provinces were accustomed to choose their conqueror for their patron. This patronship procured him the distinctive character of a 'citizen king.' Thus he is called 'the good Ancus' by Ennius (Ap. Fest. p. 301, Scal.); and by

[1] Buch xiii. § 4.

Virgil he is described as 'Nimium gaudens popularibus auris' (Æn. vi. 817). By virtue of this double part which Ancus Marcius has to play, there is something contradictory in his nature; he unites disparate qualities; and it is characteristic of this double nature that he founds, or more accurately regulates, the institution of the Fetiales, or the ceremonies of conducting war. It is probable that the old tradition discovered in the name of Ancus Marcius an indication of this two-fold part, and on this ground made Ancus Marcius the fourth Roman king. For as the name of Marcius expresses the spiritual and pontifical character of the king, so also might be found in the name of Ancus some relationship to the father of the working class, or the *plebs*. For properly his name is *Martius*, and is commonly written Marcius, because the Gentile name of the Marcii, who traced their descent from Ancus, was usually so written. But the name Martius is derived from the prophetic god Mars, whose oracles were delivered at Tiora Matiena by a woodpecker. The name *Ancus* (comp. the diminutive *ancilla*) signifies 'help,' 'servant' (Paul. Diac. p. 19, *Ancillæ* et ibi, Müller; Non. p. 71, *Ancillantur*), and thus answers to the name of *Servius*, that of the other plebeian king. But the ancients for the most part derive his name ἀγκών, *a bracchio adunco*, or because he was deformed in the elbow. Viewed in this way, the figure of Ancus Marcius shows itself to be an invention, the product of historical construction. It is not impossible that a king of this name once ruled at Rome; but that he was just the fourth king, and played just the part which tradition attributed to him as the fourth king, must be decidedly questioned."

The improbability therefore of the history of Ancus arises from two causes. The first of these—that he is the very image of Numa—we have already examined.[1] The second cause of improbability attaches not to Ancus absolutely, but only relatively; namely, that he is represented as the *fourth* king, and performs the acts which he does *as the fourth king*. If we inquire into the nature of those acts, we do not find much difference between them and those of his predecessors. Like them, he institutes some ceremonies, wages some wars, transfers the inhabitants of some conquered towns to Rome. This is all that ancient authors tell us of his acts; and it does not seem to affect the credibility of

[1] Above, p. 180, sq.

them, whether they should have been done by the first king, or the fourth, or the seventh.

The charge of improbability, however, is founded, not on anything that the ancient writers tell us, but on a theory of Niebuhr's,—that Ancus Marcius was the founder of the *plebs*.

On which we shall observe, first, that to call him their *founder* seems a very odd conception, and, in fact, a contradiction in terms. We can conceive of Romulus founding the Senate, the Equites, and even the Populus, for all these were endowed with certain rights and privileges; but to found the *plebs* is to found a negation. The plebeians having no civil privileges were founded only by nature, and cannot be regarded as an order.

And hence falls to the ground the idea of any popularity that Ancus may have enjoyed on this account. For as the *plebs* could not thank him for their foundation, so neither could they have felt grateful to him for any privileges bestowed upon them. Ancus seems to have gained his popularity rather for remitting his own privileges than for any that he conferred. Among these we might mention the right of declaring war. Neither Romulus nor Tullus appears to have consulted the Senate on such occasions. But by the Fetial law Ancus referred the matter to the Senate, and was governed by the majority. Cicero also tells us that he divided among the people the territory which he had taken, and made the woods on the sea-shore—which he had captured from the Veientines—public property.[1] It was by these acts, and others perhaps of the like kind that have not come down to us, that Ancus seems to have gained his popularity; for anything that he might have done particularly in favour of the *plebs*, as a class, would probably have rendered him unpopular with the other orders. Hence also fall to the ground the ingenious speculations founded on the name of *Ancus*. That the name of Martius, or Marcius, may be connected with Mars, in his prophetic character, seems sufficiently probable. There was a famous soothsayer of that name who predicted the overthrow of the Romans at Cannæ.[2] But the name of Marcius borne by Ancus—which, however, has nothing to do with his popularity—may, we think, be probably accounted for in a more simple manner. It is universally agreed that he was the grandson of Numa by his daughter; and though Cicero, in a passage before quoted, says that the name of

[1] De Rep. ii. 18.   [2] Liv. xxv. 12.

his father was unknown, yet as there was a family of the Marcii at Rome, who seem to have been in favour with the king, since he made one of them Pontifex, it is no extravagant supposition that he may have given his daughter to one of them. They may even have been related to Numa, as they bore his name.[1] The same passage shows that *Marcius* was not derived in this instance from Mars, but from Marcus, the Pontifex being the son of Marcus; and so Julius comes from Iulus, and Tullius perhaps from Tullus.

Nor, secondly, was it under Ancus Marcius that a plebeian population first began to exist. Such a supposition is not only contrary to the whole tenor of the history; it is also contrary to all probability that a state like Rome should have existed a century without a plebeian or proletarian class. But we shall have to examine this whole question of the *plebs* presently, when we come to speak of the Servian constitution, and shall therefore content ourselves with observing here that it is on the ground of Ancus having been their creator that the whole charge against the history rests. He is said to have been invented, as the fourth king, as their creator; but as this creation is itself an invention of the critics, no argument can be drawn from it as against the ancient writers, who ignore such a creation; nor consequently against the probability of the history.

"The wars with the neighbouring Latin states," continues Schwegler,[2] "which tradition ascribes to Ancus Marcius are certainly in the main historical. We must indeed not regard the circumstances that it is the fourth Roman king who wages them, that they last only a few years, and are ended so quickly and victoriously as tradition relates; they probably lasted many generations, with varying fortune. Under Tullus Hostilius, the Roman territory still only extends to the fifth mile-stone; and yet his successor founds Ostia; the conquest of the whole left bank of the Tiber falls consequently in the interval; an addition of territory so considerable that it cannot be believed to have been the fruit of a few summer campaigns. But the kernel of these traditions may be received as historical; namely, that the Romans, whose original bounds were of small circumference, may have conquered in time a subject district, and that the inhabitants of this territory formed the foundation of the Roman *plebs*. The circumstance that at a

[1] "Pontificem delade Numam Marcium, Marci filium, ex Patribus legit."— Liv. i. 20. [2] Buch xiii. § 5.

very early period we no longer find any towns in the triangle which the Appian Way makes with the Tiber, is confirmatory of those traditions. Some must certainly have existed there in the oldest times; and not only Ficana, Tellenæ, Politorium, but also more towns, of which the memory has not been preserved. We may trust tradition that they were destroyed by the Romans at an early period, in order to deprive the conquered district of any military *points d'appui*. Tradition is also worthy of belief in placing the extension of the Roman dominion towards the sea, and the conquest of the banks of the Lower Tiber, at an earlier epoch than the conquest of the towns beyond the Anio, which is ascribed to Tarquinius Priscus. Policy dictated such a course, and it is therefore supported by internal probability. Only it appears incredible that the inhabitants of the conquered district should have been transplanted to Rome. For it would not only have been highly unpractical to settle the plebeians at such a distance from their lands, but also impolitic to plant them at one point, and to give them possession of a strong hill inside the city; while they would have been much less dangerous if dispersed over the level country. Nor can we see very well where the 'many thousand Latins,' whom Livy describes as transplanted to Rome, could have found room there. Tradition says, on the Aventine and in the Murcian valley. But, according to more credible tradition, the Aventine was first assigned to the city *plebs* as a dwelling-place and for building their houses by the Icilian law. Till that time it was common land; nay, even, as Dionysius relates,[1] it was for the most part still wood. And in the valley of Murcia, the narrow vale which separates the Aventine from the Palatine, and which was afterwards converted into the Great Circus, there was only room for a few hundred small houses. On these grounds it is probable that by far the greater part of the *plebs* remained in the occupation of their farms. We must draw the same conclusion from the circumstance that the plebeian Comitia, or Comitia Tributa, were, according to ancient custom, held on the *nundinæ* on which the countrymen came into town for the corn-market; and that for the same reason every law proposed must be announced three *nundinæ*, or market days, before it was discussed, and must be publicly exhibited for this period.

"Only this much is correct, that the Aventine and the valley of

[1] Lib. x. 31.

Murcia were at a later period plebeian quarters. And it was this circumstance that gave occasion to the tradition that the *plebs* which dwelt there was compelled to do so by the fourth king.

"Besides the wars of conquest which, according to concordant tradition, Ancus waged with the surrounding Latins, and which in the main may pass for historical, Dionysius represents him as also fighting with the Fidenates, the Sabines, the Volsci, and the Veientines. Of these wars the same cannot be said; they are a literary invention. The capture of Fidenæ especially, which is effected by a mine, resembles the capture by Romulus of this so frequently-taken town. It is copied from the historical time, and the capture of Fidenæ by means of a mine by the Dictator Servilius A.U.C. 319."

On this we will observe that if it took the Romans "many generations," which, we suppose, must mean at least two centuries, to conquer Latium, how many must be allowed for the conquest of all Italy? and how many for the conquest of all the world?

If we divide the history of Rome from its foundation to the establishment of the empire into three periods of rather more than two centuries each,—namely, from its foundation to the expulsion of the kings, a period of nearly two centuries and a half, according to the common chronology; from the expulsion of the kings to the year B.C. 264, another period of something less than two centuries and a half; and from B.C. 264 to B.C. 44, a still shorter period,—we shall find that in the first of these periods Rome had subdued, but not finally, the greater part of Latium, an extent of territory about equal to a middling-sized English county; that in the second she had subdued the whole of Italy; and that in the third she had conquered the greater part of the known world. Now if any one were asked which was the most extraordinary of these achievements he might perhaps waver between deciding for the second or third, which are facts established on the best historical evidence; but nobody, we think, would decide for the first, though even that, in regard to other nations, may be considered a somewhat extraordinary achievement. But the Romans were an extraordinary people. We must not measure their history by that of other nations, and sit down in our closets and say what they might have done, or what they might not have done. The impulse given by Grecian blood and intellect to Sabine sturdiness made them the first people in the world. They extended their empire not less by their institutions than by their arms, and especially by their policy of receiving into their city the peoples whom they had conquered, as we are told was done by the kings with the Latins and other nations. And if they had not made a tolerably rapid progress in the early period of their history, we may safely affirm that they would never have been able to achieve what they afterwards accomplished.

We may further remark, that Schwegler supports his view of the difficulty of the Latin conquests by placing them in a false light. They did not last only a few years, but through three successive reigns: nay, we may say five successive reigns; for the Romans did not acquire a complete ascendency over Latium till the time of Tarquinius Superbus. If Tullus Hostilius did not extend his boundaries, he at all events weakened the power of the Latins by the capture of their metropolis, and the addition of its population to that of Rome. The portion of Latium subdued by Ancus Marcius appears to have been that which might be comprised between the Tiber, the sea, a line drawn from the sea to Alba Longa, and from Alba Longa to Rome, or a space about twelve or fifteen miles in extent on every side. Yet it is deemed impossible that the extent of country just described should have been acquired in a few campaigns! While at the same time Schwegler allows that the towns in that district must have disappeared at a very early period, and that it was good policy on the part of the Romans to destroy them; circumstances which confirm the truth of the traditional history.

To ask whether the whole of the inhabitants of the conquered district were transferred to Rome, whether some of them may not have been left to cultivate their lands, is to press questions on these primitive and scanty annals which they are of course not competent to answer. We must content ourselves with a general outline of the main facts, and this there is nothing to shake. It is probable that the rural population may have been left to cultivate the ground, but the towns people must have been carried to Rome; or otherwise, their own cities having been razed, they would have had no shelter. But we must conceive of these primitive towns as very small places,—in fact, little more than villages, with perhaps three or four thousand inhabitants, and some of them still fewer.

To say that the Aventine was first assigned to the *plebs* for a dwelling-place by the Icilian law in B.C. 456, that it had till then been common land, and was still *for the most part* covered with wood, is a complete misrepresentation of the account of Dionysius. From Dionysius's words, "*all of it* was not at that time inhabited,"[1] we may infer just the contrary—that by far the greater part of it was inhabited. The remainder of it was public land, covered with wood, and it was this that Icilius proposed to give to the *plebs*, as well as some of the houses already upon it, by eviction of those who could not produce a good title. And as this statement is unfounded, so also must be the inference from it, that it was from the plebeians being afterwards found on that hill—that is, of course, after the asserted first location of Icilius — that the tradition arose of the Latins having been planted there by Ancus. The Aventine is of considerable size, according to Dionysius twelve stadia, or a mile and a half, in circumference, which may be about right; and it would therefore, with its adjuncts and valleys, have accommodated some thousands in the humble manner then customary.

Whether Dionysius may have drawn upon his imagination for some of the wars of Ancus we will not undertake to say. It is not improbable that he may have invented some that are not mentioned by Livy, or taken them from dubious sources; but we have already shown that Ancus must have had a war with Veii.

Schwegler then proceeds[2] to attack the tradition which ascribes the Carcer Mamertinus to Ancus, as follows: "It is difficult to say why the building of the *carcer* was ascribed to Ancus Marcius; but it would not be at all doubtful if it could be shown that this state prison bore the name of Martius in antiquity. But such a name is not found in the ancient writers, who call it only *Carcer*, or from its lower part *Tullianum*. But the name of Carcer Mamertinus, which it bore in the Middle Ages, is much too learned to have been invented in the time of the *Mirabilia*, and must have come down from antiquity. Moreover, the name of Marforio (Forum Martis), which has been given to the statue of the river-god which stood over against the Carcer Mamertinus, points to an ancient sanctuary of Mars in this neighbourhood. Hence it is possible that the prison bore the name of Mamertinus in antiquity; and it might thus be easily explained how the foundation of the Carcer Martius was attributed to Ancus Marcius. Nay, one is even tempted to see in this traditional connexion of the Carcer with the name of Ancus Marcius a proof that the by-name in

---

[1] ἧς (λόφος) οὐχ ἅπας τοτ' φκητο.—Lib. x. 31.   [2] Buch xiii. § 6.

question is antique. There is the same connexion with the Tullianum, the 'lower dungeon.' This dungeon, from an analogous explanation of the name, is commonly attributed to Servius Tullius. But the original destination of the Tullianum was not for a prison, but a fountain-house, and this is testified by the name, since *tullius* signifies a spring;[1] Tullianum, consequently, the house of the spring. The common tradition, according to which Ancus built the upper part of the dungeon, and Servius Tullius the lower, contains moreover an actual impossibility, as it is impossible to see how the Tullianum could have been built under the Carcer without destroying it: it is inconceivable that the upper room should have been built first, and then the lower. Moreover, the whole structure was evidently executed at once from one plan, and not at different times. Thus it may be shown that the reputed connexion of the Carcer with the two kings in question rests solely on a false etymology; but it certainly belongs to the regal period. It is probably a work of Tarquin; since, as a fountain-house, it is connected with the *cloaca*, into which the water runs."

We may here admire that nicety of criticism which can distinguish whether so ancient a monument as the Carcer was built in the reign of Ancus, or, twenty years later, in that of Tarquinius; though, as there must have been fountains at Rome before the Cloaca Maxima was built, we may be unable to perceive any necessary connexion between that drain and the spring in the Tullianum. Whoever has visited this place, which may still cause a shudder from its subterranean gloom, and a recollection of the scenes that have passed in it, will see that it could never have been intended for anything but a dungeon, the use which ancient authors unanimously ascribe to it. Lying at the foot of the Capitoline Hill, and hollowed out of the rock, it was natural enough that a spring of water should gush forth, which still flows to this day. From what it derived its name, we will not attempt to determine. Nor shall we follow Schwegler in his super-subtle speculations about the name of Mamertinus,[2] having already shown that Ancus's name of Marcius is probably derived from Marcus, and not from Mars. But the impossibility of constructing the

---

[1] Festus, p. 352, Tullios; Suet. Fragm. de Flum. ap. Fest. (ed. Müll. p. 382); cf. Plin. N. H. xvii. 26, Tullii Tiburtes.

[2] The name of Marforio was probably derived from the Temple of Mars Ultor, in the Forum Augusti.

Tullianum without destroying the Carcer we must deny, as it is nothing but a cellar scooped out of the rock.

Sir G. C. Lewis makes no remarks of any importance on the reign of Ancus Marcius.

SECTION VIII.

ACCESSION OF TARQUINIUS PRISCUS.—HIS FIRST ACTS.

THE sons of Ancus were nearly grown up at the death of their father; wherefore Tarquinius pressed on all the more hastily the Comitia for electing a king. When these had been appointed, he sent the boys on a hunting-party at the time when they were to meet. Tarquinius is said to have been the first who canvassed for the crown, and to have made the following speech for the purpose of gaining the favour of the plebeians. He observed, "That what he sought was no new thing; that he was not the first foreigner at Rome who had aspired to the throne—which might be a just subject of wonder and indignation—but the third; that King Tatius had not only been a foreigner, but even an enemy; that Numa, though a stranger to the city, and without seeking the honour, had been spontaneously elected; that with regard to himself, he had migrated to Rome with his wife and all his fortune as soon as ever he had become his own master; that he had lived longer in Rome than in his former country, during that portion of his life in which men are capable of official duties; that both in peace and war he had learnt the Roman laws and customs from no master whom he need be ashamed of, from King Ancus himself; that he had yielded to nobody in duty and attention towards the king, and that he had vied with the king himself in good offices towards others."

These were no false or idle boasts, and the Roman people by a great majority conferred upon him the crown. But the same ambition which he had displayed in soliciting it accompanied him in wearing it, and is a blot upon his otherwise

ACCESSION OF TARQUINIUS PRISCUS. 231

well-merited reputation. It was as much with a design to establish his own power as to improve the constitution that he chose a hundred new senators, who obtained the name of the " minor families;" a faction he might rely on, as they had entered the Senate-house through his favour.

The first war which Tarquinius waged was with the Latins, in which he took by assault the town of Appiolæ. Here he obtained a much larger booty than was commensurate with the fame of the expedition; by the aid of which he exhibited the games much more splendidly and expensively than any of the other kings had done. It was then that a site was first marked out for the Circus, which is now called the Circus Maximus. Spaces, called *fori*, were allotted to the patricians and knights, where every man might construct for himself seats or scaffolding for viewing the games. These scaffoldings were supported on poles twelve feet high. The show consisted of horse-races and pugilists, brought for the most part from Etruria. Henceforth these games were celebrated annually, and were called indifferently the Great Games or the Roman Games. Tarquin also allotted spaces round the forum to private individuals for building on; in consequence of which shops and porticoes were erected. He was also preparing to surround the city with a stone wall, when he was interrupted by the breaking out of a Sabine war.

REMARKS.—With the accession of Tarquin, as Schwegler observes,[1] a new epoch begins in Roman history. The assertion, however, of that writer, that no interregnum took place after the death of Ancus, is unfounded. It is true that neither Livy nor Cicero expressly mentions an interregnum; on the other hand, they do not say that it was laid aside; while Dionysius, who is usually a favourite author with Schwegler, positively states that no alteration was made, and that the Senate appointed Interreges as usual.[2] In fact, Tarquin, as yet a private individual, could have had no power to make any change in the constitution in this respect. But after his accession he effected a great innovation, and

---
[1] Buch xiv. § 1.
[2] ἡ βουλὴ μένειν ἐπὶ τῆς αὐτῆς (πολιτείας) ἔγνω, καὶ ἀποδείκνυσι μεσοβασιλεῖς.—Lib. iii. 46.

almost swamped the Senate by the addition of a hundred new
members of a lower class than the old ones. This is the grand
characteristic of the Tarquinian dynasty, or at least of its first two
kings—the courting of the popular party. The first Tarquin
secured his election by flattering and soliciting the plebeians; and
Servius Tullius, his successor, put the constitution on a broader
and more popular basis by the reforms which he effected. But of
this, as well as of the regal constitution in general, we will speak
under the reign of Servius Tullius.

In his observations on the history of Tarquinius Priscus,
Schwegler remarks:[1] "The first question which occurs respecting
the Tarquinii, and on which the decision of much else depends, is
this: What is to be thought of their reputed origin from Tarquinii,
and remotely from Corinth? At the first glance, this tradition has
a seductive historical appearance; not only because it is so decidedly
connected with authentic historical events, as the rise of
Cypselus and fall of the Bacchiadæ, but also because it corresponds
so accurately with chronology. Cypselus seized the supreme power
about the 30th Olympiad, B.C. 660, and about forty-four years later,
or according to Roman chronology in B.C. 616, the son of the exiled
Demaratus became king of Rome. This chronological agreement
is the more remarkable, and appears the more to vouch for the
historical value of the tradition in question, the more certain it is
that the older Roman annalists were not, as Niebuhr has shown,[2]
in a condition to make out any synchronism between the Tables of
the Pontiffs and the history of Corinth. How little they were
capable of making such a reckoning appears from the gross chronological
errors committed by even the later and more instructed
historians, such for instance as Licinius Macer, where the synchronism
of Roman and foreign history is concerned. Thus the
writer just mentioned makes Coriolanus a contemporary of the
elder Dionysius![3]

"Nevertheless, the chronological agreement in question is but a
deceptive appearance. A synchronism of the events of Greek and
Roman history is, in the present case, only possible when the
chronology of the Roman kings is accurately ascertained; that is,
that Tarquinius Priscus actually reigned thirty-eight years; Servius
Tullius, forty-four; and Tarquinius Superbus, twenty-five. But

---

[1] Buch xv. § 8. [2] Rom. Gesch. B. I. S. 359.
[3] Dionys. vii. 1.

if Tarquinius Priscus, as the old and genuine tradition uniformly and consistently relates, was the father of the younger Tarquinius, which last, according to the Annals, died A.U.C. 259, he could not have ascended the throne in the year 138, but half a century later, seeing that when he assumed the government he was about forty years old. In short, as the traditional chronology of the Roman kings cannot be maintained, and is nothing but invention, so also the synchronism of Cypselus with the father of Tarquinius Priscus falls to the ground, and with it the main prop of the tradition in question.

"The following consideration also renders the tradition improbable. The stranger who settles at Rome is called Lucius Tarquinius Priscus: Tarquinius, on account of his origin from Tarquinii; Lucius, from Lucumo: Priscus, as distinguishing him from the younger Tarquin. According to this, the whole name would have signified nothing more than the Lucumo from Tarquinii. But it cannot be thought that Tarquinius himself would have adopted such a description as his proper name, and borne it as king. 'The distinguished man of Tarquinii' is a mode in which we might speak of a stranger, but nobody would name himself so. Moreover, in any event we must assume that Tarquin had previously no proper name, and was entirely nameless: as the name of Lucumo, which the Roman writers say he bore before his immigration, is no proper name, but a title of rank. If, however, he brought a proper name with him to Rome, the name of Tarquinius, taken from the place of his birth, could have been applied to him only as a cognomen, and not as a gentile name.

"The common tradition by which Tarquinius, a stranger settled at Rome, became king by the free choice of the people, and this, moreover, when the last king had left sons, appears, when viewed in connexion with the uncommonly rigid and exclusive spirit of the oldest Roman citizens, as not even probable. Such an elevation in a peaceable and lawful manner must have been opposed by prejudices and obstacles not to be overcome by the most brilliant personal qualities, or the greatest liberality and officiousness. Thus it appears more credible on this ground—which, however, is not decisive—that the Tarquins were by birth Roman citizens.

"The pretended origin of the Tarquins from Tarquinii is consequently nothing more than an etymological myth, for which also presumption speaks. The Tarquins were a Roman *gens*, and the resemblance of their name to that of Tarquinii is only accidental.

At the same time, we do not mean to contest the tradition respecting Demaratus, and his immigration to Tarquinii, nor the connexion which it indicates between that place and Corinth. This narrative may rest on national Etruscan tradition. But the connecting of the Roman Tarquin with this Corinthian Demaratus is, according to all presumption, without historical foundation, and as groundless as the connecting of Numa with Pythagoras.

"With this vanish also all those accounts and traditions which evidently only proceed from the assumption of the Etruscan origin of the Tarquins: such as that Tarquinius Priscus introduced the insignia of royalty, the golden *bulla*, and the pomp of triumph; evidently because these ornaments and this pomp passed for having been originally Etruscan. That the wife of Tarquin was called Tanaquil is to be viewed in the same light. Thana (whence Tanchufil) is one of the female names most frequently met with in Etruscan sepulchral inscriptions. Tanchufil is also frequently found; and it is possible that this name is merely a title of honour, like *donna*. According to another and evidently older tradition, the wife of Tarquin, moreover, was not called Tanaquil, but *Gaia Cæcilia*. Tradition also lends Etruscan names to the sons of Tarquin: they are called Lucumo (Lucius) and Aruns—two names which are also evidently invented, since Aruns (in Etruscan, Arnth) is probably as little a real proper name as Lucumo. Moreover, the contrast of the overbearing Lucius and the suffering Aruns is so strikingly repeated in the narrative of Livy about Clusium,[1] that we can hardly doubt there is some mythico-symbolical reason for the choice of these names."

The accession of the Tarquins and the consistency of their chronology are no doubt most important points in the early history of Rome, and deserve the most careful examination. Schwegler has of course put everything in the worst light for the credit of the history, and we must therefore inquire whether he has always done this fairly and on sufficient grounds.

When that writer states that "the old and genuine tradition uniformly and consistently relates that Tarquinius Priscus was the father of the younger Tarquinius," he makes an assertion for which he has no adequate reason. For, first, he has no means of knowing what the "old and genuine tradition" was. The statement in question no doubt comes from Fabius, the most ancient writer of

[1] Lib. v. c. 33.

history; but this neither proves that it was the most ancient nor the most genuine tradition. He has still less grounds for asserting that the old tradition was "uniform and consistent;" on the contrary, it appears from the historical writers, from whom alone we can know anything about it, that it was precisely the reverse. Thus, Livy says, that it was very uncertain whether L. Tarquinius —afterwards Tarquinius Superbus—was the son or grandson of Tarquinius Priscus, though most authors called him the son.[1] It appears, by implication, from a passage in Cicero, that the same doubt existed in his time. Schwegler, indeed, by quoting this passage falsely, claims it in his own favour. Thus, he writes:[2] "Tarquinius, qui admodum parvos tum haberet *filios*." But the real words are, "tum haberet *liberos*." This makes all the difference, and shows that Cicero was in doubt. Had he been certain, he would either have used the word *filios* or *nepotes*. But *liberi* may mean either children or grandchildren, and is indeed used in the latter sense by Cicero himself.[3] The doubt, therefore, was not first raised by Livy or Dionysius, though the latter is the only author who discusses it formally and at length, and comes to the conclusion that Piso Frugi, an old historian, was right in calling the boys whom Tarquinius Priscus left behind him his grandsons.[4] There is, however, as Dionysius intimates, another method of escape from the difficulty; for Tarquinius Priscus may have made the boys his sons by adoption. And thus we see that there is no force at all in the objection.

Schwegler, however, repeats it in the case of Collatinus, who is represented as the son of Egerius, the nephew of Tarquinius Priscus;[5] which he could no more have been than Tarquinius Superbus could have been his son. "In this point," he says,[6] "tradition is consistent with itself. As it makes the sons of Tarquinius Superbus the grandsons of Tarquinius Priscus, so it makes Lucius Tarquinius Collatinus, the contemporary of the latter, the grandson, and not the great-grandson, of Aruns, the elder brother of Tarquinius Priscus; though many historical impossibilities arise hence." A candid critic would here have said, not that tradition was consistent with itself, but that the error was

---

[1] "Prisci Tarquinii regis filius nepusne fuerit, parum liquet; plurimis tamen anctoribus filium crediderim."—Lib. i. 46.
[2] Band i. S. 48, Anm. 2; cf. Cic. De Rep. ii. 21.   [3] In Verr. L. 15.
[4] Lib. iv. c. 6, sq.   [5] Liv. i. 57.   [6] B. i. S. 49.

consistent with itself. Both mistakes may be traced to Fabius Pictor, who, having made the one, naturally fell into the other. We know that Fabius wrote in Greek; he may not have been a perfect master of that language, or, what is more probable, his transcribers at Rome may have corrupted his manuscript, and made Collatinus υἱός, instead of υἱωνός, of Egerius. But it must be confessed to be a mistake, however it may have arisen. And what does this prove? That the history was invented or forged? Far from it; it is an honest blunder. A forger would have taken care that no such chronological slip should be alleged against his handiwork. Or that there was no such thing as record? That there was no public record of such matters may be allowed. The private history of Egerius would not have appeared in the public annals, nor even, perhaps, the genealogy of Tarquinius Superbus, though these annals would no doubt have recorded the deaths of the kings, and of the principal members of the royal family. These annals could have recorded, and that only briefly, the great public events; and it is the truth of such events alone that we are here concerned to establish.

If we reduce the civil chronology of Rome to astronomical years, there is nothing extraordinary in the chronology of the Tarquins. Tarquinius Priscus is said to have come to Rome in the eighth year of Ancus, which would be, in the common chronology, 632 B.C.; and if he was then thirty years of age, he would have been born in B.C. 662. As he died in B.C. 578, he was then eighty-four years old; but to reduce these to astronomical years, we must deduct one-sixth, which would leave him at seventy. In like manner, if his grandson, Tarquinius Superbus, was a boy of ten at his death, he would have been forty-seven when he began to reign; an age at which he might well have been strong enough to hurl Servius down the steps of the curia; he would have been sixty-seven at the time of his expulsion, and seventy-nine when he died at Cumæ.

Tanaquil might have been ten years younger than her husband, Tarquinius Priscus, and, therefore, twenty when she came with him to Rome, and sixty at the time of his death. That she should have lived to bury her son Aruns, in the fortieth year of Servius Tullius[1] (that is, thirty-three astronomical years), when she would have been ninety-three, is barely possible; but the only authority for this fact is Fabius again; no other author appears to have

[1] Dionys. iv. 30.

mentioned it, nor is it indeed of much importance. The objections made to the chronology of Brutus we shall examine when we come down to his period.

It will be perceived, however, that if the Roman civil years are to be reduced by one-sixth, in order to bring them into astronomical years, then Tarquinius Priscus must have been the grandson, and not the son, of Demaratus. For the expulsion of the Bacchiadæ from Corinth is commonly placed in B.C. 655, and, allowing ten years for his wanderings and his settling at Tarquinii, he might have married in B.C. 645; and it is not possible that Tarquin could have been the issue of this marriage, though his father might. It is very possible, therefore, that the old annalists made a mistake of a generation respecting the father of Tarquin, just as they did respecting his sons.

Schwegler's argument from the name of Tarquin is of little value. It is quite evident that he could not have borne the name of Lucumo as a title of honour, or to denote that he was a "distinguished man," because his reason for leaving Tarquinii was that he could obtain no distinction there. As a Greek by descent, he probably only bore one name, which was Latinized by the Romans into Lucius; but it is very possible that, after settling at Rome, he adopted the name of Tarquinius from the place of his birth. The full name of L. Tarquinius Priscus could not have been given to him till the time of Tarquinius Superbus at least. That there should have been a Roman *gens* Tarquinia at Rome before the time of the Tarquins, and that the resemblance of the name to Tarquinii should have been accidental, are both highly improbable; while, on the other hand, that the Tarquins founded a *gens* Tarquinia at Rome is evident from the name of L. Tarquinius Collatinus, the descendant of Egerius, and from the mention of such a *gens* by Livy and Cicero.[1]

Tarquin, though a stranger, had as good a chance of the Roman

---

[1] Liv. ii. 2; Cic. Rep. iii. 25, 31. When in the last of these passages Cicero says: "Nostri majores et Collatinum innocentem suspiciosa cognationis expulerunt, et reliquos Tarquinios offensione nominis;" if he meant by the "reliqui Tarquinii," persons who were not blood relations, as Schwegler supposes (S. 677, Anm. 4), then he must have meant clients or liberti of the Tarquins, who bore their name. For that there was only one *gens* Tarquinia appears from the preceding passage, "civitas, exulem gentem Tarquiniorum esse jussit." If there had been two, Cicero would have said *gentes*. Livy also speaks only of one.

crown as any Roman; nay, a better one, from his intimacy with
Ancus, the high position which he held, and the popularity which
he had acquired by his liberality and affability. The circumstance
that Ancus had left sons was no bar to his claim. The Roman
crown was not hereditary, and had never yet passed from father to
son. On the whole, therefore, it does not appear that Schwegler
has any incontrovertible grounds for asserting that the pretended
origin of the Tarquins from Tarquinii is nothing more than an
etymological myth, and that the connecting of Tarquin with
Demaratus is as groundless as the connecting of Numa with Pythagoras. Sir G. C. Lewis supplies an answer to this charge: "It is
not," says that writer, "like the story of Numa and Pythagoras, a
chronological absurdity."[1] The remarks which Schwegler makes
concerning the name of Tanaquil are confirmatory of the truth of
the history, since they show the name to have been Etruscan.
When Schwegler says that, "according to another and evidently
older tradition, the wife of Tarquin, moreover, was not called
Tanaquil, but Gaia Cæcilia," this is a grossly-uncandid way of stating
the matter. It is impossible for him to tell whether one tradition
is older than another; but the fact is that in this case there were
not two traditions. Tanaquil changed her name when she came to
Rome, just as her husband did, and adopted a Latin one.[2] Tanaquil
and Gaia Cæcilia are one and the same person; and Schwegler has
not the shadow of an authority for stating in his note here that Gaia
Cæcilia is originally entirely different from Tanaquil, and not considered an Etruscan woman. And even if there was any foundation
for Schwegler's remarks on this subject, such an appeal to trifling
circumstances affords no argument against the general truth of the
early history. Of the same nature is the remark about the regal
insignia, &c.,—a mere antiquarian matter, in the above respect of no
value. We need only add that there is no resemblance whatever
between the story of Lucius and Aruns Tarquinius and that of
Lucumo and Aruns at Clusium, except in the names, which seem
to have been common in Etruria; and, therefore, because in these

[1] Credibility, &c. vol. I. p. 477.
[2] "Gaia Cæcilia appellata est, ut Romam venit, quæ antea Tanaquil vocitata
erat, uxor Tarquinii Prisci regis Romanorum."—Paul Diac. p. 95 (ed. Müll.).
Gaia Cæcilia. "Tanaquil, quæ eadem Gaia Cæcilia vocata est."—Plin. H. N.
viii. 74, § 194. There is nothing contrary to this in the other passages cited
by Schwegler, S. 678, Anm. 7: viz. Festus, p. 238, Prædia, and Val. Max.
De Nom.

two cases Aruns appears to have been the injured party, to draw thence, without any other reason, a general conclusion that the names were mythico-symbolical, does not seem to be a very sound critical method, even though Buttmann may have adopted it.[1]

Schwegler then proceeds (Section 9) as follows: "Modern inquirers also,—as Levesque, Müller, Michelet, Arnold,—reasoning from the Etruscan origin of the Tarquins, have considered the Tarquinian dynasty as the Tuscan epoch of Rome, and have referred to the Tarquins everything Etruscan which they thought they found in Roman customs and institutions. To this I cannot accede: partly because the Etruscan origin of the Tarquins is not true; partly because the Etruscan influence on Rome was not by far so great as it is assumed to be; but particularly because the epoch of the Tarquins, so far as it exhibits traces of foreign influence, shows this influence to have been Greek."

We might have thought that the first of these reasons would have been sufficient; because, if the Tarquins came not from Etruria, they could not have introduced any Etruscan influence. On this point, however, we differ with Schwegler, though on the others we are inclined to agree with him. We think that the Tarquins came from Etruria; but from their Greek descent, they brought with them Greek habits rather than Etruscan.

Schwegler has examined this question in another part of his work,[2] from which we give the following results. He is of opinion that the Etruscan settlers at Rome were not sufficiently numerous to have any decided influence on the population, which always remained Sabino-Latin: and that this is shown by the language, which has but few traces of Tuscan. Further, the Roman always regarded the Tuscan as of a distinct and foreign race. Even the natural boundaries between them are sharply marked, whilst those between the Latins and the Sabines, or the Volscians, are imperceptible. Thus, "Trans Tiberim vendere," was equivalent to "to sell to foreigners:" and Cicero even calls the Tuscans "barbarians."[3] Many things which the Romans are said to have borrowed from the Etruscans, were common to them with the Italians. The *atrium* of the Roman house is said to be Etruscan, but there can be no doubt that this was old Italian.[4] The Atrium Tuscanicum was only a particular species of *atrium*, and the very term shows that there

[1] Mythol. II. 302.   [2] Buch iv. § 32.
[3] Nat. Deor. II. 4, 11.   [4] Abeken, Mittel-Italien, S. 186.

were other *atria* which were not Tuscan. So also the Roman *toga*, and the Roman doctrine of the Lares, Penates, &c., are said by Müller, Becker, and others, to have been Etruscan. But *toga* is a Latin word, rightly derived by Varro [1] from *tegere*; and is further shown to be Latin by the Gabine cincture. So, also, the worship of the Lares is Italian and Sabine, for Tatius consecrates altars to Larunda and the Lares.[2] In fact, not a single Roman worship can be shown to be derived from Etruria; for even the Capitoline Triad, established by Tarquinius Superbus, had its prototype in the old Sabine capitol on the Quirinal.[3] But a very essential and characteristic feature, that of the statues of the gods, was undoubtedly introduced in the time of the Tarquins. Before the accession of the Tarquinian dynasty, the shrines were without images.[4] It cannot, however, be doubted, that from the earliest period the gods were at least represented by symbols. Jupiter was at first worshipped in the form of a stone, whence the oath "Per Jovem Lapidem;" Mars was represented by a spear; and Vesta by the fire which burnt upon her hearth.[5] These symbols were probably adopted rather from want of skill to make a statue, than, as Schwegler thinks, because the gods were not yet conceived of as anthropomorphous, or personal beings;[6] and this view is supported by a passage in Clemens of Alexandria, quoted by Schwegler himself.[7] In fact, Schwegler's supposition involves a contradiction in terms, for a symbol refers to something; and if this was not a personal god, what was it? The same writer is of opinion that image-worship was introduced among the Romans rather through their intercourse with Magna Græcia than from Etruria; but he gives no reason for this opinion, and allows that the Tarquins may have employed Tuscan artists and workmen. It was not, however, necessary that the Tarquins, whose ancestral home was Corinth,

[1] Ling. Lat. v. 114. [2] Ibid. § 74.
[3] "Capitolium Vetus quod ibi sacellum Jovis, Junonis, Minervæ, et id antiquius quam ædis quæ in Capitolio facta."—Ibid. § 158.
[4] "Varro dicit antiquos Romanos plus annos septem et septuaginta deos sine simulacro coluisse."—St. Aug. Civ. Dei. iv. 31.
[5] Cic. Fam. vii. 12; Polyb. iii. 25; Serv. Æn. viii. 641; Paul. Diac. p. 92, Feretrius, &c. p. 115, Lapidem; Plut. Camill. 20; and the authorities collected by Ambrosch, Studien, I. S. 5, Anm. 17, S. 6, Anm. 26, S. 9, Anm. 36, &c.
[6] B. i. S. 680, Anm. 8.
[7] ἐν Ῥώμῃ τὸ παλαιὸν δόρυ φασὶν γεγονέναι τοῦ Ἄρεως τὸ ξόανον Ὀλύμπου ὁ συγγραφεύς, οὐδένα τῶν τεχνιτῶν ἐπὶ τὴν εὐπρόσωπον ταύτην ἀκοτεχνίαν ὡρμηκέναι. ἀνειθῆ δὲ ἀνθρώποις ἢ τέχνη, ψεύδεται ἢ πλάνη.—Protrept. 4, 46.

where art had already made considerable progress, should have borrowed this custom from the Greeks of Southern Italy. The statues set up by the Tarquins were of terra cotta, and not of marble, and in works of terra cotta the Corinthians excelled. But no argument, perhaps, can be drawn from this circumstance; for terra cotta statues of the gods are found at Herculaneum at a much later period: as for example, the statues of Æsculapius and Hygieia, otherwise called Jupiter and Juno, now in the Neapolitan Museum. But it is significant that the first statue we hear of as being erected at Rome is that of Attus Navius, the augur in the time of the first Tarquin.

The Etruscan influence upon Rome can be pointed out with confidence only in the following things. First, the discipline of the Haruspices. The Haruspices at Rome were always Etruscans, and were employed on three occasions: the inspection of the entrails of victims, the interpretation and expiation of prodigies, and the performance of the rites concerning thunderbolts. Secondly, the doctrine concerning augural temples, in its application to the building of temples, the foundation of cities, the measuring of land, &c. appears to have been of Etruscan origin; though this last indeed may also have been old Italian. Thirdly, the Etruscans had a great share in the buildings and works of art of ancient Rome, as well as in their public spectacles.[1] According to Varro,[2] Tarquinius Priscus entrusted the execution of the statue of Jove for the Capitol to Volcanius, who was sent for from Veii for that purpose. Lastly, the insignia of the Roman magistrates, such as the twelve lictors, the *apparitores*, the *toga prætexta*, the *sella curulis*, also the pomp of triumphs, and the triumphal dress, as the golden diadem, the *tunica palmata*, and *toga picta*, appear to have been borrowed from the Etruscans;[3] which may partly perhaps be explained from the circumstance that the preparation of such ornaments was a main branch of Etruscan art.

So that, after all, the Romans derived not many things from the Etruscans, and fewer still through the Tarquins. But that Greek learning and art was abundantly introduced among them by that

[1] "Fabris undique ex Etruria accitis," Liv. I. 56; "equi pugilesque ex Etruria acciti," Ibid. 35; "ludiones ex Etruria acciti," id. vii. 2. Cf. Plin. H. N. xxxv. 45, s. 157.
[2] Cited by Plin. H. N. xxxv. 45, s. 157.
[3] Liv. L 8; Strabo, v. 2, 2, p. 220; Dionys. iii. 61; Sil. Ital. viii. 484, *sqq.*; Macrob. Sat. L 6; Plin. H. N. viii. 74, s. 195, ix. 63, s. 136, &c.

dynasty, is sufficiently attested by ancient authors; for we may suppose that whatever portion of Greek culture Romulus may have brought with him had now been pretty nearly obliterated by long mixture with the Sabines. Corinth, to which the Tarquins traced their origin, was at that time one of the politest cities in Greece Cicero says that Demaratus carefully instructed his children in Grecian learning and art; that through their means an abundant stream of it flowed into Rome; and that Tarquinius Priscus brought up Servius Tullius after the most exquisite manner of the Greeks.[1] But that writing was among the Grecian arts introduced by the Tarquins, as Schwegler supposes,[2] is quite contrary to the best testimony, as we have shown in the Introduction, and need not therefore again enter into the subject here. The Tarquins had no doubt improved by their intercourse with Magna Græcia the Greek learning which was hereditary in their family. This intercourse is attested by the last Tarquin having taken refuge at Cumæ, as well as by the Sibylline books having been brought thence to Rome. But to suppose, with Schwegler, that the Romans got the art of writing from Cumæ, is to suppose that the Tarquins also must have done so; which is highly absurd, since it cannot be doubted that letters were known at Corinth when Demaratus was expelled.

The Tarquins especially increased the pomp of religious worship, and made more magnificent the temples of the gods. Although Numa had introduced the frequent practice of religious rites, he had rendered them as simple and as little costly as possible, in order the more to spread them among the people. The sacred utensils were chiefly made of wood and earthenware, and to avoid the expense of animal victims he allowed cakes and fruits to be sometimes substituted for them.[3] We say "sometimes;" for Schwegler's assertion[4] that the oldest religious worship at Rome, as instituted by Numa, admitted only bloodless sacrifices, is evidently incorrect. Plutarch, the only direct authority that he adduces for this assertion, does not bear him out; for that author only says that *the greater part* of the sacrifices established by

---

[1] De Rep. ii. 19, 21. [2] B. L. a. 680.
[3] Hence the "capeduncula Numæ."—Cic. Nat. Deor. iii. 17. "Numa instituit Deos fruge colere et mola salsa supplicare."—Plin. H. N. xviii. 2.
"Aut quis,
Simpuvium ridere Numæ, nigrumque catinum,
Et Vaticano fragiles de monte patellas,
Ausus erat?"
—Juv. Sat. vi. 342. Cf. Dionys. ii. 23, 74. [4] R. 681.

Numa were bloodless[1]; while Livy describes Numa as teaching with what victims (*hostiis*) the different sacrifices should be made.[2] The Tarquins, therefore, cannot be regarded as the introducers of animal sacrifices at Rome. Roman weights and measures on the Greek model are supposed to have been adopted by Servius Tullius.[3] In like manner we find Tarquinius Superbus sending magnificent gifts to the Delphic Apollo, in conformity, says Cicero, with the institutes of those from whom he was descended,[4] and sending his son to consult that oracle, also giving a Greek name, after Circe, the daughter of the Sun, to the colony which he founded on the coast of Latium.[5] Schwegler thinks that it was also owing to the influence of the Tarquins over Latium that many Latin towns may have begun to claim a Greek origin, and especially to refer it to some of the Homeric heroes. We are of opinion, however, that many of these towns were really Greek foundations, though not, of course, by the eponymous heroes whom they claimed. But it seems very probable that the Romans, from the Greek impulse derived from this source, may have now first begun to trace their descent from Æneas, instead of that obscurer man who landed on the coast of Latium only a generation or two before the foundation of their city. All these, however, are material or extrinsic things. The Tarquins must undoubtedly have also given a vast impulse to the moral and political ideas of the Romans, and have contributed much to refine and polish their manners. These things, however, are not so easily traced in those early times, except perhaps in the effect which they produced on the Roman constitution; and therefore the ancient writers are silent about them. But before we consider the political reforms of Tarquinius Priscus, we will conclude the remainder of his reign.

SABINE WARS.—BIRTH OF SERVIUS TULLIUS.—MURDER OF TARQUIN.

The attack of the Sabines was so sudden, that they had already passed the Anio before the Romans could march to oppose them. Rome was in consternation, especially as the

---

[1] ἀναίμακτοι ἧσαν αἱ πολλαί, δι' ἀλφίτου καὶ σπονδῆς καὶ τῶν εὐτελεστάτων πυπαομένοι.—Num. 8. [2] Lib. I. 20.
[3] Böckh, Metrol. Untern, S. 207. [4] De Rep. II. 24.
[5] Liv. I. 56. The rock on which Circeii was built appears, however, to have been previously the reputed abode of Circe.

result of the first battle, though a very bloody one, was indecisive. But as the enemy recalled his troops into camp, the Romans got breathing time to prepare afresh for the war. Tarquinius was of opinion that his army was principally deficient in cavalry, and therefore he resolved to add other centuries to the Ramnenses, Titienses, and Luceres enrolled by Romulus, and to designate them by his own name. But Attus Navius, a celebrated augur of those times, proclaimed that nothing could be altered or innovated unless the birds consented. The king's anger was roused thereat, and, by way of bantering the art of augury, he is reported to have said: "Come, prophet, augur whether what I am now thinking can be done." Then Attus, having tried the matter by augury, assured him that it could. "I was considering," replied Tarquin, "whether you could cut this whetstone with a razor. Take them, and do what your birds portend you can." Then Attus, without hesitating a moment, is said to have cut the whetstone. A statue of Attus, having the head veiled, long stood in the Comitium, on the steps to the left of the Curia, the scene of the occurrence; the whetstone is also said to have been deposited in the same place, to serve as a monument of the miracle to posterity. All that is certain about the story is, that from this time auguries, and the College of Augurs, grew into such repute that nothing henceforward was done, either at home or abroad, without taking the auspices; so that assemblies of the people, armies that had been enrolled, in short, all the most important affairs of State, were dissolved and suspended if the augural omens were adverse. Tarquinius, therefore, made no change in the centuries of the knights; but he doubled their number, so that there should be eighteen hundred knights in the three centuries. These bore the same names as the former ones, only they were called the later, or second knights; which being doubled are now called six centuries.

Tarquin, having thus increased this part of his forces, again took the field against the Sabines. But he was not satisfied with having only increased his strength; he also resorted to stratagem. He directed a vast quantity of wood that was lying on the banks of the Anio to be set on fire and to be thrown into the river. The wind helped to ignite it, and a great part of it was in boats, which, driving against the piles of the bridge, set it on fire. The sight of the burning bridge during the battle struck the Sabines with terror, and not only this, but also hindered their flight, so that many of them were drowned in the river. Their arms were carried down the stream into the Tiber, and so to Rome, where they were recognised, and thus proclaimed the victory before the news could be brought. The chief glory of the day belonged to the knights. These had been stationed on each wing; the Sabines had broken the main body of the Roman foot and were in hot pursuit, when the cavalry, charging from each side, not only arrested the Sabines, but compelled them in turn to fly. They made for the mountains in complete rout, but only a few succeeded in gaining them; the greater part, as we have said, were driven by the cavalry into the river. Tarquinius determined to pursue the Sabines. He therefore sent the prisoners and the booty to Rome. The spoils of the enemy he had devoted to Vulcan; and having collected them into a great heap, and set it on fire, he proceeded with his army into the Sabine territory. Here he was again met by the Sabines, who had rallied their forces as well as they could, but without much hope of making a successful stand. The result was another defeat, which reduced them almost to the brink of destruction; so they sent to beg a peace.

As the price of this they were obliged to cede Collatia and its territory; Egerius, son of the king's brother, was left there with a garrison. The Collatines surrendered according to the following form, which became the established one. The king inquired of the envoys from Collatia: "Are you the ambassadors and orators sent by the Collatine people to surrender yourselves and them?" "We are." "Are the Collatine people their own masters?" "They are." "Do you surrender yourselves and the Collatine people, their city, lands, waters, boundaries, temples, utensils, and all their property, religious and secular, to me and to the Roman people?" "We do." "And I receive the surrender."

Having thus terminated the Sabine War, Tarquinius returned in triumph to Rome. He then made war upon the Prisci Latini, and subdued the whole Latin nation by attacking every city separately, and without once fighting a regular pitched battle. The cities thus reduced, or recovered from the Prisci Latini, were Corniculum, Old Ficulea, Cameria, Crustumerium, Ameriola, Medullia, Nomentum. A peace was then granted to the Latins.

Tarquin now applied himself to the works of peace with even greater ardour than he had conducted those vast wars, and thus kept the people in constant employment. He resumed the preparations for building a stone wall around the city, which had been interrupted. He drained the lower parts of the city about the Forum and other valleys between the hills; drawing off the water by means of drains running with a slope into the Tiber. He began also to lay on the Capitol the foundations of a Temple of Jupiter, which he had vowed in the Sabine War; already anticipating with prophetic mind the future greatness of the spot.

While he was thus employed a prodigy happened in the palace, which turned out no less wonderful in the event. It is related that the head of a boy named Servius Tullius seemed on fire while he slept, and that the prodigy was witnessed by many persons. The clamour they made at the sight of such a spectacle attracted the attention of the king. Meanwhile one of the servants had run for water to extinguish the fire, but was prevented by the queen. She bade them be still, and not to touch the boy till he should awake of his own accord; and when he did so, the flame immediately departed. Then Tanaquil took her husband aside, and thus addressed him: "Do you see this boy whom we are bringing up in so humble a manner? Know that he will hereafter be a light in our dubious fortunes, and the safeguard of our afflicted house. Let us, therefore, educate him with every care and indulgence, as he will cause us much honour both publicly and privately."

From this time the boy was regarded in the light of a child, and was instructed in all those accomplishments which befit so high a fortuna. The interposition of the gods was manifest throughout. The youth turned out of a temper truly royal; insomuch that when Tarquin was looking about for a husband for his daughter, there was no youth at Rome that could in any way be compared to him; so the royal maiden was betrothed to him. A mark of so much honour, from whatever cause bestowed, forbids the thought that he was the son of a slave, and when young a slave himself. I am rather of the opinion of those who think that the father of Servius Tullius was the chief man in Corniculum; that he was killed when the town was taken, leaving his wife pregnant; who was recognised among the other captive women, and rescued from slavery by the Roman queen on account of her rank. She was brought to bed at Rome, in the palace of Tarquin; hence a great friendship sprung up between the women, and the boy, having been brought up in the palace from his infancy, was loved and honoured. It was, probably, the fate of his mother, who, on the capture of her native city, fell into the hands of the enemy, that occasioned the belief of his being the son of a slave.

In about the thirty-eighth year of the reign of Tarquin, Servius Tullius was held in the highest esteem, not only by the king, but also by the patricians and plebs. The two sons of Ancus Marcius had long been indignant that they should have been kept out of the crown worn by their father, through the fraud of their guardian, and that a foreigner, not even of Italian, much less Roman, race should reign at Rome. But their anger was wonderfully increased when they saw that they had not a chance of the crown, even on the death of Tarquin; that it would be dragged through the mud, and that about a century after Romulus, the son of a god, and himself a god, the sceptre which he had held while he was on earth would fall into the hands of a slave. They held that it would be disgraceful to the whole Roman nation, and particularly so to their house, if, while the race of Ancus was still in existence, the Roman kingdom should be thrown open, not only to foreigners, but slaves. Such a contumely they resolved to avert by violence. But the injury which they had received at the hands of Tarquin stimulated them rather against him than Servius. It also occurred to them that, if the king should be left alive, he would avenge the murder more severely than a private person; also that, if Servius were slain, Tarquin would make any other son-in-law whom he might choose heir to the crown. For these reasons a conspiracy was formed against the king himself. Two of the most ferocious shepherds were selected to perpetrate the deed. Armed with the rustic weapons of that class, they feigned a quarrel in the very vestibule of the palace, and by the loudness of their strife attracted the attention of all the royal attendants. Then both began to appeal to the king, and the noise having penetrated into the interior of the palace, they were called into his presence. Here both began to vociferate together, as if trying which could make the most noise; till being stopped by a lictor, and told to speak in turn, they at last desisted; and one of them began to narrate the cause of quarrel. While the king's attention was thus absorbed, the other man struck at his head with a hatchet, and, leaving the weapon in the wound, both rushed forth from the palace.

The bystanders supported the dying king in their arms, while the lictors pursued and apprehended the fugitives. A noisy crowd soon gathered round, wondering what was the matter. Amidst the tumult, Tanaquil orders the palace to be cleared, and the gates to be shut. Then she busily prepares some medicaments, as if there were still hope, and at the same time contrives some means of safety if that hope should fail. She hastily summons Servius, shows him her husband on the point of dissolution, and, seizing his right hand, beseeches him not to let the death of his father-in-law pass unpunished, nor suffer his mother-in-law to be the prey and sport of enemies. "Servius," she exclaimed, "the kingdom is yours, if you are a man; not theirs who, by hired assassins, have perpetrated this horrible deed. Bestir yourself, follow the gods who lead you, and who formerly portended your fortunes, by the divine fire that played around your head. Let that celestial flame arouse you: up and be doing. Have not we also reigned, though foreigners? Consider who you are, not how you were born. And if you are at a loss to act on so sudden an emergency, then follow my counsels."

The clamour and stir of the crowd had now become insupportable; so Tanaquil, addressing the people from a window in the upper part of the house, which looked towards the Nova Via—for Tarquin dwelt near the Temple of Jupiter Stator—spoke as follows:—"Be of good cheer," she said; "the king was stunned by the suddenness of the blow; the weapon has not penetrated deep; he is already recovering his senses. The blood has been wiped away, and the wound inspected; the symptoms are good; and I trust you will soon see the king again. In the mean time he commands the people to obey Servius Tullius. He will administer justice, and discharge the other functions of the king."

Hereupon Servius comes forth in a robe of state, accompanied by lictors; and taking his seat on the throne, decides some causes, and pretends that he will consult the king about others. In this manner, the death of Tarquin being kept concealed during several days after he had expired, Servius confirmed his own power under the appearance of discharging the duties of the king. At length the death of Tarquin is announced, amidst great lamentation in the palace, and Servius, supported by a powerful guard, ascends the throne with the goodwill of the patricians, but without being nominated by the people. The sons of Ancus, after the apprehension of their hirelings, hearing that the king was alive, and that the power of Servius was so strong, fled to Suessa Pometia.

REMARKS.—Schwegler, after having pointed out that the institutions of Tarquinius Priscus were not borrowed from Etruria, but rather manifest a Grecian influence, comes to the singular conclusion, after Niebuhr, that Tarquin was a Latin.[1] Niebuhr's principal reasons for this opinion seem to be that Priscus, the name borne by the elder Tarquin, is evidently a national name; that therefore the name Tarquinius Priscus would mean Tarquin the Priscan (Latin); and that, after the expulsion of the kings from

[1] Schwegler, Buch iv. § 10; cf. Niebuhr, Röm. Gesch. B. i. 398.

Rome, we find some Tarquinii settled at Laurentum,[1] just as Collatinus settled at Lavinium; which they would not have done had Tarquinii been their home. But the opinion that *Priscus* was a national name is, we believe, now universally exploded,[2] and to call Tarquinii the home of the Tarquins, when the whole family had quitted it in disgust a century before, seems a very singular idea. We say the whole family; for Tarquinius Priscus had evidently brought away with him his brother's widow and her child, or Egerius could not have been in his service. Under these circumstances, Tarquinii, we might imagine, would have been the last place they would have thought of returning to.

Schwegler then proceeds to remark that tradition ascribes to Tarquinius Priscus three innovations in the existing constitution: the doubling of the three ancient stem-tribes, or, as he calls them, patricians; the doubling of the centuries of knights; and the addition of a hundred new senators.

"Concerning the motives for these reforms," he observes, "we may conjecture as follows. Through the subjugation of the adjoining Latin district, the Roman state had obtained so great an increase of population that the former constitution was no longer suitable to the present state of things. Together with the original citizens, who, divided into three tribes and thirty curiæ, were in the exclusive possession of all political and religious rights, there now existed a far more numerous *plebs*, but unorganized, undistributed, and without any privileges. Under these circumstances it became a political necessity organically to incorporate this *plebs* in the state; to give it a recognised position and function in political life; and in some degree to reconcile the dangerous inequality between the old and the new citizens. Another motive was that the kings, who had in the *plebs* a natural ally against that aristocracy of race which cramped the kingly power, could not but be disposed to elevate it and to endow it with political rights. Tarquin comprehended this state of things, and the necessity for a new organization of the citizens. We do not, indeed, accurately know the nature of the

---

[1] Dionys. v. 54.
[2] It is rejected by Schwegler, who observes in a note,—"*Priscus* means *ancient, previous,* in opposition to *modern* (cf. Prisci Latini). Tarquinius Priscus, therefore does not mean 'Tarquin the elder,' but 'Tarquin the old, or ancient.' He is *priscus* so far as he represents a more ancient order of things, a different phase of Tarquinian rule, from 'Tarquinius the despot.'"

reform which he contemplated; though it certainly concerned not only, as Livy represents, the institution of new centuries of knights, but also, as we see from other historians, the creation of new tribes: were it that Tarquin contemplated constituting out of the *plebs* a corresponding number of new tribes, and placing them by the side of the existing three stem-tribes of Ramnes, Tities, and Luceres, or a completely altered organization of the whole population. But the plan failed through the opposition of the old citizens. Attus Navius objected that the existing number of three tribes, firmly established by a previous taking of the auspices, rested on divine sanction, and could not therefore be altered at human pleasure: that is, the old citizens carried their opinion, that an innovation like that contemplated by Tarquin would be an upsetting of the whole subsisting order of things, and of the religious foundations of the state. And such it actually was. The old citizens were at the same time a sort of political clergy. The auspices rested with them, and consequently the exclusive consecration and right of mediation between the gods and the state, and of filling all spiritual and temporal offices. This consecration, resting on hereditary capability to receive it, could be transmitted only by birth, and not by an act of the human will; a transmission of it to those not qualified was a violation of the divine law. In short, all the objections which were afterwards raised from the religious point of view against the admission of the *plebs* to *connubium*, to the curule offices, and to the priesthood, would have been then pressed much more strongly and emphatically. In this view it is quite characteristic that, according to the old tradition, the gods themselves intervened to protect the threatened religion, and to accredit the divine right of the old citizens by a miracle. Tarquin did not feel himself strong enough to break through the opposition offered; and was compelled to content himself, instead of creating new tribes, with increasing the three existing ones, by receiving into them the leading plebeian families. To each of the three ancient tribes he added a second division equally strong, through which the number of the patrician races was doubled, while nominally the old number of three tribes remained. These three new halves of tribes were called *secundi* Ramnes, Tities, and Luceres, and the former tribes *primi* Tities, Ramnes, and Luceres. Through this innovation the old citizens lost at all events the former exclusiveness of their political position; but, in principle

at least, the existing priesthood was not overthrown, in so far—
as there is cause to suppose—the younger tribes did not obtain
full possession of the *jus sacrorum*; and thus the creation of these
younger half tribes bore predominantly a political character. The
newly created patrician races also stood politically below the
others: they were called the smaller races (*patres minorum gentium*)
by way of distinction from the old races, which from this time
were called *patres majorum gentium*: a distinguishing name from
which we must also conclude a difference of rights. For the rest,
much remains dark in this Tarquinian reform. We do not learn[1]
how the existing distribution into Curiæ was brought into accordance with the doubling of the stem-tribes, nor what measures
Tarquin adopted with regard to the remainder of the *plebs*; or
whether he permitted it to continue an unorganized mass; which,
from the point of view of military service and organization of the
army, is scarcely credible.

"The doubling of the centuries of knights undertaken by Tarquin—or, at all events, ascribed to him—is immediately connected
with the doubling of the stem-tribes. Tarquin proceeded in the
same manner in both cases; he added to each of the existing centuries, as recorded to have been instituted by Romulus, a second
division of the same strength, so that the whole number of the
centuries remained nominally the same. The knights newly added
were distinguished from those of the three ancient centuries by
calling them *posteriores*, or *secundi*. Thus the division into *primi*
and *secundi* equites Ramnenses, Titienses, and Lucerenses entirely
corresponds with the division of the tribes into *primi* and *secundi*
Ramnes, Tities, and Luceres. Both institutions evidently had an
original connexion, and the new citizens received into the three
stem-tribes would have had to furnish the *secundas equitum partes*."

Schwegler then goes on to the difficult question of the number of
the knights, which we have touched upon in another place, and
which will, perhaps, never be satisfactorily settled. Respecting the
doubling of the Senate, he says: "From the doubling of the Patres,
or the creation of the minor races, must be distinguished, as we
have already remarked, a third measure of Tarquinius Priscus, the
naming of a hundred new senators, which is ascribed to him. Tarquin thus brought up the Senate, which till then had contained only

---

[1] It would indeed have been singular if we did. Three difficulties would
have suggested to a sensible critic the error of the view he was taking.

two hundred members, a hundred from the tribe of the Ramnes, a hundred from that of the Tities, to the subsequent normal number of three hundred. If we inquire for the motives and original connexion of those measures, the historians leave us without any explanation, since we must decidedly reject their erroneous opinion that the election of these hundred senators and the creation of the minor races were one and the same act. Nevertheless, there might have been an original connexion between the two measures; as, for instance, that Tarquinius may have given the newly-created races a hundred seats in the Senate; while the old races, the *primi* Ramnes, Tities, and Luceres held two hundred of them. But this assumption is contradicted by the circumstance that the previously existing two hundred senators, *if we are to believe the historians*, represented only the Ramnes and Tities, and not the Luceres; and thus, if the hundred new senators were taken from the minor races, the *secundi* Luceres would now have been represented, while the *primi* Luceres were still without that right. This is not probable, and hence it appears more credible, if we accept the accounts of the historians respecting the successive augmentations of the Senate, that the hundred new senators added by Tarquin belonged to the Luceres, who thus, through this king, first attained complete political equality with the other two races. It is true that by this assumption we fall into other difficulties; since if the three hundred senators of the Tarquinian time were a representation of the three ancient tribes, then—since the number of three hundred appears to have been the standing one, which was never exceeded—there remains no place in the Senate for the minor races; although, as the nature of their relations compels us to assume, and as appears from a distinct account of Cicero's (De Rep. ii. 20), these races were represented in it, and that thus their senators were included in that number. No completely satisfactory method presents itself of reconciling this contradiction. We might assume, with Niebuhr, that, at the time of the Tarquinian reform, the original number of the races had been long incomplete, and that the old citizens of the three-stem tribes could no longer supply, as formerly, three hundred, but only two hundred senators; to which number Tarquinius Priscus added another hundred from the minor races. But even by this hypothesis there still remain gaps in the tradition; namely, in so far as tradition is wholly silent about the summoning of the Luceres to the Senate. Hence, therefore, it must be questioned in general whether the accounts of the ancients respecting the successive increase of the Senate, and the representation of the first two races by a hundred members each, are to be regarded as genuine and credible tradition.

"To Tarquinius Priscus is also ascribed another regulation closely connected with the representation of the stem-races: he is said to have raised the number of the Vestals from four to six. This was evidently done with the object of placing the third race on an equality with the other two with relation to the priesthood of the Vestal virgins, since the previous number of four Vestals represented only the first two races. If we connect this increase of the Vestals from four to six with the analogous increase of the members of the Senate from two hundred to three hundred, the conjecture that the last measure related to the tribe of the Luceres gains in probability, and that, consequently, the third tribe first obtained its full political rights through the elder Tarquinius, who perhaps belonged to it.

"For the rest, if Tarquin really belonged, as there is some appearance, to the tribe of the Luceres, his elevation to the throne was an innovation; for the kings before him alternate only between Ramnes and Tities. It is not impossible that this innovation was carried out by force. Tradition has preserved a trace of this, since Tarquinius Priscus is the first of the Roman kings who ascends the throne without a previous interregnum, and without being created by an Interrex, and consequently in an illegitimate manner."

On this we will remark that the notion of Tarquin's wishing to double the three *tribes* is only a Teutonic one, not to be found in any of the ancient writers, though built upon a misconstruction of some passages in them. Probability is entirely against it; for, first, Tarquin must have been an exceedingly bad political doctor to apply to a disease a remedy which could only have aggravated it. The disorder under which Rome laboured was, we are told, that it had a superabundance of patricians in proportion to the *plebs;* and, to cure this state of things, Tarquin creates as many patricians again! still leaving an immense plebeian mass unenfranchised, as is evident from the necessity of the subsequent reform effected by Servius Tullius. We do not, indeed, believe, with the German school, that Tarquin could have converted plebeians into patricians merely by distributing them among the Curiæ, because we hold that the majority of the members of the Curiæ were plebeian; but this point we have examined in another place, and, as the Germans believe the reverse, the absurdity of their view remains.

Secondly, it is in the highest degree incredible that, if Tarquin had really contemplated so important a measure as a doubling of the ancient *populus*, it should have been passed over in complete silence by Livy, Cicero, and even Dionysius, although they distinctly mention the increase made by Tarquin in the Senate and in the equestrian order. Passages, indeed, of the last two of these authors, as well as of other writers, have been adduced in proof of the hypothesis in question, which we will now proceed to examine. And first we will take the authorities adduced by Becker, who is also an advocate for the doubling of the tribes. That writer observes:[1] "The alteration which the high-minded king (Tarquin) had in view was certainly not confined to the creation of new centuries of knights; but probably new tribes were to be instituted, in addition to the three ancient ones, out of the Alban and other Latin population; or perhaps some regulation adopted similar to the subsequent one of Servius Tullius." To which he appends the following note: "It is, at all events, striking that Dionysius, in speaking of Tarquin's view, uses the word φυλαί (iii. 71) : Οὗτος ὁ Νέβιος βουλομένῳ ποτὲ τῷ Ταρκυνίῳ τρεῖς φυλὰς ἑτέρας ἀποδεῖξαι νέας ἐκ τῶν ὑπ' αὐτοῦ πρότερον κατειλεγμένων ἱππέων, καὶ ποιῆσαι τὰς ἐπιθέτους φυλὰς ἑαυτοῦ τε καὶ τῶν ἰδίων ἑταίρων ἐπωνύμους, μόνος ἀντεῖπε. (cap. 72) : ὁ Νέβιος ἐκεῖνος, ὃν ἔφην ἐπιτραπῆναί ποτε τῷ βασιλεῖ πλείονας ἢ ἐλασσόνων ποιῆσαι τὰς φυλὰς βουλομένῳ. Florus says still more strikingly (i. 5) : 'Illic et senatus majestatem numero ampliavit et *centuriis tribus* auxit, quatenus Attus Navius *numerum* augeri prohibebat;' where the missing word to *numerum* cannot well be supplied except by *tribuum*. Lastly, Festus says expressly (p. 169, *Varia*) : 'Nam cum Tarquinius Priscus institutas *tribus* a Romulo mutare vellet,' &c. Zonaras also says (vii. 8) : Πάντως δ᾽ ἂν ἄλλα πλείω ἐκαινοτόμησεν ἄν, εἰ μή τις Ἄττος Ναούιος τὰς φυλὰς αὐτὸν βουληθέντα μετακοσμῆσαι ἐκώλυκεν. The foundation of the passage of Dionysius seems to be an account, which he misunderstood, that Tarquin wished to place the population incorporated into the Roman state by Tullus Hostilius and Ancus Marcius as new tribes by the side of the old; which is quite natural, and is confirmed by the subsequent regulations of his successor. That Tarquin, moreover, wished to name the new divisions after himself

[1] Röm. Alterth. ii. 1. 241.

and his friends offers no good meaning, if we consider these divisions
to have been only centuries of knights, since what Cicero says,
'nec potuit Titiensium, Ramnensium, et Lucerum mutare quum
cuperet nomina,' is certainly erroneous. All authors, Livy, Dionysius, Festus, Florus, Valerius Maximus (i. 4, 1), Zonaras, agree that
he wanted to make a thorough alteration. Aurelius Victor also
(iii. 6) says, like Cicero, 'nomina mutare non potuit.'"

Now let us examine these passages in their order. First of all,
it is manifest, from the allusion to Attus Navius, that Dionysius
is speaking of the very same event as that related by Livy;[1]
namely, the adding of three more *centuries* to the knights, because
his army was deficient in cavalry. But if Dionysius meant that
Tarquin wanted *to create* three new *tribes*, not cavalry, then his
account is at direct variance with Livy's; and in that case we cannot
hesitate a moment which author we should follow. But we do not
believe that he meant any such thing. He tells us that Tarquin
after having enrolled some knights, wanted to *declare them* three new
tribes, and to name them after himself and his friends. Now this
account agrees substantially with Livy's. The operation contemplated by Tarquin is confined entirely to the *knights;* but instead
of enrolling his three new centuries under the existing names of
Ramnenses, &c. he wanted to call them *Tarquinienses*, &c. *as if
they had belonged* to some new tribes. They who adopt any other
interpretation of this passage must suppose that Dionysius was
absurd enough to think that tribes could be created out of the
equestrian order.

Next, with regard to the passage in Florus. That the missing
word to be supplied is *tribuum*, is just one of those dashing assertions which Becker is accustomed to make when he has a desperate
case. The *equites* were divided into *centuriæ*, while the *tribes*
were divided into *curiæ;* and, therefore, as Florus says, "*centuriis
tribus auxit*," it is evident that the missing word to be supplied is
that suggested by Pighius, "*auxit equites*." And thus Florus also
agrees with Livy.

The passage in Festus cannot by any mode of interpretation be
made to imply that Tarquin wanted to create new tribes. Festus
merely says that he wanted to *alter* the Romulean tribes,—that is, he
wished to change their names; and in this Festus agrees with Cicero.
The same remark applies to Zonaras's expression, μετακοσμήσαι,

---

[1] Lib. I. c. 36.

which cannot signify the creation of *new* tribes; though, indeed, it is of very little consequence what such an author wrote.

The use of the words φυλαί and *tribus* for *centuriæ* by Dionysius and Festus has led some critics to consider that the ancient stem-tribes were identical with the equestrian centuries; that the Ramnes, Tities, and Luceres served on horseback, and that the infantry consisted of clients.[1] But this view is altogether inadmissible.

The centuries of knights, or their names, came at last to be almost confounded with the primitive Romulean tribes. The original distinction between those tribes, which was one of race, must in the course of a century or two have become completely obliterated; the equestrian order was the only institution which perpetuated their names; and thus we see that in the time of Servius they were completely ignored, and the reforms of that king were framed on the principle of a territorial, not an ethnic, distribution of the population.

We may here further remark that the ancient division of the Roman territory among the three tribes may have helped to promote the confusion between the terms *tribus* and *centuria*. The land originally assigned to each tribe, whether consisting of one or two acres for each head of a family, was called *centuria*. Thus Paulus Diaconus:[2] "Centuriatus ager in ducena jugera definitus, quia Romulus centenis civibus ducena jugera tribuit." And Varro: "*Centuria* primo a centum jugeribus dicta, post duplicata retinuit nomen, ut *tribus* multiplicatæ idem tenent nomen."[3] Hence *centuria*, as the name of the land apportioned to each tribe, and as the name of the body of knights representing each tribe, might easily come to be confounded with the word *tribus* itself.

Thus the fancied intention ascribed to Tarquin of creating new tribes rests on no authority whatever; and, so far from being confirmed by the regulations of his successor, is controverted by them. For the *comitia centuriata* and *tributa* went a great way to overthrow the *comitia curiata*, which Tarquin is conjectured to have enlarged, and were founded on an entirely different principle. Why Tarquin might not have wished to give his name to a century of knights as well as a tribe it is impossible

---

[1] Puchta and Marquardt, ap Schwegler, i. 686. [2] P. 53.
[3] Ling. Lat. v. 35.

to divine; especially seeing that the names of the tribes scarcely survived except as the names of the equestrian centuries. And now we will ask, Why is Cicero in error in saying (De Rep. ii. 20) that Tarquin wanted to change the names of the centuries? Cicero does not say that he wanted *only* to do that, as Becker's words would lead us to think. He had said just before: "Deinde equitatum ad hunc morem constituit, qui usque adhuc est retentus." In fact, there seem to have been two versions of Tarquin's method of proceeding in this matter. According to one view, he wanted, besides increasing the number of Equites, to abolish the names Ramnenses, Titienses, and Luceres, and substitute for them his own name and the names of some friends: according to the other view, he intended to retain the ancient centuries and their names, and to add to them three other centuries with new names. The former seems to have been the view of Cicero, Festus ("tribus *mutare*") Zonaras, and Aurelius Victor in the passages cited; the latter, of Dionysius and Florus; perhaps also of Livy, whose language however appears to indicate that *both* schemes had been agitated: "Id quia inaugurato Romulus fecerat, negare Attius Navius, inclutus ea tempestate augur, *neque mutari neque novum constitui*, nisi aves addixissent, posse" (Lib. I. 36).

These passages, therefore, do not afford any ground for the assertion of Schwegler, Becker, and other German writers, that Tarquinius Priscus contemplated the creation of new tribes; they refer only to the creation of new centuries of knights. But, not content with asserting the creation of these new tribes, Schwegler also says[1] that they were called *secundi* Ramnes, Titics, and Luceres, and also *Patres minorum gentium;* thus confounding the increase of the knights with the increase of the Senate, and regarding both as an increase of the tribes. In support of this view he quotes the following from Cicero: "Duplicavit pristinum patrum numerum" (De Rep. ii. 20); taking of course the *patres* to mean here the patricians who formed the Curiæ, agreeably to his view of the ancient *populus*. Now, though *patres* may sometimes denote the whole patrician body, yet there are cases in which, from the context, it cannot possibly do so; and this is one of them, for the passage in its integrity runs as follows: "Isque ut de suo imperio legem tulit, principio duplicavit illum pristinum patrum numerum; et antiquos patres majorum gentium appellavit, quos priores sen-

[1] S. 687, f.

tentiam rogabat; a se ascitos minorum." Here the words, "sententiam rogabat," show that Cicero is speaking of the Senate; for it is hardly to be supposed that the king asked, singly and in order, the opinions of 3,000 or 4,000 men in the Curiæ, or, after he had doubled them, 6,000 or 8,000! It is further incontestably shown from the mention of "minorum gentium" that Cicero is speaking of the Senate: for Livy, in relating the same event, says: "Centum *in patres* legit, qui deinde *minorum gentium* sunt appellati: factio haud dubia regia, cujus beneficio *in curiam venerant.*"[1] Now these must have been senators; first, because the choosing of a hundred men could not possibly have been a doubling of the tribes; and secondly, because "in curiam"—not "in *curias*"—must mean the Senate-house; and therefore the "Patres minorum gentium" were senators.

We see then, from these passages, that it was not through the *plebs*, but through the Senate that Tarquin sought to strengthen his government, that it was in that body he considered the political power of the state to lie. Tarquin also doubled the knights; but this was merely a military measure, as appears from the narrative of Livy. His army was deficient in cavalry.

In support of his opinion that Tarquin doubled the tribes, Schwegler also adduces the following passage from Festus:[2] "Sex Vestæ sacerdotes constitutæ sunt, ut populus pro sua quaque parte haberet ministram sacrorum, quia civitas Romana in sex est distributa partes: in primos secundosque Titienses, Ramnes, Luceres." And to this passage he adds further on[3] the following, to show that Tarquin also increased the number of the Vestals to six, in order that they might correspond to the new number of tribes: ταῖς ἱεραῖς παρθένοις τέτταρσιν οὔσαις δύο προσκατέλεξεν ἑτέρας.[4] From Valerius Maximus:[5] "(Tarquinius Priscus) cultum deorum novis sacerdotiis auxit." Though according to Plutarch,[6] the addition was first made by Servius Tullius.

On these passages let us observe: first, that whilst Schwegler writes *Tities* in his text, as of a tribe, his author writes *Titienses*, as of an equestrian century: showing the confusion which existed between their appellations in later times, when the names of the tribes had been long disused, except as designations of the equestrian

---

[1] Lib. i. 35. [2] P. 344, Sex Vestæ. [3] S. 693, Anm. 3.
[4] Dionys. iii. 67; cf. ii. 67. [5] Lib. iii. 4, 2. [6] Num. 10.

centuries; a confusion also observable in Varro, who uses both forms indifferently; as for example, in the following passage, where they appear in the most admirable disorder: "Ager Romanus primum divisus in parteis tris, a quo *tribus* appellata *Titiensus*, Ramnium, Lucorum, nominatæ, ut ait Ennius, *Tatienses* a Tatio, *Ramnenses* a Romulo, Luceres, ut Junius a Lucumone;"[1] where we see that the forms *Ramnenses*, *Tatienses* (or Titienses) might be used of tribe just as well as *Ramnes* or *Taties;* and that this practice must have been at least as old as Ennius.

But we must confess our inability to understand Schwegler's reasoning on this subject. At p. 687, he writes, as we have already translated: "These three new halves of tribes were called *secundi* Ramnes, Tities, Luceres, and the former tribes *primi* Ramnes, Tities, and Luceres:" referring to the above passage in Festus. Again, at p. 693, he writes: "To Tarquinius Priscus is also ascribed another regulation *closely connected with the representation of the stem races:* he is said to have raised the *number of the Vestals* from four to six. This was evidently done with the object of placing the third race *on an equality with the other two*, with relation to the priesthood of the Vestal virgins, since the previous number of four Vestals represented *only the first two races.*" To this last passage he appends a note, in which he again quotes the passage in Festus at full length, and remarks upon it: "Where, however, three of the Vestals are wrongly referred to the three younger tribes; for in this case there should only have been three, not four, Vestals in office before the creation of the younger tribes." Nothing can be juster than this remark: for if the Vestals are to be referred to these (supposed) six tribes, then we have the absurdities that two tribes, the Ramnes and Tities, must have been *originally created primi* and *secundi*, to correspond with the original four Vestals; that even the *secundi* Ramnes and Tities were preferred to the Luceres, who were not represented in the Temple of Vesta at all, though they were worthy enough to be called one of the three stem-tribes, and to be represented, like the other two, by ten curiæ and a century of knights; and that these Luceres, or third stem-tribe, were first raised to their proper dignity, according to Niebuhr's untenable hypothesis, by Tarquinius Priscus, and also at once divided like the others into *primi* and *secundi*. For that the Luceres were first *created* by Tarquin is contrary to all evidence.

[1] Ling. Lat. v. 55, where there are no *variæ lectiones*.

What Schwegler says in his note is a flat contradiction to what he says in his text. In fact, there is no ground whatever for supposing that the Vestals were in any way connected with the number of the tribes. Even Dionysius, in the passage cited, says no such thing, but only that two Vestals were added, because the occasions of performing their public functions had so much increased that four no longer sufficed. For, in continuation of the extract given above, he says: πλειόνων γὰρ ἤδη συντελουμένων ὑπὲρ τῆς πόλεως ἱερουργιῶν, αἷς ἔδει τὰς τῆς Ἑστίας παρεῖναι θυηπόλους, οὐκ ἐδόκουν αἱ τέτταρες ἀρκεῖν. The only author who affords the least colour for such a supposition is Festus, in the passage in question; but, though this is evidently only a guess, or after-construction, founded upon number, yet this German critic, who on other occasions often wrongly accuses the best authors of such a process, here eagerly seizes the passage, and arrays it against the best testimony on the other side. Nor can the following passages from Cicero and Livy, which Schwegler adduces in his next note to prove that the number of places in the priestly colleges, and consequently the number of the Vestals, corresponded with the number of the stem-tribes, serve his purpose: Cic. De Rep. ii. 9, "Romulus ex singulis tribubus singulos co-optavit augures;" Liv. x. 6, "Inter augures constat, imparem numerum debere esse, ut tres antiquæ tribus, Ramnes, Titienses, Luceres, suum quæque augurem habeant." In fact, they show just the reverse of what they are brought to prove: for thus, according to analogy, there ought to have been originally only *three* Vestals, as there were only three augurs, whereas there were *four*. All this hopeless confusion arises merely from an unwillingness to accept the testimony of the best authors, and a readiness to adopt in preference that of any obscure writer, if it can only serve to muddle matters. Schwegler flounders in inextricable difficulties, merely because he will not adopt the plain statements of Cicero and Livy, that Tarquinius Priscus doubled the number of the knights, and also that of the senators; for we have shown in another place that the addition of 100 new members, *minorum gentium*, was in fact a doubling of it, whatever Dionysius may dream to the contrary, and that the subsequently normal number of 300 was not attained till after the expulsion of the kings. A doubling of the tribes is only a dream.

It is not worth while to enter into the question whether Tarquin belonged to the Luceres. This is precisely one of those "cobwebs" so often found in the brains of German critics. Of course the kings before Tarquin alternated between the Ramnes and Tities, which is only saying that they alternated between the Romans and Sabines, and, of course, Tarquin's elevation to the throne was an "innovation;" but, if we follow right reason and good authority, we know where he came from, and how he obtained the throne.

Schwegler then proceeds to examine the peculiar political character which marked the Tarquinian dynasty, as follows:—

"In general we cannot fail to recognise that the reign of the Tarquins bears a different political character from the epoch of the preceding kings; that contemporaneously with the rise of this dynasty appears a political change, a new order of things. This change is reflected in legend, or tradition, in the conflict of the innovating king with the augur Attus Navius. This was doubtless no merely temporary altercation, as it appears in the narrative, but a deeper and more general conflict of principles. In this scene is merely symbolized the contest of a new political idea with the old state. This last was a state composed of families bound together in the straitest chains of religion and an established church, which not only prevented all progress and development, but also, by the priestly character which it bore and the exclusive spirit that sprung from it, hindered the political unity of the nation. It was the object of the Tarquinian dynasty to convert this theocratical state into a political one, to remove the trammels which separated the different portions of the state from one another, to make it a whole, and thus, with regard to foreign policy, to render it stronger and more capable of conquest. It is this policy that is represented as despotism in the younger Tarquin, perhaps only through patrician hate. Perhaps the fall of the Tarquins is in part to be referred to this policy. According to all appearance it was caused by a reaction among the old families; and, as the political and religious innovations of the Tarquins were partly influenced by Greek culture, so this reaction was an assertion and restoration of the old national characteristics. This contest of principles may, perhaps, have been founded on the contrast of the Latin and Sabine elements. Nothing certain can be determined on this subject; but it is remarkable that the transfer of the Albans and the incorporation of the neighbouring Latin territories is followed by the revolution which we find in the Tarquinian period; that Attus Navius appears as a Sabine; that the Sabine sanctuaries on the Capitol are compelled to yield to the Capitoline Temple and worship; and that after the fall of the Tarquins, the Sabine families, such as the Valerii, Fabii, Claudii, appear more prominently on the political stage."

With a good deal of what precedes we are disposed to agree, though, as is not unusual with German writers, the main idea is frittered into subtleties which are merely imaginary, as those respecting the Sabine sanctuaries, and the Sabine families that appear after the fall of the Tarquins. The Tarquins, from their Greek descent and education, may very probably have entertained a secret contempt for the narrow bigotry and superstition of the Sabines, and the scene with Attus Navius is, perhaps, only one of many of the same sort, or rather a type of them. Whether it ever occurred may be very doubtful, and the miraculous part of it, if not a falsehood, is of course a trick. This is only one of those stories which are found in the early annals of all nations, and especially of theocratic nations, which Rome was to a certain extent. Even in the sixteenth century, during the reign of Calvin at Geneva, it was pretty generally believed that a man had been carried away bodily by the devil over hedges and ditches and cast into the Rhone, and Calvin was very wroth with those who had no faith in the story.[1] Livy relates the scene between Tarquin and the augur in a way which betrays his disbelief of it; and if the statue of Attus, with the miraculous whetstone, was ever erected on the Comitium, it had certainly vanished long before the time of Livy, and even of Cicero,[2] though earlier monuments were still in existence. All that is certain is that there was some conflict between Tarquin and the College of Augurs, which ended in the decided victory of the latter.[3] And it must be remembered that to attack the augurs was not only to attack religion, but also to declare war against the patricians, who were in possession of the auguries. It was therefore a political, even more than a religious movement, and we shall see it continued under Tarquin's successors.

The increase of the population through the Latins settled at

[1] See Dyer's Life of Calvin, p. 205, *seq.*

[2] Cicero says: "Cotem autem illam et novaculam defossam in comitio, supraque impositum puteal *accepimus.*"—De Divin. I. 17. "Statua Attii in gradibus ipsis ad levam curiæ *fuit*: cotem quoque eodem loco sitam fuisse *memorant.*"—Liv. i. 36.

[3] "Auguriis certe sacerdotioque augurum tantus honos accessit, ut nihil belli domique postea, nisi auspicato, gereretur."—Ibid.

Rome, and especially after the conquests of Tarquin himself, by creating a vast plebeian body without political rights, no doubt occasioned a necessity for those reforms which were afterwards effected by Servius Tullius. And here let us pause a moment to remark how consistent the old tradition is with itself, what a genuine historical character it bears in its main outlines. After the great addition to the Roman population, through the wars of Ancus and Tarquin the Elder, of a class that had no political rights, it would have been impossible for Rome, or any other state, to have maintained unaltered the old order of things. A revolution necessarily followed under Servius—for the reforms of Servius were nothing less than a revolution. Yet all this is related by the ancient writers in a simple, unaffected way, without any pretence to historical deduction or political philosophy. They are merely transcribing what they found in those simple, primitive annals. And yet it is thought that all this is nothing but invention!

It may be doubted, however, whether Tarquinius Priscus, the founder of a usurping dynasty, had anything more at heart, in the alterations which he made, than the consolidation of his own power. The creation of a new body of knights—that is, of cavalry—seems to have been necessary for military purposes; though Tarquin, in the selections which he made, may possibly have been influenced by views of personal interest. He would willingly have given them his own name, a natural vanity in any ruler; but that he had any idea of creating three new tribes, as Niebuhr and Schwegler suppose, seems to be totally unfounded and unproved. His other reform, the increase of the Senate (not of the patricians) was evidently made, as Livy says, with the view of supporting his own power.

We think that Schwegler's remarks about Roman and Sabine elements are very much overstrained. The two races, after cohabitation during more than a century, must have been pretty well amalgamated. If the Sabine shrines on the Capitol were compelled to give place to the new temple, the worship for which it was erected was certainly also Sabine. But this brings us to Schwegler's next section.

"The political tendency of the Tarquins, above described," continues that writer, "is expressed in the most evident and characteristic manner in the worship of the three Capitoline deities established by them, and so closely connected with the Tarquinian name.[1]

"The divine Triad of the Capitoline commonly passes for Etruscan,[2] and the foundation of the Capitoline Temple for a monument of the Etruscan descent of the Tarquinii. But this Triad was certainly not borrowed from the Etruscans. The grouping of Zeus, Hera, and Athene appears also in the religion of Greece.[3] The worship of Jupiter is found among the Latins in the remotest times: the Jupiter Latiaris attests the universality of it in Latium. The same holds of the worship of Juno, which was also common among the Sabines; and thus Tatius places an altar of Juno Quiritis in every Curia. Lastly, Minerva, according to the testimony of Varro,[4] was a deity of the Sabines, and introduced by them at Rome. We also find in the Sabine religion the united worship of these three deities. On the Quirinal, the original seat of the Sabines, stood the old Capitol, Capitolium Vetus, said to have been founded by Numa, a temple of Jupiter, Juno, and Minerva.[5] It was also in a war against the Sabines that Tarquinius Priscus vowed a temple to the Capitoline deities, evidently as being the gods of the enemy.

"If we further remark that each of the three deities was separately reverenced by the Latins and Etruscans as well as by the Sabines, we shall perceive that the Capitoline worship was a religious centre for the different component parts of the Roman nation; and this was no doubt the original motive for founding it. And thus it became a bond of union."

With the above remarks, so far as they relate to the Capitoline worship and Temple, we entirely concur. Only, as Schwegler himself shows that the worship was introduced at Rome long before the time of the Tarquins, and assumes that even the new Capitoline Temple was vowed by Tarquin the Elder in a war against the Sabines,

---

[1] Schwegler, in a note (p. 696, Anm. 1), adverts to an etymological resemblance or connexion which some German critics have pointed out between the name of Tarquinius and Tarpeius, the *p* being changed into *qu*. Then follows the usual German process of induction : "But *if* Tarquinius means the same as Tarpeius, we may easily suspect that the name of that sovereign family is directly derived from the Tarpeian Hill. What if the Tarquinians were so named by the legend as if they were the Capitoline dynasty?" Thus we may have them as a Latin family, a Roman family—anything but what they really were.
[2] According to a passage in Servius, Æn. l. 422.
[3] Pausan. vii. 20, 2; x. 5, 2.   [4] Ling. Lat. v. 74.
[5] Ibid. 158.

because the Triad to be worshipped in it were Sabine deities, we are unable to see the connexion of all these remarks with his opening proposition: that the establishment of this worship characterised the political tendency of the Tarquins. For it might just as well be said to characterize the political tendency of Numa, who is thought to have first established it at Rome, or of the following kings, who maintained it.

"To the policy of the Tarquins," continues Schwegler,[1] "Rome owes the elevation which she attained at that epoch. How considerable was the extension of the Roman dominion under the younger Tarquin is known from credible and partly contemporary records. But that under the elder Tarquin Rome must have already reached a high degree of power is shown by the buildings of this king, which could not have been undertaken without the resources of a powerful state. Tradition supplies us not with data for explaining this state of things. For the extent of the Roman territory, even after the conquests of Ancus Marcius, was still very moderate; and the national wealth of a people that lived only by agriculture and pasturage, that was without trade and maritime commerce, cannot have been considerable. Connecting links are here wanting. From the Tarquinian works, those gigantic buildings, which are comparable to the Pyramids in magnificence, those dumb witnesses of a time that has disappeared, we may measure how deep a night still rests on the history of that epoch."

The concluding remarks are only too true. We know but little of the regal times; first, because, as Livy says, letters were rare at that period, that is, as compared with after times; and secondly, because of that little some no doubt perished through the effects of time and the Gallic conflagration. But the little that we have is, we think, for the most part genuine; and especially we cannot agree with some modern writers, that the memory of kings capable of executing those magnificent works perished so entirely in a few centuries that even their names and their very existence may be doubted.

But in the preceding passage Schwegler is guilty of two opposite faults, exaggeration and extenuation. It is certainly exaggerating to compare the Tarquinian works with the pyramids. During the period of about a century through which their dynasty lasted, those works were: the Cloaca Maxima; the Tabernæ Veteres on the

[1] Buch xv. § 15.

northern side of the Forum; the Temple of Saturn; the rudiments of the Circus; these in the reign of Tarquinius Priscus, who also prepared the ground for the foundation of the Capitoline Temple, and formed the plan of and partly executed the wall afterwards finished by Servius. Besides completing this wall, Servius also built a Temple of Diana on the Aventine, and two or three other temples, and added the Tullianum to the prison of Ancus. The chief work of the younger Tarquin was the completion of the Capitoline Temple.

Now, without denying that these were magnificent works, we see no improbability in their having been executed in the time given, when we find that Numa had already founded several temples, and that Tullus Hostilius had built the Curia, which served for the Senate-house during several centuries. The only Tarquinian works that deserve the epithet gigantic are the Cloaca, the wall, and the Capitol. How long the first was in executing we have no means of knowing; but it is certain that the wall was in hand during two reigns, and the Capitol perhaps three. And the Servian walls did not after all much exceed in compass those of the neighbouring city of Veii.

With regard to the means for the execution of these works, which Schwegler extenuates, we may observe, first, that the elder Tarquin brought with him enormous wealth to Rome, besides the taste and intelligence which led him to project them: secondly, that the national wealth was not only derived from agriculture and pasturage, as Schwegler states, who seems unwilling to let the Romans get on too fast. Although we cannot agree with Mommsen that Rome was a great maritime and commercial city, yet it is evident that she began to have some maritime commerce at least as early as the time of Ancus, who would otherwise have had no reason for founding Ostia; and that her trade had very considerably increased before the expulsion of the kings is shown by the treaty made with the Carthaginians in the first year of the Republic. Besides these sources there was also the booty taken in long and successful wars, which must have been very considerable, and perhaps tribute from some of the conquered cities. Thus we are expressly told that the younger Tarquin devoted the spoils taken at Suessa Pometia to the completion of the Capitoline Temple.[1]

"Dionysius relates,"[2] continues Schwegler, "that the elder Tar-

---

[1] Liv. i. 53.   [2] Lib. iii. c. 62—65.

quinius reduced all Etruria under his dominion by his great victory at Eretum, and ruled thereafter as the acknowledged head of the twelve Etruscan states. If this was so, if Rome was then the capital of a king of Etruria, the Tarquinian buildings may be explained without much difficulty. But it cannot be doubted that this account, which is found only in Dionysius, is in this form unhistorical; and the more certainly so, because Dionysius relates the same thing of Servius Tullius, without mentioning, at a later period, the dissolution of this domination over Etruria. Cicero and Livy are ignorant of this Etruscan connexion, or are purposely silent about it: Livy, indeed, indirectly excludes it, by mentioning under the reign of Servius Tullius that the treaties with Veii had expired:[1] [meaning, of course, those which Ancus Marcius must have made with them when they ceded the Mæsian Forest.] The later tradition[2] seems to have connected the Roman Tarquin with the Etruscan Tarchon, the eponymous hero of Tarquinii and mythical founder of the twelve cities. Hence, perhaps, the origin, as Niebuhr has conjectured,[3] of that fabulous legend which represents Tarquin as the head of Etruria.

"Modern inquirers (Niebuhr, Levesque, Müller) have built upon the account of Dionysius the hypothesis that Rome in the Tarquinian period became a city of the Etruscan confederation, having been conquered by a Tuscan prince, who made it his residence, and adorned it with those magnificent buildings.

"But there is too little ground for such a conjecture. That there was once a period when Rome and Latium were subject to Etruria is, indeed, not improbable; an obscure memory of it is connected with the names of Mezentius and Porsena. But, according to all traces that we possess, the Tarquinian period was not

---

[1] "Jam enim indutiæ exierant."—Lib. i. 42. The term of this truce is not mentioned; but it was probably for fifty years (or forty-two solar years), when it would have expired early in the reign of Servius.

[2] By the "later tradition," Schwegler seems to mean the account in Dionysius. But there can have been no earlier or later *tradition*; all tradition must have ceased with the first annalists. The account in Dionysius was most probably an *invention*, for, writing for the Greeks, he sometimes amused himself in that way; or it was at all events taken from an unauthorized source. The story of the conquest of Etruria by Tarquin may just as probably have arisen from his successes against them when serving under Ancus as from the confounding of him with the Etruscan Tarchon.

[3] Röm. Gesch. i. 401.

subject to Etruscan influence and dominion. The political reforms of the first Tarquin are entirely foreign to the spirit of Etruscan aristocracy; while the rule of the younger Tarquin resembles a Greek tyranny. In their foreign policy, too, both the Tarquins, and particularly the younger one, are exclusively occupied with Latium, and Etruria during their rule falls completely into the background. Lastly, Gaia Cæcilia, the mythical prototype of a Roman housewife, is evidently regarded in the myth as a Roman by birth: as it would be difficult to discover how the legend should have ascribed the part of a pattern of domestic manners to an immigrant Etruscan woman. She is evidently no historical personage, and her marriage with Tarquinius Priscus must be put on the same footing as that of Egeria with Numa, or Fortuna with Servius Tullius."

Schwegler has, no doubt, come to a right conclusion in rejecting altogether Dionysius's story of the conquest of Etruria by Tarquinius Priscus. The absurdity of it is shown at once by the simple fact that this conquest of a large and powerful confederacy is ascribed to a single victory, and that, too, achieved not within the limits of Etruria but at Eretum, a Sabine town on the other side of the Tiber! It is by such inventions as this that Dionysius has brought discredit on the early Roman history; at all events with those critics who count authorities instead of weighing them, and place Dionysius, Plutarch, Florus, and Zonaras on the same line with Cicero and Livy. Sir G. C. Lewis has also pointed to another absurdity,[1] that Tarquin, after reducing the Etruscans to subjection, "treats them with the most romantic magnanimity, exacting from them nothing more than an acknowledgment of his nominal suzerainty." This reproach applies properly only to Dionysius and not to the history; but Sir G. C. Lewis does not draw this distinction. Niebuhr also ridicules the narrative of Tarquin's wars in Dionysius. "Of the wars," he writes, "ascribed to L. Tarquinius, Dionysius, adopting the forgeries of very recent annalists, has given an intolerable newspaper account."[2] Yet though Niebuhr rejects the Etruscan wars as wholly unhistorical, he founds a conjecture upon them[3] that a Tuscan might have seized the Roman throne;

[1] Credibility, &c. vol. i. p. 472.
[2] Röm. Gesch. l. 374 (vol. i. p. 358, Engl. transl.). That Dionysius wrote after Annals is inferred by Niebuhr from the Fasti Triumphales (ibid. S. 396).
[3] Ibid. 397.

thus reversing the account, and founding, upon what he considers to be totally unworthy of belief, another and different hypothesis!

The question about Tanaquil and Gaia Cæcilia we have already examined,[1] and shown them to be identical; therefore the "myth," as Schwegler styles it, could not have regarded her as a Roman; and it would be just as "difficult to discover" why an Etruscan woman naturalized at Rome might not become the pattern of a good housewife, as why she might. These are barren subtleties, but we are compelled to answer them, or it would be said that they are unanswerable. Nor is it easy to see, according to ordinary lights, why a marriage with an Etruscan woman should be on a par, as regards credibility, with a marriage with a fabulous deity, or a personified accident.

Schwegler's sixteenth section, and last of this book, is devoted to the story of Attus Navius. In it he explains at length, with that confidence which marks the German writers of his school, the origin of the story, as if he had been actually present at the whole process. We need not follow him into this profundity, because, as we have before said, the whole matter was a bit of priestcraft, and evidently so considered by Livy. But this forms no objection to the general credibility of the history of Tarquin.

Sir G. C. Lewis's objections to this history, besides his ordinary one of want of historical attestation, are the following:[2]—"The wars of Tarquinius Priscus are described at considerable length by Dionysius; but, although he is acquainted with some of their minutest details, and narrates them as if he had a series of official despatches before him, other writers omit all mention of the majority of them, and appear scarcely to have heard of their occurrence. The stories again which connect the name of Tarquin with certain monuments and public works, such as the statue of Attus Navius, are liable to the same suspicion of a legendary origin which we have found in other similar accounts. They, moreover, fluctuate between him and other kings, as in the legend of the foundation of the Temple of Capitoline Jupiter. His alleged introduction of the *fasces* and other royal insignia, from Etruria, appears in an equally unsteady light. Even if the narrative of his reign were better attested, many circumstances in it would raise a doubt of its credibility: the story of the eagle flying away with his cap, and the cutting of the whetstone by Attus Navius, are purely marvellous;

---

[1] Above, p. 238, seq. [2] Credibility, &c., vol. i. p. 478.

the manner of his introduction into Rome, and of his election to the royal dignity, is improbable, and his triumphant wars against the Latins, Sabines, and Etruscans, without a single important reverse, lie beyond the limits of credibility."

Dionysius's narrative of the wars of Tarquinius Priscus is, as we have already seen, a reflection only upon that historian himself, and not upon the history; and for the same reason these wars must be struck out of the catalogue of "triumphant wars" with which Sir G. C. Lewis concludes his paragraph. There remain then only the wars with the Sabines and Latins. The statement that those are conducted "without a single important reverse," is incorrect. At the beginning of the Sabine War, Tarquin met with a reverse so important that the enemy approached the walls of Rome, and the Romans trembled for the safety of their city.[1] Tarquin was glad of a respite to recruit his army, and especially to strengthen his cavalry. The conquest of Latium, as we have seen, is effected by the reduction of its cities one after the other; the Latins made no united effort for their defence,[2] a fact which shows, as we have already had occasion to observe, that there was not much political cohesion in the Latin League; and what little there may once have been must have been diminished by the capture of Alba Longa, its metropolis, in the reign of Tullus. Where, then, is the incredibility, or rather even the improbability, of these wars? Are we not to allow to the Romans some superiority of race and organization? And if not, how are we to account for their final conquest of the world? We may confidently affirm that this could not have been achieved unless Rome had made some such beginnings as we read of in her early history.

We abandon the story of Attus Navius, that of the eagle flying away with Tarquin's cap, and all the other miraculous parts of his history, as they were abandoned by all sensible Romans two thousand years ago. Cicero rejects these stories,[3] but he does not, therefore,

---

[1] "Idemque Sabinos, quum a mœnibus urbis repulisset, equitatu fudit belloque devicit."—Cic. De Rep. II. 20. "Itaque tropæatum Romæ est; et dubia victoria magna utrimque cæde pugnatum est."—Liv. i. 36.

[2] "Ubi nusquam ad universæ rei dimicationem ventum est."—Liv. i. 38.

[3] "Sed tamen nonnulli isti, Tite, faciunt imperite, qui in isto periculo non ut a porta, sed ut a teste veritatem exigant. Nec dubito quin lidem et eum Egeria collocutam Numam, et ab aquila Tarquinio apicem impositum putent."—De Leg. i. 1. And of Attus Navius: "Omitte igitur lituum Romuli, quem in maximo incendio negas potuisse comburi; contemne cotem

uncritically reject all the early history in a lump; because he knew that the invention and the belief of such stories were in unison with the manners of those early times; and may, perhaps, even have considered that the presence of them was a proof of its genuineness; for, as we have before observed, a wholly rationalistic history which pretended to have come down from those times would assuredly have been false and forged.

When it is said that the monuments and public works connected with the name of Tarquin are liable to the suspicion of a legendary origin, this is not saying much, because everything may be liable to suspicion, especially from critics inclined that way; and because nothing is adduced to justify it with regard to the public works, though they are invidiously connected with the statue of Attus Navius; unless it be meant as a ground of suspicion that the stories "fluctuate between him (Tarquin) and other kings, as in the legend of the foundation of the Temple of Capitoline Jupiter." But there is no fluctuation whatever. The authorities unanimously say that Tarquinius Priscus vowed the temple in the Sabine War, and prepared the foundations of it.[1] Whether anything was done by

---

Attii Navii. Nihil debet esse in philosophia commentitiis fabellis loci."— De Div. ii. 38.

[1] "Ædemque in Capitolio Jovi Optimo Maximo bello Sabino in ipsa pugna vovisse faciendam."—Cic. De Rep. ii. 20. "Et arcem ad ædem in Capitolio Jovis, quam voverat bello Sabino ... occupat fundamentis."—Liv. L 38. ἐκτίσει γὰρ, ἐν τῇ τελευταίᾳ πολέμῳ μαχόμενος πρὸς Σαβίνους εὔξατο τῷ Διΐ καὶ τῇ Ἥρᾳ καὶ τῇ Ἀθηνᾷ ἐὰν νικήσῃ τῇ μάχῃ, ναοὺς αὐτοῖς κατασκευάσειν· καὶ τὴν μὲν ἐνίκησεν ἵνα ἱδρύσεσθαι ἔμελλε τοὺς θεοὺς, ἀναλήμμασί τε καὶ χώμασι μεγάλοις ἐξεργάσατο, κ. τ. λ.—Dionys. iv. 59; cf. iii. 69. "Voverat Tarquinius Priscus rex bello Sabino, jeceratque fundamenta."—Tac. Hist. iii. 72. Why Becker should assert that it is not probable the elder Tarquin should have prepared the foundations is incomprehensible. It is a gross misinterpretation of Dionysius to say that he represents the elder Tarquin as having completed the substructure ("sollst den Unterbau vollendet"). On the contrary, that author says expressly in the latter passage: τοὺς δὲ θεμελίους οὐκ ἔφθασε θεῖναι τοῦ νεώ. The word ἀνάλημμα is not to be taken in its architectural sense, i.e. in its general sense, meaning an elevating, raising. This is shown, first, by its being followed by χῶμα. According to Becker's method the foundation would first have been laid, and then the earth heaped up! For the foundations of the actual building, the stones, Dionysius uses the word θεμέλιοι. Also being understood. Second, by the fact that the temple was built on a huge platform, or podium, like some of the temples at Pompeii. This podium was what Tarquin the Elder prepared. Third, because if Dionysius had here meant that this king finished the foundations, he would have been guilty of a gross con-

Servius Tullius seems doubtful. The completion of the war would probably have engrossed all his resources, and what he did to the temple was perhaps little. Tacitus is the only author[1] who mentions his participation in the work; the rest may have omitted his share from its unimportance. But all the authorities are agreed that the temple was finished, or very nearly so, by Tarquinius Superbus.[2] The only author from whom a doubt could be extracted is Pliny the Elder, who in one place represents Tarquinius Priscus as employing Volcanius of Veii to make the statue for the temple; whilst, inconsistently with himself, in another very doubtful and perhaps corrupt passage, he calls the artist Turranius of Tregellae.[3] That the stories fluctuate is therefore a random assertion, made "stans pede in uno," and without that caution which the ancient writers are entitled to from their critics.

The question about the introduction of the *fasces* and other royal insignia is a mere piece of antiquarianism, a question of millinery and upholstery, about which ancient authors might easily differ without damaging the credibility of the history in its more important points; though, after all, there is not even here so great a difference among them as is asserted. Livy, rightly construed,[4] says only that Romulus took the twelve lictors from the Etruscans; and even that, as he shows, was doubtful, for some thought the number of them derived from the twelve augural birds. Tarquinius Priscus may have subsequently introduced a greater pomp from Etruria—the *sella curulis*, the ivory sceptre, the embroidered robe, the golden crown: not, however, from having conquered the Etruscans, but, more probably, because having lived among them in his youth, he felt a satisfaction in assuming at Rome insignia to which he had been forbidden to aspire at Tarquinii. But the whole question is unimportant. That the manner of Tarquin's introduction into Rome, and of his election to the royal dignity, is improbable, is a more serious objection. But we confess that we cannot see it in this light. That hospitable city which had received into its bosom, without inquiry or choice, refugees from all parts, that

tradition; which, however, it may be said, would not be wonderful in that author. It is this podium, or basis, that Livy and Tacitus mean by the word *fundamenta*.—Rom. Alterth. B. i. S. 395, Anm. 767.

[1] loc. cit.
[2] Cic. De Rep. II. 24; Liv. l. 53, 55; Dionys. iv. 61; Tac. loc. cit.
[3] Plin. H. N. xxviii. 4; xxxv. 45, s. 157; cf. lil. 9, s. 70. [4] Lib. i. 8.

was daily augmenting its population by admitting among it the conquered peoples around, may well have opened its gates readily to a rich stranger like Tarquin; and those who read Livy attentively will see that it was his knowledge of this readiness that induced him to go thither. The way in which he obtained the crown has been already related; we have nothing further to add to it, by way of convincing those who hold it to be improbable. But for our own parts—the Roman king being elective, however much the children of a king may seem to have had a claim of preference—we see no more improbability in the election of Tarquin than in that of any of his predecessors or successors.

We will now proceed to consider the miraculous circumstances attending the birth of Servius Tullius.

We have given above from Livy the commonly-received account of his birth and education. There were, however, several other traditions respecting it, one of the most remarkable of which was the following:—As one day Ocrisia—such was the name of the captive of Corniculum—was offering cakes to the Lar at the hearth of the palace, he appeared to her in the midst of the fire in the shape of a *phallus*; a sort of extemporary marriage took place, and Ocrisia became pregnant with Servius Tullius.[1] There are several other versions of the story, but we need mention only two. Thus Servius is said to have been the son of a female slave of Tarquin's by one of his clients;[2] and another account of his genealogy is that given by the Emperor Claudius in a speech to the Senate, fragments of which, engraved on bronze tablets, were found at Lyons, of which place Claudius was a native, in 1528, and are still preserved there in the Palais des Beaux Arts.[3] In this speech he says: "If we follow our own authors, Servius Tullius was the son of the captive Ocrisia: but according to the Tuscans he was the faithful friend of Cœlius Vivenna, and the companion of all his adventures. Driven at length by the vicissitudes of fortune from Etruria with the remainder of the Cælian army, he occupied Mount Cœlius, which he named after his general; and having changed his name, for his Tuscan one was Mastarna, he called himself, as I have said, Servius Tullius, and obtained the kingdom, to the great advantage of the state."

The true history of the birth of Servius Tullius we cannot hope

---

[1] Plin. H. N. xxxvi. 70, s. 204; Ov. Fast. vi. 627, sq.; Dionys. iv. 2.
[2] Cic. De Rep. ii. 21.   [3] They are printed in Gruter. Thes. p. 502.

o discover. It was a secret of the palace. The testimony of the Emperor Claudius may be accepted for the fact that the Tuscans believed Servius Tullius to have been one of their own *condottieri*. Claudius was a learned man. He is said to have invented three new letters of the alphabet, and to have written in Greek a Tyrrhenian history, in twenty books, and a Carthaginian history in eight. How he prided himself on them may be inferred from the fact that he founded at Alexandria a new museum, in which, and the old one, these histories were to be alternately recited every year.[1] This, no doubt, brought the history of Cæles Vibenna, and his lieutenant Mastarna, into fashion, and accounts for Tacitus ascribing the colonization of that hill, though in a hesitating way, to the time of Tarquinius Priscus;[2] while on the other hand he appears to have no doubt about the Vicus Tuscus having been founded at this time. It is highly improbable that the Cælian Hill should have been left uninhabited till the time of Tarquinius Priscus, and we have already shown that it was most likely colonized in the time of Romulus. That Tarquin, however, through the connexion of his wife Tanaquil with Etruria—and it is she who plays the prominent part in bringing forwards Servius Tullius—may have been assisted in his wars by an Etruscan *condottiere* with his band, that this band may have been cantoned about the Vicus Tuscus, and have been of no slight service in aiding Servius to usurp the crown, is not altogether improbable. Livy says that he was supported by a strong guard, and Dionysius states the same thing.[3] But this seems to point to the mercenary band of a *condottiere*; relying upon which, he was able to set the patricians at defiance, especially as he was also supported by the affections of the plebeians, now a numerous and powerful body, whom he had gained by bribery and by paying their debts.[4] He was the first king who was able to dispense with an election in the regular

---

[1] Suet. Claud. 42.

[2] "Mox Cælium appellitatum (montem Querquetulanum) a Cæle Vibenna, qui dux gentis Etruscæ, quum auxilium appellatum ductavisset, sedem eam acceperat a Tarquinio Prisco, seu quis alius regum dedit: nam scriptores in eo dissentiunt; cetera non ambigua sunt, magnas eas copias per plana etiam ac foro propinqua habitasse, unde *Tuscum vicum* e vocabulo advenarum dicta."
—Ann. iv. 65.

[3] "Præsidio firmo munitus."—Liv. L. 41: λοχαγοὺς χεῖρα περὶ αὐτὸν ἔχων.— Lib. iv. c. 5.

[4] "Obæratosque pecunia sua liberavisset."—Cic. De Rep. 21.

form; that is, through an Interrex who proposed him to *the people;* which term, being still confined to the Comitia Curiata, included only a small part of the whole population. He, however, took care to have his usurpation confirmed some time afterwards in the regular way by proposing himself to the people, and procuring a *lex curiata de imperio*.[1]

The Emperor Claudius was not the first who brought forwards this account of the Etruscan origin of Servius Tullius. Such an origin had been adverted to by Trogus Pompeius, who flourished in the reign of Augustus. The passage occurs in a speech of Mithridates, which Justin has inserted literally, as it stood in Trogus, and runs as follows: "Hanc illos (Romanos) regibus omnibus legem odiorum dixisse: scilicet quia ipsi tales reges habuerint, quorum etiam nominibus erubescant, aut pastores Aboriginum, aut haruspices Sabinorum, aut exsules Corinthiorum, aut servos vernasque Thuscorum, aut, quod honoratissimum nomen fuit inter hæc, Superbos."[2] It is impossible to doubt, from the connexion in which the words "servos vernasque Thuscorum" stand to the sentence, that Servius Tullius is here meant; and therefore the tradition must not only have been known, but even have gained some acceptance, at the time when Livy and Dionysius wrote, though these authors have neglected to notice it.

Professor Newman remarks: "Unless we are to discard, as totally false, the tradition that *the sons of Ancus* instigated the murder of Tarquin, we ought apparently to regard it as meaning that a violent faction of the greater clans had conspired to recover their lost supremacy by this atrocious means. Hereditary succes-

---

[1] Such appears to be Cicero's meaning, De Rep. ii. 21, "Non commisit se patribus:" that is, he did not permit the Senate to appoint an Interrex. This agrees with the account of Dionysius (iv. 8, seqq.), the details of which, however, are evidently a rhetorical invention. The account of Livy (i. 41) is somewhat different. He agrees with the other two authorities in stating that Servius seized the crown "injussu populi,"—that is, without proposal of him by an Interrex to the people, and therefore without their choice; but says that he reigned "voluntate patrum," which seems hardly to have been the case. Yet *voluntas* is very far from *auctoritas*, and may mean only acquiescence, connivance. They ventured not to take any steps against the usurpation, but they did not give it their sanction. Livy also says that Servius obtained a vote of the people (i. 46), but at a later period, after waging some successful wars, and reforming the constitution. And this seems most probable.

[2] Justin. xxxviii. 6; cf. Schwegler, B. i. S. 718.

sion had not once been acted on in Rome; and it is not probable that the sons of Ancus, if prompted by personal motives, could have hoped to profit by the crime."[1]

There seems to be a good deal of truth in these observations; and, if we regard the conspiracy of the sons of Ancus as an attempt of the patricians to get rid of the Tarquinian dynasty, it will serve to explain many circumstances of the narrative. It shows why Servius could not commit himself to the Senate or Patricians—*non commisit se patribus*—and allow them to appoint an Interrex for electing a king; why he surrounded himself with a guard, and courted the plebeians; why Tanaquil, though she had sons, or grandsons, of her own growing up, wished to make him king; because these youths were not old enough to assert their pretensions, and Servius might keep the throne for them.

It is true, however, that all those things might have been equally done by Servius had he been no Etruscan, but only a Latin, an obliged and humble dependent of Tarquin and Tanaquil ; though, in that case, we do not so well see whence his guard—his *præsidium firmum*, as Livy calls it—can have come. For there is nothing to show that he had a guard as *præfectus urbi*, or warden of the city. Schwegler's objections to his being an Etruscan, drawn from his reforms,[2] are of no weight, because we do not know much about the Etruscan constitution ; and because, whatever it may have been, a king of Rome must have dealt with the Roman people and constitution according to the materials which he found, and not have gone to Etruria for a model. The same may be said of the argument drawn from his conciliating the Latins ; which is only what any politic prince would have done, and is not of the least force in proving him a Latin by birth. Nor can any argument be derived from the name of Servius Tullius, which may have been merely an adopted one, just as Tanaquil called herself Gaia Cæcilia. But the whole subject is involved in obscurity. All that we can see plainly is that there was an attempt to overthrow the Tarquinian dynasty; that it was favoured by the patricians; that Servius Tullius frustrated it, partly by a display of force, partly through the favour of the plebeians, and succeeded in seizing the throne. But Sir G. C. Lewis is hardly justified in saying that he "acquires the royal office as son-in-law of the late king, and by the assistance

---

[1] Regal Rome, p. 138. Professor Newman, however, takes Servius to have been a Latin. [2] R. L. S. 718.

and favour of Tanaquil his queen."[1] His relationship to the late king would have given him no title to the crown, nor would the favour of Tanaquil, though she undoubtedly aided him in seizing it by her encouragement, and stratagem.

SECTION IX.

FIRST ACTS OF SERVIUS TULLIUS—HIS NEW CONSTITUTION.

Servius proceeded to fortify his newly-acquired power no less by his private than by his public policy. And, lest he should experience the same fate at the hands of Tarquin's children as Tarquin had from those of Ancus, he betrothed two of his daughters to the princes Lucius and Aruns Tarquin. But human counsels could not prevail over the laws of fate, nor prevent the jealousy and envy which accompany that high station from filling even his own family with disloyalty and hatred.

A war undertaken against the Veientines and other Etruscans—for the truce with Veii had now expired—served very opportunely to maintain tranquillity at home. The valour and fortune of Tullius shone forth conspicuously in that war. By the defeat of a vast army of the enemy he assured his throne, and under the prestige of this victory returned to Rome, no longer doubtful of the issue, whether it might be necessary for him either to test the disposition of the patricians towards him, or that of the *plebs*. For he now undertook by far the greatest of any work that can be accomplished in time of peace; in order that, as Numa had been the author of religious law, so he himself might go down to posterity as the founder of the various orders of the state, as they are marked out by the different degrees of rank and fortune. For it was now that he instituted the census, an institution which was to prove the greatest benefit in so vast an empire. By this the various offices of war and peace were not to be discharged indiscriminately, and by the head, but according to the means and fortune of those who under-

[1] Credibility, &c. vol. I. p. 483.

took them. Hence the distribution of the people into classes and centuries, and that order of things arising from the census, adapted to both peace and war.

REMARKS.—We are now arrived at the most important epoch of the reign of Servius, and indeed of the whole regal period—the Servian Reform. But before we enter upon this, which will demand a review of the whole Roman constitution, we will say a few words on the transactions which preceded it.

At p. 723 Schwegler remarks: "The common tradition that Servius Tullius obtained the throne more particularly by being the son-in-law of the king, and by being advised and supported by Tanaquil, is clogged with difficulties in another respect. As the sons of Tarquin, Lucius and Aruns, are married to daughters of Servius Tullius, they would, if Servius had been wedded to a daughter of Tarquin, have taken to wife their nieces, the daughters of their sister; although, according to the Roman view, this was incest. Even in the imperial times, when the Emperor Claudius gave the first example of such a marriage, it excited great and universal disapprobation. We must, therefore, relinquish either the one account or the other; and doubtless the first, of Servius having been the son-in-law of Tarquin: since the marriage of the younger Tarquins with the daughters of Servius has incomparably a more historical character."

We must confess that we cannot arrive at the same conclusion. There were not two conflicting accounts respecting Servius having been the son-in-law of Tarquin, though Cicero, it is true, does not mention that circumstance. But there were two conflicting accounts whether the younger Tarquins were the sons or grandsons of Priscus; and probability would show them to have been his grandsons. In this case they would have married their cousins; to which there would have been no objection, and especially in a royal family. In fact, these marriages may be regarded as a further proof that the younger Tarquins were the grandsons of Priscus.

The Etruscan war of Servius Tullius, which Livy and Cicero mention only briefly,[1] was probably of longer duration than one campaign. The Fasti Triumphales appear to mention three triumphs. But that it lasted twenty years, as Dionysius states,[2]

[1] Liv. L 42; Cic. De Rep. ii. 21.   [2] Lib. iv. c. 27, seq.

and that the result of it was nothing less than the confirmation of the Roman empire over all Etruria, it is impossible to believe.

Before we describe the political reforms introduced by Servius Tullius, we will take a view of the Roman constitution as it existed before those reforms, and then proceed to consider the alterations made by Servius.

THE ROMAN CONSTITUTION UNDER THE KINGS.

The Roman constitution as it existed under the kings is a most intricate subject. Volumes have been written upon it, yet scholars are not yet agreed even upon the nature of some of the most prominent institutions; as, for instance, the early *populus* and *plebs*, the Comitia Curiata, the Auctoritas Patrum, &c. It would, perhaps, be impossible to give an account of the early constitution that should not be liable to some objections. We have attempted in the following sketch only to give what seemed to us the most probable description of it; that is, which appeared liable to the fewest objections, and therefore the most consistent. Whether this object has been attained the reader must judge; all that it becomes us to say about it is, that it is the result of a careful inquiry, instituted without any previous theories or prejudices, and conducted to the best of our judgment and knowledge.

We will first consider the composition of the Roman people.

The population of Romulus, the original inhabitants of the Palatine city, consisted only of his own immediate followers, called Ramnes; to whom were afterwards added the Luceres, composed, as some think, of the fugitives who had taken refuge in the Asylum, augmented probably afterwards by some Etruscans who had aided him in his wars against the Sabines. At a later period a still greater increase took place by the addition of the Sabines themselves; who, as we have already related, became incorporated with the earlier settlers, and ultimately formed with them the Roman nation. Other additions subsequently took place by the incorporation of conquered peoples; but it was the three races before mentioned, the Ramnes, the Luceres, and the Tities, or Sabines, that are regarded as the original and genuine stem-tribes of the Romans.

From these three races naturally arose a division of the whole nation into three tribes, bearing their respective names; whence the term *tribus* to denote a division of the people for political purposes, afterwards applied to any such division, without respect of number. This term would not, of course, have come into use before the Sabine union; but it seems natural to suppose that, before this period, the Ramnes and Luceres were subject to certain political divisions; and it appears certain that the Ramnes, at least, must have been previously divided into *gentes* and *curiæ*. For what else could have been the *curiæ veteres*, which were situated on the Palatine Hill, but the halls where the Ramnian *curiales* met? It is impossible that the Romulean state could have gone on without some such organization; but, for a general view of the constitution, it suffices to regard the state after the Sabine union.

The three tribes then formed were, as we learn from Varro, connected with a similar division of the *ager Romanus*, or Roman territory.[1] At the head of each tribe was a *tribunus*, who may be considered as their commander in war;[2] for the whole Romulean constitution was doubtless contrived, in the first instance, for warlike purposes—the forming of a militia; but, as the men capable of bearing arms alone enjoyed civil rights, the arrangement was also political. The members of the same tribe were called *tribules*, and those of the same curia, *curiales*.[3]

The curia was a subdivision of each tribe into ten parts; and thus the whole *populus*—that is, the whole army, and consequently the whole population enjoying the *jus suffragii*, or vote —was contained in thirty curiæ. At the head of each curia was a patrician priest, called *curio*, who performed the sacred rites proper to it, in its house of assembly, or hall, called *curia*.[4] In each of these halls was a statue of Juno Curitis, with a *mensa*, or altar.[5] There were also other curial priests, called *flamines*.[6] On feast-days, the curiales appear to have dined together in these

[1] "Ager Romanus primum divisus in partes tris, a quo tribus appellata Tatiensium, Ramnium, Lucerum."—Ling. Lat. v. 55.
[2] "Tribuni militum quod terni tribus tribubus Ramnium, Lucerum, Titium olim ad exercitum mittebantur."—Ibid. 81.
[3] "Curiales ejusdem curiæ, ut tribules et municipes."—Paul. Diac. p. 49.
[4] "Curiones dicti a curiis, qui fiunt ut in his sacra faciant."—Varr. L. L. v. 83. "Curionium æs dicebatur, quod dabatur curioni ob sacerdotium curionatus."—Paul. Diac. p. 49 (Müll).
[5] "Curiales mensæ, in quibus immolabatur Junoni, quæ curis appellata est."—Idem, p. 64. Dionysius also mentions these tables, τραπέζαι, as placed there by Tatius (ii. 50), but distinguishes them from the altars; cf. Ib. 66.
[6] "Curiales flamines curiarum sacerdotes."—Paul. Diac. loc. cit.

halls.¹ That the curiæ were subdivided into decuriæ rests only on the authority of Dionysius. Of the political functions of the members of the curiæ we shall speak presently.

Besides these curiæ, or halls, there was also the Curia Calabra, which seems to have been a sort of House of Convocation, or place of assembly for the priests; where they proclaimed on what day of the month the Nones would happen.²

The third and last subdivision of the people was into *gentes*, for which we can find no better English name than *clans*.

The members of a *gens* were not necessarily blood-relations: the institution was political, like the curiæ, though we cannot so easily point out for what purpose, but also most probably with a view to military organization. The principal passage respecting the *gens* is the following one of Cicero:³—" Gentiles sunt qui inter se eodem nomine sunt. Non est satis. Qui ab ingenuis oriundi sunt. Ne id quidem satis est. Quorum majorum nemo servitutem servivit. Abest etiam nunc. Qui capite non sunt deminuti. Hoc fortasse satis est."

This being a formal, logical definition, of course pretends to the greatest accuracy. We see, then, that the general mark of recognition was the *same name*, and that blood-relationship had nothing to do with the matter, except in so far that blood relations bear the same name. Cicero begins from the most general term. The same name includes all belonging to the *gens*, or clan, but the same blood would not. Hence the members of a *gens* were not necessarily any more related by blood than the members of a curia. The qualifications for a *gens* were not blood, but to have been born free (*ingenuus*), and not to have forfeited civil rights (*non capite deminutus*).

Paul the Deacon gives another definition much to the same purpose: " Gentilis dicitur ex eodem genere ortus, et is qui simili nomine appellatur, ut ait Cincius: gentiles mihi sunt, qui meo nomine appellantur."⁴

This definition is not so logical and accurate as Cicero's; but it shows still more clearly that blood-relationship was not necessary, because it includes *both* blood-relations (*eodem genere orti*) and those

---

¹ Dionys. loc. cit.
² "Calabra curia dicebatur, ubi tantum ratio sacrorum gerebatur."—Paul. Diac. p. 49; cf. Varr. L. L. v. 13, vi. 27.   ³ Top. 6.
⁴ Paul. Diac. p. 91 (Müll.)

who are only called by the same name (*qui simili nomine appellantur*).

The truth of these definitions, however, is contested by Becker,[1] who opposes to it the following passage from Varro:[2]—"Ut in hominibus quaedam sunt agnationes ac gentilitates, sic in verbis: ut enim ab Æmilio homines orti Æmilii, ac gentiles; sic ab Æmilii nomine declinatæ voces in gentilitate nominali."

"This passage," says Becker, "which Niebuhr gets rid of so easily,[3] shows, however, this much: that Varro figured to himself an Æmilius as stem-father of the whole *gens* Æmilia; and not that it could have been constituted of quite different persons, not related by blood, but bearing a common political name. That might have been possible at Athens, but not at Rome."

The objection is quite futile. The passage cannot be tortured into meaning "that Varro figured to himself an Æmilius as stem-father of the *whole gens* Æmilia." Of course those descended from Æmilius would bear his name, and be gentiles; but the question is, would these include *all* the Æmilii? Were there not other Æmilii, who did not trace their origin to a man named Æmilius? For Varro's purpose, it was not material whether there were such or not; it sufficed for his illustration to compare the cases of a noun to the family of a man. Such a passage, therefore, cannot weigh for a moment against the two before quoted, the purpose of which is to give an accurate definition of the word *gentilis*.

Becker then proceeds to argue, after Göttling, as follows:—It is not to be supposed that the Latins and Sabines gave up their family names when they were admitted into the Roman patriciate. Thus we find the Tullii, Servilii, Quinctii, &c., admitted as patricians, and consequently into the curiæ, without changing their names, though, being admitted into other *gentes*, they should have given them up.

Here we may ask, Why was it necessary that they should be admitted into *other gentes*? It was necessary, of course, to have a *gens*, in order to belong to a curia; but these Latins might have been made into Roman *gentes*, and yet have been suffered to retain their original names.

[1] Röm. Alterth. B. ii. Abth. i. S. 37; cf. Göttling, Staatsv. S. 62.
[2] Ling. Lat. viii. 4.
[3] "Aber so gleichnissweise wie er hier redet, würde wahrlich er selbst es sich verbeten haben ihm eine solche Erwähnung buchstäblich als eine historische Behauptung anzulegen."—Niebuhr, Röm. Gesch. i. 329.

The argument seems to be, that to be admitted into a curia they must first have been admitted into a gens, as each curia consisted of only ten gentes. But this rests upon nothing at all, except an inference of Niebuhr's, from a passage in Dionysius,[1] where it is said that the curiæ were divided into decuriæ, or decads. Dionysius is the only author who says this; but, though he is not a very good authority on the Roman constitution, still it is not improbable that as each tribe was divided into ten curiæ, so each curia may have been divided into ten decuriæ. Niebuhr conjectured that these decuriæ were the same as the gentes, and that there was thus in each tribe ten curiæ, and a hundred gentes. But there is no method of connecting decuria with gens. Dionysius must have known the difference, if there had been any; and if there was none, why two names? It is impossible to say how many gentes there were in a curia, or whether there was the same number in each. The number may have varied according to the numerosity of the gentes which composed it; for we must assume that some gentes were more powerful and numerous than others. And though these divisions by tens and hundreds may have been those originally established, yet we may presume that they were not unalterable, if political necessity demanded a change.

It is not improbable that the Ramnes, for instance, were first divided into a hundred gentes. It seems to have been necessary to a gens that a patrician family should have been at its head; and when Romulus appointed his first Senate of a hundred members, he made, by that act, so many patrician families.

"That the gentes," says Becker,[2] "were not a mere political institution appears to follow from their having sacra privata. Had it been a political division like the curiæ, the sacra, like those of the curiæ, would have been public."

We believe that in its origin the institution was political, and that, agreeably to the Greek descent of Romulus, it was taken from a Greek custom. On this subject Schwegler says:[3] "This view (that the institution was political) is recommended by the analogy of the old Attic constitution. In this, each of the twelve phratriæ was divided into thirty gentes (γένη), so that the whole number of them amounted to three hundred and sixty. These fixed numbers show that we cannot here think of natural relationship, or kindred; and further, it is expressly handed down that the bond of union of

---

[1] Lib. II. c. 7.   [2] S. 39.   [3] R. i. S. 613.

these *gentes* was not blood relationship, or a common descent, but a communion of holy rites. Nevertheless those communities are called. γένη, the members of them γεννῆται, and even ὁμογάλακτες, as if they had been family relations."[1]

But though the institution was most probably political, yet the connexion between the members of a *gens* was much more intimate, and as it were sacred, than that between the members of a curia. These, with regard to one another, were merely *curiales*; while the members of a *gens* were not only *gentiles*, but also bore the same proper name, as if they had belonged to one family.

It is hardly possible that all the families belonging to a *gens* were patrician, though this has been assumed. Indeed there are passages which contradict such an assumption. Livy, describing the *gens* Fabia going forth to the Veientine war, says: "Sex et trecenti milites, *omnes patricii, omnes unius gentis*, quorum neminem ducem spernere egregius quibuslibet temporibus senatus, ibant, *unius familiae* viribus Veienti populo pestem minitantes."[2]

The Fabii are here described as not only of one *gens*; it is also added that they were all patricians, all of one family. Now unless a *gens* might have contained different families, not related by blood, and plebeian families as well as patrician, these additions would have been unnecessary. It would have sufficed to say that the Fabian *gens* went forth to the number of three hundred and sixty, and every Roman would have understood that they were all patricians, all of one family.

So also the well known decree of the *gens* Manlia, after the condemnation of M. Manlius Capitolinus, " Decreto gentis Manliae *neminem patricium* M. Manlium vocari licet."[3] There were therefore plebeian families of the same *gens*.

Now, in the original constitution of Romulus, what were those plebeians that made part of a *gens*? Might they not have been the clients?

The client appears to have borne the name of his patron, and therefore, if he was an *ingenuus*, he was the *gentilis* of his patron. Docker allows that the client belonged to the *gens*, but adds,

---

[1] καὶ οἱ μετέχοντες τοῦ γένους γεννῆται καὶ ὁμογάλακτες, γένει μὲν οὐ προσήκοντες, ἐκ δὲ τῆς συνόδου οὕτω προσαγορευόμενοι.—Poll. viii. 111. Γεννῆται: οἱ (γένους) οἱ μετέχοντες ἐκαλοῦντο γεννῆται, οὐ κατὰ γένος ἀλλήλοις προσήκοντες, οὐδὲ ἀπὸ τοῦ αὐτοῦ αἵματος, ἀλλὰ κοινωνίαν τινὰ ἔχοντες συγγενικῆς ὁρμῆς, ἀφ᾿ ἧς ὠργιάσας ἀνομάσθησαν.—Etym. M.

[2] Liv. ii. 49. [3] Cic. Phil. i. 13; cf. Liv. vi. 20.

probably without being a *gentilis;* but how, bearing the name of the *gens*, and belonging to the *gens*, he was not a *gentilis*, Becker does not explain;[1] nor does he adduce any authorities in support of his opinion. But it was necessary for him to make this assertion; because, as the curiæ were composed of *gentes*, the client, as a *gentilis*, would have been a member of them, and have had the *jus suffragii:* whereas, after Niebuhr, he holds the theory that the Curiate Comitia were composed entirely of patricians. We have already shown, however, and shall still further show, that there must have been plebeian families in the *gentes;* and if these were not the clients, there must have been a plebeian population besides the clients. But Cicero's expression, that Romulus had the *plebs* enrolled in the clientship of chief men, or the patricians,[2] seems to indicate that he meant *the whole* of the *plebs;* otherwise he would have pointed out some distinction.

But this brings us to one of the most important and difficult questions respecting the ancient regal constitution. The thirty curiæ, comprising about three thousand persons, formed the whole Roman *populus*, entitled to take a part in the government by giving their vote. Did this *populus* consist entirely of patricians, or of patricians and plebeians mixed?

First, if it consisted entirely of patricians, what was the use of two names? For the terms *populus* and *patricii* must have been identical.

Secondly, we have endeavoured to show that, in the reign of Romulus, three thousand men must have comprised pretty nearly the whole population capable of bearing arms. But the title of *patricii* was bestowed by way of distinction; and if it was common to the whole population, it would have been no distinction at all. That one-tenth part of it should have been thus distinguished is surely a very fair proportion. But if the part thus distinguished was three thousand in number, then there must have been ten times as many men not so distinguished, or thirty thousand; and the whole population, including women, children, persons not

---

[1] "Wie der Client den Gentilnamen des Patrons führt, so war er mit seinen Nachkommen an dessen Familie und mithin an die gens gebunden."—Röm. Alterth. ii. 130. "Denn der Gens gehörte der Client an, wahrscheinlich ohne selbst Gentile zu sein."—Ibid. 131. Dionysius says that the clients were to defray any extraordinary expenses of their patrons, δε τους χλυτι σροοδ αστεται.—ii. 10.

[2] "Habuit plebem in clientelas principum descriptam."—De Rep. II. 9.

enfranchised, &c., must have amounted, at the very lowest estimate, to 100,000 in the reign of Romulus; a number wholly incredible.

These are arguments only from probability, but passages of the ancient writers show that the curiæ contained a large proportion of plebeians. We will adduce a few of these.

After the death of Romulus, the plebeians are described as indignant at the long duration of the interregnum: "Fremere deinde *plebs*, multiplicatam servitutem, centum pro uno dominos factos: nec ultra nisi regem, *et ab ipsis creatum*, videbantur passuri."[1] Here the plebeians plainly appear as a large and powerful body in the state, having the power to elect a king ("*creare regem*") in their assembly; for *creare* is the proper technical phrase for such a mode of election. Livy then proceeds: "Quum sensissent ea moveri *Patres*, offerendum ultro rati, quod amissuri erant, ita gratiam ineunt, summa potestate *populo* permissa, ut non plus darent juris, quam retinerent. Decreverunt enim, ut, quum populus regem jussisset, id sic ratum esset, si Patres auctores fierent."

The word *Patres* is now and then rather ambiguous. Its primary meaning is, the Senate, though sometimes it denotes the whole patrician body; but, by attention to the context, we shall, if not in all cases, certainly in most, be able to distinguish the sense in which it is used. It cannot be doubted that in the present instance it means the Senate. First because it was the hundred senators of Romulus who had seized the interregnum; secondly, they *made a decree* on the subject in dispute ("decreverunt enim"); thirdly, at the termination of the affair, the plebeians leave it to the *Senate* to elect a king: "Adeo id gratum *plebi* fuit, ut, ne victi beneficio viderentur, id modo sciscerent juberentque, ut *senatus* decerneret, qui Romæ regnaret."

The Interrex communicates the determination of the Senate to leave the election in the hands of the people in a *concio* which he has called, the members of which he addresses as *Quirites*. But it is in no such irregular assembly that the election is actually made, but in the regular Comitia Curiata. This we learn from Cicero, in a passage to which we have already adverted: "Regem alienigenam, *patribus auctoribus*, sibi ipse *populus* ascivit.... Qui ut huc venit, quamquam populus *curiatis* eum *comitiis* regem esse jusserat, tamen ipse de suo imperio curiatam legem tulit."[2]

[1] Liv. l. 17.   [2] De Rep. li. 13.

In like manner on the death of Numa Livy says: "Numa morte ad interregnum res rediit. Inde Tullum Hostilium... *rex* populus jussit. Patres auctores facti."[1] It seems to us that the intellect must be peculiarly constituted which could imagine the *populus* and these *Patres* to be the same persons. Cicero relates the same event as follows:—"Mortuo rege Pompilio, Tulla Hostilium populus regem, interrege rogante, comitiis curiatis creavit; isque de imperio suo, exemplo Pompilii, populum consuluit curiatim."[2] Here he omits the Patres Auctores as Livy does the Lex Curiata; but this seems to be merely accidental, for we have seen by a preceding passage just quoted that Cicero knew it to be necessary.

Before proceeding any further we will make one or two remarks on the passages relating to the interregnum on the death of Romulus.

First, it is impossible to believe that, if the *populus* was identical with the patricians, it would have made so determined a resistance to them in this instance. The Patres and the patricii are identical as a party, and always act together; and if the Patres deemed it to their interest to keep on the Interregnum, we may be sure that they would not have been opposed by the patricii,—that is, by their own families and connexions. The opposition must have proceeded from a body with different interests, and this could only have been the plebeians.

Second, it is maintained by those who hold that the curiæ were composed only of patricians, that the phrases *Patrum auctoritas* and *Patres auctores fiunt* mean the assent of the Comitia Curiata to any measure, and not that of the Senate, and that the *lex curiata de imperio* is only another phrase for the same thing. But in Livy's account, in which, as we have shown, it is the Senate that acts and not the patrician body, it is said that they resolved not to give the people a greater share of right than they retained themselves; and therefore they decreed that the election of a king made by the people should be valid only if they authorized it—*si Patres auctores ferent.*

Livy's account of the proceedings during the interregnum shows that the Patrum Auctoritas and the Lex Curiata could not have been the same thing. At the death of Romulus there was no Lex Curiata in existence. Romulus, as we have shown, reigned *jure*

[1] Lib. L 22. [2] De Rep. II. 17.

divino. His *imperium* could not have been confirmed, on his accession, by the curiæ, because the curiæ were not yet in existence. It was he who created them; and it would be absurd to think that he should require a confirmation of his power from those who were the creatures of his power. It was Numa Pompilius who introduced the Lex Curiata; and so Cicero tells us in a passage just quoted (De Rep. ii. 17), respecting the election of Tullus, that this king obtained a Lex Curiata not "exemplo Romuli," but "exemplo Pompilii." Indeed it was necessary that the elected king, or magistrate, should propose the Lex Curiata in person;[1] and before the election of Numa it could not even be told that he was going to do this. When, therefore, Livy alludes to the Patres Auctores during the previous interregnum, he could not possibly be alluding to the Lex Curiata.

That the *auctoritas* lay with the Senate and not with the Comitia Curiata, is still more clearly shown by the passage in Cicero quoted in p. 287,[2] because the three acts are there separated from one another: the election by the people in the Comitia Curiata; the approval of the election by the authority of the Senate; the confirmation of their own act by the curiæ through a *lex curiata de imperio*. Comparing this passage with Livy, it is impossible to dispute that "Patribus auctoribus" refers to the Senate; and, comparing the clauses of the passage with one another, it is equally plain that the Auctoritas Patrum and the Lex Curiata are different things done by different persons at different times. Yet, in spite of this clear evidence of their difference, Becker and others maintain that they are the same thing, by some singular arguments which we shall examine further on. First of all we will adduce one or two more passages to show that the *plebs* really had a voice in the government in the early regal constitution.

Livy, in his account of Tarquin's canvassing for the crown, says that, as the sons of Ancus were nearly arrived at puberty, "eo magis Tarquinius instare, ut quam primum *comitia regi creando* fierent. Quibus indictis, sub tempus pueros venatum ablegavit; isque primus et potisse ambitiose regnum, et orationem dicitur habuisse *ad conciliandos plebis animos* compositam."[3] Hence we learn that the *plebs* took part in the "Comitia regi creando," which could then have been only the Comitia Curiata; and hence we may infer that, as Tarquin took such pains to conciliate the *plebs*, they

[1] See Rubino, p. 376, *seq.*   [2] De Rep. ii. 13.   [3] Lib. i. 35.

must have formed the majority of that assembly. Yet these Comitia, though thus in a great part plebeian, formed the Roman *populus*; for Livy immediately afterwards adds: "Hæc eum haud falsa memorantem ingenti consensu *populus Romanus* regnare jussit." In like manner Cicero says: "Cunctis *populi* suffragiis rex est creatus L. Tarquinius;"[1] adding: "isque de suo imperio legem tulit;" that is, he obtained a confirmatory Lex Curiata.

In like manner Livy describes Servius Tullius, who had seized the crown without any election, returning to Rome after defeating the Etruscans without any doubts about his being confirmed in the royal dignity both by the *Patres* and the *plebs*: "Fusoque ingenti hostium exercitu, haud dubius rex, seu *Patrum* seu *plebis* animo periclitaretur, Romam rediit."[2] Here again Livy is supplemented by Cicero, whose account, however, is on this occasion rather different from Livy's. For while this historian makes Servius defer an election till after he had gained a victory, Cicero represents him as elected soon after Tarquin had been buried; though a dispensing with the usual mediation of an Interrex as well as with the authority of the Senate: thus passing over that body altogether. For he proposes himself to the people, and, having been elected by them, immediately obtains a Lex Curiata, without the Patres having been *auctores*.[3] And this account, it must be confessed, is not inconsistent with the democratic and popular character of Servius.

It may be observed that on all these occasions Cicero mentions the king's obtaining a Lex Curiata, whilst Livy says nothing about it, contenting himself with recording that the king was elected by the people, and confirmed by the authority of the Senate. It seems to be this circumstance that has induced many German critics to regard the *Patrum auctoritas* and the *lex curiata de imperio* as identical; arguing, we suppose, that Livy would certainly have mentioned the *lex* had it not been the same as the *auctoritas*. But we have already shown from Cicero himself that they were different, being mentioned by him as distinct things. It would seem that Cicero, an advocate by profession, looked on the matter with a lawyer's eye; while the historian contented himself with recording the two essential things,

---

[1] De Rep. II. 20. [2] Lib. I. 42.
[3] "Sed, Tarquinio sepulto, populum de se ipse consuluit; jussusque regnare, legem de imperio suo curiatam tulit."—De Leg. II. 21.

the election by the people and the confirmation by the Senate, without troubling himself about the *lex*; which indeed, except in the very improbable case of the people changing their minds, was little more than a matter of form and routine. And indeed in the whole course of Roman history there is not a single example of the Lex Curiata having been refused.[1] We say a matter of form and routine in so far as it was not likely that a public body should refuse to confirm the magistrate whom they had chosen; though, technically speaking, the *lex* was something more than a confirmation, as without it the person elected could not exercise the *imperium* or *potestas* belonging to his office. To obtain this *imperium* was the ostensible reason for the application of the magistrate; but virtually the granting of the *lex* by the curiæ was a confirmation of their choice.

If there is any truth in the preceding reasoning, then there was a *plebs* from the earliest times of Roman history, and a very powerful one too. We will not dispute that it was a *plebs* of a different kind from what sprung up afterwards. All that we contend for here is, that it was plebeian as opposed to patrician; that is, that it had not the right of the auspices, and other patrician privileges. But it had the right of voting in the Comitia of the curiæ, and therefore formed part of the tribes, and belonged to the *gentes*. As belonging to the curiæ it partook of the *sacra publica* of the curiæ, and as belonging to the *gentes* it participated in their *sacra privata*. Those who partook not of these *sacra* were not, at least before the time of Servius, full citizens. Now we learn from Cicero that the Sabines were admitted to the *sacra*, and therefore became full citizens: "(Romulus) cum T. Tatio rege Sabinorum fœdus icit ... quo fœdere et Sabinos in civitatem ascivit *sacris communicatis* et regnum suum cum illorum rege sociavit."[2] But Cicero does not say so much of the Latins admitted into the city by Ancus Marcius, but only "ascivit eos in civitatem."[3] Unfortunately the manuscript of the De Republicâ is mutilated in the reign of Tullus Hostilius, and therefore we have not Cicero's testimony as to what that king did with the Albans transplanted to Rome. But from Livy's account we may infer that they were admitted to the full citizenship, for Tullus promises "civitatem dare plebi,"[4] which is the technical expression for that admission. And after mentioning the admission of several Alban families among the Patres, he

[1] See Rubino, Staatsv. S. 333.
[2] De Rep. ii. 17.
[3] De Rep. ii. 18.
[4] Liv. L. 28.

proceeds to say: "Et, ut omnium ordinum viribus aliquid ex novo populo adjiceretur, equitum decem turmas ex Albanis legit." Here "omnium ordinum" must mean all the *three orders;* namely, Senate, knights, and *populus,* or members of the curiæ. But there is nothing in Livy's account of the treatment of the Latins transferred to Rome by Ancus that should lead us to think that they obtained at once the full rights of citizens. He merely speaks of them as "in civitatem accepti,"[2] which is about equivalent to Cicero's "ascivit," and seems only to mean that they were to have all the immunities of a Roman, but not to enjoy his privilege of the vote.

We may then, perhaps, assume that to the original *plebs* of Romulus enrolled in the curiæ, or rather to their descendants, had been added by Tullus a part at least of the Albans transferred to Rome. We say a part, because, as he appears to have admitted only six Alban families into the patriciate, we may suppose that he admitted only a proportionate number of plebeian families into the curiæ. The remainder would have formed the nucleus of a *plebs* without political rights, which would afterwards have been vastly increased by the Latins transferred to Rome in the reigns of Ancus and Tarquin, and thus have ultimately occasioned the necessity for the reform made by Servius Tullius.

Professor Schömann, in the programme to his course of lectures delivered at Greifswald in 1831, of which a short account is given by Becker in his "Handbuch der Römischen Alterthümer,"[3] with the view of refuting some of its leading points, appears also to have been of opinion, in opposition to the theory of Niebuhr, that there was a *plebs* in the Romulean curiæ; that this *plebs* consisted at first only of clients, but that afterwards all the conquered Latins and Etruscans were admitted. But, though we concur in the first view, that clients were the only plebeians in the curiæ, we agree with Becker in rejecting the second, that the entire conquered populations were admitted into them. This obviates Becker's objection to Schömann's hypothesis, that in later times, during the Republic, the Curiate Comitia appear to be wholly patrician, because the clients would have formed a very small minority in comparison with the whole plebeian body, and being necessarily attached to the interests of their patrons would, on most occasions, have been influenced by them.

It might be objected to this view, Why then did the clients

[1] Liv. L 80.   [2] Ib. 33.   [3] Th. ii. Abth. I. S. 300, Anm. 611.

make so determined an opposition to the Patres, on the occasion of the interregnum after the death of Romulus? To this we reply, that the cases are not parallel. The clients were in a very different position under Romulus and his first four successors to that which they occupied after the Servian reform, which, as it were, swamped them. To belong to the Curiate Comitia would then have become a sort of distinction, and would thus have engendered, over and above the natural ties by which the clients were bound to their *patroni*, an *esprit de corps*, and sort of aristocratic feeling with regard to the vast mass of plebeians who were not in the same position. Besides, in these later times no constitutional question could arise of such vast importance as whether there should be one king or a hundred. This was a grievance which came home to them practically. The frequent change of masters might have become very galling and inconvenient; and though even with respect to their own *patronus*, they might serve him willingly in that character, yet they might not have liked to see him, or the head of his house, become their king. However intimate may have been the bonds between patron and client in domestic life, yet they do not appear to have extended to political life; and though in most public questions, especially after the time of Servius, the client would most probably vote with his patron, yet there was nothing that actually obliged him to do so. However, if the opposition to the interregnum did not proceed from the clients, it must have proceeded from the patricians, which is a hundred times more improbable.

But the whole question of the Curiate Comitia, or Romulean *populus*, is so intimately bound up with the phrases *Patrum auctoritas*, *Patres auctores sunt*, that it will be necessary to examine the passages which Becker has adduced in support of his opinion that the *populus* was in fact the patricians.

Becker, as we have said, maintains that the Patrum Auctoritas is nothing more than the approval, or confirmation, of the Curiæ, or *populus*, and that therefore *Patres auctores facti* means just the same thing as a *lex curiata de imperio*. Upon this he very justly remarks (S. 324): "At the first glance, it will indeed certainly appear surprising that if the election (of a king or magistrate) was made by the Patres, that is (according to Becker) by the assembly of the curiæ, a confirmation by a resolution of the same curiæ should still be considered necessary. But the phrase *Patres auctores* must not, in the most ancient times, be understood in the sense of confirmation. Because, if from a comparison of the passages before cited from Cicero, in which it is expressly said of every election of a king that the same curiæ afterwards bestowed the *imperium* by a Lex Curiata, with the passages of Livy and Dionysius relating to the same subject, in which, instead of mentioning the *lex*, it is as expressly said, *Patres auctores facti*, τῶν πατρικίων ἐπικυρωσάντων τὰ δόξαντα τῷ πλήθει,—if, I say, from such a comparison it becomes plain that this *auctorem fieri* is nothing else but the Lex Curiata itself, in like manner in other places we are still more clearly directed to the same conclusion."

Before passing on to these "other places," we will examine for a moment what we have before us.

The passages from Cicero here alluded to, are those which we have already quoted a little before.[1] But will it be believed? the most material of them—namely, the first of those mentioned in the note beneath—is given by Becker in a garbled manner (S. 314, Anm. 628), the words which are necessary to a truthful interpretation of it being entirely omitted! The whole passage runs as follows:—

"Quibus quum esse præstantem Numam Pompilium fama ferret, prætermissis suis civibus regem alienigenam *patribus auctoribus* sibi ipse *populus* ascivit; eumque ad regnandum Sabinum hominem Romam Curibus ascivit. Qui ut huc venit, quamquam *populus* curiatis eum comitiis regem esse jusserat, tamen *ipse de suo imperio curiatam legem tulit.*"

Now Becker entirely omits the first sentence, which, as we have already shown, in conjunction with the second, so clearly indicates *three* acts, viz. an election by the Comitia, an authorization by the Senate, and again a confirmation by the Comitia; and begins his quotation in the second sentence, "quamquam populus," &c. It is impossible, we fear, to attribute so important omission by so acute and elaborate a critic to anything but wilful mutilation.

Here, then, instead of a proof, as Becker asserts, that *auctores fieri* and *lex curiata* are the same things, is a proof, as we have before shown, that they are different things. About the passages in such an author as Dionysius we need not trouble ourselves; only we will observe, in passing, that even here Becker's horse breaks down with him; for the πλῆθος and the πατρίκιοι were assuredly not the same persons.

[1] See above, p. 287, *seq.* viz. De Rep. ii. 13, 17, 20, 21.

Becker then proceeds as follows: "Cicero represents it as the essential purpose of the Lex Curiata, or at all events as a great advantage connected with it, that the people was thereby enabled to revoke a perhaps hasty choice, or had by it what is called the *potestas reprehendendi*. This occurs in the well-known passage, De Lege Agr. ii. 11: 'Majores de singulis magistratibus bis vos sententiam ferre voluerunt. Nam cum centuriata lex censoribus ferebatur, cum curiata cœteris patriciis magistratibus, tum iterum de eisdem judicabatur, ut esset reprehendendi potestas, si populum beneficii sui pœniteret. Nunc quia prima illa comitia tenetis, centuriata et tributa, curiata tantum auspiciorum causa remanserunt. Hic autem tribunus plebis, quia videbat, potestatem neminem injussu populi aut plebis posse habere, curiatis en comitiis, quæ vos non sinitis, confirmavit: tributa, quæ vestra erant, sustulit. Ita, cum majores binis comitiis voluerint vos de singulis magistratibus judicare, hic homo popularis ne unam quidem populo comitiorum potestatem reliquit.'

"The separate propositions of this important passage will be examined further on; at present it is only necessary to advert to the most material part: that Cicero represents as the most essential purpose of the Lex Curiata the *potestas reprehendendi comitia*, the *bis judicare de singulis magistratibus*. But this *potestas* is nothing more than the right of confirmation possessed by the curiæ: because, whether the *patres auctores fiunt* or not, the second decision, the *bis judicare* takes place, and in the hands of the Patres lies the *reprehensio comitiorum*.[1] If that is of itself quite clear, and a further *reprehensio* is not to be thought of, yet this also most decidedly appears to be Cicero's meaning in a parallel passage, forming a kind of commentary on the above words (Pro Planc.' 3): 'Nam si ita esset, quod patres apud majores nostros tenere non potuerunt, ut reprehensores essent comitiorum, id haberent judices; vel quod multo etiam minus est ferendum. Tum enim magistratum non gerebat is, qui ceperat, si patres auctores non erant facti: nunc postulatur a vobis, ut ejus exilio, qui creatus sit, judicium populi Romani reprehendatis:' with which may also be compared a similar passage of

[1] This passage is so puzzling that we subjoin the original German; to show that, to the best of our apprehension, we have rightly translated it. "Diese *potestas* ist nun eben nichts weiter, als das Bestätigungsrecht der Curien: indem die *patres auctores fiunt* oder nicht, findet die zweite Entscheidung, das *bis judicare* Statt, und in den Händen der *patres* liegt die *reprehensio comitiorum.*"

De Rep. ii. 32 (concerning the founding of the republican constitution): 'Quodque erat ad obtinendam potentiam nobilium vel maximum, vehementer id retinebatur: populi comitia ne essent rata, nisi ea patrum approbavisset auctoritas.' When Cicero thus places the essence of the Lex Curiata in the *potestas reprehendendi comitia*, when he just as decidedly ascribes this *reprehensio* to the Patrum Auctoritas, that is, to the *auctores fieri*; when it is said at one time of the Lex Curiata, and then again of the *patres auctores fieri*, that therein lay the *iterum judicare*, it must appear quite decided that both are only different expressions for one and the same thing. For it is altogether inconceivable that the resolutions of the Comitia should have been subject to a *reprehensio* first by the refusal of the Patrum Auctoritas, and when this has been accorded, again by the refusal of the Lex Curiata; and by such a nonsensical assumption it would not have been a second *judicium* that took place, but a third, which is quite contrary to Cicero's words."

This passage is a good specimen of what a hopeless puzzle even an acute critic may find himself in if he starts from wrong premises, and is obstinately bent on pursuing the same route he has once entered on. We believe that we have given a correct version of the passage, yet we must confess that the process of the argumentation does not appear quite clear to us; and we are rather inclined to doubt whether Becker himself had a distinct idea of it in his own mind. The main drift of it, however, appears to be to show that the *reprehensio*, or *potestas reprehendendi comitia*, or the *iterum judicare*, is, in some of the passages quoted, ascribed to the Patrum Auctoritas, in others to the Lex Curiata; that the Patrum Auctoritas and Lex Curiata must therefore be one and the same thing. But we must confess that we cannot see where the *reprehensio* is connected by Cicero with *patrum auctoritas*.

The passages, properly construed, appear to us to prove precisely the reverse of what Becker proposes to establish by them. In that from the De Lege Agraria, Cicero is addressing the people, and tells them that they used to have the *reprehendendi potestas*. He does not once mention the name of the *Patres*; while in the second passage, quoted from the Oration for Plancius by way of commentary on the first, Cicero distinctly denies that the *Patres* ever had the *potestas reprehendendi:* "Quod (viz. ut reprehensores essent comitiorum) *patres* apud majores nostros *tenere non potuerunt.*" It follows, therefore, as a necessary consequence, that the *Patres* mentioned in the extract from the Oration for Plancius, must have been a body distinct from the *populus* mentioned in the extract from the De Lege Agraria; otherwise Cicero could not have known what he was talking about, and fell into a gross and absurd contradiction. But if these *Patres* were a body distinct from the *populus*, we suppose it will not be maintained that they could have been anything else but the Senate. They are mentioned again in the following sentence of the second extract:—"Tum enim magistratum non gerebat is qui ceperat si patres auctores non erant facti." Therefore these *Patres*, though they had not the *potestas reprehendendi*, or, what is the same thing, the power of passing a *lex curiata de imperio*, had, nevertheless, the power of setting aside a magistrate who had been elected by the people. Now, what could this have been but the Auctoritas Patrum—the authority of the *Senate*—given to the election of a magistrate by the people ? without which his election was not complete; but, having which, he could again appear before the people to have his election ratified by them, and to receive the *imperium*. Cicero is contrasting the power proposed to be accorded to the *Judices* with that anciently enjoyed by the Senate.

"For if it were so," he says, "then the *Judices* would have (a prerogative) which (even) the *Patres* (i.e. the Senate) could not obtain in the time of our ancestors, namely, that they should be the reviewers of the Comitia; or rather they would have (a prerogative) which is still more insufferable. For in those times he who had been elected a magistrate was merely debarred from entering on his magistracy if the Patres had not been *auctores* (that is, if the Senate had not approved his election); while, in the present instance, it is required of you to *reverse the decision of the Roman people* (that is, instead of merely, like the Senate, withholding your consent) by the banishment of him who has been elected (that is, instead of merely debarring him from office)."

Now here it is first said that the Patres could not revoke an election; that is, of course, after the election had been completed; for it was not complete till they had given their authority. But if they had once given their authority they could not recall it. They had, however, in the first instance, the power of withholding this authority—"si patres auctores non erant facti"—and then the person elected did not obtain his magistracy. The *populus*, on the other hand, or what is the same thing, the Comitia Curiata, had the power of virtually cancelling their election, even after it had been completed by the sanction of the Fathers. For when the king or other magistrate, came to them for a *lex curiata de imperio*, they might refuse it. And this was the *bis judicare*.

We hope it is now tolerably clear that, in the opinion of Cicero at least, the Patrum Auctoritas and the Lex Curiata were not the same thing. And the matter will appear still clearer from the third passage from Cicero, cited by Becker; which, however, as is too frequent with him, he has mutilated to serve his ends. The passage, in its integrity, runs as follows:—" Tenuit igitur hoc in statu senatus rempublicam temporibus illis; ut in populo libero pauca *per populum*, pleraque *senatus auctoritate* et instituto ac more gererentur: atque uti consules potestatem haberent tempore duntaxat annuam, genere ipso ac jure regiam. Quodque erat ad obtinendam potentiam nobilium vel maximum, vehementer id retinebatur, populi comitia ne essent rata, nisi ea patrum approbavisset auctoritas" (De Rep. ii. 32).

Becker here omits the first sentence, in which is set forth the great power and *authority* of the *Senate*, as opposed to the power of the *populus*; and thus the context shows that in the last sentence the Populi Comitia could not have been Comitia of patricians, and that the Patrum Auctoritas could not have been a Lex Curiata, which would only have been an authority of the *populus*, but a ratification *by the Senate* of what had been done in the Comitia; for the *patres* mentioned in the second sentence are indisputably the same body as the *senatus* mentioned in the first. And thus all these passages show directly the reverse of what Becker proposes to prove by them.

When Becker concludes his argument by saying: "It is altogether inconceivable that the resolutions of the Comitia should have been subject to a *reprehensio*, first by the refusal of the Patrum Auctoritas, and when this has been accorded, again by the refusal of the Lex Curiata; and by such a nonsensical assumption it would not have been a second *judicium* that took place, but a third, which is quite contrary to Cicero's words"—it is only his own opinion that is "nonsensical;" which amounts, in fact, to this, that one and one do not make two. Otherwise he must assume that if A gives a decision, and B gives a decision, this is to count for two given by A. It was only the *populus* that *bis judicabat*.

In the later times of the republic it was provided by the Lex Mænia, passed probably in the year B.C. 287, that the Auctoritas

Patrum should be given to the elections of magistrates by anticipation, and before the elections took place; or, in the words of Livy, "Prius quam populus suffragium ineat, in incertum comitiorum eventum Patres auctores fiunt:"[1] thus reducing the *auctoritas* to a mere form. But since, as we have seen, when Livy thus speaks of it, the Lex Curiata was not yet in existence, he could not have thought that the abolishing of the *auctoritas* also abolished the Lex Curiata. Indeed, Becker is forced to admit that "if through the Leges Publilia and Maenia it was ordained that thenceforth the Patrum Auctoritas, or the acceptance by the Patres, was to *precede the resolutions and the elections* of the Comitia, and thus, without it, no magistrate could be chosen, and, if at the same time, there is no doubt that the Lex Curiata still continued to be given *after the election*, it must be allowed that this seems to speak against their identity. But the contradiction is only apparent, and may be satisfactorily explained from the history of the Lex Curiata."[2]

Becker endeavours to reconcile the contradiction as follows: During the early republic *he supposes it to be probable* ("es erfolgte wahrscheinlich") that the Patrum Auctoritas—that is, according to him, the Lex Curiata—was given immediately after the election, at the rogation of a magistrate still in office; so that the *imperium*, like the *auspicia*, was given by anticipation, though it went over to the new magistrates only after the abdication of the old ones: yet at the same time he allows that when a magistrate immediately entered on office, as in the case of a dictator, it was he himself who demanded the Lex Curiata. After the introduction of the Lex Maenia, he thinks that, as the *imperium* could not be given to a person unknown—that is, "in incertum comitiorum eventum"[3]—though he has, according to his own view that Patrum Auctoritas is the same as the Lex Curiata, virtually assumed that it could—the *lex* must have contained a determination (*Bestimmung*) with regard to the *lex curiata de imperio;* and that the Patrum Auctoritas given before the election was only an assurance that the result of it would not be hindered, that no opposition would be offered; and hence the legitimately-elected magistrate was irrevocable, and

---

[1] Lib. I. 17.   [2] S. 320.

[3] Yet Livy says that the *auctoritas* was so given: "in incertum comitiorum eventum Patres auctores fiunt."—Lib. I. 17. Another proof that the *auctoritas* was not the Lex Curiata. For as Paul the Deacon says (p. 50), in a passage quoted by Becker: "Cum imperio esse dicebatur apud antiquos, cui *nominatim* a populo dabatur imperium." But a person not *elected* could not be *named*.

remained so without the bestowal of the *imperium* by the Lex Curiata; which legally, in consequence of the assurance before given, could not be refused; but which might be delayed and hindered by manifold chicanes, and especially by intercession of the tribunes. And this brings Becker to his conclusion, which he gives in large type: "And thus it is quite naturally explained how, indeed, originally the *lex curiata de imperio* signified entirely the same thing as the Patrum Auctoritas, that is, the *auctores fieri* of the patricians; but that after the Lex Mænia the two must have appeared as separate acts."

On this argument we shall remark, first, that it proceeds entirely on assumption without any proof. The assertion that the Lex Mænia "*must* have contained a determination regarding the Lex Curiata" is entirely gratuitous, for we know only the general drift of that law, and not its particular provisions: and hence all the conclusions which Becker draws from the assumption are mere conjectures, made to bolster up a theory otherwise untenable. Second, it is most singular and surprising that what originally was one thing should become eventually two things; and that the framers of the Lex Mænia should be such bunglers as to make the term *Patrum auctoritas*, which had before stood for the Lex Curiata itself, to signify only the assurance of it. We may be quite sure that if, as Becker supposes, by the Lex Mænia the *Patres auctores fieri* meant only their promise beforehand that the Lex Curiata should not be withheld, it would not have used the equivocal phrase of *Patrum auctoritas*, which by long usage must have acquired quite a different meaning, but would have adopted a new term to designate the new practice. But it is quite evident that Becker's ingenious invention is, to use a favourite expression of his own, only an *Ausflucht*, or evasion. If, guided by the authority of all the passages on the subject, and by the plain sense of the words, we take "in incertum comitiorum eventum patres auctores fieri," to mean that it was the *Senate* who now gave their authority *before* instead of after the election, but that a *lex curiata de imperio* passed by the *populus* was still necessary afterwards to the magistrate elected, everything becomes clear and intelligible.

Having thus endeavoured to show that the Patrum Auctoritas and the Lex Curiata were two distinct things, that the first related to the Senate and the second to the *populus*, and that therefore the argument founded on their identity, to prove that the Patres and the *populus* were also identical, falls to the ground, we shall now proceed to examine some of the passages which have been adduced to prove the same thing, on the assumption of their showing that the *populus* was in fact the *patricii*. First of all, however, we must make a few preliminary remarks.

The two grand divisions of the Roman nation were into patricians and plebeians. But, besides these, there was a third division of the *populus*, or people properly so called, consisting, till the time of Servius, of those who had a right to vote in the Comitia Curiata; and this division, as we have before endeavoured to show, contained both patricians and plebeians. The term *plebeius*, as opposed to *patricius*, ran through all the relations of life, domestic as well as political. But the term *populus* was purely political, and, indeed, that only in a general or collective sense, denoting a body. For we cannot say *vir popularis*, in the sense of a man belonging to the people; but we may say *vir plebeius*, or *vir patricius*, or even *femina plebeia*, or *femina patricia*, in the sense of a person belonging to the plebeian or patrician orders. That part of the *plebs*, therefore, which did not belong to the *populus*, or which had not the vote, was thus distinguished in one way from the patricians, and in another way from the *populus*; so that the terms *plebs* and *populus* might be as properly used in opposition to each other as the terms *plebs* and *patricii*, or *patres*; and, indeed, they are frequently so employed. Thus, in the Marcian prophecy:

"Ils ludis faciendis præerit prætor
Is, qui jus *populo plebeique* dabit summum."[1]

So also in the prayer of Scipio: "Divi deæque maria terræque qui colitis, vos precor quæsoque, uti, quæ in meo imperio gesta sunt, geruntur, postque gerentur, ea mihi, *populo plebique* Romanæ, sociis nominique Latino . . . bene verruncent."[2] And in Cicero's Oration for Murena:[3] "Ut ea res mihi, magistratuique meo, *populo plebique* Romanæ bene atque feliciter eveniret." The phrase thus appears to have been used in solemn invocations; it descended, probably, from a very high antiquity, and continued in use long after the marked distinction between *populus* and *plebs*, which first occasioned it, had disappeared.

From these and similar passages, Niebuhr, who has been followed by many other critics, assumed that the Romulean *populus* was com-

[1] Liv. xxv. 12.   [2] Ib. xxix. 27.   [3] Cap. i.

posed wholly of patricians; and, to establish this view, he adduces the following passages.[1] Livy, after relating the story of the augur Attus Navius, says: "Auguriis certe sacerdotioque augurum tantus honos accessit, ut nihil belli domique postea, nisi auspicato, gereretur: concilia populi, exercitus vocati, summa rerum, ubi aves non admisissent, dirimerentur."[2] On this passage Niebuhr observes, that as *concilia*, which must be different from the general *comitia* of the centuries, or the *exercitus*, are nevertheless named along with them, and as we cannot think of a *concilium plebis*, because that would not be held under augury, a *concilium populi* must here be the same as an assembly of the patricians.

On this we may remark, first, that *exercitus* is here to be taken in its ordinary sense of *an army*. For Livy is talking of the affairs both of peace and war; and as *concilia populi* certainly relate to peace, there would be nothing to be referred to war if *exercitus vocati* also related to peace. Besides, we doubt whether Livy (though such a usage may be found in old forms) ever speaks of the Comitia Centuriata under the name of *exercitus*, except in his description of their first institution by Servius. For though their original organization was, no doubt, partly military, yet when assembled in Comitia, as Niebuhr here views them, it was for civil business.

Such a council it was, continues Niebuhr, to whom Publicola did homage by lowering the *fasces:* "Vocato ad concilium populo, summissis fascibus, in concionem ascendit."[3] But Livy adds: "Gratum id *multitudini* spectaculum fuit; summissa *sibi* eam imperii insignia;" and the term *multitudo* means the *plebs*, or populace, rather than the patricians. This example, therefore, is against Niebuhr, instead of for him, and shows that the term *populus* may include plebeians.

Such a council, proceeds Niebuhr, decided between the Aricians and Ardeates—"concilio populi a magistratibus dato."[4] But that it consisted, at least partly, of plebeians, appears from Livy's saying, "Consurgit P. Scaptius *de plebe;*" and, indeed, the whole

---

[1] Röm. Gesch. B. i. S. 413. [2] Lib. i. 36.
[3] Livy, ii. 7. We are aware that Livy's authority for the use of the word *concilium* is rejected by those who maintain that he did not understand his own language; but we do not participate in that opinion. We have adverted to this question in the Introduction, when speaking of Livy's merits as an historian. [4] Ib. iii. 71.

tenor of this and the following chapter shows that the *concilium* in question was the people assembled by tribes.

Another passage on which Niebuhr very much relies is Livy's account of the inquiry into the murder of the military tribune Postumius: "Iis consulibus principio anni senatus consultum factum est, ut de quæstione Postumianæ cædis tribuni primo quoque tempore ad plebem ferrent; plebesque præficeret quæstioni, quam vellet. A *plebe* consensu *populi* consulibus negotium mandatur," &c.[1] But we really cannot see any difficulty here. The tribunes of the *plebs* consulted on the matter the plebeians, either in a *contio*, or, more probably, in the Comitia Tributa; the *plebs* entrusted the investigation to the consuls, and this decision was agreed to by the *populus*, in the centuriate assembly. For, after the reform of Servius, the orders composing the Comitia Centuriata obtained the name of *populus*, which had previously been borne only by those belonging to the Comitia Curiata. And thus Cicero, in describing the operation of the vote in the Comitia Centuriata, says: "Quibus ex centum quatuor centuriis (tot enim reliquæ sunt) octo solæ si accesserunt, confecta est vis *populi* universa."[2] The people assembled by tribes, but not in Comitia Tributa, was also called *populus*. And it was from this wider extension of the meaning of the term *populus*, that it began to lose much of its former distinctive character; so that at last, in general usage at least, there was virtually but little difference between it and *plebs*.

Becker[3] has pointed out another passage in which the term *populus* must certainly comprehend a large portion of *plebs*. It respects the dedication of a temple by the plebeian curule Ædile Flavius: "Ædem Concordiæ in area Vulcani summa invidia nobilium dedicavit; coactusque *consensu populi*, Cornelius Barbatus, pontifex maximus, verba præiro,"[4] &c. Here, as Becker remarks, the consent of the patricians is not to be thought of, and therefore *consensus populi* means in this place nothing more than the universal desire of the people. We think, however, from the word *coactus*, that it means something more than this; namely, a resolution of the people in the Comitia Centuriata.

According to the testimony of all antiquity, the patrician class arose from those whom Romulus had elected into his Senate. But Becker will not allow this, and argues thus: "If Romulus chose the

[1] Livy, iv. 51.
[2] De Rep. II. 22.
[3] Röm. Alterth. Th. ii. Abth. l. S. 137.
[4] Liv. ix. 46.

senators out of the nobles (*Edelgeborenen*), and if only they and their families, or their posterity, were *patres* and *patricii*, we may very naturally ask, What position in the state had then the other nobles who had not been able to obtain the same distinction, and in what class of the population were they to find a place? For it is not conceivable that there were in the curiæ two classes with unequal rights, patricians and non-patricians; they are entirely patrician: and yet it cannot be meant, either that the senators alone with their families constituted the curiæ, or that the nobles who had not attained the patrician dignity passed for *plebs*. For they would thus have stood between the patricians and the clients, or plebeians, without name or signification."[1]

The question whether the curiæ contained patricians and non-patricians we have already examined. To the question, What became of the other nobles? we answer, there were none. It was only by the act of being chosen into the Senate that Roman nobles, or patricians, were at first created. One hundred heads of families in that small population of the Ramnes, one-tenth of the whole, must have more than exhausted those who had anteriorly any pretensions to nobility. Livy does not mention that the senators were made from nobles, and intimates the probability that there were no more than a hundred who were fit for the office.[2] Nor does Cicero say that the Patres were chosen from nobles, but only from the leading men, or *principes*.[3] It is only Dionysius who, with his frequent preposterous absurdity, makes the *patres* chosen out of the *patricii*![4] thus putting the cart before the horse. Yet it is on this author that Becker founds his reasoning!

We have here been speaking only of the patrician families created by Romulus. How after that period patricians were made is a difficult question; but there can be no doubt, we think, that the following kings possessed the prerogative of conferring that dignity. Thus Dionysius says that Ancus Marcius made Tarquin a senator and patrician; and his account is confirmed by Dio Cassius, a better authority than himself.[5] In like manner we learn from Suetonius

---

[1] Röm. Alterth. ii. 1. 145.
[2] "Centum creat senatores; sive quia is numerus satis erat, sive quia sol' centum erant, qui creari Patres possent."—Lib. i. 8.
[3] "In regium consilium delegerat principes."—De Rep. ii. 8.
[4] ἐκ τῶν πατρικίων ἄνδρας ἑκατὸν ἐπιλεξάμενος.—Lib. ii. 12.
[5] καὶ αὐτὸν ὁ Μάρκιος ... εἰς τὸν τῶν πατρικίων τε καὶ βουλευτῶν ἀριθμὸν

that the *gens* Octavia, originally of Velitræ,' a Latin or Volscian city, was first chosen by Tarquinius Priscus into the Roman *gentes*, and then transferred to the Senate and to the patrician order by Servius Tullius. We here insert the sentence, because it has been made a matter of dispute from the misplacing of a comma: "Ea gens a Tarquinio Prisco rege inter Romanas gentes allecta, in senatum mox a Servio Tullio in patricias transducta, procedente tempore ad plebem se contulit."[1] In the editions the first comma is placed after *senatum*, making the sense to be that the Octavians were elected among the Roman *gentes* and into the Senate by Tarquin, and afterwards into the patricians by Servius Tullius; and Becker remarks that the placing of the comma after *allecta* gives a much worse sense, or none at all.[2] But we are so far from agreeing with this dictum, that, on the contrary, we think the comma after *senatum* makes neither sense nor grammar. For, first, it is not probable that Tarquin would have created the Octavians senators without making them patricians; nor do we believe that there were any plebeian senators under the kings. Secondly, "allecta *inter* Romanas gentes *in* senatum," is a very peculiar construction to denote the two acts of election into the *gentes* and into the Senate, and a copula would at all events seem necessary—"*et* in senatum." Thirdly, it is more agreeable to the Latin idiom that the two clauses should end with a participle, *allecta, transducta*. But, however we may read the passage, it still shows that the Octavians were made senators and patricians either by Tarquin or Servius. The act of electing a new family into the patricians was called *co-optatio*. This act does not seem to mean, as Becker supposes,[3] an election by the curies, that is, according to him, by the patricians, into that body. The act might be done either by the king, or, during the republic, by the people. This is clearly shown by the speech of Canuleius in Livy: "Quid? hoc si polluit nobilitatem istam vestram, quam plerique oriundi ex Albanis et Sabinis, non genere nec sanguine, sed *per co-optationem* in Patres habetis, aut *ab regibus lecti*, aut post reges exactos jussu populi," &c.[4] The contrary view seems to be

ἀπίγραφαν.—Dionys. iii. 41. *οὕτω τὸν Μάρκιον διάθεσθαι, ὥστε καὶ εἰς τοὺς εὐπατρίδας καὶ εἰς τὰς βουλὰς ὑπ' αὐτοῦ καταλεχθῆναι*.—Dio Cass. Fragm. xxii. 1, l'airesc. [2] Suet. Oct. 2.
[1] Hom. Alterth. ii. 1. 148, Anm. 321; cf. Rubino, S. 197, Anm., who adopts the ordinary punctuation.
[3] S. 148, Anm. 323. [4] Lib. iv. 4.

founded on a passage of Dionysius, who says that the Romans thought proper to raise Servius by their votes from the plebeians into the patrician order; as they had before done with Tarquinius Priscus, and before him with Numa Pompilius.[1] But Dionysius, as is often the case, here contradicts himself: for he had before said that Tarquin was made a patrician by King Ancus, and not by the people.[2]

Becker, following up his idea that there were in the early population nobles who were not patricians, asks how the patricians could assert that they only had *gentes*; an assertion that was only possible as opposed to the plebeians, because these were not included in the curiæ, and the *gentes* were in the curiæ.[3]

To this it may be answered that, even if there were nobles in the Romulean population who were not patricians, which is the height of improbability, still that alone would not give them *gentes*; because the *gentes*, as we have shown, were a political institution of Romulus. Tarquin was a noble before he came to Rome; but that did not make him and his family a Roman *gens* before they were constituted into one. The family or families at the head of a *gens* were no doubt patrician; and, though they had plebeian *gentiles*, the former only could properly be said "habere gentem;" because it was they who had the power of admitting other clients into it, because it was they who possessed the *sacra*, &c. Their clients may be said to have *belonged* to a *gens*; but they could hardly be said to *have* a *gens*.

In p. 130,[4] Becker says that, in spite of all misapprehensions, the knowledge of the true meaning of *patrician*, and, along with it, of the original *populus*, has not altogether perished. Those who invented the derivation of the name from *patres*, only grammatically wrongly, were not ignorant that in the old times all *ingenui*, without distinction, were *patricii*. For so speaks Decius in Livy (x. 8): "En unquam fandi audistis patricios primo case factos, non de cœlo demissos, sed qui patrem ciere possent, id est nihil ultra quam

---

[1] καὶ διὰ ταῦτα 'Ρωμαῖοι μὲν αὐτὸν ἐκ τοῦ δήμου μεταγαγεῖν ἠξίωσαν εἰς τοὺς πατρικίους, ψῆφοι ἐνεγκόντες, κ.τ.λ.—Lib. iv. 8.

[2] In the passage from Lib. iii. 41, quoted in p. 304.

[3] Röm. Alterth. ii. i. 159. The assertion referred to is the following: "Semper ista audita sunt eadem, penes vos auspicia esse, vos solos gentem habere, vos solos justum imperium et auspicium domi militiæque."—Liv. x. 8.

[4] Anm. 328.

ingenuos." He then adverts to passages to the same effect in Dionysius and Plutarch, and especially to the following one in Festus (p. 241): "Patricios Cencius ait in libro de comitiis eos appellari solitos, *qui nunc ingenui vocentur.*"

But this is a mere grammatical subtlety. It matters not whether Livy and Cicero are right in deriving *patricius* from *patres*, or senators, or whether it did not rather at first signify any man who could name his father, that is, any freeborn man, or *ingenuus*. The important point is, that it came by use to signify only senatorial families. Our word *peer* may, in one sense, signify any man whatsoever; as when Bacon says, "Amongst a man's peers, a man shall be sure of familiarity;" but in a political sense it means only a nobleman. And therefore no inference can be drawn from the etymology of *patricius* with regard to the composition of the *populus;* because, on a political subject, it must be used in its political sense. But, in fact, the passage in Livy, properly viewed, proves just the reverse of what Becker would have it to prove. The argument of Decius is, Have you ever heard that the *Patricii* were at first *made*, not sent down from heaven; that they were nothing more than those who could cite a father, that is, nothing more than free born? But this implies that, *after being made,* they became a great deal more than *ingenui;* and therefore that *after* the institution of the patriciate, it would be the grossest of all errors to say "that all the *ingenui,* without distinction, were patrician."

Let us remark, moreover, that this passage militates terribly against Becker's notion of a non-patrician nobility in the time of Romulus. For it tells us that the patricians themselves were made from nothing more than *ingenui.*

It remains to examine some passages from which it has been inferred that all the patrician body—that is, according to Becker and his school, the curiæ and their comitia—possessed the *auctoritas;* which, therefore, it is maintained, was not confined to the Senate. But it will be necessary first to inquire what is the real value of some terms.

The Latin authors, from a more familiar knowledge of their own history and language—for we must be pardoned for thinking that after all they knew more about these matters than the most learned of the moderns—often employ words in what appears to us a somewhat equivocal sense, though the real meaning of them would probably be at once apprehended by a Roman. Such, for instance, is the word *Capitolium*, which, from its being used to signify both the whole Capitoline Hill, and also only that part of it more properly called the "Capitol," has introduced a vast deal of confusion into our ideas of Roman topography, though probably it would not have puzzled a Roman for a moment. The same remark applies to the words *patres* and *patricii*. It can hardly be doubted that the word *patres* originally designated the members of the Senate; and some modern critics, like Rubino,[1] have maintained that it never means anything else. But Becker has shown that it must also have been used of the whole patrician body;[2] and, therefore, in some cases, *patres* is equivalent to *patricii*. Becker, however, though he establishes that *patres* and *patricii* may mean the same thing, yet contends that *patricii* cannot be applied to senators, and, indeed, that in a passage of Livy which we are about to examine it is purposely used by way of contrast to senators. And as in the same passage *auctores* is employed, or appears to be employed, in connexion with *patricii*, he draws an argument thence in support of his view that the whole patrician body, or, what are in his opinion identical, the curiæ, might be *auctores*. But *patricii* properly means the whole patrician body, or the senators and their families; hence it sometimes might be rendered "the patrician party," when, in their contests with the *plebs*, the senators and their connexions act together; and in later times *patricii* seems to be used, in reference to the Senate itself, to signify its patrician members. The former of these meanings, or *patricii*, as denoting a party, is convertible with *nobilitas*, and is sometimes found thus converted. With this explanation, it will perhaps appear that the signification of these terms, though sometimes seemingly obscure and perplexing, may be easily determined by means of the context.

A long and important passage in Livy, serving to illustrate this subject, is adduced by Becker,[3] who prefaces it with the following

---

[1] Röm. Verf. S. 185, ff.

[2] Röm. Alterth. ii. i. S. 141, ff. The following passage, which is not among those cited by Becker, appears to us sufficient to prove his point: "Recusantibus id munus ædilibus plebis, conclamatum a *patriciis* est *juvenibus*, se id honoris .... libenter acturos, ut ædiles fierent : quibus cum ab universis, gratiæ actæ essent, factum senatus consultum, ut duos viros ædiles *ex patribus* dictator populum rogaret."—Lib. vi. 42. Here it is the patrician *youth*, therefore certainly not Senators, who desire to be ædiles; but the S. C. designates them as "*ex patribus*."

[3] Ibid. S. 303, Anm. 611.

remarks: "If in a hundred places *patres* means the same as *patricii*, if both terms are used by one and the same author as synonymous, with what justice can it be asserted that precisely where the *auctoritas patrum* is spoken of, these Patres must always without any further definition be taken for the Senate, nay, that even *auctores patricii* must immediately become senators! But I shall speak of this further on, and content myself here with further instancing a well-known passage of Livy (vi. 42), but which can never be sufficiently urged. I here insert it at length: 'Vixdum perfunctum eum (dictat.) bello atrocior domi seditio accepit, et per ingentia certamina dictator senatusque victus, ut rogationes tribuniciae acciperentur, et comitia consulum, adversa nobilitate habita, quibus L. Sextius de plebe primus consul factus. Et ne is quidem finis certaminum fuit. Quia patricii se auctores futuros negabant, prope secessionem plebis res terribilesque alias minas civilium certaminum venit, cum tamen per dictatorem conditionibus sedatae discordiae sunt, concessumque ab nobilitate plebi de consule plebeio, a plebe nobilitati de praetore uno, qui jus in urbe diceret, ex Patribus creando. Ita ab diutina ira tandem in concordiam redactis ordinibus, cum dignam eam rem senatus censeret esse, meritoque id, si quando unquam alias, deum immortalium causa libenter facturos fore, ut ludi maximi fierent, et dies unus ad triduum adjiceretur; recusantibus id munus aedilibus plebis, conclamatum a patriciis est juvenibus, se id honoris deum immortalium causa libenter acturos, ut aediles fierent: quibus cum ab universis gratiae actae essent, factum senatus consultum, ut duos viros aediles ex patribus dictator populum rogaret; patres auctores omnibus ejus anni comitiis fierent.'"

Becker then proceeds to remark: "I will not here repeat, what Niebuhr has rightly characterised as striking, that *the Senate* has consented to the election of a plebeian consul, and the *patricians* withhold their consent, *negant se auctores futuros;* nor will Schömann's evasion detain me long, who considers that the patricians themselves must here have been the senators; wherefore he assumes that the Senate had indeed consented to the election of a plebeian, but as their choice fell upon Sextius (which it was difficult forsooth to foresee!) it revoked its consent: nobody will easily assent to this. I will only ask what opinion we should form of Livy's capabilities as a writer, if we consider that he used the terms *senatus, nobilitas, patricii,* and *patres,* in variegated confusion within the compass of a few lines, and without any further distinction, now for the Senate, now again for the patricians (for the *juvenes patricii*, who are to be chosen ædiles *ex patribus*, can hardly be also senators!); I will only ask whether it is not plain that he has purposely chosen the terms *senatus* and *patricii* in order to avoid a misunderstanding. Lastly, with regard to the words, 'Factum senatus consultum ut . . . patres auctores omnibus ejus anni comitiis fierent:' it would be beyond measure absurd that the Senate should prescribe to itself, by a formal *senatus consultum*, that it would give its consent! So much here: what is further to be said will be found in the sequel."

Becker then resumes his examination of the passage at p. 318. He is there endeavouring to prove that *Patres auctores fierunt*, or *Patres auctores facti*, is nothing more than the consent of the patricians in the Comitia Curiata. This, he says (p. 317), may be proved in two ways: partly by the testimonies which clearly distinguish between the Patres Auctores and the Senate, and even name the patricians as the confirmers, or authors; and partly from the original identity of this confirmation with the *lex curiata de imperio*. The latter question we have already examined; we will now proceed with the former of them, or the argument from testimonies, in support of which the passage from Livy in question is the principal *cheval de bataille*.

"As regards the first method of proof," continues Becker, "the principal passage is that from Livy, vi. 42, already produced. In order to avoid every false interpretation and evasion, we must remember that it was precisely L. Sextius, who aimed at the consulate, who reproached the people that he had sacrificed himself as a tribune during nine years, without receiving the reward which might recompense him: 'Quæ munera quando tandem satis grato animo æstimaturos, si inter accipiendas de suis commodis rogationes, *spem honoris latoribus earum* incidant?' (c. 39.) There could be no doubt that so soon as ever a plebeian could be elected, the choice would fall on none but him. The Senate after a long contest yielded at last, and the election ensued against the will of the nobility, that is, of the patricians: 'Per ingentia certamina dictator *senatus* que victus, ut rogationes tribuniciæ acciperentur; et comitia consulum *adversa nobilitate* habita, quibus L. Sextius de plebe primus consul factus' (c. 42). But the contest was not yet at an end, as the patricians refused to confirm the election: 'Et ne is quidem finis certaminum fuit, quia patricii se auctores futuros negabant;' till the dictator effected an agreement by separating the judicial power from the consulate, and creating a new office, the prætorship, for the *nobility*, that is, for the *patres*: 'Quum tamen per dictatorem conditionibus sedatæ discordiæ sunt, concessumque *ab nobilitate* plebi de consule plebeio, a plebe nobilitati de prætore uno, qui jus in urbe diceret, *ex patribus* creando.' For him who does not recognise herein the difference of the *patres* or *patricii auctores* from the Senate, for him especially who does not perceive that in the whole narrative Livy purposely uses *senatus* and *patricii*, or *patres*, as antithetical, I have indeed no further proof. But let him who will not recognise this explain the difficulty which arises, under any other interpretation, from that most extraordinary *senatus consultum*: 'Factum *senatus consultum*, ut duos viros ædiles ex patribus dictator populum rogaret: *patres auctores omnibus ejus anni comitiis ferent*.' As already remarked, it would have been quite absurd that the Senate should prescribe to itself by a *senatus consultum* that it should give its consent; and the evasion employed (by Wachsmuth and Huschke), 'it is no command of the Senate directed to a curial-community independent of itself, but an indication or advertisement of the contents of the agreement' (*Inhaltsanzeige des Vergleichs*), I do not understand. If Livy were speaking of a protocol of the Senate, this might pass; but a *senatus consultum* is always a resolution that prescribes ('Quod verba fecit Cos. ... de ea re quid fieri placeret, de ea re ita censuerunt'): and this lies in the word *ferent;* if only the inclination of the Senate were expressed it would have been written *futuros*.

"But as Livy here expressly calls the assembly that is to confirm *patricii*, so, a little before, he has put the same explanation into the mouth of Appius Claudius. Claudius, appealing to a passage which has been already explained (Liv. vi. 41), that the auspices lay exclusively with the patricians, and that the plebeians had no share in them, says: 'Quid igitur aliud *quam tollit ex civitate auspicia, qui plebeios consules creando a patribus qui soli ea habere possunt, aufert?* ... Vulgo ergo pontifices, augures, sacrificuli reges creantur: cuilibet apicem dialem, dummodo homo sit, imponamus: tradamus ancilia, penetralia, deos deorumque curam, quibus nefas est. *Non leges auspicato ferantur, non magistratus creentur: nec centuriatis, nec curiatis comitiis patres auctores fiant.* Sextius et Licinius, tamquam Romulus ac Tatius in urbe Romana regnent,' &c. The principal meaning of these words is not so much that the election of plebeian consuls would be the destruction of the auspices, and therefore would have for its result that there would be no more *auctores comitiorum:* rather Claudius says with bitter irony: 'Now, let everything be profaned; let the auspices be neglected, the priestly dignities desecrated; let no more elections of magistrates, no new laws be made under the sanction of the auspices; let the Patres no longer be Auctores of the Comitia; may the plebeians Sextius and Licinius tyrannize over Rome:' that means, in short, may all the sacred privileges of the patricians be done away with, since it is only plebeians and patricians that are here opposed; the Senate by itself does not come into question. And thus has the author of the speech Pro Domo quite correctly conceived the matter when he demonstrates what would be the result if any patrician could at his own will go over to the plebeian order (cap. 14): 'Ita populus Romanus neque regem sacrorum, neque flaminem, nec Salios habebit, nec ex parte dimidia reliquos sacerdotes; *neque auctores centuriatorum et curiatorum comitiorum;* auspiciaque populi Romani, si magistratus patricii creati non sint, intereant necesse est, cum interrex nullus sit; quod et ipsum patricium esse, et a patricio prodi necesse est:' only that here the *auctores centuriatorum et curiatorum comitiorum* are nothing but a declamatory phrase, probably taken immediately from the, at all events, very similar speech of Claudius in Livy, without regard whether there were any actual Curiate Comitia in the time of Cicero. But this much is certain that the author, by *auctores comitiorum,* meant not the Senate, but the patricians."

The passage of Livy here discussed is no doubt a very difficult and important one, and we have therefore given it, with Becker's commentary, at full length. To those who have already made up their minds that *patres auctores fieri* is identical with a *lex curiata* the passage must appear decisive; but as we have endeavoured to show that there may be some reason to demur to that conclusion, so we shall now inquire whether Livy's narrative may not be reconciled with the opposite opinion.

First, then, we agree with Becker, that *nobilitas* signifies the same thing as *patricii;* only we would extend the meaning a little further than he appears to do, so as to include the *patricii* who were *in the Senate.* For when Livy says, "Concessum ab *nobilitate* plebi de consule plebeio," it cannot be supposed that this could be done without the consent of the Senate: that the younger patricians, or even the Curiæ, should take upon themselves so important an alteration in the constitution as the exchange of a plebeian consul for a patrician prætor, without even asking the advice of the senators. The *nobilitas*, therefore, or the *patricii*, both the senators and those not in the Senate, are here acting together *as a political party*, without regard to their official functions. It is in this character of a party, including the senators in their non-official capacity and the rest of the patricians, that negotiations are entered into with the leaders of the *plebs*, and the agreement in question made.

Now let us review the passage under this light. The senators after a great struggle are conquered (*victi*), that is, in fact, they are frightened—for they, and not the outside patricians, are the responsible persons—not exactly, as Niebuhr says, into consenting to the election of a plebeian consul, but that such comitia should be held. The non-senatorial patricians violently oppose the measure: the senatorial ones repent, and are carried away by the passions of their connexions; and when Sextius is elected, the patrician party affirm that they will not accord him their authority; meaning, that is, in the only way in which it could be accorded—through the Senate. Then the dictator proposes a compromise: that the nobility, that is, as we have said, the patricians, including the Senate, should consent to appoint a plebeian consul, in return for a patrician prætor. We see that all this must have been done by unofficial negotiations. It would have been beneath the dignity of the senators to enter personally into these. They would have been carried on by non-senatorial patricians, who, however, speak in the name of their body, *we* will do this, *we* will do that, *we* will give our authority, &c. Those who reject this interpretation are bound to show that patricians, not senators, or even the Comitia Curiata, could make the most vital changes in the constitution without the consent of the Senate.

With regard to the *senatus consultum*, and Becker's remark on it, "that it would have been quite absurd that the Senate should prescribe to itself that it would give its consent," we shall observe that we see no absurdity whatever in a body of men saying what they would do. On the other hand, according to Becker's interpretation, this *senatus consultum* was to bind the Comitia Curiata. Now see what absurdities arise out of this. According to him, it is these Comitia that give the *auctoritas* to a law or to an election. It is they who, according to his interpretation of Livy, could give or withhold their assent to measures so important as the creation of a plebeian consul, or a patrician prætor, without so much as consulting the Senate, for the *patricii*, he says, are carefully to be distinguished from the senators, and not to be mixed up with them. Yet this powerful and independent body is to be bound beforehand by a *senatus consultum!* If this was the case, whatever may be said about the technical meaning of the Patrum Auctoritas, it is evident that the virtual power of it, in contradiction of all Becker's elaborate arguments on the subject, lay with the Senate, and that the *auctoritas* of the curiæ was only the shadow of a name.

This *senatus consultum*, therefore, rightly viewed, only affords another proof that the "patres auctores fieri" was the prerogative of the Senate.

We must confess that we do not very clearly apprehend the drift of the latter part of Becker's reasoning. But if he means to say that in the following words in the speech of Claudius, "Nec centuriatis, nec curiatis comitiis patres auctores fiant," there is no allusion to the Senate, we differ from him altogether. If *patres* here means the *patricii*, and if the *patricii* are the same as the *curiata comitia*, then we have the absurdity of their giving their own authority to their own act. But any Roman would have known, in spite of the double meaning of *patres*, that when used with respect to the sanctioning of the Comitia, and with the adjunct of *auctores*, it could not mean anything else but the senators. Nor do we perceive, whether it be a declamatory phrase or not, that the author of the speech Pro Domo understood the formula, "auctores centuriatorum et curiatorum comitiorum," in any other manner.

The array of authorities which Becker musters to support his interpretation of this passage of Livy is very poor and meagre indeed. The first is a corrupt fragment of Sallust, which we will give according to Becker's reading, though we cannot make any sense of it: "Ne vos ad virilia illa vocem, quo tribunos plebei, modo patricium magistratum, libera ab auctoribus patriciis suffragia majores vestri paravere." On which Becker observes: "Whether the speech of the tribune Licinius himself be the groundwork of this, or whether the expression belongs entirely to Sallust, the one or the other has incontestably written *patricii* designedly, in order to avoid the term *patres*, which in his time was only customarily used of the Senate, and therefore little understood."

The passage, so far as we can make it out, seems to refer to the transfer of the elections of tribunes from the Comitia Curiata to the Comitia Tributa, the elections by the last of which do not appear to have required the Auctoritas Patrum. The speech, which according to some is that of the tribune M. Lepidus, is intended to incite the *plebs* against *all* the patricians as an order. How unfounded is Becker's remark that the author purposely avoids the term *patres*, in the sense of patricians, because that term was then only commonly understood of the Senate, is shown by the very opening of the speech: "Si, Quirites, parum existumaretis quid inter jus a majoribus relictum vobis, et hoc a Sulla paratum servitium interesset, multis mihi disserendum fuisset, docendumque, quas ob injurias et quotiens *a patribus* armata plebes secessisset:" where *patribus* evidently stands for the whole patrician body, and may be taken as another example of that usage. But the short answer to Becker's criticism is, that it is altogether beside the point. The passage is not a parallel one to that of Livy. There *patricii* is used substantively, whilst in Sallust it is an adjective. Though we may say "patribus auctoribus" by apposition, yet Sallust could not have written in this passage, "libera ab auctoribus patribus suffragia," to signify "free from patrician authors:" that is, free from the necessity of being authorized by patricians. It is in the quality of patrician, not of senator, that the sting lies, though only senators could be *auctores*.

This very unsatisfactory passage is the only one, besides that from Livy, from a Latin author, which Becker adduces in support of that branch of his argument which is to show by examples that the *patres auctores* may be separated from the Senate, and that the non-senatorial *patricii* may be designated as *auctores*. But he quotes, in addition, the following passage from Dionysius concerning the election of Numa (ii. 60): ἐκκλησίας δὲ μετὰ τοῦτο συναχθείσης, ἐν ᾗ διήνεγκαν ὑπὲρ αὐτοῦ τὰς ψήφους αἱ φυλαὶ κατὰ φράτρας, καὶ τῶν πατρικίων ἐπικυρωσάντων τὰ δόξαντα τῷ πλήθει, κ. τ. λ. The ἐκκλησία, or the φυλαί voting κατὰ φράτρας, are here evidently the Comitia Curiata, called by Dionysius τὸ πλῆθος, and therefore the πατρίκιοι ἐπικυρώσαντες must be the Senate; for at that time there were only these two public assemblies at Rome. But Becker asserts (p. 321) that Dionysius here means the non-senatorial patricians;

yet he allows, at the same time, that this could not have been his opinion, because it appears from other places that he regarded the Senate as the confirming body (see ii. 14, iv. 12). Now, as in these places he expressly affirms that the Senate had the *auctoritas*, and as in the passage before quoted he makes the *patricii* authorize, as well as in the following, τοὺς πατρικίους πείσαντες ἐπικυρῶσαι τὴν ἀρχὴν, ψῆφον ἐπενέγκαντας (vi. 90), we can only arrive at one of two conclusions: either that Dionysius considered that *patricii* could be used as equivalent to *senatores*; or that he did not know what he was talking about, and that therefore his testimony is utterly valueless.

Becker, indeed, affirms that in the passage last quoted (vi. 90) the words τοὺς πατρικίους are used in such a connexion that they cannot possibly be referred to the Senate, which has already conceded everything. But this is one of those dashing assertions customary with Becker, founded on a few isolated words, without taking the trouble to compare what goes before and what follows after, or relying that his readers would not. What the Senate had done was to make a treaty with the *plebs* that they would concede the points demanded; but this treaty had still to be carried out and made into a law in the regular constitutional manner. And that Dionysius by πατρίκιοι meant senators is shown to demonstration by what immediately follows. For in the text there is only a comma after ψῆφον ἐπενέγκαντας, and the sentence then proceeds: ἐπειδὴ καὶ τούτου παρ' αὐτῶν (i. e. τῶν πατρικίων) ἔτυχον, ἐδεήθησαν ἔτι τῆς βουλῆς ἐπιτρέψαι, κ. τ. λ. And a little further on: λαβόντες δὲ καὶ τοῦτο τὸ συγχώρημα παρὰ τῆς βουλῆς, κ. τ. λ. Hence it appears, first, that the *plebs* on their return to Rome persuaded the *patricii* to confirm their new magistracy by a regular vote; second, when they had obtained this they besought the Senate (βουλή) to suffer *moreover* (ἔτι), and *in addition* to what they had *just* done, &c.; third, when they had obtained this second concession also (καὶ τοῦτο), they proceeded to choose their tribunes. All the concessions, therefore, are obtained *from the same body*, which is called indifferently the patricians and the Senate.

Becker endeavours (p. 321) to explain away the first passage of Dionysius (ii. 60) by the following "evasion." "How he could come to name the patricians here is *easily explained* when we consider that the source whence he took his narrative *probably* used he term *patricii* as equivalent to patres. The more striking par-

harps the expression was, the less he felt himself called upon to alter it, and so he rendered it literally, I will not say thoughtlessly, but without going into the explanation of it; whilst, where he found *patres auctores*, he understood the expression to mean Senate, the only signification of it which he knew."

We feel ourselves bound to insert this "explanation;" for though we do not find much weight in it ourselves, perhaps others may. Upon the whole, the impression left upon our mind by this investigation is, that Dionysius certainly thought that *patricii* might be used as equivalent to *senatores*. And if, to adopt Becker's conjecture, he found it so used in his sources, it is not impossible that Livy used it in the same way from the same sources in the passage which we set out with.

Upon the whole of this question, therefore, we must confess our opinion that Becker has failed by both methods to prove his hypothesis, that the composition of the curiæ was entirely patrician, without any plebeian admixture; namely, either by showing that the *lex curiata de imperio* was originally identical with the *patrum auctoritas*, or that the *patres auctores comitiorum* were no other than these patricians of the curiæ. Nor do we think that his view of the identity of the *patres* and *populus* will derive any aid from such a passage as the following of Servius, which he catches at in his summing up (p. 332), like a drowning man at a straw: "Ideo autem Calabra, quod, cum incertæ essent Calendæ aut Idus, a Romulo constitutum est, ut *ibi patres vel populus* calarentur, id est vocarentur a Rege sacrificulo," &c.¹ Servius is here giving a definition of the Curia Calabra, and there was nothing that made it necessary for him to show that the *patres* and *populus* were the same, admitting, for the moment, Becker's view that they were. In such a case he would have used only one of the terms, and by using the two he shows that he is distinguishing between them, instead of identifying them; either because he did not know which body was called, or because both might have been called, but at different times. Macrobius, on the other hand, says that it was the *plebs* that was called—"calata, id est vocata, in Capitolium plebe juxta curiam Calabram."² The account of the curiæ in Paulus Diaconus is much more to the purpose: "Curiæ etiam nominantur in quibus uniuscujusque *partis* populi Romani quid geritur, quales sunt hæ, in quas Romulus populum distribuit,

Ad .En. viii. 654.   ² Sat. l. 15.

numero triginta."¹ For here we see that the *populus* was not homogeneous, or, according to Becker, "entirely patrician without any plebeian admixture;" for then it would have had no parts in its composition. Lastly, we would request those who hold that the *populus* was identical with the Patres, or patricians, to reconcile their opinion with the following passage: "Neque enim ad jus regni quicquam prætor vim habebat (Tarquinius); ut qui *nec populi jussu, neque auctoribus Patribus* regnaret."² Where the *jussus* of the populus and the *auctoritas* of the Patres, are clearly separated as two distinct acts by two distinct bodies; the one having the right technically called *jubere*, the other the right *auctoritatem dare*, or to authorize the *jussus*. And that those last were the senators has, we hope, been shown by what has been already said. To which passage we may add the following, also from Livy: "(Servium) non *comitiis habitis*, non *per suffragium populi*, non *auctoribus Patribus*, muliebri dono occupasso regnum;"³ where it is impossible, if *populus* and *Patres* meant the same thing, that he or any other writer should have used three phrases to denote their action, when one, or at most two, would have sufficed. Also, among others, the following from Cicero: "Quæ *cum populo*, quæque *in patribus* agentur, modica sunto."⁴

Schwegler has also brought forward⁵ several objections to the view that the curiæ contained plebeian members, which it will be necessary to examine. After remarking that this view pervades the whole history of Dionysius, he proceeds: "It is nevertheless erroneous, as it stands in contradiction to a number of incontestable facts. How, for example, if plebeians were members of the curiæ, and thus stood in strict community of worship with the patricians, could the difference of *sacra* be alleged as the chief obstacle to *connubium* between the two estates? ('Quam enim aliam vim connubia promiscua habere, nisi ut, qui natus sit, ignoret, cujus sanguinis, quorum sacrorum sit? dimidius patrum sit, dimidius plebis!' —Liv. iv. 2.) Could not even *curiales* have the right of marriage with one another?"

Such an objection as this arises from a wilful misunderstanding of the force of the word *sacra* in the passage cited. These were of various kinds: as, for instance, the curiæ had their *sacra*, which

---

¹ P. 49 (Müll.). ² Liv. i. 49. ⁵ Ibid. 17.
⁴ Leg. iii. 4. ³ B. L S. 622, ff.

were public, and the *gentes* theirs, which were private: yet it is neither of these kinds that is pleaded as a bar to matrimony between patricians and plebeians. It was the privilege of the auguries, of being the interpreters between gods and men, which constituted the patricians a distinct class. Schwegler himself observes more than once, that the patricians were a sort of priesthood; yet, when the time arrives for applying his remark, he either forgets it or ignores it.[1]

"How," he proceeds to inquire, "if there were plebeians in the curiae could their confirmatory resolution be called *auctoritas patrum* or *patriciorum*?"

We have already shown that the *auctoritas* is wrongly attributed to them.

"How could the doubling of the three old stem tribes, or the creation of the *secundi* Ramnes, Tities, and Luceres, be called a *duplicatio patrum*, if those three tribes consisted not of patricians?"

We have shown elsewhere[2] that the tribes were not doubled, that the *secundi* Ramnes, &c., were knights, and that the *duplicatio patrum* refers to the Senate.

"How could it be said of the plebeians, in case they were members of the curiae, that they had no *gentes* (Liv. x. 8), since the *gentes* were only organic subdivisions of the curiae, and he who was in a curia must necessarily belong to a *gens*?"

This remark was made at a period when the plebeians in the curiae bore but a very small proportion to the whole plebeian population. These, too, were only *attached* to some patrician family,

---

[1] Take especially this passage (B. xiv. § 11, S. 636): "The immediate consequence of this theory (viz. that the auspices belonged to the patricians) was the exclusion of the plebs from all those magistracies which were connected with the State auspices. Only those belonging to the old citizens" (read, to the patricians), "or to the State Church, were esteemed mediators by birth between the State and its gods: wherefore the pretensions of the plebeians to the consulate were continually met by the objection that the State auspices belonged only to the patricians, that no plebeian had the auspices. Thus the possession of the *jus sacrorum* defined the possession of all the other higher rights, and especially the *jus magistratuum*. Another consequence of this exclusion was that no *connubium* existed between the two orders," &c. It was wholly on account of the auspices that *connubium* was forbidden between patricians and plebeians: "Ideoque Decemviros connublum dirimisse, ne incerta prole auspicia turbarentur."—Liv. iv. 6.   [2] See p. 254, *sq*.

and could not properly be said *habere gentem.* Such a phrase could be used only of patricians who stood at the head of a *gens.*

"Lastly, it is well known that the curiæ, after the greater part of their earlier functions were long since extinct, still retained as their principal business the care of the family affairs of the patricians. Even in the imperial times a curiate law was still necessary when a plebeian was elevated to the rank of a patrician, or when a patrician went over to the plebeians, or when an *arrogatio* took place among the patricians. How is this to be explained if the Comitia Curiata were not connected with a difference of rank, if they had not been originally and essentially an assembly of the patrician estate?"

It is easy to see that all these functions might have belonged to the Comitia Curiata, from their having been the *earliest* public assembly at Rome. And from their constitution they continued to be the *most aristocratic* of those assemblies. If it was necessary that an *exclusively aristocratic* body should watch over those family affairs, why was not this function assigned to the Senate? But the making a patrician a plebeian, or a plebeian a patrician, concerned *both* these estates, and was therefore best done in an assembly composed of both.

"But the internal grounds are of still more weight. According to the assumption that the Curiæ were a division of the whole nation, and included the *plebs,* the history of the development of the Roman constitution becomes a veritable riddle, which, indeed, merely on account of this fundamental error, it became for Dionysius. For first, in that case the patricians would have had no assembly of their own; since the Comitia Tributa were assemblies of the *plebs,* and the Comitia Centuriata assemblies of the whole people. But how can one really believe that the *populus* of patricians, which originally formed, as the proper body of citizens, so strong and exclusive a whole, and so abruptly separated in every relation from the *plebs,* had not its own Comitia? In what kind of Comitia, then, did it give its confirmation, the so-called *auctoritas patrum* or *patriciorum,* to the resolutions of the other Comitia? In what assemblies did it choose the Interreges; whose election in the time of the republic, as appears from the most precise testimonies, was undertaken by the whole patrician body?"

Schwegler then refers to these testimonies, as collected by Becker in his "Römische Alterthümer."[1] They are the following: "(Sententia) quæ *patricios coire* ad prodendum interregem jubebat," Liv. iii. 40 ; "*Patricii*, quum sine curuli magistratu respublica esset, *coiere et interregem creavere*," *id.* iv. 7 ; "Nam *coire patricios* tribuni prohibebant," *ib.* 43, and, "prohibentibus tribunis *patricios coire ad prodendum interregem*," *ib.*; "(Ut) nos quoque ipsi (*i. e. patricii*) sine suffragio populi auspicato regem prodamus," *id.* vi. 41 ; "(Quum Pompeius et Munatius) referri ad senatum de *patriciis convocandis*, qui interregem proderent, non essent passi," Ascon. in Mil. p. 32. Or, that is, I propose a *senatus consultum*, that the patricians should be assembled to name an Interrex. "Hence," continues Becker, "what Appian says about Sulla is quite right: τῇ δὲ βουλῇ προσέταξιν ἑλέσθαι τὸν Μεταξὺ βασιλέα,[2] and applicable to every period, as the *senatus consultum* must first be passed. And thus Dionysius says : τόν τε μεσοβασιλέα προχειρισθῆναι—ἐψηφίσαντο, xl. 49."

Now, it is most extraordinary if, as Schwegler and Becker think, the Comitia Curiata were composed of patricians, and consequently therefore that the terms *patricii* and *comitia curiata* were equivalent, that in none of the passages adduced do we find the latter phrase employed, but only the word *patricii*. One would think that, merely for the sake of variety, if the Interreges were really elected in the Comitia Curiata, that assembly would have been named as the electors. But no: not even when the form *patricios coire* is repeated within five lines, as in Livy (iv. 43), is any change made, and in Livy (vi. 41), *populus* is expressly distinguished from *patricii*. These passages, therefore, instead of showing that the Interreges were chosen in the Comitia Curiata, afford the strongest possible ground for inferring that they were not so chosen; but in an assembly of patricians specially summoned for the purpose.

The objection that if the Comitia Curiata were not composed of patricians that body would have had no assembly of its own, is unfounded. They had the Senate. The objection about the Auctoritas Patrum has been already answered.

"Moreover," continues Schwegler, "if the *plebs* could vote in the Comitia Curiata, it had the majority in them, as the votes were taken by the head. But this agrees not with all that we know respecting the constitutional position of the *plebs* in the most ancient times. It would have been a real political suicide on the part of the patricians if they had admitted the populations of the neigh-

[1] B. ii. S. 299, Anm. 610.   [2] B. Civ. I. 98.

bouring towns which they had conquered to an equality of voting in the assembly of the people."

That the *plebs* had the majority under the earliest or Romulean constitution we have already seen from the court paid to them by Tarquinius Priscus when canvassing for the throne. But this was the *original plebs*, and not the populations of the conquered towns; which, with the exception perhaps of the Albans, were not admitted into the curiæ.

"On the assumption in question," proceeds Schwegler, "the Servian constitution becomes incomprehensible. If Servius Tullius transferred the functions of the Comitia Curiata, in which the votes were given by the head, and in which consequently the *plebs* had the majority, to the Comitia Centuriata, in which the vote was measured by property, and the preponderance was to all appearance in favour of the patricians, then this entire reform was in favour of the patricians and against the *plebs*, and Servius Tullius only curtailed the political rights of the *plebs*. But how does the traditional portrait of this king agree with this view? How in this case can we explain the devotion of the people to him? Or the hatred of the patricians towards him, of which Dionysius says so much? And how can it be believed that Servius Tullius introduced a constitution through which, as he must have foreseen, the influence of his adversaries would be increased and that of his own party weakened? Lastly, by the assumption in question, the rise of the Comitia Tributa also becomes enigmatical. If the plebeians had the majority in the Comitia Curiata, what need had they of that new kind of public assembly? Why did not the tribunes cite the *plebs* according to their curiæ? And as the Comitia Tributa, after they had ceased to be assemblies of the plebeian estate, also became national assemblies without a census, just like (according to the assumption in question) the Comitia Curiata, there would have existed by the side of one another two Comitia completely alike,—a useless multiplication of constitutional forms which we cannot credit of the Romans."

"On all these grounds we must hold to the opinion that the Curiæ in ancient times were only a division of the patrician citizens, or *populus*, and that only patricians had the right of voting in the Comitia Curiata."

All the questions here raised arise only from a misunderstanding of the nature of the ancient curiæ. They contained both patricians and plebeians, but of the latter only a limited number, the descendants of the ancient Romulean population, with the addition perhaps of some Albans. But beyond these had sprung up, as we have already shown, a vast plebeian population, chiefly from the conquered Latin towns, but also through those means of natural increase, by settlement, &c., which take place in every city. It was by enfranchising these that Servius became unpopular with the patricians and the idol of the *plebs*. Numbers of the plebeians thus enfranchised were no doubt persons of property—for Rome had now entered upon a commercial career—and thus money was admitted to share the privileges which before had belonged only to birth. And thus it was that Servius incurred the hatred of the patricians and won the love of the plebeians. For by his constitution every plebeian of moderate property obtained a vote, and even to the lowest order of proletarians was assigned the casting vote when those of the other centuries were equally balanced.

Schwegler then proceeds as follows: "When the defenders of the opposite view appeal to 'the testimony of the ancients' and to 'tradition,' we may remark that testimony and tradition can, strictly speaking, be cited only when we have before us the relation of a contemporary concerning things of which he might have had a trustworthy knowledge. It is quite a different thing when an historian, as for example in a history of law, undertakes to represent the legal constitutions of a time long since passed, of which only a slight knowledge remains; as, for instance, if such an historian should at the present day undertake to describe the political relations of the Carlovingian or Hohenstaufen period. Such a representation, in which, from the very nature of the thing a great deal must be mere combination and reflection, is plainly to be distinguished from immediate and contemporary testimony. This remark applies accurately to those authors of the Augustan period who have written concerning the laws and constitution of that of Romulus. We may always ask about their accounts: Are they derived immediately from the best and oldest sources? or are they more inference and reflection? That the latter is to be assumed of their assertions and representations concerning the nature of the Curiæ, the Auctoritas Patrum, &c., is certain. In the oldest historical sources, or annals, only the events of each year were set down; the political institutions were not described. When the author of such a chronicle recorded a confirmatory resolution of the curiæ and wrote 'Patres auctores facti,' it did not occur to him to explain this expression, because he presumed that it was understood, and thought not of the possibility that at some time or other it might be misunderstood, as happened not only to Dionysius, but also to Livy. Hence, when the historians give us representations supported by reasoning, or describe in detail historical occurrences, we must take good care not to give to their assertions the value of documentary evidence. This applies particularly to Dionysius, who as a foreigner describing the long past constitution of another people can plainly have no pretensions to the presumption of having never gone wrong, of having never erroneously apprehended any legal or constitutional institute of the earliest period. His history is not to be differently estimated from the history of a foreigner, say of a Frenchman, who should now undertake to explain the public legal relations of Germany in the Middle Ages from German sources, and who should interweave in his representation, as Dionysius has done, long reflections, but make no distinction between these reflections and what he finds in the sources. Who would maintain that the foreigner has nowhere misunderstood the ancient legal expressions of the documents, never made a false combination?

"Now properly it is only Dionysius who precisely certifies that the *plebs* were members of the curiæ, and had a vote in the Comitia Curiata.[1] He relates, for example (ii. 7), that immediately after the foundation of the city Romulus divided the whole population into three tribes and thirty curiæ. But this assertion is demonstrably a false reflection: for in that case, as indeed Dionysius expressly says, the Sabines, after their incorporation, must have been distributed among the tribes and curiæ which already existed: which for many reasons could not have been the case. As in this, so also in numberless other places, Dionysius gives as a fact and a real occurrence, what in truth is only his own subjective representations of the occurrences, derived from pure abstraction. Thus, for example, he represents almost regularly the inhabitants of conquered towns as distributed among the tribes and curiæ of the old citizens. But it must not be thought that these accounts rest on actual tradition, or are derived from documentary sources. From what should they be derived? From chronicles or legal documents of

[1] And besides him, Aurel. Vict. De Vir Ill. ll. 12, "(Romulus) plebem in triginta curias distribuit."

the regal period? No written line of the epoch of the kings lay before even the oldest annalists, much less before a contemporary of Augustus. Or from the histories of the Annalists? But these, as Dionysius himself says, were merely summary records of the most important events. These accounts therefore are nothing but arbitrary descriptions of Dionysius; they only prove that this historian has very consistently pursued through his whole work the erroneous theory which he had fancied for himself concerning the curiæ."

A stranger piece of criticism than the preceding we have scarcely ever perused. From what did Schwegler derive his own opinion, which he so confidently asserts, that all the members of the curiæ were patricians, and that their confirmatory vote was the *Auctoritas Patrum*? Whence could he have formed it except by *inferences* from passages of those ancient authors that have come down to us? For he pretends not to set against the assertion of Dionysius, that the curiæ contained plebeians, any counter-assertion, that they were composed exclusively of patricians. And are we to assume that Schwegler and his brother critics are more capable of making, from the present wreck of Latin literature, sounder inductions than could be made by Livy, or Cicero, or even Dionysius, when that literature was in a perfect state, and a hundred-fold more ample than we now possess it? Putting aside, however, the direct testimony of Dionysius and of Aurelius Victor, which we are content to do, though on this occasion we believe them to be right, the question whether the curiæ were wholly patrician, or patrician and plebeian, must be decided by inferences from the best authorities. These we have already examined, and by the conclusion to be drawn from them we are willing to abide.

We shall not here reopen the question of the sources of Roman history, which we have discussed in another place, and will only remark that our silence is not to be construed into assent to what Schwegler says on the subject. With much of what that writer observes about Dionysius we entirely agree; but the mistakes of this "foreigner," who lived at Rome in the palmy days of Roman literature, might well teach us moderns, who are living two thousand years later, a little caution and modesty, and lead us not too hastily to accuse such writers as Livy and Cicero of "misunderstanding" some of the most important parts of the constitution of their country.

Schwegler then proceeds to examine[1] what he calls "the origin of the *plebs*;" a most singular expression, since it is almost impossible to conceive of a state that in its origin should have consisted of nothing but patricians, that is to say, of nobles. "Concerning the origin of the *plebs*," he observes, "the ancients leave us without any explanation. They tacitly represent the Roman nation to have consisted from the beginning of patricians and plebeians, but take no account of the origin of this difference of rank; with the exception indeed of Dionysius, who attributes it, perversely enough, to a legislative act of Romulus. On this question, therefore, we are entirely confined to conjectures, among which the following most recommends itself."

On this we may remark that it is the most natural thing in the world that the ancient writers should give no account of the origin of the *plebs*, that is, of the people; the wonder would have been if they had done so. It is only the higher orders of the state, the nobles, priesthood, &c. who are *created* by a political act, and whose origin therefore can be ascertained; that is, in so far as they are distinguished from the mass of the people by certain privileges and honours. Now, to say that the origin of this difference of rank at Rome is mentioned only by Dionysius is one of the boldest and most absurd statements that ever was made: for both Livy[2] and Cicero[3] mention the creation of the patricians by Romulus. And from whom were they created but plebeians? Consequently there must have remained a mass of plebeians not so distinguished, as the ancient writers, as well as common sense, tacitly assume. Yet though Schwegler allows that those writers assume a *plebs* from the very origin of the city, yet he considers himself driven to conjecture how it arose!

We shall refrain from following him through the five or six pages in which he pursues his conjecture. It will suffice to say that it is nothing else but that of Niebuhr, that the Roman *plebs* first arose out of the populations of the Latin cities transferred to Rome. But though a large body of *plebs*, unenfranchised till the time of Servius Tullius, no doubt arose in this manner, yet there previously existed, from the time of Romulus, a *plebs* that enjoyed the franchise and voted in the Comitia Curiata.

Schwegler then proceeds to consider the subject of the *Patres*,[4] as follows: "The acquisition of a subject territory, or the addition

[1] Buch xiv. § 9.   [2] Lib. I. 8.   [3] De Rep. ii. 8.   [4] B. xiv. s. 10.

of a *plebs*, was naturally not without influence on the form of the Roman constitutional relations. The first result was that the ancient body of citizens acquired the position of a privileged estate with regard to the new citizens. The fathers of families (*patres*) belonging to the old citizens now formed a sort of nobility in relation to the *plebs;* and as, according to the constitutional view of the ruling estate, there were no families according to the sense of the word in Roman law, that is to say, *patres familias*, with all the rights belonging to a Roman family, except in the body of the old citizens—for plebeians, so far as they participated not in family rights as defined by public law, were not *patres familias* in the legal Roman sense of the word—so henceforward the name *patres* became a distinguishing and honourable appellation for the heads of families belonging to the old body of citizens, and in general for their relations. The knowledge of this fact—namely, that the patricians did not originally form an estate of nobles, but became so only in process of time—was preserved till the times of the historical writers and antiquaries.

"In later language, at the time when the patriciate had long lost its political meaning, the expression *Patres* is the usual title of honour for the Senate. This has occasioned the writers and antiquaries of that epoch to assume the same of the most ancient period, and not only to explain the name of *patres* according to this assumption, but also to deduce the historical origin of the patriciate from the appointment of the most ancient Senate. The senators elected by Romulus were, we are frequently told, called *Patres*, and their descendants *Patricii*. But, not to mention that this explanation of the term *patricius* is destitute of all grammatical foundation, the word *patres* according to the usage of ancient times—as shown by numerous passages of the historians, and particularly by the legal forms handed down from the time of the struggle between the two orders—signifies predominantly not the Senate, but the whole patrician body; while on the other hand there is wanting a correspondingly old and certain attestation that *Patres* was originally the technical name for the Senate. The right notion of the original relation between the Senate and the patriciate was never entirely lost among the Romans. Dionysius, for example (ii. 8, 12), who expressly appeals to the most trustworthy Roman authors in support of his account, represents the population of Rome as first divided into nobles, or *patres*, and commonalty or plebeians, and afterwards the Senate elected from among the first of these estates. This assertion cannot of course have the value of an historical testimony—in a question like the present such a thing cannot be expected—but it may be taken as a correct inference."

It is curious to observe here how, in the compass of a single page, the value of authorities, and even of the same authorities, varies, according as they are supposed to support or contravene the writer's opinion. First we are told that "the historical writers and antiquaries," such, we suppose, as Cicero and Varro, Livy and Verrius Flaccus, knew that "the patricians did not originally form an estate of nobles." And a little further on: "The right notice of the original relation between the Senate and the patriciate was never entirely lost among the Romans." Yet we are told, almost in the same breath, that these writers and antiquaries of a later epoch were mistaken in their explanations of the origin of the patriciate and Senate, because they interpreted the word *patres* according to the meaning which it bore in their own times! That is to say, they were ignorant of a matter the knowledge of which, as we are told twice over, had been preserved down to their times!

Schwegler's argument that the term *patres* became only in process of time a title of honour for the heads of families among the old citizens, and that originally all *ingenui* were *patricii*, is taken from Becker,[1] and has been already examined; together with the passages (Liv. x. 8, and Festus, p. 241, *Patricios*) by which it is pretended to be supported. We have shown that Livy's meaning has been completely misunderstood; and indeed the opinion attributed to him is directly contrary to what he tells us in another place[2] respecting the origin of the patricians. Are we then to set a passage in Festus containing a vague extract from Cincius against the express testimony of this historian, as well as that of Cicero (De Rep. ii. 8, 12), Paterculus (i. 8, 6), Sallust (Cat. 6), Eutropius (i. 2), Zonaras (vii. 3), who are cited here by Schwegler himself as vouchers to the contrary of what he asserts? and to whom, according to his own admission, a knowledge of the origin of the patricians had come down? And can we not set against this vague testimony of Festus the more precise one of Paulus Diaconus, that it was the senators who were called *fathers*?[3] At the same time we mean not

---

[1] Röm. Alterth. ii. 1. 150. See above, p. 306 sq.   [2] Lib. i. 8.
[3] "Patres senatores ideo appellati sunt, quia agrorum partes attribuerant anuonibus ac si liberis propriis."—P. 247.

to deny that the privilege enjoyed by the Romulean *plebs* of voting in the curiæ placed them a great deal above the subsequent *plebs*. All we assert is that it made them not patricians.

There is no force in the observation that the term *patricius*, as applied to the descendants of the *patres*, is destitute of all grammatical foundation. On this subject Schwegler remarks (S. 635, Anm. 3): "The derivative suffix *icius* signifies not physical descent, but the idea of belonging to some stock or body (*die Zugehörigkeit zu einem Stammbegriff*), as tribunicius, novicius, gentilicius, adventicius, adscripticius, &c. Thus *patricius* has the same relation to *patres* as *plebeius* to *plebs*." Well, be it so; and what more can we require? The Romans did not want to express physical descent, but political descent, or rather relationship. The *patres* were an order just as the *plebs* were an order; and therefore if *patricius* answers to *plebeius*, it is exactly what we expect of the word. So we find at Rome a temple of Pudicitia Patricia, and another of Pudicitia Plebeia.

That the word *patres* signifies sometimes only the Senate and sometimes the whole body of patricians, we have already allowed; but both meanings stand on equally good authority. The catching at the testimony of Dionysius, an author whom, only a few pages before, Schwegler has most justly abused, is noteworthy. We have already adverted to the passage here cited as remarkable for its absurdity,[1] and shall only further observe that, if it is to be taken at all, it must be taken as a whole. And then what does it show? Why, that from the very beginning there were at Rome two orders, patrician and plebeian; the very thing that Schwegler has been labouring to disprove.

On Schwegler's next section (11), in which he examines the distinctive rights of the patricians and plebeians, we have no remarks to make, except that, as usual, he confounds the patricians with the original body of citizens. In the 12th section he enters upon the subject of patron and client. We give his remarks at length.

"There is a third portion of the oldest Roman population, to be distinguished from the patricians and the *plebs*, though closely connected with the former, the class of clients.

"The origin of clientship is more ancient than the origin of the *plebs*; for there was a time when the Roman nation consisted only of patricians and clients. In its nature, clientship was a condition

---

[1] Above, p. 301.

of personal dependence; the clients were not, like the *plebs*, subject as a body to the ruling class of citizens, but were distributed among the different patrician races, and every client belonged to the *gens* of his patron.

"Dionysius describes more particularly (ii. 10) the relation between patron and client as analogous to that between father and children, relation of protection on the one hand, and filial piety on the other. The patron had to explain the law to his client, to represent him before the tribunal of justice, to take care of his domestic affairs and property like a father; in short, to give him every possible protection. On the other hand, the client had to be faithful and affectionate towards his patron; to do him every service that he could; to contribute to the dowry of his daughters, so far as the patron was without means; to ransom him if made a prisoner of war; to help to defray his damages if cast in a lawsuit, or condemned to pay a public fine, as well as to assist him in paying the expenses connected with public offices and dignities. Patron and client were not to bring one another before a court of justice, or to bear witness against one another. Dionysius, from whom this account is taken, is not the only author who thus describes the relations of the ancient clientship. There was a very old law which directed that the patron who should occasion hurt to his client should be accursed;[1] and, according to Cato's testimony, the client was to be preferred to the relation by blood.[2] It is not at all to be doubted that the relation of clientship once existed in this purity, and that the duties which it imposed on both parties were conscientiously observed.

"Respecting the origin of clientship, which reaches back beyond the historical time, of course no historical evidence has been preserved, and we can therefore only form conjectures on the subject. Among these the far most probable is, that the clients, whose relation to their patrons was an hereditary one, were at first the original inhabitants of the country who had been subjugated. Deprived of their territory by conquering races, they were received in exchange into a peculiar relationship of protection, sanctioned by religion. We find in Greece the same relationship of hereditary subjection amongst various peoples, and where it occurs we may assume that it originated in the subjugation of a more ancient population by conquering races. But whilst in Greece the subjugated

---

[1] Virg. Æn. vi. 609, et ibi Serv.   [2] Ap. Gell. v. 13, 4.

populations are mostly found as hereditary renters of farms or day labourers, the Roman clientship bore a much nobler character, that of a relationship sanctified by religion; the reason of which we must probably seek in the pious disposition of the conquering race; which descending from the Sabine mountains and the high lands about Reate into the valley of the Tiber settled in Latium.

"It follows from what has been said, and is also confirmed by other indications, that the clients originally possessed no property in land. They were, so long as clientship existed after the old fashion, mere tenants of the patricians; they held only precariously such portions of the *ager publicus* as the patricians permitted them to cultivate; and when they were not hereditary farmers on the lands of their patrons, they followed handicrafts or trades. To obtain freehold land would under the most ancient agrarian system have been almost impossible, since every portion of land was an *hereditum*, or hereditary possession. Hence we find not that they were liable to military service in the classes of the Servian constitution. On the contrary, according to the account of Dionysius, the clients remained in Rome during the first secession of the *plebs*, and therefore served not in the rebellious legions who retired to the Mons Sacer. When we find here and there in Dionysius the clients doing military service, it is only as vassals or feudatories of their patrons.

"That the clients are to be distinguished from the *plebs* appears from what has been already said. The Roman clientship has a different historical origin from the *plebs*, and rests on different laws. The clients of the oldest period are hereditary subjects, which the *plebs* are not. It is undoubtedly incorrect that all the plebeians were clients, as Ihne has recently re-asserted in his 'Forschungen auf dem Gebiete der röm. Verfassungs Geschichte.' All that we know concerning the sanctity of the ancient clientship, and which at one time was certainly a truth, speaks against this assumption. If the plebeians were clients, how shall we explain the continual bitter contests of the two orders, the character of their reciprocal relations, founded, as it were, on public law, the heavy oppressions which the patricians exercised towards the plebeians, particularly by means of the cruel law respecting debt, and the creation of the tribunate, which arose from the need of some protecting patrons? Further, we perceive that the plebeians appeared in person before the tribunals, while the clients were represented by their patrons.

But the assumption in question is especially contradicted by numerous passages in the ancient historians, in which the clients are not only distinguished from the *plebs*, but formally opposed to it: passages which decisively exclude the possibility that the whole of the plebeians were clients.

"Other scholars do not indeed completely identify the clients with the *plebs*, but declare them to be a portion of the *plebs*. They hold that the clients mentioned in the passages just quoted[1] are not any peculiar order different from the people, but plebeians, who from motives of private interest had voluntarily become clients, and sided with their patrons against the *plebs*; that clientship from the first was not a state institution, but a voluntary and personal connexion. But this is the character of the later clientship. Originally, and in the old time, clientship was not, according to all accounts, an arbitrary and conventional relation, but an indissoluble and hereditary one, resting on religious grounds, a convention founded on piety, of which the later clientship is a mere shadow. Dionysius, to whom we are indebted with reference to this for the most numerous and most definite notices, often expressly distinguishes the clients from that part of the *plebs* which held with the patricians; and thus he cannot have considered the clients as part of the *plebs*.

"Briefly, as it is undeniable that the clients became in course of time amalgamated with the *plebs*, of which they thenceforth formed a part, so, on the other hand, we must decisively hold that the clients of the most ancient period were in their origin and their legal relations a different order from the *plebs*."

This account of the earliest Roman clientship is little more than a tissue of conjectures, not only unsupported by evidence, but actually against evidence.

That "there was a time when the Roman nation consisted only of patrons and clients" is quite true; but the patrons must have been patricians, and the clients plebeians; for with reference to the especial privileges of the patricians, and particularly the sacred character with which they were endowed, which, through the auspices, made them the interpreters between gods and men, we

---

The passages alluded to are quoted (S. 643, Anm. 1) from Livy and Dionysius to show that the clients were distinct from the general body of the *plebs*, and often sided with their patrons against the *plebs*; a point which we have admitted.

can recognise only these two classes. In this view, Schwegler's conception of a *tertium quid*, something neither fish nor flesh, neither patrician nor plebeian, is utterly incomprehensible. There must, consequently, have been plebeians at Rome from the very beginning; and instead of the origin of clientship being more ancient than the origin of the *plebs*, the case was just the reverse; for the clients must have been made out of the *plebs*.

It is quite true that "every client belonged to the *gens* of his patron." But what follows from this? That he must have had political rights, that he must have belonged to the curiæ, and must therefore have been entitled to a vote on public matters. For we have shown that the *gentes* were a political institution, that they constituted subdivisions of the curiæ, and this view is accepted by Schwegler himself.[1] And if the *gentes* were a political institution, then clientship must also have been a political institution, since the clients belonged to a *gens*; and as there must have existed materials out of which to institute the clients, there must, as we have already said, have been a *plebs* before there was clientship.

Dionysius has probably given a correct account of the relations between patron and client, as it tallies with what may be inferred from Latin authors, who only incidentally mention the subject, and have not given any detailed account of that relationship. But to suppose that a connexion of this close and sacred kind could have sprung up between a conquered race and their conquerors is one of the wildest and absurdest of conjectures. There is not the slightest resemblance between the Roman clients and the Thessalian Penestæ, the Attic Thetæ, the Spartan Helots, and other Greek serfs, whom Schwegler mentions in a note,[2] by way of making some show of authority in support of his opinion. But this opinion we need not discuss, because Schwegler himself stultifies it by observing that "the Roman clientship bore a much nobler character, that of a relationship sanctified by religion." It is also refuted by what Schwegler himself assumes of the Latin populations conquered by the Romans, and transferred to Rome—in which view we concur —that these populations—with the exception, perhaps, of some of the Albans—were not admitted into the curiæ, therefore not into the *gentes*, nor into clientship, and consequently the Roman method of treating subjugated populations was not to admit them into clientship. And the Albans admitted into clientship, doubt-

[1] Buch xiv. s. 4. [2] S. 640, Anm. 4.

less became the clients of those Alban nobles who had been made Roman patricians; for in those days a patrician without clients would have been as great an anomaly as, in former times, a Highland laird without a tail.

So far from the clients having been a conquered race, we believe them to have belonged to the race, first of Roman conquerors, and then of Romans and Sabines united. Their condition very much resembled that of vassals of the Middle Ages. They were bound to do military service when summoned by their liege lords, the patricians; and both connexions are characterised by very similar reciprocal duties and obligations. Schwegler's inferences on this point are most extraordinary. He admits that we sometimes find the clients doing military service as vassals or feudatories, which is all that we are trying to establish.[1] To assert that the clients were not liable to military service under the Servian constitution proves nothing with regard to the Romulean constitution; but even this assertion we take to be erroneous. The following passage in Livy undoubtedly refers to the Comitia Centuriata, in which the consuls were elected:—"Irata plebs intercesse consularibus comitiis noluit. Per patres clientesque patrum consules creati T. Quinctius, Q. Servilius."[2] But we have seen that in the Comitia Centuriata only those who had a vote who were liable to military service. That the clients did not join the remainder of the *plebs* against the patricians in the first secession, as Dionysius[3] relates, is exactly what might have been expected, and proves nothing at all with regard to their original rights. The Servian constitution naturally rendered them a comparatively aristocratic body, and, in political matters, bound them more and more to their patrons, since as members of the patrician *gentes*, and of the curiæ, they possessed privileges not enjoyed by the remainder of the *plebs*.

"It follows from what has been said," observes Schwegler, "and is also confirmed by other indications, that the clients originally possessed no property in land." But if what has been said has no reasonable foundation, then the conclusion drawn from it is also

---

[1] πρὸς δὲ τοὺς ἥσσω πολεμίους αὐτοί τι χωρῶμεν ἀνδρῶν προθυμίᾳ, καὶ τοὺς πελάτας ἔχοντας ἐσσομεθα, καὶ τοῦ δημοτικοῦ τὸ νεαρόν, κ.τ.λ.—Dionys. vi. 63; cf. vii. 19; ix. 15; x. 27, &c.

[2] Lib. li. 64. Schwegler in a note (S. 642, Anm. 1) promises to return to these two passages, and, we suppose, explain them away; but we do not find that they are noticed in the account of the Servian constitution.

[3] Lib. vi. 47, 51.

without any reasonable ground. And for the other indications which were to confirm it we look in vain. For the following passage from Paulus Diaconus:[1] "Patres senatores ideo appellati sunt, quia agrorum partes attribuerant tenuioribus ac si liberis propriis," cannot be construed to mean that "they held only precariously such portions of the *ager publicus* as the patricians permitted them to cultivate:" *attribuere*, especially, as here, coupled with the words "ac si liberis propriis," rather means *gave, bestowed*; namely, two *jugera* a-piece. And this agrees with what has been already said about the term *centuria* as applied to land, and *heredium*.[2] Nor can it be supposed that the holders of so small a portion of land as two *jugera* were patricians.

This is the only passage adduced by Schwegler to support his view; while, on the other hand, "indications" from Livy, Plutarch, and Dionysius, which are incontestably as good as any from Paulus, lead quite the other way. On this subject, Schwegler says:[3] "That the clients were really landowners in ancient times has been inferred from Livy (ii. 16), and Plutarch (Popl. 21), where we are told that land was assigned by the state to the clients of the immigrant Appius Claudius, two *jugera* to each client. But such details are as little to be held strictly historical as the 5,000 clients of Appius. Moreover, that district beyond the Anio is described by Dionysius (v. 40), not as given up immediately to the clients, but to Appius Claudius to distribute among them, ὡς ἔχοι διανεῖμαι κλήρους ἅπασι τοῖς περὶ αὐτόν; which very well agrees with our assumption."

This piece of criticism proceeds on the usual German method of depreciating even the best authorities, if they make against a favourite theory. But, whatever may be their historical value — and, if they had been on the other side, they would have been eagerly caught at — they are assuredly more valuable than no authority at all, and none appears on the other side. As to the 5,000 clients, that probably is only one of the usual exaggerations of Dionysius. Livy merely says, "magna clientium comitatus manu." But the boldness with which Schwegler claims the words quoted from Dionysius as being in his own favour is something extraordinary, even for a German critic. Κλῆρος does not mean a piece of land let out on lease — which is Schwegler's theory of

[1] P. 247. [2] Above, p.
[3] S. 611, Anm. 2, 97.

clientship—but a piece assigned as an hereditary freehold. And, though the whole tract was in the first instance assigned to Claudius to distribute among his clients, this does not alter the matter, but seems rather to have been in accordance with the ancient Roman practice. For, in like manner, the Roman territory seems to have been first assigned to the tribes, then divided among centuries, and finally among individuals; so that the share of each client seemed to be a gift from his patron, and was at all events received at his hands. Livy, in the passage just cited, represents the land as given to the clients, who nevertheless may have received their allotments through Appius. But it is hardly to be believed that this new body of clients were put on a better footing than the clients of the time of Romulus, by being made landowners, while their predecessors were only tenants.

"That the clients," observes Schwegler, "are to be distinguished from the *plebs*, appears from what has been already said." It is more satisfactory to find that this fact appears from classical authority. When Livy says, in a passage recently quoted, that the irritated *plebs* refused to take any part in the consular Comitia, and that consequently the consuls were chosen by the patricians and their clients, it appears plainly that the clients formed a peculiar section of the *plebs*. This is also shown by the passage from Dionysius quoted on the same occasion, where the πελάται, or clients, are distinguished from the rest of the *plebs* (τοῦ δημοτικοῦ τὸ περιόν).[1] We have already explained the reason of this distinction. But we do not believe the clients to have been a sort of hereditary bondsmen; and, according to what we have already said, we of course do not believe, with Ihne, that all the plebeians were clients.

When Schwegler, in the note just referred to, says: "It proves nothing to the contrary (viz. that the clients were distinct from the *plebs*), if Cicero says (De Rep. ii. 9): 'Romulus habuit plebem in clientelas principum descriptam;' and if the same view is expressed in Festus, p. 233: 'Patrocinia appellari cœpta sunt, cum plebs distributa est inter patres, ut eorum opibus tuta esset' (cf. Dionys. ii. 9: Plut. Rom. 13). Since, without urging that accounts like these concerning the original institutions of Romulus do not rest upon historical knowledge, but arise from construction and in-

---

[1] For other passages to the same effect see Schwegler's note already referred to (S. 613, Anm. 1).

inference" (*sondern construirt sind*), "nothing compels us to accept in these passages the expression *plebs* in the strong and technical sense which it bore in the period of the struggle between the orders. In itself it signifies 'the undistinguished mass,' 'the common people,' and might thus be very properly used to signify the yet undistributed mass of clients in contradistinction to the patricians, and may even be reconciled with the assumption that originally the Roman people consisted only of patricians and clients."

That the passages from Cicero and other writers cited at the beginning of this extract are merely inferences, or constructions, we do not admit; but, even if they were, Schwegler has nothing but inferences and constructions of his own to oppose to them; which, in the present wreck of Roman literature, are not likely to be a hundredth part so well founded. And the concluding sentence is a virtual admission of the point at issue. For if originally the Roman people consisted only of patricians and clients, and if these clients were the "undistinguished mass," the "common people," then there was originally a *plebs*, which is all that we are contending for. All Schwegler's views and reasonings are founded on two main oversights: first, that the grand characteristic of the patricians, besides superior wealth, was their sacred character, the possession of the auspices; and that in this view there could be but two classes, patricians and plebeians: though of plebeians there might be different ranks, according to wealth and political privileges. And even under the Servian constitution wealth would make a distinction between plebeians, as determining the class in which they were to vote; but it would make no distinction between them and the patricians, because the privileges of the latter rested on quite a different test, namely, religion and the auspices: and in this respect the wealthiest plebeian was as widely separated from a patrician as the poorest. But, secondly, the Romulean *plebs*, or at all events the clients, who originally perhaps formed nearly the whole of it, were further distinguished from the subsequent *plebs* by being members of the Comitia Curiata; a privilege which, besides the bond between patron and client, naturally inclined them, after the establishment of the Servian constitution, to side in most cases with their patrons. Unless we keep these distinctions in view, we shall never clearly understand the early Roman history. And Schwegler loses sight of them only because he persists in rejecting the best and most decisive testimony, and in preferring to it his own inferences and conjectures.

There still remain to be examined the remarks of another authority on this question, which cannot be passed over, even at the risk of repeating what we have before said perhaps more than once. It may be better to be tedious in these repetitions than to incur the charge either of superciliously disregarding the opinion of an eminent scholar, or of neglecting to answer his remarks because they were unanswerable; and fortunately they are short.

Professor Newman, in a paper on the Comitia Curiata, published in the "Classical Museum,"[1] has observed: "Niebuhr has done service to the early Roman history (against the admirers of Dionysius) by establishing that the curies were essentially patrician. The fact is so very clear to one who studies Livy only, that probably nothing but the attempt to reconcile him with Dionysius can have misled previous inquirers. Nor does it appear requisite in this matter to affect to learn more out of Livy's words than Livy himself knew. Nothing at least is let drop by him which would imply that he, as Dionysius, looked on the curiate assembly as plebeian and democratical. On the contrary, the very first time he refers to the Auctoritas Patrum he uses words which seem distinctly to imply that he understood by it 'the assent of the curies.' It has reference to the election of Numa, Liv. i. 17. He says: ' Patres decreverunt, ut cum populus regem jussisset, id sic ratum esset, si Patres auctores fierent.'"

We have before adverted to this passage, but we will view it again under this new light.

The Patres first mentioned in this sentence are, as we have already said, undoubtedly the Senate. This appears not only from the word *decreverunt*, but also from the whole context of the chapter. For first, it is the *centum* Patres, or senators, that seize the whole power of the state; and when the people murmur, it is these same *centum* Patres who make the decree just quoted ("Quum sensissent en moveri patres, offerendum ultro rati, quod amissuri erant, ita gratiam ineant, summa potestate populo permissa, ut non plus darent juris quam retinerent. Decreverunt enim," &c.) But the Patres last mentioned ("si Patres auctores fierent") are, according to the view of Niebuhr and Professor Newman, the members of the curies. And further, according to the view of the same

[1] Vol. i. p. 101, *sqq*.

writers, the *populus* is also the same members of the curiæ. Now see what absurdities follow. For, in this view, the sentence of Livy amounts to this: "The Fathers decreed, that when the *populus* (or Comitia Curiata) had elected a king, the election should stand good if the *populus* (or Comitia Curiata) authorized it!" Which is about as rational as if we should say: "The House of Lords permitted the Commons to choose a king, and the act was to be valid if the Commons authorized it."

Further: we are told by Livy in the sentence immediately preceding,' which we have quoted in brackets, that the Senate, though they permitted the people to elect a king, retained in their own hands as much constitutional privilege as they gave ("ut non plus darent juris quam retinerent"). This of course could only be done by retaining a *veto*, that is, by withholding their *auctoritas*, if they should see fit. But if this *auctoritas* was to be exercised not by them but by the electing body, or Comitia Curiata, how could Livy say that they retained as much power as they gave?

The Latin language is sufficiently ambiguous in using Patres both for the Senate and for the whole patrician body; but if it applied that term also to the curies, we should have confusion worse confounded.

It is only fair to add that a little further on Professor Newman subjoins the following note:—"In the passage quoted from Livy, i. 17, by *populus* Livy must have meant the mass of the community (whether called clients or plebeians) as he contrasts them to the patrician curies and to the Senate. It would be hardly to maintain that he was correct in supposing this multitude to receive formal authority to elect a king; and perhaps we must necessarily impute error here."

The error, we fear, lies with the critic. For the assumption in question is entirely opposed not only to the accounts of all subsequent elections, which are evidently made by the *populus* in their Comitia Curiata, but even to Cicero's account of this very election of Numa. For that writer says: " Regem alienigenam patribus auctoribus sibi ipse *populus* ascivit. . . . Qui ut huc venit, quamquam *populus curiatis* cum *comitiis* regem esse jusserat, tamen ipse de suo imperio curiatam legem tulit " (De Rep. ii. 13). Whence it appears that Numa was elected not by "the mass of the community," or unenfranchised plebeians, but by the Comitia Curiata. Nor can any other meaning be fairly extracted from Livy; and that there is any "contrast" in his words, except between the *populus* and the Senate (not the curies), is a gratuitous assumption.

Professor Newman proceeds as follows: "Then, in order to explain the last words, he (Livy) subjoins" (viz. to the sentence which the Professor had before quoted): "'*Hodieque* in legibus magistratibusque rogandis usurpatur idem jus, vi adempta : priusquam populus suffragium ineat, in incertum comitiorum eventum *Patres auctores fiunt.*' It is perfectly clear, first, that this illustration is his own, and is not slavishly copied from an old annalist; and next that he refers to the shadowy assembly of the curies (of which Cicero speaks, In Rullum ii. 11), as the existing body, which, before the Comitia voted, gave the Auctoritas Patrum to that which was about to be proposed; for no one can imagine that he meant the Senate. It may almost be inferred that in Livy's day the beadles of the curies gave the assent of that body by the formula, 'Patres auctores sumus:' and if so, it is unreasonable to question that the law of the Dictator Publilius (Liv. viii. 12) was well understood by the historian, who reports it in the words, " Ut legum, quae comitiis centuriatis ferrentur, ante initium suffragium Patres auctores fierent."

From what is here said, the reader who had not looked into the oration against Rullus might conclude that Cicero said plainly that the then shadowy assembly of the curies actually gave the Auctoritas Patrum, or, at all events, that such an inference necessarily followed from his words. But nothing of the sort. Almost the only use of the Curies at that late date was for conferring the *imperium*, a mere formality. It was the possession of the auspices that enabled them to do this. There can be no doubt that Romulus originally established the curies by augury, like all his other institutions, and the patricians at the head of each curia and each *gens* continued to retain the auspices. And to this effect Cicero says, in the following passage of the speech in question: " Sint igitur decemviri, neque veris comitiis, neque illis ad speciem, atque ad usurpationem vetustatis per xxx lictores, *auspiciorum causa*, adumbratis, constituti" (In Rull. ii. 12). In which passage he speaks not of any authority *given beforehand*, or, in the words of Livy, "*in incertum comitiorum eventum Patres auctores fiunt,*" to elect the decemvirs, but of the election itself.

It would be beside our purpose to enter into the remainder of Professor Newman's article, which is a refutation of Niebuhr's views respecting the Comitia Curiata. The next two paragraphs alone have a direct bearing on our subject, and these have been already answered in the preceding examination of Schwegler's remarks. The first of them relates to the curiæ having retained in later times a connexion with certain patrician interests,—as, for instance, when a patrician was to be adopted into another family. The second affirms that nothing would have been gained by the plebeians by the Servian constitution if they had already had votes in the 'Comitia Curiata. For what we have said on these points see above, p. 320, and p. 322.

Sir G. C. Lewis enters not at any length into the questions which we have here discussed; but we are happy to quote the opinion of this distinguished scholar in support of the views that we have advocated. He remarks:[1] "The arguments by which it is attempted to prove that the curiæ were aristocratic bodies, and consisted exclusively of patricians, are all indirect and conjectural; no trace of any such idea can be found in any ancient writer, or even in any modern writer prior to Niebuhr." And in a note he says: "The non-existence of the right of marriage between patricians and plebeians, which Schwegler uses as a proof that both were not in the original curiæ, has no bearing on this question, as the prohibition is stated to have been introduced by the Twelve Tables.[2] The identity of the *auctoritas patrum* with the *lex curiata de imperio*, which is the main support of this hypothesis, is itself a hypothesis, and is not proved by the argument of Becker (ii. i. pp. 314-26)." (This argument we have examined above in detail.) "The celebrated passage of Cicero (De Lege Agr. ii. 11) shows that the *lex curiata de imperio* was originally the subject of a popular vote, and that it was different from the confirmation either of the Senate or the patricians. (See Marquardt, Handbuch, iii. 3, p. 186.) The *lex curiata de imperio* was proposed to the Comitia Curiata, according to the regular practice, in 308 B.C. (Liv. ix. 38.) Camillus is described by Livy as having been recalled from exile by the Comitia Curiata, and appointed dictator 'jussu populi' (v. 46). The latter was irregular. Camillus afterwards describes the Comitia Curiata as relating to military affairs: 'Comitia Curiata quæ rem militarem

[1] Credibility, &c., vol. i. p. 542.
[2] This may have been the first prohibition *by law*; but the custom must have been observed previously, and we have already given another answer to Schwegler's argument.

continent' (v. 52). Appius Claudius, in his speech at the time of Licinian rogations, speaks of the Senate as confirming the act of the Comitia Curiata: 'Nec centuriatis nec curiatis comitii Patres auctores fiant' (iv. 41). The latter passage is a clear proof that Livy conceived the Auctoritas Patrum to be distinct from an act of the Comitia Curiata."

The same author remarks,[1] with regard to the word *populus*: "It is possible that the word *populus* may have originally signified the patricians without the plebeians; it certainly seems to require this sense in the oracle in Livy (xxv. 12): 'Prætor is qui jus populo plebique dabit summum.'[2] (See Newman, *ib.* p. 114.) But it is equally certain that *populus* in Livy and other Roman historians, and δῆμος in Dionysius, is used by them in the received acceptation of these words; and we are not entitled to assume that they did not understand their own language, or that of the historians whose writings they used."

Having thus endeavoured to show of what elements the early Roman population was composed, and that it consisted of patricians and *plebs* distributed into tribes, curiæ, and gentes; that the persons thus distributed, both patricians and plebeians, were called by the general name of *populus*; that, besides these, there was, even perhaps in the reign of Romulus, a certain portion of the *plebs* not so distributed, and therefore without any political rights; and that this last class was enormously increased, in the reigns of Ancus Marcius and Tarquinius Priscus, by the settling of a great many Latins at Rome; we will, before proceeding to give an account of the new constitution established by Servius, advert to a few more points in that of Romulus. And first of the nature of the kingly power.

We have already endeavoured to show[3] that Romulus reigned as an absolute king by divine right; that the law lay in his own breast; that everything proceeded from his prerogative and grace, and that even the Senate was only a kind of royal council, whose function it was to advise, but not to direct him. After the Sabine union, however, and particularly after the death of Romulus, a change takes place. The Senate appear to have become weary of the absolute dominion of the king, and even perhaps to have com-

[1] Credibility, &c., note 219.
[2] We have endeavoured to explain the meaning of *populus* and *plebs* in this prophecy. Above, p. 301.   [3] Above, p. 131.

passed his death with the design of establishing a revolution. The Interreges which they set up are a sort of foreshadowing of the consular system afterwards introduced, and the establishment of an aristocratic republic; at the head of which were to be magistrates invested with the kingly power, but enjoying it only for a limited period. The first attempt, however, proved abortive. Mutual jealousies induced the Senate to shift the *fasces* too often; the frequent change of masters was felt by the people to be galling and inconvenient, and they compelled the Senate to return to the regal system. The same result may have been promoted by the as yet imperfect amalgamation of the Roman and Sabine elements. There was still a jealousy between the two races, as is shown by the agreement now come to, that a king should be alternately elected from each. It can scarcely be doubted that this was the origin of the elective Roman crown, though Dionysius absurdly represents Romulus, after he had built his city, called it by his own name, and exercised all the prerogatives of an absolute monarch, submitting his title to the crown to the election of the people.[1] And for the same reason it is, perhaps, that we hear of no heirs of the first three kings; but when the people has become more amalgamated, and this alternation of the crown is no longer necessary, nor perhaps even possible, we begin to hear of the sons of Ancus Marcius laying claim to the crown on the strength of their royal descent. But this claim is counteracted by the usurpation of Tarquinius Priscus.

It is impossible to say precisely what limitations were set to the royal prerogative by the revolution which introduced Numa. The very act of his election, however, and the confirmation of his authority by a *lex curiata de imperio*, were acknowledgments that he owed all to the people, and that the claim of divine right was virtually abandoned; though he was still installed with augural ceremonies, as the elect of the gods. The most essential characteristic of the Lex Curiata was that it conferred the military command;[2] for in a nation of warriors, and among a population the organization of which resembled that of an army, the king was regarded as their general or leader in war. But it also conferred the judicial power, as we learn from the express testimony of Dion

[1] Lib. ii. 3.
[2] "Comitia curiata, quae rem militarem continent."—Liv. v. 52; cf. Cic. De Leg. Agr. ii. 12, s. 30.

Cassius.[1] It has further been inferred from a passage in Tacitus,[2] in which the Lex Curiata is spoken of as regulating the appointment of quæstors by the kings, that on this law the rights and powers of the king were separately enumerated. It appears, from the account of the proceedings of Tullus, after Horatius had murdered his sister, that, in cases of high treason at least, the king had, under the new system, given the staff of justice out of his own hands, and that a law had been passed to submit such cases to the decision of duumvirs, whose judgment, however, still admitted of an appeal to the people. The Senate, also, would appear to have gained more authority, since in Livy's account of the forms for declaring war introduced by Ancus Marcius, he is represented as not merely consulting that body, but as being guided by the decision of the majority.[3] Schwegler objects to this formula that it cannot be a genuine document of the regal period, because only the Senate and people are named in the declaration, and the king is not once mentioned.[4] But there is no force in this objection. Throughout the kingly period, wars and treaties are regarded as waged between peoples, and not between kings. Thus, in the earliest example of a treaty made under Tullus, we find, "Illis legibus *populus Romanus* prior non deficiet;"[5] and again: "Tu illo die, Jupiter, *populum Romanum* sic ferito," &c. without a word about the king. But before the making of the treaty, the Fetialis asks Tullus: "Jubesne me, *Rex*, cum patre patrato populi Albani fœdus ferire?" showing that the document belonged to the regal period.

The king not only led his armies in person; he also personally administered justice. This appears from the account of the pretended dispute between the assassins of Ancus Marcius, who are brought before the king in order that he may hear and decide the case; also from the proceedings after the murder of Tarquin, when, while it is pretended that he is still alive, Servius Tullius discharges vicariously his functions as judge. The same thing also

---

[1] Lib. xxxix. 10. On the whole subject, see Rubino, S. 367, f.

[2] Ann. xi. 22; cf. Schwegler, R. L. S. 658.

[3] Ann. xi. 32. We of course take the term *patres* here to mean the senators. It is hardly possible that in any other case the king could ask all their opinions in turn ("Inde ordine alii rogabantur"). Besides, the Fetialis in declaring war says: "Senatusque populi Romani Quiritium censuit, consensit, conscivit, ut bellum cum Priscis Latinis fieret."

[4] R. L. S. 662, Anm. 3.   [5] Liv. I. 24.

appears from the express testimony of ancient writers, and especially the following passage in Cicero:—"Jus privati petere solebant a regibus;.... nec vero quisquam privatus erat disceptator aut arbiter litis, sed omnia conficiebantur judiciis regiis."[1] The king, however, in the administration of justice, appears to have been assisted by a council, and especially in capital causes; at least it has been thought that we may infer this from what Livy says of Tarquinius Superbus: "Ut metum pluribus incuteret, cognitiones capitalium rerum sine consiliis per se solus exercebat:"[2] though perhaps it may only mean without consulting the Senate; for we do not hear that the kings had any other council: and Livy tells us in the same place that the neglecting of the Senate was one of the crimes charged against the tyrant; "Hic enim regum primus traditum a prioribus morem *de omnibus senatum consulendi* solvit."

As the Roman king was the lawgiver of his people, the supreme judge, and the commander-in-chief in war, so also he was the high priest of the State. This appears from all the religious institutions of Rome being attributed to the kings, and especially to Numa. Nor was he a more superintendent of religion; he discharged in person the functions of a priest. Romulus himself was an augur;[3] Numa officiated as a priest in the service of several gods, and especially as Flamen Dialis;[4] and of Ancus Marcius we are told, that when he went to war he handed over to the priests the care of divine worship,[5] which implies, as Schwegler has observed, that he himself previously officiated.[6] And when the celebration of public worship had long been transferred to the Pontifices, Flamines, and other priests, certain functions still belonged personally to the king, for the discharge of which, after the fall of the monarchy, it became necessary to create a Rex Sacrificulus.

Becker remarks on this subject: "It may appear that the making of treaties and alliances was not carried out, like declarations of war, in the name of the Senate and people, but of the king. At all events it is frequently related that foreign nations, after the death of Roman kings, considered themselves released from treaties, as having been concluded only with the kings; and though we may say that this was an unjust pretext for faithlessness,

[1] De Rep. vi. 2.   [2] Lib. I. 49. See Becker II. L. 335, f.
[3] Cic. De Rep. II. 9.
[4] "Quamquam ipse plurima sacra obibat."—Liv. l. 20.
[5] Ibid. 33.   [6] B. i. S. 649.

yet it could not have been alleged if the treaties had been made in the name of the Senate and people."[1]

That treaties were made in the name of the people is shown by the example just adduced from Livy. The only author who says that they were broken on pretence of the death of the king with whom they were made is Dionysius; and his account is no doubt only one of those pragmatical inventions with which his history abounds.[2] We may add here that Becker, contrary to the opinion of Schwegler, considers the formula for declaring war as undoubtedly belonging to the regal times.[3]

The magistrate next in power and dignity to the king was the Tribunus Celerum, or commander of the Equites, whose office in relation to the king seems to have been much the same as that of the Magister Equitum to the Dictator. He was the representative of the king in military matters, and appears also to have had the right of assembling the people and holding the Comitia. Thus Livy: "Præco ad tribunum celerum, in quo tum magistratu forte Brutus erat, populum advocavit."[4]

As the Tribunus Celerum was the military representative of the king, so the Præfectus Urbis, or Urbi, represented him in his civil capacity during his absence from the city. Denter Romulius, Numa Marcius, and Sp. Lucretius, are respectively said to have been appointed by Romulus, Tullus Hostilius, and Tarquinius Superbus to this office. ("Namque antea profectis domo regibus, ac mox magistratibus, ne urbs sine imperio foret, in tempus deligebatur qui jus redderet, ac subitis mederetur; feruntque ab Romulo Dentrem Romulium, post ab Tullo Hostilio Numam Marcium, et ab Tarquinio Superbo Spurium Lucretium impositos."—Tac. Ann. vi. 11.)

It was a prerogative of the kings to elect the Senate. The account of Dionysius,[5] that they were elected by the tribes and curiæ, the only author who asserts this, is just as false as his account of the election of Romulus, and, as is not unusual with that writer, it is contradicted by other passages in his own work. Thus, for instance, he represents Tarquinius Priscus as admitting many plebeians into the Senate by his own choice;[6] nor does he

---

[1] Röm. Alterth. ii. L 350.
[2] See the passages cited here by Becker, and by Rubino, S. 175.
[3] Ibid. S. 349. [4] Lib. L 59.
[5] Lib. ii. 12. [6] Lib. iii. 29, 47; cf. iv. 42.

mention that the Latin senators admitted by Tullus Hostilius
were subjected to an election by the curiæ. That the senators
were appointed by an exercise of the royal prerogative appears
from many places in Livy[1] and Cicero, and from the testimony of
Festus.[2]

With respect to the progressive increase in the number of the
senators, authorities vary. Livy states the original number of
senators chosen by Romulus, before the Sabine union, to have been
one hundred, and makes them consist of the same number at the
interregnum which followed upon the death of that king.[3] Cicero
describes the first Senate as having been elected after the Sabine
union, but does not mention of how many it was composed. Festus
also gives the Romulean Senate at a hundred.[4] Livy adds,[5] that
Tarquinius Priscus added a hundred new members, who were called
minorum gentium. This account agrees with that of Cicero, who
says that Tarquin *doubled* the number of senators;[6] and his words
seem to show that this was the *first* increase, since he calls it a
doubling of the *pristine* number. It seems likely, therefore, that a
Senate of one hundred had been chosen, as Cicero says, *after* the
Sabine union, for it is not probable that the Romulean Senate
should have contained no Sabines at the time of the death of
Romulus. Or rather, it appears most probable that the original
Romulean Senate, before the Sabine union, contained only fifty
members, which accords better with the scanty population; and
that the fifty added from the Sabines, after the union made up the
number of one hundred senators. And this seems to agree with a
tradition mentioned by Dionysius, that only fifty Sabines were
then admitted;[7] for as the Sabines seem to have obtained at least
an equal share of the government with the Romans, so it is likely
that they comprised half of the senatorial body. Plutarch[8] appears
also to have followed this tradition, but to have added the fifty to
the one hundred senators already constituted; so that when the
Senate was doubled by Tarquinius Priscus, its number amounted to

---

[1] See Lib. I. 8, 30, 35, 49; Cic. De Rep. ii. 8.

[2] "Reges sibi legebant sublegebantque quos in consilio publico haberent."—
P. 246. "Præteriti Senatores."—Cf. p. 339, "Senatores." [3] Liv. L 8, 17.

[4] "Quos initio Romulus elegit centum."—P. 339. [5] Lib. L 35.

[6] "Duplicavit illum *pristinum* numerum patrum; et antiquos patres
majorum gentium appellavit, quos priores sententiam rogabat; a se ascitos
minorum."—De Rep. ii. 20.

[7] Lib. ii. 47. [8] Num. 2.

three hundred. But we prefer the testimony of the Roman author. Hence we are inclined to think that during the reigns of the kings the Senate was never more than two hundred in number. It does not follow, from Livy's account[1] of Brutus having filled up the number of the Senate to three hundred, that Tarquinius Superbus had found that number on his accession. It was the object of Brutus to render the Senate powerful by its number (*frequentia*), and hence he not only filled up the vacancies occasioned by Tarquin's having murdered some of the leading senators (*primores*)—for which surely a score or two would be a liberal allowance—but he also added a fresh body of one hundred Patres Conscripti. *Ad summam*, or *numerum, explere*, does not necessarily mean to fill up to any *former* number; and if the regular number of the Senate had previously been three hundred, Livy would have said, "Patrum numerum explevit ad *pristinam* trecentorum summam," or something equivalent. Livy, in describing the constitution of Servius, says, "Nec mirari oportet, hunc ordinem, qui nunc est, post *expletas quinque et triginta tribus*,"[2] &c., where he cannot mean the filling up of any existing tribes, but the making of them up to their whole eventual number of thirty-five, which did not happen till three centuries after the time he is speaking about. And it is not at all improbable that Dionysius and Plutarch were led to a statement of the numbers of the Senate at variance with that of Livy and Cicero, from a wrong apprehension of the word *explere*. According to Festus,[3] one hundred and sixty-four senators were added by the first consuls; but it can hardly be supposed that more than half the Senate had perished. It is more likely that the sixty-four replaced those who had died out naturally or been murdered by Tarquin, and that the remaining one hundred were an entirely fresh addition. For in this way all the *Latin* sources will agree; namely, that the Senate under Romulus comprised one hundred members, and under Tarquinius Priscus two hundred; about the Greek writers we need not trouble ourselves. The raising of the Senate to three hundred by Brutus we must take on the authority of Livy alone, so far, we mean, as it was then first made three hundred; for there can be no doubt that this was its number thenceforth.

We will now proceed to consider the functions of the Comitia Curiata, the only popular assembly at Rome till the time of Servius Tullius. We must, however, avoid taking our description from the

[1] Lib. ii. 1.   [2] Lib. i. 43.   [3] P. 254, "Qui patrem."

account of Dionysius, who evidently made the whole out of his own head. Thus, that writer not only tells us that Romulus submitted to the decision of the majority of the Senate, but also that he allowed the people the choice of the magistrates, the acceptance of laws, and the decision respecting war, so often as the king proposed the question to them.[1] These privileges, which would have reduced the king's prerogative to a minimum, are nothing but pragmatic inventions, and we must be guided respecting the early constitution by what little we can extract from the Latin writers.

It is difficult to decide what were the exact boundaries between the king's prerogative and the power of the people. The extremest opinions have been adopted on both sides. Some writers, like Rubino, have attributed to the king an absolute authority, founded on divine right; others, like Niebuhr, Göttling, and Puchta, have represented the people as the source of all power. It appears to us that this irreconcilable diversity of opinion sprung from confounding together all the different epochs of the regal period, and that both theories are partly true. When Becker says[2] that the first is contradicted by the election of the alternate kings, and by the whole constitution of the curiæ, he is evidently looking at the post-Romulean times. A change was no doubt introduced by the Sabine infusion; but we believe Romulus to have been an absolute king. The curiæ were instituted by him more for military purposes than anything else; that the fighting men, who in times of peace were occupied with their daily occupations, might, on the alarm of war, be easily summoned together under their proper leaders. The members of the curiæ formed the *exercitus* which Romulus was reviewing in the Field of Mars, whither he had summoned them to a *contio*, at the time of his death.[3] Cicero says that Romulus governed "*singulari* imperio et potestate regia,"[4] the *vis dominationis* being tempered only by the authority of the aristocracy in a *quasi-senatus*, which, however, in effect was only a council. ("Quo facto primum vidit judicavitque idem, quod Spartæ Lycurgus

---

[1] Dionys. II. 14. Dionysius adds that the decision of the people was not final unless confirmed by the Senate, that is, by the Auctoritas Patrum (οὐδὲ τούτων ἔχοντι τὴν ἐξουσίαν ἀνεπίληπτον, ἂν μὴ καὶ τῇ βουλῇ ταῦτα δοκῇ). Dionysius repeats his account of the privileges of the people, iv. 20 and vi. 66.

[2] Rom. Alterth. ii. 1. 355.

[3] "Quum ad exercitum recensendum concionem in Campo haberet."—Liv. i. 16.

[4] De Rep. ii. 9.

paullo ante viderat, *singulari imperio et potestate regia* tum melius
gubernari et regi civitates, si esset *optimi cujusque* ad illam vim
dominationis adjuncta *auctoritas*. Itaque hoc *consilio et quasi
senatu* fultus et munitus," &c.—De Rep. ii. 9.) So far, then, from
all springing from the people, even the Senate had only the power
of advising, and not of determining. Again, further on we are
told that Romulus *alone* not only founded the new people, but
also directed it during his whole reign. ("Videtisne igitur, *unius
viri* consilio non solum ortum novum populum, neque ut in cunabulis vagientem relictum, sed adultum jam et pœne puberem?"—
Ibid. 11.) Cicero seems to repeat the same thing over and over
again in order that there may not possibly be any mistake.
Thus, in another passage he says, that though Romulus had instituted a Senate, like Lycurgus, yet he reserved for himself the
highest authority, and that the royal power, the royal prerogative,
and the royal name were supreme. (Lycurgus γέροντας Lacedæmone appellavit, nimis is quidem paucos, xxviii., quos penes
summam consilii voluit esse, quum *imperii summam rex teneret:*
ex quo nostri, idem illud secuti atque interpretati, quos senes ille
appellavit, nominaverunt senatum: ut etiam Romulum, patribus
lectis, fecisse diximus; *tamen excellit atque eminet vis, potestas nomenque regium."—Ibid.* 28.) And it is plain, from the whole treatise,
that Cicero considered a very large share of this power to have
remained with the kings down to the time of their expulsion;
though the introduction of an elective monarchy, and the policy of
Tarquinius Priscus and Servius Tullius in courting the people, must
have introduced some limitations. The former change, indeed,
the passing at once from divine right to popular election, is one of
the most momentous that can be conceived in any constitution.

Becker, holding fast to his opinion that by *populus* we are to
understand only patricians before the time of Servius, says,[1] "He
who remembers that the *populus*, which alone can be meant in
those early times, was the ancient kernel of the people forming the
curiæ, will be inclined to allow a greater degree of independence
to this *populus*, and to regard the public rights which it exercised,
not as a concession of the king, but as original rights resting upon
a contract or treaty."

But if it has been shown that the original *populus* was not composed of patricians, then the force of this argument vanishes; nor

[1] Röm. Alterth. ii. 1. 857.

is the assertion of an original contract confirmed by the passages quoted by Becker in his note. For if Cicero says that Romulus *allowed* a little power to the people, this shows that it depended on his inclination and not on a contract. Such are the following passages: "*Imperti* etiam populo potestatis aliquid, ut et Lycurgus et Romulus."—De Rep. ii. 28. "Et ut advertatis animum quam sapienter jam reges hoc nostri viderint, *tribuenda* quædam esse populo."—*Ibid*. 17. The important concession on this occasion was, that Tullus Hostilius consulted the people, whether he should use the ensigns of royalty! And lastly, another passage, which we shall give at full length: "Nam in qua republica est *unus aliquis* perpetua potestate, præsertim *regia*, quamvis in ea sit senatus, ut tum fuit Romæ, quum erant reges; ut Spartæ, Lycurgi legibus; et ut sit *aliquod etiam populi jus, ut fuit* apud nostros reges; tamen illud excellit regium nomen; neque potest ejusmodi respublica non regnum et esse et vocari."—*Ibid*. 23. Here the *aliquod jus* does not seem to be any very liberal allowance, and the *unus aliquis perpetua potestate*, points, if not to a tyrant, at all events to an absolute sovereign.

The members of the Comitia Curiata appear to have been summoned to that assembly by lictors, while the Comitia Centuriata were summoned by the sound of a horn.[1] Each member had an equal vote, that is, the votes were taken *viritim*, or by the head;[2] but, if we are to believe Dionysius,[3] the voting took place separately in each curia, and thus the question was carried by the majority of the thirty curiæ. It was determined by lot which curia should give its vote first, which was hence called *principium*.[4] Varro says that they met in the Comitium;[5] but by this, perhaps, he only means the leaders of the different curiæ to report the result of their proceedings to the king; for the Comitium certainly could not have contained three thousand persons, a number that would have filled the whole Forum.

It remains to say a few words about the knights, or *ordo equester;* though it was not till in later times that it became an *ordo*. The Equites appear to have been first instituted after the Sabine union, when 100 were enrolled from each of the three tribes, or ten

[1] Lælius Felix, ap. Gell. xv. 27.
[2] Liv. i. 43.
[3] Lib. ii. 14; iv. 84; v. 6.
[4] Liv. ix. 38.
[5] "Comitium, ab eo, quod coibant eo comitiis curiatis et litium causæ."—Ling. Lat. v. 155.

from each of the thirty curiæ.¹ For military purposes they seem to have been divided into ten troops of thirty each, consisting of ten men from each tribe; each ten, or decuria, being commanded by a decurio.² The whole corps, as we have already shown, bore originally the name of *Celeres*.³

The accounts of different authors respecting the increase in the number of the knights vary so much that it is difficult to ascertain the truth. It is said by some writers that Tullus Hostilius doubled their number. This rests on a passage in Livy, where he says that Tullus chose ten turmæ from among the Albans;⁴ and if he understood by *turma* the usual quantity of thirty, the number added would have been 300, or as many as those originally instituted. But, first, it is hardly probable that Tullus should have made as many Alban knights as there were Roman, when he appears only to have added about six Alban families to the patrician order. Secondly, so large an addition hardly agrees with Livy's phraseology, when he says: "Ut omnium ordinum viribus *aliquid* ex novo populo adjiceretur, equitum decem turmas ex Albanis legit." To add *something* to a body is not the way in which we express the doubling of it. So also the words of Valerius Maximus,⁵ "Equestrem ordinem *uberiorem* reliquit," hardly suit so large an increase. We are inclined to think that Livy only meant ten decuriæ of Albans were added in all, or 100; thus making the total number of knights 400. But the whole question, from the corrupt and varying nature of the texts, is lost in inextricable confusion; it would demand too much of our space to discuss it, especially as it could not after all be brought to any sure and satisfactory conclusion.

We will now proceed to describe the new constitution established by Servius Tullius.

THE SERVIAN CONSTITUTION.

The following is Livy's account of the Servian constitution:—Out of those who possessed a *census*, or property, of 100,000 ases, or more, were constituted eighty centuries, forty of seniors, forty of juniors. These constituted the FIRST CLASS. The seniores were to be prepared to defend the city, the

¹ Liv. l. 13; Paul Diac. p. 55, Celeres.
² Varr. Ling. Lat. v. 91; Festus, p. 355, "Turmam."
³ See above, p. 111. ⁴ Lib. l. 30. ⁵ Lib. iii. 4, 2.

juniores to go on military service abroad. Their arms were to be a helmet, a round shield (*clipeum*), a breastplate, and greaves, all of brass. Such were their defensive arms; their offensive weapons were a spear and a sword. To this class were annexed two centuries of engineers, who were to serve without arms, their duty being to bring and conduct the warlike machines. The SECOND CLASS had a property of from 75,000 to 100,000 ases, and contained twenty centuries of seniores and juniores (ten of each). Their arms were an oblong shield, or *scutum*, instead of the *clipeum*; the rest being the same, except the breastplate. In the THIRD CLASS were enrolled those who possessed from 50,000 to 75,000 ases, with the same number of centuries as the preceding one, and the same divisions as to age; also with the same arms, except that they had no greaves. The FOURTH CLASS was to have a *census* of not less than 25,000 ases: it had the same number of centuries; but the arms were different, consisting of nothing but a lance and a javelin. The FIFTH CLASS was larger, and comprised thirty centuries (in equal divisions of seniores and juniores): their arms were slings and stones. Among them were *accensi*, or supernumeraries, hornblowers and trumpeters, distributed into three centuries. The *census* of this class was 11,000 ases. The rest of the population that had a less property than this was comprised in one century, and not liable to military service. Such was the distribution, such were the arms of the foot-soldiers. Of the horse were enrolled TWELVE CENTURIES, the chief men of the city. SIX CENTURIES more were added to the three instituted by Romulus, under the same names with which they had been inaugurated. Ten thousand ases were allowed to them out of the public treasury to buy horses; and, to defray the expense of their keep, certain widows were assessed to pay two thousand ases a year. Thus the burthen of taxation was shifted from the poor to the rich. But the latter enjoyed a more honourable distinction; for votes were no longer taken by the head, so that all should give their suffrages promiscuously, and that of each man have the same value and legal force; but certain degrees were made, so that nobody should seem excluded from the right of voting, while all the power virtually remained in the hands of the aristocracy. For the knights were first called, then the eighty centuries of the first class of foot. If these did not agree, which seldom happened, then the centuries of the second class were called; but the votes were hardly ever taken so low as to arrive at the lowest class. Servius Tullius also divided the city into four parts according to the regions and hills which were inhabited. These parts he called *tribes*, probably from *tribute*, for the same king also established a method of paying tribute in fair proportions, according to the census of each citizen.

REMARKS.—One of the first things that strikes us in reading this account of the redistribution of civil rights, is the great weight given to property. Under the Romulean constitution, birth was the chief title to distinction and influence; but neither birth nor money was regarded as a passport to the right of suffrage, which was enjoyed by the whole of the original *populus*. In this view the Servian constitution must be regarded rather as a curtailment than an extension of popular rights; for, though it gave the suffrage to a vast number of plebeians who had not before enjoyed it, yet from the division into classes and centuries, and the method of voting by centuries, instead of *viritim*, or by the head, as formerly, the privilege was little more than nominal. For though, under the Romulean constitution, it was the votes of the thirty curies that were ultimately taken, yet *all* the citizens had previously voted in them, and there was no distinction between one curia and another, except by lot. But in the Servian constitution the first class, with the knights, contained more centuries than all the rest put together; and hence we may readily believe Livy's account that the vote was but rarely exercised by the lowest classes. The only part of the *plebs* which could have gained anything was its wealthier members. And this leads us to infer that a large class of wealthy plebeians had now arisen, who had most probably enriched themselves by trade and commerce. Since the founding of Ostia by Ancus Marcius, it is natural to suppose that the maritime commerce of the Romans must have made great progress; a fact indeed which is testified by the treaty concluded with the Carthaginians in the first year of the Republic.

SERVIAN CONSTITUTION.

'The constitution of Servius, as Schwegler has pointed out, appears to have had three objects in view; the first military, the second political, the third financial. We place the military object, or the formation of an army, first, as the most important. For the people still formed the army. Every citizen was a soldier, and there was no such thing as a separate military profession. Even his civil rights sprung from his capability of bearing arms just as they did in the time of Romulus. For as the five *classes* into which the people were divided formed the entire army, so the centuries into which these *classes* were subdivided formed the voting population; and their votes were of more or less value in proportion to the higher or lower place which they occupied in the army: the first class, which, with the knights, formed the flower of it, and whose arms constituted them the main line of battle, enjoying almost a virtual monopoly of the suffrage. And that the vote depended on capacity for military service appears from the fact that those who had passed the age of sixty years, and were considered as no longer capable of bearing arms, lost their vote.

It should be observed here that Livy makes the whole number of the centuries 194, whilst, according to the accounts of Cicero[1] and Dionysius,[2] there were only 193. There are some other differences in the account of Cicero, which, as the text is corrupt, we shall not attempt to reconcile. With regard, however, to the number of the centuries, 193 seems more probable than 194; since, being an uneven number, it would give a majority in the event of opinions being equally divided. Hence, perhaps, we should adopt the conjecture of Sigonius, that the *accensi, cornicines,* and *tubicines* formed only two centuries instead of three.[3]

For the convenience of a synoptical view, we shall here insert tables of the arrangement, both in its military and its civil character, according to the account of Livy.

AS AN ARMY.

Class I.

	Centuries.
Knights or horsemen	18

[1] De Rep. ii. 22.   [2] Lib. iv. 18.
[3] Sir G. C. Lewis, Credibility, &c. i. 400, note.

FOOT SOLDIERS.

	Centuries
Assessment at 100,000 ases and upwards.	
Seniors (above 45 years of age to 60)	40
Juniors (under 45 years)	40

Defensive arms: a helmet, round shield, breastplate, and greaves, all of brass. Offensive: a spear and a sword. The juniors to serve in the field, the seniors to defend the city.

Engineers	2

Class 2.

Assessment from 75,000 to 100,000 ases.	
Seniors	10
Juniors	10

Arms: the same as the first class, except that they had no breastplate, and a large wooden buckler instead of a shield.

Class 3.

Assessment from 50,000 to 75,000 ases.	
Seniors	10
Juniors	10

Arms: the same as the second class, only without the greaves.

Class 4.

Assessment from 25,000 to 50,000 ases.	
Seniors	10
Juniors	10

Arms: only a spear and a javelin.

Class 5.

Assessment from 11,000 to 25,000 ases.	
Seniors	15
Juniors	15

Arms: slings and stones.

In this class were ranked *accensi*, trumpeters, and hornblowers	2

All citizens below the lowest assessment of the fifth class, or 11,000 ases, were exempt from military service, and counted as one century.

The following summary will show the relative political power of the different classes with regard to the right of voting.

	Centuries.
Knights	18
First Class	80
Engineers	2
Second Class	20
Third Class	20
Fourth Class	20
Fifth Class	30
Accensi, &c.	2
Proletarians, or below the lowest census	1
	193

Cicero[1] makes only 70 centuries in the first class, and 1 of engineers, amounting thus, with the knights, to 89, out of the 193; so that, as he says, if 8 out of these should join the first 89, these would have a majority: for $89+8=97$; and $193-97=96$.

From what has been said, it appears that the Servian constitution must not be considered, as it might appear at first sight, a mere timocracy.

The possession of a certain degree of wealth was necessary to the formation of a good soldier. First, because he was thus enabled to provide himself with the necessary arms and accoutrements, which were the more expensive according to the higher rank which he held. Secondly, because it enabled him to give his leisure to the service, which, as the soldier then received no pay, could not be done by those who lived by trades and handicrafts. Thirdly, as the military profession was no mercenary one, and as the soldier's stimulus was purely the noble one of fighting for his home and country, it was natural that those who had the greatest stake in it should devote themselves with the utmost ardour to its service.

That the Servian organization was more particularly regarded by its founder and his contemporaries as a military one, may be inferred from the name *classis* given to each of its divisions, and more emphatically to the first division. For *classis*, which in later times was used, in the affairs of war, only of a fleet, signified in the earlier periods an army. Thus Paulus Diaconus: "Procincta

[1] De Rep. II. 22.

classis dicebatur, quam exercitus cinctus erat Gabino cinctu ex-
festim pugnaturus. Vetustius enim fuit multitudinem hominum,
quam navium, classem appellari."[1] Hence in an old law of one of
the kings, quoted by Festus: "Cujus auspicio classe procincta
opima spolia capiuntur, Jovi Feretrio darier oporteat,"[2] &c. The
first division was called absolutely *classis*, without the addition of
prima, and its members *classici*, which indicates, as Schwegler has
observed,[2] that the army, properly so called, consisted of the heavy
armed soldiers. The same thing, perhaps, might be inferred from
its numbers; for the first class contained almost as many centuries
as the four others put together: and though it is true that we are
not to take *centuria* as denoting the exact quantity of 100 men—
for indeed the last century must have comprised many thousand,
and the centuries of the seniores, containing only the men aged
from forty-five to sixty years, must necessarily have been smaller
than those of the juniors—yet, on the whole, and among the *classes*,
we may suppose that some proportion was observed. For the last
century of the *capite censi* were not liable to military service, were
not therefore in any *classis*,—though Dionysius erroneously makes
them a sixth class—and therefore its number was immaterial;
while, on the other hand, it must have been necessary that the
number of the fighting men, and the force of each particular arm,
should have been pretty accurately known: how else should a general
make his calculations? Companies of a hundred men, moreover,
formed the usual divisions of the Roman legion; whence the name
of *centurio* for the commander of one. It might perhaps be
objected to this view, How then should the very richest class of the
population have furnished so large a body in proportion to the
other classes? To this we reply that the possession of 100,000
asses, the *lowest* limit for admission into this class, must have constituted only a very moderate property. We know not how much
higher the property of individuals may have risen; some may have
possessed more than ten or twenty times that sum; and thus we
have a very ample margin upwards, while downwards it is fixed

---

[1] P. 225, *Procincta classis*.
[2] P. 189, *Opima spolia*. The corrupt text says it was a law "compelli
regis," for which Augustinus suggested the emendation "Pompilii regis."
But the subject of *opima spolia* would rather suggest the emendation of
"Romuli regis." And Numa in his capacity of king is seldom called
Pompilius.   [3] S. 714.

and certain; and the property of the very last class is only about
ten times less than that of the first. If all below a census of
11,000 ases were considered as proletarians, if the class immediately
above them, having a property from that sum up to the amount of
25,000 ases, could only afford to serve with slings and stones, then
it cannot be supposed that 100,000 ases represented any very extraordinary sum. And thus our notions of the Servian constitution
as a plutocracy must be very considerably modified.

We cannot, therefore, quite agree with Schwegler, when he says [1]
that the centuries were not divisions of the army, but of the host
of voters, and had no regular number. For, first, as the *prima
classis* formed the heavy armed troops, or main line of battle, they
do not by any means form too great a proportion when compared
with the other four classes of lighter armed soldiers; while, if the
strength of the centuries of this class is to be very much reduced,
or those of the lower classes very much increased, the lighter armed
troops would be far too numerous. Again, besides the reasons we
have already suggested to the contrary, it would have been a most
crying and unbearable injustice, if, for instance, a century in the
first class was composed of only 20 men, and in the last class, say
of 200, and yet that each should have a like vote. Nor is the last
century of many thousand proletarians any argument against this;
because they did not bear the burthen of war, while those in the
classes were all liable to them. Schwegler adverts to the following
passage of Cicero in the support of his view: "Illarum autem sex
et nonaginta centuriarum in una centuria tum quidem plures cen-
sebantur, quam pæne in prima classe tota." [2] But Cicero is there
evidently alluding to the century of proletarians, whom he has just
named; and it would be absurd to think that any single century
of one of the *classes* should have borne such a proportion to the
whole first *classis*. Taking all the centuries at an average of 100
men, this would give an army of nearly 20,000 men, a very probable
number. If to this number we add 7,000 proletarians, we shall
have a total adult male population of 27,000; and the whole population, including women and children, might amount to about
80,000, without including slaves. According to the account of
Dionysius,[3] who, however, we will allow, is not a very good
authority, the census, like our modern ones, was a regular enumeration of the *whole* population, and the men were obliged to give in

[1] S. 748.   [2] De Rep. ii. 22.   [3] Lib. iv. 15.

the names of their wives and children. According to this calculation, the population would have increased about sevenfold since the time of Romulus. And so Livy states that the number of the citizens at the first Servian census was 80,000; adding, however, that Fabius Pictor says that this was the number capable of bearing arms; an evident absurdity.[1] Nothing is so easy of exaggeration as numbers. Those who have traced the outline of the Servian walls and of those of Veii, the great rival of Rome, within a two hours' ride of her, will see that the territory could not have sufficed to maintain, nor the walls to shelter, the enormous hosts of which Dionysius[2] and others speak.

We have assumed that the sums set down as the census of the different classes represent property and not income; and this, we believe, is the view of all the modern authorities who have written upon the subject. Some have gone further, and assumed that the census of each class, though valued in money, represented in fact real property. This is the view of Mommsen, who considers that the value of a *jugerum* of land was 5,000 asses; that thus the census of the fifth class was the old *heredium* of two *jugera*; and that consequently no lower census was possible; that of those who had no *heredium*, only the heads could be counted.[3] There may possibly be some truth in this view; but it rests merely on inference, and is not supported by authority. It seems, too, to clash with Dr. Mommsen's theory that Rome was a great commercial city; for commerce cannot be conducted without capital in specie; and it is not to be supposed that a rich capitalist should have been excused the burthens of war, or counted as a proletarian, if he had not invested his money in the purchase of land.

That the original organization of the people by Servius was that of an army, appears also from the fact that, even when they assembled in their Comitia for civil business, they appeared in military array, and were called *exercitus*, or *exercitus urbanus*. Thus, in the Commentarii Consulares, quoted by Varro: "Accensus dicit sic: Omnes Quirites, ite ad' conventionem huc ad Judices. Dein Consul eloquitur *ad exercitum*: Impero qua convenit ad Comitia centuriata."[4] Hence properly only those magistrates who had the *imperium* could assemble the *exercitus*; but the quæstor also appears to have had the power of assembling them in Comitia in cases

[1] Liv. i. 44. [2] Lib. iv. 15. [3] Röm. Tribus, S. 111, 115, &c.
[4] Ling. Lat. vi. 88.

of capital indictments; as we learn from the formalities observed in the indictment of Trogus, related by Varro;[1] but this magistrate seems first to have been obliged to obtain the auspices from the prætor or consul. These instances are of course taken from the republican times; but the military order which continued to be then observed must have been derived from the original institution. From this military character also it was that the Centuriate Comitia met without the walls of the city, since it was not lawful for a military command to be exercised within them.[2] But it may easily be imagined that in process of time the institution lost more and more of its military character, and at last assumed a purely civil one. Hence Dr. Arnold remarks: "Whenever we find any details given of the proceedings of the Comitia, or of the construction of the army, we perceive a state of things very different from that prescribed by the constitution of Servius. Hence have arisen the difficulties connected with it; for, as it was never fully carried into effect, but overthrown within a very few years after its formation, and only gradually and in part restored; as thus the constitution with which the oldest annalists, and even the law books which they copied, were familiar, was not the original constitution of Servius, but one bearing its name, while in reality it greatly differed from it; there is a constant confusion between the two, and what is ascribed to the one may often be true only when understood of the other."[3] On which we will remark that if this be so, it at least shows that the charge so often brought against the narrative of Livy will not here apply; namely, that it is concocted from the usages of later periods, and transferred to that of the kings.

It is impossible exactly to define the political functions and privileges assigned to the Centuriate Comitia by Servius, as we have no notices of their operation till the time of the Republic. The institution of them, however, does not seem to have been a final reform in the mind of that king. From some commentaries which he left behind him, he appears to have contemplated the establishment of the consular form of government; and we are told that it

---

[1] Ling. Lat. vi. 91, seqq.

[2] Gell. xv. 27. When we find in Varro, therefore (loc. cit.), "Collegam rogem, ut comitia edicat de Rostris, et argentarii tabernas occludant," the shutting up of the bankers' shops was not ordered because the Comitia assembled on the Forum, but because business was not to detain people from proceeding to the Campus Martius.

[3] Hist. of Rome, vol. i. p. 77.

was according to the directions contained in them that the first two consuls were appointed.[1] If we may judge of the intentions of Servius by the later practice, the Comitia Centuriata were to enjoy the right of electing magistrates, of accepting laws proposed, of acting as a court of appeal, and judging capital cases. They do not appear to have obtained the right of deciding whether war should be declared till the consulship of C. Servilius Ahala and L. Papirius Mugillanus, in B.C. 427;[2] and we may therefore conclude that Servius had continued to entrust this prerogative to the Senate.

The division of the city into four tribes, by Servius, seems to have been made for financial purposes. It was merely a topographical arrangement, not one of race, like the tribes of Romulus; though these also, as we said, were connected with an agrarian division, and, as we learn from Livy, it had nothing to do with the number and distribution of the centuries. Thus, for instance, members of every *classis* and of every century may have dwelt together promiscuously in the different regions called *tribus*; it was only when they were summoned to assemble as an army, or for the Comitia, that each man fell into his proper class and century. And here at their own homes they paid the war tax, or tribute, that was laid upon them, according to the census at which they were rated.[3] Dionysius, as is frequently the case, is at variance with the Latin authorities, and represents the tribute as paid, not *singulis*, as Varro says, or *viritim*, but by centuries;[4] but his testimony is not to be accepted against that of Varro and Livy.

The Servian division of the city into four regions is a somewhat obscure subject; but we know the names of them from Varro,[5] and therefore, approximately, their boundaries. The first region was the Suburana, the second the Esquilina, the third the Collina, the fourth the Palatina. The chief portion of the first region was occu-

[1] Liv. i. 60. [2] Ibid. iv. 30.
[3] "Quadrifariam enim urbe divisa regionibus collibusque, qui habitabantur, partes eas tribus appellavit; at ego arbitror, ab tributo: nam ejus quoque aequaliter ex censu conferendi ab eodem inita ratio est. Neque hae tribus ad centuriarum distributionem numerumque quicquam pertinuere."—Liv. i. 43. But as Livy derives the name of *tribus* from *tributum*, so, *vice versa*, Varro derives *tributum* from *tribus*: "Tributum dictum a tribubus, quod ea pecunia, quae populo imperata erat, tributim a singulis pro portione censuum exigebatur."—Ling. Lat. v. 181. Both authors, however, agree in the main point.
[4] Lib. iv. 19. [5] Ling. Lat. v. 45, *sqq.*

pied by Mons Cælius and the adjoining Cæliolus; it embraced also the Carinæ and the Subura. The second region comprised the Esquilinæ and its two tongues Oppius and Cispius. It was here that Servius fixed his residence.[1] The Viminal and Quirinal hills formed the third region, and the Palatine the fourth; the last including the Germalus and Velia. In this division the Capitoline and the Aventine are striking omissions. One might be tempted to conclude, from the passage in Livy before cited, that they were omitted because they were not inhabited. But we have already seen that the Latin populations were located on the Aventine—though perhaps the greater part were proletarians; and the Capitol appears to have been at least partially inhabited, though no doubt it was chiefly occupied by temples. From the account in Varro it would appear that the distribution of the regions was regulated according to the locality of certain chapels, or *sacraria*, called *Argei*, either twenty-four or twenty-seven in number, supposed to be memorials of an Argive colonization of Rome, and which may, at all events, serve to confirm the traditions respecting an early Greek settlement in this district. The whole subject is, however, involved in great obscurity; and, as it is antiquarian rather than historical, the reader who may be curious to know more about it is referred to what the author has said in another work.[2]

On the Servian constitution Sir G. C. Lewis remarks:[3] "It is highly probable that ancient records of the constitution of classes, by which the census and the suffrage were both regulated, existed in the office of the censors; and it may be assumed as certain that this system was, at a comparatively early period, traced to Servius. But there is nothing to authorize us in supposing that an authentic contemporary account of this division of classes had been preserved. The account followed by Cicero differs materially in the numerical arrangement of the centuries from that followed by Dionysius and Livy; and even the accounts of Dionysius and Livy, though substantially equivalent, differ in some subordinate points. The assessment for the first class is stated by Dionysius and Livy at 100,000 asses; but, according to Pliny,[4] the sum was 110,000; while Festus[5] and Gellius[6] fix it at 120,000 and 125,000. Livy

[1] Liv. i. 48; Solin. L 25.
[2] See Dr. Smith's Dict. of Ancient Geography, vol. ii. p. 733.
[3] Credibility, &c. vol. I. p. 500.   [4] H. N. xxxiii. 13.
[5] The author should rather have said Paul. Diac. p. 113, *infra classem*.
[6] Noct. Att. vii. 13.

states the assessment of the fifth class at 11,000 ases; Dionysius at 12,500; Cicero and Gellius at 15,000.[1] These discrepancies negative the idea of an official record, derived from the time of Servius himself: and they rather point to later accounts, referring to different periods, and perhaps deficient in precision. That there may have been some historical ground, resting on a faithful official tradition, for connecting the name of Servius with an arrangement of the census, is possible; but there is no sufficient reason for believing him to have been the author of the matured and complex system which is presented to us as his work, or for supposing that the authorship of it is ascribed to him in any other sense than that in which Romulus is said to have founded the Senate, Numa the ceremonial law, and Tullus Hostilius the law of the Fetiales."

That is to say, Servius is only the eponymous, or imaginary, founder of the second Roman constitution, which lasted so many centuries, just as Romulus, according to the sceptical critics, is nothing but an imaginary, or invented, founder of the Senate, Numa of the ceremonial law, and Tullus Hostilius of the Fetial law. For this is the grand point on which we must fix our attention, that the regulations of Servius were a complete political revolution; in comparison of which any minor details, and especially about figures, sink into insignificance.

Now the great novelty of the constitution established by Servius, the fundamental idea of the revolution which he effected—and a more striking and important one can hardly be imagined—was the substitution of a property qualification, instead of the previous one of birth and hereditary right, for admission to civil privileges and their reciprocal obligations. For this purpose it became necessary to institute the *census;* that is, the enrolment of the entire body of citizens, classed according to their property; a thing which had not been done before, because it would have had no meaning or value before. Now Sir G. C. Lewis admits "that there may have been some historical ground for connecting the name of Servius with an arrangement of the census;" but denies that there is any "sufficient reason for believing him to have been the author of the matured and complex system which is presented to us as his work." That is, he admits that Servius may have invented the census, the very foundation of the later Roman constitution, while he denies

[1] Cic. De Rep. II. 22; Gell. Noct. Att. xiv. 10, s. 20.

that he had anything to do with the superstructure, without which the census would have had neither value nor meaning? Which is just as reasonable as to suppose that a man should invent a key for a clock or watch, without having the slightest idea of the machine to which it was to be applied. Reasoning like this, which betrays its own fallacy, proceeds from a settled determination to depreciate the civilization and intelligence of the regal period, and therefore assumes that it must have taken a much longer period, perhaps some further centuries, to produce the "matured and complex system" of the constitution ascribed to Servius.

How long the Servian constitution lasted in its original form we know not; but we know that the next reform was effected by the mixture of two of its elements; by blending the functions of the Comitia Centuriata with those of the Comitia Tributa. But there is not the slightest trace of either of these assemblies having been first instituted in the republican times. Some writers have inferred from a passage in Livy,[1] in which the *tribus prærogativa* is mentioned in the election of consular tribunes, that the mixture alluded to must have taken place as early as B.C. 396, consequently before the burning of the city, and only about a century and a half from the first establishment of the Servian constitution. But the election of consuls and military tribunes by the Comitia Centuriata is mentioned after this period, in B.C. 387.[2]

It is impossible to see what motive the historians of Rome could have had for the process imputed to them of transferring back to Servius a constitution that was not matured till a long while afterwards. And if it be merely meant that genuine and authentic records of its working were extant only in these later times, still they were quite justified in using these for their description of it, if they were satisfied that no alterations had been made in the fundamental principles. Nor could a constitution which substituted a property franchise for a birth franchise have been matured by degrees, because they are things of a wholly different kind, and admit not of degrees; and therefore the substitution of one for the other must have been abrupt and sudden. Moreover, the historians knew that the consuls, from the first, had been elected in the

[1] Lib. v. 18.
[2] "Comitia centuriata, quibus consules tribunosque militares creatis, ubi auspicato, nisi ubi assolent fieri possunt?"—Ibid. 52. It might be said, however, that this passage occurs in a rhetorical speech, and that the former ne must have been taken from a record.

Comitia Centuriata, and therefore the new constitution must have existed before the expulsion of the kings. For, if the consular elections had ever been transferred from the Comitia Curiata to the Comitia Centuriata, so important a change could hardly have passed without record, and the first consuls are expressly said by Livy to have been elected by the Comitia Centuriata. And as the plan of the consular government is even said to have been laid down in the Commentarii of Servius Tullius,[1] it is only an arbitrary assertion to say that "there is nothing to authorize us in supposing that an authentic contemporary account" of the alterations made by Servius had been preserved.

The ancient writers are not only unanimous in referring the new constitution to Servius; they also agree as to all the essential political features of it. Cicero, Livy, and Dionysius all tell us that the people were divided into five classes, with a century of proletarians; except that Dionysius, from his imperfect knowledge of Latin, calls this last division also a *classis*, and therefore makes six. They also agree in the fact that the first class, with the knights, possessed almost a monopoly of the political power; though there is some difference between Cicero and the historians respecting the distribution of the centuries. But first: Cicero was giving a mere sketch of Roman history, or rather a dissertation upon it, and did not perhaps think it worth while to consult documents in order to be perfectly accurate; and, secondly, Cicero's text is here hopelessly corrupt. Nevertheless, he gives a total of 193 centuries, like the other writers; for Livy's statement, as we have said, should be reduced to that number from 194. The difference in the census of the various classes, which after all is not very great, may have arisen in a great measure, as Böckh supposes, from the different estimate of money in different times.

We will now return to the course of the history.

THE FIRST LUSTRUM—THE SERVIAN WALLS—THE LATIN HEADSHIP.

Servius, having completed the census, which he had pressed on by promulgating a law with penalties of imprisonment and death against those who evaded enrolling themselves

---

[1] "Duo consules inde comitiis centuriatis a præfecto urbis ex commentariis Servii Tullii creati sunt."—Liv. I. 60.

he issued a proclamation that all the Roman citizens, both
horse and foot, should assemble in the Campus Martius
at daybreak, every one in his proper century. There he
purified the whole army, by offering up the expiatory sacrifices called *suovetaurilia*, the victims being a swine, a sheep,
and a bull. This ceremony was called the *lustrum conditum*, because it was the finishing act in taking the census.
At this *lustrum* 80,000 citizens are said to have been included
in the census. Fabius Pictor, the most ancient of our writers,
adds that this was the number of those capable of bearing
arms. It seemed necessary, therefore, to enlarge the boundaries of the city, so that it should be able to contain so great
a multitude; and with this view Servius added two hills, the
Quirinal and Viminal; and made a further increase by taking
in the Esquiline. And in order to confer some dignity and
importance on this last district, he fixed his residence there.
He also enclosed the city in a wall, and partly with an *agger*,
or rampart and fosse. Thus it became necessary to extend the
pomœrium; which is etymologically defined to be *postmœ-
rium*, or space behind the walls. But in reality it is rather a
space all round the walls, both within and without, which in
ancient times the Etruscans left when building their cities,
marking out its boundaries with terminal stones, and consecrating it by augury; so that in the inside the buildings
should not adjoin the wall, which at present generally touch
it; and that on the outside a space should be left free from
cultivation. This space, which could neither be built upon
nor ploughed, the Romans called *pomœrium*, not rather because
it was behind the wall, than because the wall was behind it.
And in enlarging a city these consecrated boundaries were
carried forwards in proportion as the circuit of the wall was
to be extended.

The dignity of the state being thus augmented by the
size of the city, and all the citizens being prepared by the
regulations before recounted either for peace or war, Servius
laid schemes for increasing his empire by means of counsel
rather than arms; and at the same time to add something to
the splendour of the city. At that time the Temple of the

Ephesian Diana was in high renown; which, according to report, had been built by the cities of Asia at their common expense. Servius, when in company with the chief men of the Latins, whose society and friendship he sedulously cultivated, both publicly and privately, was always extolling the benefits of union and a league under the auspices of the gods till by perseverance and reiteration of the same arguments, he at length persuaded the Latin peoples to build at Rome, in conjunction with the Romans, a temple to Diana. This was nothing less than an acknowledgment that Rome was at the head of Latium; a matter which had been so often contested with arms. The Latins, indeed, from their many unsuccessful struggles, seemed to have abandoned all care about the matter. But a singular accident seemed to present to a Sabine a chance of recovering the lost supremacy. A certain head of a family in the Sabine country had a bull born on his farm of wonderful size and beauty; and indeed the horns, which during many generations were hung up in the vestibule of the Temple of Diana, served as a monument of the miracle. The bull was regarded, what indeed it was, as a prodigy; the matter was taken up by the soothsayers and prophets, who proclaimed in their verses how that city would have the supreme command whose citizens should sacrifice the bull to Diana. The Sabine, when a proper opportunity for such a sacrifice offered itself, drove the bull to Rome, led it to the Temple of Diana, and placed it before the altar. But the Roman priest, struck by the size of the victim, which was well known by report, and remembering the oracle about it, thus addressed the Sabine: "What, my friend, are you going to make an impure sacrifice to Diana? Will you not wash yourself in the stream? The Tiber flows there at the bottom of the valley." The countryman was struck with these religious scruples; and being desirous that the sacrifice should be properly made, so that the promised event of the prodigy should be realized, he immediately went down to the Tiber. Meanwhile in his absence the Roman sacrificed the bull, to the great delight of the king and citizens.

REMARKS.—As Servius promulgated a law, with capital penalties, to enforce the accomplishment of the census, we may infer that the king still retained absolute legislative power. For such a law would hardly have been proposed to the Comitia Curiata, then the only popular assembly; as the patricians were averse to the new constitution, as well, perhaps, as the majority of the plebeian members of the curiæ, whom it would in a great measure deprive of their exclusive privilege.

It is rather puzzling to conceive how, according to Livy's account, Servius should have added the Quirinal Hill to the city; because, as we have seen, that hill must have been long since occupied by the Sabine portion of the population. Strabo[1] and Dionysius[2] say that he only added the Viminal and the Esquiline, about which there is no difficulty. Perhaps the best way in which we can interpret Livy's meaning is, that the Quirinal was now, for the first time, surrounded with a wall or fortification; while the Capitoline, the Palatine, the Aventine, and the Cælian, were more or less fortified. A considerable part of the Quirinal in its north-eastern extension may, however, have now been added; while the Viminal, and particularly the Esquiline, were new additions. This view would derive some confirmation if we should consider that Servius's part of the work was more peculiarly the *agger*, or rampart, which runs at the back of those three hills, through which may have been effected an enlargement of the boundaries, as marked out in the original, and perhaps partly executed, design of Tarquinius Priscus.

That the pomœrium of the Servian city should have been inaugurated with Etruscan rites is a very natural circumstance, when we consider that the walls were planned by the elder Tarquin, to whom these rites were suggested by his Etruscan education, as well as by his Etruscan wife, Tanaquil. But that they were adopted at the foundation of the Palatine city, though asserted by Tacitus, may admit of some doubt. By this inauguration of the pomœrium, the whole city became, as it were, a *templum*. Another proof of foreign influence through the Tarquinian dynasty, which serves to confirm the truth of the history, is the regulation of Servius by which certain widows were taxed for the keep of the knights' horses. For we learn from Cicero that the same thing used to be done at Corinth,[3]

[1] Lib. v. p. 231.　　[2] Lib. iv. 13.
[3] De Rep. ii. 20.

and Servius no doubt took the idea from the history and traditions of the originally Corinthian family into which he had been adopted.

The walls of Servius thus enclosed the seven hills which came to be regarded as forming the real Septimontium; namely, the Palatine, the Capitoline, the Quirinal, the Viminal, the Esquiline, the Cælian, and the Aventine. But the original Septimontium, the traditions connected with which were celebrated by the festival called Septimontiale Sacrum, embraced a different list of places, some of which can hardly be regarded as hills; namely, Palatium, Velia, Fagutal, Cælius, Germalus, Oppius, and Cispius. The subject is an obscure one, as the chief authority concerning it, which is a passage of Antistius Labeo in Festus,[1] mentions, besides these places, the Suburn, which was certainly not a hill; while Paul the Deacon also inserts the Suburn, and omits the Cælian.[2] But as we learn from Varro[3] that the Cælian Hill constituted the principal part of the Suburan region, and as it seems to have had some of the Argive chapels, which were the principal objects of these divisions, it cannot well be omitted.

The account of the manner in which Servius obtained the consent of the Latin peoples to the erection of a temple to Diana on the Aventine, in token of Rome's headship, shows that the conquest of Latium by Tarquinius Priscus could not have been absolute. From the scanty notices of these times which have come down to us, we must be content to take the general outline of events. By attempting to fill up the details, writers like Dionysius of Halicarnassus have brought discredit on the early Roman history; but there is no good reason for believing that the main outline is invented.

Respecting the Temple of Diana on the Aventine, as a sign of Roman hegemony, Schwegler remarks:[4] "This proceeding of Servius Tullius does not accord very well with what we are told about Tarquinius Priscus having reduced all Latium; but the policy which he adopted appears quite clear if the representations of the historians, according to which Tullus Hostilius had already made pretensions to the supremacy in Latium, which Tarquinius Priscus made good by arms, are anachronistic inventions. And that they

---

[1] P. 348 (Müll.).
[2] P. 341, ibid. Some MSS., however, have Celio Opplo.
[3] Lib. v. 46. See more in Smith's Dict. of Anc. Geog. II. 734.
[4] S. 780, ff.

are so cannot be doubted: since the larger and more important cities of Latium—as Tusculum, Gabii, Aricia, Ardea, Tibur, Præneste—were certainly not at that time subject to the Romans, as, with regard to Gabii and Tusculum, the subsequent history shows; but there existed, independently of Rome, a Latin federation, which held its diets at the grove and fountain of Ferentina. Thus Cincius (in Festus, p. 241, *Prætor*): 'Albā dirutā usque ad P. Decium Murem coss. populos Latinos ad caput Ferentinæ, quod est sub Monte Albano, consulere solitos, et imperium communi consilio administrare.' With this Latin confederation, to which Rome had hitherto been a stranger, and for the most part hostilely opposed to it, Servius Tullius concluded a treaty, much on the same grounds as Sp. Cassius did afterwards, by which he entered upon a confederate relationship with it;[1] for that this only was the aim of his endeavours appears plainly enough from his proceedings and behaviour as represented by tradition. A recognition of the Roman hegemony lay not, at all events, as the Roman historians erroneously represent, in the building of the Dianium on the Aventine, at the expense of the League. There were in Latium many of these common resorts of worship and holy places of the League—as the Dianium in the grove of Aricia; another on the hill called Corne; while in Lavinium and Ardea were Aphrodisia, or temples of Venus, which served the same purpose[2]—yet these did not give the places where they were found any political ascendency. We should have reason for believing this only if the Latian diets had been transferred to Rome; but these were subsequently held, as before, in the grove of Ferentina. According to all indications, it was the younger Tarquin who first procured for Rome the hegemony over the Latins."

On this we will remark that the history does not pretend that the larger and more important towns of Latium were *subject* (*unterthan*) to the Romans. The very method in which it is related that Servius acted in order to procure the building of the temple at Rome shows that he could exercise no command over the Latins; that he effected his object by persuasion. The history tells us that Tarquinius Priscus defeated the Latin peoples, not that he subjected or reduced their cities, as Tullus had reduced and destroyed Alba Longa, or Ancus Marcius Politorium, Tellenæ, and Ficana: for

[1] Liv. viii. 4.
[2] Cat. ap. Prisc. p. 629; Plin. H. N. xvi. 91; Strabo, v. 3, 5.

though Tarquinius Priscus captured several of their cities, he then accorded them a peace. The place where the diet was held was in no city at all, but in a grove; and therefore proves nothing. Yet if there was a league, there must have been a nominal head, or metropolis, of it: and if, after the fall of Alba, it was not at Rome, what other place was it?—that is, from the time of Servius; for before that period the honour had often been contended for in the field:[1] a passage, by the way, which shows how fragmentary are the accounts of those wars; though that circumstance should not discredit the notices that have escaped the obliterating hand of time. Schwegler has mutilated the passage of Cincius in Festus, by cutting off its head and tail. In its integrity it runs thus: "Albanos rerum potitos usque ad Tullum regem: Alba deinde diruta usque ad P. Decium Murem coa. populos Latinos ad caput Ferentinæ, quod est sub Monte Albano, consulere solitos, et imperium communi consilio administrare: itaque quo anno Romanos imperatores ad exercitum mittere oporteret jussu nominis Latini complures nostros in Capitolio a sole oriente auspiciis operam dare solitos; ubi aves addixissent, militem illum qui a communi Latio missus esset, illum quem aves addixerant, Prætorem salutare solitum, qui eam provinciam optineret Prætoris nomine."

Now we learn from the suppressed part of this passage that the Latins were accustomed to send to Rome for generals to command their armies when wanted; which is a pretty good proof that she had succeeded, as we are told by Livy, to the leadership or hegemony of Latium. Such a general, we are told, was called "Prætor," the name of a chief magistrate among the Latins, and in military affairs so called because he "went before," or led, the army.[2]

The assertion that Tarquinius Priscus made good by arms his pretensions to the supremacy over Latium is not to be found in Livy, though Dionysius says something to that effect;[3] and therefore the accounts of that sovereign's and of Tullius's transactions with the Latins are not anachronistic inventions. The assertion that Servius only made such a treaty with the Latins as admitted Rome into their confederation is an "invention" of Schwegler's, unsupported by a single scrap of authority. Is it likely that Rome, which had

---

[1] "De quo totiens armis certatum fuerat."—Lib. i. 45.
[2] "In re militari *prætor* dictus, qui præiret exercitui."—Varr. L. L. v. 87.
[3] ταῦτα δὲ ψηφισαμένων εἶναι φίλους Ῥωμαίων καὶ συμμάχων, ἄχρις ἂν ὁ ὀρθὸς αὐτοῖς ἐν Λατίνοις κελεύσωσιν.—Lib. iii. 54.

so long contended for the supremacy, should sue to enter the Latin
League merely as a subordinate member, and thus of course place
herself under the hegemony of some other city, which city—however,
cannot be named! The passage in Livy to which Schwegler refers
proves directly the reverse of what he asserts. It is shown by the
speech of Annius that for two hundred years, and therefore, as
Schwegler says, since the reign of Servius, the Latin forces had
been under the control of Rome: "Sin autem tandem libertatis
desiderium mordet animos, si fœdus est, si societas æquatio juris
est, si consanguineos nos Romanorum esse, qnod olim pudebat,
nunc gloriari licet, si socialis illis exercitus is est, quo adjuncto
duplicent viros suas, quem secernere consules ab se bellis propriis
sumendis ponendisque nolint; cur non omnia æquantur? cur non
alter a Latinis consul datur? *ubi pars virium, ibi et imperii pars est?*
Est quidem nobis hoc per se haud nimis amplum, quippe conce-
dentibus, *Romam caput Latio esse.* . . . Quis dubitat exarsisse eos,
quum plus ducentorum annorum morem solverimus?" &c.

Now this agrees with what Livy had before said, that Rome had
obtained the hegemony of Latium in the reign of Servius. It also
agrees with the suppressed part of the passage from Festus, that
the Latins were accustomed to receive their generals from the
Romans. It matters not whether the Latins had several places
for their assemblies: the Dianium on the Aventine was the only
temple common *both* to Romans and Latins; and being built at
their joint expense at Rome, which claimed the hegemony, was a
clear confession that Rome was "caput rerum."

Livy's intimation that the plan of this temple was suggested by
that of Diana at Ephesus shows that the Romans had a knowledge
of what was going on in Greece, which they may have derived from
the cities of Magna Græcia or from the Massaliots. The latter way
is perhaps the more probable one, as the Massaliots appear to have
paid particular devotion to the Ephesian Artemis, and their friendship with the Romans has been already recorded. The wooden
image of the Aventine Diana is said to have been a copy of that at
Ephesus.[1] The time of the foundation of the temple at Ephesus
cannot be accurately mentioned, but it was certainly in existence
in the time of Crœsus, who is supposed to have ascended the throne
in B.C. 560, and, according to the reduced chronology, Servius Tullius
began to reign in B.C. 531. The story of the sacrifice of the bull

[1] Strabo, iv. 1, 4. *seq.*

is of course one of those superstitious legends which the priests delighted to propagate. In such stories we are not to look for consistency, and therefore it would be needless to inquire why the sacrificer should be represented as a Sabine instead of a Latin. A temple of Diana, erected in token of a Latin confederacy, would naturally enough have been placed upon the Aventine, where the populations of the conquered Latin towns had been settled. According to one very improbable definition, even the name of the Aventine was derived from the *advent*, or concourse, of men which it occasioned.[1] Servius also erected several temples to Fortune, in commemoration probably of the favours which she had showered on him. One of these is known to have been in the Forum Boarium; another was outside the city, on the right bank of the Tiber.[2]

We will now conclude the history of Servius.

CONSPIRACY AGAINST AND MURDER OF SERVIUS.

The title of Servius to the crown seemed to be confirmed by his long wearing of it. Nevertheless, hearing that the youthful Tarquin sometimes gave out that he reigned without the assent of the people, he determined to confirm his title by a legal act. With which view he first conciliated the good-will of the *plebs*, by dividing among them the territory taken from the enemy; and then he proposed to the people a resolution in the usual form, whether they wished and commanded that he should reign. And, on taking the votes, he was declared king with a greater unanimity than any of his predecessors. This, however, did not diminish the hopes of Tarquin of obtaining the crown; nay, it rather seemed to afford him an opening. For he seized the occasion still more violently to denounce Servius to the Patres, and of thus increasing his party in the Senate-house; for he perceived that the division of land among the plebeians was quite contrary to their wish. Tarquin was himself ardent and violent enough, and his restless mind was still further stimulated by

[1] "Alii Aventinum, ab adventu hominum, quod commune Latinorum ibi Dianæ templum sit constitutum."—Varro, L. L. v. 43. [2] Ibid. vi. 16.

his wife Tullia. Hence the Roman palace became the scene of tragic crime; so that liberty came at last all the riper and more welcome from the disgust which the Romans had of their kings, and a reign wickedly acquired was the last which they endured. The Lucius Tarquinius of whom I speak—whether he were the son or grandson of King Tarquinius Priscus is not clear; but, if I should trust the greater number of authors, I should call him the son—had a brother, Aruns Tarquinius, a youth of gentle disposition. These two young men, as I have already related, had married daughters of King Tullius, who also, like their husbands, were very different in temper. It seems to have been through the good fortune of the Roman people, in order that the reign of Servius might be prolonged, and that he might have time to establish his constitution, that the couple whose tempers were so ferocious were not in the first instance united. But the violent Tullia was filled with vexation at seeing that her husband possessed not the same ambition, the same audacity, as herself. Her thoughts now centred entirely on her brother-in-law: he alone was worthy of admiration; he alone a man, and of royal blood: and she despised her sister, who, having such a husband, was not his counterpart in female daring. A similarity of temper brought the violent pair together, for there is a strange affinity in evil; but it was the woman who was the originator of all the mischief. In the clandestine interviews which she had with her brother-in-law she gave vent to all manner of contumelies, abusing her husband to his brother, her sister to the man who had married her. Better it were, she said, that she should be a widow, and he a single man, than be united with an unequal yokefellow, and languish through the cowardice of another. Had the gods given her that husband who was worthy of her, she might soon see herself in possession of the rule now held by her father. By such discourses she soon filled the youth with her own temerity. Lucius Tarquinius and the younger Tullia, after making themselves free to contract another marriage by murders which followed quickly on each other, were wedded, rather with the tacit acquiescence than the approbation of Servius.

After this every day seemed to render the old age of Tullius more unbearable, his reign more hateful. From one crime his daughter began to contemplate another; she suffered not her husband to rest day or night, lest their former murders should seem fruitless for want of perpetrating a parricide. It was not, she whispered, her former husband, with whom she had served without complaining, who had been wanting to himself; it was he who was wanting to himself, who before he had accepted her hand had thought himself worthy to reign; had remembered that he was the son of Tarquinius Priscus, and preferred having the kingdom to hoping for it. "If thou art he to whom I believe myself married, I recognise thee as a husband, but also as a king; otherwise things are changed for the worse, for we have now not only cowardice, but crime also. Wilt thou not set to work? Thou hast not to seek a foreign kingdom, like thy father, as if thou camest from Corinth or Tarquinii. Thy household gods, the bust of thy father, thy royal palace, and the throne which stands in it, and thy very name of Tarquin, create and proclaim thee king. Or, if thou hast not courage for this, why dost thou frustrate the hopes of the city? why show thyself as a royal prince? Betake thyself hence to Tarquinii or Corinth; return to thy original obscurity, for thou art liker thy brother than thy father."

With such reproaches did she instigate the youth; nor could she find any rest when she reflected that Tanaquil, a foreign woman, could achieve so much as to procure two continuous reigns, first for her husband, and then for her son-in-law; while she, though born of royal lineage, had no power in such matters. Instigated by this female fury, Tarquin went about and solicited the senators, chiefly those of the Gentes Minores. He admonished them of his father's benefits —solicited a return for them; the younger ones he enticed with gifts; and thus he formed everywhere a party, as well by vast promises as by incriminating the king. At length, when the time for action seemed to have arrived, he broke into the Forum with a band of armed men; and there, while all were paralysed with terror, he took his seat on the royal throne before the Curia, and directed the Fathers to be summoned by a herald to the senate-house, " to King Tarquinius." They immediately assembled; some of them having been prepared for the event beforehand, others through fear lest their non-appearance should prove injurious to them, as well as from astonishment at the novelty and, as it were, miracle of the thing, and thinking that all was over with Servius. Then Tarquin inveighed against the king, beginning his abuse from his very origin: "That the son of a female slave, himself a slave, should have seized the throne by a woman's gift, after the lamentable and undeserved death of his father, without any interregnum or holding of the Comitia, without the vote of the people or the authority of the Fathers. Such a king, so born, so appointed, the benefactor of the basest order of men, to which indeed he belonged himself, out of his hatred of the nobility of others, had divided the land of which he had deprived the patricians among the lowest of the low; had shifted those burthens, which before were borne in common, upon the necks of the chief men in the state; had instituted the census with a view to hold up the fortunes of the rich as an object of envy, and a source whence, at his own good pleasure, he might draw to benefit the needy."

In the midst of this speech arrived Servius, who had been summoned by a trembling messenger, and from the vestibule of the Curia he exclaimed with a loud voice: " How now, Tarquin? What audacity is this? How hast thou dared to assemble the Fathers, and sent thyself on my throne, while I am still alive?" To which Tarquin ferociously replied: " I occupy my father's seat. The son of a king is a much more lawful successor to the throne than a base-born slave. Thou hast insulted and wantonly mocked thy masters long enough." At these words the partisans of each raised a clamour and shout; the people rushed towards the Curia, and it was manifest that he would reign who was strongest. And now Tarquinius—for necessity compelled him to dare the last extremity—being by youth and strength the better man, seizes Servius round the waist, and, carrying him forth from the Curia, hurls him down the steps towards the Forum;

then he returns into the Curia to hold a Senate, whilst the
officers and attendants of the king take to flight. Servius
himself, half dead, and unaccompanied by any of the ordinary
royal suite, was making his way homewards, and had arrived
at the top of the street called Cyprius, when he was overtaken and slain by some men whom Tarquin had despatched
after him. It is thought that the deed was done at the instigation of Tullia, as it accords with the rest of her wicked acts.
It is, at all events, pretty certain that she proceeded in her
chariot into the Forum; and there, with unblushing effrontery,
in the midst of that crowd of men, she called her husband
forth from the Curia, and was the first to salute him king.
Tarquin bade her betake herself out of that crowd; so she
drove homewards, and when she had arrived at the Summus
Cyprius Vicus, at the spot where the Temple of Diana lately
stood, and was turning to the right to ascend the hill called
Urbius, and so to gain the summit of the Esquiline, the
affrighted driver suddenly pulled up the horses, and pointed
out to his mistress the body of Servius, which lay weltering
in its gore. It is related that a most foul and inhuman crime
was then committed—and the place itself is a record of it, for
it is still called Vicus Sceleratus, or the Street of Crime—
when the maddened Tullia, goaded on by the furies of her
sister and her husband, is said to have driven her chariot
over the body of her father, and to have brought home to her
household gods some of her parent's blood, with which the
chariot, and even her own person, had been sprinkled and
contaminated. But, through these offended gods, an end was
soon to follow of the reign thus wickedly begun. Servius
Tullius had ruled forty-four years in such a manner as to
render it difficult even for a good and moderate successor to
emulate his reign. His glory was further augmented by the
circumstance that with him perished all just and legitimate
kingly government. Yet some authors say that he had thoughts
of laying down even that mild and moderate command which
he exercised—namely, because it was vested in one person—
had not domestic crime cut him off whilst he was meditating
the liberation of his country.

REMARKS.—On the end of Servius Tullius Schwegler remarks:[1] "That Servius was hurled from his throne by the younger Tarquinius with the help of the Patricians, and that in this revolution he lost his life, may pass for historical. But all beyond this, all the detail with which this revolution is related, must be rejected as altogether uncertified; and the crimes of Tullia belong rather to poetical popular legends than to history. The name of Vicus Sceleratus, at least, proves nothing for the historical nature of the legend attached to it; as it is well known how often the Romans arbitrarily connected events with the names of places. The name of 'Accursed Street' (cf. Porta Sceleratu) might have had another origin, and bear some relation to that of the Vicus Cyprius adjoining, which signified just the contrary."[2] With a good deal of this we are inclined to agree. The more important revolutions in the early Roman state naturally attracted the attention of the people, became the frequent subjects of conversation, and hence by degrees were embellished with fictitious additions. In these early times, as we have often remarked, we must be content to take the general outline; though even in the guilt of Tullia and her husband there may be some foundation of truth; and their crimes have more probably been exaggerated than entirely invented.

"The reign of Servius Tullius," continues Schwegler, "lasted, according to the common tradition, a long while—namely, four and forty years. But this is impossible if the second Tarquin was, as the old tradition with remarkable agreement and consistency relates, the son of Tarquinius Priscus. In this case, in order to avoid the greatest absurdities, Servius Tullius can have reigned only for a very short period; and this is the more probable solution.[3] We do not mean to say by this that the tradition which represents Tarquinius Superbus as the son of Tarquinius Priscus is quite historical and certain; but at all events it is older and relatively more credible than the fictitious chronology of the Roman kings. It is remarkable that Laurentius Valla and Beaufort, as well as Dionysius, argue from the traditional chronology against the sonship of the younger Tarquin, though the opposite course was readier; namely, to question the thirty-eight years' reign of Tarquinius Priscus and the forty-four years of Servius Tullius."

[1] Buch xvi. § 15.   [2] Varr. Ling. Lat. v. 159.
[3] On these inconsistencies see, among modern authors, Bayle, Dict. art. Tanaquil; Beaufort, Dissertation, &c. p. 110, seq. 222, seq.

We also should feel inclined to argue from the chronology against the sonship of Tarquinius Superbus; because the Annales Maximi would undoubtedly have recorded the accession and death of Tarquinius Priscus and of Servius Tullius, while of the genealogy of the Tarquinian family they would have taken no cognizance. The probabilities of this genealogy we have discussed in another place, and shall not again enter upon the subject. We shall only remark that we cannot see, with Schwegler, any great "agreement and consistency" in a tradition which gives us the choice of two versions.

Sir G. C. Lewis remarks:[2] "Although the reign of Servius is two centuries after the foundation of Rome, it is yet more than 300 years before the time of Fabius, and a century and a half before the burning of the city by the Gauls. The events referred to it present no trace of contemporary registration, or of a narrative derived from the testimony of well-informed witnesses. The accounts of the census, as has been already observed, though taken, directly or indirectly, from official and authentic sources, cannot be considered as ascending to the time of Servius; nor indeed can we be satisfied that the date of the inscription relating to the federal festival of the Latin towns in the Temple of Diana on the Aventine was known with certainty. That a full contemporary account of the constitution of Servius, with statistical details of the assessment and obligations of the several classes, should have been preserved, and that all accurate memory of the other events of the reign should have perished, is in the highest degree improbable. With respect to the internal evidence for the narrative portion of the reign, it does not stand higher than that of the previous part of the regal period. The legend of the birth and infancy of Servius is made up of marvels: the former part is obviously a mere etymological mythus, intended to furnish an explanation of the name *Servius*. The legends which connect him with temples of Diana and Fortune have no claim to historical truth; and the final tragedy (which incidentally furnishes an origin for the name of the Vicus Sceleratus) breathes a lofty and poetical spirit, but can hardly be considered as a recital of real facts. The chronological inconsistencies pointed out by Dionysius show that the relations of Servius to the Tarquinian family could not have been as they are described to us, and stamp the whole story with a legendary character."

[1] See above, p. 234, sqq.   [2] Credibility, &c. ch. xi. § 31.

We shall not here inquire into the objections drawn from the magical epochs of Fabius and of the burning of the city, as we have already examined these points in the introductory dissertation on the sources of Roman history. We shall only observe that in a paragraph which occurs two pages afterwards,[1] Sir G. C. Lewis is forced to admit that there are sources which carry the tradition considerably higher up than Fabius. It is as follows: "A mention of the name of Servius Tullius can be traced (though not with entire certainty) in the Greek historian Timæus. Timæus died about 256 B.C.—that is to say, about 280 years after the time fixed for the death of Servius; and if his name was known to Timæus, this carries the tradition higher up than the account of any Roman historian. We know, from the testimony of Dionysius, that Timæus wrote on the early Roman history."

This paragraph is supplemented by the following note:—

"Pliny has these words: 'Servius rex primus signavit æs: antea rudi usos Romæ Timæus tradit.' (H. N. xxxiii. 13.) Elsewhere Pliny says: 'Servius rex ovium boumque effigie primus æs signavit' (xviii. 3). The former passage would, if strictly construed, imply that Timæus described the Romans as having used uncoined copper for money before the time of Servius. If so, he must have named Servius. It is, however, possible that Pliny found it stated in some Latin writer that Servius was the originator of coined money at Rome, and that Timæus only reported that the early Romans used uncoined copper; out of which two statements he formed the passage above cited."

This last remark has more the character of special pleading than the usually fair criticisms of Sir G. C. Lewis. But it will not serve the purpose for which it is intended. Pliny had no need of two authorities to make up his account. For, first, if he had found it stated in a Latin writer that Servius first coined money at Rome, and had adopted that statement, it followed as a matter of course that the previous money must have been uncoined; and he would have felt no necessity to refer to the authority of Timæus, or anybody else, to confirm so obvious a conclusion of common sense. Secondly, even if he had consulted Timæus on the subject, he would have taken nothing for his pains unless that author mentioned the name of Servius; for so vague a phrase as "the early Romans" would have proved nothing at all: whereas it is Pliny's

[1] P. 509.

purpose to denote the very reign in which coinage was introduced. Thirdly, Pliny would hardly have suppressed the name of the Latin writer from whom he derived his positive information, and have given that of an authority from whom he learnt nothing definite. Lastly, from the words of Pliny, not "as *strictly* construed," but as fairly and rightly construed, according to the ordinary idiom of the Latin tongue, *antea* can only mean "ante Servium."

It may be considered as certain, therefore, that Timæus mentioned in his history the reign of Servius; and, as he mentions it in connexion with the coinage, it is a highly probable inference that he also mentioned the census. And when it is considered that a cultivated people like the Cumæan Greeks had existed in Italy three centuries before the foundation of Rome, that the Tarquins were in communication with them, and that Timæus, a native of Tauromenium in Sicily, could hardly have failed to draw much of his information from their writers, we are justified in supposing that his work may have contained a good many particulars not only respecting Servius, but also respecting the other Roman kings.

Sir G. C. Lewis tells us that Timæus died about B.C. 256, and thus makes him 280 years posterior to Servius. But he does not tell us that he lived nearly a century, and died at the age of ninety-six;[1] having therefore probably been born about the year B.C. 352. This will fairly bring him, *as a writer*, at least half a century nearer to Servius; and if we admit the reduction of Roman civil years into astronomical, we may say that he flourished only about two centuries after Servius. And thus there must have been writers upon Roman history a century before the time of Fabius and the annalists, and there must have been sources from which they could draw their information.

The admission that the accounts of the census were taken from official sources is a strange contrast to the assertion in the preceding sentence, that the events of the reign of Servius "present no trace of contemporary registration;" for we have already shown that it would have been a moral impossibility to refer back the accounts of the census of the republican period, "by construction," to the reign of Servius. And when we find such a writer as Livy, who is anything but a stickler for the authenticity of the early history, stating without qualification, and as an undoubted fact, that the first consuls were created according to the Commentaries of Servius,

[1] Lucian, Macrobii 22.

it seems nothing but a hap-hazard conjecture to assert that there was then no contemporary registration. But it is plain that no sort of evidence whatever would satisfy Sir G. C. Lewis, since he will not believe the evidence as to the Servian Temple of Diana, though the particulars relating to it were engraved on a brazen column, and had been perused by Dionysius himself. With criticism like this it is impossible to reason, as it rejects the very best evidence that can possibly be afforded by antiquity. Such a critic might with equal justice reject in a lump the whole of Roman history, even that of the empire; for it is supported, for the most part, by nothing but the authority and good faith of the historian: and if the critic please to say, "This authority I do not accept," there remains nothing by which we can force his assent, by means of demonstration. It then becomes a question only of probability. But the common sense of mankind will revolt against so unreasonable a scepticism. Public buildings and temples like those of Diana and Fortune attributed to Servius are among the very best historical records. They are durable and unalterable, they carry their own story with them, they are known to the whole population from generation to generation, and cannot therefore, like written documents, be tampered with and misrepresented.

To consider it as improbable that the details of the Servian constitution should have been preserved while the general events of the reign have for the most part perished does not, we think, show any very just critical view of the matter. On the contrary, this is exactly what, *à priori*, we might have expected to happen. The accounts of the census were founded, as Sir G. C. Lewis admits, on official documents, which were more likely to be preserved than the scattered memorials of political transactions either at home or abroad. It is by the deficiency of such memorials, and not by their forgery or invention, that the history of the reign of Servius, like those of the other kings, has suffered. Letters, as Livy says, were rare at that period, and even of the literary documents which existed a great part perished in the Gallic conflagration; and thus we are unable to trace the connexion of events and their causes with that accuracy which is necessary to perfect history. The fabulous incidents which accompany the birth of Servius were doubtless the contemporary figments of a superstitious age, and are not likely to have been invented three centuries afterwards. There were doubtless many more events in the reign of Servius than what we find related in the historians; but there is no good reason for doubting the general truth of those that are mentioned: such as the manner in which Servius seized the crown, his war with the Etruscans, the establishment of his constitution, his enlargement of the city and completion of the walls, his establishment of the Latin League and building of the Temple of Diana, and his final overthrow through a conspiracy conducted by his successor. The details of that conspiracy, and of the murder of Servius, may very probably be exaggerated; but on the whole we can hardly agree in the verdict that they "breathe a lofty and poetical spirit." Tullia is too execrable a fury even for a tragic heroine, and the murder, with its circumstances, except the rank of the persons implicated, is one of those brutal deeds which we might expect to find in the annals of the Old Bailey.

SECTION X.

ACCESSION OF L. TARQUINIUS—LATIN COUNCIL—VOLSCIAN WAR.

L. TARQUINIUS now began to reign, who obtained the surname of Superbus, or the Proud, an appellation which is attributed to his having forbidden his father-in-law to be buried, giving out "that Romulus also perished without sepulture." He put to death the leaders of the Patricians whom he suspected of having favoured the cause of Servius; and feeling conscious that his own example of seizing the throne unlawfully might be used against himself, he surrounded his person with a body of armed men. For on force only could he rely in support of his domination; as he had obtained it neither by election of the people, nor authority of the Senate. Moreover, as he could not rely on the affections of the citizens, through fear alone could he hope to secure his reign. So, in order to strike terror into as many as possible, he took cognizance alone of all capital cases, without taking any counsel. And thus he was enabled to put to death, to banish, or to fine, not only those whom he hated or suspected, but also those against whom he had no other motive than the booty he might gain by confiscating their estates. Having by these means diminished the number of the Senate, he resolved to elect none into that body, in order that its fewness might render it contemptible, and that its members should be less indignant at not being consulted on public affairs. For he was the first king who departed from the method observed by the preceding ones of consulting the Senate on all public matters. His whole council, in ruling the state, was contained in his palace; he made peace and war, treaties and alliances, with whom he pleased, and broke them off in the same manner by himself alone, without asking the consent of the Senate or the people. And chiefly he took care to conciliate the Latins, in order that, through his power and influence abroad, he might be the safer among his subjects at home. He not only formed friendships, but family alliances also, with the chief men of that nation. Thus he gave his daughter in marriage to Octavius Mamilius, of Tusculum, who was far the foremost man among the Latins, and, if we are to believe report, descended from Ulysses and Circe. And, by means of this marriage, he conciliated to himself many of the relations and friends of Mamilius.

Tarquin had already acquired a great authority among the Latin chiefs, when he appointed them to meet on a fixed day at the grove of Ferentina, as he wished to confer with them on certain affairs which concerned their common interests. They accordingly met in great numbers early in the morning; while Tarquinius, though he kept the appointed day, did not appear till near sunset. During that wearisome day, as may be imagined, many and various were the discourses in the expectant council. Turnus Herdonius, of Aricia, inveighed fiercely against the absent Tarquin. "It was no wonder," he said, "that Tarquin had obtained the name of Superbus at Rome. (For he had already begun to be commonly so called, though the reproachful epithet was only secretly muttered.) What could be haughtier than thus to trifle with the whole Latin nation? Though the Latin chiefs had been brought a long way from their homes, yet he who had summoned the council did not make his appearance! It was done merely to try their patience, so that, if they put their necks under the yoke, he might oppress those obnoxious to him. For who did not perceive that he affected empire over the Latins? If his own subjects were inclined to trust him, or if, indeed, his power was intrusted rather than seized by a parricide, well and good; let the Latins also trust him, though this was no rule for them with regard to a foreigner. But if his own subjects were weary of him, one after another having either been killed, or banished, or robbed, what better hope remained for the Latins? If they would attend to him, he would recommend every one of them to return home, and pay no more attention to the council-day than he who had appointed it."

While this seditious and daring man, who had by like methods attained great power at home, was uttering these and similar invectives, Tarquin arrived, and put an end to his discourse. All turned away from him to salute the Roman king; who, when silence had been obtained, in compliance with the admonitions of those near him that he should excuse himself for having come so late, explained how, having undertaken to arbitrate between a father and son, he had been detained by the pains he had taken to reconcile them; and, as the day had been thus wasted, he would to-morrow bring before them what he had to propose. But not even this excuse was accepted in silence by Turnus, who is said to have exclaimed: "That nothing could be shorter than to decide between father and son; that such a matter might be settled in a few words; that if the son obeyed not his father, woe would betide him."

Having thus upbraided the Roman king, the Aricinian quitted the council. Tarquin took the matter more seriously than he seemed to do. He began at once to contrive the death of Turnus, in order that he might inspire the Latins with the same terror with which he had filled the minds of his own subjects. And, as he had not the power to put him to death openly, he effected his ruin by bringing against him a charge of which he was innocent. Through some Aricinians of an opposite faction, he bribed a slave of Turnus to allow a grea quantity of swords to be carried secretly into his lodgings. All this was done in a single night; and a little before daybreak, having summoned to his presence the chief Latins, Tarquin, as if agitated by a recent discovery, addressed them to the following effect:—"That his yesterday's delay, as if occasioned by the providence of the gods, had proved their safety as well as his own. He had been told that Turnus was meditating the murder of himself, and of the chiefs of the different peoples, that he might enjoy alone the empire over the Latins. That he would have attempted this the previous day during the council; but the stroke was postponed on account of the absence of the caller of the council, whose life it was that he chiefly sought. Hence the motive for the invectives on his absence, because the delay had frustrated his hopes. There could be no doubt, if he had been truly informed, that at the dawn of day, when the council assembled, Turnus would come armed, with a body of followers. It was said that a vast number of swords had been carried to his lodgings, and it might be at once discovered whether or not this was true. He therefore requested them to accompany him to the inn where Turnus lodged."

The ferocious disposition of Turnus, the speeches that he had made, and Tarquin's delay—as it seemed that the massacre might have been postponed on that account—all conspired to awake suspicion. They went, therefore, with minds prepared to believe the charge; not, however, unless it should be confirmed by the discovery of the swords. On arriving, Turnus was awakened, and guards placed over him; the slaves, who out of affection for their master were preparing a forcible resistance, were seized; and then swords were brought forth which had been hidden in all parts of the inn. At this discovery everything appeared plain; Turnus was cast into chains, and a council of the Latins was immediately summoned amidst great tumult. On the production of the swords, so violent was the hatred occasioned against Turnus, that, without hearing his defence, he was put to death in a new fashion, by being cast into the fountain of the Aqua Ferentina, a basket filled with stones being thrown over him.

Then Tarquin, having re-assembled the Latins in council, and eulogised those who had visited Turnus with a punishment befitting the manifest parricide which he had contemplated, addressed them as follows: "That it was in his power to act in pursuance of his ancient right; since, as all the Latins had sprung from Alba, they were included in the treaty in which, as made by Tullus, the whole of the Alban state, together with its colonies, had fallen under the Roman dominion. But, with a view to the good of all, he thought it better that that treaty should be renewed; so that the Latins should rather participate in and enjoy the prosperous fortune of the Roman people, than be always expecting or suffering the destruction of their towns and the devastation of their fields, as they had done, first in the reign of Ancus, and then in the reign of his own father (grandfather)." The Latins were persuaded without much difficulty, although the treaty gave the Romans the superiority. But the heads of the Latin nation seemed to side with and partake the opinion of Tarquin; and Turnus afforded to every one a recent example of the danger which he would incur by opposing the king. So the treaty was renewed; and the younger Latin men were directed that, agreeably to its tenor, they should assemble in arms, on a certain day, at the grove of Ferentina. They met, according to the edict of the Roman king, from all the Latin states; when Tarquin mingled all the maniples together, and thus confounded the Latins with the Romans, so that they should not have their own officers, nor any secret command or peculiar ensigns. And over the maniples, thus doubled, he set his own centurions.

Nor was Tarquin a bad commander in war, however unjust a king he may have been in civil matters. In this department he might have equalled his predecessors, had not his warlike glory been obscured by his degeneracy in other respects. He it was who began the war with the Volsci, which was to last more than two hundred years after his time; and he took by assault the Volscian town of Suessa Pometia. By the sale of the booty taken there he realized forty talents of silver and gold, which caused him to conceive

TARQUIN SUBJECTS THE LATINS. 389

the plan of a temple of Jove of that magnitude which should be worthy of the king of gods and men, of the Roman empire, and of the majesty of its situation; so he appropriated the money he had captured to the building of it.

REMARKS.—The critics have found little or nothing to object to that portion of the reign of the younger Tarquin contained in the preceding narrative. Schwegler remarks:[1] "The foreign policy of Tarquin had for its object the supremacy over Latium; and it may be considered as historical that he succeeded in converting what was hitherto a confederate relationship on equal terms into one of dependency. But the historians differ as to the means by which he accomplished this. Cicero says[2] that he subdued Latium by force of arms; while Livy (as we have seen) says that he compassed its subjection through his connexions with the nobles of the Latin cities. The last account is incomparably the more credible one. It is probable that he incited those different nobles to seize the absolute power in their respective cities, as he himself had done at Rome; that he aided them to do this; and then by means of these despots, who were obliged to look to him for support, he made the cities themselves obedient to him. Another circumstance which compelled the Latin states to seek the leadership of Rome and to subordinate themselves to her was, it appears, the onward pressure of the warlike Volsci: the same cause which again at a later period, in spite of the equal rights stipulated for both parties in the treaty made by Sp. Cassius, brought the Latins into virtual dependence on Rome.

"When Dionysius[3] ascribes to the younger Tarquin the institution of the Feriæ Latinæ, this is certainly an error. The festival is doubtless as old as the Latin League; since all the confederacies of ancient peoples were founded on a community of worship. That the origin of the festival reaches back into hoar antiquity is also seen from the remaining tradition, which ascribes it to King Faunus, or to Prisci Latini, or to a period immediately following the death of Latinus and Æneas.[4] But this part of the account of Dionysius may be true, that the younger Tarquin was the first Roman king who, as head of the League, performed the usual sacrifice."

It would have been difficult to dispute that Rome under the

[1] Buch xviii. § 12
[2] De Rep. ii. 24.
[3] Lib. iv. 49.
[4] Schol. Bob. in Cic. Planc. p. 256.

younger Tarquin obtained the practical headship of the Latin League. Such a consummation formed a natural sequel to the efforts of Servius Tullius in the same direction, and is confirmed by the treaty with Carthage made in the first year of the Republic, and recorded by Polybius,[1] in which Rome stipulates for the citizens of Laurentum, Ardea, Antium, Circeii, and other Latin cities subject to her (ὑπήκοοι). But the exact forms and limits of their dependence cannot be ascertained.

With the scanty notices which we have of these early times, we must, however, content ourselves with the bare fact of Tarquin having achieved this supremacy, without inquiring too minutely into the means which he used. We agree with Schwegler in thinking that Livy's account is the more probable one,—that he effected it by means of his alliances, and by the terror which he struck by the example of Turnus into those leaders who were opposed to him. It is possible, however, that he may have reduced some of the outlying Latin cities by arms. It is somewhat doubtful whether Suessa Pometia belonged to the Latins or the Volscians: Cicero seems to have held the former opinion by the way in which he relates its capture,—" Nam et omne Latium bello devicit, et Suessam Pometiam, urbem opulentam refertamque, cepit" (De Rep. ii. 24); and hence he may have been led to mention Tarquin as the conqueror of Latium. And that all the Latin cities were not reduced peaceably under his dominion may be seen from Livy's narrative of the siege of Gabii. That he accomplished his purpose by making the Latin princes tyrants like himself, is nothing but an unnecessary and improbable conjecture, made by Peter,[2] a German writer; nor is the supposition that the Volscians were then pressing on the Latins any better founded.

The assertion of Dionysius that the Feriæ Latinæ were founded by Tarquin is doubtless erroneous; and we may reject it with the less scruple, as that author gives a different account in another place.[3] Dionysius also gives more details than are found in Livy of the illegal and tyrannical proceedings of Tarquin, some of which may probably be true: as that he abolished the laws and constitution of Servius Tullius, and removed from the Forum and destroyed the brazen tablets on which his laws were engraved; that in place of the census he restored the old poll-tax; that to avoid the effects of the hatred thus occasioned he forbade all public meetings, even

[1] Lib. iii. 22.   [2] Gesch. Röm. i. 52.   [3] Lib. vi. 95.

those for sacrifices and festivals; and by means of spies discovered the discontented, and punished them severely, &c.¹

On the same events in the reign of Tarquin Sir G. C. Lewis observes:² "The story of the meeting of Latin deputies is sufficiently credible (with the exception perhaps of the contrivance by which they are persuaded to condemn their colleague, Turnus Herdonius); but it appears in the suspicious form of an introduction to the origin of the Feriæ Latinæ. The amicable arrangement, moreover, by which Tarquin establishes the ascendancy of Rome over Latium is quite inconsistent with the view of Cicero, who describes him as subduing the whole of Latium by force of arms."

However credible, therefore, may be the proceedings of Tarquin with the Latin League; however they may be corroborated by the tenor of the preceding history, and especially by the subsequent treaty with Carthage,—of which not a word is here said; yet Sir G. C. Lewis evidently regards the whole story, agreeably to his favourite hypothesis, as no better than an ætiological myth. But here that theory breaks down. For neither Livy nor Cicero says a word about this having been the origin of the Feriæ Latinæ; while Dionysius, the only author who does so, is evidently wrong. And the whole passage amounts to this: that Sir G. C. Lewis will accept from any author any assertion, however wrong and improbable, provided it can be used against a narrative which of itself, and except for this assertion, he considers to be credible. Whether this is a sound method of criticism we may leave the reader to determine. Of the discrepancy between Cicero and Livy we have already spoken.

But to proceed with the history.

THE SURRENDER OF GABII.

The next war which Tarquin undertook lasted longer than he had expected. It was with the neighbouring city of Gabii, which he had attempted to carry by a *coup de main*; and, as he had also been compelled to raise a regular siege, he determined to attack it by very un-Roman arts, by fraud and stratagem. Wherefore, pretending that he had laid aside all thoughts of war, and was intent only on founding his temple and other municipal works, he instructed his son Sextus, the youngest of three, to proceed to Gabii as a fugitive, and to

¹ Lib. iv. 13. ² Credibility, &c. vol. i. p. 522.

complain of the intolerable cruelty of his father. "That he
was now diverting his pride from strangers to his own family;
that he was weary of the number even of his children, and
was meditating to make at home the same solitude which he
had effected in the Senate, to leave no progeny, no heir to
his kingdom. He had escaped from the weapons of his
father, under the belief that he could find safety nowhere
else except among the enemies of L. Tarquinius. For let
them not be deceived; there was a war in store for them
which he pretended to have given up; and when he found
an opportunity he would attack them unawares. But if a
suppliant could find no shelter among them, he would wander
all over Latium; thence he would seek the Volsci, the Æqui,
and the Hernici, till he arrived among a people who had
humanity enough to protect children against the cruel and
impious persecutions of their fathers. And perhaps he might
find among them ardour enough to undertake a war against
the proudest of kings and the most ferocious of people."

The Gabines, when they saw how influenced with anger
Sextus was, kindly received him among them. They bade
him not wonder that Tarquin should at last show himself the
same to his children as he had been to his subjects and to his
allies: nay, if other materials were wanting, he would expend
his fury upon himself. They expressed a pleasure in welcoming
him, and doubted not that, with his aid, the war would soon
be transferred from the gates of Gabii to the walls of Rome.

Sextus was soon admitted into the public councils of the
Gabines: wherein he deferred in all matters to the opinion of
the elders, as having a better knowledge of them than himself; except that he was always an advocate for war, and in
this department assumed to himself a leading part, as having
a knowledge of the forces on both sides, and being aware how
hateful was the king's pride, which even his own children
could not endure, to the citizens of Roma. Thus by degrees
he incited the chief men of Gabii to renew the war; he himself at the head of the boldest youths made predatory incursions; and, contriving everything he said and did for the
purpose of deception, so imposed upon the Gabines that they

gave him the supreme command in the war. The mass of the people had no conception of his plans; and as in several trifling actions between the Romans and Gabines the latter were for the most part superior, both high and low began to think that S. Tarquinius had been sent them as a leader by a special providence of the gods. And such was the affection which he acquired among the soldiers by sharing their dangers and labours, and by munificently dividing the booty, that Tarquinius the father was not more powerful at Rome than his son at Gabii.

At length, therefore, when he thought that he had acquired strength enough for anything he might attempt, he sent one of his people to Rome to ask his father what he wished him to do, as the gods had favoured his endeavours, so that he had become the most powerful man at Gabii. Tarquin, mistrusting perhaps the messenger, gave him no verbal answer; but passing into the garden attached to his house, whither the messenger followed, and walking up and down in silence, as if in deliberation, he is said to have struck off with his stick the tallest poppy-heads. At length the messenger, weary of asking and receiving no reply, returned to Gabii, as if his mission had been a failure. Here he related what he had said and what he had seen; that the king, either from anger or hatred, or the natural pride of his temper, had not uttered a single word. But Sextus understood the wish of his father, and the command conveyed in that roundabout and silent manner. So he contrived the death of the leading men of the city; some of whom were despatched through the opportunity afforded by the hatred felt towards them, whilst others he incriminated before the people. Thus many were publicly executed; whilst others, against whom no specious charge could be brought, were privately murdered. Some were allowed to expatriate themselves; others were driven into exile: and the estates both of the banished and the slain were alike divided. Thus the sense of the public misfortune was blunted by the sweets of bribery and booty and private advantage; till at length the Gabine state, being thus deprived of all counsel and help, fell an easy prey into the hands of the Roman king.

REMARKS.—On the preceding narrative Schwegler observes: "Tarquin founded in Gabii an hereditary collateral principality for one of his younger sons, just as the elder Tarquin had done before at Collatia. This account appears to be quite worthy of credit, especially as other indications show that Gabii stood, in very ancient times, in near relationship to Rome. On the other hand, the manner in which Tarquinius is related to have got possession of the city is a complete fable. For in the Temple of Sancus at Rome there still existed in the time of Dionysius the treaty which Tarquin then concluded with the Gabines. Over a wooden shield was drawn the hide of the ox which had been sacrificed at the solemn conclusion of the treaty; and on the hide were written the conditions of the treaty in very ancient characters. Gabii, therefore, came under subjection to Tarquin not, as the tradition represents, by treachery and conquest, but through a formal treaty and an alliance concluded with the assistance of Fetiales, the document of which was deposited in a temple. With enemies who had been forced to surrender unconditionally after a long and obstinate contest no such treaty, according to all ideas of ancient international law, would have been concluded. It can be the less doubtful that the common tradition about the subjection of Gabii is falsified, as the remaining portions of it are manifest inventions,—that is, plagiarisms. The stratagem of Sextus Tarquinius is that of Zopyrus against Babylon; and the counsel which Tarquinius gives his son by cutting off the heads of the poppies, is the answer of the tyrant Thrasybulus to the tyrant Periander."[1]

On the same subject Sir G. C. Lewis remarks: "The inscription which recorded the treaty between Rome and Gabii, still extant in the time of Dionysius, was doubtless ancient; but whether it named Tarquin, or contained within itself any indication of its date, is uncertain."[2] And again: "The entire account of the reduction of Gabii is improbable, with the borrowed stories of Sextus Tarquinius's self-inflicted punishment and the decapitation of the poppies; nor can the treaty described by Dionysius be reconciled with the fraudulent and forcible means used by Tarquin for its acquisition, or with the subsequent appointment of his son as king of the town."[3] These views are further supported by the following

[1] Herod. iii. 154, v. 92; Polyæn. vii. 12; Aristot. Polit. iii. 8, 3; v. 8, 7, &c.
[2] Credibility, &c. i. p. 521. [3] Ibid. p. 522, sq

quotation from Niebuhr: "It is quite impossible that Gabii should have fallen into the hands of the Roman king by treachery. Had such been the case, no one—I will not say no tyrant, but no sovereign in antiquity—would have granted the Roman franchise to the Gabines, and have spared them all chastisement by the scourge of war.... The very existence of a treaty, though reconcilable with the case of a surrender, puts the forcible occupation out of the question."[1]

The grounds on which Schwegler infers a near connexion between Rome and Gabii in very ancient times are, first, the following passage in Varro: "Ut nostri Augures publici disserunt, agrorum sunt genera quinque, Romanus, Gabinus, Peregrinus, Hosticus, Incertus. Romanus dictus, unde Roma, a Romulo. Gabinus ab oppido Gabia. Peregrinus ager pacatus, qui extra Romanum et Gabinum, quod uno modo in his secuntur auspicia. Dictus peregrinus, a pergendo, id est a progrediendo; eo enim ex agro Romano primum progrediebantur. Quocirca Gabinus quoque peregrinus, sed quod auspicia habet singularia, ab reliquo discretus. Hosticus dictus ab hostibus. Incertus id ager, qui de his quatuor qui sit, ignoratur."[2]

The second inference is drawn from the mode of dress called the *Cinctus Gabinus*, adopted by the Romans.

The main proof of the Roman connexion with Gabii is the treaty. There can be no reasonable doubt about the existence of this treaty. Dionysius mentions it as extant in his time in the Temple of Sancus; and as he describes not only the substance and form of the materials on which it was written, but also the archaic character of the letters,[3] he must have seen it with his own eyes. The existence of the treaty is also confirmed by Horace, as well as the fact that it was made *during the time of the kings*, and Tarquinius Superbus was the last of them:

Fœdera regum
Vel Gabiis vel cum rigida æquata Sabinis."

Sir G. C. Lewis's objection, therefore, that it is uncertain whether the treaty "named Tarquin, or contained within itself any indication of its date," is nothing but a captious and unreasonable scepticism; especially as the possibility of such treaties at the

[1] Hist. vol. i. p. 512.   [2] Ling. Lat. v. 33.
[3] γράμμασιν ἀρχαϊκοῖς ἐπιγεγραμμένη, iv. 58.   [4] Epp. ii. 1, 23.

period in question is confirmed by that already mentioned between Rome and Carthage in the first year of the Republic; the terms of which are given by Polybius, and which no fair criticism can succeed in explaining away.

Neither is there any force in the same writer's objection, though supported by the authority of Niebuhr, that, if the Gabines had been reduced by force or fraud, no treaty would have been granted to them, nor would they have been admitted to Roman citizenship. For that treaties were accorded to the conquered we learn from Livy: "Esse autem tria genera fœderum.... Unum quum bello victis dicerentur leges," &c.[1] And the assertion of Niebuhr, that no sovereign in antiquity would have granted the Roman franchise to the Gabines, and have spared them all chastisement of the scourge of war, is so flatly contradicted, as the reader will have already seen, by the whole tenor of the history under the Kings, and is so diametrically opposed to a fundamental principle of Roman policy, that, had we not known the source from which it proceeds, we should have ascribed it rather to a mere tyro than to a great and profound historian.

Under these circumstances, the fact of the connexion of Gabii with Rome needs not any collateral support that may be drawn from the passage in Varro quoted by Schwegler, or the inference from the Gabine cincture. By the last method, indeed, we might as readily prove a close political connexion between London and Paris, because Londoners sometimes wear French gloves or hats. The circumstance that the Ager Gabinus is mentioned with the Roman as a distinct field of augury is more to the purpose, if we could be quite certain of Varro's meaning in the word *singularia*; for he may mean either separate and distinct, or of a peculiar kind. But in either case we do not see how the passage can be made to support an inference of Schwegler's, after Müller,[2] that the Romans received from Gabii their augural rites; founded apparently on an obscure tradition that Romulus and Remus were educated there.

The fact of a connexion between Rome and Gabii in the time of King Tarquin the Proud being thus established on the best possible evidence in a matter of such high antiquity, the manner in which it was effected is of less importance, or whether the historians in relating it have added embellishments of their own. These historians are considered to have been very ingenious inventors,

[1] Lib. xxxiv. 57.   [2] Schwegler, B. i. S. 399; Müller, Etr. ii. 121.

and capable—for instance, as in the case of Horatius—of interweaving some half-dozen monuments of the most different sorts into one connected story; yet here they appear only as stupid and barefaced plagiarists. The ground on which such accusations are founded is that it is impossible for an event ever to have repeated itself; and that therefore the second story must necessarily be a fiction. But even if no precedent can be found for a story, it is equally liable to be condemned. Thus, for instance, Sir G. C. Lewis rejects the account of the manner in which Tarquin effected the destruction of Turnus Herdonius, though it is not pretended that it has a prototype. However, all that we are contending for on behalf of this early history is the truth of the main outlines; the reality of the kings, their order of succession, and the historical nature of the principal events of their reigns. That some of the details have been now and then amplified or embellished is very possible; even modern history may not always be free from a charge like this; but it affords no ground for condemning the entire narrative in a mass.

The history then proceeds as follows.

PEACE WITH THE ÆQUI AND TUSCANS — BUILDING OF THE CAPITOLINE TEMPLE, ETC. — COLONIES OF CIRCEII AND SIGNIA.

Gabii having been thus reduced, Tarquin concluded a peace with the Æqui, and renewed the treaty with the Tuscans. Then he turned his attention to the affairs of the city; wherein his first care was to erect on Mons Tarpeius a temple of Jupiter, that might be to posterity a monument of his reign and his name; and that it might be remembered as the work of the two Tarquins,—vowed by the father and accomplished by the son (grandson). And that the whole area set apart to Jove, as well as the temple that was to be built, might be consecrated solely to him, and freed from the worship of other deities, he resolved to exaugurate some fanes and chapels which had been vowed by King Tatius during his struggle with Romulus, and had afterwards been there consecrated and inaugurated. It is related that, at the very commencement of the undertaking, the divine will of the gods inclined them to indicate the future strength of the empire. For the auguries were favourable to the exauguration of all the other fanes except that of Terminus; an omen and augury which was interpreted to mean that Terminus not having been removed from his place, and he alone of all the gods not having been evoked from his consecrated boundaries, portended the firmness and stability of the Roman state. After the acceptance of this augury of perpetuity, another prodigy followed, portending the magnitude of the empire. Those who were digging the foundations of the temple are said to have found a human head with the face perfect; an apparition which unambiguously portended that this spot would be the citadel of empire and the head of affairs: an interpretation given not only by the soothsayers who were in the city, but also by those who had been sent for from Etruria to consult about the omen. By these prodigies the king's mind was incited to spare no expense; and hence the spoils taken at Pometia, which had been set apart to complete the whole building, hardly sufficed to lay the foundations of it. This it is that inclines me to believe Fabius rather than Piso—besides that Fabius is the older author—who writes that only forty talents had been appropriated to the work; while Piso says that it was 40,000 pounds' weight of silver; a sum of money which could not be expected from the spoils of one city, such as cities then were, and which would surely have been more than enough for the foundations even of so magnificent a work as this.

Tarquin being thus intent upon finishing the temple, not only sent for workmen from all parts of Etruria, whom he paid with the public money, but also compelled the plebeians to labour at it. These were also liable in addition to military duties; yet they were less annoyed at being compelled to build with their own hands the temples of the gods than at their labour being afterwards transferred to works of less magnificence, yet more laborious; as the making of *fori* in the Circus, and excavating the Cloaca Maxima, the receptacle of all the sewage of the city: which two works are hardly

EXTENT OF TARQUIN'S EMPIRE.   399

equalled in magnificence by those of the present day. But, though Tarquin kept the people employed at these works, there was still a superfluous multitude that he could not use, and who seemed to be only a burthen. He determined, therefore, to employ them in extending the boundaries of the empire, and sent them as colonists to Signia and Circeii, where, as frontier garrisons, they might serve to protect Rome both by land and sea.

REMARKS.—The account of Tarquin having reduced to subjection the whole of Latium is corroborated by the facts of his having founded the colonies of Signia and Circeii; one of which lies a good way inland in that country, while the other, Circeii, is almost at the southern extremity of its coast, if considered as bounded by the Volscians. A further corroboration are his wars with the Æqui and Volsci, nations that dwelt on the frontiers of Latium, and with whom he could have had no concern, had not Latium been previously reduced. These wars are merely hinted at by the historians; that indeed with the Æqui can only be inferred from Livy's mentioning the peace that Tarquin made with them,—a proof how meagre were the accounts of these early times that had been preserved.

On this subject Schwegler observes:[1] "Respecting the extension of Tarquin's dominion we possess a remarkable archival document in the commercial treaty concluded between Rome and Carthage in the first year of the Republic, under the consulship of Junius Brutus and Marcus Horatius. The conditions of the treaty were as follows: The Romans and their confederates were not to sail, south or east, beyond the Pulcrum Promontorium,[2] except compelled by weather or enemies; and in this case to make only the most necessary purchases, and depart after a stay of not more than five days. But to the west of that promontory they might traffic freely, in Africa, Sardinia, and that part of Sicily subject to the Carthaginians. The Carthaginians, on the other hand, pledge themselves to abstain from injuring the people of Ardea, Antium, Laurentum, Circeii, Terracina, and the rest of the Latins, so far as they may be subject to the Romans; and if any of the Latins were not so subject, to refrain from attacking their cities; or if they

[1] Buch xviii. § 13.   [2] Now Cape Farina in Africa.

should conquer one of them, to deliver it over unharmed to the Romans; and lastly, not to erect any fortresses in Latium. Under these conditions there shall be friendship between the Romans and Carthaginians, including their allies on both sides.

"This document, the genuineness of which cannot be justly doubted, throws an unexpected light on the relations of Rome at that time; but which, it must be allowed, is not favourable to the traditional history.

"For, first, Rome appears in it as the political head of Latium, as it publicly stipulates in the name of the whole Latin people; and then as mistress of the coast from Ostia to Terracina. That she was the head of Latium we know from the common tradition, but not that she was mistress of the coast. Circeii, indeed, is named by the historians as a colony founded by the younger Tarquin; and the fortifying of so distant a point leads to an inference of the extent, as well as the maritime importance, of the Tarquinian kingdom. But when the treaty names also Ardea, Antium, Terracina, Laurentum, as cities subject to Rome, the common tradition knows nothing of this. Ardea, especially, according to this tradition, is being besieged by Tarquin when the revolution breaks out in Rome: on which the Republic, it is said, abandons the siege, and concludes a fifteen years' armistice with the city; which consequently is all a fiction. And Antium is enumerated by Dionysius among the Volscian peoples who take part in the Temple of Jupiter Latiaris founded by Tarquin: while according to the treaty Antium at that time was not a Volscian but a Latin city; not a free member of the Latin League, but subject to Rome. In short, the treaty gives us quite a different idea of the extent and power of the Tarquinian kingdom from the common tradition; it shows what a splendid legacy the young Republic had received from the monarchy, but very quickly lost.

"Further, we see from the commercial treaty in question that the Romans under the last kings had a very extensive maritime commerce. But of this also the common tradition says not a word: we could never have guessed from it that two centuries and a half before the First Punic War Roman merchant vessels visited Africa and Sicily. In the first two centuries of the Republic, at least, we find no traces of maritime commerce. It cannot be doubted that this reverse is connected with the overthrow of the Tarquinian dynasty. The maritime commerce pursued by the Romans under the Tarquins was closely connected with the spirit and the civilization of that period: it paved the way for that Grecian influence which appears very prominently at that epoch; it promoted that spirit of enlightenment, of religious and political innovation, which characterises the times of the last three kings. But, for the same reasons, it accorded ill with the spirit and the reactionary policy of the ruling families which succeeded in the place of the monarchy; and we may conjecture that the ruling order industriously endeavoured to limit it, and to bring the old agricultural system again exclusively into vogue."

The above criticism is not remarkable for vigour and consistency; and indeed the last sentences go a great way to overthrow all that has been said before.

Schwegler admits the genuineness of the Carthaginian treaty, and that it throws an unexpected light on the relations of Rome at that time, but asserts that it is not favourable to the traditional history. But if we examine what is meant here by "the traditional history," we find that it is only some passages in Dionysius which are not found in the Latin authors. It is acknowledged that the common tradition represents Rome as at that time the head of Latium; and in this, which is the main circumstance, it is in perfect accord with the treaty. Then it is objected that tradition does not represent her as mistress of the coast. But if she was the head of Latium, would not that include the coast of Latium? And does not Schwegler almost entirely demolish his own argument when he admits that the fortifying of so distant a point as Circeii argues a kingdom of maritime importance?

Objections like these spring from the unreasonable expectation of finding all the details of the history of these early times worked out with the same minuteness and accuracy as in recent history. We must be content if we find the great leading outlines confirmed, which in this case they are, by a formal and authentic document.

Ardea was doubtless being besieged at the time of the expulsion of the kings; we learn this from Livy as well as Dionysius: but the account of the fifteen years' truce, which, if true, would have excluded it from being mentioned in the treaty, is found only in Dionysius;[1] and therefore if, as it would appear, this is "all a fiction," Dionysius must bear the blame of being the author of it. We can only conclude that, if Ardea was not actually captured,

[1] Lib. iv. 85.

there must have been a treaty with Rome instead of a truce. In a note, however, Schwegler admits that Florus[1] and Orosius[2] mention Ardea among the towns of Latium captured by Tarquin: yet he arbitrarily rejects their account as inaccurate, though it is collaterally confirmed by the treaty, and prefers to it that of Dionysius, hardly a better authority, though at variance with the treaty. It is easy to see the motive for this perverse criticism; the account of Dionysius lends a handle to impugn the history.

Still more captious and uncritical are Schwegler's remarks about Antium. That city, as Niebuhr and others have shown,[3] did not fall into the hands of the Volscians till long after this period; and Dionysius, therefore, is mistaken in representing it as a Volscian city in the time of Tarquin. And indeed it is manifest that, if Tarquin had extended his rule to Circeii and Terracina, Antium, which lies midway between Circeii and Rome, could hardly have been Volscian.

We cannot, therefore, agree with Schwegler's conclusion, that the treaty gives us quite a different idea of the extent and power of the Tarquinian kingdom from the common tradition: on the contrary, we think that the treaty very strongly corroborates the tradition; adding to it at the same time a few facts and inferences which the necessary meagreness of the tradition had not supplied.

Among these additions by far the most important and valuable is the fact that Rome must have then enjoyed an extensive maritime commerce. And Schwegler allows that[4] "We know from other sources that the rest of the towns mentioned in the treaty enjoyed a maritime commerce at a very early period. Aricia had, according to Dionysius (vii. 6), numerous merchant vessels; and its connexion with Cumæ leads to the inference that it was more specially engaged in trade with the cities of Magna Græcia. Ardea had connexions with Sicily and Saguntum, which it is said to have partly colonized (Liv. xxi. 7); and its great wealth (Liv. i. 57, Dionys. iv. 64) was derived probably from its commerce. Antium exercised piracy in conjunction with the Tyrrhenians (Strab. v. 3, 5); and its galleys and navigation are mentioned on the occasion of the subsequent reduction of the town" (B.C. 335).

From these facts we are justified in making a still wider induc-

---

[1] Lib. i. 75. [2] Lib. ii. 4.
[3] See Mr. Bunbury's article *Antium*, in Smith's Dict. of Anc. Geography.
[4] S. 792. Anm.

tion. It is impossible that a people who enjoyed so extensive a commerce as is shown by the irrefragable evidence of this treaty could have been so semi-barbarous and illiterate as it pleases the sceptical critics to represent them. Maritime commerce is a late product of civilization, and contributes still further to extend it. It implies at least a knowledge of writing and arithmetic; and the Romans therefore could not have been still without the exercise of those useful arts in the time of Tarquin, except for a few monumental purposes, as inscriptions on public buildings, treaties, and so forth, as Schwegler thinks fit to assert.[1]

Further, a commerce so extensive as that indicated by the treaty in question could not have been the product of a few years, but of at least a century or two. And the first developement of it may be traced, as we have already remarked, to the foundation of Ostia by Ancus Marcius. This carries us up to a century or so from the foundation of Rome. But how improbable the opinion that a people of this sort, that had executed the great public works then extant at Rome, should have forgotten, or left unrecorded, all the particulars of its history!

We agree with Schwegler in thinking that Rome owed a great deal to her kings, and especially to the last three kings. And though the last Tarquin may have been a tyrant, he was, like Borgia, no bad political ruler. The regal period at Rome was a period of much more enlightenment and civilization than the century or two which followed its termination. This comparative decay is indicated by the loss of her maritime commerce, of her dominion over Latium, and by the little improvement that took place in the city itself; which forms a strong contrast to the magnificent works of the Tarquins. With the exception, perhaps, of the Temple of Juno Moneta, there were no public works undertaken at Rome before the censorship of Appius Claudius Cæcus, in B.C. 312, which can for an instant be compared to the Capitoline Temple, the Cloaca Maxima, and the Circus; or even perhaps to the Curia of Tullus Hostilius. It is for the historian of the early Republic to trace the causes of this retrograde movement. A few of them are obvious enough; as the war waged against Rome by Tarquin with the aid of Porsena, and the capture of the city by the Gauls. It may also have been partly owing, as Schwegler suggests, to the reactionary spirit of the great families, their ambition and mutual

[1] R. I. 8 36.

jealousies, and their contempt for and hatred of the higher class of plebeians, who had enriched themselves by commerce. After the expulsion of the kings, these feelings had full scope for their display, without let or hindrance.

With regard to the works constructed by the Tarquins Schwegler remarks :[1] "The Capitoline Temple stands at the head of them. As in most of the undertakings of the Tarquinian epoch, tradition assigns a share in this building to both the Tarquins ; ascribing to the father the laying of the foundation and preparation of the ground, to the son the completion of the building. If we consider the magnitude of the undertaking and the extent of the necessary substructions, it must at all events appear probable that so enormous a structure was the work of several generations ; if even the reign of Servius Tullius did not stand between, during which no progress was made. Hence we see that the old tradition ascribes the building merely to the Tarquins, with whose names and endeavours it is so intimately associated, without more accurately distinguishing between father and son.

"The prodigies which are said to have presented themselves during the building of the temple show how much importance tradition, even at an early period, ascribed to it. In explanation of them we may remark what follows. The finding of the human head is an etymological myth derived from the name of the hill. This name *Capitolium*—that is, *Capitulum*—signifies simply a hill-top, which forms the head (that is, the citadel) of the town (*caput urbis*). The interpretation of this prodigy by the future Roman empire of the world appears to be ancient ; perhaps the Sibylline oracles, which contained such prophecies of future universal dominion, gave occasion to it. The second prodigy, the refusal of Terminus to remove from his place, is an etiological myth. In the cell of Jupiter was a stone resembling a boundary stone ; probably the original symbol of the god as Jupiter Lapis. Later generations saw in this stone a Terminus ; and thus arose the tradition that Terminus, in consequence of his refusal to give place to Jupiter, was enclosed in his cell. To this Terminus the later tradition referred the opening in the roof of the cell of Jupiter ; for sacrifices to Terminus were to be performed in the open air.[2] But this would seem to be a mistake. The reason for this opening in the roof is doubtless to be found in the very being of Jupiter, as god of heaven.

---

[1] Buch xviii. § 14.   [2] Serv. Æn. ix. 448 ; Lact. Inst. i. 29, 40.

Besides Terminus, Juventas is also sometimes named as a deity that would not give place for the Capitoline Temple; but this tradition is evidently an allegory. It is also of later origin; the worship of Juventas having been first introduced into the religion of the Romans through the Sibylline books. Thus, according to Livy (xxi. 62), a lectisternium was prepared for Juventas (Hebe) in the year, 536, according to the Sibylline books, in connexion with a procession to the Temple of Hercules, to whom, according to the religious belief of the Greeks, Hebe was married."

It can hardly be said that tradition does not distinguish between father and son, or rather grandson, when it plainly tells us that the temple was vowed and the area for its foundation prepared by the elder Tarquin, and that the building was completed, or very nearly so, by the younger Tarquin. The exact steps in the process it is impossible now to trace; nor is it necessary to do so, as there cannot be a reasonable doubt that the main facts of the tradition are true.

We abandon all the prodigies connected with the temple, and we believe that Schwegler has properly explained the etymology of the word Capitolium. We think, however, that there was really a stone representing the god Terminus, and not Jupiter Lapis, within the precincts of the temple. Our reason for thinking so is that Ovid, who lived within five minutes' walk of the temple, describes it as existing in his time:

> "Terminus, ut veteres memorant, inventus in æde
> Restitit, et magno cum Jove templa tenet.
> Nunc quoque, se supra ne quid nisi sidera cernat,
> Exiguum templi tecta foramen habent.
> Termine, post illud, levitas tibi libera non est;
> Qua positus fueris in statione, mane."[1]

Now Ovid was more likely to know than anybody at the present time can be whether the stone in Jupiter's cell was meant for that deity or for Terminus; and it is more probable that the "mistake" lies on the side of Schwegler than on his. How Terminus got there, and whether it was an augural trick, is another question; we are only concerned for the fact. But even on this point the "old tradition" is consistent with itself; for we have already seen [2] that a shrine had been dedicated to Terminus by King Tatius. That there was also an aperture in the roof of Dius Fidius,[3] or Sancus, proves nothing. Jupiter, under this form or appellation,

[1] Fast. ii. 667, seqq.   [2] Above, p. 160.   [3] Varr. Ling. Lat. v. 66.

was peculiarly appealed to by the Romans in their oaths—which were to be taken in the open air—as we see by the common exclamation, "medius fidius." But this concerns not the Capitoline Jupiter, nor excludes the necessity for an aperture in the Capitoline Temple for the sake of Terminus, who was also to be worshipped in the open air.[1] And the passage of Ovid shows, by the way, that the Temple of Jupiter on the Capitol was not hypæthral. Into the question about Juventas we need not enter.

The Capitoline Temple is not only in itself the most striking and authentic monument and record of the Tarquinian dynasty, but it also affords collateral proof of the existence of the other kings. For in front of it stood their statues, and in the midst of them that of Junius Brutus, who expelled them. It is certain that these statues existed there before the time of the empire: for it was among them that Gracchus was slain;[2] and Julius Cæsar caused his own statue to be placed amidst them,—an act which, among others, naturally created a suspicion that he was aiming at the regal power.[3] The hatred entertained during the republican times of Rome against the very name of king is so notorious that it is impossible to suppose that their statues could have been erected by republican hands; and the only inference is that they must have been set up by the last Tarquin when he completed the Capitol. This inference is confirmed by the testimony of Pliny; who regarded them as genuine relics of antiquity, since he appeals to them as a text respecting the ancient custom of wearing rings, and observes that only the statues of Numa and Servius Tullius had rings, and that they were on the third finger, or that next to the little finger.[4] Now it is incredible that, even had there been no written records in those times, the memory of preceding kings should have perished in about two centuries from the establishment of the monarchy, or that even Tarquinius Priscus, who obtained the throne not much more than a century after that event, should

---

[1] "Terminus, quo loco colebatur, super eum foramen patebat in tecto, quod nefas esse putarent Terminum intra tectum consistere."—Paul. Diac. p. 368, Terminus. [2] Appian, B. C. I. 16.

[3] Suet. Cæs. 76, 80; Dio Cass. xliii. 45.

[4] "Nullum (annulum) habet Romuli in Capitolio statua, nec præter Numæ Serviique Tullii alia, ac ne Lucii quidem Bruti. Hoc in Tarquiniis maxime miror, quorum a Græcia fuit origo," &c.—H. N. xxxiii. t. 2. "Singulis primo digitis geri mos fuerat, qui sunt minimis proximi: sic in Numæ et Servii Tullii statuis videmus."—Ibid. 6, 6; cf. xxxiv. 11, 13.

not have introduced civilization enough to preserve a record of his
predecessors. And though the statues of the earlier kings were
most probably executed from imagination, or some faint traditions
of their personal appearance, yet that does not invalidate the
inference which we propose to draw from them; namely, that the
kings were real and not fictitious personages, and that they bore the
names which history ascribes to them.

Schwegler then proceeds to examine the question of the site
of the Capitoline Temple, and, with most German scholars, places
it on the Monte Caprino, or south-western summit of the hill.
We are happy to say that the reasons we have given in other works [1]
for thinking that it could not have been on that summit appear to
be confirmed by very recent excavations in the garden of the
Palazzo Caffarelli; the remains there discovered being quite at
variance with what we are told of the Capitoline Temple.[2] But
we need not enter into this merely topographical question; and for
the same reason we abstain from noticing what Schwegler says
about the Cloaca Maxima.

According to Dionysius and other authors,[3] it was in the time of
the younger Tarquin that the Cumæan Sibyl came to Rome, and
sold to that king the famous oracles afterwards known as the
Sibylline books; though some authorities place this event in the
reign of Tarquinius Priscus. It is not mentioned by Livy; though
he recognises afterwards the existence of these prophecies. The
tradition that they were introduced in the reign of the younger
Tarquin is not improbable, from the connexion which that king
had with Cumæ; whatever we may think of the mode in which
the purchase of them is described. We have already touched
briefly upon this subject, and add the remarks of Schwegler:[4]—

"The Roman Sibylline oracles were of Greek origin, and composed
in the Greek language. This appears from the circumstance
that to the duumvirs to whom they were intrusted were also
assigned two Greek interpreters;[5] that the prevailing tradition
assumes that they were brought to Rome from Cumæ; that when
the books were destroyed by the burning of the Capitoline Temple,

[1] See the article on Rome in Dr. Smith's Dict. of Anc. Geography, vol. ii.
p. 761, seqq.; and the Hist. of the City of Rome, p. 384, seqq.
[2] See Reumont, Gesch. der Stadt Rom. § 65, and Anm. § 800.
[3] Dionys. iv. 62; Plin. H. N. xiii. 27, § 83; xxxiv. 11, § 22; Gell. i. 19;
Solin. ii. 16, seqq.; Serv. Æn. vi. 72, seqq.
[4] Buch xviii. § 16.   [5] Zonar. vii. 11.

envoys were despatched to Greek cities in order to find materials for their restoration;[1] that the gods and worships which play the chief part in them belong to the Greek religion, and are unknown in that of Rome; lastly, that the Romans themselves regarded the religious observances and worships connected with the Sibylline books as a Greek portion of their religion. ('Et nos dicimus xvi viros'—for consulting the books—'Græco ritu sacra, non Romano facere,' Varr. L. L. vii. 88, with Müller's note.) Moreover the Sibylline oracles were in hexameters:

"'Te duce Romanos nunquam frustrata Sibylla
Abdita quæ senis fata canit pedibus;'[2]

not therefore, as might have been expected if they were of home growth, composed in the Saturnian metre. If all these indications leave no doubt of the Greek origin of the Roman Sibylline verses, the acceptance of them in Rome, and the authority which they acquired there, are a significant indication of that favourable spirit in which the Hellenistic culture and religion were regarded in the Tarquinian epoch; and all the more remarkable, as the earliest religion of the Romans otherwise betrays a spirit of rigid exclusiveness towards foreign religions.

"That the Sibylline verses were brought to Rome from Cumæ is almost the unanimous Roman tradition, and can in no respect be doubted. This circumstance is a proof of the lively intellectual commerce which was maintained between Rome and Cumæ under the Tarquinian dynasty.

"The Sibylline books exercised a considerable influence on the Roman religion. They introduced into it a number of foreign, and for the most part Greek, worships: as the worship of Apollo, to whom, in consequence of a great pestilence, the first temple was dedicated in the year 321; that of Latona, for whom, in conjunction with Apollo, Artemis, and other Greek deities, a lectisternium was prepared, in consequence of the epidemic of the year 355; the worship of Æsculapius, who was brought from Epidaurus in the year 463, to avert a pestilence which had lasted several years; the worship of Hebe (Juventas), to whom a lectisternium was decreed in 536; lastly—to pass over originally national deities, as Venus, Ceres, and Salus—the worship of the Idæan mother, who, by

---

[1] Tac. Ann. vi. 12; Dionys. iv. 62; Lact. Inst. I. 6, 14.
[2] Tibull. ii. 5, 10.

command of the Sibylline oracles, was brought from Pessinus in
Phrygia in the year 549. The Sibylline books were the occasion
and chief source of the syncretic blending of the Roman religion
with the Greek."

To these remarks we have nothing to object.

We now approach the catastrophe which led to the downfall of
Tarquin and the monarchy.

MISSION TO DELPHI—L. JUNIUS BRUTUS—DEATH OF LUCRETIA—EXPULSION OF THE TARQUINS.

While Tarquin was intent upon the affairs before related, a
terrible portent presented itself. A snake, gliding forth from
a wooden column, caused great alarm and a rush into the
palace; and though the king himself was not struck with
any sudden terror at the sight, yet it filled his breast with
anxious forebodings for the future. Wherefore, as in the
interpretation of public prodigies Etruscan soothsayers only
were employed, he determined, on the occasion of this domestic
one, to send to Delphi to consult the oracle, the most renowned
one in the world. And being unwilling to confide the response
to strangers, he despatched into Greece his two sons, Titus
and Aruns, through lands at that time little known, and seas
still less explored. And he gave them as a companion L.
Junius Brutus, the son of his sister Tarquinia, a young man
of a very different understanding from that of which he had
assumed the appearance; for, having heard that his uncle
had put to death the chief men of the city, and among them
his brother, he resolved so to act that neither his mind nor
his fortune should cause the king any alarm. He therefore
assumed the appearance of an idiot, suffered the king to do
what he liked with himself and his property, and even spurned
not the surname of Brutus, that, under the shelter of so
degrading an epithet, the soul that was to be the liberator of
the Roman people might bide its opportunity. Being thus
led by the Tarquins to Delphi, not so much as a companion
as a butt to make sport of, he is said to have carried thither,
as an offering to Apollo, a golden stick, enclosed in one of

cornel-wood, which he had hollowed out for the purpose,—a type of his own mind. After arriving at Delphi, and discharging their father's mission, the youths were seized with a desire to know which of them would obtain the Roman kingdom; and to their inquiries an answer was returned from the lowest depths of the cavern to the following effect: "The chief command at Rome, O youths, will be obtained by him among you who shall first kiss his mother." The Tarquins, in order that Sextus, who had been left behind at Rome, might not know the response, and thus lose his chance of reigning, directed the matter to be kept as secret as possible, and decided between themselves by lot which should first kiss his mother on their return. But Brutus, who thought that the Pythian oracle had another meaning, pretending accidentally to stumble, gave the earth a kiss, that being the common mother of all men. So they returned to Rome, where a war against the Rutuli was in active preparation.

Ardea was at that time in possession of the Rutuli—a people very wealthy for that age and country; which, indeed, was the cause of the war. For the Roman king, besides having exhausted his treasury by the magnificence of his public works, wanted moreover to conciliate the people by a division of booty; for they hated his reign, not only on account of his pride in general, but also because they were indignant at being so long employed in servile and degrading labour as workmen and artisans.

It was first attempted to take Ardea by assault; but as this did not succeed, regular siege was laid to the place, and an entrenched camp established. In such quarters, as always happens in a long rather than a brisk war, furloughs were freely granted, though more to the officers than men. The royal princes sometimes amused their leisure with feasting and conviviality; and it happened that as they were drinking together in the quarters of Sextus Tarquinius, where Tarquinius Collatinus, the son of Egerius, was also supping, some talk ensued about their wives, and each began wonderfully to extol his own. As the dispute grew warm, Collatinus remarked "that there was no need of words; it might be ascertained in a few hours how much his Lucretia excelled the rest. Come, if you have any youthful vigour, let us mount our horses, and ascertain the disposition of our wives by paying them a visit. There can be no better proof than what shall meet our eyes on so unexpected a call." All answered, "Come on!" for they were excited with wine; and they spurred on at a gallop to Rome. They arrived there as night was falling, and discovered the king's daughters-in-law amusing themseves, with other high-born dames, in luxurious conviviality. Thence they proceeded to Collatia, where they found Lucretia sitting late at night in the midst of her household, spinning wool with her maid-servants; and thus Lucretia carried off the palm in this trial of female worth. She welcomed the arrival of her husband and the Tarquins, and the victorious Collatinus hospitably invited the royal youths to stay. Here Sextus Tarquinius, inflamed both by the beauty and the approved chastity of Lucretia, conceived the wicked design of forcibly dishonouring her. But at present they returned to the camp after their nocturnal and juvenile freak.

After the lapse of a few days, Sextus Tarquinius, with a single companion, returned to Collatia, without the knowledge of Collatinus. As all were ignorant of his design, he was kindly received, and conducted, after supper, to his bedchamber. But being inflamed with lust, so soon as all around seemed quiet and everybody asleep, he entered, with drawn sword, the apartment of Lucretia, and, placing his left hand on her breast, said: "Utter not a word, Lucretia! I am Sextus Tarquinius. Behold my sword! if thou makest any noise, thou shalt die." Great was the fright of Lucretia at being thus awakened, and menaced with immediate death, without the hope of succour. Then Tarquin confessed his love; used prayers and entreaties, mingled with threats; tried every effort to overcome that female mind. But when he saw that she was determined to resist, and could not be subdued even by the fear of death, he added a threat of dishonour; he would place, he said, beside her dead body the naked corpse of a slave, and give out that she had been detected and slain in that base adultery. By this terrible threat lust gained as it were, the victory, and triumphed over that obstinate chastity; and Tarquin departed, exulting in his conquest of female honour. But Lucretia, overwhelmed with the sense of so great a misfortune, despatched a messenger to her father at Rome, and her husband at Ardea, beseeching them to come to her, each accompanied by a single faithful friend; something atrocious had occurred, which required action, and that speedily. Sp. Lucretius came with P. Valerius the son of Volesus; Collatinus with L. Junius Brutus, whom he had accidentally met when returning to Rome, after his wife's message. On their arrival at Collatia they found Lucretia sitting in her bed-chamber, overwhelmed with sorrow. To her husband's question whether she was well, she answered: "No; for what can be well with a woman robbed of her honour? The traces of another man are in thy bed, Collatinus. But it is my body alone that has been defiled; my mind is guiltless, as my death shall testify. Come, pledge me with your right hands that the adulterer shall not go unpunished. Sextus Tarquinius was he who, coming hither as an enemy instead of a guest, with arms and violence, ravished from me last night a fatal pleasure—fatal to himself as well as me, if you be but men." All pledged themselves in turn, and endeavoured to assuage her grief, representing that the crime lay not with her, who had been forced, but with the author of her shame; that the mind alone was capable of sin, and not the body; and that where the will was absent, no crime could be imputed. To all which she replied: "It will be for you to see what Tarquin merits; as for myself, though I absolve myself of sin, yet I will not free myself from punishment. No wanton shall henceforth live, and plead the example of Lucretia." Then suddenly she pierced herself to the heart with a knife which she had concealed under her robe, and fell upon the floor in the agonies of death, while her husband and her father vented their sorrow in unavailing lamentations.

While these were absorbed in grief, Brutus, plucking the knife from Lucretia's wound, and holding it up, all reeking with gore, before him, exclaimed: "I swear by this most chaste blood, before it was contaminated by royalty, and call you, O gods, to witness my oath, that I will pursue Lucius Tarquinius Superbus, his wicked wife, and all his children, with fire and sword, and whatever other violence I can; and that I will suffer neither them nor any other person to reign at Rome." Then he handed the dagger in turn to Collatinus, to Lucretius, and to Valerius, who all stood wondering how, by a miracle, a new intellect seemed to have sprung up in Brutus. And as he bade them, so they swore; while, anger and indignation taking the place of grief, they followed Brutus as their leader, who exhorted them at once to overthrow the monarchy. So they carried the body of Lucretia from the house into the Forum, where a crowd soon gathered round, attracted as well by the novelty of the matter as by the indignation which naturally arose in their breasts. Then each of the four in turn denounced the prince's violence and crime; and the hearts of the bystanders were equally touched by the sorrow of the father and by the bearing of Brutus, who, reproving all tears and useless lamentations, exhorted them, as became men and Romans, to take up arms against those who had thus ventured to give the signal for hostilities. The most ardent of the youth at once volunteered their services, and were soon followed by the rest. Then, having left a guard at the gates of Collatia, and appointed persons to watch and prevent any notice of the rising being carried to the royal family, the rest, having armed themselves, followed Brutus to Rome. This armed multitude, on arriving at Rome, spread terror and tumult wheresoever they appeared; but when it was seen that some of the chief men of the city were its leaders, it was concluded that, whatever the affair might be, it was no rash undertaking. The atrocity of the crime of Tarquin, when known at Rome, occasioned there no less excitement than it had done at Collatia, and a rush was consequently made into the Forum from all parts of the city; for thither a herald summoned them to attend upon the tribune of the Celeres, in which office Brutus happened to be at that time. There he addressed them in a style which very ill corresponded with the disposition and understanding which he had hitherto simulated, expatiating upon the lust and violence of Sextus Tarquinius, the unspeakable dishonour and miserable suicide of Lucretia, the bereavement of Lucretius Tricipitinus, whose grief and indignation at the death of his daughter were rendered more bitter by the cause of it. Then he proceeded to denounce the pride of the king himself, and to paint the misery and labours of the people, compelled to dig ditches and drains; that Romans, the conquerors of all the surrounding peoples, should be turned, forsooth, into labourers and stone-cutters, instead of warriors. He recalled to their recollection the cruel and undeserved murder of King Servius Tullius, and his daughter riding over her father's body in her accursed chariot, and invoked the gods who are the avengers of parents. Reciting all these things, and also others, I believe, still more atrocious, but which the present state of things under which we live makes it difficult for a writer to repeat, he goaded on the incensed multitude to abrogate the king's *imperium*, and to sentence L. Tarquinius to exile, together with his wife and children. He himself, with a chosen body of the youth in arms, who vied with one another in enrolling themselves, proceeded to the camp at Ardea, in order to incite the army against the king; leaving the command at Rome to Lucretius, whom Tarquin had previously made prefect of the city. Tullia, amidst the tumult, fled from the palace; both men and women execrating her wherever she appeared, and invoking against her the furies that avenge the violation of filial piety.

The news of these disturbances having been carried to the camp, the king, alarmed at this new aspect of affairs, set off for Rome to restore peace; while Brutus, who was travelling the same road, and perceived his approach, turned a little aside to avoid meeting him; and thus almost at the same time, but by different routes, Brutus reached Ardea and Tarquinius Rome. But Tarquin found the gates shut, and that he was, in fact, an exile; whilst, on the other hand, Brutus was joyfully received in the camp as the liberator of the city. The king's children were also expelled; two of whom went with their father into exile to Cære, in Etruria. Sextus Tarquinius, who had proceeded to Gabii, as if it were his own kingdom, was killed by the avengers of those ancient grudges which he had brought upon himself by his rapine and murders.

L. Tarquinius Superbus reigned five-and-twenty years. The whole duration of the regal period at Rome, from the building of the city to its liberation, was two hundred and forty-four years. Two consuls were now created by the prefect of the city in the Comitia Centuriata, agreeably to the commentaries of Servius Tullius. These were L. Junius Brutus and L. Tarquinius Collatinus.

REMARKS.—On the preceeding narrative Schwegler observes:[1] "That the outrage committed by one of the king's sons on the daughter of Lucretius Tricipitinus gave the external impetus to this revolution is sufficiently credible. Thus we find in the Greek cities also, and in the Italian states in the later portion of the Middle Ages, that no cause has more frequently occasioned the overthrow either of usurped or inherited principalities than the forcible dishonouring of women or boys; and the Roman history itself presents another example of a similar revolution from a like cause. But the circumstances connected in the history with the commission of the crime have no pretensions to historical credibility. They belong partly to poetical legend, and partly to literary embellishment.

"In like manner are to be regarded all the details with which the fall of Tarquin and his expulsion from the city are related. When the annalists wrote, the memory of the actual circumstances with which the catastrophe was accompanied was extinct. But we may conjecture that the revolution was not so smoothly and easily accomplished as it appears to have been in the narratives of the historians. The Tarquins had a party devoted to them, and assuredly they were not driven from Rome till after severe and bloody contests."

With much of what is here said we are inclined to agree. The tyranny and the crimes of Tarquin and his family have probably been very much exaggerated; not, however, we think, by popular legend, or even by literary embellishment, if by such embellish-

[1] Buch viii. § 17.

ment we are to understand the narratives of the professed historians of later times. We believe these narratives to have been much earlier than the time of Fabius, and to have been contained in private memoirs of the patrician families, reaching perhaps up to the times of the events which they record; and that the exaggerations which they contain were the result of party spirit.

It seems very probable, as Schwegler remarks, that the outrage upon Lucretia was the immediate occasion of the fall of the monarchy. So striking an event, in connexion with so great a revolution, and one so universally confirmed by ancient testimony, can hardly have been an invention. But it was only the occasion, and not the cause, of the revolution. The actual cause lies much deeper. An outrage, however brutal, on the part of one of the king's sons, would not have produced not only the expulsion of Tarquin and his family, but also the great constitutional change of a republic for a monarchy, unless there had been already in the state a powerful party that meditated such a revolution. We have already seen the patrician families, after the death of Romulus, endeavouring to substitute their own rule for that of a king. An aristocratic republic in the hands of the great families appears to have remained a favourite idea among the patricians, though for a long period they were unable to realize it. It was apparently by way of counterpoise that we find Tarquinius Priscus doubling the Senate, with the view of securing for himself a strong party in that assembly. The scheme for a republic appears from the Commentaries of Servius Tullius to have been subsequently adopted by that king, and was probably the cause of his overthrow by Tarquin. The reactionary policy of Tarquin led him to depress and persecute the Senate. The fall of Tarquin was produced by a counter-revolution organized by the old patrician families; and thus we find that the first care of the new consuls was to fill up and augment the number of the Senate.

The conjecture of Schwegler, that Tarquin and his party were not driven from Rome till after severe and bloody contests, is not only unsupported by evidence, but is also improbable in itself. The final decision of the matter would have lain with the army then assembled before Ardea, whose aid and suffrage Brutus hastened to obtain. Had the army—that is, in other words, the *élite* of the Roman citizens, and especially those centuries of the knights and of the *prima classis* which in the Comitia Conturiata enjoyed almost a monopoly of the suffrage—been in favour of Tarquin, the revolution could never have been accomplished; but, being adverse to him, his deposition was sudden and complete. Tarquin, no doubt, had a small party attached to his interests: what monarch has not? But of anything like a civil war we find no trace in the historians; it would, indeed, have been totally incompatible with the course of the history, and especially with the treaty of Carthage concluded in the first years of the Republic.

"How legendary in general," continues Schwegler, "is still the history of those times is particularly manifest in the person and reputed idiocy of Junius Brutus. What consistency is there in the story that Tarquin should have bestowed the dignity of a Tribunus Celerum on an idiot who was no longer master of his own property,—a dignity which was the highest in the state after that of a king,—an office which in a despotic kingdom was of the greatest possible importance, and which, moreover, from the sacerdotal functions connected with it, could not have been discharged by such a person? It is related also that Brutus accompanied the king's sons to Delphi; and if we ask how they came to take an idiot with them on such a journey, tradition gives the silly answer, 'In order to have with them somebody they might make sport of.' In Delphi, Brutus presents the god with a gold stick. We may ask, How did he find means to make so rich a present, as the king had confiscated his whole property, and had left him, as Dionysius says, only enough for his daily subsistence? But all these questions would have been in their place if we had to do with actual historical facts. The idiocy of Brutus is an etymological myth founded upon his name, and appears, moreover, to rest upon a false interpretation of his name."

So striking an event as the fall of the Tarquins and the establishment of the Republic must naturally have become the subject of popular conversation and popular legend, and hence of embellishment and exaggeration. But the main outline of the story there is no reason to doubt; that Tarquin was overthrown by a revolution conducted by Brutus, Lucretius Tricipitinus, Tarquinius Collatinus, and Valerius Publicola. The Fasti, which contain the names of these persons as the consuls of the first year of the Republic, corroborate the historical tradition. It is possible, as Schwegler remarks, that the name of Brutus may have suggested the story about his feigned idiocy. In ancient Latin, however, it seems to have denoted "severe."[1] Cicero says nothing of his pretended folly, but alludes only to his courage and understanding.[2]

The following remarks of Schwegler's[3] on the general character of Tarquin's reign are, with some exceptions, worthy of attention:—

"The general outlines of the history of the second Tarquin may pass for historical. That with the help of the patricians he hurled Servius from the throne, exercised as king a strong and glorious, but also oppressive and arbitrary rule, and was at last overthrown by a conspiracy of the patricians—all this cannot be consistently questioned. The history of the last king stands on the boundaries of the legendary and mystic period and of the transition to the historical times.

"It can hardly be denied that his image was at an early period deformed by patrician hate and painted with dark and exaggerated shades. The memory of Sp. Cassius, Sp. Mælius, and M. Manlius, consequently of men who already belong to the time of record, has in like manner been falsified and misrepresented through the hate of the ruling party. The patricians were all the more led to paint the portrait of the last king in repulsive colours, as they had the greater interest to place a moral bar to that monarchical form of government which they detested. The details of Tarquin's tyranny must therefore be rejected, and the more, as the historians have evidently taken a pleasure in painting him as the image, or special type, of a tyrant. The later writers especially have in this given the reins to their fancy. Thus one relates that Tarquin invented instruments of torture, and then that he abused boys and virgins, &c.[4] But whilst we reject exaggerations and inventions of this sort, it cannot be denied that the rule of the last Tarquin was really unconstitutional and despotic, harsh and oppressive.

"In general, Tarquin bears a great resemblance to the Greek tyrants of the older times. Like these, he is a clever and enter-

---

[1] "Brutum antiqui gravem dicebant"—Paul. Diac. p. 31. According to some authorities the month of June was named after Brutus. "Nonnulli putaverunt Junium mensem a Junio Bruto, qui primus Romæ consul factus est, nominatum; quod hoc mense, id est, Calendis Juniis, pulso Tarquinio sacrum Carnæ deæ in Cælio monte voti reus fecerit."—Macrob. Sat. l. 12.

[2] "Tum vir ingenio et virtute præstans L. Brutus depulit a civibus suis injustum illud duræ servitutis jugum," &c.—De Rep. ii. 25.

[3] Buch xiii. §§ 10, 11.

[4] These stories are taken from such authors as Theophilus (Bishop of Antioch), Hieronymus, John Lydus, &c.

prising prince, a lover of art and splendour, but without consideration, and reckless of the means which he uses. But he particularly recalls the Hellenic tyrants by the magnificence of his buildings. For the older Greek tyrants also sought reputation by encouraging the arts, and to perpetuate their name by splendid or useful monuments. Aristotle enumerates among the arts of rule exercised by despotic monarchs the erection of great and costly buildings: a people who had been robbed of their freedom would be thus kept employed, and at the same time rendered poor. But this was certainly not the only motive which influenced the Greek tyrants or the Roman Tarquin in these buildings and creations of art, but chiefly the view of giving their reign a certain appearance of something out of the common, and of marking it by magnificence and splendour. Tarquin also resembles the Greek tyrants of that epoch in the circumstance that he seeks to support his dominion by foreign alliances, marriages, hospitality, and connexions with the princes or ruling families of neighbouring cities. Lastly, like the Greek tyrants almost universally, he incurs the hatred, not so much of the *demos* or *plebs*, as of the patricians, by whom he is at last overthrown.

"It is particularly remarkable that, in spite of the apparent estrangement between Italy and Greece, a certain parallelism may still be traced in the political development of their inhabitants. As the old Roman constitution, founded on families, answers to the old Attic, so the Servian constitution, resting on the census, corresponds with the contemporary one of Solon; the Servian division of tribes with that made by Clisthenes. And so the younger Tarquin resembles Pisistratus, who follows Solon, just as Tarquin follows Servius Tullius.

"If we examine more closely the political character of the reign of the younger Tarquin, its main tendency seems to be the realization of that idea of which the creation of the Capitoline Temple and worship is the symbolical expression—the formation of the monarchy into a unity, the removal of the bars which had till then divided the nation both in religion and politics, had hindered its development, and crippled its power of action. In this view Tarquin follows up the endeavours of his immediate predecessor, but by different means; not, namely, by the development of the existing constitution, but by founding an unlimited monarchy. Tarquinius also evidently aimed at converting the Roman kingdom, which had hitherto constitutionally been an elective monarchy, into an hereditary one. Hence it naturally followed that through these endeavours, and this system of government, he drew down upon himself the implacable hatred of the patricians."

"It is more doubtful what attitude Tarquin assumed with regard to the *plebs*. The Greek tyrants of the older times for the most part sought support in the *demos*, and favoured it when they could. This policy was the result of their position with regard to the oligarchical party, as well as of their own origin; for the greater part of them rose from being demagogues. But the younger Tarquin obtained the throne in another manner: according to all indications, he sought to support his monarchy by foreign alliances, though indications are not wanting which show that his relations to the *plebs* were no hostile ones; nay, even perhaps that they were friendly. When Porsena, as Livy relates,[1] appeared before the walls of the city, the Senate directed all its attention to the commonalty: corn was bought in different places, the price of salt was reduced, the tolls and taxes were lightened, in order to win them over and conciliate them with the Republic, so that they might not be led to prefer the restoration of the exiled royal family to a war. The property of the deposed king had been previously given up to the *plebs* to be plundered, in order, as Livy expresses it, by this robbery of the royal family to render all reconciliation between it and the *plebs* impossible;[2] while, on the other hand, as Livy relates further on, when the news of Tarquin's death arrived at Rome, the patricians began to misuse the plebeian order, which they had hitherto courted by all the means in their power.[3] That these oppressions of the *plebs* began with the year of Tarquin's death, A.U.C. 258, is indeed scarcely credible, as only two years afterwards (260) the variance between the two orders came to a complete breach; they must, therefore, have begun earlier. (Why!) But hence the true character of that revolution appears all the less doubtful, which did not, as it afterwards became the mode of talking of it, produce the freedom of the people, but, on the contrary, substituted in the place of a popular monarchy, or at all events one which repressed the exclusive pretensions of the patricians, the most oppressive despotism of the great families. The kings had always been the natural patrons of the *plebs*; their

[1] Liv. ii. 9.   [2] Ibid. 5.
[3] Lib. ii. 21; cf. Sall. Hist. ap. Aug. C. D. ii. 18.

interests were easily united with those of that class, as the latter could not, like the noble families, make any pretensions to share the government with them; and it cannot be doubted that the *plebs* always found in the kings a help and protection against the oligarchs. Between the plebs and the great families, on the contrary, there existed an abrupt opposition of pretensions and interests.

"Dionysius had already formed this judgment of the position of the *plebs* towards the kings, and of the overthrow of the monarchy. He represents the spokesman of the seceding plebeians as thus addressing, on the Mons Sacer, the deputies from the Senate: 'Rome was during seven generations a monarchy, and in the course of all these reigns the plebeians were never prejudiced by the kings in anything, and least of all by the last. By all manner of favours they sought to befriend the plebeian order, and to set it at enmity with you. Nevertheless, when the last king introduced a despotic government, by which, however, he injured not the people, but you, we deserted our good kings, and attached our interests to yours.'[1] In the same writer, the banished Coriolanus tells the Volscians: 'The Roman constitution was originally a mixture of monarchy and aristocracy: when Tarquin sought to turn it into a despotism, the heads of the noble families rose up against him, drove him from the city, and took possession of the power of the state.'[2] It is, of course, understood that these assertions rest not on positive tradition; they are the products of subjective reflection; but betray a correct judgment of these relations. They were, perhaps, taken from the experienced Licinius Macer, who, we know, interwove long speeches into his history.

"That the overthrow of the Tarquins was not, as tradition represents it,[3] a liberation effected by the whole nation, but the victory of a patrician conspiracy, a work of patrician reaction, also appears from the fact that the leaders of the conspiracy were all patricians, and indeed of the highest rank. Brutus was Tribunus Celerum, Lucretius prefect of the city.

"Niebuhr, indeed, has claimed L. Brutus for the *plebs*, and, accordingly, sees in the four leaders of the conspiracy—Lucretius, Valerius, Collatinus, and Brutus—the representatives of the three

[1] Dionys. vi. 78.   [2] Ibid. viii. 5.
[3] Tradition represents it as what it really was: how else could Schwegler have formed his opinion about it?

patrician stem-tribes and of the *plebs*.[1] But this assumption has no other support than the fact that the later Junii, who traced their descent from the founder of the Republic, were plebeians. This, however, proves nothing as to the plebiscity of Junius Brutus, since—as it is expressly handed down—the two families of the Junii are not genealogically connected; for the posterity of Brutus was extinguished with his two sons, whom he caused to be executed when mere youths. Dion Cassius says this expressly (xliv. 12), and declares the pretended descent of M. Brutus from the ancient L. Brutus to be an invention. So also Dionysius (v. 18), who appeals to the testimony of the best Roman historians, as well as the authorities quoted by Plutarch (Brutus 1). Dionysius accordingly (vi. 70) distinguishes the plebeian L. Junius, who plays a part in the first secession, and afterwards becomes tribune, from the family of the founder of the Republic, and remarks that the former had quite arbitrarily assumed the surname of Brutus. Hence, if this last Brutus is not a fictitious personage, there was in the earliest time of the Republic a plebeian line of the Junii, as well as the patrician, which died out with the consul Brutus. It is only the philosopher Posidonius who mentions that the ancient Brutus left a third and minor son, the progenitor of the race of the Junii (Plut. Brut. 1). But this account is evidently invented in their favour. At all events, the Brutus of the old tradition is decidedly a patrician: he is the son of Tarquinia, the sister of the last king; his wife belongs to the patrician race of the Vitellii (Liv. ii. 4; Suet. Vit. 1). Besides, if a plebeian, he could scarcely have become Tribunus Celerum, and still less consul, a century and a half before the Licinian rogations. It would at least have been strange in this case that the plebeians did not afterwards appeal to this precedent. But, on the contrary, the patricians, as represented by Livy, make it an objection to the law proposed by Canuleius, that since the fall of the kings there had been no plebeian consul; and the spokesman of the *plebs* admits it (Liv. iv. 4).

"There is another circumstance which still further confirms the conjecture before made as to the character of the revolution which overthrew the monarchy. We find, for instance, that the banished royal family has a numerous party, which is implicated in its fall, and follows it into banishment. In the battle of Lake Regillus,

[1] This is one of those numerous crotchets, founded on nothing at all but imagination and conjecture, which disfigure the history of Niebuhr.

these exiles form a peculiar cohort;[1] and even in the year 262, when the Romans send ambassadors to buy corn in Lower Italy, we find among the Volsci and in Cumæ a great number of Roman refugees, who bitterly oppose these ambassadors, and among the Volsci excite the people, at Cumæ the tyrant Aristodemus, against them.[2] The exiles who in the year 294 seize the Capitol, under the leadership of Herdonius, were perhaps descendants of these banished partisans of the Tarquins. We further find that the overthrown dynasty has still a party in Rome itself. Livy, at least, relates that at the breaking out of the Latin War a Dictator was chosen because the consuls of that year were regarded with some suspicion as belonging to the Tarquinian party.[3] From all these indications it follows that the overthrow of the monarchy did not only concern the expulsion of a flagitious tyrant, hated alike by the patricians and the people, but that the revolution was the result of more general causes. The same conclusion must be drawn from the circumstance that no other king is chosen in place of the banished Tarquin; for the revolution concerns, consequently, not only the person of Tarquin, but the monarchy as a political principle. And this brings us back to the conjecture before propounded, that the overthrow of the monarchy was the work of the aristocratic families."

On the same subject Sir G. C. Lewis remarks:[4] "The narrative of the reign of Tarquinius Superbus so far differs from that of the former kings that there is a much closer agreement between Livy and Dionysius, and more appearance of a fixed version of the events in the different writers from which they drew their accounts. But there is nothing which leads to the inference that the materials from which the narrative is constructed were derived from contemporary registration, or were written down from fresh and authenticated oral traditions, like the account of the Pisistratidæ in Thucydides. The interval which separated the historian Fabius from this reign is as great as that which separated Hermippus or Phylarchus from the time of the Pisistratidæ. The inscription which recorded the treaty between Rome and Gabii, still extant in the time of Dionysius, was doubtless ancient; but whether it named Tarquin, or contained within itself any indication of its date, is uncertain."

[1] Liv. ii. 19, *sqq.*; Dionys. vi. 5.
[2] Liv. ii. 18, 21.
[3] Dionys. vii. 2.
[4] Credibility, &c. xi. § 38.

Of the treaty with Gabii we have already spoken. To the objection about contemporary registration it may be answered, as we have before suggested, that it is impossible to suppose that a nation arrived at that cultivation, splendour, and commercial activity which characterised Rome at the time of the last Tarquin, should have been without all annals or records; that indubitable traces of record appear as early as the reign of Tullus Hostilius, which, therefore, à fortiori, must have existed under the subsequent kings; and that, as we have shown in the Introduction, there is historical evidence of its existence. But a great part of the records perished in the Gallic conflagration; and hence the early history has necessarily a fragmentary character, which has afforded the sceptical critics a handle to depreciate it. And their arguments have been aided by the circumstance that some of the later historians, and particularly Dionysius, have endeavoured to breach over these chasms by pragmatical inventions of their own; and also, as the narrative was necessarily bare and dry, to embellish it by working up dramatically the more prominent events, as the death of Servius Tullius, the capture of Gabii, the mission to Delphi, the rape of Lucretia, and other incidents of the like kind. But, nevertheless, under all these events we are of opinion that there is a solid foundation of truth.

"With respect to the internal evidence," continues Sir G. C. Lewis, "we may first remark that the chronology is not consistent with itself. The life of Tarquinius Superbus, as we have already seen, is extended to an impossible length, if we suppose him to have been the son of Tarquinius Priscus, and to have died at Cumæ in 496 B.C. The same may be said of Collatinus: and Brutus, who is described as a boy at the beginning of the reign of Tarquinius Superbus, and a young man at its termination, appears immediately after the expulsion of the kings with two grown-up sons."

We have before examined these chronological objections respecting the Tarquins, and shall only remark here, that Sir G. C. Lewis, without inquiring for himself, servilely follows Schwegler, who, in the case of Brutus especially, has grossly misinterpreted the plainest words of Dionysius and Livy. Thus, that writer says:[1] "Brutus,

---

[1] B. i. s. 50. In order to justify our charge against Sir G. C. Lewis of servilely following Schwegler, we may remark that he adopts Schwegler's misquotation of the chapter referred to in Livy; viz. l. 16, instead of i. 56.

who at the beginning of the reign of Tarquinius Superbus appears as a boy under age (*unmündiger Knabe*), and at the end of it as a young man of the same age as the king's sons, is said immediately after the expulsion of Tarquin to have grown-up sons." The authorities quoted for these assertions are, Dionysius iv. 68, 69, and Livy i. 56. The words of Dionysius in ch. 68 are: "νέος ὢν ὁ Βροῦτος ἔτι, 'being *still* young.'" In ch. 69 the words τοῖς μειρακίοις and οἱ νεανίσκοι refer exclusively to Tarquin's sons, and cannot by any method of construction be made to include Brutus. But, even if they did, they would not prove what Schwegler wishes to prove about the age of Brutus; for among the Romans a man was *juvenis* till the age of forty-five, as we see from the *juniores* up to that age enrolled in the Servian census. And, therefore, when Livy in the chapter referred to calls Brutus *juvenis*, that would not prevent him from having been about forty at the time of the journey to Delphi. And this journey may have taken place three or four years before the expulsion of Tarquin. For, first, we may suppose that the journey itself, as travelling was in those days, might occupy the better part of a year. Then, when the travellers return, war against the Rutuli is only preparing. Next it is attempted to take Ardea by assault, which fails; and then a blockade is established, the duration of which cannot be told. So that Brutus may very well have been forty-three or forty-four when he overthrew Tarquin, and have had sons of eighteen or twenty. Livy calls them *adolescentes*, and *adolescentia* began at the age of fifteen.

The objections which follow the preceding, respecting the meeting of the Latin deputies, the public works of Tarquin, and the reduction of Gabii, we have already examined. Sir G. C. Lewis then continues: "The prodigy of the eagles building on a palm tree, and their expulsion by a flock of vultures, must be set down as fiction; but the story of Lucretia, though it has a romantic cast, might be substantially true; nor would there be any good reason for questioning its reality, if it came to us authenticated by fair contemporary evidence. The true story of the suicide of Arria, who, when she had stabbed herself, gave the dagger to her husband with the celebrated words, *Pæte, non dolet*,[1] is not more improbable than the suicide of Lucretia; though the description of Brutus

---

So that he could not have taken the trouble to refer to the authorities to see if Schwegler's attack was just.   [1] Plin. Epp. iii. 16.

brandishing the bloody dagger, and holding it in his hand while he swears vengeance against the Tarquins, savours of theatrical effect."

The prodigy of the eagles is recorded only by Dionysius[1] and his follower Zonaras. We do not, however, reject it on that account. Dionysius may probably have taken it from good authority, if not directly from the ancient Annals; and Livy may have omitted it merely for the sake of brevity. Sir G. C. Lewis's ground for asserting that it is a fiction is, that the palm-tree does not grow at Rome,—an assertion which he makes on the authority of a certain Dr. Rothman,[2] who, in his Observations on the Climate of Italy, p. 6, remarks "that Terracina is now the northern limit of the date palm in Italy, with the exception of a convent garden at Rome and a small tract of coast between Nice and Genoa." On this we have observed in another work:[3] "The testimony of Dr. Rothman is thus preferred to that of Dionysius, who spent a great part of his life at Rome, and must have been a competent judge of such a fact. The palm excepted by Dr. Rothman is probably the fine one in the garden of the Convent of Sta. Francisca, near S. Pietro in Vincoli, which must have been seen and admired by most visitors of Rome. But if such a tree can grow there in the open air, why should not others? In fact those who are acquainted with Rome know that it possesses many palm-trees besides this; as those in the gardens of the Villa Colonna, visible from the Via della Pilotta, and others in other places." Since this was written, another visit to Rome has discovered to the author a magnificent palm, transplanted in 1865 to the Pincian Hill, at the spot where the band plays, which, from its conspicuous position, cannot fail to have been noticed by the most unobservant traveller.

That the story of Lucretia's suicide should need to be supported by that of Arria, who had hardly so good a reason to slay herself, seems a strange idea of historical criticism. But, in fact, female suicides for much more trivial reasons occur every day. Hence it would appear that a story is not to believed unless it has a parallel, though sometimes it is rejected because it has one; and further, that even "a true story" may be "improbable." The objection to Brutus brandishing the dagger savours of the very essence of

[1] Lib. iv. 63.   [2] See p. 515, note 127.
[3] Hist. of the City of Rome, p. xlvii.

hypercriticism. A history written on the principles which it implies would require even the most trivial act to be certified on affidavit.

The remaining objections of Sir G. C. Lewis to the narrative of the catastrophe that produced the fall of the Roman kingdom are not of a nature to require any lengthened examination. He admits[1] the possibility "that some fragments of true and authentic tradition may be preserved in the narrative which has come down to us; but we have no means of distinguishing them: we have no test by which we can separate the dross from the pure ore." But surely "the pure ore" must be the grand outlines of the story, in which all the historians are agreed—the outrage on Lucretia by one of Tarquin's sons, her suicide, the conspiracy of her husband, her father, and their friends to avenge her, and the consequent deposition and banishment of Tarquin. In comparison of these, the little details of the story are indeed "dross," and hardly deserve the epithet of "material circumstances" given to them by Sir G. C. Lewis. "The dispute of the young men about their wives," observes that writer,[2] "and their nocturnal ride to Rome and Collatia, which is the foundation of the attempt of Sextus in Livy, is altogether wanting in Dionysius. In the latter Rome is the place of Lucretia's suicide; in the former it is Collatia. Most of the accounts represent Tarquinius Superbus as having three sons, Sextus, Titus, and Aruns; but Livy and Ovid make Sextus, the ravisher of Lucretia, the youngest, while Dionysius says that he was the eldest of the three. Other writers again speak of Aruns as having ravished Lucretia. . . . Livy moreover represents the king and his family as escaping to Cære, with the exception of Sextus, who repairs to his kingdom of Gabii, where he is put to death. Dionysius, on the other hand, says that Tarquin first took refuge in Gabii, and afterwards removed to Cære."

It is very immaterial how Sextus's visit to Collatia was occasioned, or whether Lucretia slew herself there or at Rome; but Livy, in his whole narrative, so far as Lucretia is concerned, appears to have used better sources than Dionysius, perhaps private memoirs. That the Tarquin who outraged Lucretia was named Sextus, all the best authorities are agreed; and their difference as to whether he was the eldest or the youngest of the three sons is of small importance to the story. The only writers who say that Aruns was the ravisher are Florus and Servius, whose testimony cannot be set

[1] Vol. i. p. 526. [2] P. 524.

against that of Livy, Dionysius, Diodorus, Dion Cassius, Victor, and Zonaras. To inquire whether Tarquin went to Gabii before proceeding to Cære—which he probably did, as Gabii was nearer, and belonged to his son—is really beneath the dignity either of a critic or an historian. What a singular idea must the critic have formed of the nature of such early history, and of the information which may fairly be expected from it, to make such minute circumstances an argument against its credibility!

Schwegler concludes the first volume of his history with the following review of the regal period:[1] "If, having arrived at the conclusion of the regal period, we cast upon it a retrospective glance, it would appear to have exercised the most important and decisive influence on the form and essence of the Roman state, which indeed it may be said to have produced. It converted into a united state the loose social bond of the most ancient time, when there was nothing but families and races,[2] and reduced to practice the idea of a supreme power in the state, that principle of subordination which was still foreign to a state composed of races. The Roman idea of the magistracy, to which Rome so pre-eminently owed her greatness and power, was a legacy of the monarchy. The later Romans have rightly regarded the epoch of their kingly government as a school of discipline and political education which was necessary to perfect the Roman people, and have always preserved the memory of their kings with reverential piety.

"The number of seven Roman kings cannot be accepted as historical, as the first two of them are decidedly fabulous. That number contains in itself something mythical, since it appears as a sacred number among the Romans in other things; as the Septimontium, or seven hills. At the same time the number of seven kings presents the seven principal circumstances or fundamental facts of the constitutional history before the republican times. The first three kings represent the three ancient stem-races : Ancus Marcius is the founder of the *plebs;* Tarquinius Priscus founds the *Gentes Minores;* Servius Tullius the tribes and centuries; and, lastly, with

[1] Buch xviii. § 18 ff.
[2] This remark appears to relate more to the Sabine part of the population than the Roman. See Schwegler, B. I. S. 244. According to our view, which we believe to be conformable to tradition, Romulus at once formed his state, and *created* the races (or *gentes*) by a political act, instead of uniting races or clans that already existed. And we may remark that even the Sabines had a king when they settled at Rome.

the name of the younger Tarquin is connected the fall of the monarchy. Such a coincidence, however, is, as a recent inquirer observes,[1] foreign to actual and common life, in which important matters and unimportant ones follow one another in variegated confusion; but it agrees well enough with the character of legend, which loves to assign definite names to those connected with definite circumstances and historical turning-points."

Remarks like these do not require any serious answer. The absurdities here ascribed to legend, or tradition, are only the farfetched inventions of German historians and critics; in short, criticism run wild, or, what is often the same thing, Teutonized. There are no grounds for connecting the first three kings with the three stem-tribes, or Ancus Marcius with the *plebs*. That Tarquinius Priscus created the *Gentes Minores*, in the sense here meant of new tribes, is only a German invention; and as to the last Tarquin, he, as Schwegler shows, created nothing, yet is to be ranked among the other six (reputed) founders because—he was overthrown! A writer who can publish these platitudes inspires us with grave doubts of his critical judgment.

In the last section Schwegler discusses over again the chronology of the regal period, which we have examined in the Introductory Dissertation, and need not again enter upon.

Sir G. C. Lewis sums up as follows his view of the regal period :[2] "Having completed our detailed examination of the historical evidence of the regal period, we may now briefly sum up the conclusions to which it appears to point. It may then be stated, as the result of this inquiry, that the narrative of Roman affairs, from the foundation of the city to the expulsion of the Tarquins, is formed out of the traditionary materials. At what time the oral traditions were reduced into writing, and how much of the existing narrative was the arbitrary supplement of the historians who first framed the account which has descended to us, it is now impossible to ascertain."

So far, it would seem that the history was entirely constructed from oral tradition. But Sir G. C. Lewis immediately proceeds to give us something better.

"The most ancient materials for Roman history were doubtless (as indeed we may infer from Dionysius) unconnected stories, notes of legal usages and of constitutional forms, and other entries

[1] Peter, Gesch. Röm. I. 60. [2] Credibility, &c. vol. I. p. 526.

in the Pontifical books. These were the germs of Roman history; out of these fragments Fabius and his successors constructed the primitive annals of their country. The remains of *leges regiæ* (of which a few citations occur in ancient writers, and of which a collection is even said to have existed in later times) are nothing more than ancient records of this sort."

We learn from this that there were at all events "fragments" of records which Fabius and the other annalists used in composing their works. The natural interpretation of the first sentence is, that there were also "unconnected stories" in the Pontifical books. We do not feel quite sure whether this was Sir G. C. Lewis's meaning; but we have already endeavoured to show[1] that the Pontifices were the historiographers of the city; and in that case the stories may have had more connexion than the critic is willing to allow. But he immediately proceeds to depreciate the value of his concession, as follows:

"It was easy for a pontifical scribe, who entered a rule of consuetudinary law in his register, to dignify it with the name of a *lex regia*, and to attribute it to Numa, Servius, or one of the other kings."

We, on the contrary, affirm that it is "easy" to make such an assertion, but exceedingly difficult to render it credible. What! are we to believe that the Roman law was defiled and poisoned at its very source? That the Pontifices, whose sacred duty it was to register the laws, were no better than forgers and impostors, who, without any conceivable motive—for what could have been gained by it?—but merely from caprice and levity, gave false titles, and consequently a false importance, to these laws? Was there no check upon them,—no public punishment, no public shame? In what other nation can it be supposed that this most sacred of all trusts could be thus wantonly and carelessly abused? Such an accusation shows a critic driven to his last straits, and betrays a scepticism that not even the best evidence can satisfy.

"The same origin," continues Sir G. C. Lewis, "must be assigned" (that is, we presume, from the Pontifical books) "to the curious legal forms—such as the inauguration of the kings, the making of treaties, the appointment of capital duumvirs, the declaration of war, and the surrender of a city—which are preserved in the first book of Livy. Private documents, or papers, of Numa and Servius

[1] See the Introduction.

are likewise mentioned by the same historian; but he does not say that they were preserved."

Here then we have authentic documents for the regal period, and Sir G. C. Lewis does not even insinuate that they were forged. Though Livy does not expressly say that the papers of Numa and Servius were preserved to his time, there is nothing to show that they were not; and the passage of Cicero's Oration for Rabirius (c. 5) which Sir G. C. Lewis quotes in a note affords a strong presumption that they might have been preserved: "Cum iste omnes et suppliciorum et verborum acerbitates non ex memoria vestra ac patrum vestrorum, sed ex annalium monumentis atque ex regum commentariis, conquisierit;" where Sir G. C. Lewis observes, "the words *regum commentarii* mean documents of the regal period." Yet that writer observes in the same note that the *Commentarii* of Servius Tullius were "doubtless a fiction, founded upon his reputation as a popular king." But at all events, whether these Commentaries were preserved or not to the time of Livy, it cannot be doubted that they were made; and therefore there were records in the times of the kings.

"There is no trace," continues Sir G. C. Lewis, "of any authentic chronology of the regal period; the number of years assigned to each reign is large, although the kings are elective; most of them die a violent death, and the last king is dethroned. Nevertheless a detailed chronology for this period seems to have been fabricated by the Roman antiquaries; the extant Triumphal Fasti record the triumphs of the kings; and Dionysius[1] quotes the Annals for the date of the death of Aruns Tarquinius in the reign of Servius."

Sir G. C. Lewis begins this paragraph by remarking that there is no authentic chronology of the regal period, and ends it by saying that Dionysius quotes the annals for the date of the death of Aruns Tarquinius. On these annals he observes in another place:[2] "The annals to which Dionysius alludes are called by him ἐνιαύσιοι ἀναγραφαί. They must have been some chronological work, in which the events of the regal period were entered according to years." There was, therefore, by his own admission, a chronology of the regal period, though the question may remain whether it was an authentic one. There can be no doubt that the work to which Dionysius alludes was the Annales Maximi, the preservation of which, as we have shown in the Introductory

[1] Lib. iv. 30.   [2] Vol. i. p. 505, note 95.

Dissertation, is attested by the best evidence. The handing down of a work full of dates could not have been accomplished by oral tradition; nor is this the form which popular invention takes in matters of early history. The circumstances attending the birth and the murder of Servius Tullius, of the capture of Gabii, of the idiocy of Brutus, may possibly be exaggerated and embellished, and therefore in some degree invented; but the fancy which delights in such inventions cares little or nothing for a dry detail of dates. We must choose, then, between two conclusions: either this chronological work is a deliberate literary forgery perpetrated by the first annalists or their successors, yet not forming part of their works—since Dionysius refers to it as a separate and substantive one—or it is a genuine document of the regal period. Which is the more probable of these alternatives we have already examined in the Introduction, as well as the objection about the length of the kings' reigns.

Sir G. C. Lewis then proceeds: "At what time the oral traditions relating to the period of the kings began to be reduced into writing we are unable to determine. The records of them which were made before the burning of Rome, 390 B.C., were doubtless rare and meagre in the extreme; and such as there were at this time chiefly perished in the conflagration and ruin of the city. It was probably not till after this period—that is to say, about 120 years after the expulsion of the kings, and above 350 years after the era assigned for the foundation of the city—that these oral reports, these hearsay stories of many generations, began to be entered in the registers of the Pontifices. Even when the registration began, it was doubtless principally employed about contemporary events; it had an annalistic character, and the history of the primitive time was not written till a later period."

These assertions about the time when oral tradition began to be converted into written history are founded on nothing at all. Not a single testimony is brought forward in support of them, nothing but passages from Dr. Arnold and Schwegler. Sir G. C. Lewis has here adopted the German practice of quoting a modern authority as equivalent to an ancient one; but his assertions still remain nothing more than conjecture. There is in the ancient writers both positive and deductive evidence of the existence of record in the regal period. The burthen of proof lies on the attacking party to show that this did not and could not have existed; which, we submit, has not been done.

Why should it be more probable that registration began 120 years after the expulsion of the kings than during their time? We are convinced, and have endeavoured to show, that the Romans during that period had rather retrograded than advanced in civilization. That after the Gallic fire records had more chance of being preserved we admit. The misfortune of the early history is that the records were in great part destroyed, and consequently rare; not that there were none, or that they were unauthentic. The most careless reader may convince himself of this fact by merely opening Livy, where he will find more than three centuries and a half, according to the usual chronology, recorded in the first five books of the first decade, while the last five books comprise only a period of less than a century; and the second decade embraced about seventy-five years.

In the concluding paragraph of this 39th section, which is occupied with an inquiry into the general results with respect to the historical evidence for the regal period, Sir G. C. Lewis says little that requires any formal examination. He differs from Niebuhr's opinion that the reigns of Romulus and Numa are purely fabulous and poetical, and that those of the last five belong to the mythico-historical period, in which there is a narrative resting on an historical basis, and most of the persons mentioned are real. Sir G. C. Lewis cannot discover any ground for this distinction, and thinks that the history of the entire regal period is tolerably uniform in its character. We also are inclined to dissent from Niebuhr's view, but not quite on the same grounds; and indeed it is difficult to see what Niebuhr's view exactly was: for if, as he says, "the names of the kings are purely fictitious; no man can tell how long the Roman kings reigned, as we do not know how many there were,"[1] it is difficult to see how any of the reigns can deserve the epithet even of mythico-historical, or can be considered to rest on any historical ground. We differ from Niebuhr's opinion that the first two kings were fabulous personages; but we agree with him in thinking that a line may be drawn between their reigns and those of the subsequent kings; because the events of the first two reigns rest only on tradition, though the main facts of them were shortly afterwards recorded, while with the reign of

[1] Lect. vol. I. p. 41.

Tullus Hostilius, the Pontifices having been established by Numa, contemporary record had begun. We agree with Sir G. C. Lewis's remark, in contravention of Niebuhr, "that the names of the kings after Romulus are real is highly probable," though we would include also that of Romulus; for it is hardly possible that the name of the person who founded Rome at a comparatively late epoch, and when all the surrounding country was thickly peopled and tolerably civilized, should have been unknown or forgotten. Besides, as we have seen, his name was commemorated by his statue on the Capitol, erected only about two centuries after his time. We also agree with Sir G. C. Lewis in thinking that "the circumstance that the two King Tarquins were both named Lucius, and that it was necessary to distinguish them by the epithets of Priscus and Superbus, raises a presumption that the names were real." To which we will add that Numa's name must have been inseparably connected with the sacerdotal system of the Romans, that of Tullus Hostilius with the Curia Hostilia, and that of Servius with the wall and *agger*, and with the census. And in fact the names of all the kings must have been connected with some great public monument or institution.

In the 40th section of his 11th chapter, Sir G. C. Lewis reviews the nature of the regal government, and the difficulty of reconciling the history with the accounts of it. On this subject he remarks:[1]

"It is expressly stated that the constitutional powers of the Roman king were very limited, and that no measure of legislation, no decision of war or peace, and not even any important administrative or judicial act, could take place without the consent of the Senate and people. The constitution of Servius, with its elaborate system of voting, implies a complete development of the popular power; and the system which it superseded is described as having been still more democratic. Yet the history is exclusively concerned with the king's exploits; not even in the annals of an Oriental state could he occupy a more exclusive attention: there is no independent action in the Senate or the people; the Romans are undistinguished units, mere passive and unnamed instruments in the king's hands. If the first six kings had been as absolute and uncontrolled despots as the last Tarquin, they could not, to all appearance, have enjoyed a more ample authority. They make

[1] Vol. i. p. 534.

laws, they wage wars, they govern the state, without the smallest sign of opposition, or of a conflicting will, or of a dissentient voice from a single citizen. If the constitution had been as it is described to us, such a state of things could not have occurred. Powers such as those which are attributed to the Senate and people under the kings never slumber: if we had an authentic history of the period, and the form of government had been such as is represented, some traces of the active exercise, as well as of the legal existence, of these powers would infallibly be visible."

On these observations we shall remark: first, that they are partly unfounded; secondly, that they spring from a misconception of the nature of the government; and thirdly, from a misconception of the nature of the history.

That there are no traces of independent action in the Senate and people is not true. The people compel the Senate, after the death of Romulus, to restore the regal form of government, which they had endeavoured to abolish. The Senate under Ancus Marcius obtain the privilege of deciding upon peace or war. A declaration of war can be made only with the consent of the majority of the Senate;[1] and therefore it is not surprising that the kings wage war "without the smallest sign of opposition," because the majority of votes had overborne the opposition, if there was any. The kings, no doubt, also took the opinion of the Senate as to the making of laws, though our knowledge of the early Roman constitution is too fragmentary to enable us to say whether they were bound by that opinion. That he acted without taking counsel is one of the charges on which the tyranny of the second Tarquin is founded. Tarquinius Priscus is prevented from making any alterations in the constitution by the intervention of the High Church and State party, through their mouthpiece, Attus Navius. It was, no doubt, under considerable pressure, though we know not the details, that Servius Tullius was obliged to produce his new constitution, which was, in fact, a revolution. But to describe that constitution as a "complete development of the popular power" is utterly to misconceive it. And how it could have been so complete a development when, as we are told in the same breath, the system which it superseded was "still more democratic," exceeds our comprehension. But here again the critic misconceives the nature of the Comitia Curiata; which, though sufficiently popular in their origin, had become, in

[1] Liv. i. 32.

the progress of time, and through the vast increase of the unenfranchised *plebs* in the reign of Servius Tullius, like many an English borough, a close corporation. And, in general, Sir G. C. Lewis's notion, that the constitutional powers of the Roman kings were very limited, seems to be derived from the erroneous accounts of Dionysius.

That "the history is exclusively concerned with the king's exploits" is a natural consequence of the nature of the government. The king reigns *jure divino;* he is the inaugurated of the gods; everything is conducted under his auspices, and therefore everything is connected with his person. The consuls play the same part in after-times; but they rule only for a year, whereas the kings rule during their natural lives, and thus become the only persons, or almost the only persons, whom the history mentions. And the nature of the history further tends to produce this result; for the only historical writers, or rather annalists, are the Pontifices, whose annals are but brief and dry, and who, being themselves emanations of a theocratic state, would naturally centre everything in their divinely-appointed ruler. The Commentaries of the Pontifices were the only sources of *connected* history, though there were detached documents and monuments which served to confirm particular facts; and to these, probably, we owe such stories as the mission to Delphi, the rape of Lucretia, and others of the like kind.

"The shutting of the palace by Tanaquil after the murder of Tarquinius Priscus," continues Sir G. C. Lewis, " is an event sufficiently probable, if we suppose the government to be despotic. But it is an incident unsuited to an elective kingdom; nor is there any sufficient explanation of the means by which Tarquinius Superbus converts a limited royalty into a despotism. For such a change something more is necessary than the mere will of the ruler."

Tanaquil's act was a mere ruse to gain time for Servius to seize the crown in the manner we have already described;[1] and it is difficult to see why under the circumstances pretended—namely, the imminent dissolution of the king, and the necessity that he should be kept quiet—the palace might not have been shut up under any form of monarchy, as Servius in the interim comes forth, and vicariously discharges the king's functions.

Tarquinius Superbus had something more than "the mere will"

[1] Above, p. 245.

of the ruler" to support him in establishing his despotism. For first, as Servius had before accomplished his usurpation, he surrounded himself with an armed force—"armatis corpus circumsæpsit."[1] Secondly, he had a tolerably strong party, as we have already seen by the numbers who accompanied him into exile. These, of course, did not wish to see established the consular republic projected by Servius. Thirdly, he supported himself against his own subjects by his alliances with the chiefs of the Latins: "Ut peregrinis quoque opibus tutior inter cives esset."[2] Fourthly, he had every reason to rely—and so his subjects might have thought—on the aid of his relative, who had a sort of principality at Collatia, and subsequently on that of his son Sextus, who ruled at Gabii. He might have had other aids which we know not of; but that even these are not a "sufficient explanation" of what Tarquin accomplished can be affirmed by no man who possesses only that knowledge of the state of things at that time which can be drawn from the extant sources. His overthrow was no doubt facilitated by the accidental circumstance that the army—that is, the principal citizens in arms—was assembled before Ardea.

Sir G. C. Lewis then proceeds to remark upon the Roman constitution as described by Dionysius; but we need not examine these observations, because the writer on whose account they are founded did not understand the subject. Nor need we enter into the opinions of Cicero, Livy, Sallust, and other writers respecting the effects of the abolition of the monarchy, as they are not connected with the credibility of the history. Sir G. C. Lewis has a singular idea that it is difficult to account for the creation of such an office as that of the Rex Sacrificulus if the royal family was expelled by a forcible revolution, and seems to conceive that it rather indicates the gradual extinction of the regal power by easy steps and voluntary concessions.[3] Niebuhr also conjectured that the change from the royal to the consular form of government was made gradually, and by a mutual compromise.[4] But, with all deference to these eminent writers, we unhesitatingly affirm that such a revolution as that from a tyranny to a republic effected by slow degrees, through voluntary concessions and mutual compromise, is contrary to all historical experience. Nor do we perceive what consolation it would have been to a deposed tyrant, or what he

[1] Liv. i. 19.   [2] Ibid.
[3] Vol. i. p. 538.   [4] Hist. vol. i. pp. 518, 538.

would have gained by the compromise, that, after he was sent about his business, the priest who performed the sacrifices which belonged to his dignity should be called Rex. We are, therefore, of opinion that the old tradition is a great deal more consistent and probable than the conjectures of the critics who find fault with it, and would either abolish or amend it. Livy's account of the reasons for creating a Rex Sacrificulus, which Sir G. C. Lewis has only partially quoted, is quite satisfactory: "*Rerum deinde divinarum cura habita: et quia quædam publica sacra per ipsos reges factitata erant, necubi desiderium regum esset, regem sacrificulum creant. Id sacerdotium pontifici subjecere, ne additus nomini honos aliquid libertati, cujus tunc prima erat cura, officeret.*"[1] Whence it appears that the grounds for creating this priesthood were entirely religious, and not political; in fact, a salve for the tender consciences of the more bigoted part of the population; who, seeing in a king the elect of the gods, were content, as such consciences frequently are, with the word instead of the thing, and accepted the shadow for the substance.

"The detailed history of the Roman kings," continues Sir G. C. Lewis, "represents them as elective, with limited and not with arbitrary power, and as the heads of a constitution in which the Senate and people each bear an important part. Nevertheless we meet at other times with statements founded on a different view of the Roman royalty. Thus Appius alludes to the plebeians having been relieved from the taxes which they formerly paid to the kings, and from the bodily punishments which were inflicted upon them if they did not speedily obey the orders given them.[2] We are likewise told, in reference to the decemviral legislation, that the kings used to exercise an arbitrary jurisdiction, without written laws;[3] and again, that their power was irresponsible.[4] The accounts moreover of the influence by which Tarquin was put down do not quite harmonise: thus at one time we are told that he was expelled by the heads of the aristocracy,[5] at another that the people assisted the patricians in effecting his expulsion."[6]

These divergent accounts, it will be seen, are taken from Diony-

---

[1] Lib. ii. 2.   [2] Dionys. Hal. vi. 24.   [3] Ibid. x. 1.
[4] Dionys. Hal. xi. 41. Tacitus (Ann. III. 26) considers the powers of the Roman kings to have been unlimited till the reign of Servius.
[5] Dionys. Hal. viii. 5, in the speech of Coriolanus.
[6] Ibid. v. 65; vii. 41; x. 38.

sius, whose habit of contradicting himself we have already exposed; though after all, perhaps, the inconsistencies here alleged may be more apparent than real. For granting that the Roman kings were elective, and their power in some degree constitutionally limited—though in this respect the view of Dionysius is quite false—yet nevertheless their personal power, like that of the consuls after them, and especially in time of war, was very arbitrary and extensive, notwithstanding that it was conferred upon them constitutionally—that is, by the *lex curiata de imperio*. Thus we find even so popular a king as Servius threatening with imprisonment, and even death, those who should evade the census,[1] not to mention the tyrannous acts of Tarquin which Appius may include in his view of the regal times. Contradictory views of the Roman constitution in the time of the kings often arise, as we have before endeavoured to show, from jumbling together its different periods, and regarding, for instance, the reign of Romulus as identical with that of Ancus Marcius with regard to the royal prerogative. There is nothing contradictory in Dionysius saying in one place that Tarquin was expelled by the heads of the aristocracy, and in another that they were assisted in that expulsion by the people. The conspiracy of the patricians was the first and main cause of Tarquin's deposition, and therefore, without doing much violence to the propriety of language, they may be said to have expelled him. That they must have been aided by the people *va sans dire*, as the French say. Had the people been adverse, or even perhaps neutral, the conspiracy could not have succeeded; and therefore Brutus proceeded to the camp before Ardea, and procured their assistance. But this army did not contain the lowest class of *plebs*.

Then follows a paragraph[2] containing a sort of parenthetical attack on the history of the regal period in general, instead of the accounts of the government, which is the professed object of the section. But as it only reiterates charges before urged more than once, there will be no need to examine it.

"The constitutional accounts of the regal period," continues Sir G. C. Lewis, "are peculiarly confused and contradictory: not only are the descriptions of the constitution inconsistent with the account of the successive kings, but the general characteristics attributed to the government are inconsistent with each other. It has been supposed that the oral traditions of the Roman con-

[1] Liv. I. 44. [2] Vol. i. p. 540.

stitution were more faithful and trustworthy than the oral traditions of particular events and exploits. It seems, however, on the contrary, that the traditions of the constitution were indistinct and inaccurate; whereas individual acts of generosity, courage, and patriotism, or of cruelty and oppression, were more likely to live in popular memory."

It is impossible to enter into these general charges, as they are not substantiated by producing instances and illustrations. It is quite evident, however, that Sir G. C. Lewis takes his view of the Roman constitution from Dionysius, and therefore it is not surprising that he cannot reconcile it with what he finds in the Latin authors. That he took his view from Dionysius we infer from his mentioning "descriptions of the constitution;" for Dionysius is the only author who gives a professed description of it. And the same thing appears from the next page,[1] where he observes: "The Roman kingdom, therefore, was alternately conceived as democratic and despotic. The former is the view taken by Dionysius." Much of the alleged confusion, too, arises from a confusion in the ideas of modern critics, who as we have before observed, confound together the different epochs of the regal period.

In the remainder of this section, Sir G. C. Lewis examines and condemns Niebuhr's hypothesis that the curiæ consisted exclusively of patricians. With Sir G. C. Lewis's view of this question we entirely agree, and have indeed quoted a portion of what he here says, by way of confirming our opinion. The last section of this chapter and volume is devoted to the topography of Rome under the kings; into which subject we need not enter.

[1] P. 541.

THE END.

www.ingramcontent.com/pod-product-compliance
Lightning Source LLC
Chambersburg PA
CBHW031937290426
44108CB00011B/588